W0008754

THE FOUR AGES
OF AMERICAN
FOREIGN POLICY

Also by Michael Mandelbaum

The Rise and Fall of Peace on Earth (2019)

Mission Failure: America and the World in the Post-Cold War Era (2016)

The Road to Global Prosperity (2014)

That Used to Be Us: How America Fell Behind in the World It Invented and How We Can Come Back (with Thomas L. Friedman) (2011)

The Frugal Superpower: America's Global Leadership in a Cash-Strapped World (2010)

Democracy's Good Name: The Rise and Risks of the World's Most Popular Form of Government (2007)

The Case for Goliath: How America Acts as the World's Government in the Twenty-first Century (2006)

The Meaning of Sports: Why Americans Watch Baseball, Football, and Basketball and What They See When They Do (2004)

The Ideas That Conquered the World: Peace, Democracy, and Free Markets in the Twenty-first Century (2002)

The Dawn of Peace in Europe (1996)

The Global Rivals (with Seweryn Bialer) (1996)

The Fate of Nations: The Search for National Security in the Nineteenth and Twentieth Centuries (1988)

Reagan and Gorbachev (with Strobe Talbott) (1987)

The Nuclear Future (1983)

The Nuclear Revolution: International Politics Before and After Hiroshima (1981)

The Nuclear Question: The United States and Nuclear Weapons, 1946–1976 (1979)

THE FOUR AGES OF AMERICAN FOREIGN POLICY

WEAK POWER, GREAT POWER, SUPERPOWER, HYPERPOWER

MICHAEL MANDELBAUM

OXFORD
UNIVERSITY PRESS

OXFORD
UNIVERSITY PRESS

Oxford University Press is a department of the University of Oxford. It furthers the University's objective of excellence in research, scholarship, and education by publishing worldwide. Oxford is a registered trade mark of Oxford University Press in the UK and certain other countries.

Published in the United States of America by Oxford University Press 198 Madison Avenue, New York, NY 10016, United States of America.

Library of Congress Cataloging-in-Publication Data
Names: Mandelbaum, Michael, author.
Title: The four ages of American foreign policy : weak power, great power, superpower, hyperpower / [Michael Mandelbaum].
Description: New York, NY : Oxford University Press, [2022] | Includes index.
Identifiers: LCCN 2022003360 (print) | LCCN 2022003361 (ebook) | ISBN 9780197621790 (hardback) | ISBN 9780197621813 (epub) | ISBN 9780197621820
Subjects: LCSH: United States—Foreign relations.
Classification: LCC E183.7 .M287 2022 (print) | LCC E183.7 (ebook) | DDC 327.73—dc23/eng/20220217
LC record available at https://lccn.loc.gov/2022003360
LC ebook record available at https://lccn.loc.gov/2022003361

DOI: 10.1093/oso/9780197621790.001.0001

1 3 5 7 9 8 6 4 2

Printed by LSC Communications, United States of America

To My Esteemed Classmates

Daniel B. Badger Jr.

Michael G. Berger

H. Neil Berkson

Merrill T. Boyce

James N. Gardner (1946–2021)

Andrew T. Hingson

Peter C. Kostant

James L. Kugel

Richard B. Stoner Jr.

Robert A. Stults

James R. Vivian

Steven R. Weisman

Jack M. Weiss III

Mark L. Wolf

Yale College, 1968;

and to my esteemed wife, Anne Mandelbaum, Yale MA, 1968

CONTENTS

———◦◦◦◦———

The Second Age: Great Power, 1865–1945   113

The Third Age: Superpower, 1945–1990   233

The Fourth Age: Hyperpower, 1990–2015   375

PREFACE

WHY PUBLISH A HISTORY of American foreign policy? After all, good ones are already available.[1] There are three reasons for the existence of *The Four Ages of American Foreign Policy*. First, it offers a fresh perspective on the history it covers. The discipline of history is, as the Dutch historian Pieter Geyl aptly put it, "an argument without end." The book that follows is intended to contribute to that ongoing argument. Second, this book takes the story further than other volumes—because of when they were written—were able to do: up to the year 2015.

Third, and most important, *The Four Ages of American Foreign Policy* offers readers a new framework for understanding the history of the foreign policy of the United States. It divides that history into four distinct periods—four ages—defined by the consistent increase in the power the country has had at its disposal in its relations with others. In addition, it records three striking continuities in the 250 years it covers, in the goals and the instruments of American foreign policy, and in the way that policy was adopted and implemented.

Although every work of history identifies both continuities and changes in the period with which it deals, it is in the selection of continuities and changes in the history of American foreign policy that it specifies as the most significant ones that *The Four Ages of American Foreign Policy* differs from previous accounts.

The present work portrays the United States, in its ascent, first as a weak power, then as a great power, next as a superpower, and, ultimately, as the world's sole hyperpower. The three distinctly American features of that foreign policy are its ideological goals, the use of economic instruments in pursuit of them, and a democratic process for formulating and implementing decisions about it. These are the distinguishing features of the foreign policy in the quarter millennium between 1765 and 2015.

ACKNOWLEDGMENTS

I AM GRATEFUL TO Nicholas X. Rizopoulos and Paul M. Kennedy for helpful conversations about World War I and World War II, respectively.

I owe thanks to Starr Lee and to the staff of the Mason Library of The Johns Hopkins University School of Advanced International Studies for research assistance and to Michael Frimpong for technical assistance.

I am indebted to the two anonymous reviewers for Oxford University Press, who provided useful comments on the manuscript.

I profited greatly from reading the volumes in the Oxford History of the United States series, originally edited by C. Vann Woodward and now by David M. Kennedy. They are, collectively, a splendid monument to historical scholarship.[1]

It has been a pleasure to work again with David McBride of Oxford University Press.

My greatest debt, as always, is to my wife, Anne Mandelbaum, for her peerless editing, her keen wit, her wise counsel, the joy of her companionship, and the constancy of her love.

Introduction

THE THEME THAT unites the foreign policy of the United States of America during the 250 years between 1765 and 2015 may be simply stated: expansion and ascent. Over the course of those two and one-half centuries the American republic rose in the ranks of independent countries from an obscure, unimportant collection of small European settlements scattered along the eastern seaboard of North America to a continent-spanning colossus with a global presence that towered over all other sovereign states. It achieved this status through the expansion of its power; of its wealth, which is the foundation of power; and of its influence, which is the shadow that power casts.

Its ascent did not come about deliberately. Americans did pursue the conquest of their own continent in a consistent, determined, and sometimes even ruthless manner, and by the middle of the nineteenth century the country's territory had reached 3,000 miles to the Pacific Ocean. Expansion of this kind had a central place in American life from the first. For relations with other countries on issues other than continental settlement, however, the United States did not make the global supremacy that it ultimately achieved a consistent goal. Often it was not a goal at all, coming about instead as the result of policies— frequently, in American eyes, defensive ones—undertaken in response to a variety of challenges and opportunities.

Not only did the American ascent not take place deliberately, but also it did not proceed in a uniform way. It took place, rather, in four distinct stages. Consequently, the account of American foreign policy that follows is divided into four parts.

* * *

The most important condition that determines a country's foreign policy is the power—economic and especially military power—that it can deploy. Power, in turn, is relative: that is, every country is more or less powerful in relation to others.

Power has always been unevenly distributed. Some states are strong, others weak; and the challenges and opportunities the weak face differ from those confronting the strong.[1] Just as wealthy individuals have a wider array of options in life than do poor people, so strong countries enjoy a greater range of options for their foreign policies than do weak ones. The history of American foreign policy, as recounted here, is a series of responses to the changing circumstances in which the country's increasing power has placed it.

The United States began life as one of many weak powers, then became one among several great powers, next attained an even higher status as one of only two states whose resources and ambitions distinguished them from traditional great powers and made them superpowers, and finally, with the collapse of the rival superpower, towered far above all other countries as the world's only hyperpower. In each of these four historical eras, American foreign policy bore a resemblance to the foreign policies of other countries with similar degrees of power.

Yet America's power was never the sole determinant of its foreign policies. The values, preferences, hopes, and fears of the people responsible for them were also contributing factors. American foreign policy in all four periods thus bore the marks of several particular and enduring features of the country itself.

For this reason, the history of American foreign policy exhibits both continuity and change. The changes come from the country's increasing international power over 250 years. The continuity arises from three characteristic features of American society and public life that have been present, and politically potent, from the very beginning. The account of the nation's foreign policy that follows incorporates both.

* * *

Historically, three distinctive properties of American foreign policy stand out. First among these is the American desire to disseminate a set of political ideas to be embodied in institutions and practices. Second has been its repeated recourse to the use of economic leverage to pursue these goals. The third has been the characteristic way the American republic has made and carried out foreign policy, which has reflected the nation's democratic character: an unusually wide range of groups, individuals, and viewpoints has been able to exert influence on the policy makers. The foreign policy of the United States, that is, has been unusually ideological, unusually economic, and unusually democratic. None of the three originated in the United States or has been unique to American foreign policy. All have been found, historically, in the foreign policies of other sovereign states. At one time or another, for example, all have formed part of the foreign policy of Great Britain.[2] Still, all have played more prominent roles—appearing more frequently and exercising greater influence—in American foreign policy than in the foreign policies of any other country.

• The Ideological Basis of American Foreign Policy

The United States has carried beyond its borders the ideas on which the country was founded: liberty, popularity sovereignty—that is, free elections—and the spirit of reform, a belief in the possibilities of social and political improvement. Americans have directed their efforts to promote these ideas at three different targets. The ideas have influenced policies aimed at groups of individuals in other countries, the protection of whose human rights became a goal of the American superpower and then the American hyperpower. American ideas have affected its policies toward sovereign states: the hope of converting others to democratic politics animated American leaders and the American public from the eighteenth century, initially by the force of the American example and then, in the twentieth and twenty-first centuries, through the exercise of the nation's by then far greater military and economic power. Finally, the country's dominant political ideas have on occasion shaped its approach to the international system itself, which Americans, notably their twenty-eighth president, Woodrow Wilson, have sought to reform to make it more peaceful.

Why have these ideas had such importance? The founders of the country justified the successful effort to secure independence from Great Britain as a way to preserve and protect them, which made them central to America's political identity.

America's strong religious tradition also contributed to the ideological character of its foreign policy. The original Protestant settlers from Europe crossed the Atlantic to establish godly communities in the North American wilderness, and periods of religious revival in the eighteenth and nineteenth centuries known as "Great Awakenings" fortified the faith of their descendants.[3] Ideas central to that faith—individualism and the rejection of the principle of hierarchy—reinforced the more explicitly political principles of liberty and self-government.[4] The founding American religious tradition was not only Protestant but also evangelical, with its adherents seeking to spread their religious beliefs and practices.[5] That missionary spirit carried over into foreign policy, with Americans seeking to spread their country's political ideas, and the institutions and practices based on them, as widely as possible.

Scholars of international relations divide the driving force of foreign policy into two broad categories: "realism," in which countries seek to enhance or defend their power and territory, and "idealism," in which ideas shape relations with other countries. Virtually all sovereign states for almost all of history practiced some version of realism; historically, it was the main impulse behind foreign policy everywhere. With the advent of the United States, however, the alternative approach gained increasing prominence. "Idealism" is in fact a characteristically American approach to foreign policy—or more properly an Anglo-American approach, since Great Britain adopted some of these ideas as well.

Notwithstanding its importance, over 250 years the United States did not make idealism its exclusive or even its principal approach to relations with the rest of the world. Considerations of power have, on the whole, weighed more heavily on the foreign relations of the United States than the propagation of American ideas. When the imperatives of realism and idealism have come into conflict, Americans have usually opted for realism. Still, the wish to spread liberty, popular sovereignty, and reform have had an impact, and a more pronounced impact than on the foreign policy of any other country.

• Economic Measures in American Foreign Policy

From the eighteenth century to the twenty-first the United States has periodically imposed trade sanctions in an effort to influence the behavior on the part of other countries. Using trade as an instrument of foreign policy appealed to the United States when it was weak because the military measures it could mount were unlikely to be effective. Sanctions continued to be attractive even after America became strong, both because it had also become wealthy and thus had greater economic leverage over others and because military operations, although they could now succeed in achieving the country's aims, often seemed likely to be too expensive to be desirable.

In the twentieth century, having built the largest economy on the planet, the United States employed the export of capital in addition to access to the American market for the purpose of affecting the domestic and foreign policies of other countries. In the second half of that century and into the next one it pursued even broader goals with economic instruments. The American superpower regarded trade and investment with its allies as a mechanism for binding those alliances, which had originated in considerations of security, more tightly together. For the American hyperpower, commerce and foreign investment had an even more ambitious purpose: to promote American-style political and economic institutions and practices around the world.

• The Role of Democracy in American Foreign Policymaking

Finally, the United States has devised and conducted its foreign policy more democratically, with the public having a greater impact on it, than other countries. Public opinion has had considerable influence, especially in the matter of war. Dramatic events that threatened the United States or simply troubled Americans recurrently aroused public pressure for the government to respond as well as public support, at least for a time, when such responses took military form. In addition, every American war has provoked domestic opposition, sometimes sufficiently widespread and intense to make it impossible for the government to continue them.

The American political system is also democratic in that it is open to public influence. It affords multiple points of access for those seeking to bend or prod public policy in a particular direction. Interested parties routinely organize themselves to promote their preferences, including in foreign policy.

In these ways the United States differs from the great powers of Europe, in which a small circle consisting of the monarch and the aristocracy traditionally dominated foreign policy. The United States had neither and so lacked as well the culture of deference that they tend to foster. From the very beginning American citizens, unlike their European counterparts, exercised major influence over their country's activities abroad. While the American government has often had broad latitude to conduct the nation's foreign policy, and has occasionally done so secretly, in general public sentiment has weighed more heavily on it than has been customary in other countries.

Citizens have had influence, as well, because of the American Constitution of 1788. That document divides power between the executive and legislative branches, giving both the president and the Congress a claim to set the nation's foreign policy and furnishing the public with two institutions to which to convey its wishes and concerns. The Constitution also protects public participation in the policymaking process by guaranteeing to Americans the right to write and speak freely and to assemble peacefully on behalf of their preferred causes—rights of which, since the eighteenth century, they have regularly taken advantage.

* * *

To summarize: an ascent to the pinnacle of international power and prestige through the expansion of territory, military and economic power, and influence and prestige in the world beyond the North American continent; the passage through four different stages in this ascent, as a weak power, a great power, a superpower, and the world's hyperpower—each stage defined by the country's relative power; and three persistent features throughout—ideological goals, the use of economic instruments, and a democratic process for formulating and implementing decisions: these are the themes of the pages that follow, the distinguishing features of the foreign policy of the United States during the twenty-five decades between the Stamp Act of 1765 and the Iran deal of 2015.

The First Age

Weak Power, 1765–1865

Europe's distress became America's advantage.

Samuel Flagg Bemis[1]

The international system of sovereign states is sometimes compared to a jungle. In both, fierce and often deadly competition takes place. In jungles, some animals (predators) stalk, kill, and eat weaker ones (their prey). In the international system strong states prey on weaker ones, sometimes inflicting the political equivalent of death—the loss of sovereign independence.[2]

The United States began life as a weak power and spent the next one hundred years in that position in the international system, at least in comparison with its chief antagonist, Great Britain. The thirteen colonies originally had no effective military forces of their own and no political mechanism to coordinate their policies. On every metric of power, the British far surpassed them. Yet the United States survived continuing political friction and two full-fledged wars with its onetime colonial master. It did so by employing three principal means by which the weak can preserve their independence against the strong: difficulty of access, active defense, and the diversion of the attention of the strong by rivalry with other powerful countries. As it happens, each of the three has a parallel in the natural world.

Small, weak members of the animal kingdom avoid their predators by camouflage. Many have evolved to blend in with their surroundings. Their predators do not see them and so lack access to them. Difficulty of access in the international system comes about by virtue of geography, and here the United States has been well endowed. The world's second-largest ocean separates it from the great powers of Europe. Europeans could and did cross the Atlantic of course; but the voyage was long and uncertain. Reaching North America for the purpose of war-making, even for Great Britain, the greatest naval power of the era, was far more difficult than crossing a border with an army. In addition, the distance from the northern tip of the northernmost colony, Massachusetts (which then included what became the state of Maine), to the southern border of the southernmost one, Georgia—about 1,500 miles—made occupying them a formidably expensive proposition. Finally, the vast wilderness to the west of the colonies offered suitable terrain for hiding, regrouping, and launching attacks on European soldiers.

In nature, animals that predators hunt have developed, thanks to evolution, mechanisms of defense. A familiar example is the quills of the porcupine. Not only quills but also claws, teeth, hooves, and hard outer coverings give prey the means to resist and indeed to harm predators so that the predator may give up the attack or even be deterred from an assault in the first place.

Similarly, weak states can muster enough military power to inflict damage on strong ones even if the weak cannot ultimately prevail in a prolonged war. In the 1960s, for example, France equipped itself with a nuclear arsenal modest in comparison with that of the Soviet Union not in order to be able to win a nuclear war between the two but to give itself the means to wound its more powerful adversary and thus prevent a Soviet attack. In the next decade, the Vietnamese communists defeated the far mightier United States because they exacted a higher toll in the lives of American troops fighting in Southeast Asia than the American public proved willing to sanction—while the communists accepted far heavier losses than the Americans suffered.

Unlike animals, weak countries do not automatically use their mechanisms of pain infliction against the strong. The weak must decide to fight and persuade the strong that they are not only willing to fight but also willing to persist in fighting. In its first half century the United States did manage to persuade Great Britain of its determination to secure and retain its independence.

Finally, predators may be diverted from pursuing their prey by fighting among themselves. Predatory mammals do fight others of the same species, for control of territory, access to females, and food. In the international system, rivalry between and among the strong can afford the weak a respite from the dangers that the strong pose to them, and even give the weak some room to maneuver. Moreover, while intramural fighting among the big beasts of the jungle is episodic, great-power rivalry tends to be constant. It was so during the first hundred years of American foreign policy and the United States took advantage of it.* Indeed, this proved to be the single most potent determinant of the success that American foreign policy achieved in the country's first fifty years.

* * *

In nature, while caterpillars do become butterflies, deer cannot turn into lions, but weak powers can strengthen themselves and thereby escape the problems that weakness imposes. This the United States managed to do in the course of its first hundred years. Geographic, demographic, and economic expansion promoted America, in the wake of its mid-nineteenth-century Civil War, into the ranks of the world's great powers.

Growth occurred in large part through the uncoordinated initiatives of individuals. Settlers moved westward to claim land for themselves and reclaim it for agriculture or ranching. The country's population expanded through natural increase—Americans had consistently high

---

* The quotation making this point from the historian Samuel Flagg Bemis, "Europe's distress was America's advantage," misleads in the sense that the great-power rivalry of which the United States took advantage between 1765 and 1865 was not simply a bad period in European history, although the wars of the French Revolution and Napoleonic conquest from 1792 to 1815 were bloodier and more prolonged than conflicts of the past, but rather a fundamental and continuing condition of that history.

birth rates in this era—and large-scale immigration, mainly from northern Europe.

Population growth spurred economic growth: more workers produced more output. The reverse was true as well: economic growth created opportunities that attracted immigrants. Such growth came as well from the ongoing Industrial Revolution—at its core the substitution of machine for human power—which began in Great Britain at roughly the same time that the United States achieved independence and whose technologies migrated across the Atlantic Ocean. In the second half of America's hundred-year career as a weak power, the innovations that laid a new basis for military power began to arrive: the telegraph, Bessemer process steel, and the steam engine and its offshoots—steam-driven ships and railroad locomotives. The American mastery of these industrial processes and products, even more than the growth of its territory and population, underlay its transition to a higher status in the international system.

Public policies also contributed to American expansion. The federal government brought large parts of North America into the United States, which, by 1865, stretched all the way to the Pacific Ocean. Americans settled in the territories that their government added, sometimes preceding, and agitating for, their annexation.

The thirteen colonies that initially formed the United States added the Louisiana territory in 1803, Florida in 1819, Texas in 1845, the northern part of Mexico in 1846, Oregon that same year, parts of what became Arizona and New Mexico in 1853, and Alaska in 1867. The threat of military activity helped persuade Spain to relinquish Florida, but the American government also paid the legal claims of Americans against Spain in exchange for the land and purchased Louisiana from France as well as the land that was incorporated into Arizona and New Mexico—the Gadsden Purchase—from Mexico. In the first two instances of expansion, the conditions of European politics, and specifically Spanish and French relations with the great powers of the continent, worked to the advantage of the United States, which also expanded its territory in another way: by war.

* * *

The hundred-year American experience as a weak power divides into two fifty-year periods. In the first, from 1765 to 1815, the United States functioned as a classic weak power, with the urgent and overriding goal of surviving the predations, actual and potential, of stronger states. In the second, from 1815 to 1865, the country remained weaker in military terms than the European great powers but did not face threats of the magnitude that it had confronted in the previous fifty years and with which weak states typically must cope.

In the hundred years between 1765 and 1865 the United States fought four wars, two in the first half of that period and two more in the second. The first two pitted Americans against the British, and American independence was—or was thought by the Americans to be—at stake in both. The last two were waged between and among peoples of the Western Hemisphere and determined the country's borders, not its independent existence. The United States emerged victorious—or, in the case of the War of 1812, not defeated—from each of them; and the outcome of each conflict increased the country's strength.

As the result of what they came to call the Revolutionary War of 1775 to 1783, the Americans secured their independence from Great Britain. In this war they made use of all three strategies of the weak—difficulty of access, defense, and diversion. Great-power rivalry in Europe generally worked to the advantage of the United States, but it had the opposite effect in 1812 when the ongoing conflict between Napoleonic France and Great Britain provoked the second American war against the British. The three measures that weak states can employ in conflicts with stronger powers also figured in the War of 1812.

In the fifty years between the end of the War of 1812 and the end of the Civil War, between 1815 and 1865, European politics became less violent and the United States grew more detached from them. America's relations with Great Britain, the one European power of continuing importance to American security, occasionally became strained, but the two never again came to blows.

In the Mexican War of 1846–1848 the United States assumed an unfamiliar role as the stronger of the two combatants. This was the most imperial of America's wars in that it was waged for the purpose of territorial expansion. The fourth war of America's first hundred years, the Civil War of 1861–1865, counts, along with the Revolutionary War and

World War II, as one of the three most consequential the country has ever fought. While it was waged exclusively by Americans, the shadow of Great Britain hung over it throughout. Had the British supported the South they could have inflicted serious damage on the United States. They might have done to America what America did to Mexico: reduce its size and therefore its power through the detachment of a large part of its territory. But Britain did not support the Confederacy and the Union prevailed.

While the outcome of the Civil War settled the territorial dimensions and political and economic character of the United States, it had consequences for American foreign policy as well. The process by which the country grew out of its initial position in the international system culminated with the Union's victory. By 1865, the United States became a great power; and in the next century American power changed the world.

I

Independence, 1765–1788

The Origins of the American Revolution

In the year 1765 the thirteen British colonies that stretched along the Atlantic coast of North America for almost 1,500 miles from Maine, then a part of Massachusetts, to Georgia were flourishing. Their collective population was soaring. Numbering about 250,000 at the turn of the eighteenth century, natural increase and immigration had pushed that total to around two million. Economically the colonies were thriving, with trade, especially with the mother country, growing rapidly.[1] By one estimate, the Americans enjoyed a standard of living as much as fifty percent higher than that of the inhabitants of Great Britain.[2] The colonials considered themselves loyal subjects of the British Crown and proud members of Great Britain's overseas empire. They shared a language and a political culture with the British. Americans thought of the British Isles as "home" even if they had never set foot there.[3]

Yet in ten years the colonials would go to war to sever their ties with Britain and escape the British Empire. The seeds of that dramatic shift lay in the outcome of a war the Americans and the British waged and won together, a war that had ended two years before, in 1763.

In the Seven Years' War[4] Great Britain and France fought each other for the fourth time since 1689. That war has a good claim to being the very first world war because it involved major battles on three different continents—North America, Europe, and the Indian subcontinent. It was the only one of the five global conflicts waged over the course of two hundred years—the other four being the Wars of the French

Revolution,[5] World Wars I and II, and the Cold War—to begin in North America. It started on May 28, 1754, with a skirmish in the Ohio Valley in what is now western Pennsylvania between French soldiers and a detachment of the militia of the Virginia Regiment led by a twenty-two-year-old lieutenant colonel named George Washington.[6] The Seven Years' War ended in a sweeping victory for Great Britain, driving France from North America[7] and giving the British control of the continent from the Atlantic Ocean to the Mississippi River.[8] The outcome of the war completed the rise of Great Britain from a relatively minor country off the northwest coast of Eurasia in 1688 to a status greater than that of the dominant European power of the seventeenth century, Bourbon France.

With victory came new responsibilities.[9] The British had to police North America, which involved riding herd on both the Americans, on whose behalf, among other motives, they had waged the war, and the indigenous peoples, then known as Indians,[10] who had sided with the French. As they moved outward from the Atlantic coast into the North American interior, European settlers were displacing Indian tribes, who were determined to resist. The British also had to be able to check French and Spanish designs on the territory they had won.[11] The government in London decided to keep a larger garrison of British troops across the Atlantic than before the war. The garrison would be expensive to maintain, creating the need for more revenue. More revenue was needed, as well, to pay off what the British government had borrowed to wage the Seven Years' War. That war had nearly doubled the national debt,[12] which stood at 137 million pounds with an annual interest cost of 5 million pounds, a heavy burden in light of the government's normal peacetime budget of only 8 million pounds.[13]

The level of taxation that the government believed it could prudently place on the people of Great Britain having reached its limit, it was all but inevitable for London to look to its colonial subjects to contribute part of the required revenue. The Americans were both prosperous and lightly taxed. They had benefited greatly from the victory in the war while contributing very little to its costs. The colonies would draw further benefit from the enhanced British presence in North America. Moreover, as the sovereign power, the British government had the right to tax the people living under its rule.[14]

The taxes that His Majesty's government sought to impose in the colonies did not raise the revenue it expected. Instead, they led to resistance, rebellion, and, ultimately, war. The war that began in 1775 concluded in 1783 with Britain recognizing the thirteen colonies as an independent country. The emergence of that country, the United States of America, would ultimately prove to be the most important development in international politics of the next 250 years.

The Path to War

On March 22, 1765, the British Parliament passed a revenue-raising measure known as the Stamp Act.[15] It required Americans to purchase government-issued stamps for a wide array of paper products: newspapers, legal documents, even playing cards. The law evoked a powerful, widespread, negative response in the colonies, which the British had not expected. Americans engaged in protests and demonstrations, some organized by a loose network of groups that called themselves the Sons of Liberty. "Taxation without representation is tyranny" became their slogan. Mobs intimidated the agents licensed to sell the stamps in North America. Nine colonies sent representatives to a Stamp Act Congress in New York in order to draft petitions objecting to the measure. American merchants agreed not to import British goods in an effort to force Parliament to repeal the law.

The Stamp Act began the sequence of events that would culminate in American independence. It also inaugurated a pattern that would recur in American foreign policy for the next two and one-half centuries: an act endangering American security or affronting American sensibilities—or both—provoked a strong reaction among the public and a demand for a response of some kind. Eventually in this case, and often on subsequent, similar occasions, the response would be a military one.

On March 19, 1766, after a change in government in London, Parliament did repeal the Stamp Act, partly in response to pressure from British merchants whose profits suffered from the American boycott.[16] At the same time, the British government insisted on its right to impose any tax it chose in the colonies. In the short term, repeal soothed American anger. It also gave birth to the idea, which was valid in this particular case[17] and was to have a long life in the history of American foreign policy, that trade sanctions against other countries can serve as an effective instrument for achieving both economic and political goals.

In 1767 and 1768 the British government tried again. The Townshend Acts, named for Charles Townshend, the Chancellor of the Exchequer, placed duties on imports of glass, lead, paint, paper, and tea, which were not produced in the colonies and thus had to be purchased from Britain. The Townshend Acts evoked, if anything, a stronger negative American response than had the Stamp Act. Boston merchants organized another boycott of British goods, which merchants from other colonial ports joined. In 1770 Parliament repealed all the Townshend tariffs except the one on tea. In the meantime, however, the British government had sent troops to Boston, the hotbed of resistance. On March 5, 1770, some of them fired on a group of protesters, killing five, in what became known as the Boston Massacre.

Three years later Parliament passed the Tea Act, which gave the East India Company a monopoly on the sale of tea in the colonies. The main purpose was to shore up the East India Company's then-parlous financial position,[18] but it had the effect of discriminating against colonial tea merchants. In protest, in Boston on December 16, 1773, a group of Americans, disguised as Indians to conceal their identities, seized a shipment of East India tea worth 10,000 pounds and threw it into the harbor.

The Boston Tea Party proved to be a turning point in relations between the colonies and the government in London. Appalled and alarmed by the vandalism and destruction of property as well as by the continuing colonial defiance of its lawfully enacted measures, Parliament, to punish the Americans and assert its imperial authority, passed what came to be known as the Coercive Acts, which the Americans called the Intolerable Acts. One of them closed the port of Boston until all the colonists paid for the tea that a few of them had destroyed. Another revoked the colonial charter of Massachusetts and brought it under the control of the British government. A third allowed for moving the trials of accused British officials in Massachusetts to Britain if it was decided that a fair trial was impossible in America. A fourth, which applied to all the colonies, provided for the housing of British troops in America, which some colonials interpreted as a license to install the soldiers in private homes against the wishes of the homeowners.

The resulting American outrage spurred the convening of the First Continental Congress in Philadelphia on September 5, 1775, to plan and coordinate resistance. Twelve of the thirteen colonies—all but Georgia—sent representatives. As the Americans had done in reaction to the Stamp Act and the Townshend duties, the Congress voted to respond to the latest British outrages by prohibiting the import of British goods. Neither side wanted or expected its actions to trigger an armed conflict with the other,[19] but that is what happened.

The king declared Massachusetts to be in a state of rebellion, and on April 19, 1775, the commander of the British troops that controlled Boston got word of the existence of an unauthorized armory in the nearby town of Concord. He sent a detachment to seize it that encountered armed colonists determined to prevent this. Shots were exchanged between the two forces, first in the town of Lexington and then in neighboring Concord. The death total for the day included 275 British soldiers and 95 Americans. The war for American independence had begun.

The pattern by which the war came about—a series of events creating increasing suspicion, hostility, and a sense of threat—anticipated the way that, between 1945 and 1950, another wartime American ally, the Soviet Union, turned into an adversary.[20] The Cold War rivals, however, had radically different political systems, different aspirations for the global order, and different and conflicting views of Europe. In retrospect, the causes of the twentieth-century rivalry are obvious. That is not the case for the thirteen colonies and their mother country. Why, then, did the Anglo-American solidarity of 1765 turn into an armed conflict only ten years later?

The Americans believed that they were fighting to defend a sacred political principle: liberty. The ideological character of American public life, and therefore of American foreign policy, had its origins in the American Revolution. By levying taxes on them for which they themselves had not voted, His Majesty's government was, in the colonials' view, violating their liberty by denying rights they had always enjoyed—the rights of Englishmen, as the Americans viewed them. Many Americans further believed the British were actively conspiring to deprive them of those rights, with the conspiracy's headquarters in London.[21] Moreover, familiar as they were with English history, they justified their own rebellion by comparing it to the rebellions in the mother country of the preceding century—the overthrow of King Charles I in 1645 and especially the "Glorious Revolution" of 1688 that removed his son James II from the throne.[22] In defending liberty, the Americans saw themselves as following in the footsteps of the British themselves.

The colonials considered what they were doing to be not only defensive but also revolutionary. Drawing on the tradition of American uniqueness—later to be called American exceptionalism—and the belief in the special mission of its people to embody and exemplify virtue that began with the first English settlers in North America in the early seventeenth century,[23] they were convinced that the success of their enterprise would reverberate throughout the world.[24] Thomas Paine, the most widely read pamphleteer in North America at a time and in a place in which the political pamphlet served as the major vehicle of political argument and persuasion, wrote, in his most widely circulated work *Common Sense*, that "we have the power to begin the world anew." Thus began the missionary spirit in which Americans were frequently to conduct their foreign policies over the next two and one-half centuries.

Beyond the matters of political principle that stood at the center of the conflict for the Americans, they had specific grievances against the government in London. One concerned land. In 1763, for the sake of peace with the Indians, Britain had issued a Royal Proclamation prohibiting settlement west of a line drawn along the Appalachian Mountains. The Proclamation Line not only rendered worthless land grants given by the British to subjects who had fought against the French in the Seven Years' War but also transgressed a fundamental feature of eighteenth-century American life. Americans were, either themselves or by descent, settlers. The right to claim and settle land and develop it for farming was integral to the culture of British North America from its beginning. With the Proclamation Line, Britain proposed to restrict settlement for a purpose that, as the Americans saw it, did not take precedence over their right to acquire virgin territory.[25]

In addition, the Americans chafed at some of the constraints on their economic activities imposed by Britain's mercantilist laws, principally the Navigation Acts that dated from the seventeenth century. By these laws the colonists were, among other things, forbidden to trade freely with countries and their imperial possessions other than Great Britain and the British Empire. The restrictions made the colonies marginally poorer than they would have been without them; but the costs were not particularly high and certainly not high enough to prevent the prosperity that they enjoyed in the second half of the eighteenth century.[26]

Of particular relevance to these restrictions and the American attitude toward them was the fact that they were not at all rigorously enforced. The Proclamation Line failed to bring order to the territories reserved for the Indians or even prevent Americans from moving there,[27] and the colonials evaded the restrictions of the Navigation Acts through smuggling.[28] This had a major implication for the measures that Parliament enacted beginning in 1765 and the American responses to them. In the decade leading up to the outbreak of war each side believed that the other was violating, and that it was itself defending, the status quo in North America; and by its own lights each was correct.

The British were defending the de jure—the legal—status quo, according to which the imperial government in London had the right to make and implement laws for North America just as it did in Great Britain. The Americans, however, were insisting on preserving the de facto—the actual—status quo, in which, whatever their putative prerogatives, the British authorities had in fact historically exercised very little control over their North American colonies.

While London for the most part appointed colonial governors, real power—including the power to tax—resided in the local elected assemblies. Moreover, while in America as in Britain eligibility to vote depended on the ownership of property, in the colonies a far greater percentage of the male population did own property and so took part in elections. Proportionally, therefore, more people in North America than in the British Isles governed themselves through their votes.

The general British disengagement from North America, which the Anglo-Irish parliamentarian Edmund Burke called "salutary neglect" and from which the Stamp Act and the measures that followed represented a sharp break, had several sources, distance foremost among them. In the 1760s it took at least six weeks, and sometimes two or even three months, to cross the Atlantic. Moreover, the colonies stretched for 1,500 miles from north to south, outside the coastal cities the population tended to be widely scattered, and the thickly forested North American interior between the coast and the Mississippi River, over which the British had title as a result of the Seven Years' War, was, for practical purposes in the eighteenth century, largely impenetrable.

In truth, before that war London had had little incentive to try to exercise tighter control over the Americans. While begun with royal charters, colonies were largely private undertakings. The benefit from them about which the British cared most—insofar as they cared about the colonies at all—was economic; and for the first seven decades of the eighteenth century the economic returns from North America were more than satisfactory.[29] Finally, whatever attention and resources the British government had to devote to the world beyond the British Isles were invested in the recurrent wars with its cross-channel rival France, wars in which interests far more important than any in North America were in play.[30]

Because of the different definitions of the status quo, when the British decided to impose new taxes on the colonies, what came into dispute was the question of who would govern them. An old saying about private disputes has it that when the parties concerned say that the dispute is not about money, it is, in fact, about money. At its core, however, the dispute between the colonies and the British government over taxation was not in fact about money. It was about a fundamental political principle. What was at stake was nothing less than sovereignty. A central sovereign prerogative is, after all, the power to tax. Each side claimed that power for itself. While at least initially proclaiming their loyalty, in principle, to the British Empire, by asserting that Britain had no right to levy taxes on them the Americans were effectively declaring that they were, always had been, and forever ought to be sovereign—that is, independent. They went to war to protect that independence. The British, for their part, went to war to preserve what was just as vital to them—their imperial prerogatives, without which, they feared, they might lose all their imperial possessions and become vulnerable to the other European powers.[†]

[†] The British willingness to fight "must be found in the equation of sovereignty with the preservation of those interests that were considered indispensable to

Because they ended imperial control over the colonies, or at least Britain's claim to it, the war and the political disputes leading up to it have sometimes been seen in retrospect as the first instance of the kind of anti-imperial rebellion and emergence into independent statehood that became common in the twentieth century. The comparison misleads in an important respect. Twentieth-century anti-colonial movements claimed the right to independence on the basis of the principle of national self-determination, according to which every self-identified national group is entitled to its own independent state. That principle became a global norm in the course of the twentieth century, due in no small part to the efforts of the twenty-eighth American president, Woodrow Wilson.[31]

The principle did not, however, have anything like that status in the eighteenth century. Far from being an aberration, let alone politically unacceptable, the multinational empire was then the predominant, almost universally accepted form of political organization worldwide. Nor were the Americans challenging the principle of empire. In waging war against Great Britain they were not so much seeking independence as, in their own eyes, defending the independence that they already had and that the authorities in London were trying to revoke.[32]

Taxation being the essence of sovereignty, and sovereignty being the definition of statehood, the thirteen colonies were therefore acting as a state before the world recognized them as one—indeed, even before they themselves declared themselves to be one. In going to war against Great Britain, they were doing what weak states have so often done: seeking to defend their independence. Not surprisingly, in what the Americans came to call their Revolutionary War, they employed the typical strategies of the weak for this purpose.

Britain's status as a great power and without which not only the nation's leading position among the powers but also its very security and material well-being would be jeopardized." Robert W. Tucker and David C. Hendrickson, *The Fall of the First British Empire: Origins of the War of American Independence*, Baltimore and London: The Johns Hopkins University Press, 1982, p. 196. See also Brendan Simms, *Three Victories and a Defeat: The Rise and Fall of the First British Empire*, New York: Basic Books, 2007, pp. 629–630, 654–655.

The North American War

Two months after the skirmishes at Lexington and Concord the first important battle of the war took place, in Charlestown, just outside Boston. Colonial troops had laid siege to the British forces in the city and learned that the British were planning to send a detachment to fortify the surrounding hills, which would give them control of the Boston harbor. In anticipation of this maneuver, 1,200 of the colonial soldiers stealthily occupied two of the hills.[33] Early on June 17, the British became aware of the colonial positions and launched an attack. In the end they got the better of the fighting, as they usually did in battles that both sides chose to fight during the war. They captured the positions the rebels had held because the Americans ran out of ammunition and had to retreat to Cambridge, another town near Boston.

Yet in the larger scheme of things the battle counted as a success for the Americans. A number of officials in London and not a few in North America had believed that the American forces, untrained and ill-organized as they were, would be unable to stand up to the British redcoats and that with their inevitable humiliating defeats the rebellion would collapse. The Battle of Bunker Hill demonstrated this belief to be incorrect. The Americans gave a good account of themselves, inflicting, in fact, more casualties than they incurred.[34] They showed the British—and themselves—that, while outgunned and often outnumbered, they were willing and able to fight, an indispensable condition for resisting a stronger adversary.[35]

In June the Second Continental Congress, now functioning as a kind of government of the colonies, authorized a campaign to liberate Canada from British control. In late December, a small force led by Benedict Arnold, a gifted commander later to earn infamy in the annals of American history by going over to the British side, reached Quebec after a long and arduous journey. It was joined by another small American force led by Richard Montgomery. On the last day of 1775 they attacked the city but failed to capture it. They had hoped that the Canadian people would welcome, and even assist, them. This did not happen, which contributed to their failure. Ultimately the Americans had to retreat back across the border.[36]

On this occasion it was the Americans who fell victim to overconfidence. They made a mistake that was to be repeated at the end of the nineteenth century in the Philippines, in the twentieth century in Vietnam, and in the twenty-first century in Iraq. They overestimated the affinity of a foreign people for American intervention and American tutelage. The majority of Canadians in Quebec were French Catholics whose enthusiasm for joining their fates to armed English Protestants turned out, then and on subsequent occasions, to be severely limited.

The Continental Congress appointed George Washington as the head of the American army. This was the same George Washington who had taken part, two decades previously, in the skirmish in the Ohio Valley wilderness that had set in motion the long chain of events that had produced the war it became his duty to wage on behalf of the thirteen colonies. He had a major qualification for the job in the eyes of some members of the Congress: he was an important citizen of Virginia, whose full participation in a war triggered by events in Massachusetts was crucial for the success of that enterprise. Selecting a Virginian to lead an army largely composed of New Englanders would, it was hoped, help to ensure Virginia's commitment to the war effort.[37]

Washington had military experience, of course, but not in commanding troops or supervising logistical operations on the scale that his new position required. Nor, over the course of eight years, did he establish himself among the ranks of history's most daring, imaginative, or successful battlefield commanders. He turned out, however, to be the ideal man for the job he was given. Indeed, he proved to be indispensable for the success of what he called "the glorious cause" because of his personal qualities.

He was a man of iron integrity, considerable personal courage,[38] an unflagging commitment to hard work including tedious administration,[39] and shrewd judgment about both people and situations. His greatest achievement was to keep a rag-tag, often battered army in the field and fighting despite military setbacks, harsh living conditions, and only sporadic pay.‡

---

‡ "Six foot four inches tall and mounted on a white charger, he became a living legend during the war. He inspired the loyalty of his men, and showed humility in allowing junior commanders to vent their frustration. He was equally

The army that Washington commanded consisted entirely of volunteers. In comparison with the forces they were fighting they lacked experience, training, and discipline. Colonial militias sometimes augmented the Continental Army, although they often went home when the spirit moved them; and the American side benefited from partisan warfare, especially in the southern colonies in the latter part of the war. Still, the British forces in North America almost always outnumbered the American ones.[40] Thanks in no small part to Washington, the American forces sustained their will to fight, and their ability to fight improved over time.[41]

Another of Washington's major achievements was to maintain proper relations with the Continental Congress, which did not reliably provide him with the troops and supplies he needed. He always deferred to its ultimate authority, thereby establishing for the new country the essential democratic principle of civilian control of the military.

His personal virtues made George Washington the symbol of the country his efforts did so much to create. As early as 1779 Americans were celebrating his birthday. His appointment in 1775 began a fortunate pattern. In each of its three major wars—the Civil War and World War II being the others—the United States had a commander-in-chief well suited to the task that confronted it and him. George Washington belongs in the select company that includes Abraham Lincoln and Franklin D. Roosevelt. As a strictly military leader—with the confidence he inspired among his troops, his integrity and good judgment, and his knack for maintaining good relations with a variety of difficult allies and subordinates—the figures in American history he most closely resembles are the commander of the Union Army in the Civil War, Ulysses S. Grant, and the supreme commander of Allied forces in Europe in the Second World War, Dwight D. Eisenhower. All three

---

dispassionate in his often trying dealings with the French. He showed the same equanimity and diplomacy in working with Congress. He understood the politics of warfare. Most importantly, he kept his army intact and mostly out of reach of the British." Andrew Jackson O'Shaughnessey, *The Men Who Lost America: British Leadership, the American Revolution, and the Fate of the Empire*, New Haven and London: Yale University Press, 2013, p. 359.

generals served, in the wake of the wars they won, as president of the United States.

It was entirely appropriate for the United States to name its capital city after George Washington. Without him, the country for which Washington, D.C., served as the capital beginning in 1790 would not have come into existence, at least not when and as it did.

Washington had originally become a soldier because he wanted to win glory for himself, which could only be achieved in battle. He did fight a major battle against the British early in the war, on Long Island on August 27, 1776, in which the British side prevailed. Thereafter he abandoned his personal preference and settled on a defensive strategy, which was appropriate for the militarily inferior party to the conflict. He called it "a war of posts," which involved fighting from strong fortifications.[42] He relied on maneuver and speed to avoid a decisive blow from the British army, with the hope that the British would eventually abandon their efforts to subdue the colonies—as they eventually did. Popular hostility to the British among American civilians gave rise to harassment of British forces through guerrilla tactics, which supplemented the efforts of the Continental Army.

For their part, the militarily superior British went on the offensive. They sought to defeat and disperse the American forces and to deploy their own troops in order to divide the colonies. Also part of their strategy, although not always explicitly stated, was the expectation, or at least the hope, that once the rebel forces were defeated in battle London would be able to govern the colonies through the Americans who remained loyal to the Crown.[43]

British officials understood that they needed the colonies' acquiescence to reassert imperial control. Their troops could occupy the major port cities, although their experience in Boston showed them that this would be no easy task if the population actively opposed them. As a naval power without a tradition of a large standing army,[44] however, Britain would never be able to muster sufficient manpower to subdue all the towns, villages, and farms where ninety percent of the population lived,[45] let alone police the vast North American interior where rebels could find sanctuary and from which they could mount resistance.[46] The British recognized, at least tacitly, the truth of the assertion by a French observer that "though the people of America might be conquered by well-disciplined European troops, the country of America was unconquerable."[47] Geography made available to the Americans one of the major ways that the weak can thwart the strong: difficulty of access.

The loyalists on whom the British counted did make up a substantial part of the population of the colonies—twenty percent by one estimate. As in all the country's wars, some Americans opposed the government's policies. Unlike subsequent wars, however, in the Revolutionary War almost all of the dissenters actually favored the other side and perhaps 20,000 of them fought in regiments of the British army. Also unlike the succeeding American conflicts, at the war's end many of those who had opposed the rebels against British rule—between 60,000 and 100,000 of them—fled to still-British Canada.[48] The loyalists were not the majority, however, and during the war the British did not manage to put their sympathies to effective use. To secure the political goal for which they were fighting—the maintenance of effective control over their colonies—the British had, to use a phrase that became popular during the American war in Indochina two centuries later, to win the hearts and minds of the Americans. This they did not manage to do.

In strictly military terms, however, in the initial stages of the war Great Britain enjoyed appreciable success. After the Battle of Bunker Hill the main British force moved, by ship, to New York, which its commanders considered the American center of gravity. After the British victory at Long Island Washington's troops retreated, first to Manhattan, then to New Jersey, and ultimately to Pennsylvania. The British commanders did not pursue them vigorously, however, thereby missing what seems in retrospect to have been their best chance to crush the colonial army. Moreover, after the defeat Washington conducted successful raids on British encampments in New Jersey: in Trenton in December 1776 and in Princeton in January 1777. While of little military value, these sallies, like the first battle outside Boston the previous year, fortified American morale and demonstrated that the Continental troops were, despite their defeat in New York, willing and able to continue the fight.

While the army was fighting, the Continental Congress took a major political step. In the month before the Battle of New York, on July 4, 1776, it issued a declaration of independence. It proclaimed that "these united colonies are, and of right ought to be, free and independent states; that they are absolved from all allegiance to the British Crown, and that all political connection between them and the state of Great Britain is and ought to be, totally dissolved. . . ." Over the years the Declaration, the bulk of which listed the colonials' grievances against the British sovereign, George III, came to be regarded as the founding document of the country that became the United States of America. It assumed a status in American public life in some ways comparable to the Bible in American religious life.[49]

For much of the nation's history, most Americans were familiar with the opening words of the document's second paragraph: "We hold these truths to be self-evident: that all men are created equal; that they are endowed by their Creator with certain inalienable rights; that among these are life, liberty, and the pursuit of happiness. . . ." The words encapsulate the ideology that has pervaded American politics and strongly influenced American foreign policy for 250 years. On July 4, 1776, the American Revolution had its most ideological moment.

While the members of the Continental Congress who signed it certainly believed what the Declaration said, they had an ulterior motive for issuing it when they did, a motive central to their hopes of securing the independence they announced. They had known from the beginning that, as with all weak powers, their chances of successfully resisting a stronger adversary would increase to the extent that they could enlist on their side other countries—the more the better and the stronger the better. They also realized that, while the continental powers that were Great Britain's geopolitical rivals would be happy to see the British suffer a defeat in North America, and might themselves be willing to contribute to administering such a setback, they would not extend themselves on behalf of rebellious provinces of the British Empire that aspired merely to better treatment within it.[50]

By declaring independence, the Americans hoped to make themselves a more attractive recipient of European assistance by showing their seriousness and determination. The proclamation of the goal of complete separation from Great Britain demonstrated that they were staking everything—their lives, their fortunes, and their sacred honor, as the text of the Declaration put it—on the struggle with their imperial overlords.[51]

The Americans did gain European support, thereby employing, along with defense and difficulty of access, the third strategy of weak powers: diversion. The assistance they obtained proved to be crucial for the successful outcome of their war. Declaring independence did not by itself, however, suffice to secure that assistance. The European powers gave the Americans important support after, and because of, the Americans' first significant military victory, which did not come until a full fifteen months after July 4, 1776.

The British planned two major military campaigns for 1777, with the aim of ending the war on their terms. General William Howe moved his troops from New York to Philadelphia, defeating Washington's forces at Brandywine and Germantown and occupying the city on September 26, 1777. (In anticipation of the British initiative, the Continental Congress had moved to Baltimore the previous winter.)

In the second campaign the British general John Burgoyne led an army south from Canada along a route passing across Lake Champlain and down the Hudson Valley. The objective was to cut off New England from the other colonies,[52] with the expectation that this would help to bring the rebellion to an end. Burgoyne's army encountered logistical difficulties and harassment by American irregulars on its march south.[53] At Saratoga the British troops met an American army commanded by General Horatio Gates. For the first time in the war, in a major battle the Americans got the better of the fighting. On October 17, Burgoyne surrendered.

Although less well known than other military engagements in this and subsequent conflicts over the next two and a half centuries, Saratoga counts as one of the three most important battles Americans in arms ever won. It proved to be the turning point in the Revolutionary War, as did Gettysburg in the Civil War and the Battle of the Atlantic did in World War II.[54] The victory crystallized a decision by the government of the French monarch Louis XVI formally to enter the war on the side of the colonies. The French entry transformed the conflict, changing it from one that the weaker Americans had to devote all their efforts to avoiding losing to one that, with a major assist from others, they could hope to win.

The European War

In a poem written sixty-two years after the event, Ralph Waldo Emerson called the opening salvo of the skirmishes at Lexington and Concord "the shot heard round the world."[55] Emerson exaggerated: no evidence has come to light suggesting that the beginning of the war of American independence registered at, for instance, the imperial Chinese court in Peking. The rebellion did, however, arouse intense interest, and considerable sympathy for the Americans, in Paris.

As an absolute monarchy the French government had no use for the principles on which the colonials based their rebellion. Indeed, six years after the end of the war a revolution far more sweeping, and with much wider global and historical consequences, was to overthrow King Louis XVI and his regime.[56] The French did, however, have a compelling reason, rooted in the great-power politics of Europe, for wishing for Great Britain to suffer a defeat in North America. The greatest European power of the seventeenth century, France had seen Britain emerge as its chief rival in the eighteenth and score a major victory in the Seven Years' War. In the Anglo-French rivalry a loss for one counted as a gain for the other. If the colonists prevailed in their contest with the British Empire, this would weaken Britain's global position and reduce British prestige, to the advantage of France. The French thus had a strong motive to hope for, and to work for, American success.

The Americans had begun to look abroad for support as soon as hostilities broke out.[57] In November 1775 the Continental Congress established a secret committee of correspondence for the purpose of communicating with potential friends abroad.[58] It appointed two agents in France (Arthur Lee and Silas Deane) and in December 1776 dispatched a far more important representative, Benjamin Franklin, to Paris. Born in Boston in 1705, Franklin had had a distinguished career in Philadelphia as a printer, editor, scientist, and inventor. He had founded several civic organizations, including one that became the University of Pennsylvania. He had also had considerable diplomatic experience, as the agent in London for the Pennsylvania Assembly and then for several other colonies as well. Franklin did more than any other individual to win French support for the American cause. He charmed the French, who treated him "as something between a hero and a saint,"[59] and was able to coax arms and substantial loans[60] from their government. He was by far the most important diplomat of the Revolutionary War and thus, because the stakes in that war were so high and the need for foreign support so acute, arguably the most important diplomat in all of American history.

Soon after the rebellion broke out, France began a clandestine program of assistance to the Americans, supplying arms that were crucial for keeping the Continental Army fighting and especially in winning the Battle of Saratoga.[61] In the wake of that battle the British offered the colonials a settlement that conceded most of their demands but stopped short of granting them independence. Franklin deftly used this offer as leverage to persuade the French government to sign a formal treaty of alliance with the Americans, which it did on February 6, 1778.[62] By the terms of the treaty, France officially joined the war against Great Britain.[63]

The next year Spain became allied with France against Britain. The Spanish monarchy had no more reason to wish for the triumph of America's republican—that is, anti-monarchical—principles than did the French and indeed had good reason to fear the rise of a country that could compete with it for territory in North America, as the independent United States soon did. Spain entered the war nonetheless, to gain the return of the Mediterranean island of Gibraltar, located off its coast, which it had ceded to the British in 1713. The Netherlands traded with the colonies, angering the British, who declared war on the Dutch in 1780, thereby broadening the coalition against them. Russia organized a league of neutrals among the European states to protect their shipping against the Royal Navy, thus indirectly aiding the colonials' cause as well.[64]

The French alliance and the diplomatic alignment that followed transformed the war, to the advantage of the Americans, in two ways. It enhanced the fighting power of the colonials' armed forces. After signing the treaty the French sent not only arms and money but also troops and ships to North America, which enabled a joint Franco-American force to win the decisive battle of the war in 1781.

Just as important for American success, the formal, full-fledged French entry into the war dramatically broadened its geographic scope, compelling the British to disperse their own forces, including their navy.[65] This reduced its presence off the North American coast. Great Britain had to defend its possessions, and its naval positions, in the Caribbean and the Mediterranean. It had to take seriously the prospect of a seaborne assault on its home islands: the French and the Spanish made serious plans for such a campaign in 1779, although they failed to follow through on it.[66] North America became, for the British, merely one theater of war among several, and not necessarily the most important one.

After 1778, in fact, the geopolitical alignment of the Seven Years' War and of the previous Anglo-French conflicts, which had favored Great Britain, was reversed.[67] In the previous war France had had to contend with Britain's ally Prussia on the European continent in addition to confronting Britain overseas. The diversion of attention and resources that this imposed on the French contributed significantly to the British victory. In the wake of the Franco-American alliance, by contrast, it was the British who had to wage war in multiple theaters— on the North American continent but also in several of the world's seas and oceans. Whereas Britain had had an ally willing and able to fight on land in the earlier conflict, it was France that had one in the later war in the form of the Continental Army. As had been the case with France between 1756 and 1763, this handicap weighed on Britain's military efforts in the Revolutionary War, with ultimately decisive results.

In the wake of the Franco-American treaty, the British shifted the emphasis of their North American military operations to the southern colonies, which had greater economic importance than the others for Britain and were believed to harbor more robust loyalist sentiment.[68] The southern campaign enjoyed some success. The British army captured two major port cities—Savannah, Georgia, in August 1779 and Charleston, South Carolina, in May 1780. On the second occasion an American army of 5,500 surrendered, the greatest loss of soldiers for the Continental Army in the entire war. The British also, however, encountered serious guerrilla resistance.[69] By the summer of 1781 Americans had regained control of most of the lower south. The campaign for their hearts and minds had failed where it had been deemed most promising.[70]

In 1781 the British forces in the south, commanded by Lord Charles Cornwallis, moved north into Virginia. There, at Yorktown, they came into contact with a combined French and American army almost twice their size: George Washington and his French counterpart, Count Jean Baptiste Rochambeau, had skillfully marched their troops rapidly south from New York,[71] displaying a talent for logistics that would become a hallmark of American military affairs thereafter. Crucially, taking advantage of the dispersal of the Royal Navy, French ships under the command of Admiral Francois de Grasse controlled the waters off the Virginia coast. Cornwallis was trapped. On October 19 his army marched out from its fortifications to lay down its arms. As it did, a band played "The World Turned Upside Down."[72]

The British defeat at Yorktown, painful and humiliating though it was, need not have ended the war. His Majesty's forces retained a powerful position in North America. The king himself favored fighting on. But the government in London fell and the new one sought peace. Or rather, the dominant figure in the new government, the Earl of Shelburne,[73] wished to end Britain's confrontation with the broad coalition it confronted and decided to try, by diplomatic means, to eliminate the Americans from it, the better to cope with his country's European adversaries. No doubt the colonies were important, important enough to have waged war for six years to try to retain them. By 1781, however, other global and imperial interests had come to seem more important, at least to Shelburne. Thus began a pattern, which recurred over the next hundred years, in which a more powerful Great Britain nonetheless conciliated a weaker United States for the sake of British interests apart from the issue dividing the two countries at the moment.

Although, like a number of his colleagues—Edmund Burke prominent among them—Shelburne had opposed the measures that had led to the American war, he had also opposed granting independence to the colonies. He came to realize in the course of negotiations with Benjamin Franklin, however, that independence had become the indispensable condition on the American side for settling the conflict. He finally conceded it in July 1782.[74] While the Americans, for their part, had promised the French not to make a separate peace with Great Britain, in effect Franklin did just that.

The negotiations dragged on for another six months, but on January 20, 1783, the British came to terms with all the other belligerent parties. The Americans, the French, and the Spanish (acting on behalf of the Dutch as well) concluded an armistice and preliminary peace agreement with Great Britain. The final treaty was signed in Paris on September 3, 1783.

Its crucial clause read: "His Britannic Majesty acknowledges the said United States . . . to be free Sovereign and independent States. . . ."[75] Great Britain officially recognized the sovereignty that the Americans had been claiming, sometimes without fully realizing that that was what they were doing, since 1765. The treaty established the borders of the new country: as well, of course, as the Atlantic Ocean to the east they included the line of the Great Lakes to the north (a line close to the twenty-first-century boundary with Canada), the thirty-first parallel (now part of the northern border of Florida) to the south, and the Mississippi River to the west.[76]

As a result of the war the French regained some of the prestige they had lost twenty years earlier but made few tangible gains. Spain received some territorial compensation, but not Gibraltar.[77] The loss of the American colonies aside, Great Britain did reasonably well by the settlement.[78] Moreover, while the British had gone to war because of the fear that the loss of the colonies would seriously degrade their standing as a great power,[79] in the ensuing decades this fear was not borne out. A little more than three decades later, in fact, after a long series of European wars triggered by the French Revolution, Britain emerged as the greatest of the great powers.[80]

The weaker party to the Revolutionary War, the American side, managed to defeat—that is, to gain its objective against the armed opposition of—the stronger one partly because of British weaknesses and mistakes. The British political class was divided from the outset about the confrontation with the colonies, with some important figures believing that the effort to impose taxes on them was unwise and more of them critical of their government's war policy that colonial resistance to those taxes triggered.[81] The military men on the ground in North America had apparently mixed feelings about fighting against people of British stock and fellow Protestants who were claiming to be defending the rights of Englishmen.[82]

Those commanders made some tactical misjudgments. Howe should have pursued Washington's army after defeating it on Long Island in 1776, for example, and should have made it a point to try to reinforce Burgoyne from the south the next year. The military leaders, whose aristocratic backgrounds qualified them for their positions—as distinct from their American counterparts, for whom merit and achievement on the battlefield mattered much more—seem, in retrospect, to have been at times timid, complacent, and unimaginative when the opposite qualities would have better served their cause.

Still, the credit for the outcome of the war belongs mainly to the Americans, and in particular to their ability to make use of the three strategies the weak can hope to employ to oppose the strong. First and foremost among these was defense—the willingness to fight. Without this the colonials would not have been able to take advantage of the other two. Fight they certainly did, not always effectively and seldom with clear battlefield success but persistently and at considerable cost. The death toll on the American side was 25,000, a large number for eighteenth-century warfare that amounted to nearly one percent of the population of the thirteen colonies. It stands, proportionately, as the highest toll for any American armed conflict except the Civil War.[83]

Just why they fought is not easy to determine: the motivation no doubt varied among those who took up arms, who themselves probably had more than one reason for the risks they ran. It does seem likely, however, that the principles for which its architects said the war was being waged, above all the defense of liberty as they defined it, had something to do with the sacrifices Americans made. In this way ideology played an important role in the first American war.

The Americans' determination to fight, and the increasing prowess on the battlefield that they displayed, especially at Saratoga, convinced the French government that entry into the war against Britain would pay geopolitical dividends. Without French participation the Americans could not have won the Battle of Yorktown. More broadly, the war against the European powers that Britain had to wage after the Franco-American treaty of 1778 diverted and diluted the attention and the resources that London could devote to the conflict with the colonies. This ultimately persuaded Shelburne of the need to conciliate the colonials; and he came to accept that conciliation required conceding independence.

The British had another reason for ending the war on American terms, which the American commitment to active resistance to their rule also triggered. Even if they had persisted after Yorktown, even if they had managed to win subsequent battles against the American and French forces, the British had no feasible way of achieving their goal, which was the restoration of the pre-1765 status quo in North America. So vast was the territory that the colonies covered, so widely scattered was the American population, and so palpable was the evidence of their rejection of rule from London that in order to govern America the British would have had to deploy there permanently an army far larger than any that they had ever raised or had any prospect, given the British political system, of raising.[84]

In the nineteenth century and through the first half of the twentieth, the British were able to control their imperial possessions in India, which were far larger in both territory and population than the thirteen colonies, with very few officials and British soldiers. The social, political, and cultural conditions in India made this possible. By 1783—indeed by 1765—the comparable conditions in North America, in combination with the facts of geography, were such that imperial governance of the kind Britain was willing and able to impose there was no longer possible. By their determination to resist, the Americans thus activated the third strategy of the weak: difficulty of access.[85] Along with defense and the diversion of having to fight other European powers, it brought them victory in their war against the richer, more populous, and militarily more formidable British Empire.

The Constitution and Foreign Policy

The new sovereign state that Great Britain and other countries recognized as independent in 1783 was also a weak power. It was weak both in comparison to the great powers of Europe and in its political capacity to muster resources for collective efforts, including war. In 1781 the Continental Congress had adopted the Articles of Confederation to govern their relations among themselves, and the Articles served as the charter for the first government of the United States. They vested virtually all power in the governments of the thirteen colonies that became the first thirteen states. The new country had almost no effective central authority capable of the functions that central governments have typically performed: raising revenue through taxation, enacting laws applicable to all citizens, regulating its relations with the rest of the world, and defending the country.

The assembly for which the Articles provided did manage to pass one important piece of legislation: the Northwest Ordinance of 1787 set out the procedures by which other states could be added to the original thirteen. In general, however, the design of the Articles left the United States vulnerable to a variety of perils, which soon became apparent.

Trade had played a major role in the economic life of the thirteen colonies, and the new country expected that role to continue. Indeed, Americans expected their trade to expand since they had freed themselves from the restrictions imposed by the Navigation Acts. Great Britain remained by far the largest trading partner, but the British closed their West Indian possessions to American commerce.[86] Nor were the other European powers more forthcoming.[87] Independence did not bring prosperity—quite the opposite.[88] Without an effective government the United States had no means of negotiating with or retaliating against other countries in matters of trade. It had, that is, no means of conducting a trade policy.

It faced difficulties from the original inhabitants of North America as well. Settlers moving westward threatened the Indians' lands, their livelihoods, and sometimes their lives, and those who were threatened fought back. Soon after independence the Americans confronted what amounted to a full-scale war in the west,[89] but, inasmuch as the volunteer force that had fought for independence had disbanded, they lacked both an army to fight it and the mechanisms needed to raise one.

The challenge from the Indians was all the more ominous because the European powers provided some assistance to them.[90] Moreover, the Europeans had wider ambitions than simply enhancing the Indians' capacity for resisting the settlers. Since historically almost every republic—which was what the Americans, having disavowed a monarchy, had established in North America—had proved perishable,[91] it was widely anticipated that the United States would not endure as an independent country.[92] If and when it failed, at least some in France, Spain, and Great Britain hoped to seize parts of it for themselves.[93] Each of them already held territory in the Western Hemisphere—the French in the Caribbean, the Spanish to the south and west of the new United States, and the British in Canada.

By the terms of the 1783 Paris Treaty the British promised to evacuate their military outposts south of the new border between the United States and Canada. They did not do so, however, maintaining garrisons from Lake Champlain to Lake Superior, ostensibly because the new American government had failed to pay its debts to Britain.[94]

To compound the perils to the new country, in 1786 and 1787 a military threat arose from an American source. Daniel Shays, a wounded veteran of the Revolutionary War, led an armed uprising in western Massachusetts to protest economic conditions there.[95] To these economic, political, and military challenges the infant republic, with its all but nonexistent central government, had no effective way of responding. The fear spread among Americans that without dramatic changes in its governmental arrangements the United States of America, a weak state in a hostile world, would not survive.[96]

Accordingly, a convention assembled in Philadelphia on May 25, 1787, with the intent of strengthening the American system of government. It eventually produced a constitution, which has governed the United States, with some modifications, ever since. In keeping with the spirit of democracy, the participants worked out the final document through compromise. The most important series of compromises addressed the central dilemma the delegates to the Constitutional Convention confronted. On the one hand, they knew that the country needed a more powerful central government to deal with the problems it faced then and would continue to face in the future. On the other hand, Americans had recently fought for independence precisely in order to free themselves from what they considered a too-powerful central authority in London. The delegates therefore had to strike a balance between an oppressive and an impotent public authority.[97]

They sought to guard against the danger of tyranny by dividing power. They divided it horizontally, dispersing it among the legislative, executive, and judicial branches of the federal government through what came to be called the separation of powers. They divided power vertically as well, with authority vested in both the federal and the various state governments, a design known as federalism. The Convention decided to give the federal government the power to regulate trade, the better to be able to negotiate favorable agreements with other countries.[98]

The delegates to the Convention also struck compromises between the large and small states over the formula to be used for legislative representation, with membership in one chamber of the Congress, that of the House of Representatives, apportioned according to population and the other, the Senate, allotting two members to each state no matter its size. They compromised as well on the issue of slavery, which divided the Southern and Northern states and grew so bitter and contentious over the decades that it provoked a great civil war in 1861.[99]

After it was drafted, the Convention decided that the Constitution would have to be ratified by nine of the thirteen states. Its opponents, the anti-federalists, believed that it gave too much power to the central government and that, as it stood, it placed at risk the liberty that Americans had gone to war against Great Britain to protect. To reassure the critics, ten amendments were added to the original document, which were chiefly devoted to enumerating the individual rights on which the government was forbidden to trespass. On June 21, 1788, the ninth state, New Hampshire, voted for ratification and the Constitution went into effect.

It became the central text and framework for American public life. Over the next two centuries most Constitutional issues involved one or another aspect of domestic American politics and economics; but in its origin the document had a great deal to do with the country's relations with the world beyond the United States.

A leading goal in negotiating and adopting the Constitution was to ensure the capacity of the infant republic to defend itself. In its first sentence, which states the purposes in drafting it, providing for the common defense is listed third, after forming a more perfect union and ensuring domestic tranquility but before promoting the general welfare and securing the blessings of liberty. Of the eighty-five essays in *The Federalist Papers*, a series of essays written by James Madison, Alexander Hamilton, and John Jay—the nation's fourth president, first secretary of the treasury, and first chief justice of the Supreme Court, respectively—to persuade their countrymen to ratify the Constitution, the first twenty-nine dealt with foreign policy.[100]

The Constitution achieved its main foreign policy goal: it strengthened the United States. A principal theme of American history, and the principal theme of the 250-year history of American foreign policy, is the expansion of the country's power: a century after the protests against the Stamp Act it, had graduated from the category of weak power to the more exclusive ranks of the planet's great powers, and in subsequent decades ascended to even loftier positions in the international system. The exponential increase in American power came about through territorial expansion, population growth, the mastery of the Industrial Revolution, and success in war. The first self-strengthening exercise, however, and perhaps the most important one of all because without it the subsequent increases in power might never have occurred, was the reorganization of the government of the United States through the writing and the adoption of the Constitution.

The delegates at Philadelphia designed a structure of government strong enough to preside over the remarkable expansion of the nation's geographic scope and economic production and to win a series of wars, but without the permanent encroachment on individual liberty that so many eighteenth-century Americans feared, although occasional encroachments did occur. The governmental architecture the Constitution put in place lent itself, moreover, to one of the principal recurrent features of American foreign policy: its democratic character. The separation of powers made room for a plurality of voices and viewpoints on all issues of public concern, including issues of foreign policy. The Constitutional design encouraged a pluralist process of foreign policymaking by providing multiple places in the government where citizens could make their opinions known and urge officials— the right of petition being constitutionally protected—to adopt them.

Having first achieved independence and then put in place a political system suitable for defending and taking advantage of it, the Americans hoped they could now be free to concentrate on their own internal affairs. This was not to be. In the year after the Constitution went into effect and the first government to be formed under its auspices was chosen, the most important European political event in a thousand years took place. The shock waves from the massive political earthquake known as the French Revolution reverberated around the world. That epochal event gave rise, among other things, to more than two decades of war in Europe on a very large scale. The wars following the French Revolution reached across the Atlantic Ocean and drew in a reluctant United States.

2

In the Shadow of the French Revolution, 1788–1815

The New Republic

As mandated by the newly adopted Constitution, the United States chose a national government in 1788. It elected its first Congress, which sat for two years. George Washington performed yet another service for the country he had done so much to create by becoming the head of the executive branch—the first magistrate, or president. The distinguished citizens drawn from the thirteen states who formed what came to be called the Electoral College chose him unanimously for the position, the only occupant of the office ever to be honored in this way.[1]

Although the Constitution had, Americans hoped, better equipped them than had the Articles of Confederation to meet challenges to their security, indeed to their national independence, it had not eliminated those challenges. Actual or potential threats in North America came not only from Great Britain, ensconced in Canada to the north, and from Spain, with its vast territories to the south, but also from Native Americans determined to protect their own land to the west.

While wary of these hostile presences on their home continent, and while creating three executive departments relevant to international affairs—State, Treasury, and War—the new government hoped that its foreign policy would consist entirely of commercial matters. It hoped, specifically, to expand trade as substantially as it could. These hopes were not fulfilled. Instead, for the first quarter century of its formal national existence, the foreign policy of the United States was dominated by a European event that Americans, like almost all Europeans, did not anticipate and over which the new country, as a weak and distant power, had no control: the French Revolution.

Just as the Seven Years' War led to the American Revolution, so, too, the Revolutionary War in North America led to the French Revolution in Europe, and in the same way. Like the British government in the earlier conflict, the government of France ran up debts to finance its contribution to the later one.[2] Just as the British government passed the Stamp Act in 1765 to raise the needed funds, so King Louis XVI convened a long-dormant assembly, the Estates-General, in 1789[3] for the same purpose. The body quickly became radicalized, sparking disorder and violence in Paris and across France. In 1791 it adopted the country's first written constitution and the next year it sent the king himself to the guillotine. There followed a period of terror in which 17,000 people were executed. In 1799, France's most successful general, Napoleon Bonaparte, seized power in a coup d'état and in 1804 proclaimed and crowned himself emperor.

At its outset, Americans saw the French Revolution as a replay of their own, with some even concluding that what they had accomplished had inspired the French.[4] The two events did have features in common. Both ended monarchical rule. The makers of both revolutions declared that power properly resided with the people, not with a hereditary monarch, and proclaimed fealty to certain inalienable individual rights.

The French Revolution had much greater global and historical significance, however, and far more potent consequences than did its American counterpart. It took place not 3,000 miles from the western shore of Europe but in Europe itself, which by the late eighteenth century had become the richest and most powerful part of the planet. The world experienced what happened in North America as a minor tremor, the events in France as a massive earthquake. Moreover, while the American Revolution detached several remote provinces from the British Crown but left King George on his throne and the British political system intact, the French Revolution entirely eliminated the French monarchy—in the seventeenth and eighteenth centuries the most important one in Europe—and thus threatened hereditary rulers everywhere. It also dispossessed France's aristocracy and the

French branch of the wealthy, powerful, and long-established Catholic Church.

The international consequences of the American and the French Revolutions differed as well. While the Revolutionary War in North America proved to be simply another episode—and hardly the most consequential one—in the long-running Anglo-French rivalry that would persist through the nineteenth century, the French Revolution convulsed all of Europe and much of the world beyond, dislodging long-ruling regimes and redrawing borders on a scale never before seen. It turned out, along with the process of substituting machines for human power known as the Industrial Revolution that began in Great Britain at roughly the same time, to be one of the two defining developments of the modern age, with its influence continuing to the present day.[5]

The French Revolution had an impact far beyond France's borders through the force of its example but also, beginning in 1792, by war, which raged almost uninterruptedly for almost a quarter century. Throughout this long spell of warfare France once again confronted Great Britain. The British pursued their familiar strategy of seeking to establish and maintain maritime supremacy while helping to forge and sustain a continental coalition to oppose the French army. Ultimately this approach achieved victory, but only after twenty-three years of fighting, the formation of seven different coalitions (France having defeated or frustrated the first six), and five million deaths.

France proved more difficult to defeat than in the past. It managed to conquer more of Europe and the world than previously because of the social and political effects of the Revolution, which made possible a more extensive mobilization for war of French society—"the nation in arms"—than ever before. The Revolution supplied new motives for French soldiers, who fought on behalf of ideological principles— liberty, equality, and fraternity—as well as the power and the glory of the French nation. It furnished able commanders, with the ablest of all being Napoleon himself. Rather than eighteenth-century-style campaigns of maneuver employing professional soldiers and directed by aristocrats who owed their positions to their noble lineages, France waged wars of unlimited conquest. It fielded the largest European army since the time of ancient Rome, an army that eagerly sought and won battles under the direction of daring and resourceful generals who had proved their merit as commanders in the field.[6]

The United States played a distinctly minor role in this great upheaval. To Europe's warring powers the new country was only a pawn in their game, but it was a part of that game. It was, that is, a weak power on the fringes of an epochal clash between and among the great powers. While the United States had no effect on the course of the French Revolution and a very limited effect on the wars that followed it, however, the reverse was not true: they had a powerful impact on both American domestic affairs and foreign policy.

At home, as the Revolution in France became more radical, it polarized American opinion, and the rift it created became the basis for the first great cleavage in American politics. For America's relations with the rest of the world, the European earthquake and its aftershocks had contradictory consequences. On the one hand, the wars led to expanded trade. While America strove to avoid taking sides, its merchants traded with the warring countries wherever and whenever they could. Americans also benefited from the demands for their ships to transport food and finished goods among ports in the Caribbean and in Europe.[7]

Moreover, the European powers' preoccupation with one another during this period allowed them less time and attention and fewer resources to pursue schemes they might otherwise have hatched to expand their influence in North America.[8] On the other hand, the young republic found itself unwillingly drawn into Europe's deadly quarrels, by both sides. Eventually the American government felt compelled to go to war with Great Britain.

Early American foreign policy arose from the impact of the French Revolution in combination with a great domestic political divide that opened after independence was won, a divide based on radically different visions of the new country's future that underpinned its first two political parties—the Federalists and the Republicans. The visions had mainly to do with American domestic arrangements but encompassed the new republic's relations with the world as well. Two major figures in the American Revolution and the affairs of the early republic became the leading architects of and spokesmen for these two visions: the Federalist Alexander Hamilton and the Republican Thomas Jefferson.

Hamilton served with distinction in the Continental Army and became a close advisor to George Washington, who appointed him the first secretary of the treasury. He foresaw the United States growing into a mighty commercial and industrial republic, the peer of the European great powers.[9] He took as his model for the American future Great Britain's progress in the century after 1688, and was particularly impressed with that country's financial strength.[10]

Jefferson was the principal author of the Declaration of Independence of 1776 who served as governor of Virginia and then minister to France and became the first secretary of state, in which role he squabbled with his fellow cabinet member Hamilton. Jefferson had a different vision for the American future. He wanted to create a republic of yeoman farmers, perhaps in a series of agrarian republics stretching across North America.[11] What he valued above all, and sought to cultivate in the new country, was virtue, not power. He believed that the commerce, manufacturing, cities, and debt that Hamilton favored corrupted virtue, and so he opposed them. The expansion of government that Hamilton's vision inevitably required, Jefferson was convinced, threatened the precious liberty that the thirteen colonies had fought a war against Great Britain to protect.

Jefferson promoted continental expansion so as to have ample land for Americans to farm. Hamilton also supported American expansion, but with an emphasis on commercial expansion.[12] Hamilton saw society as naturally and properly hierarchical, while Jefferson was a radical egalitarian, which was ironic given their social origins: Jefferson came from the closest American equivalent to a European aristocracy. He was a gentleman farmer and slave owner from Virginia. Hamilton was born illegitimate on the small Caribbean island of Nevis and made his way in the world through ambition and ability.

Jefferson became the nation's third president. The political party that he founded, known initially as the Republicans, dominated American politics for most of the first half of the nineteenth century and sustained a continuous and influential existence thereafter, although for most of that time under a different name—the Democrats. Hamilton, by contrast, never held another significant public position after leaving the Treasury Department. His life ended prematurely when he was killed in a duel with the onetime vice president Aaron Burr in July

1804. Yet Hamilton's ideas have done a great deal to shape public life in the United States ever since. Hamilton is, along with Martin Luther King Jr., one of the two Americans who have exerted the most influence on the country's public affairs without ever having held elective office.

The urban, industrial United States that developed in the second half of the nineteenth century, and by virtue of its industrial prowess became a great power, more closely resembles his vision than Jefferson's. In the Civil War, the Union embodied Hamiltonian economic preferences, while the Confederacy conformed in important ways to the Jeffersonian model. The Union, of course, prevailed, and its values and institutions predominated thereafter.

In fact, in the more than 200 years since the two men set out their differing visions, the United States has incorporated elements drawn from each, a trend illustrated by the presidency of America's most important twentieth-century chief executive, Franklin D. Roosevelt. Roosevelt did a great deal to elevate Jefferson in the pantheon of American leaders. It was he who presided over the creation, in 1943, of a memorial dedicated to the third president in Washington, D.C. Roosevelt was also the architect of the greatest expansion of the federal government in American history, a development that would presumably have appalled Jefferson, who feared and resisted federal power all his life.[13] In 1943, however, the United States was waging war against powerful dictatorships and Jefferson commended himself to Roosevelt as the most conspicuous champion in the nation's history of the political value on behalf of which America was then fighting: liberty.[14]

So Franklin Roosevelt, and most Americans, could fairly be characterized as both Hamiltonian and Jeffersonian. Unlike Jefferson, Hamilton lacks a full-scale monument in the nation's capital. He is remembered by a statue in front of the Treasury building, next to the White House. Yet the twenty-first-century city of Washington, where the statue is located, with its many departments and agencies, its formidable financial apparatus, and its status as the capital of the most powerful country in the world, can stand as a monument to Alexander Hamilton.

Hamilton and Jefferson differed on foreign policy as well. Hamilton assumed that international politics would proceed as it always had, with rivalry and sometimes war the normal condition of relations between states. Given this enduring reality, he believed, the United States should aim to strengthen itself in order to survive, and thrive, in the inevitably competitive and dangerous international system.

Jefferson, by contrast, pioneered the alternative approach to foreign policy, which, since his day, has recurred in the conduct of the nation's foreign relations. He advocated reforming the international order in two ways: by encouraging the spread of liberty—that is, democracy—and by transforming the rules and procedures of interstate relations so as to eliminate the age-old practice of war. The first of these reforms, he thought, would lead to the second: in common with a number of his prominent contemporaries, in particular the pamphleteer Thomas Paine, and Jefferson's close colleague and successor as president James Madison, he believed the abolition of war to be feasible by replacing war-prone monarchies with pacific republics like the United States.[15]

Unlike Hamilton, Jefferson had the opportunity to conduct American foreign policy himself and, committed though he was to transforming international relations, he pursued some distinctly Hamiltonian policies. He authorized war against the Barbary pirates off the Mediterranean coast of Africa to combat their practice of capturing Americans and holding them for ransom, for example, and was not above threatening war against the European powers,[16] a threat that his successor as president James Madison actually carried out.

In fact, as with its domestic affairs, the foreign policy of the United States has incorporated both approaches. It has, like other countries, routinely (and with considerable success) followed the kinds of policies that Hamilton envisioned. Since 1783 it has engaged in eleven significant wars[17] and many other lesser skirmishes. From the 1950s it has maintained large military forces, even in peacetime—indeed the most powerful forces in the world. At the same time, however, not least during the Jefferson and Madison administrations and to a greater degree than in other countries, the desire to promote liberty and to abolish war has influenced America's relations with others, particularly in the wake of World War I through the initiatives of the twenty-eighth president, Woodrow Wilson. American foreign policy has had a persistently ideological component.

Throughout the wars of the French Revolution the United States remained, in comparison with Britain and France, a weak power, incapable of defeating either in an all-out war. During this period the strategies available to the weak on which the Americans had capitalized during their war of independence were once again in evidence.

The two contrasting approaches both to domestic affairs and to foreign policy shaped the American approach to the problems and opportunities that the Wars of the French Revolution created for the United States. Hamilton and the Federalists were first dismayed and then appalled by the radical turn the French Revolution took;[18] and they had felt, since independence and despite the war they had fought to secure it, an affinity for France's main adversary, Great Britain. Jefferson and the Republicans, by contrast, greeted the great upheaval in France with enthusiasm and Jefferson continued to support it even during the Terror. While his enthusiasm eventually cooled, he retained a powerful aversion to all things British.[19]

For the first three presidential terms, from 1789 to 1800, Hamilton's Federalists held power and their foreign policies followed, roughly speaking, a Hamiltonian path. This meant making accommodation with Britain and its superior power. In the succeeding four terms, from 1800 to 1816, Jefferson and Madison occupied the presidency. They attempted to make the nation's foreign policy conform to their ideological principles, which turned them away from conciliation of Great Britain and, ironically for men who shunned war, ultimately toward military confrontation with the British. In the foreign policies of the Republican presidents of those years the penchant for promoting domestic conversion and international transformation, which distinguishes the foreign policy of the United States from those of other countries, was on vivid display.

Federalist Foreign Policy

When war broke out in Europe in 1792, the United States decided to remain neutral. The young country had little to gain and a great deal to lose by placing itself squarely in either the French or the anti-French (effectively the British) camp. Jefferson and Hamilton agreed that neutrality was the best policy, but Jefferson wanted a neutral stance that leaned toward France. He asserted that neutrality was compatible with maintaining the treaty the thirteen colonies had made with the French in 1778. Hamilton disagreed and wanted to abrogate the treaty.[20]

President George Washington issued a proclamation of neutrality on April 22, 1793, but without formally ending the French accord. His proclamation set an important precedent. By taking the initiative in formulating the American response to the European war he helped to establish the primacy of the president in matters of foreign policy, a prerogative claimed, usually successfully, by subsequent chief executives.[21]

The observation of the twentieth-century Russian revolutionary Leon Trotsky that "you may not be interested in war but war is interested in you" applies to the United States and the European wars of the late eighteenth and early nineteenth centuries. Contrary to the intent that lay behind it, the declaration of neutrality did not spare the United States difficulties with both France and Britain. In 1793 the revolutionary French government sent a representative to America in the person of Edmond Genet, known, in the new egalitarian style, as "Citizen Genet." He received a cordial reception from a public still well disposed to the Revolution. He soon made trouble, however, by trying to pull the United States into the war on the side of France. He fitted out French privateers in American ports for the purpose of launching attacks on British merchantmen. He sought to bypass the executive branch and appeal for support to what he assumed was the pro-French public.[22] He succeeded in stirring up a debate among Americans about whether and to what extent the United States should side with the Revolution against its enemies.[23]

Jefferson initially established close ties with Genet but then distanced himself from the Frenchman as Washington's government declined to fall in with Genet's schemes and his attempts to steer American policy became ever more blatant. Ultimately, Genet lost favor with the increasingly radical government in Paris and opted to remain in the United States (of which he became a citizen) rather than return home to risk accusations of disloyalty to the Revolution and possible execution.

The Genet affair offered an early demonstration of the democratic character of American foreign policy. The French envoy's activities showed the susceptibility of that foreign policy to influence from a wide variety of interested parties, not all of them necessarily American citizens.[24] It was the first but not the last time the French Revolution and the wars it triggered divided Americans. The controversy he aroused illustrated, as well, the far greater potential in the democratic United States than in monarchical Europe for matters of foreign policy to become contentious issues in domestic politics.

The American dispute with Great Britain centered on the definition of neutral maritime rights. The United States embraced an expansive one, which afforded wide latitude for profitable trade. The British, locked in a mortal struggle with France in which their military advantage lay in their mastery of the seas—and that they used to try to weaken their adversary by shutting down its trade—insisted on more restrictive terms.

Specifically, while both countries agreed that neutral ships should not be allowed to carry contraband—that is, illegal goods—the British defined the term more broadly than did the Americans to include food as well as guns and ammunition, and claimed the right to seize American ships transporting such cargo. In addition, the United States insisted on the principle that "free ships make free goods," meaning that the private property of belligerents aboard neutral ships was immune to seizure. The British did not accept this principle, and acted accordingly.

They began seizing and searching American ships in the Caribbean and confiscating cargo that violated their particular definition of neutrality.[25] The American government protested, and public opinion in the United States turned sharply against Great Britain. Under pressure to take countervailing measures, the Washington administration began military preparations.[26] Aware of Britain's decisive military advantage at sea, however, President Washington strongly preferred to avoid war and decided to try to negotiate an agreement with the British. He sent John Jay, the Chief Justice of the Supreme Court, to London for this purpose.

Jay secured an accord that made some gains for his country.[27] The British agreed to vacate the forts on American territory that they had retained after 1783 and opened their possessions in the West Indies to wider American trade than they had previously permitted. Jay failed, however, to obtain any modification in the British definition of neutral rights, in effect conceding the British position—which the United States lacked the military means to challenge.[28]

When Washington received the treaty, he decided to accept it; but because he anticipated that it would occasion controversy, he made the process of ratification by the Senate, which the Constitution required, a secret proceeding. The Senate did furnish—barely—the required two-thirds majority, by a vote of twenty to ten, the closest treaty ratification vote in American history.

The terms of the treaty, when they became known, did cause a public outcry. Once again, foreign policy became a heated issue in domestic politics as Americans decried what to many of them appeared to be a surrender to the British on a matter of American sovereignty. Jefferson and the Republicans, whose hostility to Britain predated the dispute over neutrality, harshly criticized what became known as Jay's Treaty. Jefferson called it "a monument of folly and venality."[29] No American international accord has ever received a more hostile reception.[30]

For all its unpopularity, however, the Treaty brought the United States considerable benefits. Suspecting, wrongly, that it portended an Anglo-American alliance that could be turned against Spain's possessions in the New World, the government in Madrid sought to appease the United States. The result was the October 1795 Treaty of San Lorenzo, negotiated by the American minister to Spain Thomas Pinckney and thus known as Pinckney's Treaty. By its terms Spain rec-ognized for the first time the boundary with Spanish Florida claimed by the United States since 1783 and granted Americans access to the Mississippi River, a crucial outlet for western farmers.

The news of Pinckney's Treaty reduced the public anger at Jay's Treaty, as did the fact that, partly as a result of British concessions, American trade increased substantially over the next several years.[31] Federalist foreign policy, while it aroused domestic opposition and failed to enshrine the preferred American standard of neutral maritime rights, markedly strengthened the position of the United States on its home continent.

Two years after the Jay Treaty, George Washington performed his final service to his country by declining to run for a third term as president. In addition to establishing the tradition that no presi-dent serves more than two terms—a tradition violated by Franklin Roosevelt in 1940 and subsequently written into the Constitution in 1951 as the Twenty-second Amendment—Washington's decision to step down confirmed that the United States would remain a republic and not become a quasi-monarchy in which one person governed for life. The president decided to impart to the Congress and his countrymen some thoughts on the nation's future and, with help from Alexander Hamilton, compiled what is known to posterity as Washington's Farewell Address. (Because it was never delivered orally it is technically a state paper, not an address.)

It had two parts. The first concerned domestic affairs and warned against the dangers to the United States of its increasingly prominent and often bitter political divisions, then called "factions," which turned into political parties. Washington saw the presidency as an office standing above partisan politics and wanted the country as a whole to avoid them as far as possible. Whether any democracy can function properly without explicit and, inevitably, sometimes acrimonious formal divisions represented by political parties seems doubtful.[32] Whatever the case, despite Washington's publicly expressed misgivings, this is not what happened in the United States. From his day to the present, such parties, although not part of the Constitution, have played a major role in American public life.

The second part of the Farewell Address, on foreign relations, contained another warning, this one against alliances on a more than temporary, ad hoc basis. Washington decried "passionate attachments" to other countries.[33] During the Revolutionary War, while he had welcomed French military assistance and cooperated with French officials, he had remained wary of the danger, as he saw it, of the colonies throwing off British rule only to come under the undue influence of Britain's fellow great power and continental rival.

This part of his message has had a long life. Beginning in 1862 and becoming an annual event in 1893, the whole address has been read aloud in the United States Senate. In the twentieth century the opponents of military intervention abroad invoked it to justify the policy of nonintervention that they preferred, an approach widely but inaccurately called "isolationism."*

---

* Neither George Washington nor any other American president ever believed that the United States could or should isolate itself from the rest of the world. What is meant by isolationism is, properly understood, nonintervention,

In fact, Washington was not offering foreign policy advice for all time. He delivered his message in a particular context. He disapproved of the efforts of Jefferson and the Republicans to commit the United States to an alliance with revolutionary France on the basis of history, ideology, and sentiment because the adversarial relationship with Great Britain that this would inevitably create could do serious damage to American interests. More broadly, his prescription applied to the United States in its then-current international position as a weak power. He firmly believed, however, that the country would not always be weak. When it became strong—and his associate Hamilton's domestic program was designed to make it a great power as rapidly as possible—it would have wider options. "The time is not far off," Washington said, "when we may choose peace or war, as our interests, guided by justice, shall counsel."[34] The advice he gave for one set of circumstances would not necessarily be valid for all time. The expansive global role that the United States came to play in the twentieth century did not, therefore, traduce the principles of its first president.

George Washington's vice president, John Adams of Massachusetts, who had served as one of the peace commissioners in Paris in 1783, succeeded him as president in 1797. Adams had to deal with a difficult relationship with France. Angered by the Jay Treaty, which they interpreted—not wrongly—as tilting the United States geopolitically in Great Britain's direction, the French began seizing neutral American ships carrying British goods.[35] As Washington had done toward Britain in similar circumstances, Adams responded to the French assaults by authorizing military preparedness while also seeking an accommodation with France.

In 1799 he dispatched a negotiating team to Paris. Talleyrand, the French foreign minister, initially refused to receive its members. The putative representatives of the French government with whom they did meet, whose names were kept secret and who were known as "X," "Y,"

with intervention implying the dispatch of American fighting forces abroad. George C. Herring, *From Colony to Superpower: U.S. Foreign Relations Since 1976*, New York: Oxford University Press, 2008, p. 83; Walter A. McDougall, *Promised Land, Crusader State: The American Encounter with the World Since 1776*, Boston: Houghton Mifflin, 1997, pp. 39–40, 43.

and "Z," demanded bribes from their American interlocutors as a condition for proceeding. The Americans refused. When news of what had transpired in Paris became public, many Americans, as with the Jay Treaty, were outraged, but this time at France, not Great Britain. What became known as the "XYZ Affair" gave rise to the popular slogan "Millions for Defense but not one Cent for Tribute."[36]

There followed two years of sporadic maritime conflict between the two countries, which Adams called a "half war." In response both to the conflict and to the fears it raised, particularly among Federalists, that some Americans were not only sympathetic to France but also actively in league with the French in an effort to subvert the American government, the Congress, at the behest of Adams and the Federalists, passed two pieces of what can only be called repressive legislation. The Alien Act of 1798 gave the president the power to expel from the country resident non-Americans whom he deemed dangerous to the United States, a power common to autocracies but hardly in keeping with the spirit of republican governance.[37] The Sedition Act of the same year made it a crime to publish "false, scandalous, and malicious writing or writings"[38] about the American government, which violated the intent of the First Amendment to the Constitution.

The Federalists believed that pro-French elements posed a genuine threat to the republic. The laws to which that conviction gave rise established a pattern that would recur during the course of the nation's history. At moments when foreign threats have seemed acute, the American government has sometimes adopted, usually with considerable public support, measures against those considered to have connections with the adversary and who therefore imperil the country, measures that have infringed on the basic American value of liberty. Other such episodes after 1798 include Abraham Lincoln's suspension of the legal principle of habeas corpus during the Civil War, the "Palmer Raids" on suspected radicals in the immediate aftermath of World War I, the interning of Americans of Japanese descent during World War II, and the search for communists in the government and other positions of responsibility and influence in American society, led by Senator Joseph McCarthy, in the 1950s. In all of these cases, including the Alien and Sedition Acts, the infringement on liberty proved to be temporary. On each occasion, when the sense of danger passed, the restrictions were relaxed.

In 1800 the United States and France did manage to reach a settlement of their differences. In 1798 Adams decided, against serious opposition within his own Federalist Party,[39] to send another delegation to Paris. Napoleon, now fully in charge of the French government, saw advantages in conciliating the United States.[40] The Convention of 1800 between the two tacitly put an end to their alliance of 1778 and included a statement of neutral rights that did not conflict with the Jay Treaty. The French leader staged an elaborate signing ceremony at Mortefontaine, twenty-five miles northeast of Paris, on October 3, 1800.[41]

While arousing serious controversy at home, and notwithstanding disputes within the Federalist camp, by following a sober, Hamiltonian approach to foreign policy and keeping in mind the limits of American power in comparison with that of Great Britain and France, Federalist diplomacy under the aegis of George Washington and John Adams made some major gains for the country. It improved the position of the United States in North America; paved the way for the expansion, albeit unevenly, of American trade; and avoided a major conflict with both of the far more powerful principal belligerents in the European wars.

The last Federalist diplomatic accord, the Convention with France, was ratified in December 1801, during the presidency of Thomas Jefferson, who had defeated Adams in the election of 1800. This election proved to be, for both domestic affairs and foreign policy, one of the most consequential in all of American history. For the first time a member of one party succeeded a sitting president of another, which established a pattern of the peaceful transfer of power that has characterized American democracy ever since, as well as leading to changes in the policies of the federal government. This was all the more notable because by 1800 the political divisions had become very deep indeed,[42] with the Republicans fearing that the Federalists sought to restore a monarchy and the Federalists afraid that the Republicans would bring the practices and policies of the French Revolution to the United States. These suspicions made the Federalist era one of the three most politically polarized periods in American history, along with the pre–Civil

War era with its conflict over slavery, and the post–Cold War period and its disputes over culture.

In relations with other countries, a change of direction, if anything even more pronounced than the one in domestic affairs, also took place after 1800. Jefferson and his successor James Madison had an intense dislike of Great Britain that the Federalists did not share. In addition, the Republicans were committed, as the Federalists had not been, to a foreign policy embodying the ideological principles on behalf of which, in their view, the colonies had fought for independence and on which the republic that they had created rested. Jefferson and Madison also believed that the United States, notwithstanding its modest armed forces, was far better placed to have its way in disputes with the British than the Federalists had thought possible. The two presidents launched what amounted to an experiment in the conduct of an ideological foreign policy.

The Republican foreign policy did not achieve the results for which its architects had hoped. The experiment did not succeed, and despite the persistence of an ideological strain in American thinking about international affairs, the country would not repeat it for a hundred years—and then, after World War I, under very different geopolitical circumstances. In a related endeavor, however, that had an even higher priority for the third president, Jefferson did accomplish his goal. Indeed, he accomplished more than he had initially sought, with profound consequences for the United States. He secured the most important expansion of the nation's territory in American history.

Louisiana

The major theme of the nineteenth-century history of the United States is territorial expansion. In that period, and mainly in its first half, the country extended its borders to the Pacific Ocean. The desire for land is embedded in the DNA of American culture,[43] and the impetus for expansion came initially and most powerfully not from the government but rather from individuals. While the first European immigrants crossed the Atlantic in search of religious freedom, their descendants, and the millions who followed them, saw in the New World an unparalleled opportunity for economic betterment. Before the nineteenth century and well into it, this meant the opportunity to own land. North America had more accessible, cultivable land than anywhere else on the planet and Americans, both native-born and arrivals from Europe, moved steadily westward to claim it and plant and build on it. They staked their claims even where the land did not formally belong to the United States, and the American government encouraged, supported, and followed them.[44]

The federal authorities in Washington added territory in several large pieces through the use of two time-honored instruments: guns and money. War, or the threat of war, made other countries that had land in North America that the United States wanted willing, although sometimes reluctantly, to part with it. The American government invariably proved willing, for its part, to pay for the territory that it acquired.

Of all the American presidents, none surpassed Thomas Jefferson in the desire to expand.[45] Adding territory was integral to his political outlook. The United States needed, he believed, as much territory as possible on which to establish what he foresaw as an "empire of liberty." To sustain liberty required the predominance among the citizenry of land-owning farmers rather than merchants and middlemen, and the more extensive America's territory was, the greater the number of cultivators it could support.[46]

It was Jefferson who, from 1804 to 1806, sent an expedition led by Meriwether Lewis and George Clark on an epic journey from St. Louis up the Missouri River and all the way west to the mouth of the Columbia River on the Pacific Ocean, and then back. (The trip began an American tradition of government-sponsored exploration that led, in the twentieth century, to the space program and the moon landing.) The route that Lewis and Clark took, while gathering information of scientific and commercial value, ran through territory that the United States had very recently acquired; and as an architect of American expansion, the acquisition of that territory—Louisiana—proved to be Jefferson's foremost accomplishment.

The Louisiana territory, named after Louis XIV—the king in whose name France had claimed it in the seventeenth century—stretched, north to south, from Canada to the thirty-third parallel (just south of the present border between the states of Louisiana and Arkansas) and, east to west, from roughly the Mississippi River to the Rocky

Mountains. Unlike the pattern in Canada, few immigrants from France had settled there before 1763, when the French formally ceded it to Spain as part of the settlement of the Seven Years' War.[47] In 1800, Napoleon decided that he wanted it back, and through the initially secret Treaty of San Ildefonso of October of that year Spain, which was in no position to refuse the leader of its far more powerful neighbor, complied.[48]

Renewed French possession of Louisiana posed a serious threat to American aspirations for westward expansion, and even to the United States itself, as President Jefferson recognized. He and others had assumed that their country would be able to gain control of it over time, piece by piece, and American settlers were already moving there.[49] This made sense when it was a Spanish property. In decline since the sixteenth century, Spain was the least of the European great powers—if it still counted as a great power at all. Napoleonic France, by contrast, was indisputably the mightiest country on the continent. Fully capable of standing up to, indeed defeating militarily, the United States, it made for a far more dangerous neighbor than did Spain.

France was all the more dangerous because Napoleon, not a man of modest aspirations either for himself or for his country, had in mind the establishment of a French empire in the New World, of which Louisiana would be an important part. Jefferson was sufficiently alarmed to entertain, or at least to be seen to entertain, ideas previously unthinkable for him: an alliance with his hated enemy Great Britain and even war with France.[50] He also launched another initiative for coping with what had the potential to become a mortal threat to the United States. He authorized James Monroe, the governor of Virginia who had served as the American minister to France, and Robert Livingston, who currently held that position, to try to negotiate the purchase of New Orleans, the port located where the Mississippi River flowed into the Gulf of Mexico that had great economic importance for the American west.

In the meantime, fortune smiled on Jefferson and the United States. Napoleon abandoned his North American project. The necessary first step in his plan was the pacification of the Caribbean island of Sainte Domingue, the site of the present country of Haiti.[51] A rebellion of former slaves had overthrown the government there. Napoleon dispatched 20,000 troops to regain control. The French force encountered far more resistance than it had expected and suffered severely from disease, principally yellow fever, as well. Ultimately the French abandoned the effort at reconquest. The fortitude of the former slaves rendered a huge service to the United States,[†] which the American government repaid poorly by refusing to recognize the republic that they established until 1862.

Another development contributed to Napoleon's change of mind. His plan depended on peace with Great Britain, and in March 1802 the two countries signed a treaty for that purpose in the northern French city of Amiens; but the Peace of Amiens did not hold. A year later, in May 1803, the two were at war again, and the peace had begun to break down even before then. Because the British enjoyed naval superiority over France, and the establishment of a French North American empire required unfettered seaborne communication with the New World, the British, as adversaries, could thwart Napoleon's scheme.[52] So he abandoned it, which was not particularly difficult for him since his strategic priority was Europe rather than a thinly populated continent 3,000 miles away. From his decision the United States reaped an extraordinary windfall.

The French government surprised the American negotiators in Paris by offering to sell not only New Orleans but also all of Louisiana that France controlled. Napoleon seems to have reckoned that with the resumption of the war with Great Britain he would likely lose it anyway, and he preferred that the Americans rather than the British have it. Then, too, he could use the payment he received to finance his future campaigns.[53] The Americans had been prepared to pay up to

---

[†] According to Alexander Hamilton, "To the deadly climate of St. Domingo, and to the courage and obstinate resistance made by its black inhabitants are we indebted for the obstacles which delayed the colonization of Louisiana. . . ." Quoted in Robert W. Tucker and David C. Hendrickson, *Empire of Liberty: The Statecraft of Thomas Jefferson*, New York: Oxford University Press, 1990, p. 91. "What disrupted the French plans time and again, causing delays in sending an expedition and reductions in the force that was to be sent, were the voracious demands of the campaign on Santo Domingo. Had it not been for these demands, there is every reason to believe that New Orleans would have been occupied by a French force by the end of 1802 and that this force would have been one of substantial size." *Ibid.*, p. 120.

$10 million for the port. The asking price for the entire territory was $15 million. They quickly agreed to it. The Louisiana Purchase of April 30, 1803, doubled the size of the United States at a cost of roughly 15 cents per acre.

The sale faced two obstacles in the United States. First, the Federalists opposed it, but Jefferson and the Republicans overrode them. Second, the Constitution did not clearly vest in the presidency the authority for such a transaction, and Jefferson, more than any other figure in the early republic, insisted on a strict construction of that document and on binding limits on federal power. Setting aside those convictions, he went ahead with the purchase.[54]

The acquisition of Louisiana completed a trio of epochal developments, occurring at twenty-year intervals, that determined the geopolitical structure of North America. In 1763, the agreement concluding the Seven Years' War evicted France from the continent, leaving Great Britain and Spain with the largest possessions there. In 1783, the Treaty ending the Revolutionary War reduced the British holdings to Canada while establishing, in the territory the British relinquished, a new political entity, the United States of America. In 1803, with the Louisiana Purchase, the United States took a giant step toward primacy on the continent. Spain retained considerable land but even then it was becoming apparent that the Spanish would lack the strength to defend it against American power.

The United States gained Louisiana in much the same way that it was able to prevail in its war of independence. It confronted a stronger power that found itself diverted by other, more important threats and so was willing to make concessions to the Americans: in the first instance, war with France weakened Great Britain; in the second, war with Great Britain weakened France—on both occasions to the American advantage. In both, the Americans made good use of one of the strategies of the weak: the diversion of the attention and the resources of a stronger adversary.

They effectively borrowed power to achieve their goals—independence in 1783, expansion twenty years later. They did so explicitly and actively in the earlier case, fielding an army to fight Great Britain and signing a treaty with France. They did not have to be either explicit or active on the later occasion: the dynamics of great-power rivalry conferred on the United States an enormous benefit without the American government having to do anything to bring it about. In the matter of Louisiana, the United States was a third-party beneficiary of the collapse of the Peace of Amiens.

Of the four presidents whose likenesses are carved into Mount Rushmore in South Dakota—George Washington, Abraham Lincoln, and Theodore Roosevelt being the other three—Thomas Jefferson is the only one who took no active part in any American war. The Louisiana Purchase stands as his greatest monument; and as a contribution to the history of the United States it is as significant as most of the wars the nation has fought.

Jefferson differed from the other three not only in his lack of experience of war but also in his attitude to it: in addition to disdaining war as an instrument of statecraft, he thought that the United States could make its way in the world, and achieve its often-ambitious goals, without having to fight. He believed in victory without war.[55] With the resumption of Anglo-French hostilities in 1803 the United States once again came into conflict with Great Britain over the rights of American ships. In presiding over the American side of that conflict he and his fellow Republican and successor as president, James Madison, adopted a different approach from the one their Federalists predecessors, Washington and Adams, had followed. They did not achieve victory, but they did get a war.

Republican Foreign Policy

When war between Britain and France began again, the British deployed their maritime superiority to put pressure on France by limiting French trade to the greatest extent possible. Once again, as in the 1790s, this brought the British into conflict with the United States over the definition of neutral rights. Once again, the United States adopted a broad definition, in order to maximize its own commercial opportunities. Once again, Great Britain insisted on a far narrower understanding of neutrality, with the goal of minimizing the goods and precious metals reaching France.

Two issues in particular came into dispute between the British and the Americans. One stemmed from the British denial of the right of

neutral nations, such as the United States, to trade with ports in countries with whom Britain was at war that had been closed to Americans
in peacetime, as ports in the French and Spanish empires had been.
The Americans got around this by taking French and Spanish goods
from their imperial ports to the United States, deeming them neutral
cargo and thus not subject to British seizure, and then sending them
to France and Spain. Having for a time permitted this, the British
changed their position.[56]

The other contentious issue, which aroused widespread anger in the
United States, was the British practice of impressment—forcing men
to work on their ships. British sailors left their British ships, sometimes
even deserting, for safer and better-paying berths on American ones.
As America's neutral trade boomed, the demand for sailors increased,[57]
and more and more British seamen followed this course. Desperate for
skilled personnel to man their warships, the British began intercepting
American ships and seizing crew members they suspected, often correctly, of desertion, or merely of being originally British subjects who
had taken American citizenship, and compelling them to work on
British vessels.[58]

To the British this seemed a justified tactic in their life-and-death
struggle with Napoleon, in which their survival depended on their naval
prowess.[59] The Americans, however, regarded it as an insult to, and indeed a gross violation of, the national sovereignty that they had, within
living memory, wrested from Great Britain. After the breakdown of
the Peace of Amiens, as before, the American government strongly
preferred to steer clear of the European conflict; but the seizures of
American ships, and especially impressment, turned the United States,
in American eyes, into a country whose very independence had come
under attack.[60]

Something had to be done. The Jefferson administration initially
followed the Federalist precedent. It sent William Pinkney as a special
envoy to London in June 1806, and he and James Monroe, who was
then serving as the American ambassador there, managed to reach an
agreement with the British in December of that year. By its terms the
British promised to reduce impressment, granted concessions in the
American re-export trade, and reaffirmed Jay's Treaty. Departing from
the Federalist approach, however, President Jefferson and Secretary of

State Madison rejected the Monroe-Pinkney accord, on ideological grounds: it did not fully satisfy American principles.[61]

After the rejection, on June 22, 1807, off the coast of Norfolk, Virginia, the British warship *Leopard* attacked the American frigate *Chesapeake*, which had four deserters from the Royal Navy on board. The assault killed three and wounded eighteen, and touched off an explosion of indignation in American opinion, putting substantial pressure on Jefferson to take serious steps to respond to British outrages.[62]

The way he responded represents perhaps the most extraordinary moment in the long American tradition of employing trade as an instrument of foreign policy. In 1806 he had taken steps to prohibit imports to the United States but discovered that Americans depended heavily on goods from Great Britain.[63] So he then signed the Embargo Act of 1807, which prohibited all American exports.[64] It made sending goods to other countries illegal and barred American ships from leaving port. Blockades of enemy countries had long been part of warfare. Jefferson blockaded his own country.

He chose an embargo in part because, in the face of British provocations and public anger at them in the United States, he could not do nothing but found the two other potential courses of action unacceptable. He ruled out war not only because of Britain's superior naval forces but also because armed conflict violated his own basic political principles. War, he and Madison firmly believed, was the scourge of liberty, and the American republic therefore had to avoid it at all costs.[65] The alternative to war, which the Federalists had chosen in similar circumstances, was a negotiated settlement, and Pinkney and Monroe had obtained one. Here, however, Jefferson's ideological approach to the conduct of foreign policy came into play. He refused to compromise what he regarded as basic American principles in order to advance the nation's interests.

That left him relying on economic instruments of statecraft, a reliance all the more attractive to him because he believed that the embargo would work. That is, he believed that imports from the United States had such significance for Great Britain that the British government would make major concessions to avoid having to do without them. Jefferson had, of course, lived through the decade of mounting political conflict with Britain between 1765 and 1775 when American boycotts of British goods had activated British merchants to lobby their governments to withdraw the measures that had triggered the American protests; so he had a very high estimate—too high, as it turned out—of the power of economic sanctions.[66]

Finally, Jefferson saw the embargo as part of an effort to change the character of international relations. This would occur, he hoped and believed, by substituting economic for military measures in conflict between and among sovereign states. The prohibition of American exports was an exercise in peaceful coercion.[67] Jefferson's embargo represents one of the historical moments when this ideological strain has dominated the nation's foreign policy. By imposing the embargo, the nation's third president was conducting an experiment in transcending the familiar, age-old instruments of statecraft: armed forces and war.[68]

His experiment failed. Although seriously inconvenienced by the loss of access to American exports,[69] the British were not about to abandon a practice they considered crucial for their survival in order to regain it. Moreover, Americans suffered more in economic terms from the embargo than did the British, especially in the Northeast, where many depended on trade for their livelihoods.[70] By one estimate it cost the country five percent of its gross domestic product.[71] What was intended to be a major step toward a revolution in international affairs turned out to be a self-inflicted economic wound.

Not surprisingly, many Americans did what they could to evade the embargo. They followed in the footsteps of their predecessors in colonial times who had gotten around the array of British mercantilist laws and established a precedent for their many successors in the twentieth century who flouted the prohibition against alcohol mandated, between 1920 and 1933, by the Eighteenth Amendment to the Constitution.[72] In an effort to prevent their evasions, Jefferson imposed various restrictions that were inconsistent with his often-expressed opposition to a powerful central government that could threaten individual liberty. He called out the army, for example, to enforce laws against smuggling.[73]

Because it penalized Americans while having no visible impact on British maritime practices, the embargo became increasingly unpopular and in 1809 Congress repealed it. By that time James Madison had succeeded Jefferson as president.[74] The problem that the embargo had been imposed to address, however—British violations of what Americans considered their neutral rights, amounting to an assault on American independence—remained. During the Madison presidency the United States mounted another response to that problem, one that the Federalists, in confronting it, had scrupulously avoided; that both Jefferson and Madison opposed in principle; and that weak powers, when facing stronger ones, almost always eschew: it declared war on Great Britain.

The War of 1812

Jefferson's embargo was replaced, in 1809, by the Non-Intercourse Act, which permitted trade with all countries except Great Britain and France. The Congress then passed a piece of legislation known as Macon's Bill No. 2, which allowed trade with those two powers with the stipulation that if one of them revoked its restrictions on neutral commerce, the United States would restore its ban on trade with the other. France promised—disingenuously—to lift the restrictions that it had imposed, and President Madison, over considerable opposition, announced the reimposition of American restraints on trade with the British.[75] This set the stage for war.

Great Britain, preoccupied with the challenge that Napoleonic France posed to them, had little attention to spare for the United States and its grievances.[76] By contrast, the American side, or at least the Republicans, became increasingly indignant at the British violations of their country's neutrality. Madison, despite the principled opposition to armed conflict that he shared with Jefferson, and despite his inability to persuade the Congress to supply funds for increasing military preparations, became resigned to fighting Great Britain.[77] Finally, in June 1812, the United States declared war.

The Congressional divisions on the issue were, by the standards of such votes in American history, relatively close: seventy-nine to forty-nine in the House of Representatives and nineteen to thirteen in the Senate. Both votes divided along party lines, with Jefferson and Madison's Republicans in favor and the Federalists opposed. Thus the War of 1812 was, from the start, a sharply partisan affair rather than a unified national effort. Moreover, the legislators who voted for war came overwhelmingly from the South and the West, regions that had the least directly to do with maritime trade, the issue that precipitated the conflict.[78] This led to an early manifestation of a particular aspect of America's singularly democratic style of foreign policy: dissent during wartime. The Federalists and their northeastern constituents never became reconciled to fighting the British, and many actively opposed it, which set a precedent for conflicts in the future and made the War of 1812 perhaps the most unpopular one in the nation's history.[79] It also has a claim to being an unnecessary war in that before it was declared the British had, in fact, revoked the decrees the Americans found most objectionable. Word of this decision, however, reached North America only after the Congress had voted for war.[80]

Wars often have complicated causes and occasionally opaque ones, but the causes of the War of 1812 seem, in retrospect, unusually obscure and hard to fathom. Neither country wanted it. The Americans responsible for it had a horror of war, the issues at stake seem to have been eminently susceptible to compromise, and the country formally initiating the conflict was the weaker party. Why, then, did the United States choose war?

Some Americans believed that their side would win it, and win easily. Britain's preoccupation with the great European conflict provided some basis for this belief, which turned out to be an overconfident one. Others saw war as a way to annex Canada, a recurrent American aspiration. Pressure for war came from the fact that the Republicans had protested what they deemed British maritime outrages since 1794 and had held power for the last twelve of those eighteen years without doing anything about them: they had backed themselves into a political corner.[81] Madison, for his part, insisted that, because of the British violations of the American understanding of neutral rights, the two countries were already at war but that the United States was not fighting back.[82]

The impetus for war drew most of its force, however, from the conviction that the British disregard for American maritime rights threatened the nation's hard-won sovereignty. Republicans, at least, persuaded themselves that what the British were doing placed in jeopardy their country's independent existence.[83] For them, the War of 1812 had the same cause as the Revolutionary War. At the time, and even more so afterward, they considered it a necessary measure to defend their sovereignty. The need to preserve its independence is the circumstance in which a weak state, which ordinarily, prudently, indeed logically seeks to avoid armed conflict with a stronger one, may nevertheless go to war against such a power, as the United States did against Great Britain.

At the outset of the War of 1812, as at the beginning of the Revolutionary War, the Americans attacked Canada. Even if they could not conquer all of British North America and incorporate it into the United States, the Americans were determined to strike the British in some way, and this was the only way available. They also hoped at least to secure enough Canadian territory to gain leverage on their British adversary.[84] On the second occasion, as on the first, the attack failed. The Canadians had not become better disposed to joining their republican neighbors to the south. Moreover, the United States had failed seriously to prepare for war, and the lack of preparedness led to poor results on the battlefield.[85] The British, in response, imposed a maritime blockade that inflicted serious harm on the American economy.

In 1814 the global context of the war changed dramatically, and to the disadvantage of the United States. A few days after the Congress had declared war, in June 1812, Napoleon had mounted an invasion of Russia that turned into a disaster for France. The severe Russian winter, the vast distances his troops had to march, and harassment by Russian forces took an immense toll on the French army, which staged an ignominious retreat while losing most of its men.[86] The anti-French coalition finally defeated Napoleon and forced him into exile in April 1814 on the Mediterranean island of Elba.

When they had declared war in 1812, the Americans had been able to count on the diversion of British military power to wage its war against France, a reprise of the circumstances of the Revolutionary War in which the British conflict with France had functioned as an indispensable strategic asset for the Americans.[87] The French defeat after the disastrous Russian campaign freed the British to concentrate their military attention on North America, and they launched offensives that met with considerable success. In the North, they won several victories in a campaign that, if it had been sustained, could have cut off New England from the rest of the country and resulted in the annexation of

American territory to Canada.[88] The Americans finally stopped them at the Battle of Plattsburgh at Lake Champlain.

In the Chesapeake Bay region the British staged an amphibious invasion, defeated the American troops at Bladensburg, occupied Washington, D.C., and burned most of the public buildings in the capital, including the White House. Only the Post and Patents Office remained standing. President Madison fled to Virginia. British troops reached Baltimore, where Fort McHenry, on the city's harbor, managed to hold out against them.[89] On the Gulf Coast the British attacked New Orleans at the beginning of 1815 but suffered a defeat there at the hands of an American force commanded by Colonel Andrew Jackson.[90] In fact, by then the war had ended but word had not reached New Orleans.

In August of 1814 peace negotiations between the United States and Great Britain had begun in the city of Ghent. Madison had had an interest in a negotiated settlement almost from the beginning of the war.[91] By the second half of the year the British were occupying eastern Maine,[92] and that and the military reverses and economic distress the United States had suffered had made the American government eager for an end to the conflict.[93] As for the British, they had secured an important strategic aim: the security of Canada under British rule.[94] The actual conquest of the United States was an even more forbidding prospect in 1814 than it had been during the war for American independence: the difficulty of access, which had played a crucial part in the outcome of that conflict, had become even more acute, with the United States considerably larger territorially and more populous than it had been in 1783.[95]

Moreover, although Napoleon had been defeated, Europe remained unsettled: the continuing diversion of British armed forces across the Atlantic would have weakened the British in Europe.[96] As in the past, Europe had a higher strategic priority for London than did North America. Indeed, many in Britain did not even know that their country was at war with the United States.[97] The Duke of Wellington was offered command of the British forces in North America but declined, which made him available for the decisive Battle of Waterloo on June 15, 1815, in which Napoleon suffered his final defeat after escaping from Elba and reconstituting the French army. Finally, the British had never wanted a war in the first place. It had been the Americans, after all, who had declared it.

The terms of the Treaty of Ghent, signed on December 24, 1814, restored the status quo before the war. Two and one-half years of fighting, at a cost to the United States of 2,260 killed and 4,505 wounded,[98] had changed nothing. Madison had wanted the American negotiators to demand an end to the British practice of impressment, but they decided not to make this demand. Impressment did in fact end, however. The British ended it unilaterally because, with the defeat of Napoleon, they no longer had a military reason for it. So the United States did at last receive satisfaction on its principal reason for going to war—through the military victory of the country that it was fighting.[99]

Although there is competition for the distinction, in retrospect the War of 1812 stands out as perhaps the most misbegotten and ill-advised war the United States has ever fought,[100] and the third and fourth presidents as the least competent managers of foreign policy in American history. While the British harassment of American shipping took a toll on the nation's economy, the blockade that Jefferson ordered inflicted far more damage. While Republicans, especially, may have believed that British disregard for what Americans considered their neutral rights threatened American independence, it was the war that the United States launched in defense of those rights that brought genuine peril to the nation. The greatest danger to the integrity of the republic came not from British armed forces, however, but from the deep divisions among Americans that the war both created and exacerbated.

The conflict became so unpopular in Federalist-dominated New England, which was already alienated from Jefferson and Madison's Republicans on a number of domestic issues, that it stirred talk of secession. In December 1814 five of the New England states sent representatives to a meeting in Hartford, which became known as the Hartford Convention, to discuss their grievances. They drafted a report proposing several amendments to the Constitution and appointed a three-man delegation to take them to Washington. By the time the three arrived, news of the victory at New Orleans and the Treaty of Ghent made their mission superfluous. The Convention did not propose that New England secede from the United States, but the fact that it took place denoted serious disaffection with the federal government that could, had the war continued, have jeopardized their membership in the union.[101]

The War of 1812 thus created substantial risks.[102] The thirteen colonies had also run risks in their war against the British, but in order to secure a major reward: independence. No comparable reward was in prospect in the later conflict, even if the United States had managed a better military performance.

By eschewing compromise with Great Britain in order to vindicate neutrality as the Republicans understood it, finally, Madison, like Jefferson with his embargo, was pursuing the American version of an ideological foreign policy and thereby arguably sacrificing national interest for the sake of principle. Yet the war served neither its ideals nor its interests. It aligned the United States, a country whose purpose, in the view of its founders, was to embody and exemplify liberty, with one of history's greatest tyrants, Napoleon Bonaparte,[103] and against the country that, unlike the other European powers, had a commitment to political freedom and representative government. In addition to violating American principles, the war was inconsistent with the country's long-term interests, properly understood. Had he been able to overcome the British, after all, Napoleon planned to establish a North American empire that would, as Jefferson recognized, have posed a threat to the United States.[104] In the European war, therefore, America had a vital interest in precisely the outcome that its policy in the War of 1812 undercut, but that came to pass despite its efforts.‡

Americans, however, regarded the outcome of the war not as a fortunate escape from worse damage but rather as a victory.[105] The second war against Great Britain entered the nation's collective memory as a triumph. A Baltimore lawyer, Francis Scott Key, witnessed the British bombardment of Fort McHenry and wrote a poem celebrating the flag's survival during the attack that was set to music and ultimately

---

‡ Ironically, a far more powerful United States would enter the two world wars of the twentieth century primarily for the purpose of checking the ambitions of the strongest power on the European continent that, if it was not stopped, could ultimately threaten the United States. Great Britain opposed Napoleon precisely for this purpose in the Wars of the French Revolution, but America, at least when the Republicans were in power, effectively took the other side.

adopted as the national anthem—the "Star-Spangled Banner." Sung at public occasions throughout the country, it is the single enduring feature of the War of 1812.

Andrew Jackson became a national hero after his troops' success at New Orleans, setting him on the path to becoming the seventh president in 1828, although the battle turned out to have no military significance. The Republican Party, which had initiated the war because it had run out of alternatives to fighting and had then presided over it incompetently, dominated American politics for a generation thereafter. The Federalists, who had warned against and then opposed armed conflict with Great Britain, faded out of existence.

While the United States gained nothing tangible from the peace agreement, the war evidently bestowed some psychological benefits on Americans.[106] It boosted the nation's confidence. It did away with such doubts as there were, presumably on both sides of the Atlantic, about America's long-term viability as an independent, sovereign state. It came to be seen as the nation's "second war for independence."[107] It also put an end to any serious consideration of secession in New England. Over the next four decades opposition, and ultimately armed resistance, to membership in the union passed to the southern states.

The war marked two other noteworthy endings in American history. The year 1814 was the last time hostile foreign troops managed to set foot on American soil. And the War of 1812 was the last one the United States fought against a militarily superior foe.

3

The Continental Republic, 1815–1865

The United States and Great Britain

The downfall of Napoleon ushered in a new order in European and international affairs. The United States remained a lesser power, having emerged from the War of 1812 with its territory intact and its independence preserved but without the military might of the great imperial states of Europe. It was still, compared to them, a weak power.

The new order defined the opportunities and challenges the country would confront for the next half century, and those opportunities proved to be broader, and the challenges less taxing—at least in international terms—than those the country had faced in the previous fifty years. In the earlier period America fought two wars against a stronger adversary, Great Britain, to secure and then (in its own view) to preserve its independence. Over the succeeding five decades the United States waged two other consequential wars, but with the borders, not the sovereign existence, of the country at stake and against adversaries less formidable than imperial Britain. In general, the new, post-Napoleonic order afforded the United States the two most valuable opportunities available to a weak state: to be free of the urgent threat of attack from stronger rivals and to use that freedom to become more powerful.

Two features defined the new international order. The great powers of the European continent looked inward. The French Revolution and its consequences had driven their monarchical governments to the brink of extinction. Seeking above all to preserve their regimes, the rulers cooperated among themselves to an unprecedented degree with the aim of avoiding the recurrence of destructive warfare and preventing another French bid for dominance. The arrangement came to be known as the Concert of Europe.[1] The great powers made major changes in their foreign policies in order to avoid major changes in their internal affairs. Their preoccupation with European matters left them with less time, energy, and resources to involve themselves in North America than at any time since the beginning of the eighteenth century.

The other defining feature of the new world order after 1815 also served to minimize the continental powers' engagement in the New World: the unchallenged maritime supremacy of Great Britain,[2] which limited the other Europeans' access to North America. British naval mastery, in turn, stemmed from the outcome of the Napoleonic Wars, in particular Britain's defeat of France. Two other important developments in the course of the nineteenth century bolstered it: the British lead in the ongoing Industrial Revolution and its related dominance in global commerce and finance.[3] The Royal Navy's supremacy created a more peaceful maritime order than in the previous century, a "Pax Britannica" comparable to the "Pax Romana" that the Roman Empire had imposed in Western Europe and throughout the Mediterranean region in ancient times.

For the United States, this new order had three particular consequences. First, America had more distant relations with Europe politically, but at the same time closer ties economically, than in the preceding decades.[4] Second, the new international circumstances afforded the American republic the geopolitical space to pursue what became its principal national project in the fifty years between the end of the War of 1812 and the end of the Civil War: territorial expansion.[5] Third, while the country's relations with the rest of the world were different and, from the American point of view, more agreeable in the second half of the century from 1765 to 1865 than in the first half, there was one major element of continuity between the two: because Great Britain continued to be its biggest trading partner; because the British continued to have, in Canada, a major presence in North America; and because British naval forces controlled the Atlantic Ocean, relations with Great Britain had greater importance by far for the United States than its relations with any other country.

In this era that relationship was a mixed one, combining elements of tension with some common interests and other sources of mutual restraint. On the spectrum running from enmity to friendship it fell somewhere between the hostility of the period of the Revolution and the early republic, at one end, and the solidarity of the twentieth century at the other.

Mutual suspicion lasted to mid-century and beyond. The Americans continued to be wary of an empire with a robust presence on their borders in three directions: militarily in Canada to the north and the Atlantic Ocean to the east, and economically, increasingly as the century wore on, in Latin America to the south.[6] The two wars that the Americans had fought against Great Britain did not vanish from their collective memory.

Indeed, Americans defined their own nationalism, their sense of what it meant to be an American, in no small part by resistance to the erstwhile mother country.[7] As late as 1908, Albert Spalding, a sporting goods manufacturer, organized a commission to determine the origins of the country's national game, baseball, and directed it to find that the game had been invented by the Union Civil War general Abner Doubleday in the typical American small town of Cooperstown, New York. This genealogy, which became the sport's official origin story, was false: baseball evolved from the English game of rounders, which had its roots in the equally English game of cricket. Spalding felt that baseball needed an impeccably American pedigree, however, because the association with England would diminish its popularity and therefore his profits.[8] For their part, the British saw the relentless territorial expansion of the United States as creating a potentially formidable geopolitical rival and worried that their former colonies had not entirely abandoned their ambition to bring Canada into their Union—as, for much of the nineteenth century, they had not.

On the other hand, the two wars the two countries had fought against each other brought about a mutual respect; and while the British retained their military superiority over the Americans, they were eager to avoid, if possible, a third such conflict, which would have diverted attention and resources from their imperial responsibilities and

European interests. The military advantage that the British enjoyed in naval power, moreover, was not easy to apply on the North American mainland. In addition, the two countries had robust commercial relations, and their trade enriched them both.[9]

Finally, the major interests that each country pursued were not in conflict. The British sought to expand their political influence and their economic presence beyond their shores, including in the Western Hemisphere, but not by formally subjugating more territory than they already governed. They preferred, rather, to enlarge their informal empire, where they exercised influence and held major positions in trade and investment, without assuming the responsibility for governance. They did so in Latin America in particular.[10]

This aim was compatible with the American drive in the first half of the nineteenth century to expand the scope of the territory that it governed directly to the west and the south in North America. In fact, since the Royal Navy could block any of the continental powers from intervening in the New World, while at the same time it protected transatlantic trade, with respect to British maritime power the United States qualified as what economists call a "free rider," reaping the benefits of London's naval supremacy without having to pay for it.[11]

Still, the territorial contiguity of the United States and Canada, despite the fact that the Americans and the British did not have identical goals and aspirations, did create points of friction between the two countries. It was a cardinal feature of the most important foreign relationship the United States had in the five decades after the Treaty of Ghent that the two managed on several occasions to deal with those differences through diplomatic compromise.[12]

In the wake of the War of 1812, they signed the Rush-Bagot agreement of 1817, which restricted naval armaments on the Great Lakes. The agreement has the distinction of being the first formal American accord to limit arms, and therefore the forerunner of the far more complicated arms control accords, covering much more powerful weapons, of the 1970s and 1980s.[13] The Convention of 1818 established the border separating the United States from Canada between the Lake of the Woods in Minnesota and the Rocky Mountains at the forty-ninth parallel, where it remains, while providing for joint control, for ten years, of the Oregon Territory, which was located between the Rockies and the Pacific Ocean.[14]

The Webster-Ashburton Treaty of 1842, named for its principal negotiators—the American secretary of state (and more renowned historically as a senator) Daniel Webster and the British ambassador to the United States Alexander Baring, Lord Ashburton, the scion of a major banking family—resolved other Canadian-American border issues.[15] In 1846, after considerable controversy and even the threat of war, the two countries drew that border through the Oregon Territory, extending it along the forty-ninth parallel to the Pacific.

Finally, in 1850 the two countries signed the Clayton-Bulwer Treaty—like Webster-Ashburton named for the American secretary of state and the British minister who negotiated it, John Clayton and Henry Bulwer, respectively. It stipulated joint control over the isthmian canal linking the Atlantic and the Pacific Oceans that the two countries expected—prematurely—to be built through Panama.[16]

Three of these agreements—Rush-Bagot, the Convention of 1818, and the Oregon accord—were negotiated during the presidencies of the Democrats James Monroe and James K. Polk. Although they were political descendants of Thomas Jefferson and James Madison (with Monroe being Madison's immediate successor in the White House), neither was as averse to making agreements with Great Britain as their two predecessors. In the wake of the War of 1812, the alternate, Federalist approach to diplomacy prevailed.

The best-known and perhaps the most significant instance of Anglo-American cooperation in this period did not yield a formal agreement. It took place tacitly. It found expression in a unilateral presidential declaration in 1823 that became known, in succeeding decades, as the Monroe Doctrine.

The Monroe Doctrine had its origins in the political uprisings that, inspired by the French and American Revolutions and taking advantage of Spain's steady decline as a great imperial power (which Napoleonic France's occupation of the country in 1808 made evident), swept over Latin America between 1811 and 1824.[17] These upheavals created a series of independent republics in what had been the Spanish empire in the New World.

The United States welcomed the end of monarchical rule to its south, as it did almost everywhere, but Secretary of State John Quincy Adams prevailed upon President Monroe not to extend formal recognition to the new governments immediately because Adams was in the midst of delicate negotiations with Spain about the extent of Spanish claims in North America.[18] As committed as Americans were in principle to the propagation of liberty and republican government, in practice, Adams believed, the promotion of these political ideas and institutions had to give way to the pursuit of concrete geopolitical interests. Encouraging democracy in Latin America, while perhaps desirable, carried less weight with him than expanding the territory of the United States in North America.[19] Adams had a distinguished diplomatic career and then a notable spell in the House of Representatives as the most out-spoken opponent of slavery, between which he served a disappointing term as president between 1825 and 1829, making him the only person in American history for whom the presidency was not the highlight of his political life. From him came the most frequently cited statement in favor of avoiding active efforts to promote the American form of government abroad, in a speech on July 4, 1821: "Wherever the standard of freedom and Independence has been or shall be unfurled," he said,

> there will [America's] heart, her benedictions, and her prayers be. But she goes not abroad in search of monsters to destroy. She is the well-wisher to the freedom and independence of all. She is the champion and vindicator only of her own.[20]

In that spirit he argued that Monroe should not express support for the Greek nationalist revolt against the Ottoman Empire in 1822, and the United States did not in fact recognize Greek independence;[21] and while the continent-wide uprisings against the European monarchies in 1848 evoked considerable sympathy among Americans, the American government did nothing to try to assist the anti-monarchical movements.[22] The country did not entirely abandon its ideological predilections in foreign policy; but for most of the nineteenth century Americans expressed their commitment to the spread of their political ideas almost exclusively by rhetoric.

To be sure, the country's relative weakness, as distinct from a lack of faith in its founding ideals, had a great deal to do with this restrained approach. The American government frequently disregarded Adams's advice in the twentieth and twenty-first centuries, when the United States had become a far stronger member of the international system.

The Monroe administration did ultimately recognize the new Latin American states, including Mexico, in 1822, and found itself confronting a potential threat from that part of the world. Americans suspected that the European powers would intervene there to restore Spanish rule. The continental monarchies had formed the Holy Alliance, with Russia, Austria, and Prussia the founding members, an association within the Concert of Europe that was dedicated to resisting challenges to monarchical rule. In retrospect it became clear that Europe's royalists never seriously contemplated dispatching an expeditionary force to the Western Hemisphere to reimpose Spanish sovereignty.[23] At the time, however, the Americans could not be sure of this.

The American government strongly opposed the return of European military forces to what it regarded as its neighborhood, a neighborhood toward which it had adopted an increasingly proprietary attitude. When, in 1821, the Russian tsar announced an exclusive maritime zone extending more than 100 miles from the Pacific coast from the Bering Strait and Alaska southward to the fifty-first parallel, which passes through Canada, Adams was quick to reject the legitimacy of the imperial edict.[24]

The British, too, had an interest in maintaining the independence of the Latin American republics, with several of which they had established profitable economic ties[25] that the return of Spanish rule would jeopardize. British Foreign Secretary George Canning therefore proposed to the Monroe administration that the two countries issue a joint statement declaring their common opposition to such an initiative. Jefferson and Madison, despite their long-standing hostility to Great Britain, recommended agreeing to the proposal.[26] Adams, however, convinced Monroe not to do so but rather to act unilaterally.[27] Accordingly, in his presidential message to Congress of December 2, 1823, Monroe included a section on Europe and the Western Hemisphere. He distinguished between the Old World and the New and asserted that neither should impinge on the other, that the Americas were henceforth not to be the objects of European colonization, and that the Europeans should never undertake the kind of military intervention that the Americans feared they were planning.[28]

The message was not regarded as a diplomatic landmark when the president issued it, but later in the century it came to be seen as a declaration of the country's diplomatic independence and of American predominance, to be enforced militarily if necessary, in the Western Hemisphere. Twentieth-century presidents—Truman, Eisenhower, and Carter—promulgated "doctrines" that declared a special American interest in a particular part of the world and an intention to defend that interest by military means. At its inception, and unlike its successors, however, the Monroe Doctrine denoted no such thing. Like Washington's Farewell Address, it subsequently took on a political significance that it did not have when it was first presented.

As a weak power, the United States lacked the military means to keep the Europeans out of what Americans later came to regard as their geopolitical sphere of influence. Only Britain, with its naval supremacy, could do that; and British naval power did in fact guarantee that the era of European colonization on the other side of the Atlantic had come to an end. While Adams made sure that His Majesty's government did not formally join with the United States in posting the Monroe Doctrine's "no trespassing" sign for the Western Hemisphere, through the middle of the nineteenth century it was the Royal Navy, not the modest American military forces, that backed it up.[29]

By the second half of the century, however, the Americans came to regard the Monroe Doctrine as a central pillar of their foreign policy. They were able to do this because, in the preceding decades, taking advantage of the protection that British naval supremacy and the post-Napoleonic preoccupation of the European governments with the affairs of their own continent afforded, the United States had accumulated the elements of geopolitical strength, thus ultimately ending its career as a weak state and graduating to a more powerful international status.

Growth

America acquired the basis of great international power through three kinds of growth: demographic, economic, and territorial.[30] In the modern era, as before, a country or empire's relative strength rested on the size of its population, the size of its territory, and its wealth. Between the end of the War of 1812 and the end of the Civil War all three expanded substantially in the United States.

Continuing the pattern of the colonial era and the period of the early republic, the American population increased rapidly during this era. In 1815 the country included 8.4 million people; in 1830, 12.9 million; in 1840, 17.1 million—approximately the population of Great Britain; in 1850, 23.2 million; and by 1860 there were 31.5 million Americans, an almost 300 percent increase in forty-five years.[31]

Most of the growth came from natural increase: Americans continued to have lots of children.[32] The process that began what became the United States in the seventeenth century, immigration from Europe, also contributed to that growth. Between 1820 and 1840, 700,000 people made the transoceanic journey. In the succeeding two decades the pace accelerated: 4.7 million immigrants arrived.[33] Most of them settled in the North and Midwest, many in cities, where more and more Americans came to live during these years.[34]

The expansion of the nation's population helped to drive another trend that ultimately lifted the country into the ranks of the planet's most formidable countries: economic growth. The Industrial Revolution, which began in Britain in the eighteenth century and spread around the world thereafter, brought more sweeping change to human life than any development since the agricultural revolution of the Neolithic age, more than 10,000 years before. One of the Industrial Revolution's consequences was that, by employing the power of machines, for the first time the production of food and goods increased steadily,[35] making individuals healthier, longer-lived, and more prosperous. Another was that it transformed the character of military power. For almost all of history military might had depended on the number of soldiers a government was able to recruit and pay. Henceforth, it stemmed as well from the volume and quality of a country's industrial output, and in these the United States came, eventually, to surpass all others.

It was able to take early and extensive advantage of the Industrial Revolution's possibilities because of its relatively high standard of education, its open and egalitarian—rather than rigid and hierarchical—social structure (except in the South), its abundance of natural resources, its sturdy regime of laws including strong property rights, its culture of mobility and innovation, and not least its growing population, which supplied ever more farmers, workers, merchants, investors, and inventors.

Growth has three ingredients: land, labor, and capital; and the United States had all three in abundance. In the first half of the nineteenth century the country sustained an economic growth rate of 3.7 percent,[36] despite the fact that financial crises and slumps, especially between 1837 and 1843, depressed economic expansion.[37] This was a remarkable achievement in light of the economic stasis of almost all of history before then, and in comparison with the economic growth of Britain, the pioneering country of the Industrial Revolution, which had a rate of 2.2 percent.[38]

In the quarter century between 1815 and 1840 the cotton cultivated in the American South served as the engine of the country's economic growth. Exported mainly to Great Britain, it brought in revenue that spread around the country, lifting economic activity everywhere.[39] Between 1840 and 1860 the locus of economic dynamism shifted to the North, where manufacturing expanded rapidly,[40] and to the Midwest. There the settlement of the Great Plains, the sowing and harvesting of grain and its export in increasing quantities to Europe, and especially to Britain, thanks to the construction of railroads in North America, faster transatlantic shipping, and the 1846 repeal of Britain's protectionist Corn Laws, together produced substantial earnings.[41] In both periods, foreign markets made major contributions to American growth, as would be the case in the second half of the twentieth century in East Asia. There, too, rapid increases in output stemmed substantially from exports—of manufactured goods rather than, as in nineteenth-century America, of agricultural products—to overseas markets, foremost among them the United States itself.

Internal American developments also spurred economic expansion in this period. The Industrial Revolution yielded three revolutionary innovations in transportation and communication: the steam engine, which made possible steamships far faster than vessels powered by wind and sail and able to carry more cargo; the railroad; and the telegraph.[42] These three drew the different parts of the geographically expanding country closer together for economic purposes: goods and information could move much more rapidly than ever before. Complementing the acceleration of travel, and thus the shipment of goods, on land was the increase in the speed and ease of waterborne transport through the construction of canals. The most notable was the Erie Canal, completed in 1825, which linked the Great Lakes with the Atlantic via the Hudson River.[43] Canals supplemented the navigable rivers with which nature had endowed the American republic.

Steam power and the telegraph knitted together what had been loosely connected regions into a single national market. All other things being equal, the larger an internal market it has, the larger a country's economic potential will be; and so it was for the United States in the first half of the nineteenth century. In addition to markets for American products, Europe—and again mainly Great Britain—furnished much of the capital necessary for economic expansion.[44] All these ingredients of economic growth combined to put the United States, even before the Civil War, well on its way to becoming an economic giant, the country with the world's largest economy.

Trade not only fueled economic growth in the decades after 1815 but also became permanently entangled in domestic politics. Of all the aspects of America's relations with other countries, cross-border commerce became the most democratic in the sense that public opinion, interest groups, and partisan considerations permeated it. Unlike in the previous fifty years, however, the federal government did not attempt to use that commerce as leverage to achieve political goals in the half century after 1815. Instead, at the heart of the politics of trade, beginning in the second decade of the nineteenth century and continuing for most of the next 200 years, stood the issue of tariffs—taxes on imports.

The government relied on tariffs for the revenues it needed for everything that it did; for much of American history almost no other form of taxation was feasible.[45] Just how high the tariffs should be, however, and what purposes, if any, they should serve beyond revenue collection became contentious issues soon after the War of 1812. On these questions the country divided along geographic lines because different economic activities dominated different regions, which created different regional political and economic interests that the politics of trade reflected.[46]

In the economic geography of the United States of the early nineteenth century, the South depended heavily on agricultural production, above all of cotton, which dominated its economic life. Cotton growers sent most of what they grew elsewhere—to the Northern states but especially abroad.[47] Southerners used their earnings from "King Cotton" and other agricultural products to buy the other goods they needed and desired. For that reason, the South, and therefore the political party that chiefly represented it, Thomas Jefferson and Andrew Jackson's Republicans (who became known in the nineteenth century and thereafter as Democrats), strongly favored low tariffs. They tended to be, in the parlance of the politics of commerce, free traders. Tariffs harmed them in two ways: by making what they bought abroad more expensive and by encouraging other countries to erect retaliatory barriers to trade, which jeopardized the exports on which they depended.

The Northeast, the Middle Atlantic states, and the Midwest (originally called the Old Northwest, which included most of what became Ohio, Indiana, Illinois, Michigan, and Wisconsin) became, during this period, the industrial heartland of the United States. This made the people of these places better disposed than their Southern counterparts to tariffs. For one thing, Northerners welcomed more revenue from tariffs because they looked more favorably on government expenditure for the purpose of promoting economic activity. More importantly, tariffs afforded their industries protection from European competition in industrial products—above all from Great Britain, for much of the nineteenth century the world leader in manufacturing. While tariffs made Southerners poorer, barriers to trade tended to make many Northerners richer. Consequently, the political party that emerged to represent their interests, the Whigs, gave more support to tariffs than did the Democrats.[48]

In 1816 the Republican-Democrat James Madison, breaking with his party's previous policy, called for, and Congress enacted, tariffs for a purpose other than raising revenue. They were designed to reduce the country's dependence on Great Britain by keeping out British products, a consideration that the War of 1812 had placed on the national agenda.[49] The debate over that measure revealed two opposing factions—roughly speaking the North and the South—based on the country's regional economic differences, which would thereafter battle over tariff legislation.[50]

In 1824 a tariff increase passed the Congress narrowly, over Southern objections.[51] Four years later what Southerners called the "tariff of abominations" provoked some politicians in South Carolina, including the most prominent of them, Vice President John C. Calhoun, to propose the doctrine of "nullification," according to which individual states could nullify federal acts they disliked.[52] A compromise in 1833 defused what had become a political crisis[53] and led to twenty-five years of steadily lowered tariffs because the South held the upper hand in national politics during this period.[54] Still, trade politics remained fraught because the regional cleavages on which they were based coincided with the division over a more explosive issue, one that came to dominate the political life of the nation in the 1850s: slavery.

Population growth, economic growth, territorial growth—all these enriched and improved the lives of those living in North America, with the conspicuous exception of slaves and Native Americans. The forces that made the United States a thriving and ever more powerful country diminished and dispossessed the American Indians. If the nineteenth century was an era of progress in and for the American republic, the Europeans were its beneficiaries and the Native Americans its principal victims.

When the first settlers arrived from Europe, they had varying relations with the people who had preceded them by at least 11,000 years. Friendly meetings and cooperation took place, symbolized by what became the American holiday of Thanksgiving, along with outbreaks of armed conflict.[55] Cooperation and coexistence ultimately failed because at the heart of the encounter between the two groups lay an irreconcilable conflict. The European settlers wanted land, their appetite for which was satisfied only when they had come to control the North American continent from the Atlantic to the Pacific Oceans. Their drive for ever more land came, and was bound to come, at the expense of the Indians, whose way of life depended on unfettered access to that land, which the European settlers were bent on denying them.

The Indians asserted themselves when and as they could. For many of them warfare was part of their culture, but the tactics and the weapons with which they were accustomed to fighting proved, in the end, to be no match for those the Europeans could employ. As a further handicap, the indigenous population was fragmented, by some estimates, into as many as 600 tribes and subtribes, many with their own languages, customs, and social structures.[56]

As the European settlers pushed outward from the Atlantic coast and into the interior of North America, the Indians did make serious efforts to unite against those they experienced as invaders. The tribes fought, and lost, several significant battles: American forces commanded by the Revolutionary War general Anthony Wayne defeated an Indian contingent at Fallen Timbers, in northeast Ohio, in 1794;[57] and General William Henry Harrison overcame another Indian confederacy at Tippecanoe in the Indiana territory in 1811.[58] By his victory Harrison, like another successful "Indian fighter," Andrew Jackson, earned a heroic reputation with the American public that led, as it did for Jackson, to the presidency.

In resisting the settlers, the Indians, not surprisingly, adopted one of the principal strategies of the weak, which the American colonists had used to good effect in the Revolutionary War: alliance with a stronger power with which they had common interests. Because Frenchmen in North America in the eighteenth century came for economic purposes and planned to return home—they were mainly trappers in search of furs to sell—whereas those who arrived from England stayed to create families, build communities, and claim land, in the Seven Years' War the tribes sided mainly with the French.[59] In the Revolutionary War they again aligned with the warring party that was less threatening to them—the British; but their allies lost both wars and after 1783 they had to deal with the government of the now-independent United States.

That government adopted several approaches to the Native Americans. Sometimes it treated them as sovereign in their own right and signed treaties with them, although it was not always scrupulous about observing the treaties' terms.[60] The Americans also tried, in a number of ways and with some success, to promote the Indians' assimilation into the Europeans' culture through schooling and the provision of opportunities for employment.[61]

Many of the tribes, however, retained their attachments to their original ways of life and sought to defend them. As European encroachment proceeded, and the world they had known steadily contracted, revivalist movements swept through the Indian communities, inspiring fervent although ultimately futile bouts of resistance.[62]

The War of 1812 marked a watershed. As in the Revolutionary War, the Native Americans sided with Great Britain, and to the peace negotiations at Ghent the British brought a proposal for the establishment of a neutral Indian barrier between the United States and British Canada. During the course of the negotiations, however, they dropped the proposal, and the Indians' last chance for a safe haven in North America disappeared.[63]

In the wake of that war the Americans' treatment of the Indians became harsher.[64] They forced the tribes to sell land to the federal government. They evicted Indians from their ancestral homelands in large numbers, driving them westward. The process came to be called "Indian removal"[65] and was similar to the brutal evictions in twentieth-century Europe known as "ethnic cleansing." Sporadic resistance continued for much of the nineteenth century, with the highlight, from the Indian point of view, being the defeat of American troops commanded by Colonel George Armstrong Custer at Little Bighorn in Montana in 1876. Even with the occasional success, however, the resistance was in vain. By the end of the century the Native Americans had suffered total defeat. They had lost their access to the land, and with it their ability to lead the lives they had known for thousands of years.

The Indians lost on the battlefield because they, unlike the settlers, had not mastered the techniques of the Industrial Revolution and so were deficient in the weaponry that the machine age made possible.[66] The difference in power between the two communities, however, stemmed more fundamentally from the much earlier agricultural revolution, which had never fully arrived in North America before the English settlers brought it in the seventeenth century. It was that revolution that produced what has come to be called, broadly and perhaps not entirely fairly, civilization: large populations, cities, economic and social specialization (and with them social stratification), trained military forces, and written language: that is, the basis of power in the preindustrial world.

The Indians' lack of these things made the gap in power between them and the European settlers a cavernous one, and that gap condemned them to defeat and dispossession. Few outcomes in history can plausibly be said to have been predetermined, but the fate of the native population of North America is one of them. With the Europeans implacably resolved to dominate the continent, and in the absence of allies who could stand up to the settlers, the Native Americans, for all their rearguard resistance, were doomed from the start.

Territorial Expansion

The territorial expansion of the United States in the first half of the nineteenth century took place on two mutually reinforcing levels. Individual Americans moved westward beyond the borders of the republic and staked claims, built homes, and created farms. They then agitated for the territories that they had settled to be incorporated into the American republic. Indeed, in migrating beyond the territorial limits of the United States they had some expectation that the places where they were settling would sooner or later become part of their home country. The government in Washington was usually happy to accede to the appeals of its citizens west (and sometimes south) of the country's existing borders; and these citizens were often willing to take up arms to bring about the incorporation they sought.[67]

The federal government was also willing to pay the previous owner for the new territories; but the payment was usually part of what came, in the last quarter of the twentieth century, to be described—drawing on the 1972 film *The Godfather*—as "an offer it couldn't refuse." Behind the offer of payment, that is, lay the usually implicit but seldom unclear threat of force. To obtain the last great addition to American territory, the Mexican cession of 1848 that brought California and most of the Southwest into the Union, the United States did in fact go to war.

In 1845 a newspaper editor, John O'Sullivan, coined a term to describe the American march westward: "Manifest Destiny." The term gave a name to what had become the national project of the United States and implied that expansion was predestined, with at least a hint of divine sanction and the suggestion that Americans were entitled to the land they were in the process of acquiring. It tapped into the country's ideological predispositions, implying a mission to spread republican government and liberty across North America.[68] While it was a new term when O'Sullivan coined it, Manifest Destiny referred to a long-established pattern in American life. Continental expansion dated back to the Louisiana Purchase, and indeed to the establishment of the first European communities on the North American continent.

The principal acts of annexation provoked a measure of partisan controversy.[69] The Democrats strongly favored bringing in as much territory as possible, and the major additions to the country took place during Democratic presidencies. The Whigs, who became the second major party in the late 1830s, had less enthusiasm for expansion although they were not opposed to it in principle. They emphasized economic development in what was already the United States and the acquisition of more territory through moral and economic example and voluntary, peaceful means rather than through coercion and conquest;[70] but they never advocated relinquishing any territory once the United States had formally acquired it. In addition, the Whigs tended to oppose the expansion of slavery in the new territories. The Democrats, a party dominated for most of the first half of the century by slaveholders, generally took the opposite position.

No nineteenth-century American had a greater commitment to territorial expansion than did John Quincy Adams. He believed, and said, that the United States should and would establish its western border on the Pacific Ocean.[71] His own principal contribution to the achievement of this goal came in the form of the agreement he made with the Spanish diplomat Luis de Onis in 1819, which is known to history as the Transcontinental Treaty.

The United States had emerged from the War of 1812 intact, and with enhanced confidence in its military capacity and its appetite for expansion whetted by the addition of Louisiana. Spain, by contrast, had been weakened by the Napoleonic Wars and the insurrections in its American possessions that would lead to the dissolution of its empire there. With the European great powers unwilling to intervene to protect that empire, the Spanish government decided to cede some of it to the growing republic to the north. Adams, then secretary of state, agreed with Onis on a line of demarcation between the United States and New Spain that zigzagged in a northwesterly direction from the westernmost point on the Gulf of Mexico of the Louisiana Purchase all the way to the Pacific Ocean on the southern border of what was then the Oregon territory.[72]

Under the treaty, Spain relinquished territory that it had no hope of keeping from the Americans over the long term while preserving as Spanish, temporarily as it turned out, Texas and California—which, with Mexican independence in 1821, became provinces of Mexico. The United States gained a large part of what became the middle of the country, much of it then known as the Missouri territory, and achieved Adams's goal of reaching the Pacific.[73] The American government agreed to pay the claims on the Spanish government of residents of the annexed territory up to $5 million. Not least important, the Treaty, which went into effect in 1821, gave the United States full control of Florida.

The present-day state of Florida was, before the United States acquired it, divided into two Spanish provinces: West Florida consisted of what became the Florida panhandle and the Gulf Coasts of Alabama and Mississippi; the peninsula jutting south from the Georgia border into the Caribbean was East Florida. After the acquisition of the Louisiana territory from France, the two Floridas had all of their land borders with the United States. They seemed to Americans to be the unfinished business of the Louisiana Purchase.[74]

American settlers filtered into Florida and expressed their unhappiness with Spanish rule there.[75] The Spanish possession also attracted former slaves and Indians fleeing oppression in the United States, giving the Americans a double motive for incorporating it.[76] As president, Thomas Jefferson unsuccessfully tried to do so, but his successor, James Madison, did manage to annex two segments of West Florida in 1813.

In the acquisition of the rest of Florida, the use of force by the United States did not remain in the background as a tacit threat. In 1818 Andrew Jackson led an army into East Florida, ostensibly to pacify a group of Seminole Indians, and, in effect, conquered it for the United States. President James Monroe had not explicitly authorized him to do so, but neither had he or Secretary of State Adams actively discouraged what they certainly suspected were Jackson's intentions.[77] Adams was already negotiating with Onis, and Jackson's invasion served to strengthen his hand.[78] By the terms of the Transcontinental Treaty, Spain ceded all of both Floridas to the United States.

Next on the list of major acquisitions came Texas. The new Mexican government passed a law in 1823 welcoming American settlers to its sparsely populated province.[79] By 1836 they outnumbered Hispanics by a ratio of ten to one.[80] The Americans proved to be a collective Trojan Horse. They rebelled against the government and, with assistance from the United States, secured independence in 1836: once again force, although not used directly by the American government, contributed to the addition of new territory to the United States. Its transfer, however, took a decade to consummate. Almost all the settlers strongly preferred incorporation into the United States to open-ended independence for Texas, and Democrats and Southerners (and many people, of course, were both) wanted it to become a state. Other Americans, however, objected to adding more territory where slavery could flourish. Not until the first year of the presidency of James K. Polk, in 1845, did the annexation of Texas finally take place.

The final episode in the process of filling in the map of the United States in North America through settlement by individual Americans and negotiations conducted with the prospect of war hovering in the background occurred in the Pacific Northwest. With the Oregon territory the United States confronted not Spain, which had renounced its claim there in the Transcontinental Treaty, but Great Britain, which was far more formidable in military, political, and economic terms and occupied a strong position in Canada.

In 1827, the Americans and the British had agreed to leave Oregon open indefinitely to citizens of both countries.[81] During that period and thereafter, as in Florida and Texas, Americans moved there in far greater numbers than any other nationality.[82] What became known as the Oregon question concerned the location of the border between the United States and Canada. Polk had made a public commitment to draw it at fifty-four degrees forty minutes latitude, a line farther to the north than the British were willing to concede. An American political slogan of the time was "54-40 or fight," and as tension between the two countries rose, armed conflict over Oregon began to seem altogether possible.[83] Then, in 1846, Polk agreed to compromise and accepted the already-existing Canadian-American dividing line east of Oregon at forty-nine degrees latitude as the final border stretching to the Pacific, where it has since remained.[84]

Polk backed down because a majority of the members of Congress, both his own Democrats and the opposition Whigs, made it clear that they would not support a war with Britain over Oregon.[85] He retreated from his initial position as well because he had begun another war, one that would bring into the federal Union territory comparable in scope to the gains of the Louisiana Purchase and the Adams-Onis Treaty, a war that would set the borders that would define the continental United States thereafter—a war with Mexico.

The Mexican War

The 1844 presidential election proved to be one of the most consequential in American history.[86] Polk, the winner, was the first "dark horse" candidate, a relatively obscure Democratic governor of Tennessee who defeated the better-known and more accomplished Whig candidate, Henry Clay of Kentucky. Polk turned out to be, with Thomas Jefferson and John Quincy Adams, one of the three greatest American expansionists of the first half of the nineteenth century. As president, he acted as the agent of Manifest Destiny.

His election led directly to the annexation of Texas and as he took office he said that he had four major goals. They included settling the Oregon question in order to extend the country's border to the Pacific Ocean, which, during his single term in office, he did, and acquiring California, which he also did.[87] Clay would almost certainly not have proceeded as he did.[88] Polk might have been content to acquire California in the same way that Florida, Texas, and Oregon became part of the United States: by letting the influx of American settlers incline the territory politically in that direction and then negotiating from a position of strength with Mexico to acquire it.[89] As occurred so often in the first hundred years of American foreign policy, however, the policies of Great Britain—actual, potential, and imagined—affected an American leader's calculations. Polk worried that the British might have designs on California or at least would help Mexico keep it.[90] For that and other reasons he adopted an aggressive policy toward Mexico, which led to war.

Like other presidents who led the United States into armed conflict, Polk was accused at the time, and thereafter, of having deliberately provoked the Mexican War.* The charge is not entirely fair. Polk was certainly willing to go to war—after all, that is what happened—and took steps that brought it about; but he hoped to obtain California without fighting.[91] In November 1845 he sent a special emissary, John Slidell, a former congressman from Louisiana, to Mexico to try to persuade the Mexican government to sell the province. At that point, however, and not for the last time, the United States ran afoul of fervent nationalist sentiment in a poorer, weaker country. The Mexicans refused to consider parting with what was legally their territory, although they exercised little control there.[92] The authorities in the Mexican capital refused even to meet with Slidell. Some Mexicans believed, incorrectly as it turned out, that if war came they could count on assistance from Great Britain, which, when the war did break out, was still embroiled in the dispute over Oregon with the United States.[93]

The president believed that forceful tactics yielded success in negotiations[94] and so, in order to put pressure on his Mexican counterparts, he dispatched an armed force led by General Zachary Taylor to the border between the recently annexed Texas and Mexico. The two countries disagreed, however, about the location of that border. Texans claimed territory as far south as the Rio Grande River; the Mexicans insisted that the boundary ran along the Nueces River, to the north and east of the Rio Grande. In April 1846, when the American troops entered the disputed territory, skirmishes with Mexican forces took place. Asserting that American soldiers had been attacked on American soil, Polk asked the Congress to declare war. As had happened before and would happen again in American history, the news of the fighting aroused public opinion, which supported retaliation. In an atmosphere of patriotic indignation, and by a healthy majority,[95] in May 1846 Congress passed a war resolution.

Since the purpose of the war was to acquire territory for the United States, soon after its outbreak Polk dispatched modest military

---

* Franklin Roosevelt was accused, for example, of knowing in advance of the Japanese assault on Pearl Harbor in 1861 and doing nothing to thwart it. Critics of the attack on Iraq in 2003 said that George W. Bush had lied about the presence in that country of weapons of mass destruction, one of the reasons for launching the attack. See pp. 206, 428-430.

detachments to the places in question, where Mexico was the legal authority but exercised little or no effective control, to establish an official American presence. He sent Colonel Stephen Kearny to New Mexico, which, encountering no resistance there, he declared to be part of the United States.[96] Kearney moved on to California where, at roughly the same time, two American military officers, Commander Robert Stockton and Captain John C. Fremont, took advantage of a small-scale uprising known as the "Bear Flag Revolt" to proclaim that Mexican province to be American territory as well.[97] Polk still needed Mexican acquiescence in a formal treaty for the United States to take legal title to the northern part of Mexico, which the Mexican government showed no sign of being willing to furnish.[98] The formal American military campaign in and against Mexico, which had begun shortly before the expeditions to New Mexico and California, therefore continued.

Taylor defeated a larger Mexican force at Monterrey in northern Mexico in September 1846.[99] After a two-month armistice and the evacuation of the city by the Mexican troops he pushed southward and, in February 1847, held his own at Buena Vista, in which the Mexican forces again outnumbered those of the United States—by a ratio of three to one.[100] Both demonstrated American military prowess—the use of artillery proved crucial at Buena Vista—but neither battle proved decisive: the Mexicans did not sue for peace.

Polk decided to open another front in the war, in the heart of Mexico. At Vera Cruz on the Gulf of Mexico in March 1847, an American land and sea force under the leadership of General Winfield Scott, one of the most accomplished commanders the United States ever produced,[†] staged an amphibious landing—perhaps the most complicated and hazardous of all military operations. It anticipated two other major American military undertakings of this kind in the twentieth century: at Normandy in World War II and at Inchon in the Korean War.

[†] John S. D. Eisenhower, *So Far from God: The U.S. War with Mexico, 1845–1848*, New York: Random House, 1989, p. xxv. Scott was less highly esteemed by the public than he was militarily accomplished. His nickname was "Old Fuss and Feathers." Zachary Taylor had a better reputation. He was known as "Old Rough and Ready" and it was he, not Scott, who was elected president in 1848.

Having successfully put ashore, Scott's troops laid siege to the heavily defended city, conquered it, and proceeded to march inland while cut off from the coast and therefore from reliable sources of supplies.

His army won another major battle at Cerro Gordo, in which a member of the Engineering Corps, Captain Robert E. Lee of Virginia, distinguished himself, and finally reached and occupied Mexico City in September. The United States finally had sufficient leverage to achieve its war aims: ending the conflict while acquiring the Mexican territory Polk and other Americans coveted.

Like other American wars, the one with Mexico generated opposition at home. The geographic center of dissent, as with the War of 1812, was New England,[101] where the writer Henry David Thoreau spent a night in jail for refusing to pay his taxes in protest against the conflict.[102] Most of the political opposition to the war came from the Whig Party, one of whose subsequently well-known members, Abraham Lincoln, then serving his only term in the House of Representatives, introduced a series of Congressional resolutions designed to show that the war had not begun with a clear-cut act of aggression by Mexico, as Polk had insisted.[103]

The critics charged that it was the United States that bore responsibility for starting the conflict and that the object of the war, the acquisition of territory, made it nothing more than attempted theft.[104] They also objected to the prospect of adding to the Union more territory in which slavery might be permitted.[105]

Few Whigs in Congress voted against the initial war resolution, an act that, given the public enthusiasm at the time for teaching Mexico a lesson, would have been politically risky.[106] That enthusiasm made it possible to recruit volunteers to supplement the small professional army that the United States maintained in 1845, without whom the army would probably not have fared as well as the American armed forces actually did.[107] As the war continued without reaching a decisive conclusion, however, it lost popularity, and the Whigs took political advantage of this trend. They identified the conflict with the president, calling it "Mr. Polk's War."[108] They managed to block or delay two of the president's war-related initiatives.[109]

In the end their opposition, and its timing, paid political dividends for the Whigs. They avoided the opprobrium of voting against the war at its outset, when it was popular. They gained control of the House of Representatives (although not the Senate) in the midterm election of 1846. And they won the presidency in 1848 with Zachary Taylor, a leading general in a war they had opposed, as their candidate.

In April 1847, with Scott making progress toward the Mexican capital but the war becoming increasingly unpopular, Polk, seeking to end it, sent a representative to Mexico to attempt once more to negotiate with the government there. Nicholas Trist was the senior civil servant in the State Department, a man with connections to the founder of Polk's political party, Thomas Jefferson, and considerable experience in Latin America.[110] Meanwhile, a segment of American opinion began to demand that peace terms include a larger part of northern Mexico than the president had initially intended to annex, a demand that, if fulfilled, would have brought many Hispanic, Catholic Mexicans into the Union. Some Americans even favored making all of Mexico part of the United States.[111]

Accordingly, Polk decided to expand his territorial requirements for peace and in October his secretary of state, James Buchanan, ordered Trist to return home. There followed the most spectacular act of insubordination in American history. Trist declined to return[112] and instead worked out a settlement with Mexico based on the earlier and more generous terms that he had initially been assigned to deliver, with the United States annexing less of the country, with far fewer Mexicans.[113]

On February 26, 1848, Trist and his Mexican counterparts signed the Treaty of Guadalupe Hidalgo, which embodied these terms. In exchange for a payment of $15 million, Mexico ceded what would become the state of California, most of Arizona, half of New Mexico, a quarter of Colorado, and a small section of Wyoming. Although angry at Trist, Polk calculated that submitting the treaty to the Senate for ratification served his interests.[114] Despite opposition from some senators who thought it too harsh and others who regarded it as yielding insufficient territorial gains, on March 10, 1848, it was approved.[115] Whether the Mexican government would ever have accepted Polk's later and more extensive territorial demands, and what the consequences of making all of Mexico (and all Mexicans) part of the United States would have been, cannot, of course, be known; but in retrospect Trist's decision to disobey orders seems to have rendered a considerable service to the president personally—although Polk did not regard it as such at the time—and to the United States more generally.[116]

If Oregon and Texas are included, James K. Polk acquired more territory for the United States than any of his predecessors or successors as president. That and his expansion of the presidential power to make war[117] are his enduring achievements. The settlement of the Mexican War filled out the southwestern part of the map of the United States[118] and gave the country, in California, what would become its most populous and sometimes its economically most dynamic state.

By expanding its territory, the war helped to lay the basis for the country's emergence as one of the world's great powers in the latter decades of the nineteenth century. So, too, did the American military performance. The Mexican War marked the American debut as a country capable of mustering and using military power for purposes beyond defense, which great powers have but weak powers lack.[119] It put on display what came to be America's military strengths: an unsurpassed logistical capability—projecting power all the way to Mexico City was an impressive feat—and the capacity to develop and utilize the most advanced military technology, which enabled Taylor and Scott to overcome Mexico's numerical advantage in manpower.[120]

The morality of the war on the American side remains contested, as it was at the time. It is difficult not to see it in retrospect, and notwithstanding the dispute over the circumstances of its outbreak, as a war of aggression; and its outcome made it plainly a war of territorial expansion, of the kind the great powers of Europe had waged for centuries but of which the American republic had consistently disapproved. In this sense the war did not advance the values Americans had aspired to spread beyond their borders since the republic's founding.‡

On the other hand, territorial expansion was the central theme of American history in the first half of the nineteenth century, supported, in one way or another, by almost all Americans; the territory that the

---

‡ Ulysses S. Grant, whose credentials as an American patriot can hardly be questioned, said of the Mexican War that it was "one of the most unjust ever waged by a stronger against a weaker nation." Kori Schake, *Safe Passage: The Transition from British to American Hegemony*, Cambridge, Massachusetts: Harvard University Press, 2017, p. 70.

United States acquired was largely uninhabited; and historically the people who have populated it have lived freer and more prosperous lives than their counterparts on the other side of what became the border with Mexico—who might, but for Trist, have become Americans as well. Certainly, once the Senate ratified the peace treaty, the issue of returning the territory to Mexico did not arise.[121] Perhaps it may be said of the conflict that it was successful by the standards of the nineteenth century and dishonorable by those of the twenty-first.

One other feature of the war offered a preview of things to come for the United States. In 1846 David Wilmot, a Democratic congressman from Pennsylvania, offered a proposal to prohibit any of the funds for the purchase of land ceded by Mexico from being used to incorporate territory where slavery was permitted. The Wilmot Proviso passed in the House of Representatives but failed in the Senate and did not become law. It demonstrated that the Mexican War had made the question of slavery, already a contentious matter, even more important in the national life of the United States and that the issue divided the country on sectional rather than on partisan lines.[122] Ultimately, the dispute over slavery came to dominate American politics. It was only resolved by a war between the nation's sections, the bloodiest and most destructive war ever fought in North America.

The Civil War

The two developments that made the United States a great power in the international system—the Industrial Revolution and territorial expansion—also caused the Civil War. In the eighteenth century, Americans believed, or at least hoped, that slavery would somehow die out.[123] The Industrial Revolution, however, transformed, by making far more productive, the textile industry, for whose now cheaper and more plentiful products—clothing—the global demand was all but inexhaustible. The transformation made cotton the industry's basic raw material.[124] Much of the territory acquired through the Louisiana Purchase was ideally suited to growing cotton, which became enormously profitable;[125] and slave labor turned out to be, from the standpoint of profitability, superior to free labor.[126] So the demand for slaves increased.[127]

While the institution of chattel slavery became well entrenched and popular in the cotton-growing South, in other parts of the country Americans increasingly considered it an abomination—an inhuman, intolerable violation of the principles on which the United States had been founded. States outside the South outlawed slavery within their own borders, and sentiment in favor of abolition grew. That meant that, as the country expanded, the addition of each new state provoked a fight over whether slavery would be permitted there.[128]

The first half of the nineteenth century produced a series of efforts at compromise on the issue. The Missouri Compromise of 1821 admitted Maine as a free state, admitted Missouri as a slave state, and prohibited slavery north of the thirty-six degrees thirty minutes parallel—part of the southern border of Missouri. The Compromise of 1850 defused, for a time, the disputes that the territorial acquisitions from the Mexican War provoked. The Kansas-Nebraska Act of 1854 (which repealed the Missouri Compromise) allowed the people of those two prospective states to decide for themselves whether to allow slavery.

The polarization of the country over the issue, however, became ever more acute. A virtual war broke out between proponents and opponents of slavery in what became known as "bleeding Kansas." The Supreme Court's Dred Scott decision of 1857 deeply offended Northerners by holding that people of African descent had no rights as American citizens, seeming thereby to establish slavery as unchallengeable in perpetuity. Southerners, for their part, were alarmed when John Brown, a fervent abolitionist, seized a federal arsenal in Harper's Ferry in what is now West Virginia in an effort to spark a slave uprising across the South. Brown was apprehended, tried, convicted, and hanged, but he became a hero and martyr to many in the North.[129]

In the 1850s the Republican Party, which opposed slavery, supplanted the Whigs as the nation's second major political party. When its candidate, Abraham Lincoln, won the 1860 presidential election, eleven southern states announced that they were seceding from the United States to form the Confederate States of America. In one of those states, South Carolina, on April 12, 1861, local forces fired on Fort Sumter, a federal military installation in the Charleston harbor. As with other American wars, the attack galvanized public opinion—on both sides. Thus began the Civil War.

The warring parties, the Union and the Confederacy, differed on more than slavery and in ways that proved crucial for the outcome of the conflict. The Northern states had become increasingly industrialized; the South remained largely agricultural. The North had seventy percent of the country's wealth as well as eighty percent of its banking assets.[130] The Union had a larger population—18.5 million people compared with 5.5 million free whites and 3.5 million slaves in the Confederacy.[131] The North therefore had a far greater potential for military power.

Each side regarded the other as aggressive and itself as the aggrieved, assaulted party that was acting to defend itself. Northerners saw the South as attempting, through measures such as the Dred Scott decision and the Fugitive Slave Act of 1850, which required that slaves be returned to their owners even from free states and that the federal government enforce this, to impose slavery on them. The South feared the addition of more free states to the Union heralded the day when the North would control national politics and impose abolition on them.[132]

Both sides, finally, saw themselves as defending fundamental American values: the Civil War was perhaps the most ideological conflict Americans have ever waged. Each believed that it was protecting the liberty on behalf of which Americans had rebelled against Great Britain in the eighteenth century, although they defined liberty differently.[133] The Union fought for the individual liberty that the South was denying to slaves.

For some Northerners, however, including Abraham Lincoln, the stakes were even higher than that. For them the United States represented an experiment in self-government of global significance. If the experiment failed through the breakup of the country, they believed, the political values that it embodied would suffer a devastating blow worldwide.[134] At the conclusion of his tribute to the Union soldiers who had fallen at the Battle of Gettysburg in July 1863—the most famous oration in all of American history—Lincoln exhorted his listeners to "resolve that these dead shall not have died in vain" so that "government of the people, by the people, for the people, shall not perish from the earth."

The Confederacy, by contrast, sought to preserve the liberty of its communities and states to live their lives as they—that is, the nonslaves—preferred and as they always had. The Southerners saw themselves as repeating the American Revolution, when the thirteen colonies had seceded from the British Empire.[135] The kind of liberty they believed they were defending would come in the twentieth century to be called self-determination, and Southerners fought for it with comparable determination to, and at even greater sacrifice than, their Northern counterparts.[136]

In its basic strategic form the Civil War resembled the Revolutionary War. The Confederacy, like the thirteen colonies in the earlier conflict, was the weaker party but possessed several advantages: its soldiers were defending their home region and consequently had shorter supply lines as well as a powerful incentive to fight. Many of the best officers and most experienced soldiers of the national army came from the South and put themselves at its service.[137] Not least important, in order to win, the Southern states had simply to avoid losing. Their goal was to compel, or to persuade (or to persuade by compelling), the North to give up its military effort to bring them back into the federal Union and concede independence to them. The North, like the British in the 1770s, was the stronger side but faced the task of mobilizing its military resources, projecting and sustaining its armed forces over long distances, and mustering the political will to absorb the costs of fighting on until victory.[138]

The course of the war was a tale of two theaters, two chronological periods, and two generals. The Union Army of the Potomac opposed the Confederate Army of Northern Virginia in the eastern theater— the states of Virginia, West Virginia, Maryland, and Pennsylvania. Much of the fighting took place in Virginia, where, in Richmond, the Confederacy established its capital. It was here that the war was finally decided. The western theater, on the other side of a line running north and south through the Appalachians, consisted of Alabama, Georgia, Florida, Mississippi, Kentucky, South Carolina, and Tennessee, as well as Louisiana east of the Mississippi River.

At first, between 1861 and the middle of 1863, the South had the upper hand in the fighting, especially in the east. From the middle of 1863 the North, in the face of continued and often fierce resistance, ground down the forces of the Confederacy and finally secured their surrender on April 9, 1865, at the village of Appomattox Courthouse in central Virginia.

The two leading generals, Robert E. Lee for the Confederacy and Ulysses S. Grant for the Union, had both graduated from the United States Military Academy at West Point (Lee ranked second in his class of forty-five, Grant twenty-first out of thirty-nine) and had served in the Mexican War. Lee came from a prominent Virginia family and had had the more distinguished pre–Civil War military career. He proved to be a master tactician, a daring commander, and an inspiring leader. He, rather than the Confederacy's president, Jefferson Davis (another West Point graduate who had also served in Mexico), became the symbol of the Southern cause; and in the wake of the war memorials to him were created all across the South.

Grant came from humbler origins—his father was a tanner in Ohio—and had had a less successful career in the army before the Civil War. In 1861 he had left the military and was working for his father in Illinois. He joined the Union army and rose quickly in its ranks, ending the war as its commanding general in charge of the Army of the Potomac. Grant had the disposition and the talent, as many of the other Union generals did not, to do what achieving the North's goals required: pursuing the Southern forces relentlessly and fighting and winning battles, even at great cost to his own forces. With the exception of the president, he did more than any other individual to win the war.

When the war began, neither side was well prepared for it and each believed that it could win quickly.[139] The first year of the war, culminating with the Battle of Shiloh in Tennessee, disabused them of this idea. Shiloh was the bloodiest engagement in American history to that point and made it clear that the war would be a long, difficult, and costly one.[140]

The South owed its early military success to Lee's tactical virtuosity and the timidity of his Northern counterparts. He achieved notable victories in the Peninsular Campaign, at the Second Battle of Manassas, at Fredericksburg, and especially at Chancellorsville, all of them in Virginia.[141]

In the second half of 1862 the North's war aims changed dramatically. In July, Lincoln disclosed to two cabinet members his intention to free all the slaves in the states of the Confederacy and on January 1, 1863, officially issued the Emancipation Proclamation.[142] It marked a sharp departure for both the Union and the president himself. While believing slavery to be morally wrong, Lincoln had not entered the presidency as a fervent abolitionist. His overriding goal was to preserve the Union. In a letter sent to the newspaper publisher Horace Greeley before making public his plans for emancipation he wrote:

> My paramount object in this struggle is to save the Union, and is not either to save or destroy slavery. If I could save the Union without freeing any slave I would do it, and if I could save it by freeing all the slaves I would do it; and if I could save it by freeing some and leaving others alone, I would also do that.[143]

The Emancipation Proclamation carried risks. Lincoln presided over a shaky pro-war coalition, parts of which—many Northern Democrats, for example—while wishing to keep the United States intact, did not favor abolition.[144] Indeed, as in wartime in other periods of American history, Lincoln and his cabinet became sufficiently concerned about internal opposition to undertake policies that encroached on citizens' liberties, suspending for a time the right of habeas corpus.[145]

Lincoln's decision on emancipation, and especially its timing, resembled the decision to declare independence in July 1776. Just as the colonists had hoped thereby to win support from other countries, especially France—a hope that was realized—so Lincoln had his eye on constituencies important to the Union cause. The most important of these was domestic. He depended on the states to furnish troops for the Union army and concluded that emancipation would generate the kind of enthusiasm necessary to keep its ranks filled.[146] He was also concerned with foreign opinion, especially in Great Britain, which harbored influential Confederate sympathizers but where slavery was widely unpopular.[147]

Lincoln did get the troops he needed and did make headway with British public opinion. Emancipation hindered the Confederate war effort by diminishing its labor force and making former slaves available to serve in the Union army. Most importantly, it transformed the war because it transformed the war's purpose for the North. The Union was no longer fighting to restore the political status quo in the South. It was waging war to make a social revolution there;[148] and that, up to a point, is what happened.

The tide of the war turned in the North's favor in mid-1863 with two major victories. In the West, Grant captured Vicksburg with a resourceful and determined campaign, giving the Union control of the Mississippi River and effectively cutting the Confederacy in half.[149] At the same time Lee, having invaded Union territory, was stopped at Gettysburg in southern Pennsylvania. His troops came close to breaking through the Union lines at several points but the Northern troops ultimately held firm and repelled them. To Lincoln's frustration, Lee was able to withdraw his forces without being pursued, but his offensive had come to an end.[150] Because it marked the turning point in the Civil War, and because that war was one of the three most important that the United States has ever waged, Gettysburg ranks with Saratoga in the Revolutionary War and the Battle of the Atlantic in World War II as one of the three most important military successes the United States has ever had.

In March 1864 Grant took charge of the Army of the Potomac[151] and won a series of costly battles against the Confederates.[152] While he was doing so, a Union army commanded by William Tecumseh Sherman captured Atlanta: the victory boosted Lincoln's political fortunes—the president had feared that he would lose the presidency in 1864[153]—and he won re-election in November of that year. Sherman's army next set out for Savannah and then proceeded to South Carolina. It employed scorched earth tactics, burning farms, tearing up railroads and other infrastructure, and confiscating food from the local people.[154] With much of the Confederacy devastated and his army defeated, Lee surrendered at Appomattox. By that time 360,000 Northern troops and at least 260,000 Confederate soldiers had died, a loss of life as great as in all the nation's other wars combined.[155]

The North won the Civil War because it far surpassed the South in military resources. "God," Napoleon said, "is on the side of the bigger battalions." The North's battalions proved, in the end, to be more numerous and better equipped than those of the South. The British had military superiority in the Revolutionary War, however, and did not win it. The Union succeeded where the mighty British Empire had failed for several reasons.

Technology gave the Union the means to overcome the difficulties of access that had frustrated Great Britain. The railroad and the steamship enabled the North to bring its military power to bear on the Confederacy in a way that had not been possible seventy-five years earlier.[156] Moreover, despite the political cleavages that it harbored, the Union was more highly motivated to prevent the secession of the Southern states than the British government and public had been to retain the colonies. The commitment to defending the American experiment and the liberty that it embodied inspired hundreds of thousands of young men from the North to volunteer for the cause, and to keep fighting for four long and bloody years. In addition, the length and ferocity of the war, the destructive power of the machine-age weapons that were used, and the tactics that the Union armies, especially the one led by Sherman, employed brought ruin to the South. The war destroyed half the livestock of the largely agricultural Southern states and reduced the value of their real property by half.[157] Photographs of Richmond at the war's end, in 1865,[158] bear a striking resemblance to those taken in Berlin, the capital of a country that also suffered a crushing defeat eighty years later, in 1945. Southerners fought long and doggedly and endured considerable hardship, but in the end the military assaults of the North broke their will to resist.[159]

The South chose not to adopt the military approach the thirteen colonies had successfully employed during the Revolutionary War. Rather than avoiding engagements, as George Washington had generally done, Lee fought one battle after another. In part this stemmed from the South's political and military culture, which emphasized the pursuit of glory through combat.[160] The South did not follow Washington's example, as well, because the government of the Confederacy felt obliged to defend all of its territory, as the Continental Army had not.[161] The approach also had a strategic rationale: if Southern forces won enough battles and inflicted enough casualties, the Confederacy could hope to weaken the North's morale, widen its political divisions, and perhaps bring advocates of a compromise peace to power—as at one point seemed to be the likely outcome of the 1864 presidential election. The Southern emphasis on taking the offensive and fighting and winning battles did not defy strategic logic; it simply, in the end, didn't work.[162]

Another Northern asset made a major contribution to its victory. As in the other two most important wars in American history—the Revolutionary War and World War II—in the Civil War the United States benefited from superior leadership. Abraham Lincoln came from much humbler origins than either George Washington or Franklin Roosevelt. Unlike Washington he did not lead troops in battle (nor did his Confederate counterpart Jefferson Davis, who had been a professional soldier), and he entered the presidency with far less executive experience than Roosevelt had had before his time in the White House. Like them, however, Lincoln excelled at the most important and difficult task a wartime president faces: keeping the country committed to fighting.

The sixteenth president turned out to possess in abundance the qualities necessary for the job he had to do. Lacking a background as a soldier, he quickly educated himself in military affairs, came to understand the requirements for victory, and performed admirably as commander in chief.[163] He demonstrated notable courage in insisting on prosecuting the war to a decisive conclusion despite serious setbacks and constant criticism. Not least important, he shrewdly and deftly managed the political aspects of the war, assembling and tending a fractious coalition of individuals, groups, political parties, and states that disagreed sharply among themselves and making good use of a cabinet composed of able but highly ambitious people, several of whom had aspired to the Republican nomination for president in 1860 that he had won. At a time when strong and effective leadership was needed to preserve the Union, Abraham Lincoln supplied it.

The Civil War differed from the Revolutionary War in one other important respect. In the eighteenth century, the weaker party that sought independence from the stronger one secured assistance from a foreign patron. The alliance with France proved indispensable for the colonies. In the nineteenth, the party attempting to secede did not receive decisive aid from abroad, but not for lack of trying. Although the actual fighting involved only Americans, the war did have a significant international dimension.

As the world's industrial and commercial leader, and because of its dominant navy the only European country with unfettered access to North America, Great Britain's attitude toward the Civil War mattered more than that of any other country.[164] The Confederacy hoped for, and even, at the outset of the conflict, counted on, British support, which could have taken several forms. Britain could have extended diplomatic recognition to the South, in which case other countries might well have followed suit. That would have conferred a major political benefit by giving the world's blessing to secession. The British could have supplied arms on a large scale and ensured their delivery by breaking the naval blockade that the North imposed on the South in the first year of the war.[165]

Southern leaders were optimistic about receiving some or all of these benefits because they believed that they wielded decisive leverage in the form of their exports of cotton. The British economy depended heavily on its textile industry centered in Lancashire, which in turn depended heavily on cotton from the American South.[166] The Confederacy therefore resorted to one of the oldest traditions of American foreign policy, by using trade as an instrument to obtain political concessions. It imposed an unofficial, informal embargo on the export of cotton, believing that in order to lift it the British government would take steps favorable to the Confederate cause.

The tactic failed. A bumper cotton crop in 1860 generated a surplus on which the British textile industry was able to draw. That industry also proceeded to diversify its source of supply, purchasing cotton from Egypt and India among other places.[167]

The Union's policy toward Britain was, of course, the opposite of the Confederacy's. The North sought to prevent the government in London from recognizing the South as a sovereign state and from providing assistance of any kind to it. In this, Lincoln's government largely succeeded; and one reason for its success was the British government's concern that tilting toward the Confederacy would trigger a conflict with the United States, perhaps at the expense of British Canada.[168] In this way the Union effectively, if tacitly, deterred Great Britain.

Although the British political system was less democratic than the American one—the franchise was more limited—public opinion did play a role in the making of British foreign policy and at the beginning of the Civil War that opinion was divided. Members of the upper class, who exercised disproportionate influence on public policy, harbored some sympathy for the South, which, as a hierarchical and agricultural society, corresponded to their own social and political preferences.[169] In addition, the British government calculated that the division of the United States would weaken a geopolitical rival.[170] On the other hand, especially among the country's middle class and workers, opposition to slavery ran deep.[171] In the end, the course of the war had a decisive impact on British policy. The government was tempted by Lee's early victories to side with the Confederacy but held off doing so; and as the North gained the upper hand on the battlefield, intervention on behalf of the South became steadily less attractive.

On a couple of occasions diplomatic incidents threatened to bring the North into serious conflict with Great Britain. In November 1861 a Union naval captain, acting on his own, intercepted the British vessel *Trent* and seized two representatives of the Confederacy who were traveling aboard it to Europe—one of them the same John Slidell whom President Polk had dispatched on a fruitless quest to negotiate with Mexico in 1845. The North at first celebrated the capture, but the British government objected on the grounds that it violated international law. Fearful of severely worsening relations with the British,[172] Lincoln ordered the two men released after a few weeks.[173]

The Confederate navy commissioned several ships to be built in British naval yards despite Britain's official neutrality in the conflict. One of them, the *Alabama*, destroyed or captured sixty-four American merchant ships before being sunk in June 1864. This time it was the American government's turn to protest, and in 1863 the British moved to block other such ships from sailing across the Atlantic.[174]

The other European powers followed the British example and refrained from recognizing the Confederacy. France, under Napoleon Bonaparte's nephew Napoleon III, did take advantage of the American preoccupation with the Civil War as well as continuing unrest in Mexico to try to establish, contrary to the Monroe Doctrine, a French protectorate in Mexico. French troops occupied the country and an Austrian archduke was dispatched to be the country's emperor. After Appomattox the American government forcefully expressed its opposition to what France had done. The French withdrew their support for it and the putative empire collapsed in 1867.[175]

With its powerful and destructive weapons, its massive armies and large, costly battles, the practice of conscription that both sides employed, and the toll it took on civilian populations, the Civil War introduced to the world the kind of "total war" that would be waged twice, on a global scale, in the twentieth century.[176] It also underscored a lesson that had emerged from the American conflict with Mexico: through its growing population, its mastery of the Industrial Revolution, and its capacity for generating armies and weaponry in large numbers and deploying them over vast distances, the United States of America possessed as much military potential as the traditional great powers of Europe.

In addition, the way the war ended foreshadowed an aspect of the country's military future. At Appomattox the Union dictated the terms of peace to the Confederacy. As a result, "unconditional surrender" came to be seen as not only the desirable but also the normal way for America's wars to conclude, although American governments were not always able to enforce it.

The postwar period offered a preview of what would become another feature of American foreign policy in the twentieth and twenty-first centuries. The program of Reconstruction in the South represented the first foray into what came to be known as nation-building. The North sought to replace the prewar South's hierarchical political system based on racial subordination with its own more egalitarian institutions and practices. It did abolish slavery once and for all, and for a time the former slaves were able to participate fully in the political life of the communities and states in which they lived. Racial equality encountered determined resistance from the white population, however, and the presence of Northern troops was required to maintain it after the war.

Eventually the Northern states tired of keeping military garrisons throughout the South and withdrew them. Racial subordination thereupon returned, albeit in new forms: segregation and the practice of sharecropping succeeded slavery.[177] As would be the case in the next century and beyond in foreign countries, an American effort at political transformation failed for lack of a receptive cultural basis among the people to be transformed and a limit to the willingness of the American people to persist in attempting it.

The most important and enduring significance of the Civil War lies in the fact that it determined what kind of nation the United

States would thereafter be. The North's victory sealed the triumph of Alexander Hamilton's principles and preferences over those of Thomas Jefferson. The war's outcome meant that the country would be urban, industrial, and commercial, with a large financial sector and ultimately a powerful state apparatus rather than a politically decentralized republic of yeoman farmers with a minimal government. A Hamiltonian country, unlike a Jeffersonian one, had the basis for deploying military power and wielding political and economic influence all around the world, which is what the United States proceeded to do in the following century and beyond.

The outcome of the Civil War laid the basis for the country's emergence as a great power in another way. It ensured that the United States would remain united. Had the South managed to secede, had America broken into two (or even more)[178] sovereign political communities, the country that continued as the United States would likely have been preoccupied in subsequent decades with North American affairs at the cost of involvement overseas and would in any case have had fewer resources—a smaller population and economy—to use as a platform for its international activities.

Such a historical development would have had profound consequences for the rest of the world, and especially for twentieth-century Europe. The United States played an indispensable role in rescuing and protecting Europeans from tyranny three times during that century, which it might well not have been inclined or able to do if the North had not won the Civil War. A British saying, referring to the preparatory school where members of the country's upper class, including the Duke of Wellington, were educated and presumably learned the art of leadership, has it that "the Battle of Waterloo was won on the playing fields of Eton." Similarly, the two world wars and the Cold War were won on the battlefield at Gettysburg.

The Second Age
Great Power, 1865–1945

Nobody doubts any more that the United States is a power of the first class, a nation which it is very dangerous to offend and almost impossible to attack.

The London *Spectator*, 1866[1]

The world of sovereign states that the United States joined when it gained its independence has always had a defining feature: an unequal distribution of its most important property—power. Historically, most states have been weak while a few have been strong. The term for the geopolitical giants of the planet that became common in the nineteenth century is "great power." After the Civil War, America joined this select company. Its new position in the international system established the challenges and the opportunities that the country faced over the next eight decades, a period when the United States was one great power among several and its foreign policy an American version of the foreign policies that great powers typically conduct.

An abundance of power—economic but chiefly military—defines great powers. Unlike their weaker brethren, they do not have to exercise constant vigilance to preserve their sovereign independence. Unlike the weak, they can project power beyond their borders, sometimes far beyond them.

No official register of the great powers exists: the term is an unofficial designation rather than a formal title, but in certain circumstances the world has implicitly acknowledged the countries in this category. In the wake of three major wars of the modern era the most powerful states acted in concert—if only briefly and not necessarily effectively— to try to reconstruct the international order that the war had destroyed as well as to prevent future such conflicts. The European states attending the Congress of Vienna in 1815 after the Napoleonic Wars, the countries whose leaders dominated the Paris Peace Conference in 1919 following World War I, and the permanent members of the United Nations Security Council in the wake of World War II were acknowledged by the world—and acknowledged one another—as the great powers of the day.*

The status of great power is not necessarily a permanent one. The international distribution of power has changed over time and with it the cast of characters at the summit of international politics. During the period in which the United States arrived at that destination, two transformational developments—the Industrial Revolution and the French Revolution—changed that distribution and thus membership in the ranks of the great powers. Spain, Portugal, and the Netherlands, once among the titans of the international order, failed to industrialize rapidly enough (and Portugal and the Netherlands lacked the size to compete with the great powers of the day) and so dropped out of the global upper class. The nationalism that the French Revolution inspired severely weakened the multinational Habsburg and Ottoman Empires, which finally collapsed after their defeats in World War I.

While these countries left the informal club of the great powers, in the second half of the nineteenth century three other countries joined

* At the Congress of Vienna, the four great powers were Great Britain, Russia, Austria-Hungary, and Prussia. The "Big Four" at Paris included the United States, Great Britain, France, and Italy. The five permanent members of the United Nations Security Council were in 1945, and continue to be, the United States, Russia (previously the Soviet Union), Great Britain, France, and China. Each grouping incompletely represented the great powers of the day because all excluded the losers of the recently concluded war: France on the first occasion, Germany and the recently established Soviet Union on the second, and Germany and Japan on the third.

it. The United States was one of them. Territorial expansion, population growth, industrialization, and the political unity assured by the outcome of the Civil War underpinned America's new international standing. Prussia expanded its territory and population through two victorious wars, in 1866 and 1870, and rapidly increased its industrial production. Japan emerged from decades with little contact with the rest of the world and became the first Asian country to create an industrial base that supported an army and a navy comparable to those of the most powerful European countries.

Great powers conduct two kinds of foreign policies: toward weaker countries and toward one another. The history of American foreign policy between 1865 and 1945 encompasses both, in each case following the general outlines of the policies of other great powers but in both cases with characteristically American features.

* * *

In international relations the strong tend to dominate the weak, usually the weak that are located geographically close to them but sometimes in places far away. In the nineteenth century domination almost always took the form of multinational empires: hereditary monarchies ruled territories on which more than one ethnic, religious, or national group lived.

By contrast, the United States did not have or want a monarch. To the contrary, the Americans had cast aside the British Crown in the eighteenth century. In the first half of the nineteenth century, as the size of the country increased, while people immigrated to it from various parts of Europe the immigrants were expected to adopt the language and customs of their new homeland. America was emphatically not a multinational state and indeed deliberately refrained from annexing territory inhabited by people who were not white Protestants. Nor was it an imperial state. Thomas Jefferson had foreseen the United States becoming an "empire of liberty"; but by the standards of nineteenth-century imperial governance the term was an oxymoron—an empire denied liberty to many (and sometimes all) of its inhabitants, and in this sense the United States did not qualify as one.

The nineteenth century was an era not only of imperial rule but also of imperial expansion because the Industrial Revolution widened the gap in power between the strong and the weak. Their early advantages in the machines of both transportation and war gave the European empires both readier access to distant parts of the planet than had previously been possible and the means to extend their imperial reach to unconquered parts of Africa, Asia, and the Pacific.[†] The knowledge that other empires had comparable opportunities gave them an incentive to expand in order to preempt their imperial rivals.

The United States participated in what turned out to be the last great episode of imperial expansion, acquiring a formal empire in its immediate neighborhood to the south and the west. In the decades after the Civil War, the country had increased its influence in these directions and in the pivotal year 1898 it fought a war with Spain—the first of several it was to wage overseas during the succeeding twelve decades—as a result of which it took control of Cuba and Puerto Rico in the Caribbean and Hawaii and the Philippines in the Pacific.

While the United States became an imperial power, its experience as an empire differed in important ways from those of its European counterparts. Two of the recurring features of American foreign policy marked the country's imperial experience: democracy, in the form of domestic opposition to the acquisition of overseas territories, and ideology, in that Americans—some at least—believed that they had accepted an imperial vocation for the purpose of spreading liberty. Compared to the European empires, moreover, the American one had a short life.

Finally, while the fact of empire loomed large in the histories of the great powers of Europe, it had only a very modest effect on the United States. Few Americans were involved, directly or indirectly, with the country's imperial possessions while it had them, or placed much value on them, or indeed paid any attention to them. By contrast, the relations

---

[†] Great Britain enlarged its empire in South and Southeast Asia, France in North Africa and Indochina, and Russia across Eurasia to the Pacific Ocean. The great powers also carved out trading entrepôts along the coast of China and, at the end of the century, divided among themselves the last unconquered continent, Africa.

of the United States with the other great powers had, in the first half of the twentieth century, an immense impact on its national life.

* * *

Great powers have occasionally cooperated with one another, notably to try to reconstruct the international order after the Napoleonic Wars and the two world wars. In that spirit, following the Civil War, the government in Washington found ways to cooperate with the foreign country that remained, to the end of the century and beyond, the most important one for America: Great Britain. In addition, at the turn of the twentieth century America engaged in limited cooperation with the European powers that it had joined in exploiting the economic opportunities available in a weakened Chinese empire.

Historically, however, the great powers have competed rather than cooperated with one another. When they have gone to war, these conflicts have become the defining events of international history, making and breaking states and empires and rearranging the hierarchy of great powers.[2]

In matters of great-power conflict the United States followed a particular path, one established before the American Revolution and maintained thereafter by Great Britain. While imitation may be the sincerest form of flattery, the Americans did not adopt the great-power habits of the British in order to flatter them, or even because, of all the great powers, the United States stood closest to Britain in the political values to which it adhered—although this was not irrelevant to American foreign policy. What underlay the American affinity for the British approach was geography.

As an island off the coast of Europe, Great Britain had a particular and overriding interest on the continent: to prevent any single great power from achieving continental dominance, for such a dominant power might be able to invade and occupy the British Isles.[3] A similar calculation guided the United States. Like Britain it did not aspire to control territory in Europe (although, unlike the British, the Americans did not have a vast overseas empire to protect), but the United States had a strong interest in making certain that no European power could threaten North America. To be sure, the Atlantic Ocean that separated the New World from the Old afforded considerably more protection for this purpose than did the English Channel. Still, the march of technology made the Atlantic Ocean ever easier to cross (and in the second half of the twentieth century intercontinental ballistic missiles rendered it useless in protecting North America from attack from afar). So the American policy toward Europe had the same general goal as that of Great Britain, although it was, in the first half of the twentieth century, a less urgent one.

When a European power sought continental domination—Louis XIV and Napoleon of France, imperial and Nazi Germany, and, in the second half of the twentieth century, the Soviet Union—a coalition to block it formed and the British joined it. As part of these coalitions the British preferred playing the role of "offshore balancer." They sought to ensure a balance of power on the continent by means of a blocking coalition that checked the ambitions of the state seeking dominance.[4] Located offshore from Europe, Britain preferred to contribute to the "counterhegemonic" coalition by sending money to its continental allies to enable them to raise larger armies rather than dispatching British troops to fight the disruptive power directly. The British traditionally had a smaller army than the continental powers and assigned much of it to police the empire while maintaining a superior navy. Ultimately, however, the course of its wars against France and Germany compelled the British to send their own soldiers to fight in land battles on the continent in order to forestall a continental hegemony.

In the two world wars the United States, too, began as an offshore balancer, dispatching money and military supplies to the members of the blocking coalition, which on both occasions included Great Britain. In the end, however, to prevent Germany from controlling Europe— and in the Second World War to keep Japan from dominating Asia— American forces went into battle, and not only on land but also at sea and in the air.

If the Spanish-American War of 1898 marked the debut of the United States as a full-fledged imperial power, World War I began the American career—a far more consequential one for both the United States and the rest of the world—as a European power. Between the two world wars, and contrary to popular belief, America did not retreat entirely from the continent. It maintained a role in European affairs but, following the offshore balancer's preference for avoiding direct military engagement, that role was principally an economic one.

As in its brief and modest spell as an imperial power, the relations of the United States with the world's other great powers displayed both the democratic and the ideological character of its foreign policy. Public opinion resisted involvement in both world wars and had a particular impact on the second one: before the official American entry into the conflict in December 1941, President Franklin D. Roosevelt wanted to provide maximal assistance to Great Britain but public opposition restrained him. In both conflicts, the American government proclaimed the spread of liberty to be a major war aim. In both world wars the country's ideological goals did not conflict with the country's geopolitical aims. In both, America's values and interests were generally aligned—although not entirely so: the United States fought to prevent a single illiberal power from dominating Europe in both cases but in World War II allied itself, for this purpose, with another distinctly illiberal country, the Soviet Union.

In the immediate aftermath of the Civil War in 1865, the Union demobilized its military forces and had no thought of taking any part in European affairs. In the immediate aftermath of World War II, eighty years later, the United States had powerful military forces deployed all over the world, having established a major presence in Europe and in Asia as well, both of which were destined to endure into the following century. Thus the trajectory of the American global role in this period: at the outset, with the demobilization of the Union's military forces, the United States was the least of the great powers; at the end it had become the greatest of them, indeed so powerful that it achieved a new international status even higher than that of great power.

4

Great-Power Debut, 1865–1914

The Foundations of Great Power

A country's power in the international system rests on the extent of its territory, the size of its population, and, perhaps most important of all, the magnitude of its wealth.[1] Since the nineteenth century wealth has been measured in industrial terms. In the five decades between the end of the Civil War and the outbreak of World War I the population and the economy of the United States expanded at a dizzying pace.[‡] That expansion changed America more dramatically than in any other fifty-year period,[2] from a largely rural republic of farmers to an urban industrial nation[3] and from a country with a Protestant population whose origins, with the exception of African-Americans, lay mainly in the British Isles to a religiously plural society whose citizens had roots in southern and eastern Europe and in East Asia as well.

These changes created social and economic problems, and sharp political cleavages over whether and how to address them, which took up

---

[‡] "In the decades between the end of the Civil War and the outbreak of World War I, the United States became a recognizably modern society. In 1864 the country still bore the traces of the old world of subsistence. Cities contained as many animals as people, not just horses but also cows, pigs, and chickens . . . most buildings were still made of wood. By 1914 Americans drank Coca-Cola, drove Fords, rode underground trains, worked in skyscrapers . . . lit and heated their houses with electricity, flew in airplanes or at least read about flights, and gabbed on the phone, courtesy of AT&T." Alan Greenspan and Adrian Wooldridge, *Capitalism in America: A History*, New York: The Penguin Press, 2018, p. 91.

almost all of the country's political attention and energy. Little was left over for foreign policy. In the three decades after Appomattox, relations with other countries had less importance in American public life than before or afterward. Still, that thirty-year period had a major impact on the foreign policy of the United States because in those decades the foundations of the nation's role as a great power were laid.

In contrast to the first half of the nineteenth century, in the wake of the Civil War the United States did not make major additions to its territory, with one exception. In 1867 Secretary of State William H. Seward purchased the Russian imperial economic colony in North America for $7.2 million, and Congress approved the transaction. Located across the Bering Strait from Russia at the edge of the Arctic Ocean, and attached mainly to Canada, it ultimately became, almost a century later, the northernmost state of the Union.

The Russians decided to sell it for some of the same reasons that Napoleon had parted with Louisiana six decades earlier. They believed that the United States would eventually take the territory whatever they did, and the sale brought the tsar's government much-needed revenue in the wake of Russia's defeat in the Crimean War.[4] The Americans called their new northern acquisition Alaska.[5]

Thereafter their government added no territory of consequence for three decades. This was not for lack of trying by important officials. Seward in particular, the most prominent and enthusiastic expansionist since John Quincy Adams, considered the Asia-Pacific region a logical place, although not the only one, for the United States to plant its flag.[6] President Ulysses S. Grant, who served from 1869 to 1877, sought to annex Santo Domingo (subsequently known as the Dominican Republic).[7] Their efforts failed because their countrymen, and thus their countrymen's elected representatives in Congress, were dubious about adding territory that would bring with it people who were neither white nor Protestant. Moreover, what had become the normal form of territorial expansion, to areas geographically contiguous to what was already the United States, was not feasible; the Canadians were, as ever, unwilling to join the Union[8] and Americans regarded Mexicans as unsuitable for citizenship in the United States.

In the post–Civil War era, Americans moved in large numbers into the lands the country had already acquired. Between 1870 and 1900 they settled more territory than in the entire previous history of the United States.[9] Settlement took place because, among other reasons, the number of Americans grew rapidly. In 1865 the nation's population stood at 35.7 million. In 1885 it was 56.6 million. By 1900 it had swelled to 99.1 million.[10] Whereas in 1850 the United States had had roughly the same number of people as Great Britain, France, and what became the German Empire, by the eve of the First World War it had surpassed them all. Of the European powers, only the Russian Empire had a larger population.[11]

Population growth came both from a still relatively high birth rate and, increasingly in this period, from immigration. In 1865 the United States welcomed 248,000 people from abroad; in 1885, 395,000; and in 1914, 1.2 million. During five of the eight years preceding 1914 the number exceeded 1 million.[12] In 1910, 13.5 million people living in the country had been born abroad, which was 14.7 percent of the total population. Most came from southern and eastern rather than northern Europe.[13] Some of the new Americans were fleeing political or religious oppression but the majority immigrated in search of better economic opportunities, and most found them.[14]

The inflow of immigrants created a backlash among native-born Americans, whose wages sometimes fell as the labor pool expanded[15] and who often found the cultural habits the newcomers brought to be disturbing and even threatening. In this way immigration affected domestic American politics.[16] It also affected the nation's relations with other countries, as various ethnic and national groups sought to persuade the American government to support the members of their group who had remained in Europe—another example of the democratic character of American foreign policy. Irish-Americans opposed cooperation with England, the imperial power in their home island, and in the years before the two world wars German-Americans similarly attempted to weaken American ties with Germany's British adversary. In the early twentieth century American Jews lobbied for sanctions against, or at least expressions of disapproval of, the tsarist government of Russia and its antisemitic policies.[17]

Immigrants from Asia inadvertently affected foreign policy by inspiring political movements seeking to restrict their entry into the United States, which then created problems for the United States in their home countries. The vast construction project of extending the railroad to the Pacific attracted workers from China, which gave rise to political efforts to limit and ultimately to prohibit them.[18] This caused enough anger in China to trigger a boycott of American goods there, which the government in Peking tacitly supported.[19] Japanese immigration to the United States also stirred resentment, and to restrain it the governments of the two countries negotiated "Gentlemen's Agreements" that placed limits on the number of Japanese permitted entry.[20]

Immigration also had a broader, less tangible but ultimately more enduring and consequential impact on the nation's external relations. While most European and other countries consist largely of people with the same religion, language, and/or ethnicity whose ancestors have lived on its territory for generations, the United States came to be composed of people who arrived, or whose ancestors had arrived, from many different places. The newcomers had in common not religion, native language, or ethnicity, but rather a commitment, which they either brought with them to the New World or acquired once there, to the founding principles of the republic, above all liberty. This enhanced the importance of these principles in American public life and therefore in its relations with other countries. In this way, immigration reinforced the ideological character of American foreign policy.

As impressive as the country's increase in population in the decades following the Civil War, and just as important—perhaps even more so—as a component of international power, was the continuing economic growth of the United States. In the decade of the 1870s its average gross national product was an estimated $7.4 billion.[21] On the eve of World War I it had risen to nearly $40 billion, which far surpassed those of the European great powers.[22] By then Americans also had the highest per capita income in the world.[23] The advance was all the more impressive because the country suffered two financial crises during that period, in 1873 and 1893, which slowed growth.[24]

That growth followed the path begun in Britain and subsequently taken by countries around the world: people moved in large numbers from rural to urban settings and abandoned their farms for factories, where they were much more productive. They were willing to move, and able to find work when they did, because the American economy after the Civil War benefited—indeed took the lead in—what came to be called the Second Industrial Revolution. Its defining features were the widespread use of electricity and the domination of steel in construction and petroleum in energy. The United States became the world's largest producer of both.[25] The Second Industrial Revolution transformed the United States in ways that relegated to the past the nation of sturdy farmers that Thomas Jefferson had envisioned and preferred. It created one of the things that Jefferson had feared: very large private economic concerns, the most notable of which, at the turn of the twentieth century, were United States Steel and Standard Oil.

Individual initiative drove American economic growth in the second half of the nineteenth century as it had the settlement of the country in the first half and did subsequently. The country produced inspired tinkerers and organizers who invented and applied the technologies that spurred economic advance in both the United States and Europe before the Civil War, men such as Cyrus McCormick and his mechanical reaper, Robert Fulton and the steamboat, and Samuel F. B. Morse and the telegraph.[26] Thereafter such men tended not only to invent technologies but also to find ways to produce and use them on a large scale. They included Isaac Singer and the sewing machine, Thomas Edison and the light bulb, and Henry Ford and the motor car.[27]

Beginning during the Civil War, the federal government adopted policies designed to encourage and support economic growth. Even as the war was raging, President Lincoln, an admirer of the Whig leader Henry Clay's program of "internal improvements"[28] (later to be called "infrastructure"), presided over the passage of the Homestead Act of 1862, which encouraged the settlement of the lands acquired in the 1840s; the Morrill Act of 1862, which provided for the founding of universities throughout the country; and the Pacific Railway Acts of 1862 and 1864, which underpinned the surge of postbellum railroad building.[29] Abraham Lincoln did more than any previous president to implement Alexander Hamilton's vision for the United States.

American economic growth had a profound impact on the world all apart from its contribution to the country's power in the international system because it introduced previously unknown products and processes that other countries proceeded to adopt and that thus became standard features of modern life.[30] The "American system" of mass production yielded goods of high quality on a large scale at increasingly affordable prices.[31] It made widely accessible useful possessions, and food, far beyond the few necessities with which all but the most powerful and affluent had had to content themselves for generations. Plentiful and affordable consumer goods became an eagerly embraced part of modern life, first in the United States, then in Europe, and ultimately virtually everywhere.[32]

Among the things available for mass consumption that the United States introduced before World War I, that exploded in volume and popularity afterward, and that spread around the world was entertainment. With the diffusion of electricity, it no longer had to be performed live before a limited audience, as had been the case since the time of the ancient Greeks.

To the economic activity that by definition involves interaction with other countries, cross-border trade, the Civil War brought a major change. Until 1861 the United States had pursued a policy of relatively free trade because the Democratic Party had dominated politics at the national level and represented constituencies—above all southern agriculture—to which trade brought economic benefits. The war shifted the balance of power in the country. It led to the supremacy of the party of the Union and of Lincoln, the Republicans, whose domination lasted, with a few interruptions, until the 1930s. The Republicans represented northern and midwestern manufacturers, who favored tariffs to protect their industries from foreign competition.[33] The Democrats continued to favor more open trade but lacked the power to bring it about.[34]

Tariffs therefore rose, which meant, among other things, that the federal government could no longer make ready use of the policy of trying to use trade as a source of leverage to achieve political goals, a policy to which Americans had resorted since before independence.[35] Reducing the inflow of goods from abroad became a matter of economic principle and therefore difficult to employ as an occasional foreign policy tactic.[36]

Despite American tariffs, and the move to protection by most European countries after 1870,[37] the volume of transatlantic trade increased until 1914. This seemingly paradoxical trend came about because of the dramatic decline in transportation costs during this period.[38] The railroad and the steamship made it possible to sell American wheat and cotton in particular at ever-lower prices in Europe.[39] Tariffs notwithstanding, the years from 1870 to 1914 proved to be the first great age of globalization;[40] and the United States, which by then had the largest economy in the world, participated in it—exporting commodities (and ultimately manufactured goods)[41] and importing people.[42]

In this era, as well, American finance came of age. Banks, like firms in other industries, grew large. For its first hundred years almost exclusively an importer of capital, by the twentieth century the United States had begun to export it, through the large firms that came into existence in the last decade of the nineteenth century that conducted international operations.[43] Three consequential financial developments took place in this period: in 1879 the United States adopted the gold standard;[44] in 1909 it enacted the Sixteenth Amendment to the Constitution, which permitted the levying of an income tax; and in 1913 it established the Federal Reserve, the American version of a national central bank.

The last two of these made significant contributions to American power in the international system in the twentieth century and beyond. The income tax furnished the means to support a far-reaching foreign policy, something that tariffs, which had been the major source of federal revenue, could not do because they did not bring in enough money for this purpose.[45] The Federal Reserve provided a mechanism for financial stabilization, not only in the United States but also, ultimately, up to a point, in other countries as well.

The years immediately preceding the First World War saw the federal government launch a brief effort at using finance for political purposes abroad. President William Howard Taft's "Dollar Diplomacy" did not succeed,[46] but in subsequent decades the deployment of capital did come to play a significant role in American foreign policy.[47]

While the United States accumulated the demographic and economic bases for a major international role between 1865 and 1914, it was slow to translate them into power that could be wielded effectively in the international arena.[48] In part because, unlike the great powers of Europe, it did not face serious threats from its neighbors, America did not build armed forces on anything approaching the scale of which it was capable until World War I.[49] Nor, because of the deep Jeffersonian prejudice against a too-powerful state, did it have a government large enough and strong enough[50] to conduct an expansive foreign policy.[51]

Gradually, the country's actual capabilities did catch up with its potential. In the decades between the Civil War and World War I America became a great power, in important ways on a par with the strongest countries in Europe. It began by establishing, in its geographic neighborhood, what is often called a sphere of influence. As Britain had done, for example, in Latin America in the first part of the nineteenth century, the United States exerted influence without taking direct control of the countries it dominated. It also inserted itself into the great-power politics of East Asia. Then, in 1898, like Britain and the other European great powers, America acquired a formal empire, which it governed directly. Finally, with World War I, it became a European and therefore a global power, with immensely important consequences for both America and the world.

Spheres of Influence

Lacking a tradition of governing alien peoples and of annexing territory beyond North America, the United States nonetheless began, in the wake of the Civil War, to extend the scope of its influence outside its homeland. It had no master plan for this purpose; rather, a series of uncoordinated initiatives created spheres of influence in its immediate neighborhood, which encompassed Pacific islands to the west[52] and Central America to the south.

Americans took an early interest in Hawaii. Located 2,000 miles from the part of North America nearest to it, and the most isolated archipelago in the world,[53] what Westerners originally called the Sandwich Islands remained undiscovered until the British captain James Cook's third voyage of exploration in 1778.[54] The first American set foot there in 1790 and Protestant missionaries arrived in 1819. Sugar became Hawaii's cash crop, with most of it exported to the United States. By 1842 the islands had become important enough in American eyes for President John Tyler to apply the Monroe Doctrine to them, thereby expanding to the Pacific Ocean the scope of his country's claims to a privileged position beyond its borders.[55]

In 1875 the Grant administration signed a treaty of commercial reciprocity with the indigenous Hawaiian government that granted to the islands' sugar duty-free access to the American mainland, a major advantage for their predominantly American sugar growers. The two governments renewed the treaty in 1887 and the United States gained the right to use Pearl Harbor to supply coal to its ships and as a repair base.[56]

Then, in January 1893, the melodically named Hawaiian Queen Liliuokalani dismissed the legislature and announced her intention to exercise supreme power. This precipitated a successful revolt that involved, among others, the American businessmen in the islands and drew sympathy from the American government, which landed armed sailors from a ship in Honolulu Harbor. A provisional government was formed that sought annexation by the United States. As with the comparable case of Texas six decades earlier, the authorities in Washington resisted formal annexation[57]—at least for a few years. Even so, the proclamation of a Hawaiian republic on July 4, 1894, enhanced the already strong ties between the islands and the mainland.[58]

Further away from North America in the Pacific, the United States also established a presence in Samoa, a group of fourteen inhabited islands located 1,500 miles southwest of Honolulu and 4,000 miles from San Francisco that held attractions for both shipping and naval interests.[59] An American naval officer concluded a treaty with local chiefs for the use of the harbor at Pago Pago in 1872 but the Senate refused to ratify it. In 1878, however, it did approve a similar accord.

In 1889, Germany, as part of its campaign to establish an empire in the southwest Pacific, tried to dislodge the United States from Hawaii. Naval combat briefly seemed imminent but the two countries, along with the other European power in the Pacific, Great Britain, reached a tripartite agreement for a protectorate over the islands. Ultimately the British dropped out and the Americans and Germans divided predominance in Samoa, with the United States getting Pago Pago.[60]

Even more than in the case of Hawaii, American policy toward Samoa made little impact in the United States; it seems unlikely that many Americans were even aware of it. By the standards of the great powers of Europe, neither counted as a major acquisition. Unlike Hawaii, moreover, American firms and individuals had no economic motive for involvement in the Samoan islands. The attraction, which Hawaii also held out, was strategic in nature, having to do with Samoa's location.[61]

To its south, the United States had, with the Monroe Doctrine, declared a proprietary interest well before the Civil War. From the end of the nineteenth century, Washington conducted an intrusive policy toward the small countries of Central America,[62] dispatching troops a number of times to preserve Western investments, collect debt, and enforce political stability, and even helping to carve out a new country in order to build a canal linking the South Atlantic Ocean with the Pacific. If a sphere of influence is defined as a place where a country can more or less do as it wishes, then Central America qualifies as one for the United States. On occasion the American government even inserted itself further to the south, in South America proper. In 1894 Grover Cleveland, hardly a bellicose president, dispatched five ships to the coast of Brazil to intervene in an internal power struggle and to protect American interests.

The Cleveland administration suspected that the British were attempting to use the Brazilian upheaval to enhance their own position there.[63] In several other Latin American episodes as well, America encountered Great Britain, the one European power that, because of its naval and commercial prowess, had a major presence in the Western Hemisphere. The Anglo-American relationship, in the Americas as elsewhere, changed over the decades; and its trajectory reflects the transition of the American international position from weakness to strength. As the nineteenth century wore on, its dealings with Britain certified the United States as a great power.

The initial sign of a change in Anglo-American relations, and thus in the international status of the United States, came not from an incident in Latin America but rather as part of the legacy of the Civil War. In 1871 the two countries signed the Treaty of Washington, in which the British agreed to arbitration for Washington's claims for compensation for the damage inflicted during the war by Confederate ships built in England. The accord also resolved conflicts over the border between Canada and the United States and over the economically significant issue of access to Atlantic fisheries.[64] The Washington Treaty signaled the British recognition of the importance of good relations with its former imperial possession and of the need to treat the North American republic as an equal.

In 1895 Washington intruded on a boundary dispute between Britain and Venezuela over British Guiana, demanding that arbitration take place and invoking the Monroe Doctrine. In a note to the government in London, the American secretary of state, Richard Olney, gave the most expansive interpretation yet offered of the American role in Latin America, asserting that "the United States is practically sovereign on this continent" and that "its fiat is law upon the subjects to which it confines its interposition."[65] The British at first declined to respond at all, then rejected Olney's claim.[66] Tensions rose between the two countries and the government in London decided to back down, tacitly conceding the American interpretation and American primacy in the Western Hemisphere. This was a major signpost in the history of American foreign policy: the British not only acknowledged the United States as a fellow great power but also recognized an American sphere of influence in a region in which they had once held greater sway than all other outside powers.[67]

In 1902 another Venezuelan crisis erupted, over the country's refusal to pay debts owed to European creditors. A joint German-British-Italian naval force blockaded Venezuelan ports and bombarded two forts. The United States at first agreed to the action but then became alarmed at German although not British intentions in the hemisphere, Germany appearing to the American government to be the more aggressive of the two.[68] This episode portended a development in America's relations with the great powers—a favorable attitude toward Great Britain, and an unfavorable view of Germany—that would have momentous twentieth-century consequences for all three countries, and indeed for the whole world.

The second Venezuelan crisis led to a restatement, and expansion, of the Monroe Doctrine, and thus of the American definition of its role in Latin America. It became known as the Roosevelt Corollary because its authoritative articulation came in President Theodore Roosevelt's annual message to Congress in December 1904: "Chronic wrongdoing," it said,

> or an impotence which results in a general loosening of the ties of civilized society, may in America, as elsewhere, ultimately require intervention by some civilized nation, and in the Western Hemisphere

the adherence of the United States to the Monroe Doctrine may force the United States, however reluctantly, in flagrant cases of such wrongdoing or impotence, to the exercise of an international police power.[69]

Whereas in its original formulation the Monroe Doctrine had declared the Americas off limits to colonization by the European great powers, its reformulation arrogated to the United States the prerogative of intervening in the internal affairs of the countries of the region. Roosevelt's statement did not claim the right to impose full-time, formal imperial governance on Latin America, but it did assert the right to act, on occasion, as the de facto government there when and as the United States chose.

Even before the proclamation of the Roosevelt Corollary, British recognition of the United States not only as a fellow great power but also as the predominant power in the Western Hemisphere had reached another milestone. The Clayton-Bulwer Treaty of 1850 had stipulated joint Anglo-American control of a putative isthmian canal linking the Atlantic and Pacific Oceans, which would be an economic asset for America because it would reduce shipping costs between the two coasts. American opinion became dissatisfied with the idea of sharing control

and in 1900 Secretary of State John Hay and the British ambassador to Washington Julian Pauncefote negotiated a new pact, which ceded to the United States the sole right to build and operate such a canal.[70]

Anglo-American relations at the end of the nineteenth century and the beginning of the twentieth looked forward to the partnership of the two countries in the two world wars, but also backward, to the eighteenth century. Great Britain made concessions to the United States in the Western Hemisphere for the same reasons that it had conceded independence in the 1780s. The burden of empire weighed ever more heavily on the government in London, as did its commitment to the increasingly challenging task of sustaining an equilibrium of power on the European continent.[71]

In light of these responsibilities, as well as of the rapidly growing power of the United States, the British relinquished the position they had maintained in Latin America for much of the nineteenth century.[72]

They did so believing—rightly—that the United States could be counted on to respect and even safeguard their still-considerable interests there,[73] and that the sacrifice of a no-longer-tenable claim to a commanding position to the south of the United States was a reasonable price to pay for American friendship.

Such a friendship did develop. While the antagonism to Great Britain that dated from the Revolution did not disappear,[74] a growing number of Americans, some of them in positions of political influence,[75] came to see the two countries as having not only common interests but also a common destiny to dominate international politics and thus to shape the world, a destiny based on race, culture, and history that came to be known as Anglo-Saxonism.[76] The sense that they shared common values also contributed to the wartime alignments of the two countries in the first half of the twentieth century.

Anglo-American relations offered one indication of the new, post–Civil War international status of the United States. Another appeared on the far side of the Pacific Ocean. There, the United States took its place as one great power among several. There, too, in its policies toward China, the United States first undertook the approach to other great powers that it would adopt twice, in the context of world war, toward Europe.

East Asia

In East Asia, in the decades between the end of the Civil War and the outbreak of World War I, the United States neither dominated the region, as it came to do in Central America, nor absented itself entirely from its political affairs, as it did in Europe. On the far side of the Pacific, America established a presence along with other great powers—Britain, France, Germany, Russia, and ultimately the first modern Asian great power, Japan. The others treated the United States as a peer—that is, as a fellow great power.[77] East Asia thus provided the setting for the development of American policy toward comparably powerful countries.

The American engagement in East Asia went back to the eighteenth century, when it had had a strictly economic purpose. The country's first trading voyage to China, by the ship *Empress of China*, took place in 1784.[78] Then, and until the 1840s, China's trade with the West went through a small Western enclave at the edge of Canton (now known as Guangzhou) on the Pearl River. There foreigners, barred from the rest of China, were allowed to interact with Chinese merchants. The buildings that housed the Western traders were known as "factories" and the United States maintained one from the last decade of the eighteenth century through the first Opium War, in 1842.[79]

The Chinese defeat by British naval forces in that war opened the country to wider trade with the outside world.[80] The Treaty of Nanking that ended the conflict established five Western trading outposts, known as treaty ports, along the China coast. It also ceded Hong Kong to the British.[81] The United States did not take part in the military operations against the imperial Chinese government and, unlike Great Britain, America maintained no serious military forces in Asia.[82] The Americans did, however, take advantage of the British victory to expand their own commerce with China, although the volume of their trade remained smaller than that of Britain.[83] As with the Monroe Doctrine in Latin America when it was initially proclaimed,[84] so in trade with China during the second half of the nineteenth century the United States found itself in the happy position of "free rider" on British naval power, enjoying its economic benefits without having to pay for them.[85]

The mid-nineteenth-century American policy in Asia with the most consequential long-term effects concerned Japan. That archipelago had, even more than China, been essentially closed to foreigners for more than 250 years. For the sake of trade, Americans resolved to pry it open. In 1854 a flotilla commanded by Commodore Matthew Perry succeeded in doing so.[86] Japan inaugurated commercial relations with the rest of the world, which began its career as one of the world's great trading nations. That status became possible because of an internal transformation that exposure to the West triggered, known as the Meiji Restoration.[87] The term understates the magnitude of the change it brought: it was in truth a revolution in Japanese domestic affairs that made the country the first one outside the West to master the Industrial Revolution. That, in turn, laid the foundation, as it had in Europe and was doing in the United States, of formidable military strength. Japan became a major force in East Asian international affairs and, by the twentieth century, American policy in the region mainly involved trying to cope with Japanese power in order to secure American interests.[88]

In the wake of the Treaty of Nanking the United States negotiated its own bilateral accord with China, the Treaty of Wanxia. The Americans secured access to the same treaty ports as Britain had and also received other concessions. In return they agreed to the outlawing of opium, the importation of which into China had triggered the war in the first place. The American government also made clear that it supported China's territorial integrity, which was at constant risk during those years from the imperial powers. Washington would maintain that position throughout the nineteenth century and beyond.

A second war between Great Britain, with France as its ally, and China ended in another Chinese defeat. The Treaty of Tianjin (also known as the Treaty of Tientsin) that followed, negotiated in 1858 and ratified in 1860, opened ten more treaty ports.[89] Again, the United States negotiated its own follow-up treaty, this time in one of the most remarkable episodes in the history of American diplomacy. Representing China in the negotiations, which took place in the United States, was a delegation headed by the former American minister in Peking, Anson Burlingame: he negotiated the treaty with the American secretary of state William Seward.[90]

The trust that the Chinese court was willing to repose in an American recently employed by his own government fed an attitude toward China that took root in the United States in the nineteenth century and persisted into the twentieth and beyond. Americans saw themselves as having a special, benign, proprietary relationship with the Middle Kingdom. Their country had, after all, never attacked it and controlled none of its territory. They had, many Americans came to believe, a mission to uplift this old, traditional, and, by the nineteenth century, troubled civilization.

This was the belief of the American Protestant missionaries who went to China in increasing numbers in the nineteenth century to win converts for Christianity.[91] The country's economic potential intrigued American businessmen. Those two groups, and even Americans without a religious or mercantile interest in the country, also often believed, or at least hoped, that the United States could transplant its own political system across the ocean and bring the blessings of liberty to China. Here was yet another circumstance in which the ideological character of American foreign policy made itself felt. It was one strain among others in America's policy toward China, and often not the dominant one; but it endured for more than a century and a half, through tumultuous times and sweeping changes in Asia and the world.

For their part, Chinese officials down through the decades showed few signs of regarding the United States as a kindly tutor whose advice they needed earnestly to heed. They more often regarded the country on the western side of the Pacific as a potentially useful geopolitical counterweight to other outside powers, and on more than one occasion America did in fact play this role.[§]

For three decades after the Burlingame Treaty and the beginning of the Meiji Restoration in 1868, China, burdened with an archaic imperial government and having had to put down, at great cost and with the ruling Qing dynasty coming close to falling, the great Taiping Rebellion that convulsed much of the country between 1850 and 1864,[92] grew progressively weaker in its relations with other countries. In the same period Japan became much stronger. In 1894, after a dispute over Korea,[93] Japan attacked and easily defeated its larger neighbor.[94] The Treaty of Shimonoseki of 1895, which ended the war, gave the island of Taiwan to Japan. The Chinese also ceded to Japan the Liaodang Peninsula, including Port Arthur, the largest port on the Yellow Sea, but Russia, Germany, and France forced the Japanese to return it.[95]

In the wake of the Sino-Japanese war the Europeans turned their attention to China and seemed on the point of "slicing the Chinese melon"—that is, dividing the country, or at least its coastal provinces, among themselves.[96] A "scramble for China," like the "scramble for Africa" that had recently partitioned that continent among the

---

[§] In the nineteenth century, "Chinese hostility toward the West tended to be generalized and the Americans, sharing as they did in the treaty system, could not escape from this hostility. On the other hand, when it served China's purpose to make distinctions among the oppressing powers, when China needed help, the Americans looked relatively friendly and exploitable." Warren I. Cohen, *America's Response to China: A History of Sino-American Relations*, New York: Columbia University Press, Fourth Edition, 2000, p. 25.

European powers, threatened American interests there. The United States wanted no territory for itself and lacked the deployable military power to stop the Europeans or compete with them, but did very much wish to maintain its economic access to all of China, which a partition might well hinder.[97]

In these circumstances, on September 6, 1899, the American secretary of state John Hay circulated a memorandum to the other countries with positions in China that became known as the Open Door note. In it he proposed that all agree to grant equal economic access to all others in their respective spheres of influence.[98] While sometimes portrayed as yet another instance of American benevolence toward China, the United States was, rather, seeking to protect its own interests in a way consistent with the relatively modest scope of those interests and the limits on the resources it was able to devote to East Asia.[99]

The British shared the general American outlook and in fact had privately pressed Washington to adopt it publicly,[100] which is what the Open Door note accomplished. The other great powers did not fully embrace Hay's proposal, which, like the Monroe Doctrine in 1823, the United States lacked the means to enforce; but they did not flatly reject it. In March 1900, Hay announced, with some exaggeration, that he had received "full and definite acceptance" from all of them.[101] Partly to avoid offending the United States, but mainly for their own reasons, the other great powers did not do to China what they had done to Africa.[102]

Despite its modest impact, the Open Door note was a milestone in international relations. The great powers had in the past made agreements about the disposition of territory in Europe but not in Asia. Nor had the United States participated in any of these agreements; so 1899 marked the first occasion on which it took a full part in a great-power political question.

The American stance had important features in common with the traditional British approach to the European continent. Like the British in Europe, the United States did not harbor ambitions to control territory in China.[103] Like the British in Europe, however, America was not prepared to regard what happened in China with indifference. The British, for strategic reasons, felt the need to ensure that no single power dominated the continent adjacent to their islands; the Americans, for economic reasons, wanted to avoid being shut out of China commercially. The British were generally unwilling, the Americans unable, to intervene militarily to secure their goals. They both therefore opted for policies that avoided the direct use of force: the British supported, with economic and occasionally military assistance, whichever countries opposed the one that represented the greatest threat: they joined, that is, the "counterhegemonic coalition" and engaged in offshore balancing. The Americans, with less available military power and a modest economic interest in China, issued the Open Door note.

Reluctant as it was to dispatch armed forces to East Asia, the American government nonetheless did so, on a small scale, in 1900 in response to an uprising in China. A movement of mainly rural Chinese that combined Chinese folk beliefs with anti-Western sentiment, which called itself "the fists of righteous harmony"[104] and became known in English as the Boxers, began attacking Westerners, especially missionaries. It gathered strength, received the approval of the Chinese court, and besieged the foreign legations in Peking.

The European imperial powers and Japan dispatched troops to lift the siege and defeat the Boxers.[105] In response, the United States issued a second Open Door note but also decided to send 5,000 troops of its own. President William McKinley dispatched them without Congressional authorization, thereby enhancing the power of his office and establishing a precedent that would become both common and controversial in the twentieth century.[106] He acted both out of concern for imperiled Americans in China and in order to have a say in what the imperial powers did in and to that country. Again, the American intervention had as its principal purpose the maintenance of conditions in China that served the interests of the United States.[107]

Japan's victory over China in 1895 increased American respect for the country it had opened to the world four decades earlier.[108] And while the United States had taken the lead in similarly opening Korea to the West in 1882—Commander Robert Shufeldt had negotiated the Treaty of Chemulpo with the Korean authorities[109]—American officials on the whole approved of the post-1895 Japanese domination of the Korean peninsula. Russia seemed to pose the principal threat to the balance of power in East Asia and the Americans saw Japan as providing a useful check on Russian aspirations in the region.[110] The goal of ensuring a military balance in East Asia favorable to American interests, which was related to but distinct from the Open Door policy's aim of preserving commercial access to China, had taken on greater importance for the United States as the twentieth century began because of the acquisition, in 1898, of territory in the Pacific to which that balance was relevant. The conquest, occupation, and direct governance of the Philippines broke with historical precedent, which made those events a major episode in the history of American foreign policy.

Empire

The American conquest and occupation of the Philippines came about as a consequence of, and indeed almost an afterthought to, a war in Cuba. That Caribbean island, only 103 miles from Florida, had commanded the attention of the United States throughout the nineteenth century, inspiring several efforts at annexation that never, however, mustered sufficient political support in Washington to succeed.[111] Meanwhile, Spain continued to govern the island, suppressing a decade-long uprising against its rule between 1868 and 1878. Rebellion erupted again in 1895 and the Spanish authorities responded in brutal fashion,[112] which created a deeply unfavorable impression in the United States and alarmed Americans at the suffering the Spanish military forces inflicted on the Cuban population.[113]

President William McKinley tried to end the violence by offering to purchase Cuba, but the Spanish government, determined to retain its last major imperial possession in the Western Hemisphere, rebuffed him. As a sign of American concern McKinley sent the battleship *Maine* to Havana harbor and there, on February 15, 1898, it exploded, killing 266 sailors. The American public quickly concluded that Spanish sabotage had destroyed the ship—subsequent investigation suggested that this was not so, that some internal fault was instead responsible—and demanded a sharp response. The episode proved to be one of those occasions in American history when a dramatic event galvanized public opinion in favor of a more aggressive policy than had previously been politically feasible.[114] "Remember the Maine" became a popular slogan.[115] On April 20, the Congress passed a resolution calling for war with Spain, and McKinley signed it.[116]

For all its remarkable economic growth in the previous three decades, the United States had not equipped itself with a formidable land army. The outbreak of the Spanish-American War, however, triggered a surge of volunteers, as had the Mexican and Civil Wars. The army the country sent to the island did not perform with military distinction,[117] and yellow fever took a toll on the troops, but after three months the American forces prevailed. The assistant secretary of the navy, a forty-year-old New York politician named Theodore Roosevelt with a personal enthusiasm for war, organized his own battalion, nicknamed the Rough Riders. The name came from Buffalo Bill Cody's Wild West Show.[118] The battalion took part in the most important land battle of the conflict, the successful assault on the heights overlooking the island's second-largest city, Santiago, and its harbor. Roosevelt had a talent for public relations (and had acted with genuine bravery) and his exploits made him widely known and admired in the United States. America's navy was more technologically advanced and powerful than its army,[119] and the country's naval forces, by destroying the Spanish fleet in Santiago harbor, ensured victory in Cuba.[120]

The United States Navy also achieved a major triumph more than 9,000 miles from Cuba, in the Philippines. The Spanish had controlled the archipelago, which consists of 7,600 islands in the western Pacific Ocean, since the sixteenth century. While in the Navy Department, Roosevelt had ordered Commodore George Dewey, the commander of the navy's Asiatic Squadron, to attack the Spanish fleet near the Filipino capital of Manila in case of war with Cuba, and McKinley had not countermanded the order.[121] Dewey engaged and destroyed the Spanish forces with virtually no loss of American life and little damage to American ships.

As for Roosevelt, the instigator of the American campaign in the Pacific, the reputation he earned in Cuba gave a major boost to his political career. He was elected vice president in 1900 and succeeded to the presidency upon McKinley's assassination in 1901, becoming one of the seminal figures in the history of American foreign policy.[122] While he was neither the first nor the last American to gain that office in large part due to his achievements in wartime,** he remains the only one to have done so in a war that he himself helped to start.

** The others include George Washington, Andrew Jackson, William Henry Harrison, Zachary Taylor, and Dwight Eisenhower. Roosevelt did not exercise

On December 10, 1898, the United States and Spain signed a peace treaty in Paris by the terms of which the Spanish relinquished their claims to Cuba and the Philippines. In passing the war resolution in April the Congress added an amendment, introduced by Senator Henry Teller of Colorado, prohibiting the establishment of permanent and direct control over Cuba. American troops remained on the island, however, and in 1901 Congress passed the Platt Amendment, which defined the relationship between the two countries. It gave the United States broad authority over Cuban foreign and domestic policy as well as the right to establish military bases there.[123]

The McKinley administration took the occasion of the war with Spain to annex the Hawaiian Islands,[124] as well as the Spanish-held Caribbean island of Puerto Rico, where American troops received a warm welcome in July 1898,[125] and the western Pacific island of Guam. After a spirited debate the Congress voted, on February 6, 1899, to annex the Philippines as well. These events created what the great powers of Europe had long had but that the United States had previously shunned: a formal empire.

The first American overseas war, leading to an empire for the United States, had more than one cause.[126] The democratic character of the nation's foreign policy had something to do with it: President McKinley felt pressure from the public to act, in order to avenge the deaths caused by the sinking of the *Maine* and to rescue the people of Cuba from Spanish oppression. The second concern makes the Spanish-American War the first overseas conflict in American history, but not the last, to be fought in part for humanitarian reasons.[127]

The vivid and occasionally exaggerated coverage of the events on the island by the so-called yellow press—the inexpensive, popular newspapers that had become the major source of information for many Americans[128]—contributed to the public attitudes that the president had to take into account.[129] He himself was not eager for war but was willing to wage one; and his Republican Party supported a more expansive foreign policy than did the opposing Democrats. The 1896

as broad command as did those men. They were all generals while he was known as "Colonel" Roosevelt. Of the presidents whose wartime exploits substantially assisted their political careers he most closely resembles John F. Kennedy.

Republican Party platform called for, among other measures, Cuban independence from Spain.[130]

In 1898, moreover, the European powers were rushing to acquire as much territory as possible in Africa and China, among other reasons in order to deny to their great-power rivals the places they were seizing.[131] The United States could not remain wholly unaffected by this global trend.[132]

At the time, and later in retrospect, observers and critics of American policy in 1898 assigned economic motives to the imperial initiative; and economic explanations for late-nineteenth-century imperialism in general (as well as for twentieth-century foreign policy) achieved a certain prominence.[133] Some Americans did have economic interests on the island, which the instability there put in jeopardy, and so were happy to see the turmoil end and the United States establish a dominant position in Cuban affairs.[134] Those interests, however, amounted to a minuscule fraction of the total economic activity of the United States. In fact, trade and foreign investment played a much smaller role in American economic life than they did for Great Britain, and in the American case most of both involved Canada and Europe, where the United States did not establish imperial control.[135]

Another retrospective interpretation of 1898 views the attacks on Cuba and the Philippines as a way of diverting attention from the domestic conflicts—between urban and rural America and between capital and labor—that the massive changes of the Second Industrial Revolution had created.[136] Conflict there certainly was,[137] and the war did unite the country—bringing white Southern opinion on this particular issue together with that of the North in a way that had not occurred since before the Civil War.[138] Political leaders throughout history have used, or tried to use, foreign conflict to bolster their own positions at home,[139] and the Spanish-American War redounded to the benefit of McKinley's Republicans in the election of 1900. Still, the evidence that the hope of fostering national solidarity, or gaining political advantage, or both, played an important role in the calculations of the American officials who decided on war is thin at best.

Important officials and influential people outside the government did push the country toward war, but for a different reason. They believed that extending the American reach to the south and west was what a great power should do in 1898, and that the United States had become, and therefore ought to act as, a great power, following the examples of the great powers of Europe.[140] Some also saw the policies of that year as the logical continuation of the continental expansion of the nineteenth century. Empire, from this perspective, was in keeping with the spirit of Manifest Destiny.[141]

In the United States, as elsewhere, only a small part of the overall population takes an active interest in foreign policy, although what is sometimes called the foreign policy community—or foreign policy establishment, or foreign policy elite—has tended to be broader in the United States than in Europe and on matters of war and peace the sentiments of the American public as a whole have sometimes had telling effects.[142] In all countries the members of this community exercise disproportionate influence on their countries' activities abroad. By the end of the nineteenth century such an American community had taken shape, and important figures in it favored an assertive, great-power foreign policy.[143]

The individual among them whose ideas had the greatest impact was Alfred Thayer Mahan, a captain in the United States Navy who in 1890 published a widely noted book entitled *The Influence of Seapower Upon History, 1660–1783*.[144] In it he argued that naval prowess was the key to global power, from which it followed that the United States should build a powerful navy for that purpose.[145] Beginning at the end of the 1880s the American government did expand and modernize its fleet, which made possible the victories of 1898. Among those persuaded by Mahan's ideas and enthusiastic about his prescriptions were both Theodore Roosevelt and his close friend Henry Cabot Lodge, senator from Massachusetts and chairman of the Senate Foreign Relations Committee.[146] In 1898 both were in a position to promote policies in accord with Mahan's teachings, which is what they saw as the purpose of the war with Spain.

Three factors led to the war in Cuba: the century-long interest in a nearby island, American economic ties there, and public concern about a brutal, extensively reported war in the neighborhood. The Philippines also happened to be a Spanish possession and therefore a target in a war with that country. The United States had no substantial connection to the islands, however, and in 1898 most Americans couldn't find the archipelago on the map. Indeed, in the immediate aftermath of the naval victory, McKinley did not intend to take all of the Philippines; he was inclined to confine American control to Manila and its harbor, as Mahan recommended.[147] He ultimately decided, however, to incorporate all 7,000 islands and 9 million people. In an often-cited statement he explained his reasoning for this decision:

And one night late it came to me this way—I don't know how it was, but it came: 1) that we could not give them back to Spain— that would be cowardly and dishonorable; 2) that we could not turn them over to France or Germany—our commercial rivals in the Orient—that would be bad business and discreditable; 3) that we could not leave them to themselves—they were unfit for self-government—and they would soon have anarchy and misrule over there worse than Spain's was; and 4) that there was nothing left for us to do but to take them all and to educate the Filipinos and uplift and civilize and Christianize them, and by God's grace do the very best we could by them as our fellowmen for whom Christ also died.[148]

His explanation has sometimes been seen, in retrospect, as disingenuous if not cynical:[149] he was addressing a group of Methodist ministers. Yet his words probably do explain the calculations that lay behind his decision. With Spanish sovereignty gone (and returning the islands to Spain would have made the Pacific part of the 1898 campaign look foolish at best), without American control the Philippines would have been prey to other imperial powers, something that Washington did not want.[150] McKinley certainly shared the widely held late-nineteenth-century view that non-Europeans lacked the cultural requirements for effective self-rule; and he undoubtedly also subscribed to the American ideological commitment, dating back to the Revolution, to spreading the blessings of liberty as widely as possible.

On February 4, 1899, Filipino forces opposed to the American occupation—they sought national independence from all foreign powers—attacked American troops. This stimulated sufficient patriotic feeling in the Senate to secure, two days later, the ratification of the treaty annexing the Philippines by slightly more than the necessary two-thirds majority, a margin of fifty-seven to twenty-seven. The attack, however, proved to be the opening salvo of an insurrection against the American presence that lasted until 1901.[151] A total of 4,200 American troops were killed and 2,800 wounded. An estimated 15,000 rebels died, and perhaps 200,000 Filipinos perished overall.[152] The insurrection marked the first—but, as with the humanitarian motives for the war in Cuba, not the last—American experience of a military intervention in a distant land undertaken for benign purposes but meeting determined resistance from local people motivated by nationalist feelings. In this way the Philippines offered a preview of Vietnam and Iraq.

The vote in the Senate showed that not all Americans were persuaded of the wisdom of annexing the Philippines; and, like prior and subsequent American conflicts, the Spanish-American War, and in particular the creation of a formal empire to which it led, provoked dissent in the United States. As with the opposition to the War of 1812 and the Mexican War, it was strongest in New England.[153] The list of opponents included a number of prominent figures of the time such as the philosopher William James, the novelist Mark Twain, and the industrialist Andrew Carnegie—who provided the funds for an Anti-Imperialist League.[154]

The opponents argued that the acquisition of an empire violated basic American principles: the United States had no business governing other people against their will, which also risked subverting liberty at home. It followed logically that the United States should never take over territory to which it did not eventually grant statehood, and no one supposed, in 1898 or thereafter, that the Philippines would ever qualify for inclusion in the Union.[155] The proponents of annexation agreed with McKinley's defense of it, and with Lodge, Mahan, and Roosevelt that possession of the Philippines was in keeping with, indeed indispensable for, America's international status as a great power.[156] In the political conflict between the two sides the proponents prevailed. William Jennings Bryan, the Democrats' 1896 presidential candidate, advised the senators of his party, who tended to be skeptical of empire, to support the treaty of annexation;[157] and when he ran against McKinley again in 1900, the Republican incumbent, now with solid credentials as an imperialist, he won re-election.[158]

Samuel Flagg Bemis, a distinguished twentieth-century diplomatic historian of the United States, termed the Spanish-American War and its aftermath, in the context of the grand sweep of American history, "a grand national aberration."[159] Insofar as 1898 marked the debut of a formal American empire, with the direct control, without their consent, of other peoples,[160] the events of the twentieth century bear out that judgment. The annexation of the Philippines did not establish a precedent. America established direct imperial control nowhere else.[161] The imperial career of the United States, defined in this way, turned out, in comparison with those of the great powers of Europe, to be brief, modest, and generally half-hearted.

Disillusionment with the unexpectedly difficult effort to pacify and uplift the Philippines (an exercise that came in the twenty-first century to be called "nation-building") set in quickly, as did the idea, which the difficulty inspired, of disencumbering the United States of the archipelago for which it had assumed responsibility.[162] In January 1900 a presidential commission that McKinley had appointed recommended preparing the islands for self-rule.[163] Roosevelt's first message to Congress after becoming president in 1901 hoped for self-government in order to "relieve us of a great burden."[164] The Jones Act of 1916 authorized independence as soon as a stable Filipino government could be established and the Tydings-McDuffie Act of 1934 envisioned independence in twelve years. In 1935 the archipelago achieved full-scale self-government with an American high commissioner, and in 1946 the Philippines did become independent.[165]

In Cuba, the United States played a dominant economic and political role for six decades after 1898 but never exercised direct control over the island, and in 1934 repealed the Platt Amendment (while retaining the military base at Guantanamo Bay). The intrusive American presence of their northern neighbor offended some Cubans, however, and in 1958 a group of them, led by Fidel Castro, seized power on the island and established a regime dedicated to opposing the United States that, for three decades, was allied with America's chief global adversary, the Soviet Union.[166]

Hawaii (along with Alaska) eventually gained admission to the Union as the fiftieth state, and Puerto Rico landed in a kind of constitutional limbo, becoming a commonwealth with some but not all the privileges states enjoyed.[167] From Revolutionary times Americans had seen themselves as politically different from the powers of the Old

World. In the twentieth century, in the matter of empire, this proved to be the case.

On the other hand, the events of 1898 did, in major ways, set the course for America's relations with the world thereafter. For one thing, foreign policy subsequently played a consistently more prominent role in the country's public life: it took on greater importance than it had had since 1815. For another, those events sealed the country's self-image—and, not less important, other countries' perception of the United States. The great North American republic came to be seen by other countries as a great power, a major participant in international affairs whose views and preferences its fellow great powers had to respect and take into account.[168] It was not accidental that ambitious American initiatives such as the Open Door notes, the dispatch of troops to China to defeat the Boxers, the Hay-Pauncefote Treaty, and the Roosevelt Corollary all came in the wake of the Spanish-American War.

After 1871 a united Germany and after 1895 an assertive Japan had joined Britain, France, Russia, and—in Europe but not in Asia—the Habsburg and Ottoman Empires in the club of great powers. In 1898 the United States became a full-fledged member. McKinley captured the impact of the war on American and global psychology when he said, in 1899, that "in a few short months we have become a world power."[169]

The war of 1898 was the first but not the last that the United States was to wage beyond its borders, sometimes far beyond them. Even in peacetime, in the second half of the twentieth century and the early years of the twenty-first, America projected military power and political and economic influence around the world; and this pattern, a major development in world history, had its origins in the war against Spain.

Two Visions

At the end of the eighteenth century the United States, having become an independent country, had to decide what kind of country it wanted to be. At the outset of the twentieth, having emerged as one of the world's great powers, it had to decide how it wished to use its power. On the later occasion as on the earlier one, two prominent public figures propounded, and attempted to put into practice, different visions of the American future. Alexander Hamilton and Thomas Jefferson had differing ideas about the desirable foreign policy for the United States as well as about the proper domestic order, and their twentieth-century descendants adopted and elaborated those foreign-policy ideas.[170]

Theodore Roosevelt, the Hamiltonian,[171] embraced the role of a traditional great power for the United States. His country ought, he believed, to expand its global presence and influence as far as possible. Woodrow Wilson, who, like Roosevelt, served as president and therefore, like him, had the opportunity to shape America's relations with the rest of the world, followed his own political ancestor, Thomas Jefferson.[††] Wilson sought to reform the international system in which his country had come to play a prominent part, with an eye toward eliminating what he regarded as its greatest scourge: war.[172]

Neither man, as president, conducted a pure version of his preferred approach to foreign policy: Roosevelt sought to spread American values whenever possible; Wilson authorized the use of military force on more than one occasion. Nor has American foreign policy ever exclusively employed either one or the other approach. It bore the imprint of both men's ideas in the twentieth century and into the twenty-first. For much of that period, Roosevelt's ideas dominated the country's relations with the rest of the world, but Wilson's never disappeared and sometimes came to the fore.

Roosevelt's approach enjoyed greater success on the issue that most sharply divided them: the United States did, for long periods, prevent war by mustering military strength and did fight and win several wars. Neither American policy nor the course of international history ever brought about the full, permanent abolition of large-scale, organized, state-perpetrated violence; but the hope that this would somehow, someday come to pass never died out. It persisted not only because war became increasingly destructive but also because the idea of reforming the international order, and the related ambition to reform its member states to render them more peaceful, have from colonial times been

---

[††] In domestic affairs Wilson did not follow Jefferson's example. In this area he was more sympathetic to Hamilton's ideas and in fact criticized Jefferson's approach. John Milton Cooper, *Woodrow Wilson: A Biography*, New York: Alfred A. Knopf, 2009, pp. 34, 74, 335.

part of the ideological character of American political life and the international outlook of Americans.

The two presidents had a number of things in common. Both came from relatively well-to-do backgrounds: Roosevelt was a genuine American patrician, descended from the original Dutch settlers of what became New York; Wilson had less lofty origins but, as the son of a prominent Presbyterian minister in Virginia, he began life in comfortable circumstances.[173] Each saw himself as both a man of ideas and a man of action: both published extensively but each felt called to enter the public arena, Wilson later in life than Roosevelt and after a time as president of Princeton University.

In domestic affairs both played important roles in the Progressive movement, the effort to reform American institutions in order to meet the challenges caused by the impact of the Second Industrial Revolution. When they contested the 1912 presidential election, each ran as a progressive, with the former Republican Roosevelt advocating even more extensive reform than the Democrat Wilson.[174]

Both felt a personal affinity for Great Britain,[175] which had an impact on their foreign policies. They shared, as well, some fundamental beliefs: in the supremacy of the presidency in the conduct of the nation's foreign affairs; in the desirability of American global leadership; and in a hierarchy of nations, cultures, and races, with the Anglo-Saxons at the top.[176] Both thought it beneficial to other peoples to spread American values among them.

Roosevelt believed that the United States should conduct itself, as a great power, in a way similar to the behavior of the great powers of Europe. While at best a lukewarm champion of territorial expansion after the American experience in the Philippines, he always believed in exercising American influence as widely as possible.[177] He believed as well that the country needed formidable armed forces, with an emphasis on the navy, and that it had to be prepared to use them.

Indeed, he had a personal fondness for war: he considered combat to be the supreme expression, and the supreme test, of the manly virtues for both individuals and nations.[178] As president he did not, however, conduct a relentlessly bellicose foreign policy. He based his policies, especially in Asia, on the conviction that an equilibrium of military might among the great powers served American interests and conduced to peace. He aimed, that is, to help contrive a stable balance of power.[179]

Wilson did not admire the traditional foreign policies of the European great powers. He came to believe that the United States should not emulate them but should instead seek to reconfigure relations among them so as to do away with the instrument of foreign policy that Roosevelt accepted as normal, inevitable, and even in some circumstances desirable: warfare. While he shared with Roosevelt the hope that other countries would reform themselves in ways consistent with American political values and practices and so carry out peaceful foreign policies, Wilson was generally more willing to take steps actively to promote such developments than Roosevelt had been after 1898.[180] Woodrow Wilson's great chance to implement a sweeping reform of international affairs came in the wake of World War I. His chosen instrument for this purpose was an international organization, the kind of institution in which Theodore Roosevelt had far less faith.[181]

As president, in keeping with his beliefs about what wielding great power in the world required,[182] Roosevelt gave particular attention to the nation's military forces. His secretary of war, Elihu Root, set about improving the army, which had not performed with distinction in Cuba.[183] The president continued the expansion of the navy that had begun in the 1880s. Whereas in 1898 the fleet had had eleven battleships, by 1913, when he left office, the number had risen to thirty-six, giving the United States the third-largest such force in the world, after Great Britain and Germany.[184] To show that his country had become a naval power of the first rank he sent sixteen battleships, manned by 14,000 sailors, on a cruise around the world, calling at twenty ports from December 1907 to February 1909.[185] The ships were painted white rather than the grey that would later become common and so became known as America's "Great White Fleet."

Concerning Latin America, President Roosevelt not only proclaimed the Roosevelt Corollary to the Monroe Doctrine but also applied it in the Dominican Republic. The United States took over the collection of customs there to ensure payment to foreign creditors.[186] He also sent troops to Cuba and installed a provisional government on the island.[187]

Of more enduring significance, Roosevelt presided over the beginning of construction on the long-discussed isthmian canal in Central

America. In June 1903 Congress voted to build it across Panama, which was under the nominal sovereignty of Colombia, whose government balked at selling the necessary territory to the United States. A Panamanian rebellion erupted, with American approval, that made Panama independent under American protection. The new Panamanian authorities signed an agreement for the United States to build the canal, which was completed in 1914.[188]

In East Asia, Roosevelt adopted policies designed to secure a balance of power stable enough to protect American interests, which now included the safety of the Philippines as well as commercial access to China. The emergence of any single country in the region appreciably more powerful than the others had the potential to put these in jeopardy. The most important East Asian event during Roosevelt's time in office was the Russo-Japanese War of 1904–1905. At first, he hoped for Japan's success: he admired the country's rapid post-1868 modernization, thought it fitting that the Japanese should dominate more backward countries such as Korea, and considered Russian ambitions, in Manchuria and elsewhere, potentially dangerous. The sweeping Japanese victory, however, changed his mind. It raised the prospect of a too-powerful Japan endangering America's interests in the Asia-Pacific region.[189]

For the purpose of sustaining an East Asian equilibrium, and in keeping with his commitment to a major role for the United States there, Roosevelt brought Russia and Japan to a peace conference at Portsmouth, New Hampshire, in August 1905. Controlling the proceedings from Washington, he hammered out an agreement that, while fully satisfactory to neither side, did bring the conflict to an end.[190] Portsmouth marked the debut of the United States as an international mediator, and for his efforts Roosevelt became, in 1906, the first American to win the Nobel Peace Prize.

Thereafter he kept a wary eye on Japan, the clear winner of the war and the country likeliest to disrupt the political status quo in the Pacific.[191] His balance-of-power policy in East Asia relied both on the military buildup over which he was presiding and on diplomacy with Japan: the phrase for which he became perhaps best known, and that captured his approach, was "Speak softly and carry a big stick." His administration concluded two agreements with Tokyo designed, from the American point of view, to reinforce the regional equilibrium by specifying the political understandings that underlay it.

In 1905 then secretary of war William Howard Taft and Japanese prime minister Taro Katsura signed a memorandum in which the United States recognized the dominant position that Japan had created for itself in Korea and Japan disavowed any interest in the Philippines or Hawaii.[192] In 1908 Root, by then Roosevelt's secretary of state, negotiated a secret agreement with the Japanese ambassador to Washington Kogoro Takahira in which Japan pledged respect for the status quo in the Pacific. For its part the United States implicitly conceded Japanese predominance in southern Manchuria, still officially a part of China.[193] Roosevelt also had a hand in an effort to prevent war in Europe, using his good offices to organize a Franco-German conference in Algeciras, Spain, in 1905 to try to resolve their dispute over Morocco. The meeting did reduce tensions between the two rival powers.[194]

Taft succeeded Roosevelt in the White House in 1909 and during the course of a generally uneventful term in office introduced an innovation in American foreign policy. Regarding political and economic instability in Central America as a problem for the United States, and wishing to avoid military intervention there if possible, he and his secretary of the treasury, Philander Knox, launched a policy that came to be known as "dollar diplomacy." It involved using American loans to the afflicted countries as leverage to promote the introduction of experts in finance and public administration who would, it was hoped, implement changes that would place these countries on a sound economic footing.[195] The idea was to preserve and expand American influence by "substituting dollars for bullets." The Taft administration attempted a version of the policy in Asia as well.[196]

Dollar diplomacy did not achieve its goal. Neither China nor the Central American countries became models of economic propriety and efficiency or political stability; the pace of American military intervention to the south in fact accelerated.[197] The deployment of capital in order to promote political goals abroad, however, did become part of the repertoire of American foreign policy, joining trade as a twentieth- and twenty-first-century instrument that the United States sometimes used in its relations with other countries.

Woodrow Wilson entered office in 1913 planning to devote his presidency largely to domestic affairs and strongly inclined to depart from the foreign policies of his two immediate predecessors.[198] He sought to uplift the people of China rather than to help American businessmen make money there, and wanted a policy in Central America that respected the independence of its various countries. With Latin America in general he hoped for a future of friendship and sovereign equality, as the states of the region adopted constitutional, liberty-protecting forms of governance.[199]

His actual policies, especially toward Central America, did not comport with his stated goals. Instead, they followed Roosevelt's more closely than Wilson had initially expected or desired.[200] Political instability drew the United States into the internal affairs of the countries there and despite his initial intentions he made the region more firmly an American sphere of influence than ever, sending troops to it more frequently than any other president: to Cuba, Haiti, and the Dominican Republic; to Mexico twice; to Panama twice; and to Honduras five times.[201]

In particular, he became more deeply entangled in and with Mexico than any president since James K. Polk. In that country, in May 1911, a revolution overthrew Porfirio Diaz, who had ruled it for thirty-one years and had kept it friendly to American business.[202] Francisco Madero succeeded him but was soon himself overthrown, and murdered, by General Victoriana Huerta. Wilson was appalled by what Huerta had done and, breaking with precedent, refused to recognize him as the country's leader. He hoped, he said, to teach the Central Americans "to elect good men."[203]

Wilson's hostility to Huerta strained relations between the two countries and in April 1914, in the Mexican port city of Tampico, local officials briefly detained American sailors who had gone ashore for provisions. In response, Wilson sent troops to Veracruz, the city where Winfield Scott had landed his forces in 1847 to begin their march to Mexico City, in the hope of toppling Huerta.[204] The troops occupied the city for seven months: a new president, Venustiano Carranza, replaced Huerta and the American forces withdrew.[205]

Meanwhile a several-sided civil war was taking place in Mexico. One of the contenders for power, Francisco "Pancho" Villa, attempted to rally support for himself by conspicuously opposing the United States. On March 9, 1916, his troops attacked the border town of Columbus, New Mexico. In the battle, seventeen Americans and hundreds of Mexicans died.[206] It was the first foreign attack on American soil since the British invasion in 1814 during the War of 1812. Wilson responded by sending a force commanded by General John J. Pershing into Mexico to capture Villa. It never found him, and in June 1917, after six months of negotiations with the Mexican government, it withdrew.[207] The first Mexican War had brought the southwest part of the United States into the Union. The second, seven decades later, brought nothing.

After the first year of his presidency, therefore, Woodrow Wilson had not changed the pattern of American foreign policy that had taken shape over the half century following the conclusion of the Civil War. The United States had become one of the great powers of the international system. It had effectively excluded the other great powers from the Western Hemisphere and carved out an increasingly intrusive sphere of influence in Central America and the eastern Pacific. It had become as well, in a small way, an imperial power, governing the Philippines directly. It participated, with other great powers, in the affairs of East Asia and had adopted policies designed to protect its interests there without deploying armed forces on any appreciable scale. In Europe, the heart of the international system, the most heavily militarized part of it, and the home, with the exception of Japan, of the other great powers, the United States played no role at all.

That was about to change. On June 28, 1914, an event far from the United States, in a place of which few Americans had heard, set in motion developments that transformed the country's relations with the rest of the world. Across the Atlantic Ocean in Sarajevo, in the Balkans, a Serb nationalist assassinated the heir to the throne of the Austro-Hungarian Empire, which led to the outbreak of World War I. Indifferent to major political and military developments in Europe for a century after 1815, the United States could not, or at any rate did not, manage to ignore this one, ultimately becoming directly involved.

In the short run, the war furnished Woodrow Wilson with the opportunity to apply American ideological principles to international politics. At its end he tried, unsuccessfully, to implement the most ambitious reform of international politics ever seriously attempted. In the long term, World War I dramatically expanded the scope of American foreign policy. It made the United States a European and ultimately a global power.

5

The Offshore Balancer, 1914–1933

The United States and World War I

In the wake of the assassination of the heir to its throne by a Serb nationalist, Austria-Hungry declared war against Serbia. Germany promised to support its Habsburg ally. Russia mobilized to support the Serbs and France honored the military agreement it had made with the tsarist regime. What had begun as a local conflict had turned into a major European war. German war plans called for attacking France through Belgium; the Germans therefore refused to respect Belgian neutrality. This, along with previous commitments and the longstanding aim of preventing a single power, in this case Germany, from dominating the European continent brought Great Britain into the confrontation in alliance with France and Russia. A European conflict thus became a world war.[1]

Membership in the two opposing coalitions—Britain, France, and Russia joined by Italy in 1915 on one side; Germany, Austria-Hungary, and Turkey, which entered the conflict at the end of October 1914, on the other—did not come out of the blue: the international relations of the European continent had been moving toward such a division for more than a decade. The war did, however, bring a major surprise, and a grim and fateful one at that. The warring parties expected it to be short. It proved instead to be long—it lasted for more than four years—and extraordinarily costly in lives and treasure, costlier in these terms than any previous conflict.[2]

While the battle lines on the Eastern Front of the war, where Germany and Austria-Hungary fought Russia, moved back and forth, on the Western Front, where the British and French confronted the Germans, the two sides dug into parallel, well-fortified trenches that stretched across northern France from the North Sea to the Swiss border. The opposing armies there spent the better part of three years launching attacks that killed and wounded soldiers on both sides on a frightening scale but did not significantly alter the territory each side controlled. As had been the case with the Napoleonic Wars, the length and the cost of World War I created the conditions that drew the United States into it.

Americans were well aware of what was happening on the other side of the Atlantic and in the early weeks of the war many were dismayed at the suffering it caused,[3] especially to civilians. A mining engineer named Herbert Hoover organized a program of relief for displaced Belgians that earned him a national and indeed worldwide reputation as "the Napoleon of Mercy," an effective entrepreneur of good works.* Still, almost no one in the United States thought that Americans should or would become involved in the battles an ocean away. European armies had gone to war from time to time in the hundred years since the end of the Napoleonic Wars without affecting their lives and they saw no reason, at first, to believe that this war would be different. At its outset the United States declared itself to be neutral.

Neutrality had an important place in the history of American foreign relations. The United States had sought to remain neutral during the previous great European war, between 1792 and 1815.[4] It was the logical stance for a power that did not believe that it had a major stake in the outcome of the fighting. It also corresponded to the predominant desire of the American people, who, whatever their views of the

---

* George C. Herring, *From Colony to Superpower: U.S. Foreign Relations Since 1776*, New York: Oxford University Press, 2008, p. 400. An admirer wrote that Hoover was "a simple, modest, energetic man who began his career in California and will end it in Heaven." Patricia O'Toole, *The Moralist: Woodrow Wilson and the World He Made*, New York: Simon & Schuster, 2018, p. 278. Hoover went on to become the thirty-first president of the United States. While a number of his predecessors and successors attained that office partly through their exploits in war—an exercise, after all, in inflicting suffering—Hoover is the only one thus far whose initial reputation stemmed from alleviating it.

rights and wrongs of the conflict 3,600 miles away, overwhelmingly did not want their country to take part in it. Woodrow Wilson won re-election as president in 1916 with the slogan "He kept us out of war."

As the war proceeded, however, Americans developed two different and opposing views of the conflict.[5] The largest number of those who paid serious attention to and formed opinions about it came to favor the cause of Great Britain and France.[6] Some had ideological reasons: the Allies, as they came to be called, and with the conspicuous exception of tsarist Russia, had democratic governments, while the German Hohenzollern, Austrian Habsburg, and Ottoman Turkish Empires did not.[7] Others of this first group were concerned about the balance of power on the continent and worried that a German victory would give that country a dangerously dominant position there. Prominent Republicans such as former president Theodore Roosevelt and his close friend Senator Henry Cabot Lodge gravitated toward a pro-allied position,[8] as did Wilson's two most prominent foreign policy aides, his informal advisor Edward M. House (who bore the honorary title of colonel) and his second secretary of state, Robert Lansing.[9] Many who saw the war as they did became increasingly well disposed to providing assistance to the Allies, even, in some cases, to the extent of actually sending American troops to Europe to fight alongside them.

A second group considered it a matter of principle for the United States to steer entirely clear of the conflict. It numbered among its adherents influential members of the United States Senate, including Republicans William Borah of Idaho and Robert LaFollette of Wisconsin. In addition, many Irish-Americans opposed siding with the Allies out of hostility to Great Britain for its rule over the island from which they or their forbears came, and German-Americans did so because they wanted the German rather than the Allied side to win the war.[10]

Woodrow Wilson occupied a category of his own. He had personal sympathy for Great Britain[11] but did not, at least until the United States entered the war, place any particular emphasis on the political differences between democratic Britain and France and their autocratic adversaries. Nor did he fear the potentially adverse consequences for the United States of a German victory.[12] Rather, he opposed the practice of war itself; and as the fighting continued, he increasingly came to see the hostilities as offering an opportunity, when they ended, to abolish that age-old feature of relations among sovereign states.[13]

In this way he resembled his predecessor Thomas Jefferson, whose policies during the Napoleonic Wars were intended to bring about peace by transforming the conduct of international relations.[14] Jefferson had presided over a weak power, with no capacity to restructure the international system directly, and so he had sought to end the practice of war by the force of the American example. A century later Wilson led a great and growing power, one that could, he believed, directly undertake the project of remaking the world order. Wilson harbored the ambition to do precisely that, and that ambition shaped his approach to the war and, even more consequentially, the postwar settlement.[15]

When the war began, President Wilson said that the United States would be "neutral in fact as well as in name . . . impartial in thought as well as in action."[16] That is not what happened. While it did not explicitly endorse the claims of either side in the conflict, the American government did adopt policies that strongly favored the Allies. It observed the letter of the laws of neutrality as it understood them, but this produced a strong tilt toward France and, especially, toward Great Britain. It was not what Wilson wanted to do and not what he believed his country was doing, but the United States, under the banner of neutrality, in fact carried out a version of the classical British foreign policy of offshore balancing. America gave major, indeed indispensable, support to a coalition that was resisting a power, Germany, bidding to achieve mastery of the European continent.

The United States was open to trade with both sides but because Britain's navy controlled the seas it was able to restrict German commerce while trading with North America on an expanding scale.[17] As the war continued, and as it grew increasingly expensive, transatlantic trade became more important for both parties engaging in it: Britain's imports from the United States sustained the British war effort; America's exports to Great Britain contributed to prosperity in the United States.[18]

The enormous cost of fighting meant that the British had to borrow money to make their purchases. At first the American government confined the loans the warring parties could receive to credits offered by banks; but when those proved, by mid-1915, insufficient to cover

Britain's purchases of food and munitions, the Wilson administration decided to allow banks to sell securities on public markets to raise the money required.[19] In this way, and while considering itself to be neutral, the United States partially funded the British war effort.

The British used their naval superiority to impose a restrictive blockade on German shipping. The neutrality laws protected neutral property on every ship, and all property on neutral ships, with the exception of contraband. The effect of the British maritime campaign against German trade therefore depended in no small part on the definition of contraband. The British gave it a very broad definition, which inflicted serious economic damage on the Germans. The United States made only tepid and ineffectual protests against the way the British conducted the blockade and defined contraband, which afforded an advantage to the Allies.[20]

Losing the maritime war of surface ships, Germany resorted to retaliating from beneath the ocean's surface in a way that ultimately brought the United States into the war against it. The German navy made use of the recently invented submarine to attack and sink ships conducting trade with and for the Allies. The American government did not accept the legitimacy, under the laws of war, of submarine warfare. When the Germans declared that they would wage it, Wilson protested and said that Germany would be held to "strict accountability" for losses the United States suffered from its undersea raids.[21]

The German campaign began in February 1915 and on May 7 of that year a submarine attack sank the British passenger ship *Lusitania*,[22] killing 1,200 civilians including 128 Americans. The sinking shocked the American public. It proved to be one of those events in the nation's history, like the Boston Massacre, the firing on Fort Sumter, and the blowing up of the *Maine*, that turned public opinion sharply in a bellicose direction.[†] Like those earlier episodes, it paved the way for the

---

[†] "The emotion that underlay the implicit threat of war after the sinking of the *Lusitania* was not fear but outrage—a compound of moral indignation and a fierce desire to uphold the rights of American citizens." John A. Thompson, *A Sense of Power: The Roots of America's Global Role*, Ithaca, New York: Cornell University Press, 2015, p. 107. "The emotional response evoked by the sinking resembled a great tide that swept everything before it." Robert W. Tucker,

United States to go to war, although the official American entry into World War I did not come for another two years.[23]

Motivated by the public's outrage,[24] Wilson dispatched a stiff note to Berlin demanding an end to such attacks. His then–secretary of state, the three-time unsuccessful Democratic presidential candidate William Jennings Bryan, resigned in protest on the grounds that Wilson's position departed from the neutrality in which he, Bryan, strongly believed.

The sinking of the *Lusitania* affair triggered other American initiatives. It led to the National Defense Act of May 1916, which doubled the size of the regular army and expanded the National Guard, and to the Naval Appropriations Act of the following month, which established the goal of building a navy equal to the most powerful in the world by 1925.[25] Although pushed toward a break with Germany, Wilson did not want war. He had to operate in a political context shaped by what he called the American public's "double wish": to defend the country's neutral rights, which German submarine attacks violated, but also to avoid becoming directly engaged in the fighting in Europe.[26] The best way to avoid a fateful choice between abandoning American rights and entering the war, he believed, was to end the fighting. He therefore stepped up his efforts, which had begun before the sinking of the *Lusitania*, to use his good offices and American economic strength and prestige to bring about such a development.[27] He sent Colonel House to Europe, where his advisor worked out an agreement with the British foreign secretary, Lord Grey, that House believed had the potential to end the conflict.[28] It did not.

Meanwhile the Germans, anxious to avoid having the United States oppose them more forcefully than was already the case, promised that their submarines would observe "cruiser rules," which involved giving a warning to the ships they were targeting before attacking them.[29] Following these rules, however, put an effective end to submarine warfare, which depended on the underwater assault on surface ships coming as a surprise.[30]

Woodrow Wilson and the Great War: Reconsidering America's Neutrality, 1914–1917, Charlottesville, Virginia: University of Virginia Press, 2007, p. 108.

Between the outbreak of the war in August 1914 and the early part of 1917, relations between the Wilson administration and the Allies did not always proceed smoothly.[31] During that time, however, public opinion in the United States became, on the whole and with exceptions, more favorable to the Allies, with the sinking of the *Lusitania* substantially enhancing that sentiment. Then, in January 1917, the German Kaiser authorized the resumption of unrestricted submarine warfare and on the last day of that month his government announced it.

The German government had a twofold rationale for its decision. First, the British blockade was taking an increasing toll both on the country's war effort and on its civilians' daily lives, and the government felt pressure to do something to ease it. Second, the German high command reckoned that, although submarine attacks might well precipitate American entry into the war, German forces could defeat the Allies in Europe before the United States could dispatch enough troops to make a material difference in the fighting.[32] So the Germans did what in 1915 Wilson had warned them against doing, and in March, German submarines sank three American merchant ships, killing fifteen Americans.[33]

To increase the American incentives to abandon neutrality and enter the war, in February the British government gave its American counterpart a telegram it had intercepted sent by Arthur Zimmermann, the German foreign minister, to Mexican officials. It proposed, in the event that the United States entered the war, an alliance between their countries and promised that, if such a partnership were created, Germany would help Mexico reclaim territory it had lost to the United States in the war of 1846 to 1848.[34] An additional development increased the inclination of some Americans, including Woodrow Wilson, to go to war: in March 1917, the Russian tsar abdicated and a more liberal provisional government came to power. The change seemed to open the way for Russia to adopt democratic political practices, thereby making the war a clear contest between democracy and autocracy.[35] In those circumstances, by fighting on the side of the Allies, the United States would be going to war on behalf of basic, long-held American values.

Wilson's cabinet met on March 20, 1917, and took the unanimous view that war had become unavoidable and that Congress should be convened to authorize it.[36] The president asked the Congress for a declaration of war on April 2. On April 4 the Senate voted for one by a margin of 82 to 6. On April 6 the House of Representatives voted in favor by 373 to 50. For the first time in 100 years, the United States was involved in an armed conflict that had begun in Europe, that was being fought in Europe by Europeans, and in which the major stakes were located on the European continent.

To the very end, Wilson himself was a reluctant warrior. He opted for war for much the same reason that James Madison had, also reluctantly, advocated war in 1812: the violation of America's neutral rights, both presidents believed, had left them with no other choice.[37] In his war message, however, Wilson went beyond this rationale. He told the nation and the world that the United States would fight for other, broader goals, goals with deep roots in American history, goals that could justify the extraordinary step that Wilson was proposing and the sacrifices it would surely entail. "The world must be made safe for democracy," he said. "Its peace must be planted upon the tested foundation of political liberty."

The United States in World War I

In April 1917, as often in American history, the United States found itself unprepared to wage the war it had entered. Indeed, it was not entirely clear what waging that war would involve. Soon after the Congressional votes an official from the War Department, testifying before the Senate Finance Committee, said in passing that "we may have to have an army in France." The Committee chairman, Senator Thomas H. Martin of Virginia, responded, "Good Lord! You're not going to send soldiers over there, are you?" At the outset of the war even the commander in chief himself hoped that this would not be necessary.[38]

In the end, American soldiers did go to Europe, and in large numbers. In order to send them there the government first had to find soldiers to send. For this purpose Congress authorized conscription, passing the Selective Service Act on May 18, 1917. It required all men between the ages of twenty-one and thirty to register with the government for military service. On June 5, 1917, a total of 9.6 million did register.[39] Ultimately 4 million Americans, almost all of them men, served in the armed forces.

The country had to pay their salaries and the other expenses of waging the conflict. For financing the war it relied on taxation, which raised about twenty-two percent of the needed revenue, but also, and increasingly, on loans, which accounted for fifty-eight percent of expenditures. Many of the loans came in the form of "Liberty Bonds" marketed and sold to the public. Roughly half of all American families bought them.[40] Like other wars, this one proved to be more expensive than anticipated.[41] Ultimately the United States had to pay $32 billion—which came to fifty-two percent of its total annual gross domestic product at that time[42]—in order to help defeat Germany.

In addition to recruiting individual Americans to serve in the ranks of its armed forces, the country had to mobilize its resources to support them. To this end the federal government assumed a larger role in national life than ever before. On December 26, 1917, it took control of the nation's railroads and placed them under the direction of the Department of the Treasury, which was headed by William Gibbs McAdoo, a prominent lawyer who was also Woodrow Wilson's son-in-law.[43] The Wilson administration created a number of specialized agencies to oversee crucial parts of the war effort. Herbert Hoover headed one for food. Harry Garfield, son of the twentieth president James A. Garfield, directed another for fuel. A third, the War Labor Board, had former president William Howard Taft as its cochair. The administration also established a War Production Board to coordinate the different economic sectors contributing to the war effort. It had no real power and did not function well at first,[44] but when the financier Bernard Baruch took charge of it he managed to improve its performance.[45]

The experience of World War I had an impact on American society. Notably, two amendments to the Constitution emerged from the war years. The first proved transitory. The Eighteenth Amendment, ratified in 1920, restricted the manufacture and sale of alcohol. In 1933, the Twenty-first Amendment repealed it. The other Constitutional innovation had more staying power. The Nineteenth Amendment gave women the right to vote.[46] The introduction of daylight saving time in 1918 marked another enduring change in national life.[47]

From April 1917 to November 1918 Wilson and his colleagues faced the problem, common to all American presidents in wartime, of securing and sustaining public support for the war. For this purpose, they established the Committee on Public Information (CPI) to generate enthusiasm among the American people. Partly (and largely unintentionally) through its activities, anti-German sentiment in the United States grew.[48] It sometimes took odd forms: the familiar dish sauerkraut was renamed "liberty cabbage." The fear of subversion from within grew as well, and as in other wars this fear led to measures that infringed on the liberties of American citizens. In the spirit of the Alien and Sedition Acts of the 1790s, Congress passed the Espionage Act on June 15, 1917,[49] and the Sedition Act on May 18, 1918. Publications critical of the war found the rates the postal service charged for their circulation raised to prohibitive levels.[50] Prominent opponents of the war, such as the anarchist Emma Goldman and the socialist Eugene V. Debs, were imprisoned.[51]

Nor did Germany's surrender in 1918 put an end to such activities. The Bolshevik coup in Russia in November 1917, brought to power a Communist Party dedicated to fomenting revolution everywhere. The fear that its agents were active in the United States led to the roundup of several thousand suspected subversives, which the attorney general A. Mitchell Palmer ordered in January 1920.[52]

The most notable initiative the president himself took during the eighteen months when the United States was at war was the proclamation of what he believed should be the Allies' war aims, in an address to a joint session of Congress on January 8, 1918. His "Fourteen Points" speech took its name from the number of major proposals he made. (The French leader Georges Clemenceau, a cynic when it came to Wilson's idealistic global schemes, said of the Fourteen Points that "le bon Dieu n'avait que dix"—the good Lord himself had only ten.)

Wilson wanted to make clear his vision for the postwar world, and in his mind the Bolshevik seizure of power in Russia made it all the more important that he do so.[53] The communist regime published the secret treaties its tsarist predecessor, in the early months of the war, had signed with the other Allies, which delineated the division among themselves of their adversaries' territories that they expected to control after winning the war.[54] The secret treaties made it possible to portray the Allied war as simply a campaign to expand their imperial holdings, devoid of any higher purpose. Wilson did not want such an unworthy aim to contaminate the American war effort. In addition, the Bolsheviks, with their Marxist-Leninist ideology that foretold a utopia for working people, were offering the promise of a freer, more just, more peaceful world than the one the capitalist great powers had built. Wilson felt the need to present an image of a different but equally compelling future.[55] Drawing on ideas that he had previously advanced, notably in a Congressional address on January 22, 1917,[56] the Fourteen Points speech offered the most comprehensive statement he ever made of the world that Woodrow Wilson wanted to bring into existence.

The first five and the last of the Fourteen Points set out general principles for the conduct of foreign policy once Germany and its allies had been defeated:[57] "open covenants" rather than secret diplomacy; freedom of maritime navigation; free trade; the reduction of armaments; and, finally, the formation of a "general assembly of nations." The observance of these principles, Wilson believed, would make the world a far more peaceful place than it was at the beginning of 1918 or indeed had been for much, perhaps all, of recorded history.

Points six through thirteen addressed the disposition of specific territories. In September 1917 Colonel House had established a study group known as "The Inquiry" to work out the details of an optimal postwar settlement. (Its initial chief of research was a young journalist, seven years out of Harvard, named Walter Lippmann, who subsequently became America's most influential newspaper commentator on politics.)[58] The Inquiry delivered a memorandum to the president on December 22, 1917, whose contents formed the basis for the more specific of the Fourteen Points. They called for the evacuation of territory that other countries had occupied in Russia, Belgium, France,[59] Rumania, Serbia, and Montenegro; the detachment from Turkey of the non-Turkish parts of the Ottoman Empire; and the restoration of an independent Poland.

The territorial provisions of the Fourteen Points had a recurrent theme: the drawing of borders to gather together people of the same nationality. The principle of national self-determination, with which Wilson became identified, was threaded through the program he set forth. His principles and goals differed from those that the European great powers had embraced in the past and to which they continued, in some cases, to be devoted. He did not consult any of them before announcing his program. Taken together, the Fourteen Points offered not only a comprehensive statement of Wilson's vision of international relations, many of whose features were part of the ideological tradition of American foreign policy, but also a preview of what the president would try to accomplish at the Peace Conference that convened in Paris after the war had ended.

First, however, the Allies had to win the war. In the months immediately after joining it the United States was able to offer only limited help in accomplishing that task. American troops did not begin arriving in France in large numbers until well into 1918.[60] Even before then, Wilson had insisted on setting them apart from the British and French forces: the United States entered the conflict not as an allied but instead as an "associated" power. In that spirit, the commander in chief of American forces in Europe, General John W. Pershing, decreed that American soldiers would fight only in units composed of and led by Americans, rather than being inserted into French and British formations to replace killed or wounded troops who had left their ranks—although ultimately Americans did serve under European command.[61] A major purpose of separating the American forces from the European ones was to highlight the independent contribution of the United States to the outcome of the war and thus, it was hoped, maximize American leverage in the postwar period.[62]

In the year after the American entry the war did not go well for the Allies. The all-out German submarine campaign took a heavy toll on transatlantic shipping. Italy, which had entered the war on the Allied side in May 1915 with the promise, enshrined in a secret treaty, of postwar territorial gains, suffered a serious defeat at the hands of Habsburg and German armies at Caporetto in October and November of 1917.[63] The British and the French launched major offensives against the entrenched Germans along the Western Front that failed, at great cost to the attacking forces.[64] The French setbacks triggered mutinies in the ranks of the French army. In March, the new Bolshevik government withdrew Russia from the war, signing the Treaty of Brest-Litovsk with Germany that conceded tsarist territory to the Germans. The treaty freed 750,000 German troops who had been fighting in the east to transfer to operations in the west.[65] Accordingly, on March 21,

1918, the German army began a major offensive that was intended to win the war at last.

The Allies halted the offensive and launched a counterattack that, in November, finally brought the war to an end on their terms. During the last six months of fighting on the Western Front the American Expeditionary Force, as it was called, played an important role.[66] Beginning at the end of May, American units helped to stop the German advance in battles at Cantigny, Chateau-Thierry, and Belleau Wood. In mid-July about 300,000 Americans, serving in the French sector of the front, took part in a counteroffensive at Aisne-Marne.[67] The American assault at St. Mihiel in September was the first major action under American command and succeeded in pushing back the already-retreating German army. The final and most extensive fighting by American troops took place in the climactic Meuse-Argonne campaign, which lasted from late September to the end of the war in November.[68]

In the autumn of 1918, the United States had more than one million troops in France, with three million more in training.[69] A total of 60,000 were killed and 206,000 wounded.[70] American soldiers fought bravely and, on the whole, effectively.[71] It is doubtful that the Allies could have won the war when they did and as they did—if they could have won it at all—without the late infusion of soldiers from the United States. Pershing did less well as a commander. He had believed that offensive tactics, of the kind both sides had employed at great cost and disappointingly little gain for three years on the Western Front, could work for the American units. That belief was not borne out on the battlefield, where his offensives gained less ground, at higher cost in Americans killed and wounded, than he had anticipated.[72]

During America's time as an active combatant in Europe, Woodrow Wilson, who dominated American policy both before the American entry and after the guns had fallen silent, had only a modest impact on events. This was so because, lasting only half a year, the period of American combat was relatively short and because the most important strategic question—where to send American troops—had only one answer: to France.

Wilson did decide, reluctantly, to send a small American military contingent to Russia. In the wake of the Bolshevik coup and the Treaty of Brest-Litovsk, the Allied governments intervened there hoping to revive the war's Eastern Front in order to weaken Germany in the west as well as to prevent the communists from consolidating power.[73] Seeing both a threat to and an opportunity for its own ambitions in the region, Japan sent forces to Siberia. To keep watch on the Japanese, and to show solidarity with his European partners in the war effort, Wilson authorized the dispatch of a small detachment of American troops to Arkhangelsk and Vladivostok,[74] which had, however, no appreciable impact on the course of events in Russia.

Meanwhile, as the Allied forces moved forward on the Western Front in the fall of 1918, the German high command and the German government came to the conclusion that the military balance had tilted decisively against them. They decided to give up the fight, seeking an armistice that went into effect at 11 a.m. on November 11—the eleventh hour of the eleventh day of the eleventh month. What had come to be called "The Great War" was finally over. Like Great Britain in previous centuries, the United States had served as an offshore balancer. It had taken part in a coalition—first supplying money and then fighting forces—that had prevented a continental power from achieving hegemony in Europe. With this accomplished, the task of peacemaking took center stage.

The Peace Conference

The postwar Peace Conference convened in Paris in January 1919, on a continent suffering from the effects of four brutal years of widespread death, destruction, and displacement. The peacemakers had to settle accounts for the recently concluded conflict, lay the basis for Europe's economic recovery, and build new political structures from the rubble of the multinational empires that the Allies had defeated. The Czech leader Thomas Masaryk called the Europe with which they had to deal "a laboratory resting on a vast cemetery."[75] In addition, with the Bolshevik seizure of power in St. Petersburg, the specter of revolution haunted the meeting.[76]

In this conference, as Woodrow Wilson had wished from the outset of the fighting, the United States played a major role. World War I had made the great North American republic a European power. Wilson decided to represent his country personally at Paris.[77] He arrived in Europe to a rapturous reception. In the eyes of the war-battered people of the continent he came as what he himself believed he was: a quasi-messianic figure who could free the Old World, once and for all, from the scourge of war.[78]

At the beginning of the conference the important decisions fell to the leaders of the Allied countries meeting as the Group of Ten, which consisted of two delegates each from the United States, Great Britain, France, Italy, and Japan (which had formally declared war on Germany in August 1914). When that arrangement proved unwieldy it was reduced to a Group of Four: President Wilson, the British prime minister David Lloyd George, the French prime minister Clemenceau, and the Italian president Vittorio Orlando.[79]

Wilson often took the lead in these meetings but his personality did not work in his favor. Some of the leaders and representatives of the other Allied countries found him pompous, arrogant, unrealistic, ill-informed, and insensitive to their national needs.[80] The president also had an inadequate staff that, to compound his difficulties, he often ignored, relying on his own less-than-encyclopedic knowledge and his personal instincts in working out the inevitably complicated and disputed details of postwar settlement.[81]

Further limiting his effectiveness, he overestimated his own and America's influence over the others. He believed, for example, that the wartime loans America had furnished to the Allies would serve as a source of leverage. That might have been the case if he had been able to offer reductions in their debts in exchange for concessions on issues over which he and they were at odds. The American public's strong opposition to debt relief, however, which continued throughout the decade of the 1920s, made this tactic politically impossible.[82] Also contributing to Wilson's overconfidence at Paris was his conviction, which his reception on the continent encouraged, that he could appeal to the people of the Allied countries over the heads of their leaders to support him when he differed with his colleagues. This, too, did not prove possible.[83]

The Paris Peace Conference reprised a similar gathering at Vienna in 1815, when the conquerors of Napoleonic France assembled to restore order to Europe after finally defeating the French. The peacemakers at

Paris, however, faced a larger and more difficult challenge. Not only had World War I, although shorter, wrought more death and destruction than the Napoleonic campaigns, but also the victorious powers at Vienna had agreed on restoring the territories and the governments of the imperial monarchies of the continent that Revolutionary and then Napoleonic France had battered for almost a quarter century.[84] The victors at Paris did not have the option of recreating pre-1914 Europe even if they had been inclined to do so, as Woodrow Wilson certainly was not: the war had swept it away, never to return.

Moreover, as in almost all wars waged by coalitions, the Allies had differences of interest and outlook that they suppressed during the fighting for the sake of achieving their common aim of victory but that inevitably rose to the surface once they had achieved it. For example, the Americans, separated from Europe by the Atlantic Ocean and bent on using the Peace Conference to transform international relations, had different goals for postwar Germany than did France, which was fated to live next door to the defeated power and wished to use the proceedings at Paris to ensure its security in the future.[85] The Americans sought political reform, economic recovery, and international reconciliation for the defeated power. The French, by contrast, wanted a settlement that provided them, at Germany's expense, with revenge, compensation, and safety.‡

In addition, in 1815 public opinion scarcely affected the policies of the great powers. In the case of the most autocratic of them, Russia, it had no effect at all. At Paris, by contrast, none of the leaders could ignore

‡ Margaret MacMillan, *Paris, 1919: Six Months That Changed the World*, New York: Random House, 2001, p. 32. "The day after Wilson had made a speech in London reiterating his faith that a League of Nations was the best way to provide security for its members, Clemenceau had spoken in the Chamber of Deputies. To loud cheers he asserted: 'There is an old system of alliances called the Balance of Power—this system of alliances, which I do not renounce, will be my guiding thought at the Peace Conference.'" *Ibid.*, p. 23. Wilson's program contradicted British principles as well. It "was an open refutation of the British international order, with its established concepts of protecting national and international sovereignty, imperial preference for trade, and markets forced open by military might." Kori Schake, *Safe Passage: The Transition from British to American Hegemony*, Cambridge, Massachusetts: Harvard University Press, 2017, p. 231.

the public's wishes: public affairs had become far more democratic, especially in western Europe, in the intervening century. The people of the Allied powers had had to make extraordinary sacrifices to win the war and demanded that these bring tangible postwar gains. There was a good case for treating Germany with generosity,[86] a case that sometimes persuaded Lloyd George and Wilson[87] if not Clemenceau. Public opinion in Great Britain and the United States, however, insisted on relatively harsh terms for the Germans, and the leaders had to bend to their wishes.[88]

The leaders at Paris labored under a final handicap. They made many decisions but, as the conference proceeded, their capacity to enforce those decisions diminished because the ultimate mechanism of enforcement, their countries' armed forces, were steadily demobilized. The American, British, and French publics were not interested in keeping in existence and supporting huge armies. Accordingly, in the short term in some parts of Europe, and over the longer term throughout the continent, the peacemakers' handiwork collapsed.

The major business of the Peace Conference involved dealing with the defeated powers, the Habsburg, Ottoman, and German Hohenzollern Empires; and in the cases of the first two that chiefly entailed disposing of their former territories. Initially, Woodrow Wilson had hoped to keep the Austro-Hungarian empire in existence in some form, but this proved impossible.[89] From the Habsburg territories, and from parts of imperial Turkey, Russia, and Germany, emerged ten new sovereign states.[90] As his Fourteen Points had made clear, Wilson believed that such states should be composed of a single national group. Europe was to be remade according to the principle of national self-determination. The principle turned out to be more easily articulated by the American president than implemented by the peacemakers at Paris. It raised two questions, to which there were (and continue to be) no definitive answers: which groups qualified as a nation and therefore deserved a state, and how borders should be drawn when different nations were intermixed with one another. Lansing, Wilson's secretary of state, foresaw the trouble the effort to apply the principle would cause. "The phrase is simply loaded with dynamite," he said. "It will raise hopes which can never be realized."[91]

So it proved. The borders established at Paris led, in Europe and the Middle East, to political strife, outright war, and the forced mass movement of peoples that subsequently came to be known as "ethnic cleansing." That grim pattern repeated itself as late as the 1990s when an outbreak took place in Yugoslavia, a multinational country formed after the end of the war, although before and apart from the deliberations at Paris.

Still, the Peace Conference needed some rule on which to base the political reconstruction of Europe. The longstanding multinational empires could not be reassembled. No better or more popular principle than the national one was available; it had gained legitimacy throughout the nineteenth century and had underpinned the unification of Italy and Germany. In the twentieth century it became the universally accepted formula for organizing sovereign states. While the countries that emerged from Paris seldom had populations marked by ethnic or national homogeneity,[92] many of the borders that the leaders at Paris drew, despite the controversy and even bloodshed that they generated, were still in existence a hundred years later.

In the case of the Ottoman Empire, a treaty signed at the Paris suburb of Sevres[93] in August 1920 redistributed its territory among the victorious powers, but this particular dispensation did not endure. With the blessing of the Allies, Greece dispatched troops to claim a piece of Asia Minor. The Turks, under the leadership of a former Ottoman general named Mustafa Kemal, resisted, defeated the Greeks, and created a Turkish state larger than the one for which Sevres had provided.[94] The Treaty of Lausanne[95] ratified this outcome in 1923, by which time the United States had washed its hands of Europe's political affairs.

As for Germany, the Versailles Treaty that settled its fate, which a successor government to that of the Kaiser signed with great reluctance, reduced its territory,[96] limited its military power, and included what became the notorious Clause 231. The Clause stipulated that Germany had started the war and so, having lost it, would have to pay reparations to the winners. The Germans never accepted as justified the terms forced on them. They had agreed to end the war in November 1918 on the basis of Wilson's Fourteen Points, but the treatment they received departed from Wilson's program. In particular, national self-determination turned out not to apply fully to postwar Germany.

Territories populated by German speakers were included in postwar Czechoslovakia and Poland.[97]

German resistance to the terms of the Versailles Treaty poisoned the politics and economics of Europe for the next two decades. In the 1920s the Germans balked at paying the reparations they owed, which weighed on economic activity across the continent. In the 1930s the Third Reich overturned one after another of the provisions of the treaty, leading, eventually, to an even more destructive replay of the war of 1914 to 1918.

While the Peace Conference addressed issues in addition to the fate of the war's principal losers, it did not deal in any decisive way with the Soviet Union. The leaders at Paris could not decide whether to try to overthrow the Bolsheviks, to quarantine them, or to open a channel of communication with them. In the end they adopted none of these courses of action.[98]

Having declared war on Germany in 1914, Japan qualified as a member of the winning coalition and demanded a share of the spoils of war.[99] Specifically, the Japanese wanted to keep Germany's colonial possessions in China, centered on Shantung, a coastal province in the northeastern part of the country. Wilson, like other Americans, had a proprietary, protective attitude toward China and the Japanese demand violated his treasured principle of national self-determination. Nonetheless, he and the other Allied leaders gave the Japanese government what it wanted.[100]

The decision was part of a pattern. The European peoples living within the borders of the defeated empires received their own states but the non-Europeans who were similarly situated did not.[101] The former imperial territories outside Europe became "mandates" under the League of Nations, the international organization that the peacemakers authorized, that were assigned to one or another of the victorious powers. Britain and France, for example, divided between themselves the formerly Ottoman Middle East. Far from having to surrender their own non-European possessions, therefore, the British and the French, contrary to the spirit of national self-determination, actually added to them.[102] The United States was offered, but declined, a mandate for the former Ottoman territory of Armenia, which was eventually absorbed into the Soviet Union.[103]

The Paris Peace Conference has had, on the whole, a poor historical reputation, and for one main reason: the meeting's most important goal was to work out arrangements to prevent another war like the one just concluded, and in this it failed. The undoubted shortcomings of the Paris settlement, however, many of them noted at the time, had less to do with the inadequacies of the men who made it—although Wilson, in particular, did not cover himself with glory[104]—than with the larger forces with which they had to contend: the extent of the disruption that World War I had caused; the sharp differences between and among the members of the Allied coalition; and the pressures from the publics to which the leaders had to answer both to forge a settlement that could justify the costs they had had to pay for victory and to end the social and military mobilization that that victory had required.

Moreover, World War II had causes that did not go back directly to the events in Paris in 1919 and 1920.[105] During the 1920s, in fact, adjustments to the settlement, to which the United States contributed, seemed to bring political and economic stability both to Europe and to East Asia.[106]

Woodrow Wilson's reputation has had a different fate. On his foreign policy historians have returned two polarized verdicts. Some have seen him as an abject failure, others as a prophet without honor whose ideas could have prevented the disasters of the 1930s and 1940s if only his countrymen had embraced them. The dispute about the legacy of the twenty-eighth president centers on the project he valued most highly: the establishment of a League of Nations.

Wilson made the creation of the League his first order of business at Paris. As initially designed, it consisted of an Assembly of all the countries that belonged to it[107] and a Council with five permanent members (the victors of World War I: the United States, Great Britain, France, Italy, and Japan)[108] and four nonpermanent members, to be elected for three-year terms. It also had a Secretariat and two ancillary bodies: the Permanent Court of Justice and the International Labor Organization.[109] The president attached the Covenant of the League— its charter—to the Versailles Treaty so that when the United States Senate voted on that treaty it was voting, as well, on American membership in the League.

The idea of such an organization was not Wilson's alone. During the war others, including the former Republican presidents Theodore Roosevelt and William Howard Taft,[110] had advocated the establishment of an international association of some kind to keep the postwar peace. For Wilson, however, it came to be the central, indispensable feature of the postwar settlement. Its creation would, he believed, vindicate his difficult decision to take the United States to war and redeem the sacrifices Americans had made to help win it.[111] He conceived of the organization as the mechanism that would solve major international problems: mistakes or shortcomings in the terms of the peace treaties could and would be corrected in and by the League.[112] He failed, however, to persuade the necessary two-thirds of the Senate to ratify the Versailles Treaty and thus authorize American membership in the League. The United States never joined.

On the question of League membership, the Senate divided into three factions. One, following Wilson, favored unconditional membership. Another, the "irreconcilables," wanted to stay out under any circumstances. A third, led by Henry Cabot Lodge, as the result of the Republican Congressional victory in 1918 the chairman of the Senate Foreign Relations Committee, was willing to support membership under certain conditions. Lodge ultimately proposed fourteen of them.[113] In three votes of the entire Senate, the treaty failed to achieve the necessary two-thirds majority: the irreconcilables and reservationists opposed it as Wilson had submitted it, and the treaty with the Lodge conditions also failed because Wilson and his followers rejected any compromises on the League as originally designed.[114]

The United States failed to join in part for reasons of personality. Lodge had come to despise Wilson,[115] who, for his part, stubbornly refused to accept any modifications of what the peacemakers at Paris had devised.[116] In the fall of 1919 the president undertook a grueling national speaking tour on behalf of his cherished project and in September, after a speech in Pueblo, Colorado, he suffered a serious stroke. He never fully recovered and was incapacitated for the rest of his presidency.

Beyond matters of personality, serious issues of policy and principle divided the Senate and the country over the League; and at their heart lay Article X of the League charter. It read as follows:

The Members of the League undertake to respect and preserve as against external aggression the territorial integrity and existing political independence of all Members of the League. In case of any such aggression or in case of any threat or danger of such aggression the Council shall advise upon the means by which this obligation shall be fulfilled.

Lodge and his allies registered several objections to it. It entailed, they said, far too broad and open-ended a commitment, with the potential to embroil the United States in quarrels and conflicts in which it had no interest.[117] Moreover, the language implied that the League could by itself engage America in armed conflict, overriding the Constitution, which reserves the power to declare war to the Congress. As such, Article X touched on the fundamental issue of national sovereignty. By one interpretation it deprived League members of a basic sovereign prerogative, one that countries ordinarily do not relinquish unless they are compelled to do so through conquest.[118]

At one point Wilson held an unprecedented personal meeting at the White House with the members of the Senate Foreign Relations Committee[119] and argued that Article X involved a moral rather than a legal obligation, a distinction that skeptics found neither clear nor convincing. One of Lodge's reservations stipulated that the United States had no obligation to fight, whatever the League decided, without Congressional authorization.[120] Wilson refused to accept it.[121]

When America declined to join the League, and especially in the wake of a second great and terrible world war, Woodrow Wilson became, in some eyes, a martyr for the cause of peace, whose policies could have avoided the catastrophe of 1939 to 1945 if only Americans had followed his lead. If he had agreed to accept the Lodge reservations, the Versailles Treaty almost certainly would have passed the Senate and ratified League membership. The impact this would have had on the international history of the period between the two world wars cannot, of course, be known. It is unlikely, however, that the League, even with American participation, would have become a sufficiently powerful and effective organization to keep the peace and suppress aggression around the world. The United Nations, after all, the comparable international body that was successfully launched in the wake of the second war, became no such thing.

Lodge and others did favor a postwar American commitment, which Wilson had in fact offered at Paris, to support France and help protect its security if necessary. Such a commitment found expression after World War II in the North Atlantic Treaty.[122] Implementing such an arrangement, however, would have involved surmounting a major obstacle to American membership in the League: the public reluctance to become militarily engaged anywhere.[123] It took another global conflagration, and the conviction that America's post–World War I resistance to a military role in Europe had contributed to the outbreak of the second conflict, to overcome that reluctance.

In the 250-year history of American foreign policy Woodrow Wilson looms large.[124] He is the only American president to have lent his name to a distinctive approach to foreign policy. "Wilsonianism," as expressed most authoritatively in the Fourteen Points, connotes an emphasis on the promotion of values, especially democracy, rather than the protection of interests, a predilection for creating and joining international organizations, the abolition of or at least restrictions on armaments, and a general disposition to seek the transformation of international relations so as to make them more peaceful—all under American leadership.[125] This approach, like the person for whom it is named, remained controversial a century after Wilson himself had passed from the political scene.

In retrospect, a number of his personal qualities seem both unattractive and dysfunctional.[126] His shortcomings hindered him at Paris and in his campaign to secure the ratification of the Versailles Treaty in the United States. In addition, of course, his effort to secure American membership in the League of Nations, the enterprise about which he cared most and that he considered to be of supreme importance, ended in failure.

Yet some of the principles that he brought to the center of international affairs did take root, the national principle as the basis for statehood being the most influential. Moreover, while his dream of world peace and his attempt to abolish the age-old routines of power politics and substitute for them international harmony and cooperation came to nothing in his lifetime, that dream has persisted and similar efforts, although none as ambitious as Wilson's, have recurred. The aspiration to transform international relations first appeared in the United States well before the Wilson presidency, at the dawn of the republic. Along with the exaltation of liberty, it is embedded in the country's political genes. So while Americans have not fully implemented, and perhaps cannot implement, Wilsonian ideas, they also have not discarded them and probably never will.

Postwar Foreign Policy: Security

Even as he was losing the battle for American membership in the League of Nations, Woodrow Wilson believed that the American public supported him and that the 1920 election would vindicate his policies. He toyed with the idea of running for an unprecedented third term but the effects of his stroke made that impossible. The election did return a verdict on Wilson, his foreign policies, and his eight years in office, and it turned out to be a massively negative one.

The Democratic ticket—notable in retrospect mainly for its vice presidential candidate, the former assistant secretary of the navy Franklin Delano Roosevelt, a distant cousin of his namesake the former president—lost in a landslide. Three different Republicans won that and the next two presidential elections: Ohio senator Warren G. Harding in 1920, his vice president Calvin Coolidge in 1924 (Harding had died in office in 1923), and Coolidge's secretary of commerce, the celebrated humanitarian Herbert Hoover, in 1928. American foreign policy for the twelve years after Woodrow Wilson was therefore Republican foreign policy.

In popular historical memory this period of foreign policy has received the name "isolationist." Congress did pass laws restricting immigration in 1921 and 1924[127] but in most important respects the term is misleading. The United States did not seek to isolate itself from the rest of the world, or even from Europe, and in fact conducted an active foreign policy that achieved some significant successes.[128]

A more appropriate label for the period is the neologism identified with Harding. He promised the country a return to "normalcy" in the wake of the war, and his foreign policy and those of his two successors aimed at restoring what they considered normal for the United States. America, as they saw it, continued to be what it had been on the eve of World War I: a great power with important interests around the world, interests that it was the responsibility of the federal government to protect and promote.

Those interests did not, however, include what World War I, breaking with historical precedent, had involved: the presence of American troops in large numbers on the European continent. Americans had become disillusioned with the results of their country's military efforts there and opposed repeating them.[129] Moreover, during the terms of the three Republican presidents no military threats to the United States either existed or seemed likely to arise there.[130] America thus felt no need to serve as the military balancer for Europe. The political and military affairs of East Asia, by contrast, did fall within the scope of those interests, as they had in the two decades before 1914. Accordingly, the United States maintained a serious naval presence in the Pacific and pursued active Asian diplomacy.

The Republicans' foreign policy did not ignore Europe entirely. To the contrary, government officials and business leaders believed that the United States had an important stake in the economic health of the continent and the federal government, working through the private sector,[131] launched major initiatives to restore it—which, for a time, they seemed to do. The hallmark of American foreign policy after Woodrow Wilson was, therefore, continuity—not with the policies he had espoused, although his successors did adopt some Wilsonian measures, but rather with those that had preceded his presidency.

In the part of the world where the United States had had the deepest involvement for the longest time, Central America, the three immediate postwar presidents in fact changed American foreign policy. While they did not forsake the Monroe Doctrine—one of their fellow Republican Lodge's reservations had stipulated that League membership could not override it—they did soften the American approach to the countries there. They placed less emphasis on military intervention and more on neighborly economic ties.[132] In 1924 the Coolidge administration withdrew American troops from the Dominican Republic. It also withdrew Marines from Nicaragua in 1925, although they returned in 1926 and did not leave again until 1933.[133]

With the country to the south with which the United States had historically had the most troubled relationship, Mexico, the most difficult bilateral issue had become Article 27 of that country's 1917 constitution. Through it the Mexican government sought to reclaim land and resources, notably oil, that foreigners—mainly American citizens—had purchased. The owners naturally objected. Negotiations between the Mexican government and American business interests, led on the American side by Thomas Lamont, a partner at the prominent financial firm of J. P. Morgan, reached a compromise in 1923. Another Morgan partner, Dwight Morrow, helped to smooth the bilateral relationship as the American ambassador in Mexico City and brokered a final settlement in 1928.[134] Still, while their successors modified the Central American policies of Theodore Roosevelt, Taft, and Wilson, they did not abandon these policies entirely. The United States maintained a military presence in Cuba, Haiti, and Panama in the 1920s.

In Europe, political and military issues in the wake of the war, and without the United States taking part in them, became contentious. Germany refused to pay the reparations it owed France under the terms of the Paris settlement. In retaliation, in January 1923 French troops occupied Germany's Ruhr Valley.[135] Both France and Germany suffered economically, and the French withdrew in August 1925.[136]

There followed a hopeful development. With the Treaty of Locarno[137] -- signed in 1925 with some offstage encouragement from Washington -- Germany, France, and Belgium undertook not to attack one another and Great Britain and Italy guaranteed the accord.[138] The treaty appeared to go a long way toward resolving the postwar conflict between France and Germany and thereby bring a measure of political stability to the western part of the European continent.

Locarno did not, however, relieve the French of their anxieties about the threat their German neighbor posed to them or of their desire for an American security guarantee. In 1928 the French foreign minister, Aristide Briand, in an attempt to bring the United States, if only indirectly, into the European security order, proposed a "solemn declaration" by France and the United States that they would not go to war against each other. Having no interest in giving the French a bilateral commitment of any kind, Briand's American opposite number, Secretary of State Frank Kellogg, converted the French initiative into a multilateral peace agreement, open to all countries. Ultimately sixty-three of them signed it.[139]

As a global treaty to outlaw war, the Kellogg-Briand Pact was consistent with the tradition that Woodrow Wilson had codified. Signing it was a declaration of good intentions rather than the acceptance of a serious obligation, which is no doubt the reason that so many governments were willing to adhere to it. Like Locarno, however, it did have symbolic importance. It denoted the easing of the political conflict that the Paris Peace Conference had bequeathed to Europe.

Unlike its European policies, in East Asia the United States did involve itself in the security affairs of the region and in the first postwar decade American efforts helped to bring about a broad political settlement. In 1921 the Harding administration convened a conference in Washington to discuss naval armaments. Secretary of State Charles Evans Hughes, previously governor of New York and the 1916 Republican candidate for president, and subsequently the Chief Justice of the United States Supreme Court, surprised the delegates in attendance by proposing sweeping and specific limitations on warships, a proposal that led the next year to a treaty incorporating such limitations.

Political conditions within the principal signatory countries produced the restrictions.[140] All three major maritime powers in the Pacific had domestic incentives to limit their navies. In the United States, the Harding administration had come under pressure to reduce military spending both from those who rejected military engagement in general and from economy-minded Republicans;[141] and the president saw the negotiations as an arena in which to assert himself politically.[142] The British, too, felt the economic burden of conducting a global policy, including the maintenance of an expanded empire, in the wake of an exhausting war. In addition, the British, and the Japanese as well,[143] were eager to avoid a naval arms race with the United States.[144]

The Washington Conference ultimately yielded three closely related treaties.[145] The Five-Power accord established a ratio in battleship tonnage among the United States, Great Britain, Japan, France, and Italy.[146] In the Four-Power Treaty, the United States, Britain, Japan, and France each agreed to respect the insular possessions of all the others and to confer with one another in the event of any threat to them.[147] By the terms of the Nine-Power Treaty, the other European imperial powers joined the signatories to the Five-Power accord in promising not to encroach (or encroach further) on China's sovereignty and territorial integrity. The treaty reaffirmed the prewar American Open Door policy.[148]

Together the three accords made up a political and military settlement in the Asia-Pacific region that was the rough equivalent of Locarno in Europe. Unlike the European dispensation, the Asian settlement came about not only with full American participation but also through the leadership of the United States. It continued the regional policies of John Hay and Theodore Roosevelt, both of whom had sought to create a balance of power in Asia without the United States having to exert itself to sustain it.

The East Asian settlement had a Wilsonian element as well: one of the mechanisms for achieving the regional balance, limits on armaments, echoed one of Wilson's Fourteen Points. Naval arms control in the 1920s, moreover, established—or rather revealed—a pattern that would be evident during the next period of serious American negotiations to place limits on weaponry, in the 1970s.[149] Arms control in both eras was embedded in, and depended on, politics, in the sense that political considerations supplied the motive and the opportunity for such agreements. The parties to the Washington treaties observed its terms more or less faithfully throughout the 1920s, and in 1930 a conference in London renewed, adjusted, and extended the restrictions on naval armaments.[150] Then political conditions in East Asia changed.

Specifically, they changed in Manchuria. In this northeastern part of China[151] the ambitions of China, Japan, and Russia collided with one another: it became the geographic focus of their geopolitical rivalry. It had value not only for its strategic location but also because of its endowment of natural resources. By defeating China in 1895 and Russia in 1905, Japan had established its preeminence in the southern part of the territory.[152]

The Qing Dynasty, which had ruled China for three centuries and whose weakness had opened the door to Japan's encroachment, collapsed in 1911 and after more than a decade and a half of turmoil Chiang Kai-shek came to power in 1928. He began a campaign to restore Chinese control over all of Manchuria.[153] Alarmed at this, and dissatisfied with the policies toward China of the government in Tokyo, the Japanese military provoked an incident in the Manchurian city of Mukden on September 18, 1931, and used it as a pretext to extend its own grip over northern as well as southern Manchuria. Japanese forces also launched a brutal attack on the Chinese city of Shanghai, killing an estimated 10,000 to 20,000 civilians.[154] The Japanese government established a new Manchurian puppet state that it called "Manchukuo."

The Japanese assaults, the extension of their control over all of Manchuria, and the deployment of their forces into other parts of China struck a major blow at the political and military status quo in East Asia, which the American-sponsored treaties of a decade previous had codified and bolstered. The League of Nations condemned the actions (leading Japan to quit the League) but the League's members, including Great Britain, which retained a naval presence in the region, looked to the United States for a definitive response to them.

The Hoover administration reacted in an ambivalent manner. It was outraged at Japan's aggression and concerned that this would eventually lead to Japanese domination of East Asia. Yet it was also convinced that Manchuria alone did not rise to the level of a vital American interest and was aware, in any case, that it could not expect to command public support for a military initiative to stop Japan, let alone roll back its advances. Unwilling to do nothing but unable take effective countervailing action, Secretary of State Henry Stimson sent a note to the Japanese government on January 7, 1932, whose contents became known as the Stimson Doctrine. It asserted that the United States would not recognize any territorial or other gains that Japan (or other countries) made by force. The note and attendant doctrine registered American disapproval but did nothing to affect the object of that disapproval.[155]

The Manchuria episode and its aftermath prefigured the events of the 1930s in Asia and Europe. Aggressive powers destroyed the political status quo on both continents. The democracies, including the most powerful of them, the United States, condemned the aggression that unfolded but took no measures to oppose it effectively. The American public's reluctance to fight outside the Western Hemisphere, which the experience of World War I had fortified, made such opposition politically impossible for the American government. Another development of the early 1930s also constrained the United States and its World War I allies. All were preoccupied with their own internal affairs because all had, by the time of the Manchurian episode, fallen into deep economic distress.[156]

Postwar Foreign Policy: Economics

After World War I, as before, the United States had the world's largest economy. It fell into recession from 1919 to 1921[157] but recovered thereafter and grew rapidly until 1929, conferring on that decade the title "the roaring twenties." The rate of economic growth averaged five percent per year.[158] Overall, the gross national product (GNP) increased by fifty-nine percent during that period, GNP per capita by forty-two percent, and personal income by more than thirty-eight percent.[159] By 1929, American national income exceeded that of Great Britain, Germany, France, Canada, Japan, and seventeen other nations combined.[160]

Much of the growth took place in relatively new industries that made products for consumers. In the years between the two world wars the United States became a full-fledged consumer society, the first of its kind in all of history.[161] Two major inventions underpinned the American consumer revolution.[162]

The internal combustion engine made possible the automobile. By the mid-1920s the United States was home to eighty percent of all the cars throughout the world.[163] The automobile industry became, like the railroad in the nineteenth century, the leading sector of the American economy, generating employment both directly and indirectly on a large scale.[164] At the same time, electricity laid the basis for appliances for the home that more and more Americans were able to purchase and use: electric lights, the electric iron, the sewing machine, and the radio, among others.[165]

The American example of mass consumption proved powerfully attractive everywhere. It spread to Europe after the second war and, in the decades that followed, all around the world. While not a part of the nation's foreign policy, through the example of a consumer society that it was the first country to develop, the United States had an enormous impact on the world.

In matters of trade, the Republican Party carried out a policy of protection, as it had done when in power since the Civil War. In 1922 the Congress passed the Fordney-McCumber Tariff.[166] Still, the United

States became the world's largest exporter in the 1920s and while total world trade expanded by only thirteen percent between 1913 and 1929, American trade more than doubled in that period.[167]

In no area of economic activity did American prowess play a more important international role than in finance. The war turned the United States from a debtor nation into the world's largest creditor.[168] It became by far the leading source of loans worldwide,[169] and Europe's economies came to depend on American capital. American multinational firms made direct foreign investment on a large scale, much of it in agriculture and extractive industries.[170]

The three postwar Republican administrations believed that, while events beyond North America would not disturb their country's security, the United States did have a major interest in the conditions of the global economy in general and in economic conditions in Europe in particular. They therefore made indirect use of American financial strength to try to improve those conditions.[171] In the 1920s, American capital became the principal, and the most effective, instrument of American foreign policy.

Finance entangled the United States in European affairs.[172] America had lent the European allies $10 billion during the war and insisted on being repaid. The British and the French resented this insistence. As they saw it, they had paid in blood for a cause they had in common with the United States.[173] Furthermore, they took the position that their ability to pay depended on their receiving the reparations from Germany that the Paris settlement had mandated.[174] The Germans balked at fulfilling this obligation, feeling strongly that it had been unfairly imposed on them: their resistance was a major source of conflict in postwar Europe. Even with the best will in the world, moreover, Germany had to earn the money to pay reparations, and the war had severely disrupted its economy.[175] To resume growth it needed capital, which could only come from the United States: so Germany depended on American loans.[176]

Thus a politically awkward and economically precarious pattern came into existence. American loans transferred money to Germany, which sent it—some of it, anyway—to Britain and France, who used what they received to satisfy their American creditors.[177] This system, such as it was, did not function smoothly and impeded economic recovery in Europe. The United States stepped in to try to remedy the situation.

A committee of financial experts was appointed in January 1924 to reconsider the reparations question, with Charles Dawes, a Chicago banker, at its head. The committee produced the Dawes Plan, which rescheduled Germany's obligations, reorganized its monetary system in the wake of a bout of hyperinflation, and included a loan to Germany as well. It provided for a substantial de facto reduction in Germany's debt to the Allies.[178]

The Coolidge administration took no direct part in the Dawes Committee but worked behind the scenes to ensure its success: the Dawes Plan was widely and correctly seen as an American initiative.[179] As with the prewar Taft administration's program of Dollar Diplomacy, in adjusting the schedule of reparations the United States relied on private capital, not government funds. Once accepted, the Plan set the scene for the Treaty of Locarno[180] and together they brought a measure of harmony and a period of economic growth[181] to postwar Western Europe. Five years later, with the reparations question still disturbing the politics and economics of the continent, another committee, chaired by the American Owen Young, who had served on the Dawes Committee, further modified German obligations.[182]

The American government's efforts to bring stability to Europe in the 1920s returned the United States to the foreign policy it had pursued outside the Western Hemisphere before 1914. It conducted the policy of a great power seeking to protect its interests while limiting the costs of doing so. Washington accepted that it did have major economic if not political stakes in Europe; it could not ignore the financial affairs of the continent.

As with Great Britain's historical policy of offshore balancing, the United States did not intervene directly: just as the British preferred not to send their own troops to Europe when this could be avoided, so the Republican administrations successfully encouraged private banks to supply the resources required rather than having the government provide funds itself. As with the Open Door policy toward China, the United States worked to bring other countries around to a position that reduced the prospect of conflict among them while protecting

American economic interests at minimal risk and cost to American taxpayers.

The Young Plan, like the one produced by the Dawes Committee, seemed initially to improve the outlook for political conciliation and economic growth in Europe. A few months after its announcement, however, the American stock market crashed.[183] That event and those that followed had an impact on Europe comparable to the effect of the Manchurian episode in Asia. They transformed the prevailing political conditions from tentative, limited cooperation to escalating tension. The year 1929 turned out to mark the transition from a postwar to a prewar period, for in that year began a chain of events that led, at the end of the next decade, to the outbreak of World War II.

The crash was followed by banking crises, first in the United States[184] and then in Europe.[185] Banks failed in large numbers on both continents and this touched off a downward economic spiral that ultimately engulfed the whole world. Businesses could not obtain credit and so cut back their workforces or closed altogether. Economic activity stalled. Unemployment rose. Consumption plummeted as did prices, worsening the downturn. Debt became impossible for individuals and firms to service. These negative trends reinforced one another, increasing the economic distress. In the Great Depression, economic activity fell more sharply than at any time since the beginning of the Industrial Revolution. Only wars and plagues had done more economic damage to Europe, and none of the several downturns the United States had experienced since its founding had been as severe.[186]

Nine decades later historians still debated the precise connections between and among the bursting of the bubble in American stocks, the bank failures on both sides of the Atlantic, and the deflationary spirals in Europe and the United States.[187] Retrospective judgment did, however, converge on one central point: whatever the causes of the Great Depression, the policies that the major countries adopted to deal with it only made it worse.[188]

Those countries reduced spending, seeking to balance their budgets, when they should have increased government outlays. They raised interest rates instead of lowering them, in order to comply with the rules of the gold standard, which served as a straitjacket for their economies and that they abandoned too late. Toward each other they implemented what came to be called "beggar-thy-neighbor" policies, devaluing their currencies and erecting barriers to trade[189] in a vain effort to stimulate economic activity within their own borders at the expense of others: economic cooperation would have served them far better. In the grip of beliefs about the economy that were not just unhelpful but indeed positively counterproductive, the governments' policies had the effect of pouring gasoline instead of water on a dangerous fire. Mistaken ideas contributed substantially to the Great Depression.

The United States shared those ideas, and acted on them.[190] It also made three distinctive contributions to the depth of the Depression. First, the American refusal to forego or at least modify the debts its allies had incurred in wartime weighed on the European and global economies throughout the 1920s, rendering them less robust and thus less prepared than they might otherwise have been to absorb the shocks that began in 1929. Second, because Europe depended so heavily on capital from the world's leading creditor, the American banking crisis, which reduced the volume of transatlantic loans, had a crippling impact on the European economies.[191]

Third, with by far the world's largest economy, only the United States was in a position to take the initiatives necessary to contain the crisis. Only the United States, that is, could have acted, as Great Britain had acted in the past but was now too weak to do, as the global economic leader.[192] At the beginning of the 1930s, America could have, and in hindsight should have, taken Britain's place but did not. In economic as well as political terms, Americans and their government saw their country as one great power among several but not as the leader of all of them with the singular responsibilities that came with that status.[193]

President Hoover did take steps in the right direction. In 1930 he proposed, for example, a one-year moratorium on both Allied loan repayments to the United States and German reparations payments to the Allies.[194] The policies that public opinion and the ideas of the economic establishment would permit in the United States, however, were not adequate to put a stop to the downward global economic spiral.

The Great Depression had profound consequences for international relations and therefore for the foreign policies of all the great powers, including the United States. Each of them devoted almost all of its attention and political energies to coping with economic problems at home, and so had little of either available for other issues. Four years after the stock market crash, with the world still mired in depression and because of the political fallout from it, new leaders came to power in Germany and the United States. Each would remain in his position for twelve turbulent years.

Adolf Hitler, the new German chancellor, would carry out a murderously aggressive foreign policy that would put an end to the Paris settlement and start the costliest war in all of history. With far less reluctance than Woodrow Wilson in 1914, and with the perverse assistance of both Hitler and a Japanese government that conducted an equally aggressive foreign policy in the wake of the Manchurian episode, Franklin Delano Roosevelt, the thirty-second American president, would lead the United States into that war.

6

The Arsenal of Democracy, 1933–1945

The Collapse of the Peace

Franklin Delano Roosevelt, the thirty-second president of the United States and the only one to be elected to the office four times, dominated American public life, including American foreign policy, during his term of office, which ran from his first inauguration in March 1933 to his death in April 1945. The history of American foreign policy in these years is, first and foremost, the history of his ideas, his inclinations, his leadership, and his policies in guiding the international course of the North American great power.

Roosevelt came from a well-to-do family, attended Harvard College and the Columbia Law School, served as governor of New York, ran for vice president on the Democratic ticket in 1920, and attained the nation's highest political position despite suffering a bout of polio as an adult that left him largely confined to a wheelchair.

As a national leader his outstanding characteristic was confidence: he possessed it, expressed it, and inspired it.[1] He created public confidence not just in himself but also in the resilience and potential of the United States itself, in no small part through his mastery of the new medium of communication, radio, through which he delivered occasional informal nation-wide addresses known as "Fireside Chats."* The boost

---

* The novelist Saul Bellow described the experience of listening to one of the Fireside Chats in Chicago in the 1930s: "I can recall walking eastward on the Chicago Midway on a summer evening. . . . The blight hadn't yet carried off the

he gave to the morale of its citizens, along with his policies, helped the country through its two greatest twentieth-century trials: the Great Depression and the Second World War.

If his style of national leadership consistently provided uplift, however, his methods of management frequently sowed confusion. Those who worked for and with him often found the experience frustrating. He rarely set forth either clearly or candidly the motives for his policy choices, the goals at which he was aiming were sometimes uncertain, and the lines of authority emanating from his office were frequently tangled, blurred, and overlapping.[2] He had a penchant for pitting some subordinates against others as a way of maintaining ultimate control over them all. Henry Stimson, a veteran of high-level government service whom he appointed secretary of war (and who served him loyally), called him "the worst administrator I have ever served under."[3] Roosevelt said of himself in 1942 that he was "a juggler, and I never let my right hand know what my left hand does. . . . I may be entirely inconsistent, and furthermore I am perfectly willing to mislead and tell untruths if it will help win the war."[4]

To the conduct of foreign policy he brought a depth and breadth of experience unusual for an incoming American president:[5] he had traveled widely and had served as assistant secretary of the navy from 1913 to 1920. He was a distant cousin, and an admirer, of Theodore Roosevelt; and like his relative and predecessor he understood power to be at the heart of international politics, with the strongest states exercising the greatest influence. His foreign policies reflected that recognition. Yet he was also, in his way, a disciple of Theodore Roosevelt's

---

elms, and under them drivers had pulled over, parking bumper to bumper, and turned on their radios to hear Roosevelt. They had rolled down the windows and opened the car doors. Everywhere the same voice, its odd Eastern accent, which in anyone else would have irritated Midwesterners. You could follow without missing a single word as you strolled by. You felt joined to these unknown drivers, men and women smoking their cigarettes in silence, not so much considering the President's words as affirming the rightness of his tone and taking assurance from it." "In the Days of Mr. Roosevelt," in Bellow, *It All Adds Up: From the Dim Past to the Uncertain Future, A Nonfiction Collection*, New York: Viking, 1994, pp. 28–29.

philosophical antipode, Woodrow Wilson, who had appointed him to the Navy Department.[6]

Initially a supporter of Wilson's vision of the postwar world, Roosevelt had moved away from that vision, with its emphasis on membership in the League of Nations, when it became clear that the American people would not embrace it. Wilson's experience impressed him with the political danger of advocating foreign policies that lacked firm public support, a lesson that guided his conduct of American foreign policy throughout his presidency.[7]

In the years preceding American entry, his approach to the second European war of the twentieth century differed sharply from Wilson's to the first: between 1914 and 1917 Wilson had regarded the outcome of the fighting on the other side of the Atlantic as having little or no bearing on American interests. From the mid-1930s Roosevelt, by contrast, believed that the United States had a huge stake in the prevention of German domination of Europe. During his second term and through most of the first year of his third he struggled to provide support to the British (and, until their defeat in 1940, to the French) in the face of the resistance of the war-averse American public.

Roosevelt's view of the postwar world, however, bore a strong resemblance to Woodrow Wilson's. Roosevelt, too, called for national self-determination. He, too, advocated the establishment of an international organization to keep the postwar peace. In this way he also followed an older, broader American tradition of foreign policy. As the leaders of a major participant in a victorious coalition in a great global war, both Wilson and Roosevelt confronted the question of how international relations as a whole should be organized not as a theoretical exercise but as a practical problem. Both men, and indeed their successors in America's highest office, furnished answers that incorporated values and preferences dating back to the beginning of the American republic. Franklin Roosevelt, like subsequent presidents and like American foreign policy for the rest of the twentieth century and beyond, combined the power-oriented approach to the conduct of the nation's affairs of Theodore Roosevelt with a predilection for the ideas, and idealism, of Woodrow Wilson.[8]

When he took office, the Great Depression had the nation in its grip and he devoted virtually all of his time to seeking ways to revive the

American economy, sponsoring a series of programs known collectively as the "New Deal." The remedies he proposed had, for the most part, a strictly national rather than international scope.[9] His predecessor, Herbert Hoover, had encouraged the convening of an international economic conference in London in 1933, with the goal of finding cooperative solutions to an economic slump that plagued Europe as well as the United States. Roosevelt rejected any significant steps of that kind, such as coordinated currency stabilization.[10] He preferred to look for effective antidotes to the Depression at home.

During his first term he did adopt or support some international initiatives that turned out to have important consequences in later years. In 1934, for example, Congress passed, at the administration's request and with the active, enthusiastic, and effective support of Secretary of State Cordell Hull, who was a devout free trader,[11] the Reciprocal Trade Adjustment Act (RTAA), which empowered the president to reduce tariffs in trade agreements with other countries. American trade did not increase appreciably in the near term[12] because of the Depression and the war; but after 1945 it expanded dramatically.

The RTAA marked the passage from a period, beginning with the Civil War, in which the champions of protection held the upper hand in American trade policy, to an era when national policy favored free trade.[13] The new era in trade had as its principal underlying causes the political hegemony of the Democratic Party—of the two major political parties the one more favorably disposed to low tariffs—and the expanded power of the presidency in conjunction with the diminished authority of the Congress over international economic policy, which tilted the inevitable political conflict over trade policy toward expanded commerce.[14]

In November 1933 the Roosevelt administration established formal diplomatic relations with the communist government of the Soviet Union, the last major country to do so.[15] American diplomatic recognition made it easier than it would otherwise have been for the two to collaborate against Nazi Germany from 1941 to 1945.

The single reference to foreign affairs in the president's first inaugural address concerned Latin America, toward which he promised that the United States would act as a "good neighbor."[16] As such, in May 1934 the American government revoked the Platt Amendment, which had served as the charter for American intrusion into Cuban affairs after 1898.[17] It made, as well, a more general commitment to refrain from military intervention in the countries to its south[18] and in 1939 finally settled an ongoing dispute with Mexico over compensation for the nationalization of American oil companies there.[19] These measures paved the way for steps to combat German influence in the region when war came.[20] Finally, by the terms of the Tydings-McDuffie Act of 1934 the United States promised (and in fact granted) independence to the Philippines in 1946, a promise that helped to sustain pro-American sentiment there during the Japanese occupation.

Meanwhile, the world beyond North America moved toward war. Three major countries with dictatorial governments—Nazi Germany, Fascist Italy, and Imperial Japan—conducted foreign policies designed to overturn the post–World War I political and military arrangements in their regions and expand their own power, influence, and territorial control. In both Europe and Asia one aggressive initiative followed another. The democracies tried to avert a repetition of the First World War but ultimately failed to do so. The war they could not avoid, when it did finally break out, did not come, as had World War I, as a surprise, even to the distant Americans.[21] The events of what the English poet W. H. Auden called a "low, dishonest decade" had pushed the world, steadily and seemingly inexorably, in that direction. The great powers went to war again not with the naïve enthusiasm of 1914 but with feelings of resignation and trepidation.

From the mid-1930s, Germany and Italy undid, step by step, the terms of the post–World War I settlement in Europe. In 1935 Nazi Germany repudiated the disarmament clauses of the Versailles Treaty and, in the same year, Italy invaded Ethiopia. In 1936 Hitler, again contrary to the 1919 treaty, moved military forces into the Rhineland, intervened on the side of fascist-sympathizing rebels against the legal government of Spain in a war that the rebels ultimately won, and concluded agreements with the other two revisionist powers, first Italy and then Japan, that in effect declared their common opposition to Soviet Union.[22] In 1938 Germany annexed Austria and demanded the cession of German-speaking parts of Czechoslovakia, which the British and French governments successfully pressed the Czech government to concede at a meeting with Hitler in the southern German city of Munich.

Finally, in March of the eventful year 1939, Nazi Germany swallowed up the rest of Czechoslovakia. In response, Great Britain and France offered security guarantees to Poland. In August of that year, Germany and the Soviet Union, hitherto sworn enemies, concluded a treaty that, among other things, stipulated a partition of the countries lying between them. In September, Germany attacked Poland, and Britain and France honored their commitment to the Poles by declaring war on Germany. The second great European conflict of the twentieth century had begun.

On the other side of the world, in East Asia, in 1934 Japan repudiated the treaty-imposed limits on its naval forces. Then, in 1937, a clash between Japanese and Chinese armed forces in the Chinese capital of Peking triggered a full-scale war between the two countries. Japan quickly gained the upper hand and occupied north China.[23] The next year the Japanese government proclaimed a sphere of influence for itself in Asia with the title "The Greater East Asia Co-Prosperity Sphere." In 1940 the Japanese government aligned itself with Germany and Italy through the Tripartite Agreement, often called the Axis Pact.

The American public responded to the growing probability of war in Europe and the fact of war in Asia by rejecting direct participation in armed conflict on either continent. Until late in the 1930s, the more dangerous the world appeared, the more determined Americans became to remain aloof from any war that might ensue.[24] Because the nation had recently fought a European war, the domestic politics of international engagement before Pearl Harbor had a European and not an Asian focus. The label "isolationist" has never truly applied to the United States, for at no point did its leaders believe cutting their country off from all international contact to be feasible or desirable. Still, the opposition to active engagement in European (and to a lesser extent Asian) security affairs during the 1930s makes that decade the most nearly isolationist period in the history of American foreign policy; and it was during those years and afterward that the term came into common usage to describe them.[25]

At the root of the public's aversion to direct involvement in armed quarrels abroad lay the conviction, which, by the 1930s, a majority of Americans had come to share, that their country's participation in World War I had been a mistake.[26] The war had cost the United States lives and treasure—and in the postwar period the Allies had tried to avoid repaying in full the money they had borrowed in America—without making the European continent a harmonious place.[27] The negative verdict on the war, and the prospect of repeating it, spanned the American political spectrum.

The left included opponents of war under any circumstances as well as those appalled by the wartime infringement on civil liberties; the right had in its ranks opponents of the expansion of government and public spending that war invariably brings.[28] In addition, the consuming need to fight the effects of the Great Depression made battles elsewhere and of other kinds seem, if not foolish, then at least luxuries the United States could not afford. Finally, Americans were confident that geography, in the form of the Atlantic Ocean, gave them an effective layer of insulation against the geopolitical storms of Europe, as it traditionally had.

Public opinion on this issue prompted the Congress to enact a series of Neutrality Laws in 1935, 1936, and 1937. They aimed at avoiding the circumstances that had drawn the country into World War I by prohibiting the sale of weapons to warring countries as well as loans to such countries of the kind that the United States had made to Great Britain before World War I. In response to demands that the United States cease all commerce with countries at war, which raised the concern that this would penalize Americans economically, Congress devised a policy of "cash and carry." By its terms, trade in nonmilitary items could take place but only on condition that the purchasing power pay cash and carry them away from the United States in their own, rather than American, ships.[29]

President Roosevelt was far from indifferent to the gathering storm in Europe. Nazi Germany and its leader, Adolf Hitler, alarmed him, for reasons characteristic of both Theodore Roosevelt and Woodrow Wilson. He believed that German domination of the continent, which it became increasingly clear was Hitler's goal, would threaten American security.[30] He also saw Germany's rise as threatening American values by placing Europe's democracies in jeopardy. Certainly after the surrender of Czech territory at Munich in September 1938,[31] and perhaps before that, he was determined to support Britain and France; but public resistance to going to war, and to foreign policies that might lead the United States to fight, limited what he could do. In this way the 1930s, especially the decade's latter years, and the period between the outbreak of war in Europe and American entry into it at the end of 1941, provide a vivid illustration of the singularly democratic character of American foreign policy. Public opinion circumscribed that policy more narrowly than the president wished.[32]

It was not helpful to Roosevelt in advocating support for Britain and France in the 1930s that those countries did not mount either formidable or consistent opposition to Germany's aggressive initiatives. To the contrary, both because they had come to consider some parts of the post–World War I settlement unfair to the Germans and because they had a horror of going to war again, the French and the British practiced a policy of appeasement, offering concessions in the hope of satisfying German demands and thereby preserving the peace.[33] The United States could hardly adopt more forceful policies than did the powers that Germany directly threatened.

Still, the president did what he believed he could do to affect the course of events abroad.[34] He floated occasional proposals for peace. He made a number of speeches in support of the democracies.[35] He managed to get the Congress to increase military spending:[36] in particular he sought to expand the production of military aircraft, which, he hoped, when in possession of Great Britain and France might deter Hitler from open warfare.[37] In March 1938 he decided that, in order to ship arms to the Chinese fighting against Japan, the United States would not invoke the Neutrality Acts for Asia.[38] None of these measures had any appreciable effect on the outbreak of war in Europe or the continuation of the fighting in Asia.

The World at War

In September 1939, Germany quickly conquered and occupied Poland.[39] There followed six months of military inactivity in Europe, a period known as the "phoney war." Then, in the spring of 1940, the German army conquered Denmark, Norway, Belgium, and the Netherlands and, with a daring thrust through the Ardennes Forest in Belgium using "blitzkrieg" tactics that involved fast-moving, powerful tank formations supplemented by close air support, routed the army of

France that had held out against it for four long years in World War I. The British, who were fighting alongside the French, managed to evacuate and repatriate more than 220,000 of its own troops and more than 100,000 French soldiers, but France surrendered. Nazi Germany faced no active military opposition on the European continent.[40]

The sudden fall of France came as a shock everywhere, including in the United States.[41] It left Great Britain with its islands off Europe and a still-vast overseas empire but no great-power allies in combat confronting the all-conquering Germans. In London the prime minister, Neville Chamberlain, resigned and Winston Churchill replaced him. A romantic, brave, eloquent veteran of British politics who had served in the Cabinet in World War I, Churchill was determined, unlike some of his parliamentary colleagues, to resist Germany to the end. He understood that his country's hopes for salvation depended on the United States.[42†]

Churchill had made contact with Franklin Roosevelt before taking office and devoted himself to cultivating the support of America's president but also of its other political leaders and more broadly its people. The prime minister was in daily communication with Roosevelt, sending him a total of 1,300 messages during the war.[43] The two forged a close association, although not one free of disagreement, that in turn formed the core of a larger partnership between their two countries.

[†] In reporting to the House of Commons on June 4, 1940, three weeks after becoming prime minister, on the evacuation of forces from France in the wake of the German victory there, he made a speech that ended with words that expressed both the spirit of the man and his war strategy:

> We shall go on to the end . . . we shall defend our Island, whatever the cost may be, we shall fight on the beaches, we shall fight on the landing grounds, we shall fight in the fields and in the streets, we shall fight in the hills; we shall never surrender, and even if, which I do not for a moment believe, this Island or a large part of it were subjugated and starving, then our Empire beyond the seas, armed and guarded by the British Fleet, would carry on the struggle, until, in God's good time, the New World, with all its power and might, steps forth to the rescue and the liberation of the old.

The International Churchill Society, https://winstonchurchill.org/resources/speeches/1940-the-finest-hour/we-shall-fight-on-the-beaches
On this point see John Lukacs, *Five Days in London: May 1940*, New Have n, Connecticut: Yale University Press, 1999.

When the war began, the president distinguished his policy from Woodrow Wilson's at the outset of World War I. Whereas Wilson had promised that the United States would be "neutral in fact as well as in name . . . impartial in thought as well as in action,"[44] Roosevelt said that "this nation will remain a neutral nation, but I cannot ask that every American remain neutral in thought as well. . . . Even a neutral cannot be asked to close his mind or his conscience."[45] Like the president, the American public strongly favored the democracies.[46] The state of public opinion gave Roosevelt wider but still limited latitude to support them. The structure of American opinion in fact resembled its "double wish" when World War I broke out.[47] Then, the public had wanted both to defend their country's neutral rights and to avoid the war; now Americans wanted both for Britain to defeat Germany and for the United States to stay out of the fighting.[48]

Primarily because of the war in Europe, Roosevelt decided to seek an unprecedented third term as president in 1940. Primarily because of the war, he won the November election.[49] Like Woodrow Wilson during his 1916 re-election campaign, Roosevelt promised the voters that, if he were returned to office, American boys would not be sent abroad to fight in foreign wars.[50] Whatever doubts he may privately have harbored that he would be able to keep that promise, he certainly hoped to keep it. Like other Americans, he naturally preferred that his country act as a purely offshore balancer, bolstering Great Britain, in whose military prospects it had a deep interest, without having to put its own citizens on the front lines.

Ever mindful of the unhappy consequences of Woodrow Wilson's failure to muster adequate domestic political support for his foreign policies, Roosevelt moved, even before the election, to give himself and his international initiatives political protection by appointing two prominent Republicans to major foreign policy positions in his government: Henry Stimson, who had served as Herbert Hoover's secretary of state, became secretary of war, an office he had previously held in the administration of William Howard Taft; and Frank Knox, the Republican vice presidential candidate in 1936, took the post of secretary of the navy.

Still, after the outbreak of the fighting in Europe and even after the fall of France, the opposition to joining the war remained formidable.

A number of organizations dedicated to promoting nonintervention came into existence, the most notable of which was America First, whose leading spokesman was the aviator Charles A. Lindbergh, an international celebrity by virtue of having been the first person to fly alone, nonstop, from New York to Paris in 1927.[51] Like all American wars, as a consequence of the country's unusually democratic political system and political culture, World War II occasioned controversy, debate, and outright opposition. Unlike other wars, the sharpest controversy and strongest opposition came *before* the country formally entered the conflict.

As Britain's position grew more precarious, Roosevelt's warnings of the dangers that a British defeat would pose to the United States and his calls for American support for the British war effort became more urgent. "If Great Britain goes down," he said in a Fireside Chat on December 29, 1940,

> the Axis powers will control the continents of Europe, Asia, Africa, Australasia, and the high seas—and they will be in a position to bring enormous military and naval resources against this hemisphere. It is no exaggeration to say that all of us, in all the Americas, would be living at the point of a gun."[52]

While conscious of the need not to move so abruptly as to cause a backlash in American opinion, and for that reason not always advertising what he was doing, the president went beyond rhetoric in support of Britain. In the eighteen months following the fall of France, at his behest the American government took a series of steps to furnish ever-greater assistance to the British. These made the United States, by the last month of 1941, effectively if not officially a cobelligerent against Germany.[53] What Woodrow Wilson had, accidentally and unknowingly, allowed to happen in World War I, Franklin D. Roosevelt caused to happen in World War II.

In 1940 and 1941 the president succeeded in persuading the Congress to set aside the Neutrality Laws.[54] The United States began to ship war materiel across the Atlantic for the British to use in defending themselves. America had to take on the role, Roosevelt proclaimed, of the "arsenal of democracy."[55] At the same time, the increase in American defense spending accelerated, rising from 1.4 percent of gross national product in 1939 to 11.4 percent in 1941.[56] In 1940 Congress voted in favor of a military draft and the next year extended the Selective Service Act—by a single vote.[57]

The Roosevelt administration took two other major initiatives to fortify the British military effort. In 1940, without explicit Congressional authorization, the president provided the Royal Navy with old but serviceable destroyers, which he described as "surplus," in exchange for title to British military bases in the Western Hemisphere. In 1941, with the British treasury running out of funds to pay for American supplies, Roosevelt persuaded Congress, after a vigorous national debate, to enact the Lend-Lease program. By its terms the United States provided what the British needed without requiring immediate payment, in return for wartime leases on army and naval bases in territories the British and their dominions, allies, and sympathizers controlled.[58] Also in 1941, secret military staff talks between the Americans and the British took place.[59]

Roosevelt went even further in support of what had become in all but name America's British ally. He ordered a series of maritime initiatives that put American ships in direct opposition to German naval forces. The measures included American naval patrols in the Atlantic far from the East Coast of the United States, the arming of American merchant vessels, and the participation of American vessels in convoys escorting transatlantic shipping. The United States sent troops to Iceland and took control of Greenland. By these steps, without ever saying so explicitly it joined the war against Germany in the Atlantic.

In August 1941, Roosevelt held a personal meeting with Churchill—there would be eight in all during the war—at Placentia Bay in the Canadian province of Nova Scotia. At that meeting, Churchill later reported to his War Cabinet, the president "said he would wage war, but not declare it."[60] The two issued a joint statement of war aims, even though the United States was not officially at war, that became known as the Atlantic Charter. It was a thoroughly Wilsonian document, its eight principal articles repeating some of Wilson's Fourteen Points of 1917: self-determination, a lowering of trade barriers, freedom of the seas, and disarmament among them. It bespoke the recognition that the stakes in the European struggle concerned not only the distribution of power on the continent but also basic political values: the Nazis opposed, and sought to obliterate, the liberty on which American democracy rested.

More broadly, the Atlantic Charter signaled Roosevelt's ongoing allegiance, in concert with his appreciation for the realities of power politics, to the alternate, idealist tradition in American foreign policy.[61] That allegiance stemmed, in all likelihood, both from a conviction that invoking it was politically necessary to mobilize the American public in support of goals beyond their borders and from his own loyalty, shared to some degree by almost every predecessor and successor, to that tradition.

In Asia, American support for China and for its leader Chiang Kai-shek, including the provision of military assistance under Lend-Lease, aroused less controversy at home than did Roosevelt's European initiatives. The historic national fondness for China played a role, as did the widely shared perception that the Asian conflict was less likely to draw in the United States. Moreover, unlike Irish- and German-Americans vis-à-vis Great Britain, no significant domestic group objected to assisting the Chinese. In the Pacific region, however, the Roosevelt administration pursued a contradictory policy, which ended in failure, indeed—in the short term at least—in tragedy.

Because he believed that Germany posed a more serious threat to the United States than did Japan, Roosevelt wanted to avoid becoming more deeply involved in the Sino-Japanese conflict. Before the American entry into World War II as well as afterward, he sought to conduct a "Europe-first" policy. Yet his administration, making use of one of the oldest of all American foreign policies, imposed increasingly stringent economic sanctions on Japan, sanctions that, because Japan depended heavily on the United States for raw materials, presented a major challenge to Japanese foreign policies and domestic security; and the Roosevelt administration followed this course in the face of warnings from within the American government that doing so risked war with Japan.

In 1939 the United States terminated its 1911 commercial treaty with the Japanese. In 1940 the American government embargoed the shipment of scrap metal to Japan, cutting off much of its supply. In July of 1941 the administration froze all Japanese assets in the United States and banned oil and gasoline exports to Japan, a particularly severe economic blow because at that point more than eighty percent of Japanese oil came from the United States. Enacted by the American government in response to its aggression against China and then in Indochina, these measures were bound to seem to Japan to be efforts at economic strangulation. Having made a neutrality agreement with its adversary of four decades, the Soviet Union, in April 1941, the authorities in Tokyo decided to break out of the tightening economic constraints by striking to the south to take control of territories from which it could acquire the raw materials it needed. In so doing it would feed its imperial appetite and expand the scope of the Asian Co-Prosperity Sphere it had proclaimed the year before.[62] As the opening salvo of this campaign, the Japanese government decided to launch a surprise attack against the United States.

The American government intended its economic sanctions to compel Japan to abandon the activities in China to which the Americans objected, or at least to deter the extension of these policies elsewhere.[63] Yet responsible American officials were aware, and said, that the sanctions might fail to achieve their purpose, indeed might provoke Japan.[64] Why, then, did the administration proceed with them?

In part it did so mistakenly. As it was implemented, the oil embargo imposed tighter restrictions than Roosevelt had intended, but he concluded that modifying it would send a signal of weakness to Tokyo.[65] In general, and in keeping with his strategic priorities, Roosevelt paid less attention to Asia than to Europe. Perhaps most important of all, in what it did in Asia, as with its policies toward Europe, the Roosevelt administration had to operate within the constraints of American public opinion; and in Asia this produced a firmer policy than the president apparently wished. Continuing trade with Japan would have provided material support for the brutal Japanese occupation of China, of which Americans strongly disapproved. A more conciliatory policy toward Japan would have risked eroding the popularity of the Roosevelt foreign policy, which was already under attack for its escalating support for Great Britain.[66]

As Japanese-American relations were deteriorating, an event on the other side of the world changed the course of the war in Europe and ultimately did more than any other development to determine its outcome. On June 22, 1941, in violation of the nonaggression pact be-tween the two countries of two years earlier, Nazi Germany attacked the Soviet Union.[67] The three-pronged assault by the German army, the Wehrmacht, overwhelmed the poorly equipped and poorly prepared Red Army. To the north, German troops reached the former tsarist capital of St. Petersburg, which had been renamed Leningrad in honor of the founder of the Soviet Union, and laid siege to it. The siege was to last 900 days and kill an estimated 800,000 Russian civilians. The central thrust of the attack brought German forces to within twelve miles of the current capital, Moscow, and sent the Soviet government, including its supreme leader and Lenin's successor, Joseph Stalin, into a temporary panic. To the south, the Wehrmacht overran the principal Ukrainian city of Kiev and headed for the oil fields of the Caucasus.

Operation Barbarossa, as Hitler called the campaign after a me-dieval German Holy Roman emperor, took a fearful toll. By some estimates the Soviet side suffered 800,000 deaths with perhaps as many as six million troops wounded or taken prisoner.[68] Yet the attack did not achieve its goal. The Soviet Union did not collapse. Thanks to the country's vast distances, its large population, and the courage and resil-ience of that population along with the assist of the freezing weather for which the German troops were not adequately prepared—the "General Winter" that had blunted Napoleon's assault on Russia in 1812[69]—the Red Army and the Soviet regime survived and began to fight back. The Germans' experience in World War II turned out to be the opposite of what had happened in World War I: this time they won in the west but failed to win in the east.

Barbarossa brought a new and potentially powerful recruit to the anti-Nazi cause. It gave the British and the Americans the opportunity to act on one of the central tenets of traditional great-power politics: the enemy of my enemy is my friend. Churchill, an outspoken opponent of the Bolshevik regime since it had seized power in 1917, lost no time in doing so,[70] offering as clear a statement of the underlying logic as has ever been made: "if Hitler invaded hell I would make at least a favor-able reference to the devil in the House of Commons."

Roosevelt had the same inclination[71] but had to deal with do-mestic resistance to active support for Stalin's communist state.[72] For Americans, the Soviet Union was, in several ways, an unattractive candidate to be a partner of any kind. American opinion had a strong strain of anti-communist sentiment and Americans had not forgotten Stalin's war against religion in the Soviet Union, his pact with Hitler, his aggression against Poland, his annexation of the Baltic countries, and his attack on Finland. Moreover, American officials were uncertain that the Red Army would be able to make effective use of the kind of military supplies the United States was sending to Great Britain because they were uncertain that it would be able to hold out against the Wehrmacht. At the outset of Barbarossa, Secretary of War Stimson reported to the president the belief of American military leaders that Germany would conquer the Soviet Union in three months at most.[73]

Roosevelt nevertheless succeeded in furnishing military aid to the Soviet Union, as to Britain and China, under the Lend-Lease law.[74] That assistance proved militarily indispensable to the Soviet Union. In turn, Soviet survival and persistence in the war against Germany became, in December of 1941, indispensable to the United States, for in that month the United States formally entered the war as a result of a Japanese attack on the American Pacific fleet anchored at Pearl Harbor, Hawaii.

During the summer and fall of that year the American government, mainly in the person of Secretary of State Hull, conducted negotiations with representatives of Japan in an effort to resolve the deepening dispute between the two countries. The talks foundered on the issue of China. Japan would not withdraw from that country; the United States would not accept the Japanese occupation.[75] The Japanese government therefore proceeded with its plan to attack Hawaii as the first step in a military sweep to its south.

On the morning of December 7, carrier-based aircraft launched that attack. The Japanese had planned to surprise the Americans and succeeded.[76] When their bombing ended, eighteen American naval vessels, including eight battleships, had been sunk; 180 aircraft had been destroyed; a total of 2,403 Americans were dead; and 1,178 had been wounded.[77]

The attack had the same kind of galvanizing impact on the American public as other, similar episodes in the nation's history: the Boston Massacre, the firing on Fort Sumter, the sinking of the *Maine*. American reservations about, and outright opposition to, going to war disappeared.[78] On December 8, President Roosevelt addressed a joint session of Congress and, calling the day before "a date that will live in infamy," asked for a declaration of war against Japan. Both chambers voted in favor, the Senate by a count of 82 to 0, the House of Representatives by 388 to 1.[79]

Like the Germans in attacking the Soviet Union, the Japanese were counting on a short war.[80] They did not expect the United States to collapse but they did expect to buy themselves time and space for a campaign of conquest to the south and believed, or at least hoped, that the Americans would accept a compromise peace and not mobilize their far larger population and economy to wage war against Japan. These expectations proved to be incorrect, to Japan's enormous ultimate cost. Not for the first time or for the last, an enemy had underestimated American resolve.

On December 8, the United States was at war with Japan but not with Germany. On December 11, Hitler declared war on the United States. For what seemed a puzzling and unnecessary decision he had, in all probability, several motives. There is some evidence that he did not rate highly the American capacity for warfare.[81] He had encouraged the Japanese to strike the Americans and had promised to support them if they did—although consistent loyalty was not a feature of the Nazi leader's character. Perhaps most importantly, he likely calculated, as had the imperial German authorities in 1917 when deciding to resume unrestricted submarine warfare, that the United States would not for some time be able to do any more damage than it was already doing to the German war effort.[82]

At the end of 1941, therefore, the United States found itself not only at war but at war on two fronts, against two powerful enemies located on the far sides of the Atlantic and Pacific Oceans, respectively. The attack on Pearl Harbor proved to be one of the most consequential events in American, and indeed in global, history. It set in motion a series of events that would extend far into the future and bring major changes both to the world and to the American role in it.‡

‡ The Japanese attack had the immediate consequence of achieving the major short-term strategic aim of Great Britain and its prime minister. As the historian A. J. P. Taylor put it: "No greater service than Pearl Harbour was ever performed for the British cause. The doubts of President Roosevelt and the American people

America at War

In the coalition that waged World War II the United States, Great Britain, and the Soviet Union were equals in the sense that each needed the other two and had to take into account the others' needs and wishes in setting its own policies. Such coalitions are a regular feature of European history but the Second World War was the first and only occasion on which the United States had this historically familiar great-power experience: in the Revolutionary War, France was very much the senior partner, and the period of active American fighting in the First World War, in comparison with the Second, was relatively brief.

As allies do by definition, the United States, Great Britain, and the Soviet Union pursued a common goal: the defeat of Nazi Germany and, in the American and British cases, of Imperial Japan as well. The three also had, as in every alliance, differences among themselves, the deepest of all of which concerned their respective political systems: those of Great Britain and its political offspring the United States rested on individual liberty; the Soviet Union, by contrast, had as its founding principle the total and unchallengeable power of the self-selected and putatively infallible Communist officials of the Soviet Union. British and American leaders governed by consent, Soviet leaders by coercion. These fundamental differences made, in the case of the anti-German coalition, the disagreements that all coalitions display historically deep and ultimately irreconcilable ones. Geography but also ideology created divisions among the Americans, the British, and the Soviets that affected the conduct of the war, not to mention, as after World War I although even more powerfully, the peace settlement.

The United States had an unusually close relationship with Great Britain. The two forged as close a partnership as any two great-power allies have ever achieved in wartime. Nonetheless, they and their leaders found themselves at odds on some important matters.

were resolved for them: they were in the war whether they would or no. The private war between Great Britain and Germany was ended. A true World war began, and the outcome of that seemed sure. Churchill made the only appropriate comment: 'So we had won after all!' " A. J. P. Taylor, *English History, 1914–1945*, Oxford, UK: Oxford University Press, 1965, pp. 532–533.

They disagreed about the future of the British Empire. To Churchill, it formed part of the fabric of his country's glorious history. He considered it an indispensable part of Britain's greatness. Roosevelt, who had promised independence to the Philippines, believed that all empires, including Great Britain's, should be dissolved. With the war imposing more urgent issues on both of them, the president did not press the prime minister on, for example, British control of India, even though he opposed it in principle.[83] In the negotiations over the terms of financial assistance from the United States to its ally, however, American officials pushed for the end of the special trade privileges Britain enjoyed with its imperial possessions, which the Americans believed denied economic opportunities to the United States.[84] The British suspected the Americans of wishing to use the end of imperial preference as a means to bring about the end of the Empire itself, a belief that was not entirely mistaken.[85]

The American and British governments also disagreed about where and when to fight in Europe. The Americans believed that the best and surest way to defeat Germany was to mount a large invasion of France across the English Channel and proceed eastward. The British, with much more limited manpower and painful memories of German military prowess in France in 1940 as well as of the huge losses they had sustained in assaulting German positions on the Western Front in World War I, preferred a "peripheral" strategy. This involved attacking the flanks of Germany's extended perimeter on the continent, where its defenses were likely to be less formidable; the Balkans were a favored target for that purpose.[86]

Roosevelt and Churchill also adopted different approaches to two major political figures. One was Charles de Gaulle, the leader of the Free French movement that emerged outside France after the surrender to Germany in May 1940 and the formation of a German-sponsored government of most of France's European territory at Vichy. Churchill did not always find the proud and prickly Frenchman an easy person with whom to deal,[87] but he believed in and supported de Gaulle, seeing him (accurately as it turned out) as the future leader of a liberated French nation. Roosevelt, by contrast, took a strong dislike to de Gaulle and considered him a man of undemocratic political beliefs, although this did not stop the American government from providing grudging support to the Free French.[88]

Churchill and Roosevelt also differed in their approaches to Joseph Stalin. The prime minister recognized that the Soviet Union's contribution to the anti-German cause was crucial and treated the people, the armed forces, and the leader of that country with respect. He had no illusions, however, about the totalitarian character of Stalin's regime and understood that, beyond defeating Hitler, Soviet political aspirations and those of the Americans and the British were incompatible. Churchill therefore sought, as the war proceeded, to do whatever he could to minimize postwar Soviet power and influence in Europe.

Roosevelt was not naïve about Stalin or communism but believed— or hoped—that he could establish a personal rapport with the Soviet leader that would help to make the postwar settlement better, from the Anglo-American point of view, than it would otherwise have been.[89] He overestimated the influence that his personal charm, which had served him well in dealing with American politicians and the American public, would have on the Soviet dictator.[90] His efforts, on the two occasions when the three wartime leaders met, to ingratiate himself with Stalin at Churchill's expense neither furthered his political aims nor burnished his historical legacy.

American friction with the Soviet Union at first involved a single issue. Stalin insisted on, indeed was desperate for, the opening of a second front in Europe, by which he meant an invasion of France, as soon as possible in order to relieve German pressure on Soviet forces fighting in the east. Once the Americans and the British had made a firm commitment to a date for a cross-Channel assault, and the tide of war had turned against Nazi Germany, the postwar political organization of Europe, with an emphasis on the fate of Germany and the countries of Eastern and Southern Europe, ranked high on the Allies' agenda. Here the differences between the democracies and the communist power became increasingly obvious, and the efforts to bridge them—although Churchill and Roosevelt never gave up hope of accomplishing this—ever more clearly doomed to failure.

World War II put Franklin Roosevelt in the company of George Washington and Abraham Lincoln as the commander in chief during one of the three most important wars the United States ever fought. In some ways he had an easier task than they. He did not, as George Washington did, have to lead troops in battle. He faced a less severe challenge in maintaining public support for the war than Lincoln had confronted and he initially presided over a great war not, like Lincoln, as a novice but after nine relatively successful years as president. On the other hand, Roosevelt had to manage a conflict of far greater geographic scope than they and, through membership in the alliance of which the United States was a part, confronted far more complicated international political choices than any that either the first or the sixteenth presidents had had to make.

To the job of commander in chief Roosevelt brought the same combination of infectious optimism, suitably modified for circumstances in which several hundred thousand Americans were to die, and an undisciplined style of management that had marked his approach to domestic affairs. Having served as assistant secretary of the navy during World War I, he had a greater familiarity with military matters than most of his predecessors and successors.[91] Unlike Churchill, Stalin, and Hitler, he did not closely supervise the operations of the American armed forces:[92] the chief of staff of the army said that he could go for six weeks without seeing the president,[93] a statement that the principal military advisors of the other three leaders would not have been able to make about the men to whom they reported. Unlike the other three, moreover, Roosevelt never appeared in public in a military uniform.[§]

Yet he kept himself well informed about the progress of the war and made the major decisions concerning its conduct, overruling his senior military advisors when he considered it necessary.[94] Most importantly, his principal decisions seem, in retrospect, to have been the right ones. He was right in providing, before the United States entered the war, as much support to Great Britain as was politically feasible; right in treating Germany as a more pressing threat than Japan and pursuing a "Europe-first" strategy; and right in going against the prevailing sentiment of his senior military officials by rejecting a cross-Channel operation in 1942 and 1943 but then right again in contradicting the British preference for further postponement and fixing the time of that operation as mid-1944. With Washington and Lincoln as commanders in

---

[§] All three of the others had taken an active part in military operations: Churchill in late-nineteenth-century colonial wars, Hitler as a soldier in World War I, and Stalin during the Russian Civil War. Roosevelt had had no similar experience.

chief during the Revolutionary and Civil Wars, fortune had smiled upon the United States of America. The presidency of Franklin D. Roosevelt during World War II counted as another stroke of good fortune. In that war, as well, the man matched the moment.

As the largest collective enterprise the United States had ever undertaken, World War II brought major changes to the country's society, economy, and government. The impact of the federal government on daily life expanded dramatically. Many Americans went to work for it directly, as members of the armed forces. Approximately fifteen million of them served, the vast majority of them young men.[95]

As had happened during World War I, and again during the New Deal in order to fight the Great Depression, Congress authorized the creation of a number of specialized federal agencies, such as the Office of War Mobilization to supervise manufacturing for the armed forces and the Office of Price Administration to prevent inflation by freezing prices. The most important wartime federal agency, the Department of War, underwent reorganization as well as expansion. A new five-sided headquarters for it known as the Pentagon—then and now the world's largest office building—was constructed in Virginia, across the Potomac River from Washington, D.C., in only sixteen months.[96] An organization bringing together the heads of each of the armed services, the Joint Chiefs of Staff, came into existence in early 1942.[97]

Military leaders naturally became prominent during the largest war the United States ever fought, and three army generals in particular achieved widespread public recognition and considerable acclaim. George C. Marshall became the chief of staff on September 1, 1939, the day Germany invaded Poland. He had remarkable administrative talents,[98] presiding over the expansion of the army from 174,000 people at the time he assumed the position to over 11 million by the end of the war. He personally selected the principal commanders. A man of unimpeachable integrity, Churchill called him the "true organizer of victory."[99]

Douglas MacArthur, the son of a Civil War hero, had already had a prominent career in the army by the time the United States entered World War II, having served with distinction and earned a promotion to brigadier general in World War I and then having been the army's chief of staff in the early 1930s. He spent much of his career in Asia and at the time of Pearl Harbor he was living in the Philippines and acting as the chief military advisor to that country's president in preparation for its independence in 1946. Personally flamboyant, with a talent for public relations and self-promotion,[100] he had to flee the Philippines ahead of the Japanese invasion in early 1942 but made a celebrated promise to return and did so as the commander of Allied forces in the southwest Pacific.

Younger than the other two, Dwight D. Eisenhower,[101] widely known by the affectionate nickname "Ike," graduated from West Point in the class of 1915, known to history as "the class the stars fell on" because 59 of its 164 members—thirty-six percent—became general officers. Marshall appreciated his talents and promoted him, choosing him to command the campaigns in Europe. There Eisenhower excelled at controlling and harnessing the energies of the able but volatile military leaders under his authority, in particular the American general George S. Patton and the British field marshall Bernard L. Montgomery.[102] Eisenhower personally made the most important and risky military decision of the war, choosing June 6, 1944, as the day when the weather over the English Channel would be fair enough to permit the successful launching of the cross-Channel invasion of France. All three generals[103] went on to play important roles in American foreign policy after World War II: Marshall as secretary of defense and then as secretary of state; MacArthur as the head of the American occupation authority in Japan and then commander of American forces in Korea; Eisenhower as the thirty-fourth president of the United States.[104]

As important for the war effort as the armed forces was the American industrial base. Existing factories were converted from civilian to military production and new ones were built. Private firms, with large ones playing the dominant role, turned out the instruments of warfare in prodigious numbers. By the war's end these included 5,777 merchant ships, 1,556 naval vessels, 299,293 aircraft, 634,569 jeeps, 88,410 tanks, 2,383,111 trucks, 6.5 million rifles, and 40 billion bullets.[105] By 1944, the United States, one of five great powers and several lesser ones at war, manufactured fully forty percent of all the world's armaments.[106]

These did not go exclusively to American fighting men and women. The United States supplied a major proportion of the weaponry and other things its allies needed to stay in the war. Even after it had formally entered the conflict and sent its troops overseas, it remained the arsenal of democracy—although the last word of that phrase did not apply to the Soviet Union. America exported eighteen million tons of war material to Europe.[107] In the Soviet case, by the end of the war their forces held

> 665,000 motor vehicles, of which 427,000 were Western, most of them American. . . . American industry also supplied 13 million Soviet soldiers with their winter boots, American agriculture 5 million tons of food, sufficient to provide each Soviet soldier with half a pound of concentrated rations every day of the war. The American railroad industry supplied 2000 locomotives, 11,000 freight carriages and 540,000 tons of rails, with which the Russians laid a greater length of line than they had built between 1928 and 1939. American supplies of high-grade petroleum were essential to Russian production of aviation fuel, while three-quarters of Soviet consumption of copper in 1941–44 came from American sources."[108]

All this was expensive.[109] The proportion of the federal budget devoted to military uses leaped from less than half (and six percent of gross domestic product [GDP]) in 1941 to ninety percent (and thirty-eight percent of GDP) in 1944.[110] As in the First World War, the government paid for what it spent with a combination of taxation—the number of taxpayers surged from fewer than four million in 1939 to more than forty-two million in 1945[111]—and borrowing, much of it in the form of bonds sold to the public. The war provided an unexpected economic gift to the United States. It lifted the country, finally, out of the Great Depression. As production soared from $85.6 billion in 1939 to $131 billion in 1945,[112] unemployment plummeted: in 1939, 10 million Americans were out of work; in 1944 that number was less than 700,000.[113] Even with one-third of the economy devoted to the war effort, private consumption increased, in stark contrast to the privations that the people in all the other belligerent countries suffered during World War II.[114]

Like other wars in American history, finally, this one led to an infringement of the foundational national political principle of liberty.[115]

In the anxious public mood that war engenders, suspicion fell on Americans of Japanese descent living on the West Coast. They might somehow, it was feared, render assistance to Japan's war against the United States. The president issued an executive order in 1942 authorizing the War Department to exclude anyone it chose from designated areas, and with that authority it ordered 110,000 Japanese-Americans removed from their homes and sent to spartan, uncomfortable relocation camps in seven western states.[116] In the 1944 case *Korematsu v. the United States*, the Supreme Court rejected an appeal to annul the order.[117] Conceivably because of the practice of interning but more likely despite it, pro-Japanese sabotage did not take place. An infantry regiment composed largely of Japanese-Americans fought valiantly in Europe, and with the end of the war the internment camps were disbanded. Ultimately, those who were interned received an official apology and monetary compensation.[118]

The combat phase of the war for the United States began in North Africa. The American military leaders did not want to conduct a campaign there: they considered it a diversion from the main business of striking at Germany as directly as possible. Roosevelt, however, bore in mind, as had Washington and Lincoln and other wartime presidents, the importance of sustaining domestic political support for fighting the war that the country had entered. He decided that Americans had to see their army in action in 1942.[119] Accordingly, Operation Torch, a three-pronged landing in Morocco, Algeria, and Tunisia, by then all under the control of the pro-German French government in Vichy, France, took place in November of that year. The Americans joined the British forces that had been fighting in North Africa since 1940 and, after an initial setback at the Battle of Kasserine Pass in Tunisia and a British success at El Alamein in Egypt, managed to overcome the Germans, securing victory in May 1943.

In that period, however, the most important battle for the outcome of the war in Europe took place far to the north and east of Africa and did not involve any American or British troops. In 1942, Hitler launched a summer offensive, a chief goal of which was to capture the Soviet city of Stalingrad on the Volga River. The battle for the city dragged on into the winter, with the Wehrmacht coming close to success in bitter, brutal urban warfare. Then, at the end of the year, the

Red Army attacked and shattered the mainly non-German divisions that were protecting the German army in Stalingrad and trapped the Germans in the city. In early February 1943, the German commander surrendered.[120]

At Stalingrad the momentum of the war on the Eastern Front reversed. The Soviet forces demonstrated, for the first time, the capacity to execute a complicated maneuver. The German army suffered a major defeat. The reputation for invincibility that it had acquired since 1939 evaporated.[121] The outcome of the battle made clear that the war in the east would be a prolonged one; and in a long war the side with the biggest pool of manpower on which to draw and access to the largest supplies of war material had the advantage.[122] In its war in Russia, Germany had neither. From the city named for the supreme Soviet leader,[123] his army began the long, bloody campaign that would ultimately take it to Berlin.

In the other principal theater of war, in the six months after Pearl Harbor, Japan rampaged across the Asia-Pacific region. Japanese forces took over the midocean islands of Wake Island and Guam. They captured, as well, parts of New Guinea, the Bismarck Archipelago, and the Marshall and Gilbert Islands, obscure pieces of land in the Pacific that would become familiar to Americans over the next four years as they became the scenes of fighting against their Japanese occupiers. In this period Japanese forces also conquered the British possessions of Burma, Malaya, and Singapore (which the British had mistakenly regarded as impregnable), as well as the American-controlled Philippines and Borneo and Java in the Dutch East Indies.[124] By the middle of the year Japan presided over the largest empire that any country had ever assembled in the Asia-Pacific region.[125]

The Japanese position posed a serious threat to Australia, but that threat eased with the first major naval engagement of the Pacific War[126]—with Pearl Harbor not counting as an actual battle because the American forces, taken by surprise, offered little resistance. The Battle of the Coral Sea took place in the southwest Pacific from May 4 to 8, 1942. Conducted by carrier-based aircraft (the carriers of the Pacific fleet had not been present at Pearl Harbor on the preceding December 7), it was the first naval battle waged by ships that never came within sight of each other. Each fleet inflicted damage on the other, but by holding their own the Americans put a stop to the Japanese string of clear-cut military victories.

The next month brought an even more consequential maritime engagement, the Battle of Midway on June 4. The Japanese sought to capture Midway Island, 1,100 miles northwest of Pearl Harbor, to use as a base for offensive action against the west coast of North America.[127] The United States Navy sent a fleet to oppose them, which the Japanese flotilla outnumbered in carriers and planes. The first wave of American torpedo bombers attacking the Japanese ships inflicted only minor damage. Soon thereafter, however, with the decks of the Japanese carriers crowded with planes and fuel, a group of thirty-seven American dive bombers, which had gone off course earlier but managed to locate the main Japanese ships, illustrated the underappreciated role of luck in war by swooping in and delivering what an eminent military historian called "the most decisive blow in the history of naval warfare."[128] Three of the four carriers Japan had committed to the battle were wrecked. Hours later the fourth was sunk.

The Battle of Midway had the same impact on the war in the Pacific as the Battle of Stalingrad did on the war in Europe. It administered a major, prestige-sapping, morale-draining defeat to the hitherto all-victorious Japanese navy. It ensured that the campaign in the Pacific would be a long one, in which the larger and more productive country would have a decisive advantage; and the military potential of the United States far exceeded that of Imperial Japan.[129] The Japanese, like the Germans, had gambled on a short war and lost.

In January 1943, thirteen months after the United States had joined Great Britain as a formal ally, and in accord with the need for consultation and joint decisions in the coalition war that their countries were waging, Roosevelt and Churchill met in the Moroccan city of Casablanca. There they agreed on a common agenda for the next phase of the war in Europe. They demanded the unconditional surrender of their German adversary. They agreed that, a cross-Channel assault not being feasible in 1943, their armies in North Africa would have as their next objective Sicily and then the Italian peninsula.[130] They emphasized the importance of two joint military missions: winning control of the Atlantic, which meant defeating the German submarines there,[131] and conducting a bombing campaign against Germany.[132]

Air power, which had made its appearance in World War I, played an even more important role in World War II. The Allies could not have won the war without the air superiority they achieved, thanks in no small part to American prowess in designing and producing aircraft. The United States employed air power in three distinct ways: to protect and complement naval activity, especially in the Atlantic and over the English Channel at the time of the invasion of France; to supplement the efforts of ground troops through "tactical air support"; and to attack the German and Japanese homelands—the "strategic bombing" that enthusiasts for air power had believed, before the war, could be the decisive factor in winning a major war.

The British had fought a desperate campaign against the German air force, the *Luftwaffe*, in the skies over their home island in 1940. In the Battle of Britain, London and other cities suffered serious damage but the Germans failed to subdue their last remaining adversary in the European theater. Then and thereafter the British high command ordered air raids on Germany itself, concluding that nighttime "area bombing" of German cities gave them the opportunity to wreak the greatest destruction. From bases in Italy, once the American army arrived there, and from Great Britain as well, Americans mounted daylight attacks on German industrial targets, with limited success at first[133] but with greater effectiveness as the war went on. The bombing of Germany did not obviate the need for a protracted, costly ground campaign by the Allies, but it did hinder the German war effort.[134] The American aerial bombardment of Japan, launched from bases on islands that American forces captured, did even greater damage and, when the United States made use of the new and unprecedentedly powerful atomic bomb in August 1945, helped bring an end to the war in the Pacific.

At Casablanca, Roosevelt and Churchill could have greater confidence in the outcome of the war than had been possible for much of 1942. The Battle of Stalingrad made it clear that Germany would not be able to conquer the Soviet Union. The outcomes of the major naval battles of May and June made it possible for the American forces in the Pacific to go on the offensive. What Churchill had said in November 1942, after the British victory at El Alamein, described the status of the war when he met Roosevelt at Casablanca: "This is not the end. It is not even the beginning of the end. But it is perhaps the end of the beginning."[135]

Reversal of Fortune

In the year and a half after the Casablanca conference the Allies and the Axis powers exchanged the military roles they had played since the outset of the war. Germany and Japan were now fighting to defend the gains they had made, while the United States, Great Britain, and the Soviet Union fought to reverse those gains. With the weight of America's extraordinary industrial production exercising increasing influence on the fighting, the battle lines moved—slowly, unevenly, and at great cost—back toward Berlin in Europe and Tokyo in Asia.

The American army in the European theater pushed on from North Africa to Sicily, landing there in July 1943,[136] and moving next to the Italian mainland in September. Months of grinding combat followed, as the American forces proceeded slowly up the Italian peninsula.** They captured Rome on June 5, 1944, but by that time the focus of the American military effort in Europe had shifted to the far more important cross-Channel invasion of France. Eisenhower had left Italy for Britain to command it, and he launched it on June 6.

The crucial American fighting in 1943 took place not in Italy, however, but on, under, and above the Atlantic Ocean.[137] The Atlantic formed the lifeline of the anti-German alliance.[138] The military and civilian supplies on which Great Britain and the Soviet Union depended passed across it by ship. Without what the Americans sent, neither would have been able to sustain the fight against the Germans, who naturally attempted to sever this crucial lifeline by sinking the ships.

** For the United States the campaign in Italy was "an old-fashioned one of strategic diversion on the maritime flank of a continental enemy. . . ." John Keegan, *The Second World War*, New York: Penguin Books, 1990, p. 368. The campaign "began with weighty liabilities. It had formed no part of earlier planning exercises, was decided on short notice and for opportunistic reasons, and was required to go forward with severely restricted resources. Most important, it had no compelling strategic goal." David Kennedy, *Freedom from Fear: The American People in Depression and War, 1929–1945*, New York: Oxford University Press, 1999, p. 596

The principal German weapon in this effort was the country's fleet of submarines, known as U-boats. They did considerable damage in 1942[139] and in early 1943 they had reduced the volume of shipping that reached its destinations on the eastern shores of the ocean to dangerously low levels.[140] Then, in six remarkable weeks between March and May 1943, the Americans and the British managed to defeat the anti-shipping campaign.

Their success had a number of sources.[141] One was sheer numbers. The North American "arsenal of democracy" turned out merchant ships and anti-submarine platforms—escort carriers and surveillance and bomber aircraft—in impressive quantities. The Allies also improved their ability to track the movements and locations of the U-boats. Technological ingenuity made several contributions to the clearing of the Atlantic. Air cover was crucial for the safety of the ships but the Allies were plagued by a "mid-Atlantic gap,"[142] a stretch of the ocean that land-based aircraft could not reach from either North America or the British Isles. They closed the gap by adjustments to some of their aircraft that extended their range.[143] They also devised more effective anti-submarine devices, notably depth charges that exploded under water.[144]

These developments reduced the German U-boat attacks to tolerable—and ultimately to negligible—levels.[145] If the Allies' efforts had failed, they could not have prevailed in Europe when they did, if they had been able to prevail at all. For that reason, the Battle of the Atlantic ranks, along with the battles at Saratoga in the Revolutionary War and Gettysburg in the Civil War, as one of the three most consequential the United States has ever won.

Because of the need for consultation and coordination in the coalition war that the Allies were waging, face-to-face meetings of their leaders became as distinctive a feature of World War II as the submarine or the military airplane. Following the Casablanca conference in January 1943 Roosevelt and Churchill met again in Washington in May of that year and yet again, for the third time in eight months, in Quebec in August. In November the president and the prime minister traveled to Cairo to meet with Chiang Kai-shek and two days later met Joseph Stalin in Tehran.

This was the first time that Roosevelt had encountered the Soviet leader in person, and he did what he could to establish a personal connection between the two that, he hoped, would smooth wartime and postwar relations with the communist state.[146] At Tehran the three leaders agreed that the Anglo-American assault on German-occupied France would begin in May 1944: at last Stalin would have his second front. For his part, Stalin promised to enter the war against Japan after the defeat of Germany.

The three also began discussions about the political future of Europe. They proceeded with some circumspection and caution, no doubt wary of having their differences interfere with the ongoing prosecution of the war; but Roosevelt did acquiesce in Stalin's proposal to move Poland's frontier westward, into German territory, setting its western border at the Oder River. The president made it clear that he did not expect a postwar American military presence in Europe, a point that would have been of great interest, and not at all unwelcome, to the Soviet dictator.[147] Stalin also announced his intention to deal harshly with Germany. As for the details of the political disposition of the continent after the end of Nazism, these would be determined by future conferences and above all by developments on the battlefield.

In the Asian theater of operations, having stopped Japan's surging post–Pearl Harbor expansion at Midway, the United States had to decide how to design its counteroffensive against the Japanese. Washington decided to fight on three fronts—one on land, two at sea. The strategy called for pressing the Japanese in China. America had supported Chiang Kai-shek since the Japanese breakout from Manchuria into north China in 1937. Chiang's forces had received American military assistance since before Pearl Harbor.

Like previous—and subsequent—American leaders, Franklin Roosevelt had great expectations for China. In his earliest conception of the postwar global order, he foresaw that country as one of the world's "Four Policeman," along with the United States, Great Britain, and the Soviet Union, each of which would keep order in its own region.[148] The president dispatched General Joseph W. Stilwell, who had previously served in China, to work with Chiang and help to train the Chinese army. Stilwell's experience proved to be frustrating and ultimately unsuccessful.[149]

The United States hoped to act as a kind of offshore balancer on the Asian mainland, with American military equipment combining with Chinese manpower to resist the Japanese. Chiang, however, had other ideas. He displayed a greater interest in conserving his forces for his war against his domestic rivals, the communists led by Mao Tse-tung, than in attacking the Japanese occupiers of his country. He made repeated demands for more American assistance but showed only a modest inclination to make use of it against the Japanese. At one point, Roosevelt sought to put Stilwell in charge of Chiang's troops, but the Chinese leader outmaneuvered the American officer, who was finally recalled to the United States.

On the ground in Asia, a British army led by the redoubtable General William Slim managed to fight off a Japanese attempt to invade India from Burma and then to retake that country, which the Japanese had conquered in their surge of 1942. Chiang's forces did tie down Japanese troops in China that, without their presence, might have fought elsewhere, but otherwise contributed little to the outcome of the campaign in the Pacific.

For the purposes of that campaign the American government divided the ocean into two additional military sectors. In both, American forces proceeded toward the Japanese archipelago through amphibious landings on Pacific islands, relying on superiority in the air and at sea and fighting brutal and costly battles against the Japanese troops that occupied them. After consolidating control, the Americans launched further assaults on other islands located closer to their ultimate destination. Fewer American troops fought in the Pacific than in Europe and they fought a different kind of war: rather than confronting modern, mechanized armies over protracted periods of combat, they waged "a war of isolation, boredom, and disease, punctuated by long ocean crossings and brief bursts of combat, much of it in hand-to-hand struggle with poorly outfitted but ferociously motivated Japanese Imperial soldiers."[150]

In part for domestic political reasons, President Roosevelt assigned the southwest Pacific command to Douglas MacArthur and the army.[151] In 1942 MacArthur's forces began a bitter struggle for New Guinea. The central Pacific command belonged to the United States Navy, with the United States Marine Corps taking a leading role in the fighting on the ground. The campaign there consisted of "island hopping," attacks within and among a series of island chains: the Solomons, the Gilberts, the Marshalls, and the Marianas. The Americans achieved their first victory on Guadalcanal, in the Solomons, in February 1943. Once having captured the islands, the American military constructed air strips on them from which planes could take off to participate in the battles for further islands, with the goal of bringing American military might, and particularly American air power, closer to the Japanese homeland.

The second phase of America's war reached a climax with the invasion of France that began on June 6, 1944, a date known thereafter as D-Day.[152] An amphibious assault against a defended coast, as the United States, Great Britain, and Canada conducted that day, is perhaps the most difficult and risky of all combat operations. Overlord, the invasion's code name, was the largest such operation ever attempted. The Allies had two possible French sites for it. The Pas de Calais region lay closer to southern England, but Normandy, to the south, offered other advantages and that is where Overlord took place. The Allies concocted an elaborate scheme of deception that persuaded much of the German high command that the attack would come at Pas de Calais, and so the point of actual attack was less heavily defended than it might otherwise have been.[153]

D-Day required extensive and elaborate preparations. More than 156,000 troops, 6,939 ships and landing vessels, and 2,395 aircraft took part in it. The troops had to receive the appropriate training. Much of the equipment had to be specially designed and produced, the landing craft in particular. The British designed and built two large artificial harbors, known as "mulberries." The operation also required precise coordination not only among the three different national armed forces but also among all three of their branches—their armies, navies, and air forces. The military strengths of the United States were on display: the enormous production of equipment, an unsurpassed logistical capacity, and a large reservoir of civilians ready to enter military service and fight. Altogether, Overlord has a strong claim to being not simply the greatest of all American military operations but "the most prodigious undertaking in the history of war."[154]

Many things could have gone wrong, and some did: the landing on one of the five designated beaches, Omaha, for example, took a heavy toll in American casualties.[155] Overall, however, the combination of Allied maritime and aerial supremacy, meticulous preinvasion planning and preparation, the skill, courage, and fortitude of the troops involved, and the good weather in the often-stormy English Channel on the first Tuesday in June made the operation a success. The troops got ashore and established beachheads that German attacks failed to dislodge.[156] Twenty-seven years after American troops had arrived on the European continent for the first time in the nation's history during World War I, and thirty months after the United States had finally entered World War II, a substantial and soon-to-be far larger American army was encamped on French soil and prepared to fight its way to Germany. The last stage of the European war had begun.

The Endgame

The American army in Europe, joined by its British counterpart, engaged in eleven months of hard fighting against stubborn and resourceful albeit ultimately doomed German resistance between D-Day and Germany's surrender eleven months later, on May 8, 1945.[157] The Germans had the advantages of almost six years of combat experience and of fighting on the defensive, as well as the motivation, for part of this period, of defending their home country.

The Allied armies liberated Paris in August 1944 but missed a chance to shorten the war in the west when a large number of German troops managed to break through a partial encirclement at Falaise in Normandy that month.[158] The Allied offensive designed to punch through German lines and establish a position stretching well behind them, called Operation Market Garden, failed in September.[159] In December the Germans mounted a counteroffensive in the Ardennes region, where they had broken through against France in 1940, that achieved surprise and made headway toward the Belgian port of Antwerp until halted by a courageous stand by American troops at Bastogne, in what the Allies called the Battle of the Bulge.[160]

As the supreme commander, Eisenhower declined to adopt the suggestion that the Americans and the British race to Berlin to take the

German capital before the Russians could get there,[161] advancing instead deliberately along a broad front. American troops crossed the Rhine on March 26, 1945, and met Soviet forces at the Elbe River a month later, on April 25. Hitler committed suicide on April 30 and the remnants of his regime gave up the fight.

When Soviet forces entered Poland, and later when American troops crossed into Germany, they encountered horrifying evidence of the Nazis' war of extermination against Europe's Jews. Antisemitism had been a major part of Hitler's program from the beginning of his political career,[††] and upon taking power in Germany and then with even greater determination and on a much larger scale after the Wehrmacht conquered Central and Eastern Europe, where millions of defenseless Jewish people lived, he set about murdering as many Jews—men, women, and children—as he could.[162]

For this purpose, the Germans built six death camps in Poland, having already established concentration camps in Germany,[163] into which millions of Jews, as well as others the Nazis deemed undesirable, were herded and killed by starvation and gassing. Hundreds of thousands more had been shot as the Germans marched eastward.

In the years after the war the Holocaust became an increasingly important part of World War II in the eyes of posterity, and the American response to the destruction of European Jewry became, along with the fate of Poland and the use of atomic weapons against the Japanese cities of Hiroshima and Nagasaki, one of three American policies that came in for retrospective criticism, not least in the United States. The charge in this case against the American government, including Franklin Roosevelt himself, was that they had done less than they could have to save at least some of Germany's Jewish victims.[164]

[††] "Hitler's ideas about the Jews were at the center of his mental world. They shaped his world view and his political ambitions, forming the matrix of his ideology and the ineradicable core of National Socialist doctrine. They determined the anti-Jewish policies of the German dictatorship from 1933 to 1945, and they furnished the authority for the murder of the Jews in Europe during World War II." Lucy S. Dawidowicz, *The War Against the Jews, 1933–1945*, New York: Holt, Rinehart and Winston, 1975, p. 5.

From the time the Nazis took power in Germany in 1933, German Jews were desperate to leave the country, with the United States a strongly preferred destination; but the American immigration laws strictly limited the number the country received. The State Department and the Congress refused to modify these laws and Roosevelt did not press the matter.[165] Accurate reports of the death camps reached America as early as November 1942, and as the Allies pounded Germany from the air some urged the bombing of the death camps—especially the largest of them, Auschwitz—or the railroad tracks along which the victims were transported to them, or both. This, too, did not take place.[166] Exactly how many of Europe's Jews would have been saved by different American policies can never be known, but some certainly could have been.[167]

Even as the fighting continued, efforts were under way to design institutions for the postwar era that would help prevent the kinds of developments that had produced the war. A multinational conference, with the United States and Great Britain taking the lead, convened at Bretton Woods, New Hampshire, in July 1944 for the purpose of reconstructing an international monetary system to replace the gold standard, which had not survived the Great Depression. The absence of an agreed-on set of monetary rules, the participants understood, would hinder trade and economic growth. In the new system, which was chiefly the work of the Americans and the British, the American dollar effectively supplanted gold: it became the only currency for which that universally accepted metal could be exchanged.

Whereas the gold standard had provided for fixed exchange rates among different national currencies, the Bretton Woods system allowed for some flexibility. It established the International Monetary Fund, with headquarters in Washington, D.C., to oversee the world's exchange rates. Bretton Woods occasioned another dispute between the Americans and the British. The workings of the gold standard placed the responsibility for making the economically painful adjustments in the event of international payments imbalances on the countries in deficit. The British, led by the influential English economist John Maynard Keynes, proposed that countries with payments surpluses bear some of the burden of adjustment.[168] Not entirely coincidentally, the British expected to run deficits, at least in the short term, after the war. The American delegation, confident of surpluses, disagreed and prevailed.[169]

While having no impact on international economic affairs during the war, the Bretton Woods system played a major role in the decades that followed, as, to a lesser extent in international relations more broadly, did another international organization that emerged from the war. President Roosevelt, who was elected to a fourth term in 1944, was enough of a Wilsonian to want an organization of some kind to keep the peace, and a meeting of the Allied foreign ministers in Moscow in November 1943 endorsed the idea. A conference at Dumbarton Oaks in Washington, D.C., in the summer of 1944 took the first steps in bringing into being what came to be called the United Nations, or UN, and a larger gathering in San Francisco from April to June 1945 filled out the details of its structure.

Like the League of Nations, the UN was to have universal membership, but it also included a version of Roosevelt's idea of the "Four Policemen" presiding over international affairs in the form of a Security Council, whose permanent members would wield considerable authority, including the power to veto its decisions.[170] A problem arose over membership. Stalin, suspicious as always of Western initiatives and wary of being outvoted, insisted that all of the Soviet Union's fifteen constituent republics—none of them remotely independent of the communist authorities in Moscow—have separate membership. Ultimately he settled for three seats in the General Assembly[171] and agreed to take part in the organization; and unlike what had happened with the League after World War I, the United States Senate approved American membership in the UN.

The practice of holding face-to-face meetings of the leaders of the Allied powers continued in 1945. They met in the Soviet Union itself—at Yalta, on the Black Sea—in February, Roosevelt's final meeting before his death on April 9 of that year. They met again from mid-July to early August at Potsdam, a suburb of Berlin in recently conquered Germany, where the United States was represented by President Harry S Truman, who had been Roosevelt's vice president in his brief fourth term. In both conferences the shape of the postwar world dominated the agenda. The proceedings of both provided evidence—clearer, to be sure, in retrospect than at the time—that postwar Europe would not fulfill all of the democracies' hopes for it.

At Yalta, Roosevelt, Churchill, and Stalin agreed to divide Germany into four zones of occupation, one for each of them and the fourth for France.[172] Stalin promised that the Soviet Union would join the United Nations and again said that it would eventually go to war against Japan. In later years the most controversial issue at the conference, the one that occasioned retrospective criticism of the American president, was Poland.

The country mattered to all three members of the coalition. Great Britain had gone to war to defend it in 1939 but had not been able to prevent its brutal division between Germany and the Soviet Union. Nonetheless, almost a quarter million exiled Poles had fought bravely for the Allied cause in World War II. The United States had six to seven million citizens—and voters—of Polish descent, who, Roosevelt more than once told Stalin, expected the American government to protect the interests of their country of origin.[173]

The Soviet leader, for all his devotion to the principles of Marxism-Leninism (as he interpreted them), had a traditional Russian great-power attitude toward Poland. As an independent country it had disappeared at the end of the eighteenth century through a series of partitions among Germany, Austria-Hungary, and tsarist Russia; and a genuinely independent Poland seemed to the Soviet leadership, if not exactly an anomaly, then certainly not a geopolitical necessity. When the people of Warsaw rose up against their German occupiers in August 1944, the Red Army was in a position to come to their aid but conspicuously failed to do so. Perhaps most important from Stalin's point of view, Poland had served as an invasion corridor to the Russian homeland twice in the twentieth century. The Soviet Union would therefore, he surely assumed, have to control it; and Soviet control proved incompatible with the national independence and political liberty that most Poles wanted and that the Americans and British wanted for them.

Stalin agreed to free elections in all the Eastern European countries liberated from the Germans, including Poland, but the elections, if and when they took place, would be held under the auspices of the occupying power, which was the Soviet Union. Moreover, two separate groups claimed the right to act as the Polish government: one based in London and friendly to the United States and Great Britain, the other in Lublin, in eastern Poland, and a puppet of the Soviet leadership.

The Yalta declaration effectively conceded the primacy of the Lublin Poles.[174]

Roosevelt put a good face on the implications of the conference for Poland,[175] but privately he understood that Soviet rather than Anglo-American preferences would determine the politics of that country.[176] He made no public protest for a variety of reasons: his belief in the need for Soviet assistance in the final battle against Japan; his conviction that American forces would not remain in Europe after the war and that Soviet good will would therefore count for a good deal at that point; and his characteristically American belief, shared by other officials, that the United States could use its economic strength to affect Soviet policies.[177]

His later critics accused him of "selling out" the Poles.[178] In truth, he had nothing to sell. The Red Army was in possession of the country and thus in a position to enforce Stalin's wishes there. Only military measures could have changed this, and it was unthinkable that the United States would move directly from the conquest of Germany to a war against the Soviet Union. The course of World War II determined Eastern Europe's fate. The forty-five years that the countries of the region involuntarily endured under Soviet domination and communist rule after 1945 turned out to be part of the price of defeating Nazi Germany.

At Potsdam Churchill attended the first part of the meeting but midway through it a general election took place in Britain and his Conservative Party lost its majority in the House of Commons. The leader of the Labor Party Clement Attlee (who had been part of the wartime coalition government) became prime minister, and he joined Truman and Stalin at the conference in Churchill's stead.

The question of Germany dominated the proceedings. Roosevelt had at one point favored the plan of his secretary of the treasury, Henry Morgenthau, to dismantle German industry but had changed his mind.[179] Churchill wanted a revived, de-Nazified Germany to serve as a bulwark against Soviet power in Europe.[180] At Potsdam, the three leaders confirmed its division among themselves; agreed to conduct trials of Nazi officials as war criminals (the trials took place in the German city of Nuremberg from 1945 to 1949); decreed that all German territorial annexations were to be reversed; provided, at

Soviet insistence, for reparations to the victorious powers; and foresaw "orderly and humane" expulsions of ethnic Germans from Poland, Czechoslovakia, and Hungary. In fact, at least ten million Germans fled westward, often in disorderly and inhumane circumstances.[181]

Intended to be temporary, the division of Germany lasted for forty-five years, during which time the divided country stood at the heart of a divided Europe. The conquest and political disposition of Germany effectively ended World War II for the Soviet Union. For the United States, however, the war continued, in Asia.

In the southwest Pacific, MacArthur achieved his goal of returning to the Philippines in early 1945. The American navy had paved the way by defeating an outmatched but still determined Japanese fleet at Leyte Gulf in the waters off the Philippine archipelago, in the largest naval battle ever fought.[182] There followed a bitter struggle for control of Manila, the capital, in which American forces ultimately prevailed. The battle took a heavy toll in civilian casualties: an estimated 100,000 Filipinos died.

In the central Pacific, the island-hopping campaign took American forces to Iwo Jima in February and March 1945, and then to Okinawa, where the largest amphibious landing of the Pacific war took place and where the fighting lasted from April to June. American military planners intended to use Okinawa as a base for the anticipated assault on Japan itself. In both Iwo Jima and Okinawa the Americans met bitter resistance. Most of the Japanese defenders fought to the death rather than surrender.[183] In these battles the Japanese employed "kamikaze" tactics, sending planes on one-way suicide missions to crash into American ships and other targets in order to inflict as many casualties as possible.[184]

Meanwhile, from the middle of 1944 and with increasing intensity in 1945, the American air force had been pounding Japan. In late 1944 the capture of the Marianas island chain made bases available from which the largest bomber aircraft, the B-29, could reach the Japanese archipelago. Employing a technique known as firebombing,[185] the B-29s set off conflagrations that burned down large sections of Japanese cities, which contained many wooden structures. Air raids struck Nagoya, Kobe, Osaka, Yokohama, and Kawasaki as well as Tokyo. An estimated 240,000 to 300,000 Japanese died in these attacks.[186]

Committed to nothing less than an unconditional surrender, the American authorities assumed that a massive invasion of Japan's islands, costing many casualties on both sides, would be required to secure it. Fortunately for both Americans and Japanese, such an invasion proved unnecessary. Working in the secret Manhattan Project, American scientists and engineers developed and, in July of 1945, in the New Mexican desert tested, an explosive device far more powerful than any previously known. It drew its force from the energy locked in the heart—the atomic nucleus—of matter. President Truman approved the use of the two available bombs against Japanese cities. On August 6 the first one struck Hiroshima; three days later the second hit Nagasaki.[187]

Long afterward, the bombings, like American policy toward the Holocaust and toward Poland, attracted retrospective criticism, according to which the United States had acted immorally in unleashing this horrific weapon on defenseless civilians. The decision to use the bomb aroused almost no controversy when it was made.[188] The inhibition against attacking civilians, such as it was, had long since been overcome—by American and British aerial attacks against Germany and Japan and earlier and, on a much larger scale, by the mass killings in Eastern Europe and China by the Germans and the Japanese.

In August 1945 the United States was waging a brutal war that had lasted for almost four years. To finish it, the American government contemplated a campaign against the Japanese homeland in which a large number of American soldiers, and many Japanese military personnel and civilians as well, would certainly die.[189] The responsible American officials considered any measure that had the potential to make the projected invasion less costly to be entirely justified. The atomic bomb did more than that: it ended the war. On August 9, the Soviet Union, as Stalin had promised, declared war on Japan. On August 15, the Japanese emperor made a radio broadcast—the first time the Japanese people had ever heard his voice—announcing that his country would give up the fight. On September 2, on the deck of the battleship *Missouri* anchored in Tokyo Bay, Japanese officials signed a document of surrender. With that ceremony, World War II passed into history.

In that history—the long history of human civilization—it has a singular distinction: it was, and remains, by the death and destruction it wrought, the greatest war that human beings have ever fought. The value of the property destroyed is beyond calculation; the number of deaths is not: the American armed forces incurred 405,399 combat deaths. Other countries suffered far more. The Soviet Union may have lost as many as 25 million people, both civilian and military. Poland lost 20 percent of its prewar population, about 6 million people. The British armed forces lost 244,000 men and their Commonwealth and imperial forces another 100,000. Over 4 million German military personnel were killed, along with more than 500,000 civilians. Japan suffered 1.7 million battle deaths. Between 14 and 20 million Chinese were killed. All told, an estimated 50 million people died as a direct result of World War II and perhaps 25 to 30 million more from war-related disease and famine.[190]

In World War I, the United States made a crucial but marginal contribution to the outcome. In the victory in World War II it had a central role, as a full-fledged and long-serving member of the winning great-power coalition. American soldiers, sailors, and air personnel won the war in the Pacific and played an indispensable part in the defeat of Nazi Germany. Just as important, if not more so, was the American role as the arsenal of democracy, supplying the military hardware as well as the food and the fuel without which Great Britain and the Soviet Union could not have persisted in the fight against Hitler. It is perhaps an exaggeration, but not a gross one, to impute the outcome of the war in Europe to American equipment, British determination, and Russian blood.

A war of such magnitude was bound to change the world. It also changed the American role in the world. The United States had entered World War II as one of several great powers. Without this being an explicit war aim, indeed almost entirely unintentionally, it emerged from the conflict with an even more elevated international status.

The Third Age

Superpower, 1945–1990

> This war is not as in the past; whoever occupies a territory also imposes on it his own social system. Everyone imposes his own system as far as his army can reach. It cannot be otherwise.
>
> Joseph Stalin, 1945

The United States emerged from World War II with more power than ever before. It had had the largest economy in the world before the war and expanded its economic activity while waging it. Its currency had gained official recognition, through the Bretton Woods agreements, as the most important on the planet. America had, as well, formidable military forces, which included the most numerous and sophisticated war machines—ships and aircraft—as well as the most destructive weapon ever devised by humans, the atomic bomb.

Even that recitation fails to do full justice to the American global role in 1945: power in the international system is relative and World War II had severely reduced that of other countries that had begun it as great powers. Germany and Japan lay in ruins. France, although admitted to the winning coalition at the end, had incurred a humiliating defeat in 1940. Great Britain, while a full-fledged victor, had reached the limit of its resources by the end of the fighting.

The war had had a different impact on the Soviet Union. No country had suffered more death and destruction, yet it had rallied from early battlefield setbacks and had pushed the German army all the way back to Berlin while producing an ever-expanding volume of war materiel. In May 1945, the Red Army occupied Central and Eastern Europe to the middle of Germany. As a conqueror and liberator, the Soviet Union enjoyed high prestige across the continent and beyond. In the wake of the war, the United States and the Soviet Union became rivals and their rivalry dominated American foreign policy, and indeed international relations, for the next four decades.

That rivalry became the fifth global conflict to include the United States, along with the Seven Years' War, the Wars of the French Revolution, and the two world wars of the twentieth century. Like the first four, this one featured alliances, deadly weaponry, efforts at subversion on both sides, and proxy battles in which one of the two adversaries opposed forces assisted by the other. In contrast to the previous conflicts, the United States joined this one at the outset and remained central to it from beginning to end. The Soviet-American antagonism differed from the other four in one other, vitally important way: the two countries never fought each other directly. Their conflict thus inspired a new term in the lexicon of international politics. It became known as the Cold War.[1]

The new conflict gave rise to another terminological innovation. The great powers of the international system had waged the major wars of the past. The main contestants in the Cold War belonged in a different category and came to be known as "superpowers."[2] The term reflected more than linguistic inflation. The United States and the Soviet Union differed from the great powers of the past, including the recent past, in three major respects: their common possession of nuclear weapons (the Soviet Union acquired them in 1949); the global scope of their rivalry; and the fact that their conflict involved a clash not only of two large, powerful countries but also of two distinct and radically dissimilar political and economic systems.

* * *

The power of the atomic bombs that struck Hiroshima and Nagasaki was measured in the kilotons—a measure equal to a thousand tons of TNT. Subsequently, both superpowers equipped themselves with many bombs more than a thousand times as powerful, with explosive power measured in megatons: a single one of them could destroy a city; a dozen could make an entire country uninhabitable. For decades the two competed to develop and deploy these weapons. They also had to find ways to conduct their rivalry without destroying themselves and much of the rest of the world as well.[3] Several other countries did obtain them,[4] but the Soviet and American nuclear stockpiles dwarfed those of third countries. In recognition of the contribution these armaments made to their enhanced international status, the two giants of the international system were often called the "nuclear superpowers."

The United States and the Soviet Union qualified as superpowers, as well, because the conflict they waged encompassed the whole world, including the oceans and, with the launch of Earth-orbiting satellites, outer space as well. To be sure, the British Empire in the nineteenth century and the United States in World War II had had political interests, and deployed military forces, in far-flung corners of the globe. The steady improvement in the technologies of transportation and communication that had begun with the Industrial Revolution made this possible. Neither those two nor any other great power before the Cold War, however, had felt the need to be present everywhere.

The two superpowers resembled opponents in a chess match for whom every square on the chessboard has significant value because occupying it has the potential to bring victory closer. The fact that two and only two countries stood at the summit of the global order also pushed their conflict into every part of the planet. The "bipolarity" of the international system made the superpower contest akin to a zero-sum game in which any gain for one side was automatically a loss for the other.

The global scope of the country's interests and activities made the sheer volume of American foreign policy—the number of commitments, conflicts, negotiations, and diplomatic contacts of all kinds—far greater than during the two previous periods in which foreign policy had played an important part in the national life: between 1765 and 1815, and again between 1917 and 1945. It also meant that the foreign policy of the United States had a greater impact on the rest of the world than in the earlier periods. The conflict's global reach, finally, combined with the existence of nuclear weapons, raised the stakes of their rivalry for both the United States and the Soviet Union, as did the third feature that distinguished them from the great powers of the past: the ideological character of the Cold War.

Both superpowers were "idea-states." While most countries base their identity on features that their populations share—language, religion, and ethnicity—the two great rivals had both been founded on particular political principles, principles that justified their existence. The United States had declared and won independence to safeguard and promote the basic political value of liberty, which played a central role in its national life thereafter. The Soviet Union succeeded the multinational empire of the tsars and in important ways resembled its autocratic predecessor.[5] Yet it had come into existence as the result of a violent revolution and its leaders claimed, with some justification, to represent a sharp break with Russia's history—indeed with the histories of all countries—by virtue of embodying the set of ideas that came to be known as Marxism-Leninism. The term, and the ideology, fused the writings of a nineteenth-century philosopher, economist, pamphleteer, and would-be political organizer from the Rhineland named Karl Marx with the political structures created by Vladimir Ulyanov, known as Lenin, the leader of the Bolshevik Party that seized power in St. Petersburg, the tsarist capital, in 1917 and managed to consolidate it by winning the civil war that followed.

Each superpower sought to foster its founding principles beyond its borders. The United States had aspired to spread the blessings of liberty since its founding. According to Marx's teachings, the rule of the working class, known as communism, was destined to take hold everywhere. Lenin and his successors, beginning with Joseph Stalin, were eager to assist what their ideology regarded as the inevitable course of history through subversion and war.

The two sets of founding principles were polar opposites. Marxism-Leninism had no room for the individual liberty that Americans prized. The Soviet government exerted iron control over those it governed. Contrary to the theory and practice of liberty, it aspired to manage every aspect of political, economic, and even cultural life, earning it the designation "totalitarian."[6] The two superpowers also adopted markedly different ways of organizing economic activity: for the United

States, free markets with the private ownership of property; for the Soviet Union, government control over all significant economic assets and the determination of what was to be produced by government planners rather than, as in a market system, through the interplay of supply and demand driven by the free choices of consumers.

As in the great wars of the past, the United States and the Soviet Union organized supporting coalitions, and the other members of the two coalitions adopted the political and economic practices of the leader. In the case of the United States this came about more or less voluntarily, and not through deliberate design but rather by a series of ad hoc measures in the early years of the Cold War. The Soviet Union, by contrast, relied on coercion to create the communist bloc.

In this way, the Cold War became a contest of systems, as each side sought to outdo the other not only in military terms but also, and ultimately more importantly, in the productivity of its economy and the legitimacy and attractiveness of its political order. The recognition that they could not fight a full-scale war against each other made the political and economic competition all the more important. So, too, did the fact that Europe was divided between the two blocs, as were important countries—Germany, Korea, and China. These divisions made the differences in the performances of the two systems readily apparent.

The sharp ideological divergence between the two rivals contributed to the intensity of their rivalry because it meant that each considered the other illegitimate, the patron of political and economic arrangements that ought not to exist. The Cold War rivalry was thus not only geographically wider but also politically deeper than the great-power conflicts of the past.[7]

* * *

The Cold War unfolded in three stages. In the first, between 1945 and 1953, the wartime allies turned into adversaries. For both the United States and the Soviet Union this development was largely unintended, certainly unwelcome, but in retrospect all but unavoidable.[8] During these years the superpowers' defining features emerged. The United States had become a nuclear power with the raids on Hiroshima and Nagasaki in August 1945. In August 1949 the Soviet Union achieved that status as well. The Korean War, from 1950 to 1953, extended the conflict to Asia, making it global in scope. In this initial stage, as well, the political and economic institutions that bound together the two opposing systems came into existence.

The Cold War's second stage encompassed the rest of the 1950s and the two decades that followed. In retrospect, over the course of these three decades the conflict can be seen to have become relatively stable. One historian termed the period "the Long Peace."⁹ Because neither side could defeat the other militarily, moreover, the Cold War seemed destined to persist indefinitely. In its final phase, however, which spanned, roughly, the decade of the 1980s, it ended.

In its denouement, the Soviet-American rivalry differed from the global conflicts of the past in that it occurred without a shot being fired. The Soviet Union was not beaten on the battlefield and did not surrender. It collapsed from within, as the result of decisions made by its supreme leader, Mikhail Gorbachev.

In the epochal events that produced the collapse of communism in Europe and the termination of the Soviet-American rivalry, the United States played almost no direct role. Over the course of the Cold War, however, persistent American opposition to the Soviet Union and its international ambitions did a great deal to create the conditions in which the conflict came to an end. When it did end, the United States emerged from it with a new and even more powerful position in the international system.

7

The Contest of Systems, 1945–1953

Year Zero

World War II left even greater destruction in its wake than had World War I.* National economies and political systems around the world as well as the European, Asian, and global political and economic orders had to be rebuilt more or less from scratch: in that sense 1945 was, in the international history of the twentieth century, "Year Zero."[1] For the new world that had to be created, the United States had the same broad goals as it had had after the previous conflict: international harmony and global prosperity, as expressed in Woodrow Wilson's Fourteen Points and Franklin Roosevelt's Atlantic Charter.

After the second war, as after the first, America did not achieve these goals, and for the same reason: the coalition that had won the war did not survive in peacetime. The differences between and among the members of that coalition, which the wartime meetings of their leaders had begun to reveal, came to the fore with the defeat of their common enemies. Those differences turned out to be wide enough and deep

---

* "Much of Europe and important parts of Asia were wastelands. Many of the world's greatest cities—Berlin, Warsaw, Vienna, Leningrad, Tokyo—had been reduced to rubble. Tens of millions of people had no shelter. Millions more were on the road, returning home from battlefields and forced labor camps. . . ." Melvyn P. Leffler, *A Preponderance of Power: National Security, the Truman Administration and the Cold War*, Stanford, California: Stanford University Press, 1992, p. 1..

enough to cause yet another great global conflict, the third of the twentieth century.

Just as World War II grew out of World War I, so the Cold War had its roots in the outcome of World War II, but with important differences. The Cold War came sooner—in five years rather than twenty. It pitted the United States not against its adversary in the previous conflict, as in World War II, but rather against its erstwhile ally, the Soviet Union. While America had not been a party to the outbreak of the two world wars, in the Cold War it occupied a central position and assumed a leading role from the outset. The Cold War lasted ten times as long as America's participation in World War II—forty years instead of four; and while it ended, as had the two world wars, in victory for the United States and its allies, that victory came about in an unexpected and indeed an unprecedented way—peacefully rather than through success on the battlefield.

After World War I, as after the Wars of the French Revolution, the task of reconstructing the global political order fell to the victorious great powers meeting at a peace conference—in Vienna in 1815 and in Paris in 1918. After World War II no such meeting took place. Indeed, it was not clear, after the guns fell silent, which countries could usefully participate in one. While great wars invariably rearrange the hierarchy of power in the international system, this one had shattered it.

Defeated militarily, ruined economically, and occupied by their conquerors, Germany and Japan did not count as independent forces in the world, let alone as great powers. France was part of the winning coalition by courtesy but had suffered a sweeping and ignominious defeat at German hands in 1940 and had contributed very little to the Allies' ultimate military success.

Great Britain had fought the war from the beginning to the end, standing alone against the Nazi war machine for a perilous and heroic year between the fall of France and the German invasion of the Soviet Union. Britain had made major contributions to the victories both in the European and the Asian theaters. It thought of itself as a great power and in major respects it was; but the war had drained its national resources.[2] The British were to spend the next two decades liquidating the empire on which their claim to great-power status largely rested and their influence in Europe was limited by the fact that they had never had, and did not aspire to have, a major, permanent, peacetime military presence on the European continent. The traditional European powers, therefore, were either in a weak position or in no position at all to exert influence over the postwar international order.

The Soviet Union, by contrast, did have the means to shape that order. In 1941 and 1942 particularly it had suffered massive death and destruction but had rallied its productive and military forces, pushed the invading Germans back more than 1,600 miles from the Volga River to the middle of Germany, and ended the war with an army in Europe that was the largest ever deployed there.[3] Its wartime feats had gained it good will, admiration, and prestige around the world. Soviet wishes would plainly count for a great deal in 1945 and thereafter.

Those wishes were in fact the wishes of the country's supreme leader, Joseph Stalin. He had a straightforward set of priorities for the postwar world, although because of the secrecy that enveloped the Soviet political system these were not clear to other countries at the time. He sought security for himself, his regime, and the communist multinational state over which he presided. He had assured his own position at home by killing off potential opponents. Internationally, he came to regard the optimal mechanism—the only reliable one—for becoming and remaining secure to be the exercise of control over as much adjacent territory as possible.

As a convinced Marxist-Leninist, Stalin believed that history had predestined a struggle between the world's socialist nations, which he headed, and the capitalist countries. He also believed that the capitalist powers were ultimately doomed to fratricidal conflict, which is how orthodox Leninists understood the two world wars. The Stalinist, and therefore Soviet, preferences for and assumptions about the international future, therefore, had nothing in common with the visions of Woodrow Wilson and Franklin Roosevelt. However, Stalin was prepared to be tactically flexible. He had, after all, made alliances first with Nazi Germany and then, when Hitler attacked his country in June 1941, with the arch-imperialist Great Britain and the arch-capitalist United States. Although he did not expect long-term peace, let alone friendship, with the capitalist world, and did not trust its political leaders (Stalin, in fact, trusted nobody), he did hope for, perhaps even counted on, decent relations with his wartime allies in the short term, with an eye toward gaining their help in the economic reconstruction of the Soviet Union.[4]

The United States emerged from the war as the country with, potentially, more influence than any other. It had built a vast military force that was deployed in both Europe and Asia. Its navy dominated the world's oceans and it had the mightiest air force on the planet. Economically, in 1945 it accounted for one-third of all global production and one-half of all manufacturing.[5]

Yet it was far from clear that America would use these assets as the basis for shaping the new global order. It had had the world's largest economy since the late nineteenth century and had belonged to the winning coalition in World War I but had not exercised international influence commensurate with its wealth and power. Because of this history, neither the people nor the governments of any country, including the United States, could be confident about the kind of postwar role America would play.

The American public wanted to bring the troops home from their foreign postings and to resume a peacetime national existence. As after the First World War (and the Civil War as well) they got what they wanted. The United States had 12 million men and women under arms in 1945. By the end of June 1947, the number had fallen to 1.5 million. Defense spending, which had stood at $81.6 billion in 1945, had declined to $13.1 billion by 1947.[6]

During the war, the federal government had done some planning for the postwar world. The military, for example, was intent on keeping many of the overseas bases it had established during the course of the war.[7] The bureaucracy proposed, however, no overall design for American foreign policy after 1945.

While most Americans turned away from international affairs to concentrate on their American-based lives once their country had ceased to be at war, a minority of them remained interested and engaged in, and took pains to inform themselves about, the world beyond the United States. The members of this foreign policy community, including most senior government officials, generally believed, or at least hoped, as had Franklin Roosevelt, that their country could maintain friendly, cooperative relations with the Soviet Union after Germany and Japan had surrendered.[8] They also hoped—again like Franklin

Roosevelt—that the newly created United Nations could contribute to upholding international peace.

All Americans fervently wished to prevent another war. Many of those attentive to foreign policy shared the conviction that for this purpose the United States had to take a larger part in international affairs than it had done in the wake of World War I.[9] The democracies, they felt, including their own, had made mistakes in the interwar period that had paved the way for the outbreak of the terrible war that had just ended.[10] It followed that avoiding such mistakes in the future had to have the highest national priority. This conviction was to weigh heavily on American policymakers in the second half of the 1940s.

In one sector of international life the government of the United States was prepared to assume major responsibilities in the wake of the war: economics. Indeed, it launched a major economic initiative—the Bretton Woods conference and the reconstruction of the world's monetary arrangements—even before the war had ended. Such initiatives had a precedent. The United States had tried to help sort out Europe's economic problems after World War I. America also had a strong motive for international economic activism: anxious for a smooth transition from wartime mobilization to a robust peacetime economy, American officials understood that the chances of this occurring depended in part on economic conditions elsewhere. The international economic policies that the American government carried out at the end of the war and in the years immediately following it, which were, among other things, efforts to avoid the missteps of the past, turned out to have momentous and largely unanticipated consequences for the future.

The Creation of the West

Among the mistakes of the interwar period that American policymakers identified was the failure to prevent or effectively address the Great Depression. That severe economic downturn had not only damaged the lives of tens of millions of people through falling incomes and unemployment but also helped to bring to power governments in Germany and Japan that launched aggressive policies that led to war. During the Depression, cross-border flows of money and goods had dwindled, worsening economic distress everywhere. Even before World War II ended, therefore, the American government set itself the task of establishing institutions and encouraging practices that would reverse these trends by supporting postwar international economic cooperation.

The United States led the deliberations at Bretton Woods in the summer of 1944 that produced a dollar-centered international monetary system, along with the International Monetary Fund and the International Bank for Reconstruction and Development (commonly known as the World Bank) to bolster it. Also, before the war ended, the State Department, led by the ardent free trader Cordell Hull, began planning ways to avoid the tariff barriers and competitive devaluations that had stifled trade during the 1930s.[11]

For that purpose, in April 1947, representatives of eighteen countries convened in Geneva and negotiated both tariff reductions on a range of manufactured products and a series of general principles designed to foster international commerce.[12] The Geneva results encountered political opposition in the United States but President Truman weighed in on their behalf[13] and Congress ratified them.[14] The American government did not adopt the charter for an International Trade Organization written at a follow-up conference in Havana between November 1947 and March 1948; but the rules that had emerged from the Geneva meeting, known as the General Agreement on Tariffs and Trade (GATT), remained in place and governed much of global trade for the ensuing fifty years.

While the politics of trade in the United States and other democracies are inevitably contentious, with those injured by foreign competition engaging in political efforts to protect themselves from it, the level of resistance to open trade fell to historically low levels in the United States in the wake of World War II. The war had so damaged America's major trading partners, while largely sparing the United States, that almost every sector of the American economy enjoyed a trade surplus with the rest of the world. Other countries were desperate for American products and had, temporarily as it turned out, little to sell that Americans wanted to buy.

Thus it was that in the immediate aftermath of the war American trade policy underwent a historic shift.[15] The political advantage that protection had had over free trade, which dated from the Civil War, was reversed. With the American economy in the ascendant worldwide, with the Democratic Party, historically the advocate of low tariffs, dominating national politics, and with the American government increasingly seeing international economic interdependence as a strategic asset in the Cold War,[16] the United States became what Great Britain had been in the second half of the nineteenth century: the global champion of the freest possible trade. Accordingly, and in contrast to the experience of the decade preceding it, in the years after World War II trade in Europe and Asia expanded rapidly.[17]

The postwar international trade and monetary systems that owed their existence in great part to the United States were designed for normal economic times, when the national economies that took part in them were functioning more or less smoothly. That was not the situation in Europe in the immediate aftermath of World War II. Winston Churchill described the continent as "a rubble heap, a charnel house, a breeding ground for pestilence and hate."[18] These dire conditions called, the American government came to believe, for emergency measures; and so America came to Europe's rescue with large infusions of capital.

With its dollar diplomacy of the pre–World War I era and the Dawes and Young Plans of the 1920s, the United States had previously deployed capital abroad in peacetime for political as well as economic purposes. What the government did in the wake of World War II differed from those previous initiatives by providing money on a far larger scale and on more generous terms than ever before.

In 1946 an economically struggling Great Britain received an American loan of $3.75 billion. As with its past economic assistance to that country, the United States made a condition of the loan an end to preferential British trade policies that discriminated against American products. Washington insisted as well that the pound sterling be made convertible within a year. On the other hand, the loan came with low interest rates and the cancellation of Britain's Lend-Lease debt, which came to $20 billion.[19]

By 1947 the United States had sent, since the war's end, $9 billion worth of assistance to Europe, much of it for humanitarian purposes;[20] but in the first half of that year the senior officials of the American government concluded that even more was needed. In particular, a way had to be found to fill the "dollar gap" that plagued the countries of the continent: they lacked sufficient American currency to pay for imports from the United States, particularly the capital goods required to make things that they could then sell to earn dollars. In response to this emergency, the Truman administration assembled a package of large-scale grants to the countries of Europe that ultimately came to $13.2 billion.[21]

Well aware of the resolutely democratic character of American foreign policy, Truman and his colleagues were far from certain that the Congress would approve what would be the biggest program of foreign aid in American history—or indeed in the history of any country.[22] The president decided to call the European Recovery Program the Marshall Plan, after his secretary of state, the wartime military leader George C. Marshall, who had announced it at Harvard University in June 1947. Truman feared that attaching his own name to it would arouse Republican opposition. After a robust campaign to persuade the public of the Plan's merits and extensive lobbying of the people's elected representatives in Washington to authorize it,[23] Congress approved it and Truman signed it into law on April 3, 1948.

It had the desired impact. Historians have debated the precise economic effects of the American grants, but they unquestionably helped to revive European economic growth.[24] Just as significant in doing so was their psychological impact: they engendered confidence on the part of the people and the political leaders in the recipient countries that they could and would recover from the war—and confidence, of course, is an essential ingredient of economic success.[25] Over the long term, moreover, the Marshall Plan had several immensely important consequences that contributed both to the beginning and, ultimately, to the end of the Cold War.

It was, first and foremost, a crucial event in the economic and political division of Europe, which lasted for four decades and became the signature feature of the post–World War II global conflict. The Truman administration offered Marshall aid to all European countries, east as well as west. Those that the Red Army had occupied on its way to the center of Germany expressed interest, but Stalin forced them to decline to participate in the program.[26] Thereafter, two fundamentally different economic camps came into existence on the continent.

The recipients of Marshall aid in the West rebuilt their prewar free-market economies, with private property as a central institution. These countries left the important economic decisions—what to produce and invest—to individuals. Their governments did assume three major responsibilities: stabilizing the economy in times of imbalance; providing a social safety net to cushion the negative impact of unemployment and illness as well as furnishing financial support in old age; and supplying economically indispensable "public goods" such as infrastructure and education that individuals would not provide on their own. Because of these government roles, which became more extensive after 1945, the Western economies came to be called "mixed systems" or "welfare states."

The countries in the eastern part of the continent installed—or rather the Soviet leaders forced them to install—radically different economic systems, of the kind that the Soviet Union had built in the wake of the Russian Revolution of 1917. Under this system, the state had the powers that market economies vested in individuals.[27] Government planners made all the main economic decisions and the state owned all major property. Because it operated through commands from on high, this system became known as the "command economy," or, because economic activity proceeded (or was intended to proceed) according to government-designed five-year plans, as the "planned economy." Central planning hampered economic contacts with other countries and the planned economies therefore engaged in relatively little trade with and virtually no investment in similarly organized countries, let alone those in the West with market economies.[28]

In creating a planned economy during the civil war that followed the 1917 Revolution, the Bolshevik Party, which had seized power in that year, was both taking steps it deemed necessary to prevail in that conflict and implementing one of the central precepts of Marxism— the abolition of private property. By placing economic activity under the control of the government, the planned system also served the Communist Party's need to control as much of the society it governed as possible, a need that grew out of both its aspiration radically to reshape that society and the fact that remaining in power required such control because the communists had so little actual support in the Russian empire.

It became the communist claim, and no doubt belief, that because it operated according to the design of presumably sophisticated planners rather than, as with free markets, through millions of independent decisions by firms and individuals, the command economy surpassed the free market in rationality and effectiveness in achieving the universally desired goal of economic growth.[29] Comparisons between the two systems, and therefore competition between them in the promotion of economic welfare, thus became a major theme of the international history of the second half of the twentieth century.[30] This competition was especially vivid because during that period several countries—Germany, Korea, China, and for a time Vietnam—were divided, with one part adopting free-market practices and the other employing central planning. These divided countries offered the closest approximation political life can provide of a controlled experiment to determine which system performed better. The results of that experiment had a great deal to do with how the Cold War ended.

The Marshall Plan had other important long-term consequences. It spurred the economic revival of the countries that took part in it, which in turn ushered in a stretch of unprecedentedly rapid economic growth that lasted until the 1970s.[31] In this period Europe became far more urban, industrial, and above all affluent than it had been before World War II. It also became what the United States already was: a society in which consumer goods, such as refrigerators, sewing machines, and automobiles, were widely available and widely owned. In retrospect, the French termed that happy period "les trente glorieuses"—the thirty glorious years.

In addition, the Marshall Plan included the Western-occupied two-thirds of prewar Germany, marking the return of that country to a central place in the economy of the continent.[32] One lesson that had emerged from the interwar period was that a prosperous Europe required a prosperous Germany. The Marshall Plan incorporated that lesson. The next decades validated it: rapid German economic growth, which the Germans called their "wirtschaftswunder"—economic miracle—made a major contribution to growth throughout Western Europe.

Finally, but not least important, the American-sponsored European Recovery Program started what became the historic process of economic integration of the countries of Western Europe, with ever-increasing flows of trade and investment among them. The Program's terms required the European governments to coordinate among themselves in devising the requests for funding that they submitted to Washington.[33] The habit of cooperation took root. It led to the Schumann Plan of 1950, named for the French foreign minister of the day, Robert Schuman, and inspired by the Frenchman Jean Monnet, whom history would remember as the father of continental economic integration. That Plan merged the coal and steel industries of six countries, including France and Germany, to create, in 1952, the European Coal and Steel Community.[34] That, in turn, paved the way for the Treaty of Rome of 1957, which established the European Economic Community, the forerunner of the twenty-eight-member European Union[35] of the post–Cold War era. In concert with the United States, with which their economic and political ties multiplied after 1945, the countries of Western Europe formed a wider community, one that rested on common interests, common purposes, and common values and became known during the Cold War as, simply, "the West." The Marshall Plan can be seen in retrospect as the seminal event in its creation.

These three consequences of the Marshall Plan—rapid economic growth, a central Western European role for the western part of Germany, and increased economic cooperation in the region—proceeded simultaneously and reinforced one another. For example, the inclusion of Germany in the program prompted the French to seek an acceptable method of achieving their familiar goal of restraining and controlling German power. That method turned out to be European economic integration. Together, the three consequences had a powerful impact on the performance of the free-market economies in their ongoing competition with communist central planning.

In international affairs, economics and politics are never entirely separate; and they were certainly not separate considerations for American foreign policy in the second half of the 1940s. The nation's economic initiatives of that period had economic but also political purposes. Once again, the United States reverted to a long-established pattern, using economic instruments for political ends. The economic initiatives were intended not only to reinvigorate production and commerce in Europe but also to prevent the countries in the western part of the continent from falling under the sway of the Soviet Union. Their neighbors to the east had suffered that fate as a result of the course of World War II, which had brought the Red Army into their territories. The dispatch of American capital to Europe took place in, and responded to, a particular political context: the increasingly intense rivalry with the country's wartime Soviet ally.

The Truman administration had that rivalry in mind in concluding the trade agreements of the immediate postwar period.[36] It made the 1946 loan to Great Britain for the same general reason that the Roosevelt administration had given aid of various kinds to that country before December 1941: to strengthen a friendly power on which Washington was counting to sustain a robust postwar international presence, to the advantage of the United States.[37] The major impetus for the Marshall Plan came from the American fear that economic distress on the continent would open the way for increasing communist influence there; and by 1947, minimizing communist influence had become an important, indeed the single most important, American international aim.[38] As after World War I, the United States practiced a kind of "Dollar Diplomacy," but on a larger scale and in what turned out to be a more urgent political context.

In that year the policymakers in Washington did not anticipate a further thrust westward by Soviet forces that had already reached the middle of Germany. The Americans worried, instead, about communist subversion of seemingly shaky Western European governments. It did not seem far-fetched to imagine communism coming to power in the west by peaceful, legal means. Communist parties in France and Italy had numerous adherents and enjoyed the prestige of association with the great European conqueror of Nazi Germany. Communists took part in national governments in both countries in the immediate aftermath of the war.[39]

Support for the Marshall Plan arose from the conviction that the American grants could improve the desperate economic conditions that prevailed on the continent and in that way reduce the communist threat there. This tactic was preferable to what might well ultimately present itself as the alternative if the United States did not act: the costs of increased military preparedness,[40] with the possibility of going to war in Europe for the third time in three decades. The Truman administration recommended the Plan as a measure in the spirit of off-shore balancing, designed to thwart a would-be continental hegemon without having to deploy American troops for this purpose. In 1947 and 1948 the American government succeeded in persuading the American public of the plausibility of such a scenario. The American officials who did the persuading were themselves brought to this point of view by the political events, in Europe and elsewhere, that followed the end of World War II.

The Origins of the Cold War

The transformation of the Soviet Union, in American eyes, from an ally to an adversary resembled the outbreak of the Revolutionary War in the eighteenth century and the advent of the Civil War nine decades later. It came about through a series of events that revealed and aggravated fundamental differences and built on and reinforced one another to create first concern, then hostility, and finally genuine fear. American officials, and the American public, came to see Stalin's communist version of the centuries-old Russian empire as similar to Hitler's Germany: a brutal dictatorship bent on dominating Europe and extending its malign influence as far beyond the continent as possible.

The wartime meetings of the Allied leaders at Yalta and Potsdam had settled some of the questions about the organization of the postwar world but a great deal still remained to be decided when the war ended. A series of conferences for this purpose bringing together the relevant foreign ministers, including a Soviet representative, took place—six in all between 1945 and 1947 with one more in each of the years 1948 and 1949. While they produced agreement on several matters, these meetings did not resolve some major issues, notably the status of Germany, and became increasingly confrontational.[41] Meanwhile, three declarations within a month in 1946 exposed the widening rift between the Soviet government and the democracies.

On February 9, Stalin gave a well-publicized speech at the Bolshoi Theater in Moscow in which he restated the basic Marxist-Leninist precept that capitalism inevitably foments war, from which it followed that communism and capitalism were irreconcilably opposed to one another.[42] On March 5 in Fulton, Missouri, Winston Churchill, now

the head of the political opposition in Great Britain but still an authoritative, indeed heroic figure in the United States by virtue of his
wartime leadership of America's British ally, gave a public address, with
President Truman in attendance, in which he noted that the European
continent had become sharply divided. An "iron curtain" imposed by
the Soviet Union to seal off the countries its troops had occupied, he
said, had descended across it. Together the two speeches made it clear
that the cooperation among the members of the anti-Nazi coalition,
which Franklin Roosevelt had hoped would last beyond the war, had
come to an end.

Between the two speeches, on February 22, George F. Kennan, a
Russian specialist in the American embassy in Moscow, dispatched
to his superiors in Washington a 5,326-word telegram, the longest in
the history of the State Department, analyzing the present and future of the Soviet-American relationship. On the basis of his close ac-
quaintance with the Soviet Union, Kennan had never believed in the
possibility of harmonious relations with Moscow once Germany and
Japan had been defeated, and his message explained why. The Marxist-
Leninist ideology of the Soviet leaders, he said, made them irremedi-
ably hostile to the West; they would devote their considerable resources
to enhancing their own power and weakening that of the democracies,
whom they regarded as inevitably and eternally their enemies.[†] The
Long Telegram, as it came to be called, circulated in the upper echelons
of the American government and had a powerful impact: it crystallized
concerns about Stalin and his colleagues that had become widespread
and offered a plausible explanation for their words and deeds since the
war's end.[43]

Kennan's ideas reached a wider audience when presented in an article, published anonymously, under the byline "X," in July 1947 in

---

[†] In the telegram Kennan wrote, "We have here a political force committed fa-
natically to the belief that with US there can be no permanent modus vivendi,
that it is desirable and necessary that the internal harmony of our society be
disrupted, our traditional way of life be destroyed, the international authority
of our state be broken, if Soviet power is to be secure." Quoted in John Lewis
Gaddis, *George F. Kennan: An American Life*, New York: The Penguin Press, 2011,
pp. 220–221.

the journal *Foreign Affairs*, the most prestigious American publication devoted to foreign policy. Although not based directly on it, the article echoed some of the themes of his 1946 dispatch. It included the word "containment" to describe the appropriate Western goal in dealing with the Soviet Union,[44] which became the standard term for the policy of seeking to limit Soviet power and influence that the United States carried out for more than four decades thereafter.

Also in 1946, two episodes on Europe's periphery reinforced the American perception of the Soviet Union as an aggressive, expansionist power. In 1942, the Soviet and British governments had agreed to a joint occupation of Iran—in the northern and southern parts of the country, respectively—to keep Nazi Germany from gaining a foothold there. They had also agreed to leave Iran when the war ended, but the Soviet Union refused to do so. Instead, it organized a secessionist movement on the territory that it occupied, in order to separate that part of Iran from the rest of the country and ensure Soviet domination there. The Iranian government protested, the American government supported the Iranians at the United Nations, and the Soviet Union withdrew from the country.[45]

In August 1946, Moscow demanded joint control over the Turkish Straits, waterways that connect the Black Sea to the Mediterranean and the Aegean, the sole control of which the Montreux Convention of 1936 had vested in Turkey. Here, too, the country most directly affected, Turkey, protested; the United States supported the Turks and dispatched the Sixth Fleet to the Mediterranean; and the Soviets ultimately backed down.[46] The two episodes followed a course that seemed ominous to American officials. In both cases the Soviet Union had sought to enhance its power and territorial control at the expense of a weaker neighbor, which bespoke, Americans feared, a general disposition to expand wherever possible. In both cases American firmness had helped to stop Soviet expansion.

Finally, in the year after the war ended, atomic energy became an issue of contention between the two wartime allies. After the atomic attacks on Hiroshima and Nagasaki in August 1945, the American government, cognizant of the extraordinary danger posed by the successful harnessing for military purposes of the energy at the heart of matter, devised a scheme for reducing that danger by putting all aspects of atomic energy, from the mining of uranium to the fabrication of weapons, under international control. A committee cochaired by then–under secretary of state Dean Acheson and David Lilienthal, the chairman of the Tennessee Valley Authority, produced a report for accomplishing this that President Truman asked the financier Bernard Baruch to present to the United Nations. To the report Baruch added compulsory sanctions for any country that violated the terms of what became known as the Baruch Plan.

The Soviet Union rejected it, offering in its place a proposal that mandated the destruction of existing atomic weapons (which only the United States then had) that effectively gave national governments control over atomic matters.[47] Moreover, Moscow was already working on making atomic bombs of its own, and on September 23, 1949, the American government announced that it had detected a Soviet atomic explosion. Even as the Baruch Plan was being presented, therefore, the competition to develop and refine nuclear weaponry—the nuclear arms race—had begun.

Events in the year 1947 set the Cold War firmly in place at the center of American foreign policy, confirming the American perception of the Soviet Union, which had come into focus since the end of the war, as a serious, aggressive rival. The most influential of these events, from the American point of view, took place in the Eastern European countries that Soviet forces had occupied on their way to Berlin. Through subversion, persecution, and violence, full-fledged communist governments, in which communist parties completely loyal to Moscow wielded all power, were installed in Bulgaria, Romania, Poland, and Hungary.[48]

The political trajectories in these countries followed a common pattern. Immediately after the war, "popular front" governments were established, which included noncommunists. In each, however, the Soviet Union had the ultimate power by virtue of its troops on the ground. Communists controlled the interior ministries and the police and Soviet "advisors" were everywhere.[49] Still, other noncommunist political parties not beholden to Moscow were able to take part in national politics and serve in the government.[50] Relatively free elections were held, in which the local communist parties invariably fared poorly.[51] In 1947, Stalin decided to abandon any pretense of democratic politics in Eastern Europe. He ordered the eviction of noncommunists from the political systems there and the imposition of regimes that replicated the one he had constructed in the socialist motherland.[52]

Whether he had intended to foist full-scale communism on these countries all along or decided to do so only as events unfolded is not entirely clear.[53] What is clear in retrospect is that the creation of a reliably friendly, not to say subservient, buffer zone between the western border of the Soviet Union and western Germany[54] had the highest priority for the Soviet leader—and not surprisingly in view of the devastating German invasions Russia had suffered in 1914 and again in 1941.

It also became clear, in the months following the end of World War II in Europe, that the more political independence an Eastern European country had, the less responsive to Soviet wishes it would be.[55] In Poland, especially, the long decades of Russian rule in its eastern part, which spanned the nineteenth century, the Bolshevik assault on the newly reconstituted country in 1920, Stalin's cooperation with Nazi Germany in partitioning it in 1939 and 1940, and the Soviet decision to allow the Nazis to crush the Warsaw uprising in 1944 together had created a strong current of anti-Russian sentiment in Polish society. An acceptably docile Poland would have to be a communist Poland: Soviet strategic requirements and ideological inclinations coincided.[56] Imposing communism on Poland, Stalin is supposed to have remarked, would be like putting a saddle on a cow. He did it all the same. After World War II, the great land-based empires of Europe had disintegrated; but the extinction of noncommunist political forces in the four Eastern European countries in 1947, and the even more brutal repetition of that process the next year in Czechoslovakia[57]—ironically, the one country in the region in which the Soviet Union enjoyed some popularity—returned imperial rule, in the form of Soviet-imposed communism, to the European continent.

Whatever the combination of motives that lay behind Stalin's decision to reshape the countries of Eastern Europe in this way, it made a powerfully negative impression on Americans, and on Western Europeans as well. It violated promises that the Soviet leader had made about the region's future at Yalta, promises that many Americans had unwisely believed.[58] The subjugation of these countries dissolved whatever trust they had in Stalin. Even more importantly, it instilled in them the belief that the Soviet goal in Europe was the expansion, as far as possible, of its own power, influence, and control, a belief for which the revival of the prewar Comintern, an agency dedicated to spreading communism throughout the world (now renamed the Cominform), seemed to provide further evidence.[59] What Stalin had done in and to Eastern Europe, Americans concluded, he would, if not checked, do in and to Western Europe as well.[60]

That idea contributed to the passage of the National Security Act in 1947. By creating a cabinet-level secretary of defense, making permanent the wartime institution of the Joint Chiefs of Staff, establishing the National Security Council, and founding the Central Intelligence Agency, it effectively reorganized the federal government for the struggle with the Soviet Union. The solidifying of a national consensus in favor of confronting Stalin and international communism also prompted two major American initiatives in Europe in 1947 for the purpose of resisting the Soviet campaign of expansion. The second of these was the Marshall Plan. The first was the Truman Doctrine.

In 1947 a civil war was raging in Greece. Forces loyal to the pro-Western monarch were fighting, with British help, an insurgency in which communists were prominent. In March the British government, under severe financial pressure despite the American loan of the year before, informed the United States that it could no longer afford to keep British troops in the country.[61]

The Truman administration concluded that without British support the Greek government might fall and the insurgents take power, which would advance the communist cause in Europe, to the strategic disadvantage of the anti-communist forces on the continent and of the United States. The administration resolved to step into the breach by providing $400 million in aid to both Greece and Turkey. Coming as it did before the Marshall Plan, this program confronted the Congress, for the first time, with the need to decide whether to approve a large package of foreign assistance.

The administration anticipated that securing approval would not be easy and mounted a lobbying campaign that foreshadowed the one for the European Recovery Program later that year. It offered two notable arguments in favor of the program it was proposing. Dean Acheson, then the under secretary of state, deployed what would later come to be called the "domino theory"—the contention that a setback in one place would start a chain reaction of communist gains elsewhere. In 1954 then-president Dwight Eisenhower used the vivid image of a row of falling dominoes to describe the adverse consequences for the rest of Asia of the loss of Vietnam to communists.[‡] Acheson, in a private meeting with members of Congress in 1947, employed the metaphor of infection: "[L]ike apples in a barrel infected by a rotten one, the corruption of Greece would infect Iran and all the East" and perhaps spread even farther.[62]

The idea that one political defeat for the United States and its allies would likely lead to others by encouraging communist aggression, and weakening the ability and the will of the target countries to resist it, called to mind the series of events in the 1930s in which Nazi Germany overturned the post–World War I Paris peace settlement step by step, until the democracies felt compelled to go to war but had to fight from a weaker position than if they had acted earlier. The American government acted on this way of thinking about geopolitics more than once during the Cold War.

President Truman spoke on behalf of aid to Greece to a joint session of Congress on March 12, and he cast the conflict with the Soviet Union in the starkest and most ideological terms he had yet used. "At the present moment in world history," he said, "nearly every nation must choose between alternative ways of life." "One way of life," he argued,

is based upon the will of the majority and is distinguished by free institutions, representative government, free elections, guarantees of individual liberty, freedom of speech and religion, and freedom from political oppression. The second way of life is based upon the will of a minority forcibly imposed upon the majority. It relies upon terror and oppression, a controlled press and radio, fixed elections and the suppression of personal freedoms.[63]

[‡] ". . . [Y]ou have broader considerations that might follow what you would call the 'falling domino' principle. You have a row of dominoes set up, you knock over the first one, and what will happen to the last one is the certainty that it will go over very quickly. So you could have a beginning of a disintegration that would have the most profound influences." Quoted in Odd Arne Westad, *The Cold War: A World History*, New York: Basic Books, 2017, p. 151.

The stakes in the rivalry with the Soviet Union and its ruling ideology, the president implied, went far beyond those of the great-power conflicts of the past. Communism posed a mortal threat to liberty, the founding political value of the United States. America had to act accordingly. Truman told the Congress that "I believe that it must be the policy of the United States to support free peoples who are resisting attempted subjugation by armed minorities or by outside pressures."[64] The last ten words plainly referred to communists and the Soviet Union.

The policy that he proposed came to be known as "the Truman Doctrine." The term suggested not simply a program tailored to a specific situation but rather a broad approach to foreign policy around the world; and so it proved to be. The first such program of economic and military assistance the United States furnished during the Cold War, the aid to Greece and Turkey that Congress passed in May 1947 by wide margins,[65] was far from the last.

The aid to Greece inaugurated another significant feature of the post-1945 foreign policy of the United States: the replacement of British with American power in places from which Great Britain felt compelled, often by its economic circumstances, to retreat. In 1945, for example, responsibility for keeping order in the Middle East belonged to Britain and its Empire. A quarter-century later the Empire was gone from the region and so, for all intents and purposes, were the British. In political and military terms, the United States had replaced them: in a world of two and only two major powers, the American government felt pressure to fill geopolitical vacuums everywhere.

While the United States sent military and economic assistance to Greece, it did not send American troops: it was the Greeks who did the fighting, and by 1949 those whom the United States supported had won the civil war.[66] The Truman Doctrine, as formulated in 1947, thus remained faithful to the familiar policy of offshore balancing.

The newspaper columnist Walter Lippmann offered a criticism of the Truman Doctrine of a kind that would recur, in different circumstances, throughout the Cold War. He did not take issue with the general policy of opposing communism in Europe but considered the policy, as Truman had framed it, too broad. It was all too likely, he wrote, to make excessive demands on American resources by involving the country in propping up weak and embattled governments around the world.[67]

Cold War foreign policy, like American foreign policy historically, provoked dissent and opposition, which was almost always similar to Lippmann's critique. Whereas opponents of the Revolutionary, the Civil, the Mexican, and the Spanish-American Wars had generally believed that the United States should not be waging them at all, the domestic opposition to American initiatives after 1945 generally found fault with their scope or cost, not their major goals. This was true of most of the opposition to the wars in Korea and Vietnam.[68]

Principled rejection of the basic direction of Cold War foreign policy turned out to be rare and politically ineffective. It reached its zenith early on, in 1948, when Henry Wallace—Franklin Roosevelt's secretary of agriculture, and then vice president and, when Harry Truman replaced him on the Democratic ticket in 1944, secretary of commerce—offered himself as an independent candidate for the presidency. American communists played a prominent role in his campaign and he advocated a warmer relationship with the Soviet Union than the one the Truman administration was conducting. He lost decisively,[69] and no major political figure ever again embraced a pro-Soviet worldview.

After the Truman Doctrine came the Marshall Plan, which the American government put forward for strategic as well as economic reasons. Indeed, the two rationales were connected. The American funds had as their goal the reinvigoration of the Western European economies for the purpose of making those countries better able and more willing to resist the lure and the subversion of communism.[70] The implementation of the Marshall Plan marked a turning point in the political and strategic as well as the economic dimensions of the great postwar contest of systems. While aid to Greece had involved a country of at best marginal interest to Stalin (who was in fact not actively supporting the Greek insurgency),[71] the European Recovery Program bore directly on the fate of his foreign policy's central preoccupation: Germany.[72]

The meetings at Yalta and Potsdam had yielded interim arrangements for that country, dividing it into Soviet, American, British, and French zones of occupation and, in addition, dividing among the four of them the capital city, Berlin, which was located inside the Soviet sector. Under these arrangements, the Soviet Union received reparations from all four zones. The wartime allies made no significant progress toward a final peace treaty thereafter. The German occupation became expensive for the Western powers[73] and they looked for ways to lighten the economic burdens it imposed. In May 1946, General Lucius D. Clay, the American military governor in Germany, suspended reparations deliveries to Moscow from the zone over which he presided, and three months later the British followed suit.[74]

When, the next year, the Americans decided to include Germany in the Marshall Plan, Stalin excluded the Soviet occupation zone from participation. The Western powers responded by instituting a currency reform in their own zones.[75] These measures reversed the initial American inclination to punish the Germans in favor of a policy of reviving the country economically and including it—at least its western part—in Western institutions.[76]

On March 5, 1948, the three Western allies announced their intention to coordinate economic policies between the "bizone" that the consolidation of the British and American parts of the country had created at the beginning of 1947 and the French zone, as well as plans to create a federal government for these territories.[77] The division of Germany, which none of the wartime leaders had seriously contemplated at their 1945 conferences, was on the verge of becoming a reality.

Stalin found the prospect of a German state firmly integrated into an American-sponsored capitalist economic bloc in Europe deeply threatening.[78] In an effort to prevent this, on June 26, 1948, Soviet forces blocked all Western communication by land with the western sectors of Berlin, making it clear that abandoning the plans for western Germany and returning to the status quo before that day was the price of ending the blockade.[79] The Truman administration regarded the Berlin blockade as a challenge to the American position not only in Berlin but also in all of Europe.[80] Failure to protect and preserve the Western foothold inside communist eastern Germany would, the American government believed, dishearten the leaders and the people of Western Europe, which would negate what Washington hoped would be the political and psychological impact of the Marshall Plan. The Americans therefore resolved to circumvent the blockade and sustain the western part of Berlin by air.

They succeeded. The Berlin blockade evoked one of America's greatest strengths, which had proved crucial in World War II: its mastery of logistics. A total of 278,000 Western flights over eleven months brought food, fuel, and other necessities to West Berlin.[81] On the night of May 11, 1949, the Soviet Union lifted the siege.

Establishing a pattern that would persist throughout the Soviet-American conflict, during the blockade neither side fired directly on the other. The Cold War remained cold. The United States and Great Britain charted a middle course, between accepting the loss of their rights in Berlin and taking active military measures to preserve them. Without having to resort to the tactics routinely employed in similar circumstances in the past, the United States and its allies prevailed. West Berlin continued to be a Western outpost and the plans for establishing a west German state went forward, culminating in the proclamation of the German Federal Republic in May 1949. In the Soviet zone the same year, the German Democratic Republic, like the other countries of Eastern European states a political and economic replica of the Soviet Union, came into existence.

The course of events in Germany gave the leaders of Western Europe an interest in a reliable military connection to the United States. The Berlin blockade had raised the possibility that war would once again break out on the continent. While the two dominant powers did manage to avoid shooting at each other, the danger of war was present throughout. In addition, although West Germany was being welcomed into the Western political and economic community, given the history of its relations with neighboring countries, those neighbors wished to have some insurance against the revival of an aggressive German foreign policy.

For that second purpose Great Britain and France made common cause in the Dunkirk Treaty of 1947. Belgium, the Netherlands, and Luxembourg joined them in an expanded version in 1948. They persuaded the United States to take part, which produced the North Atlantic Treaty, signed in Washington on April 4, 1949, a year and a day after Harry Truman had signed the legislation authorizing the Marshall Plan.[82] It had a threefold purpose, as its first secretary-general, the British general Hastings Ismay, succinctly put it: to "keep the Americans in, the Russians out, and the Germans down."[83]

With the consummation of the North Atlantic Treaty, France finally received what it had sought but failed to gain three decades earlier, in the immediate aftermath of World War I: an Anglo-American security guarantee.[84] By the Treaty's terms the United States promised to do, if needed, what it had already done twice in the twentieth century, in the two world wars: come to the aid of the democracies of the continent. The Treaty did not, however, commit the Americans to stationing a large army there in advance of hostilities; and Dean Acheson, now at the State Department as the secretary, assured the Senate Foreign Relations Committee that no such deployment was contemplated.[85] Still, with the North Atlantic Treaty the United States embraced a formal, ongoing peacetime role in the security affairs of Europe for the first time.

The creation of a Western military alliance and then, in 1955, of a Soviet-dominated counterpart to the east, the Warsaw Treaty Organization, or Warsaw Pact, gave Europe and the world a solution to one of the great geopolitical conundrums of the modern era, which historians called the German Problem.[86] It stemmed from the inability of that country, after its unification under the aegis of Prussia in 1871, to find a role on the continent acceptable both to itself and to its neighbors. In the seventy-five years between 1870 and 1945 it produced three destructive conflicts—the Franco-Prussian War and the two world wars. The division of Germany and its occupation by two more powerful countries—in geographic terms one of them, the Soviet Union, only partly European and the other, the United States, not European at all—rendered the German nation incapable of launching another military bid for continental primacy.

West Germany also became positively unwilling to do any such thing, indeed entirely uninterested in the kind of project of conquest its predecessors had undertaken. The Western alliance to which it belonged endured longer than the transient coalitions of the past and developed far-reaching cooperation and unprecedented trust among its members, such that armed conflict between or among any of them, including a resolutely peaceful German Federal Republic, became unthinkable. The alliance that the North Atlantic Treaty created in 1949 turned into something that political scientists came to call a "security community."

As a voluntary association of democracies, this security community differed as sharply from the Warsaw Treaty Organization, which was in effect an imperial domain, as the Western free-market economies differed from the centrally planned economic systems of the Soviet bloc. The combination of the security and economic orders on each side constituted two radically different systems, the contest between which defined the forty-five years of international history after World War II.

The second half of the 1940s, the most consequential decade in the history of American foreign policy, proved to be as eventful as the first and brought comparably momentous changes. At the decade's end, the conflict with the Soviet Union had become the lodestar of the foreign relations of the United States. It was a conflict of both power and ideology, which drew on the foreign policy traditions represented and articulated by both Theodore Roosevelt and Woodrow Wilson. On the European continent, America was opposing both Soviet power and communist political and economic ideas and practices.

Could things have been different? Could the conflict have proceeded in more limited fashion, or even been avoided entirely? Historians and pundits began to address that question even before it ended and some sought to revise the reigning Western orthodoxy by taking issue with the American government's account, in which the Cold War arose from an understandable, indeed necessary, Western response to actual and potential Soviet aggression. This version of Cold War revisionism holds that the United States bears the responsibility for starting an unnecessary conflict, with its motive for doing so usually attributed to a drive for economic expansion.[87]

A different revisionist account assigns significant responsibility for what happened after World War II to what political scientists call the "spiral model," in which conflict arises from interacting misperceptions.[88] An initiative by one party—an individual, a country, or a coalition—undertaken for defensive purposes seems to another party to be aggressive. The second party reciprocates, and again, what is intended to be defensive is interpreted as aggressive. Such measures build on each other to create a spiral of hostility and a conflict where none would have existed with more accurate perceptions on both sides.

Of such a syndrome in the Cold War, particularly at its beginning, there is some evidence. In no small part because of the secrecy of the Soviet political system and the ingrained habit of mendacity on the part of its leaders, the United States did partly misread Soviet policies.

Unlike Hitler, Stalin had no firm plan for conquering all of Europe (or even Greece),[89] nor any internal timetable for doing so; and he was anxious to avoid war with the United States, at least a war involving the direct engagement of Soviet forces.[90] Stalin had his own misperceptions. A prisoner of Marxism-Leninism's understanding of the dynamics of world politics, he wrongly believed that the capitalist countries would sooner or later go to war with one another; but that mistake was just as likely to restrain as to promote Soviet aggression, on the grounds that communists had only to wait and their enemies would tear themselves apart. According to the interpretation of the events immediately after 1945 as a spiral of misunderstanding leading to mutual mistrust and fear, the United States need not, and should not, have reacted to what it saw as the Soviet threat as strongly as it did.[91]

What, if any, different results different American policies between 1945 and 1949 would have produced cannot, of course, be known.[§] In retrospect, however, especially given the deep and abiding differences between them, conflict of some sort between the democracies and the Soviet Union, and probably conflict along the lines on which it actually developed, seems all but inevitable. For one thing, World War II left a vacuum of power in the western part of Europe. If the United States had not stepped in, the Soviet Union, the only remaining continental great power, would have filled it in some fashion. Soviet influence, and especially the installation of communist political and economic systems all the way to the Atlantic, would have negated the achievements—the preservation of a European balance of power and the safeguarding of democracy there—that the United States had just gained in a bloody, expensive war.

[§] It has also been suggested that different personnel would have carried out different policies: specifically, that had Franklin Roosevelt lived to complete his fourth presidential term, relations with the Soviet Union would have been friendlier. Had he lived, however, Roosevelt would have seen his hopes for the continuation of wartime cooperation disappointed, in which case he might have adopted policies similar to those his successor carried out. Benn Steil, *The Marshall Plan: Dawn of the Cold War*, New York: Simon & Schuster, 2018, p. 9. Indeed, shortly before he died Roosevelt said, "We can't do business with Stalin. He has broken every one of the promises he made at Yalta." *Ibid.*, p. 4.

Moreover, the United States and the Soviet Union not only had radically different political values, and not only had constructed radically different political and economic orders on the basis of those values, but each also regarded its own system as universally valid and that of the other as illegitimate. Each side regarded its own creed as either destined to spread all over the world, as in the Soviet case, or worthy of spreading, as the Americans viewed theirs.

Finally, the origins of the Cold War cannot be understood without reference to the beliefs and habits of the person who dominated Soviet policy in those years.[92] As an orthodox Marxist-Leninist, Stalin had no concept of long-term peace, let alone cooperation, with the noncommunist world, nor did he repose any trust in the good faith of its leaders. In his worldview, conflict with the Soviet Union's implacable capitalist enemies might be postponed but it could not be avoided altogether.[93]

Although Stalin was capable of acting cautiously, indeed prudently, in the international arena, his basic approach to international affairs was aggressive. He made it his goal to expand Soviet power and influence whenever and wherever he could do so at acceptable cost: thus his 1946 initiatives in Iran and the Turkish Straits. When the United States resisted, he pulled back. Without resistance, however, there is good reason to believe that he would likely have proceeded.[**] Had Western Europe remained weak, vulnerable, and unprotected he would surely have found ways to expand the Soviet presence and Soviet influence there, if not Soviet control; and for Stalin, in pursuing his goals both at home and abroad the favored tactic was violence.

Yet another reason to doubt that the post–World War II contest of systems could have been avoided, or even substantially modified, is that the existence of such a conflict did not depend on the particular set of

[**] Stalin authorized the North Korean assault on South Korea, believing that it would not meet effective resistance, and with the caveat that Soviet troops would not intervene if the invasion foundered. See p. 272. Maxim Litvinov, a onetime Soviet foreign minister, told an American journalist in 1946 that if the West gave in to Soviet demands "it would lead to the West being faced, after a more or less short time, with the next series of demands." Quoted in David Holloway, *Stalin and the Bomb: The Soviet Union and Atomic Energy, 1939–1956*, New Haven, Connecticut: Yale University Press, 1994, p. 167.

circumstances that prevailed in Europe in 1945. By 1950, East Asia had also become a region divided between the two camps.

The Division of Asia

As before and during World War II, in that war's wake the United States followed a "Europe-first" policy. The American government devoted most of its attention to events on the European continent: Asia had a lower priority. In 1945, much of it remained at least nominally under European imperial control, putting it beyond the reach of potential American responsibility or, despite a long-standing objection to European empires, serious American interest. Moreover, enough was happening in Europe to consume most of whatever attention and resources Americans, focused on returning to a peacetime national life, had to spare for foreign countries.

Japan was the major exception to this pattern. The United States occupied it and, despite Great Britain's participation in the war against Japan and the last-minute Soviet entry, occupied it alone. Ultimately, Japan would follow the same course in American foreign policy and global affairs as the other major adversary of World War II, Germany. It would become a peaceful democracy, a loyal American ally, an economic, commercial, and financial leader in its region, and the eastern pillar of the Western political and economic system. In the forty-year contest of systems that the United States waged with the Soviet Union, Japan, like Germany, proved to be a considerable Western asset.

The year 1945 was "Year Zero" in Japan as well as in Europe.[94] Much of the country lay in ruins, having suffered severe and extensive destruction, virtually all of it inflicted by the United States.[95] The Japanese received their conquerors with remarkably peaceful acceptance, in stark contrast to the ferocity with which they had waged war. General Douglas MacArthur, whom President Truman appointed to be the military governor of occupied Japan, landed virtually unprotected at Yokohama in September 1945 and rode safely past 30,000 Japanese troops.[96]

MacArthur exercised far-reaching, almost unchallenged power.[97] He used that power to implement a sweeping program of reform that, in important ways, remade the country.[98] Of all the American efforts at nation-building, the one in Japan enjoyed perhaps the greatest success—although that success was possible only because the Japanese themselves embraced, adopted, and preserved the changes that MacArthur introduced.[99]

Prominent among those changes was extensive land reform, which gave Japan a large cadre of small agricultural proprietors.[100] He also presided over the installation of functioning parliamentary government, for which the Japanese emperor cleared the way by renouncing his previous status as a divinity and becoming, like the monarchs of Europe, the head of a constitutional state. MacArthur also gave Japan an American-written constitution, which included an article renouncing war.[101] In a variety of ways the American authorities elevated the status of Japanese women.[102]

The beginning of the Cold War in Europe shifted American policy in Japan. In 1947 MacArthur and the occupation authorities executed what came to be known as the "reverse course": the emphasis of the occupation changed from political reform to economic revival, as the American government began to see Japan as an Asian bulwark against communism.[103]

The Japanese economy recovered from its wartime devastation, resuming its prewar status as the largest and most dynamic in Asia. The United States made a major contribution to this recovery by opening its markets to Japanese goods, and Japan became one of the world's great trading states. The countries of Southeast Asia also became important destinations first for Japanese exports and then for Japanese capital, as well as sources of raw materials for Japan's industries: much of what the country had gone to war to achieve in the 1940s it gained peacefully in the 1950s under the aegis of American military power and political influence. A postwar version of the Greater East Asia Co-Prosperity Sphere came into being without a shot being fired or a Japanese soldier setting foot outside the home islands.[104]

Japan's impact on economic life in Asia went beyond its exports of goods and capital. The economic success it achieved—eventually building the second-largest economy (after that of the United States) in the world—through free markets, selective government intervention, and an emphasis on exports, made its economy a model for other Asian countries.[105] For them, as for Japan, that model brought rapid economic growth in the postwar decades. So Japan not only anchored but also extended the Western system, at least in economic terms, to the Asia-Pacific region. The *contest* of systems, however, arrived in Asia in China.

America's China policy in 1945 continued Franklin Roosevelt's wartime vision of the country as one of the world's "Four Policeman," serving as a stabilizing presence in East Asia.[106] Despite their frustration with Chiang Kai-shek's unwillingness or inability to fight effectively against Japan, American officials assumed that he would continue to lead China. Stalin was also willing to accept Chiang's leadership, having obtained at Yalta, in return for his promise ultimately to attack Japan, extensive concessions in that country for the Soviet Union: effective control of Outer Mongolia, the western province of Xinjiang, and Manchuria, as well as naval bases at Port Arthur and Dairen. Chiang, who was not present at Yalta, was not consulted on these concessions.[107]

He faced serious opposition within China from Mao Tse-tung's communists. The Civil War between the two sides had paused during the Japanese occupation but resumed in 1946.[108] The Truman administration supported Chiang's Kuomintang (KMT) but, hoping to end the fighting, dispatched George Marshall, who had stepped down as chief of staff of the army but whom the president had not yet appointed secretary of state, to mediate between the two sides. The Marshall Mission followed the tradition of American policy in Asia of trying to secure American interests at low cost through diplomacy. Unlike John Hay's Open Door notes and Theodore Roosevelt's successful effort to broker a settlement between Japan and Russia after their 1905 war, however, Marshall's undertaking failed.[109] The gap between the two sides proved too wide to bridge. Neither trusted the other. Both sought control of the entire country and were willing to fight to secure it. The war continued.

Chiang held the military advantage initially, but overextended his forces and suffered a serious setback in Manchuria. His army and his government began to unravel, as soldiers defected or surrendered in large numbers[110] and Chinese civilians switched their allegiance to the communists. Mao's army gained the upper hand and Chiang and his government fled to the island of Taiwan, 100 miles off the southeast coast of the mainland. On October 1, 1949, in Peking, Mao proclaimed the founding of the People's Republic of China.[111]

In August 1949, as Chiang's defeat became imminent, with an eye toward deflecting domestic criticisms that the Truman administration had "lost China," the State Department issued a White Paper that gave as the principal reasons for the communist victory the military and political shortcomings of Chiang Kai-shek's government:[112] it had suffered from massive corruption, had exercised poor military judgment, and had presided over rampant inflation, thereby losing support in urban China.

In addition to the military and political flaws in the KMT that the White Paper listed, the communists benefited from the perception in China—not, in retrospect, entirely justified by the facts[113]—that they had resisted the hated Japanese more consistently and forcefully than had Chiang's government. While communist ideology scorned nationalism as a bourgeois distraction from the true interests of the working class, the Chinese communists managed, during the Civil War and afterward, to mobilize on their own behalf nationalist sentiment,[114] which surpassed in popularity among the Chinese population fidelity to the principles of Marxism-Leninism-Maoism. Not for the last time, the United States found itself on the wrong side of nationalism, to its considerable disadvantage. Finally, but not least important, the Chinese communists received crucial military assistance from the Soviet Union, without which they almost certainly would not have been able to win the Civil War.[115]

Unhappy with Mao's victory, the American government nonetheless initially believed that it could establish businesslike, perhaps even cordial relations with the new Chinese regime. American diplomats had made contact with the communists during the war and some had come away favorably impressed, taking them to be "agrarian reformers" rather than hard-core Stalinists. The State Department foresaw strains in the new regime's relations with Moscow and perhaps even a split between the two communist governments, something that did in fact occur but not until more than a decade after the consolidation of Maoist rule. Contrary to American hopes, Mao and his colleagues proved to be dedicated Marxist-Leninists, faithful to its political and economic principles and loyal to Stalin.[116] They acknowledged the Soviet dictator

as the leader of the global communist movement, with which they en-
thusiastically identified. Mao traveled to Moscow at the end of 1949—
his only trip outside China—and, in February 1950, signed a Treaty of
"Friendship, Alliance, and Mutual Assistance" with the Soviet Union.

Thus, at the end of the momentous decade of the 1940s, East Asia,
like Europe, was divided: between Japanese democratic and Chinese
communist rule as well as between a Japanese version of free markets
and an incipient Chinese variant of central planning and state control
of industry and agriculture. In the five-year period after World War
II, American policy in the region had reversed itself: at the beginning
supporting China and opposing Japan, at the end closely tied to Japan
and alienated from the new Chinese government.

China itself was divided, with the Communists ensconced in power
on the mainland but the KMT in control of Taiwan and claiming
to be the rightful government of the entire country, a claim that the
American government was not prepared to enforce.[117] The United States
had not anticipated these new circumstances and did not welcome the
state of affairs in China. Still, the Truman administration did not feel
the need to devote a major share of its attention, let alone significant resources, to Asia, which had a lower priority for American foreign policy
than did Europe.[118] Asia was divided but not actively contested. That
changed when war broke out on the Korean peninsula.

The Korean War

A peninsula abutting China (with an eleven-mile-long border with
Russia as well) and jutting out into the Yellow Sea to the west and the
Sea of Japan to the east, Korea, in the mid-twentieth century, had had
nearly 1,300 years of cultural distinctiveness and political unity. With
a vulnerable location—within striking distance not only of China and
Russia but also of Japan—the country had suffered an estimated 900
invasions over two millennia, and five major periods of foreign occupation, the most recent of them the Japanese overlordship from 1905 to
1945.[119]

With the Japanese defeat, the United States and the Soviet Union
moved troops into the country and divided their respective zones at the
thirty-eighth parallel. In 1948 a communist regime came into existence

in the Soviet-controlled north, led by Kim Il-sung, a loyal acolyte of Stalin. In that same year, a month earlier, in the south a noncommunist government assumed power, with the pro-Western Syngman Rhee at its head.[120] Each aspired to reunify the peninsula under his own rule, and violent skirmishes between the two sides repeatedly erupted, accounting for an estimated 30,000 to 100,000 Korean deaths.[121]

Kim wanted to launch a full-scale attack, with the goal of conquering the south, but as a good communist he would not do so without permission from the leader of world communism, Joseph Stalin. Stalin rejected Kim's request several times but in the first half of 1950 he changed his mind. Mao's victory in China contributed to this change because it provided North Korea with another important local ally.[122] Accordingly, on June 25, 1950, Kim sent large numbers of troops across the border with the South.

Until that moment the American government had displayed an ambivalent attitude toward Korea. It had initially hoped to reunify the peninsula, but as the Cold War gained momentum in Europe that goal seemed increasingly unrealistic.[123] It did not entirely abandon Rhee but neither was it willing, before June 25, to direct resources on any scale to him.[124] In 1949 American troops had left the peninsula and in January 1950 Secretary of State Acheson made a speech delineating the American security perimeter in Asia that conspicuously omitted the Korean peninsula.[125]

Yet President Truman responded to the North Korean attack by dispatching American troops to the peninsula to oppose it. The administration also went to the United Nations and secured a resolution condemning the attack, which passed because the Soviet Union did not veto it, being absent from the Security Council in protest against the failure of Mao's new government to obtain China's seat there. The United States therefore fought in Korea, along with fifteen other countries, with the official imprimatur of the UN.[126] Finally, Truman ordered the American Seventh Fleet into the Taiwan Strait, between the Chinese mainland and Taiwan, thereby preventing Mao from launching the attack he was planning with the aim of bringing the island under communist control.[127] As so often in American history, domestic political considerations came into play here. One reason for interposing maritime power between the two parties to the Chinese

Civil War was to win the approval of Chiang's American supporters, who came to be known, collectively, in the 1950s as "the China lobby" and who had criticized the administration for failing to prevent his defeat on the mainland.[128]

Given Washington's previous lack of interest in Korea, the swift decision to intervene came as a surprise. It could not reasonably have been predicted beforehand, although Stalin did provide for contingencies unfavorable to the communist cause by telling Kim that if the invasion went badly, North Korea could not count on Soviet troops to come to its rescue.[129] In this way the American intervention set a precedent. On several other occasions during the Cold War—in 1962 in the Cuban missile crisis, for instance, with the Soviet invasion of Afghanistan in 1979, and in the case of Saddam Hussein's 1991 attack on Kuwait as well—adversaries of the United States underestimated the American response to an initiative that they undertook. They evidently found American politics and the American decision-making process difficult to read; and one reason for that was the fact that the democratic character of American foreign policy, with its many sources of influence and in particular the powerful impact of the country's sometimes-volatile public opinion, did in fact make it difficult to anticipate. The North Korean attack turned out to be yet another in the series of catalytic moments in the nation's history that galvanized the American public and the American government, producing a sense of imminent and serious threat that triggered an unexpectedly vigorous response.

That response, and American participation in what began as a Korean civil war, had several causes. It was an Asian version of the communist challenge to Western interests and Western values that had emerged in Europe. As such, it counted as another episode in the Cold War, which by 1950 dominated the foreign policy of the United States. The Truman administration in fact feared at first that the Korean operation was merely the opening salvo of a global communist military campaign. That proved not to be the case; the war remained confined to the Korean peninsula. Even so, it seemed to American officials vital not to allow communist aggression to go unchecked lest it ultimately encourage aggression elsewhere, particularly in Europe.

The "domino" analogy that Acheson had employed in urging aid to Greece three years earlier affected his and his colleagues' Korean policy as well.[130] That particular framework resonated with them because it accorded with their interpretation of the events leading up to World War II; and the North Korean assault seemed to reprise what Hitler had done to provoke that war.[††] The communists in Korea, like the Nazis in Europe, had committed a textbook act of aggression, sending troops across an international border.[131] Subversion in Korea rather than a direct attack might not have evoked the same American response.

The war unfolded in four distinct stages,[132] with first one side and then the other gaining what seemed to be a decisive advantage, only to have the opposing side recover its position. A year of this pattern gave way to a two-year stalemate before the fighting finally ended in late July 1953.

In the initial stage, the North Korean forces swept down the peninsula, captured the southern capital, Seoul, and pushed South Korea's defenders back into a pocket at Pusan, on the southeastern edge of the country.[133] Then the Americans counterattacked. Led by Douglas MacArthur, whom Truman had appointed commander in chief of the allied forces, in the tradition of Veracruz in the Mexican War and Normandy in World War II it mounted a daring amphibious landing at Inchon on the west coast, 150 miles behind the North Korean front line. This inaugurated the war's second phase. The troops that landed at Inchon combined with those that broke out of the pocket at Pusan to trap and destroy a large part of the communist army. The American forces regained Seoul, crossed the thirty-eighth parallel in early October, and advanced through North Korea, approaching the Yalu River, the Korean border with China. The Truman administration adopted as a war aim the reunification of Korea under the government of the South.[134]

[††] Truman said in retrospect that he had thought, when he learned of the North Korean attack, that "Communism was acting in Korea just as Hitler, Mussolini, and the Japanese had acted ten, fifteen, and twenty years earlier. . . . If this was allowed to go unchallenged it would mean a third world war, just as similar incidents had brought on a second world war." Quoted in Ernest R. May, *"Lessons" of the Past: The Use and Misuse of History in American Foreign Policy*, New York: Oxford University Press, 1976. First published, 1973, pp. 81–82.

Then came the war's third stage, which began on November 25, 1950, with the People's Republic of China sending more than 200,000 troops, which Peking claimed were "volunteers," across the Yalu.[135] Stalin had put pressure on Mao to intervene to save the North Korean regime. The Chinese leadership had hesitated but then decided on intervention, out of communist loyalty, to be sure, but also because Mao believed that a victorious United States would pose a threat to his rule.[136] China's attack caught MacArthur and the government in Washington by surprise and sent the American forces retreating back down the peninsula.

That led to the war's fourth stage, in which the American army regrouped and recovered the territory south of the thirty-eighth parallel that it had lost. General Matthew Ridgway, who had served with distinction in World War II and to whom MacArthur gave wide latitude in directing the operations of the Eighth Army, devised tactics employing American firepower and aerial supremacy that took a heavy toll on the Chinese. The administration decided not to try to retake North Korea but instead simply to defend the South. General MacArthur publicly objected to this decision[137] and Truman relieved him of his command on April 11, 1951, thereby asserting the principle of civilian control of the military that went back to the Revolutionary War and the founding of the American republic.

The war ended when, and, on the communist side because, the two superpowers acquired new political leadership. Having been unexpectedly re-elected in 1948, Harry Truman declined to run for president again in 1952 and Dwight Eisenhower, now a civilian and the nominee of the Republican Party, won the election, promising to bring the war to a conclusion. On the communist side, on March 5, 1953, Stalin died. He had resisted ending the war[138] since it was bleeding the Americans at little cost to the Soviet Union.[139] His successors saw things differently,[140] and on July 27, 1953, at Panmunjon, an armistice, but not a formal peace treaty—which the ensuing six decades failed to produce—went into effect. It divided the two parts of Korea roughly, but not exactly, along the thirty-eighth parallel. A total of 33,686 Americans lost their lives in the Korean War and 103,284 were wounded. An estimated 183,000 Chinese died. By far the most numerous victims of the war were the Koreans themselves. Their toll of killed, wounded, and missing—north and south, civilian and military—is estimated to have approached three million people, almost ten percent of the prewar population.[141]

In the decades after it ended, the conflict in Korea came to be called "the forgotten war."[142] The epic experience of World War II, and the War in Vietnam of the 1960s and 1970s, which lasted longer and had wider domestic ramifications than the Korean conflict, overshadowed it in the public mind. Forgotten it may have been, but insignificant the Korean War certainly was not. Only the impact of the Second World War had a greater effect on the foreign policy of the United States. It also had significant domestic consequences for the United States.

In the matter of control over foreign policy, the Constitution, according to a popular interpretation, furnishes "an invitation to struggle" to the executive and legislative branches of the federal government.[143] The Korean War tilted that struggle decisively toward the executive. The United States fought it without a formal Congressional declaration of war. Harry Truman sent troops to the peninsula without waiting for Congressional authorization. He did so because, with North Korean forces surging southward, time was of the essence: any delay might have meant the loss of the entire country. Even after the Americans had arrived, however, the administration declined to ask the Congress to go on record in favor of the military operations it was conducting. It asserted that the Constitution vested in the president, as commander in chief, sufficient power to wage the war without formal Congressional approval,[144] an interpretation that previous administrations had not embraced.

For the next four decades, Truman's successors frequently sent troops into action abroad without such approval, including, on a large scale and for the better part of a decade, in Indochina. It was as if the Cold War was a single long conflict, participation in which the country had approved. Its various episodes in which the United States used force were simply battles in that larger conflict, over the conduct of which the commander in chief had wide discretion. Only when the Cold War had effectively ended, with the Persian Gulf War in 1990 and 1991, did a chief executive secure an affirmative endorsement from the legislature before unleashing American military power. In Korea, in a backhanded tribute to the now-discarded practice of submitting a request for such an initiative to the legislative branch, the administration described what the United States was doing not as a war but rather as a "police action."

Like other American wars, this one generated dissent. It took the form not of explicit protests but of the conflict's growing public unpopularity as measured in public opinion polls, as the fighting dragged on and as casualties mounted without a conclusive result. Ultimately, nearly half the country considered the war to have been a mistake.[145] The public found fault not with the anticommunist American goal in Korea but rather with the cost of trying to achieve it, above all the cost in American casualties.[146]

This general pattern repeated itself in the Vietnam War and also in the second Gulf War, which took place in the first decade of the twenty-first century.[147] In the Korean War, as in the subsequent ones, the administration and the chief executive presiding over the increasingly unpopular war suffered politically. Their approval ratings in opinion polls declined. Harry Truman decided not to run for re-election and the candidate of the opposing party succeeded him.

Also as in previous conflicts, the Korean War had a negative impact on liberty in the United States. A series of developments had created a climate of anxiety before June 25, 1950: the Soviet atomic test, the fall of China to communists, and the discovery of Soviet spies working in the American government.[148] The war in Korea aggravated this public mood. Even before it broke out, Joseph McCarthy, a Republican senator from Wisconsin, caused a sensation by claiming to have lists of subversives active on behalf of global communism, a contention that subsequent investigations did not bear out. As a result, people who belonged to the American Communist Party, which was legal at the time, or suspected of membership or of disloyalty to the United States in other forms, came under public scrutiny. Tests of loyalty became fashionable. Several thousand people lost their jobs.[149]

McCarthyism, as this episode in American national life came to be called,[150] hardly compared, for savagery and the human damage caused, to the show trials and liquidation of prominent communists that Stalin ordered in Eastern Europe at the same time; but, like the Alien and Sedition Acts of the 1790s, Lincoln's suspension of habeas corpus during the Civil War, and the interning of Japanese-Americans during World War II, it did mark a departure from the normal national fidelity to the country's founding value, individual liberty.

The Korean War had even more far-reaching consequences for American foreign policy than for the domestic life of the United States. Only the impact of the Second World War compares with its effects on the nation's foreign relations, and it affected other countries as well. It had a pronounced impact, for example, on Japan, from which the allied armed forces fighting in Korea obtained many of their supplies. This gave the Japanese economy a formidable boost,[151] similar to the impact of the Marshall Plan on Western Europe. Before the war, the American government had begun negotiations for a peace treaty with Japan, which was signed by forty-nine countries in San Francisco on September 8, 1951. At the same time, the United States concluded a security treaty with Japan, which became the most important American ally in Asia for the duration of the Cold War and beyond.[152]

It was not, however, the only one. The United States also made security arrangements with Australia and New Zealand, South Korea, the Philippines, and Taiwan.[153] An American-sponsored security order with the same goal as the one in Europe—the containment of communism—came into existence in the wake, and in no small part because, of the outbreak of fighting in Korea. It differed from the European order in that it did not involve a single, multilateral security system like the one for which the 1949 North Atlantic Treaty formed the basis. Nor, with the exception of South Korea, did American troops stand guard in any country on the Asian mainland, as they came to do in Europe after the outbreak of the Korean War. Instead, the Asian design resembled a hub and spokes, with the United States at the center as the common partner in a series of bilateral accords with other countries.

The bilateral pact with Taiwan set the seal on the American estrangement from the Communist government in China that the Chinese intervention in Korea had created, which was to last for two decades. That pact effectively guaranteed Taiwan's independence under Chiang Kai-shek's Kuomintang, which the government in Peking did not accept and vowed to eliminate through the "reunification" of the island with the mainland.

What at first seemed an important consequence of the Korean War turned out to be ephemeral. The United Nations resolution authorizing resistance to the North Korean attack did not mark the beginning of a major role for that organization in keeping the peace and enforcing international law. Instead, the Cold War blocked such a role, since both the United States and the Soviet Union could veto any measure that either opposed. After Korea, and for the duration of the superpower conflict, the UN had only a marginal impact on international affairs, serving mainly as a forum in which representatives of the two opposing superpowers could denounce each other.

As an actual shooting war, Korea made the contest of systems a military as well as a political and economic one in a way that it had not been before June 25, 1950. In April of that year the National Security Council had produced a document, NSC-68, that recommended a substantial increase in defense spending.[154] Truman had shelved it, but with the outbreak of war, military spending did rise sharply, quadrupling between the fiscal years 1949 and 1953. In 1950 defense expenditures represented five percent of the national gross national product and thirty-three percent of federal spending. By 1953 those figures were twelve and sixty percent, respectively.[155]

During the Cold War, the defense budget became a barometer of the American perception of the state of international affairs. When international circumstances seemed more threatening, and not only during actual wars involving the United States,[156] defense spending increased. When the proportion of the federal budget devoted to defense declined, this signified that Americans felt more comfortable about their country's international position.

The increased defense spending that the Korean War triggered did not all go to that country, or to Asia. Some of it went to Europe, to which Truman ordered the dispatch of four divisions of American soldiers. The Atlantic Alliance changed from a guarantee pact—as a promise to send troops to Europe if and when circumstances warranted it—to an integrated military force deployed on the continent. The North Atlantic Treaty became the North Atlantic Treaty Organization (NATO),[157] and in December 1950, President Truman appointed Dwight Eisenhower its first supreme commander.[158]

Finally, Korea set a precedent for the American conduct of war. In World War II, and in the other landmark war the country had waged, the Civil War, the United States had sought, and achieved, the adversary's unconditional surrender. Korea, by contrast, proved to be a "limited war."[159] Despite the Truman administration's initial fears, unlike in World War II the fighting remained restricted to the country where it began. Nor did American and Soviet armed forces engage each other directly, at least not on any appreciable scale or in a way that either country acknowledged.[160]

The United States waged the war for limited ends. The administration abandoned the aim of conquering all of Korea, considering the expense of doing so, if it could be done at all, to be prohibitive.[161] It settled for preserving a noncommunist South Korea. In Korea, as in the Berlin blockade, the American government adopted a middle course, eschewing both all-out war to reunify the peninsula and no war at all, which would have abandoned South Korea to communist rule.

The United States also limited the means it employed to fight in Korea. It did not make use of its most powerful armament against North Korea or China. The tradition of the nonuse of nuclear weapons began with the Korean War. At several points during the conflict nuclear use seemed possible. At a press conference on November 30, 1950, a reporter asked President Truman whether this was under active consideration. Truman replied, "Always has been. It is one of our weapons."[162] His comment caused an uproar. The British prime minister, Clement Attlee, rushed to Washington to remonstrate with him. In the end Truman did not authorize any nuclear attack, for several reasons. By early 1951, the American forces had regained lost territory and stabilized the front, making liberal use of non-nuclear air strikes, so the atomic bomb did not seem militarily necessary. The global consequences of dropping such bombs in Korea were unforeseeable; they might conceivably have included the spread of the fighting to Europe, something the United States strongly wished to avoid. Not least important, the destructive power that such armaments had demonstrated at Hiroshima and Nagasaki in August 1945 endowed them with an aura of horror. This created a presumption against their use, sometimes called the nuclear taboo, which became a major cause of the decades-long tradition of not using them.[163]

When the Korean War ended in 1953, the framework within which American foreign policy would operate during the Cold War was in place. The war both reinforced it and illustrated the three significant ways in which the Soviet-American rivalry differed from the great-power conflicts of the past. First, the Korean conflict, like the Cold War as a whole, played out in the shadow of armaments that had the potential, if employed on a large scale, to destroy each of the two major rivals and much else besides. Second, the Korean War demonstrated that the Cold War was a global rivalry in the sense that each side felt compelled to vie with the other for power and influence everywhere. That logic propelled the United States into Korea, a place with little economic or strategic importance other than the fact that the West confronted communism there. Third and finally, the outcome of the Korean War, and the history of the Korean peninsula thereafter, were in keeping with the Cold War's status as a contest of systems. North and South Korea adopted two antithetical ways of organizing eco-nomic and political activity, indeed two distinct and opposed ways of life that the Soviet Union and the United States each embodied and represented. The contest was particularly sharp in countries divided be-tween the two systems and, as a result of the war there, Korea became one of them.

It was these three differences that gave the United States and the Soviet Union an international standing beyond that of the great powers of history. World War II had made them superpowers, the Korean War confirmed that status, and as such they jockeyed for advantage, and more often to avoid disadvantage, for the next three decades.

8

War Improbable, Peace Impossible, 1953–1979

Learning to Live with the Bomb

The Truman administration presided over the origins of the Cold War and for a quarter century after it left office, the structure of that conflict remained intact. For the United States those twenty-five years were, to borrow a phrase from another context, "crowded with incident":[1] wars in which America took direct or indirect part; near wars with the Soviet Union known as crises; high-stakes diplomacy; and economic upheavals. Some of these episodes were politically traumatic; some seemed at the time to bring extreme peril; some looked likely to restructure the international hierarchy.

These twenty-five years qualify as the most event-filled such period in the history of American foreign policy. Yet by its end, nothing fundamental had changed. The two superpowers continued to tower above all other countries in military might and political influence, not least because of their growing stockpiles of the most powerful weapons ever invented. The two continued to compete for primacy all over the world, with their rivalry even extending into outer space. The radically different political and economic systems that they had organized, in the case of the United States, or imposed, as the Soviet Union had done, persisted, most notably in a divided Europe.

Each side's coalition expanded between the end of the Truman administration and the end of the 1970s. Cuba, Indochina, and parts of Africa joined the communist camp; three southern European countries—Spain, Portugal, and Greece—discarded dictatorial (although not communist) governments, adopted democracy, and integrated their economies with those of the free-market democracies of Western Europe.[2] These additions, however, had little effect on the global geopolitical balance.

In 1953 Dwight Eisenhower, who had led the Anglo-American forces in Europe in World War II and was appointed the supreme commander of the North Atlantic Treaty Organization (NATO) in 1951, became the latest victorious American general to win the nation's highest political office, following in the footsteps of George Washington, Andrew Jackson, William Henry Harrison, Zachary Taylor, and Ulysses S. Grant.[3] Uniquely among American presidents, he owed his initial election almost exclusively to his credentials in foreign affairs. His Republican presidency ratified the innovations in public policy of his two immediate Democratic predecessors. He accepted the major domestic programs of Franklin Roosevelt's New Deal[4] and, in contrast to the preferences of his chief rival for the Republican presidential nomination in 1952, Senator Robert Taft of Ohio, he adopted the approach to foreign affairs that Harry Truman had initiated, with its full-scale commitment to the global contest with the Soviet Union.

A theme that persisted throughout the Cold War first made its appearance during the Eisenhower years: the impulse if not to end the conflict with the Soviet Union and international communism then at least to modify, limit, or narrow it to make it less dangerous. The impulse had its origins in the extraordinary destructive power that both superpowers wielded.[5] The death in March 1953, shortly after Eisenhower took office, of the person more responsible for the conflict than any other single individual, the Soviet dictator Joseph Stalin, inspired the hope of reducing the hostility between the two superpowers; and his death did in fact pave the way for the end of the Korean War[6] in that year and, in 1955, the signing of a treaty establishing and guaranteeing the neutrality of Austria, a small country in the middle of Europe.[7]

Eisenhower and his Soviet counterpart, Nikita Khrushchev, who consolidated supreme power in Moscow after Stalin's death, met face to face in Geneva in 1955 and again in Washington in 1959. The relatively cordial atmosphere in which both meetings took place raised hopes that some of the pressing disputes of the Cold War could be resolved, but no significant agreements emerged. The two leaders were scheduled to meet again in Paris in 1960, but two weeks beforehand a Soviet surface-to-air missile shot down an American U-2 spy plane overflying Soviet territory and the incident torpedoed the meeting.[8]

Meanwhile, the Eisenhower administration and its successors had to grapple with the questions of how, and for what purposes, to deploy, and to use, the nuclear weapons that the United States had possessed since 1945. These were questions for which military history supplied, at best, an incomplete basis for answering. No other country had ever had at its disposal weaponry remotely as powerful. Weapons serve, or ought to serve, political purposes; and at its outset the Eisenhower administration made an important start on devising a nuclear strategy by deciding on the principal political purpose of its relations with its communist adversary.

During the 1952 presidential campaign, and for their first few months in office, Eisenhower and his colleagues had declared their intention to take the offensive against communism in Europe and to liberate the countries of Eastern Europe from communist political control.[9] Because such an effort ran a very high risk of beginning a third world war, the administration abandoned the goal, settling instead for the defensive aim that its predecessor had adopted: the containment of communist power and influence. The term that came to denote the military component of containment was deterrence, which means prevention by threat.[10] The concept goes back at least to ancient Rome, which had an adage, "si vis pacem bellum para"—if you wish for peace, prepare for war.[11] American nuclear weapons became instruments of deterrence— that is, of preventing war. The American government spent the decade after the end of the Korean War working out how to achieve this goal.

The Eisenhower administration's military strategy, known as the New Look, envisioned deterring communist aggression through what the secretary of state, John Foster Dulles, in a speech in New York City on January 12, 1954, called "the capacity for massive retaliatory power," which the United States would be prepared to unleash "instantly, by means and at places of our own choosing."[12] The massive retaliation on the threat of which deterrence was to rest, the administration made clear, included, potentially, the use of nuclear weapons. The communist side would not know where or when the United States would undertake such a punishing military operation but it would know that such a spasm of violence was always possible. That knowledge, the American government hoped, would deter many forms of aggression around the world.[13]

The new deterrence doctrine incorporated the lesson the administration had learned from recent history: the need to avoid fighting the kind of costly, frustrating, limited war that the United States had waged in Korea. The threat of massive retaliation was designed to discourage the communist world from instigating such conflicts by raising the possibility of a catastrophic reprisal. It was also designed to save money. Relying on nuclear weapons reduced dependence on the far more expensive non-nuclear "conventional" forces—tanks, planes, ships, and especially the costliest component of all, military manpower.[14]

The dangers, as Eisenhower saw them, of excessive military spending concerned him more than they did any of his successors in the presidency. He considered balanced budgets to be not only a staple of good government but also an ingredient of American strength in the international arena. His best-known speech remains his Farewell Address to the nation of January 17, 1961, in which he warned of the creation of what he called a "military-industrial complex"—an informal alliance of the armed forces and the country's defense industries that, he feared, might use its influence to give undue weight to military considerations in American foreign policy and promote excessive spending on defense.

In the years following the proclamation of the strategy of deterrence through the threat of massive retaliation, a series of technological developments combined to call its effectiveness into question. Where the bombs that struck Hiroshima and Nagasaki drew their explosive power from nuclear fission—the splitting apart of the elements at the heart of matter—in 1954 the United States successfully tested a device that made use of the process of fusing those elements together. This fusion, or "hydrogen," bomb had a thousand times more power than the original "atomic" versions. Moreover, such explosives turned out to be relatively inexpensive to produce. Ultimately, America came to have tens of thousands of them, each capable of devastating a large city.[15] The decade of the 1950s also saw the development of the ballistic missile, which could deliver nuclear explosives to more distant targets more quickly and more reliably than airplanes could.

These innovations seemed to undercut the Eisenhower strategy because, although generally lagging a few years behind the United States in the development of the relevant technologies, the Soviet Union, too, was acquiring fission and fusion bombs in large numbers and preparing to mount them for delivery on ballistic missiles of intercontinental range. The possession of these technologies gave Moscow something of enormous strategic value that it had not previously had: the capacity to strike, with nuclear weapons, the continental United States.

An unanticipated and, to Americans, troubling display of Soviet technical prowess announced this imminent military reality: on October 4, 1957, the Soviet Union sent into space the first Earth-orbiting satellite, known as Sputnik. Its launch proved to be another of those events that, throughout American history, have galvanized the public by making the nation's circumstances seem suddenly more threatening, requiring a change of direction in national policy. Sputnik not only made clear North America's vulnerability, in the not-distant future, to a Soviet attack but also raised the alarming possibility that, in militarily crucial fields of science and technology, America's Cold War adversary had taken a dangerous lead.

Sputnik did not cause the United States to go to war, but it did prompt an increase in defense spending as well as a greater national emphasis on education, research, and development in the basic and applied sciences and in engineering.[16] More urgently, the imminent Soviet capacity to strike the American homeland posed two strategic challenges that the threat of massive retaliation did not seem capable, by itself, of meeting: the challenge of deterring a surprise attack and the challenge of preventing a non-nuclear attack on Western Europe by communist forces, which became known as the problem of extended deterrence.

The advent of ballistic missiles created the theoretical possibility that one side could destroy the nuclear weapons of the other with surprise attack, leaving the victim of the attack at an immense strategic disadvantage. An article entitled "The Delicate Balance of Terror," published in the January 1958 issue of *Foreign Affairs*, the journal in which George Kennan's 1947 "X" article had appeared, suggested that the American long-range striking force was in danger of becoming vulnerable in this way.[17]

Being privy to the findings of American intelligence, Eisenhower knew that the Soviet Union did not have a nuclear advantage over the United States. In fact, the opposite was the case: America had, at the end of the 1950s, many more long-range missiles and aircraft.[18] Still, it was clear that successful deterrence required ensuring that a nuclear force could survive the most powerful attack an adversary could mount against it with enough nuclear firepower intact to inflict so much retaliatory damage on the attacker that such an attack became unthinkable. Successful deterrence required, that is, the assurance of being able to visit vast destruction on an adversary in any and all circumstances. "Assured destruction" became the term for what effective deterrence required.[19]

First the United States and then the Soviet Union achieved the capacity for assured destruction in two ways: they acquired a large number of weapons. The more each side had, the less likely it was that either could destroy all of them in a surprise attack. Thus it became less likely that the other would believe it could destroy all of them in this way and therefore be tempted to try to do so. The competitive accumulation of nuclear weapons—the nuclear arms race—in which the United States and the Soviet Union engaged during the Cold War often came in for criticism as irrational, or dangerous, or both. In fact, large numbers of weapons promoted the survivability of their retaliatory forces and so reinforced the nuclear truce between the two superpowers.

The two sides also diversified their nuclear arsenals to make them more survivable. The United States ultimately deployed a "triad" of vehicles carrying nuclear explosives and capable of reaching Soviet territory: land-based intercontinental-range ballistic missiles, submarines carrying such missiles that were practically undetectable when on patrol under the oceans, and long-range nuclear-armed bomber aircraft, some of which were aloft at all times.[20] The Soviet Union matched the American nuclear arsenal and so the property of assured destruction became mutual. The condition of mutual assured destruction gave rise to an appropriately grim acronym for the new basis for nuclear stability: MAD.*

---

* Mutual assured destruction embodied a kind of strategic reversal: in the age-old contest between the offense and the defense in military affairs, nuclear weapons,

The Soviet capacity for striking North America produced a second major strategic challenge, at the heart of which lay the issue of credibility. It was widely accepted that a country would be willing to retaliate for an attack on its own territory with an attack—including the use of nuclear weapons—on the country that had launched the assault. The invulnerable American nuclear force would therefore deter a Soviet attack on American territory. But the United States also had responsibility for deterring a communist assault on its NATO allies in Western Europe; and an American response to such an assault had the potential to trigger a Soviet nuclear salvo against the United States itself. Under these circumstances, was American deterrence credible? Would, that is, the Soviet leaders believe that their American counterparts would run the risk of the destruction of their own homeland in order to protect countries thousands of miles away?[21]

The problem seemed all the more difficult because the troops and tanks of the Warsaw Pact outnumbered those that NATO fielded. If the communist side mounted a non-nuclear attack in Germany it might overrun Western defenses, presenting the American president with a choice between seeing his democratic allies conquered from the east or taking steps that could lead to unprecedented, almost unthinkable damage to his own country. This was a choice between humiliation and holocaust.[22] Credible, and therefore effective, American deterrence in Europe seemed to depend on finding a third option.

One alternative was for the European allies to acquire nuclear weapons of their own, which they could credibly threaten to use against the Soviet Union in the event of a Soviet attack. Great Britain conducted a successful nuclear test in 1952 and France became a nuclear power in the same way in 1960.[†] The logic that justified British

---

because of their extraordinary destructive power, gave a decisive advantage to the offense. When the world's two nuclear superpowers both acquired formidable, survivable nuclear arsenals, however, neither dared to attack the other, leading to the supremacy of the defense.

[†] The French had political as well as strategic motives for getting nuclear weapons. Becoming a nuclear-weapon state was part of their efforts to enhance their country's international standing and independence. See Tony Judt, *Postwar: A History of Europe Since 1945*, New York: The Penguin Press, 2005,

and French nuclear arms also supported an independent nuclear force for the Federal Republic of Germany. In the 1950s the Germans seemed interested in acquiring one, and the American government seemed disposed to permit this, perhaps even to assist it. The Soviet Union made clear its adamant opposition to such a development, however, making German nuclear weapons a potential source of dangerous instability in Europe. The American government devised what it hoped would be an acceptable compromise. The Multilateral Force that it proposed involved surface ships and submarines carrying nuclear weapons and manned by multinational crews, including Germans and Americans. In the mid-1960s, however, the scheme fell through.[23]

The United States came to favor a different way of making deterrence in Europe credible: by deploying military forces that could check a Warsaw Pact attack at all levels of violence, including non-nuclear assaults, thereby precluding the need to resort to the use of nuclear weapons in a European war. This strategy, which the Americans called "flexible response," required building up NATO's conventional forces to match those of its communist adversaries. America's European allies accepted flexible response in principle but declined to field the non-nuclear forces necessary to put it into practice. They did not wish to spend more money on defense; they resisted the larger German army that the strategy entailed; and they feared that implementing flexible response would increase the chances of a war in Europe, albeit a non-nuclear

pp. 290–291; Frederic Bozo, "France, 'Gaullism,' and the Cold War," in Melvyn Leffler and Odd Arne Westad, editors, *The Cambridge History of the Cold War, Volume II: Crises and Détente*, Cambridge, UK: Cambridge University Press, 2010; and Stanley Hoffmann, "De Gaulle's Foreign Policy: The Stage and the Play, the Power and the Glory," in Hoffmann, *Decline or Renewal? France Since the 1930s*, New York: The Viking Press, 1974, pp. 297–300. The French "force de frappe" did not have the same assurance of surviving a Soviet attack as the American arsenal did, nor could it do as much damage to the Soviet Union as could its American counterpart. French nuclear strategy assumed that the threat to do some damage—to "tear an arm off the bear"—would suffice for effective deterrence. The assumption that a small number of nuclear weapons were adequate for deterrence, which China shared with France after both tested nuclear explosives, became known as "existential deterrence," meaning that the mere existence of a handful of these weapons had a substantial deterrent effect.

one. They had already fought two such wars in the twentieth century and did not want to take any steps that might risk a third.[24]

German nuclear weapons and flexible response having been ruled out, the American government came to rely, for deterring a Soviet-led attack in Europe, on two measures designed to "couple" its military forces to Western Europe in Soviet eyes: repeated declarations, at the highest political levels, that the United States was committed to defending its allies in any and all circumstances, and the stationing, at the height of the Cold War, of more than 400,000 American troops on the continent both to defend it in case of attack and to enhance the credibility of the national commitment to doing so.[25] These measures worked, at least in the sense that no Soviet attack in Europe ever took place.

The policies designed to achieve deterrence on the continent had an important and unexpected consequence: they kept a large American army in Europe for the duration of the Cold War. The United States had not intended to maintain a major peacetime military presence there. Indeed, Dwight Eisenhower had anticipated its removal. It remained in place because it turned out to be integral to the strategy of protecting Western Europe on which the United States and NATO, in no small part by default, ultimately settled.[26]

While deterring the Soviet Union became and remained the country's paramount military goal during the Cold War, the American government had to address the possibility that deterrence would fail and that it would have to wage a war involving nuclear armaments. It would then confront the task of preventing such a conflict from causing catastrophic damage. It explored several approaches, none of which proved satisfactory.[27]

The United States deployed many short-range "tactical" nuclear weapons in Europe, but in the simulations of a conflict employing them that the American Defense Department conducted, the damage inflicted did not remain acceptably limited. Some officials proposed the idea of conducting a nuclear exchange with the Soviet Union that would avoid heavily populated areas, but there was no way to ensure that during such a war each side would, or could, avoid attacking the other's cities. The federal government recommended that American civilians build and stock bomb shelters in which they could ride out a nuclear attack, but the idea aroused controversy and the shelters that were built proved costly and seemed unlikely to provide much protection for the majority of Americans.

To the question of how to wage a nuclear war, therefore, the United States found no acceptable answer. This led to the conclusion that avoiding such a war was the overriding imperative of the nuclear age, with the corollary that the best way to avoid a nuclear war was to avoid a war of any kind in which the superpowers fought each other directly. The Soviet as well as the American leaders reached this conclusion.[28] Nonetheless, in the early 1960s, first in Berlin and then in Cuba, the two countries came close, or so it seemed at the time, to engaging in just such a direct conflict.[29]

John F. Kennedy, who succeeded Dwight Eisenhower as president, bore the ultimate responsibility for American policy during the two crises. At age forty-three the youngest man ever elected president, he came to office regarding the global competition with the Soviet Union as more urgent, and the American position in that contest more precarious, than any other Cold War chief executive. Shortly after his inauguration he delivered an unprecedented State of the Union address[30] in which he told the Congress and the country that "the tide of events has been running out and time has not been our friend" and that "the news will be worse before it gets better."[31]

As a leader, Nikita Khrushchev, his Soviet counterpart, displayed an unusual combination of qualities. He was a reformer, who presided over a relaxation of the harsh repression that Stalin had imposed. Khrushchev was also a true believer in Marxism-Leninism, convinced that that ideology held the key to human fulfillment and was destined to replace capitalism everywhere.[32] Stalin's successor was, finally, a risk-taker, prone to embarking on dangerous initiatives in foreign policy without having fully thought through their potential consequences.[33] This last-mentioned feature of his personality, more than any other single cause, brought about the perilous episodes in Berlin and Cuba.

The Berlin crisis unfolded in two stages, the first of which took place during the Eisenhower administration. West Berlin was the most vulnerable Western position in Europe. Entirely surrounded by the communist German Democratic Republic (GDR), it could not be defended against a determined communist assault except by resort to nuclear weapons, which seemed all too likely to have disastrous consequences. As such, it was a convenient spot to which to apply pressure, as Khrushchev recognized.[34] At the same time, however, the city of Berlin created a vulnerability of a different kind for the Soviet bloc. Free passage between the eastern and western sectors of the city gave East Germans the opportunity to escape to West Germany, and many took it. By the summer of 1961, 2.7 million people had fled communism for the West in this way, a number equal to fifteen percent of the GDR's population in 1950.[35] East German officials told their Soviet counterparts that without closing this hole in its borders their communist state faced collapse.[36]

In 1958, Khrushchev threatened to sign a peace treaty with the GDR, thereby jeopardizing the West's occupation rights in West Berlin, which stemmed from wartime arrangements originally intended to be temporary. The threat implied that following the signing of such a treaty, communist forces would evict the Western powers from the former German capital.[37] Eisenhower said that the United States and its allies would stand firm in Berlin, and Khrushchev rescinded the threat—but only, as it turned out, temporarily.

He renewed it during an acrimonious meeting with Kennedy in Vienna in June 1961.[38] The American president took the threat of a communist takeover of West Berlin with the utmost seriousness. On July 25 he made a televised address to the American people on the subject, one of the most alarming presidential speeches of the Cold War. He reiterated the commitment to stand fast there and announced a substantial increase in American conventional military forces and a partial mobilization of the country's military reserves.[39] Because the center of Germany was the most heavily militarized place on the planet, because American and Soviet forces confronted each other directly there,[40] and because Germany was the most valuable stake in the Cold War, the likelihood of a direct military clash between the superpowers seemed uncomfortably high.

The communist side defused the crisis by building a wall between the two parts of Berlin, cutting off the avenue of escape from East to West Germany.[41] This solved the urgent problem that the leaders of the GDR and their Soviet sponsors faced: the outflow of people stopped. Western leaders, including Kennedy, denounced the measure but took

no steps to undo it. Ugly and unjust though it was, "a wall," the president said, "is better than a war."[42] The two superpowers thus settled
the crisis through a compromise, although they did not officially acknowledge it as such. The Soviet Union reinforced (and perhaps saved)
its East German client; the United States maintained its presence in
West Berlin.

The next year, on the other side of the Atlantic, the two came even
closer to war. The origins of the Cuban missile crisis lie in the conquest of power on that island by Fidel Castro, a young radical nationalist who formed a guerrilla band in the Sierra Maestre Mountains
that succeeded, in 1959, in driving out and replacing the autocratic,
pro-American government of Fulgencio Batista. Castro thereupon
nationalized American-owned firms, accepted support from the Soviet
Union, and announced his commitment to the principles of Marxism-
Leninism. Faced with the establishment of a communist outpost in
the Western Hemisphere, only 103 miles from the coast of Florida—
a clear violation of the Monroe Doctrine, whose spirit still resonated
in the United States more than a century after its proclamation—the
Eisenhower administration recruited and trained a group of Cuban
exiles to overthrow Castro. The Kennedy administration launched an
assault by the group at the Bay of Pigs, on the Cuban coast, in April
1961, which failed miserably, acutely embarrassing the American government.[43] In order to protect the Castro regime from its powerful
and now-hostile northern neighbor, Khrushchev decided to place on
the island ballistic missiles capable of striking targets across much of
the United States.[44] Ultimately, Moscow dispatched to Cuba sixty
medium- and intermediate-range nuclear-capable missiles, along with
42,000 troops to guard them.[45]

When reconnaissance photographs from U-2 spy planes revealed the
presence of Soviet missiles to the American government on October 15,
1962, Kennedy decided that he had to bring about their removal.[46] The
underlying rationale for the decision was the same as the reasoning that
sent American troops to fight in Korea and animated the determination, by three administrations, to stand firm in Berlin:[47] regardless of
their precise strategic value,[48] the successful deployment of the missiles
in its own geographic backyard would deliver a serious setback to the
United States in its global competition with the Soviet Union and

international communism. It would weaken the American position in the world, undercut its allies' confidence in American leadership, and encourage communist aggression around the world. This his administration could not permit.[49]

While Kennedy therefore regarded doing nothing about the missiles as being out of the question, he also rejected the counsel of some of his military advisors to launch an immediate attack on the Soviet installations in Cuba. He chose, instead—not for the first or the last time in the Cold War—a middle course, imposing a naval blockade on Cuba that he coupled with a public demand that the Soviet Union withdraw the missiles. Khrushchev had ordered the missiles installed clandestinely, so he was not expecting the American government to welcome them; but the United States responded more forcefully than he had anticipated.[50] On this occasion, as on others, the leaders of another country underestimated what the United States was prepared to do when provoked.

At several moments during the second week of the two-week crisis a shooting war between the two superpowers seemed distinctly possible, even imminent.[51] A Soviet surface-to-air missile shot down an American U-2 plane over the island, but Kennedy chose not to retaliate. Soviet vessels bound for Cuba encountered American ships enforcing the blockade but opted to turn back rather than attempt to proceed. The American government assembled, in the southeastern United States, a large military force for the purpose of invading the island and Soviet officials in Washington were convinced that such an operation would in fact take place.[52] But it did not.

In the end, Khrushchev chose to comply with the American demand and withdraw the missiles. The outcome of the crisis seemed, at first glance, an unalloyed victory for the United States: its local military superiority combined with the substantial advantage it then enjoyed in long-range nuclear weaponry and its clearly communicated determination to have its way appeared to have inflicted a major defeat on the Soviet Union. In fact, like the Berlin crisis before it, the missile crisis was resolved by a compromise.

In exchange for taking the missiles off the island, the Kennedy administration made two promises to the Soviet government: not to invade Cuba, and to withdraw from Turkey some American medium-range nuclear-tipped missiles deployed there and aimed at the Soviet Union.[53] The administration made these promises secretly, but kept them.[54] As in Berlin, the standoff ended with the precrisis status quo intact, and with each side getting something that it wanted.

No Soviet-American crisis as serious as those over Berlin and Cuba occurred after 1962.[55] However close they came to fighting each other directly on those two occasions, the two superpowers never came as close again. While their rivalry continued, both observed the unwritten rule not to tempt fate by taking steps that might lead to a direct clash between them. In addition, in 1964 Khrushchev was deposed and replaced as the leader of the Soviet Union by Leonid Brezhnev, a far more conservative, risk-averse personality who remained in power until his death in 1982. In the wake of the Cuban missile crisis, therefore, the military dimension of the Cold War achieved a certain stability. The massive firepower each side deployed made a war between them improbable.

A World Split in Three

In the twenty-five years after the end of the Truman administration the political and economic rivalry between the American and Soviet systems, like the military contest between them, continued. As in the military competition, in the contest of systems during this middle period of the Cold War neither side gained a decisive advantage. During these years Europe remained divided between democracy and free-market capitalism in the west and the dictatorship of communist parties and central economic planning in the east.

The rest of the world did not, however, fully conform to Europe's bipolar division. A large number of countries outside Europe, many of them newly created out of what had been European overseas empires, rejected alignment with either superpower. These countries saw themselves as separate from the other two and came to be called, collectively, the Third World. They had two distinctive features: they were poorer, especially in comparison with the United States and its allies, and they had far less disposable military power.

The efforts of the countries that identified themselves as belonging to the Third World to cohere into an effective third force in international

politics largely failed. Nonetheless, these countries did play a significant role in the Cold War—as the arena for the kind of political and
military competition between the superpowers that, it was clear by the
mid-1960s, was not feasible in Europe.

The United States, the countries of Western Europe, and Japan,
when referring to themselves as a collective, called their bloc not the
"First World" but either the West or the "Free World," the latter to em-
phasize the central political value they had in common and that communism suppressed. While the politics and economics of the Western
countries shared a strong family resemblance, they were not identical.
Some, notably the United States and France, had strong presidencies,
while others vested supreme authority in an elected assembly. All, however, remained stable democracies at peace with one another, in stark
contrast to the experiences of many of them in the interwar period and
World War II.

Although all had free-market economies, the "social market" economic systems of Western Europe offered comparatively generous
benefits to their citizens,[56] while Japan practiced a "Confucian" capitalism in which the government played a more intrusive role in allo-
cating capital than was the case in Europe or North America.[57] In the
United States, markets functioned more independently of the government than they did in Europe and Japan.

The West achieved robust economic growth in the 1950s and 1960s,
although it did less well during the 1970s. The United States, the
world's economic leader throughout the twentieth century, recorded
overall annual growth rates of 3.5 percent in the 1950s and 4.2 percent
in the 1960s, falling to a still respectable 3.2 percent in the economically
rockier 1970s.[58]

During this period, for perhaps the first time since the seventeenth
century, the rate of economic growth in Western Europe exceeded that
of North America—4.9 percent in the 1950s and 4.5 percent in the 1960s
before dipping slightly below the American performance in the 1970s
with an annual rate of 3.0 percent.[59] The Western Europeans started
from a lower baseline than the United States, having suffered far more
damage during the war. They also benefited from incorporating new
technologies first developed on the western side of the Atlantic, from
the movement of people on a large scale from rural to urban settings

where they almost always contributed more to economic production,[60] and from the process of economic integration that began with the Schumann Plan and continued with the formation, by the same six countries, of the European Economic Community in 1957. The increase in economic cooperation augmented growth in the western part of the continent[61] as did the revival of the German economy.[62]

In Japan, out of the ruins of World War II came an economic performance as impressive as that of its fellow Axis power, if not more so: a growth rate of 8.8 percent in the 1950s, and 10.5 percent in the 1960s before declining to 4.5 percent in the 1970s.[63] Relying heavily on exports, the bulk of them at first going to the United States, Japan became a manufacturing powerhouse, moving quickly from the production of textiles to automobiles and consumer electronics.[64]

The United States continued to preside over the Western bloc, supplying military protection, capital, and a market for European and Japanese goods.[65] It also organized and led several rounds of multilateral trade negotiations involving its democratic allies as well as other countries, which lowered tariffs, thereby increasing economic growth. Unlike the Soviet Union within the communist bloc, the United States did not impose its political and economic systems in the West and did not insist on selecting or approving national leaders. When disputes arose with other members of the Free World, the American government addressed them through bargaining and compromise, the standard practices within its own democratic political system, rather than with Soviet-style repression.[66]

Its security treaty with Japan aroused opposition in the Japanese public, but the governments of the two countries successfully modified it in 1960.[67] France, under the leadership of Charles de Gaulle, who returned to power in 1958, attempted to chart an independent course in foreign policy, leaving NATO's integrated military command in 1966.[68] Although unhappy with French policy, the American government made no effort to intervene to change it. In general, while the West owed its formation in no small part to American power, its continued existence and, Franco-American political strains notwithstanding, the increasingly close political and economic ties among its members rested on Western values, above all the value that, historically, Americans most esteemed: liberty.

The year 1953 was significant for the communist bloc not for the end of the Truman administration but because of the death of Stalin. His passing had important consequences, but the basic structure of the communist world did not change. The Soviet Union remained its leader and all the countries that composed it had political systems in which the Party wielded unchallenged power and economies in which government planners made the major decisions. Every communist government on the planet had come to power through the use of force; but while it was the Red Army of the Soviet Union that had installed such governments in Eastern Europe, the Chinese and Cuban regimes had taken control of their countries through their own violent efforts and so had the potential for greater independence from Moscow, a potential that the Chinese ultimately exercised.

Like those of the West, the communist economies grew in the 1950s, 1960s, and 1970s. In those decades the Soviet Union recorded growth rates of 5.2 percent, 4.8 percent, and 2.4 percent, respectively. In Eastern Europe the comparable figures were 5.1 percent, 4.3 percent, and 3.8 percent.[69] Less industrialized and more agricultural before World War II than the countries to their west, those under communist rule also benefited from the boost to economic growth that comes from the large-scale movement of people from farm to factory. The eastern economies differed from those of Western Europe, however, in three ways: all the communist countries emphasized heavy industry; all but Poland imposed collective ownership on agriculture rather than permitting the far more productive system of private farming; and all provided their citizens with fewer consumer goods, of worse quality, than were available in the West.[70]

Although imposed by a foreign power, the Eastern European regimes did have at their disposal some sources of popular acceptance, if not enthusiastic support. The war had done a great deal to discredit their previous governments and the new communist dispensation offered opportunities for upward social mobility and presided, at first, over economic growth that was high by historical standards. However, in the decade and a half after Stalin's death three major anti-government uprisings took place in the region, fueled by political brutality and oppressive working conditions as well as nationalist resentment of the dominant influence of the Soviet Union and its ideology.

In June 1953, protests by workers in East Berlin spread across East Germany. The Soviet Union suppressed them using 20,000 troops and 350 tanks.[71] Then, in February 1956, Khrushchev delivered a speech to the Twentieth Congress of the Communist Party of the Soviet Union in Moscow in which he revealed, and denounced, the crimes of his predecessor.[72] Since Stalin had been, until then, the object of godlike veneration by communists everywhere, the address shook the communist world. In June of that year, 100,000 workers in the Polish city of Poznan gathered to demand radical changes and the unrest spread across Poland. In October, Wladyslaw Gomulka, a communist recently released from prison, became the head of the Polish Communist Party and managed to reassure the Soviet leaders, who feared that the country would spin out of control, while calming his fellow Poles.[73]

Similar unrest in Hungary that month went further. Once again, a previously disgraced communist, Imre Nagy, assumed the leadership of the local Communist Party but the demonstrations in Budapest, the national capital, continued and expanded. Soviet troops fired on some of the protesters, leading to street battles with Hungarian civilians. In response, Nagy promised to institute a multiparty democracy,[74] announced the country's withdrawal from the Warsaw Pact, and proclaimed its neutrality. Moscow sent a total of 60,000 soldiers and 1,000 tanks into Hungary and crushed the rebellion.[75] The United States and its European allies denounced the assault on Hungary but took no steps to stop it, making clear that they would not go to war to undo the division of Europe. During the uprising, a media outlet of the American government, Radio Free Europe, broadcast messages that some Hungarians interpreted as suggesting that the United States would come to their rescue.[76]

Twelve years later, in 1968, the communist government of Czechoslovakia embarked on a program of radical reform, which included something unknown in any other communist country: virtually unfettered freedom of public expression.[77] Khrushchev's successor Leonid Brezhnev, and his colleagues in Moscow, found the events of what became known as the "Prague Spring" alarming. They feared that the Czech reforms would spread across their bloc and threaten communist rule.[78] Despite assurances from the Czech leader Alexander Dubcek[79] that his country would remain in the Warsaw Pact, in August

1968 the Soviet Union led an invasion force of 500,000 drawn from five communist countries that deposed Dubcek and restored Soviet-style political orthodoxy in Czechoslovakia. Moscow also proclaimed a duty to intervene to prevent the overthrow of its system wherever it was threatened, an assertion immediately termed the "Brezhnev Doctrine."[80]

The three popular uprisings put down by military interventions demonstrated that, unlike the West, the communist bloc had to be held together by force. In 1956 and 1968 the Warsaw Pact became the only alliance in history to attack its own members rather than its putative adversary.[81] The episodes also showed that the example of the West, with its freedom and prosperity, functioned as a source of instability in the Soviet-dominated countries to the east. Finally, the uprisings in East Germany in 1953, Poland and Hungary in 1956, and Czechoslovakia in 1968 provided evidence that, while the communist bloc could match the West in military might, in the contest of political and economic systems, especially in the matter of political legitimacy, it was doing poorly.

While conceding Soviet domination in Eastern Europe, during the Cold War's middle period the United States took an active interest in the countries of the Third World. Washington did not have to deal with these countries as a single political and economic bloc. Their efforts to create one—at a conference of thirty postcolonial countries in Bandung, Indonesia, in 1955;[82] with the establishment of an official Nonaligned Movement in Belgrade, Yugoslavia, in 1961;[83] and with the unveiling at the United Nations in the early 1970s of a program for a New International Economic Order that attracted the rhetorical support of dozens of UN members[84]—did not succeed. The relevant countries were too diverse, with interests too varied, to act in a unified manner. Instead, Washington saw the Third World as an increasingly important front in the Cold War. In that global contest it was possible to make gains there—or, what loomed larger in American calculations, suffer losses—as it was not at the heart of the conflict, in Europe.

For this reason, successive administrations established political, economic, and military ties with a number of Third World countries, both to broaden the global anti-communist coalition and to prevent those countries from joining the other side. For their part, the governments that the United States befriended often sought access to American arms and money in order to consolidate their power at home and pursue regional interests that had nothing to do with the Cold War. Such was the case, for example, with Pakistan, with which the United States maintained a close relationship for most of the Cold War. The unelected generals who governed the country for most of this period used American resources to entrench their rule and conduct their ongoing conflict with neighboring, and democratic, India.[85]

In an attempt to replicate outside Europe its multilateral European military alliance, the United States organized the Southeast Asia Treaty Organization (SEATO), joining with Australia, France, New Zealand, Pakistan, the Philippines, and Great Britain.[86] America also sponsored, while not officially joining, the Central Treaty Organization (CENTO), also known as the Baghdad Pact, to which Iran, Iraq, Turkey, Pakistan, and Great Britain belonged.[87] Unlike NATO, however, neither played a significant role in the affairs of its region.

Because of the establishment of a Soviet outpost in the Caribbean, America reverted to its approach of the late nineteenth and early twentieth centuries in its Cold War dealings with Latin America. It brought its influence heavily to bear, and in Central America occasionally undertook military interventions,[88] to ensure that governments friendly to the United States held power. Between the early 1950s and the late 1970s such governments often turned out to be military regimes. In 1977, however, Franklin Roosevelt's "Good Neighbor" policy in the Western Hemisphere staged a comeback when the Congress voted to turn over responsibility for operating the Panama Canal to the government of Panama.[89]

To advance American interests in the Third World, the Eisenhower administration made occasional use of the Central Intelligence Agency (CIA), which, in addition to collecting intelligence, also conducted political operations. In 1953 the CIA helped bring about a change of government in Iran.[90] A radical nationalist prime minister, Mohammed Mossadeq, nationalized the Anglo-Iranian Oil Company. In retaliation, the British imposed an economic embargo on the country, sought to remove Mossadeq from office, and persuaded the American government to take part in that effort. The Agency worked with the opposition to the prime minister,[91] which, drawing on popular dissatisfaction with him,[92] managed to drive him from power and restore the pro-American monarch, the Shah, who had previously fled the country.

The next year the CIA played a somewhat more active role in a similar initiative in the Central American country of Guatemala. Another nationalist leader, Jacobo Arbenz, had expropriated uncultivated land, some of which belonged to the American-owned United Fruit Company, which had extensive holdings in the country. Suspecting him of communist tendencies, the American government trained rebel forces that marched into the country, and recruited pilots to fly fighter planes that strafed the capital, Guatemala City. Arbenz resigned.[93]

From these two episodes[94] there emerged an image of the CIA, which had currency in the United States but especially in anti-American circles abroad, as a kind of rapacious octopus, with tentacles reaching into, and controlling, countries throughout the Third World. In fact, the Iranian and Guatemalan coups succeeded because they took place in weak countries with underdeveloped political institutions and were mainly the work of local forces that took advantage of American support. The CIA was not a major instrument of American Cold War foreign policy and had nothing to do with the way the contest of systems finally ended. Nonetheless, it was elevated, in some imaginations, to the status of powerful, secret, global bogeyman.

In October 1956, American policy in the Third World intersected, and came into conflict, with relations with its allies during a crisis over the Suez Canal. Gamal Abdel Nasser, an army colonel and yet another radical nationalist, took power in Egypt in 1952 and in July 1956 ordered the seizure of the British-operated Canal. This infuriated the British prime minister, Anthony Eden, who had been Churchill's wartime foreign secretary. He devised a plan to reverse the seizure and humble Nasser. Joining the British in this project were France, which was aggrieved at Egypt's support for anti-French rebels in Algeria, and Israel, which had suffered repeated Egyptian border attacks after winning its War of Independence against five Arab armies, including an Egyptian one, in 1948 and 1949. In early November, the Israelis attacked Egypt and the British and French proceeded to intervene militarily, with the announced mission of protecting the Canal.

The Eisenhower administration had little affection for Nasser, who had signed an agreement to receive arms from the communist bloc.

The administration had in fact rescinded an offer to help Egypt finance a major dam on the Nile River at Aswan.[95] But the president was also angry at the French and especially the British, who, he believed, had not been fully candid with him about their plans for an invasion. More importantly, in his view that invasion risked turning Arab opinion against the West and so clearing the way for major Soviet gains in the Middle East.[96] The Suez operation was also diverting the world's attention from the ongoing and bloody Soviet repression of the Hungarian uprising, which was injuring the global reputation of the communist bloc, to the advantage of the West.[97]

Accordingly, the American government refused to make up for the loss of oil that the closure of the Canal was costing Great Britain, or to support the British currency, the pound sterling, which came under pressure in international financial markets.[98] Abandoned by the United States, the British were forced to retreat from Suez.[99]

The Suez affair turned out to be a consequential event in world history. It marked the effective end of Great Britain's centuries-long career as a great power by making it clear that the British could no longer undertake major military initiatives independently. Suez marked, as well, a climactic chapter in the history of Anglo-American relations and a final reversal of the two countries' roles. Where once Britain and its empire had towered over the North American colonies and then the infant United States, by 1956 the United States had become the colossus and Great Britain the weaker and often dependent country. Finally, Suez continued the trend, begun in Greece in 1947, of American power replacing that of Great Britain. The global imperatives of the Cold War meant that, with its British ally weakened and in the process of withdrawing from the region, the United States felt that it could not afford to be absent from the Middle East; and two years later, on the basis of a Congressional resolution that designated that part of the world as vital to American interests and came to be known as the Eisenhower Doctrine, the administration dispatched Marines to Lebanon to forestall the possibility of a pro-Soviet regime there.[100]

John F. Kennedy came to office believing the Third World to be the most important arena of Cold War competition. A 1961 Khrushchev speech extolling "wars of national liberation" waged by communist forces against noncommunist regimes made a deep impression on him.[101] He saw communist insurgencies in Third World countries as the leading threat to Western interests and was determined to equip the United States to combat them effectively, in two distinct ways.[102]

Communism had its greatest appeal, he and many others believed, in conditions of poverty. America therefore had to find ways to promote economic growth—the term commonly used was economic development—around the world.[103] The Kennedy administration signaled the importance it placed on doing so by consolidating the foreign aid programs that it had inherited and establishing a separate bureaucracy for them, the Agency for International Development.[104] The administration created, as well, a special agency to assist Latin America, the Alliance for Progress.[105] Perhaps the Kennedy administration's most enduring legacy was the Peace Corps, which sent volunteers—most in their twenties—to provide assistance of various kinds, often the teaching of English, to poor countries.[106] The program exemplified the recurrently ideological character of American foreign policy. It expressed the American commitment to spreading the country's values and institutions beyond its borders. The Peace Corps was the secular equivalent of religious missionaries, spreading far and wide the gospel of Western-style modernity.

Kennedy also believed that coping with Communist-sponsored wars of national liberation required a specialized military approach. Communists had already made use of guerrilla insurgencies to seize control of China and Cuba.[107] On the other hand, an American-supported government had turned back an insurgency in the Philippines and the British had defeated one in Malaya.[108] The president wanted the American military to study these conflicts and incorporate their lessons into its own training. The place where an insurgency posed the most urgent threat to American interests, it was clear during the Kennedy presidency, was Vietnam.

The Vietnam War

The American involvement in Vietnam, which turned into the country's greatest setback in the entire Cold War, began in the aftermath of World War II. Having been evicted from its colonial possessions in Indochina by Japan, France sought to regain them and met armed resistance from a Vietnamese nationalist movement controlled by communists. The Truman administration decided that supporting a European ally and fighting communism took precedence over the historical American opposition to European overseas empires and began to pay some of France's military costs, a policy that the Eisenhower administration continued.[109]

The Vietnamese defeated the French, winning a decisive battle at Dienbienphu in 1954. A peace conference in Geneva in that year produced an agreement to divide the country temporarily along the seventeenth parallel between a communist north and a noncommunist south. National elections, paving the way for reunification, were to take place in 1956. With the encouragement of the United States, the government in South Vietnam refused to take part in these elections and the country remained divided.[110] Shortly thereafter an insurgency against the South Vietnamese government began, with the support of the communist North.[111]

John F. Kennedy inherited, accepted, and deepened the American commitment to South Vietnam, which, he believed, the United States could not afford to lose to communism. When he took office, 1,000 American military personnel were working in the country. At the end of his presidency the number had risen to 16,000.[112]

Because the Vietnam War turned out badly for the United States, a consensus formed even before it ended that in choosing to wage it America had made a mistake. That raises the obvious question of how this could have happened. The answer is straightforward: the United States went to war in Vietnam for the same reason it insisted on remaining in West Berlin and invested lives and treasure in keeping South Korea out of communist hands.[113] It was in reference to Vietnam that Dwight Eisenhower had articulated the "domino" principle, and Kennedy affirmed that he himself considered it to be valid.[114]

While less important than Germany or China, Vietnam mattered, beyond its symbolic significance, as a major country in Southeast Asia, a region on which Japan, the principal American ally, increasingly depended economically.[115] Moreover, Kennedy, remembering the damage the Truman administration and the Democratic Party had suffered from the fall of China to Mao and his forces, was leery of the potentially similar impact of a communist victory in South

Vietnam.[116] The conflict with the insurgency was going badly for the South Vietnamese government in the fall of 1963 when, on November 22, Kennedy was assassinated in Dallas.[‡] His vice president, Lyndon Johnson, succeeded him and had to confront the seemingly imminent prospect of defeat in Southeast Asia.

The parlous circumstances in Southeast Asia with which Johnson had to cope had their roots in the failure of an enterprise that the United States would have occasion to undertake several times during the next half century, and indeed had already attempted without success a century earlier in the post–Civil War South: nation-building.[117] Waging war successfully against the Vietnamese communists required a stable, competent, legitimate South Vietnamese government to oversee that war. The officials in the Southern capital Saigon, despite the economic, military, and technical assistance they had received from the United States, had failed to build such a government in the decade since the French defeat.[118] A series of coups that changed the leadership there five times after 1963 did not help matters.

Given South Vietnam's inability to resist the communist assault with its own military resources, Johnson had an unhappy choice. If he permitted a communist conquest, the blow to the American position in the world to and the credibility of its promises to protect its allies could, he feared, send dominoes toppling around the world, as well as do grievous damage to the political standing of his administration and his Democratic Party at home.[119] On the other hand, an all-out

---

[‡] Just as the death of Franklin Roosevelt led to retrospective speculation that had he lived the relationship between the United States and the Soviet Union would have proceeded differently, so Kennedy's death in office inspired a comparable debate about whether he would have limited, or even ended, the American role in Vietnam had he served a second term. He apparently told the Senate Democratic Majority Leader, Mike Mansfield of Montana, that he planned to do so. Daniel Ellsberg, "The Quagmire Myth and the Stalemate Machine," in Ellsberg, *Papers on the War*, New York: Simon & Schuster, 1972, p. 97. For the argument that Kennedy would have pulled American troops out of Vietnam see Frederik Logevall, *Choosing War: The Last Chance for Peace and the Escalation of the War in Vietnam*, Berkeley, California: University of California Press, 1999, pp. 395–400. For the contrary argument see George C. Herring, *America's Longest War: The United States and Vietnam, 1950–1975*, New York: McGraw-Hill, Second Edition, 1986, p. 106.

military effort to defeat the communists risked bringing China into the conflict,[120] as had happened in Korea, as well as undercutting support in the United States for the president's ambitious agenda of domestic legislation, the "Great Society," which had a higher value for him than any other aspect of his presidency.

Faced with these options, the new president deferred major decisions on the war until after the 1964 presidential election—in which, echoing Woodrow Wilson's 1916 claim that he would keep the United States out of World War I, he promised not to widen the country's participation in Vietnam[121] and was returned to office by a landslide. Then, in 1965, Johnson escalated the American role in Vietnam. In the spring he sent 40,000 combat troops and by the end of that year 184,000 American military personnel had been dispatched. Eventually the total reached almost 500,000.[122] To avoid provoking the Chinese and alarming the American public, he expanded the numbers gradually, which allowed the enemy to adjust to the increasing powerful force it faced;[123] and he ruled out going to the source of the problem by invading North Vietnam.

Lyndon Johnson did not increase the American presence in Indochina with any enthusiasm. No president since James Madison in 1812 had made war more reluctantly or with lower expectations of success. At none of the moments at which Johnson authorized the dispatch of more Americans to Vietnam did he have confidence that the increases would suffice to win the war. He hoped, rather, to avoid defeat. American policy aimed not at victory but rather at stalemate.[124]

The American army that the president sent to Southeast Asia did not consistently fight battles and hold territory as its predecessors had done in Korea and the two world wars. The communist side often tried to avoid direct encounters with American forces and operated clandestinely, including in villages ostensibly under the control of the government of South Vietnam. The United States pursued a strategy of attrition, conducting "search and destroy" missions with the goal of killing or incapacitating enough communist soldiers—regular and guerrilla—to compel the communists to abandon their campaign to conquer South Vietnam.[125] The strategy proved to have two major and related flaws: first, since many of the opposing fighters did not wear uniforms, the Americans could not know how many of those they killed were combatants, so they could not gauge accurately how well their strategy was working. Second, because it was difficult to distinguish military from nonmilitary personnel, the search-and-destroy operations killed Vietnamese civilians. The most notorious such episode took place at My Lai on March 16, 1968, where between 247 and 540 unarmed civilians, women as well as men, died. One of the American commanders, Lieutenant William Calley, was court-martialed, convicted, and imprisoned.[126] The toll the American war took on Vietnamese civilians eroded public support, both in America and around the world, for what the United States was doing.

The American military also conducted a sustained campaign of aerial bombardment against North Vietnam, in addition to the bombing that supported the operations of American ground troops in the South. The bombing campaign against the North, called "Rolling Thunder," began in earnest in February 1965[127] and continued until 1968, when the Johnson administration instituted a pause in an effort to accelerate diplomatic efforts to end the war. The bombing of the North had a twofold purpose: to reduce communist military operations by destroying or crippling its sources of supply, including the flow of war materiel from the North to the South along the route through neighboring Laos and Cambodia known as the "Ho Chi Minh Trail," named for the leader of the Vietnamese communists from 1945 to 1969, and to change the political calculations of the North Vietnamese leaders by destroying part of their infrastructure. To avoid losing more and more of it, the Americans hoped, the communists would desist from their campaign against the South.

North Vietnam and its guerrilla proxies in the South could not hope to defeat their far stronger adversary. They therefore adopted a classic strategy of the weak, on which the American colonists had drawn in their struggle against Great Britain two centuries earlier—although not on behalf of the supreme value for which the colonists fought: individual liberty. The Vietnamese communists, too, waged a war of attrition, seeking to inflict more casualties than the American public would tolerate and thus compel the United States to abandon the fight.[128] Like the American colonists, the Vietnamese communists received crucial assistance from foreign powers. Their allies the Soviet Union and the People's Republic of China, while not actually taking part in the fighting as France did in the American Revolution, provided North Vietnam with a generous flow of weaponry and other assistance.

Ultimately the communist strategy succeeded. The American public did tire of the war and, through the multiple channels available in a democracy, compelled the American government to stop fighting it. The Vietnam War was, in essence, an exercise in competitive suffering and the Vietnamese communists, although suffering far more in death and destruction than the United States, proved willing to tolerate the losses the Americans imposed on them[129] while the American public proved, in the end, unwilling to continue to absorb the far lower costs the Vietnamese communists were able to inflict on the American armed forces. What Ho Chi Minh had said to a Frenchman in 1946 proved true of the United States as well: "You will kill ten of our men, but we will kill one of yours. And in the end it is you that will tire."[130] The Americans gave up first, and lost; the Vietnamese communists persisted, and won.

They were able to persist while accepting monumental losses because the communist regime exercised iron control over the population it governed. In all likelihood their victorious persistence owed more, however, to the nationalist sentiment the communist regime was able to mobilize in support of continuing the war.[131] The soldiers and the people of North Vietnam, and their numerous allies and sympathizers in the South, were fighting, as they saw it, for control of their own country, just as they had against the French. In Vietnam, as in China and Cuba, the United States found itself on the wrong side of the most powerful political idea of the modern era.

Like the other American wars, the one in Vietnam displayed a feature that democracy makes possible: domestic dissent. In the 1950s and 1960s government officials with responsibility for and experience with Southeast Asia frequently harbored reservations about the viability of the South Vietnamese government and the wisdom of extensive and expensive American support for it.[132] After Johnson's escalation, prominent figures in the foreign policy community—George F. Kennan, Walter Lippmann,[133] and the chairman of the Senate Foreign Relations Committee, the Arkansas Democrat J. William Fulbright among them—expressed opposition to the course the president had set. Well-known dissenters made headlines, but for the conduct of the war the opinion that counted most was that of the American public as a whole. Here the conflict in Vietnam followed the Korean pattern: strong initial support that declined as American casualties mounted.[134]

Unlike the Korean conflict, the war in Vietnam inspired large, noisy public protests in major cities and on college campuses.[135] Whereas the vast majority of the war's opponents among the members of the public generally approved of the country's goals in waging it but came to regard the pursuit of those goals as too expensive—above all in American lives—those who took part in demonstrations, who called themselves, collectively, the antiwar movement, considered the entire enterprise to have been wrong from the start. While most of the public objected to the failure to win the war at acceptable cost, they objected to fighting it at all.[136]

Like the Vietnamese communists, Lyndon Johnson recognized that American public opinion was the central front in the war and that he needed to maintain public support, or at least tolerance, for waging it. For this purpose, he and his senior officials repeatedly expressed confidence that success was in sight: "light at the end of the tunnel" became the phrase used to refer to the impression they were attempting to foster. That impression fell victim to a communist offensive in late January and early February of 1968, on the occasion of Tet, the Vietnamese lunar new year. Communist forces launched attacks in urban areas all across South Vietnam, even penetrating the grounds of the American embassy in Saigon.[137] The Tet offensive turned out to be, in strictly military terms, a defeat for the communist side, which suffered extensive losses among its cadres.[138] In the larger and more important political context, however, the offensive succeeded: it undercut the Johnson administration's assertions that the enemy was on its last legs and that the United States would soon achieve the goals for which it was fighting.[139] Approval of the war, and the president's performance in overseeing it, fell further.[140] He did less well than expected in the first Democratic presidential primary in March in the state of New Hampshire and, on the last day of that month, a beleaguered Lyndon Johnson announced that he would not seek another term in office.

Richard Nixon, who had served as Dwight Eisenhower's vice president, won the presidency that year with an unspecific promise to end the war and so inherited responsibility for American policy in Vietnam.

Like his predecessors, he had no basis for confidence that the war could be won but, like them, he was determined to avoid a humiliating defeat, and for the same reason: the damage to American credibility, and to the free world in its global contest against communism, that an abject failure would inflict.[141] Henry Kissinger, the Harvard professor whom Nixon chose as his national security advisor and who later became secretary of state, expressed the underlying logic in an article he published shortly before he joined the government:

> . . . [T]he commitment of five hundred thousand Americans has settled the issue of the importance of Vietnam. For what is involved now is confidence in American promises. However fashionable it is to ridicule the terms "credibility" or "prestige," they are not empty phrases; other nations can gear their actions to ours only if they can count on our steadiness.[142]

In pursuit of his goal of avoiding a disastrous outcome to the war, Nixon adopted a three-pronged strategy. His administration called the first part of it "Vietnamization." This involved turning over responsibility for fighting the war to the South Vietnamese army while withdrawing American troops, in order to reduce American casualties, the principal source of domestic opposition to the war in the United States.[143] As Vietnamization had envisioned, by the beginning of 1973 all American combat forces had left the country.

Second, the administration undertook negotiations with North Vietnam, which had begun at the end of the Johnson administration. Nixon hoped, at best, to reach a settlement that would leave South Vietnam an independent noncommunist country and, if not, at least to ensure a "decent interval"[144] between the American departure and the end of the noncommunist South Vietnamese regime.

The Nixon strategy had a third component: occasional sharp increases in the American use of force, in order to compensate for the steadily shrinking combat power that could be brought to bear against the enemy as the number of American troops declined. In late April and early May 1970, American and South Vietnamese forces invaded Cambodia in an effort to destroy sanctuaries for communist troops and military supplies located in that country.[145] In the spring of 1972 the North Vietnamese army launched a major offensive against the South, which a fierce American bombing campaign blunted. Then, in December of that year, the United States unleashed another powerful aerial assault, this time concentrated on the capital of North Vietnam, Hanoi, with the aim of compelling the North Vietnamese government to sign a peace agreement with the United States.[146] Soon thereafter, on January 27, 1973, such an agreement was signed in Paris, a city where so much American diplomatic history had taken place.[147]

The agreement did not end the war. The communist side continued its campaign against the South Vietnamese government. In March 1975, North Vietnam mounted another major attack on the South. This time the United States did not intervene and, despite possessing more military equipment and troops,[148] the South Vietnamese army collapsed. On April 30, 1975, Saigon fell to the North Vietnamese.[149] The quarter-century American effort to prevent the communist conquest of the entire country had failed. During the course of the war 58,000 Americans were killed and 150,000 had been wounded.[150] By most estimates well over a million Vietnamese, North and South, civilian and military, lost their lives.

The outcome of the Vietnam War had international consequences. As predicted by American policymakers, the dominoes did fall in Southeast Asia—but only up to a point. The component parts of French Indochina—Vietnam, Laos, and Cambodia—all came under communist control; but the march of communism in Asia stopped with them. The war affected American foreign policy by creating a strong presumption against putting American soldiers in harm's way in large numbers anywhere. In fact, the United States did not send another substantial contingent of troops abroad to fight until 1991, by which time the Cold War had effectively ended.[151] The aversion to overseas campaigns came to be known as the "Vietnam Syndrome."

All told, however, the consequences of Vietnam for American foreign policy were more modest than had been the case with the Korean War, whereas the conflict in Southeast Asia had larger and farther-reaching domestic effects than the previous war. The regularly unfulfilled assurances the Johnson administration provided about the course of the war sapped public confidence in its own government's truthfulness. The ensuing "credibility gap"[152] made implementing public policy more difficult in other areas as well, and it outlived the Vietnam era. So, too, did the divisions in American society that the war and the opposition to it created. They combined with cultural changes of various kinds that came to fruition in the decade of the 1960s to produce social and political cleavages, embodied in the political distinction between liberal "blue" and conservative "red" states, that persisted into the third decade of the twenty-first century.

The Vietnam War also had an impact on the balance of power over foreign affairs within the federal government. As in Korea, the executive branch prosecuted it—in defiance of the practice in the United States before the Cold War—without a formal declaration of war from the Congress.[§] As the war became increasingly unpopular, the Congress began to push back against untrammeled executive authority to wage it. In 1973 it passed the War Powers Act, which forbids the president to keep troops that he has sent abroad in combat beyond sixty days without formal Congressional authorization,[153] a requirement unevenly observed in succeeding decades.

In 1975, after the removal of American troops, the Congress did something that it had declined previously to do: it cut off funding for American military operations in Vietnam, which further weakened the South in the face of the ultimately decisive North Vietnamese offensive of that year.[154] In one of the supreme ironies of American history, the domestic political backlash that previous presidents had anticipated if South Vietnam fell to communism, the fear of which had helped to persuade them to persist in the war despite having no expectation of winning it, never materialized.[155]

The war, and the ill will and suspicion it generated domestically, also contributed to perhaps the greatest political scandal in American history—the Watergate affair,[156] which led to the only occasion on which a president has left office before the completion of his term for any

---

[§] Herring, *America's Longest War*, pp. 132–133. In August 1964, the Congress did vote overwhelmingly in favor of American assistance to allied countries in Asia, a vote occasioned by presumed attacks on American naval vessels in the Gulf of Tonkin. *Ibid.*, pp. 121–123. The Johnson administration sometimes pointed to the Gulf of Tonkin Resolution as the functional equivalent of a Congressional declaration of war.

reason other than death. Furious at the acrimonious opposition to his war policies and angry in particular at the unauthorized disclosures to the press and the public of classified information, the Nixon administration took extra-legal steps to try to stop the disclosures and punish their perpetrators.[157] This led to an illegal burglary on June 17, 1972, at the headquarters of the National Committee of the opposition Democratic Party in the Watergate Office Building not far from the White House. The Watergate burglars were arrested and the administration tried to conceal its connection with them, with the president himself playing an active role. The coverup unraveled, the House of Representatives voted to impeach the president, and on August 8, 1974, before the Senate could hold a trial to determine whether he would be allowed to continue in office, Richard Nixon resigned the presidency. He left a major legacy. In the preceding five and a half years, and all apart from the Vietnam War, he had initiated a series of policies that made him a major figure in the history of America's foreign relations.

The principal Nixon initiatives followed, and in important ways followed from, the war in Vietnam. In the sweep of Cold War American foreign policy it divides the period in two. In the wake of the unhappy and unsuccessful experience there, the United States retained its basic, era-defining commitment to opposing the Soviet Union in Europe and around the world. Its alliances continued, as did its basic military policy of deterrence. America did, however, make important adjustments in its foreign policy, most of them with the aim of lightening the burden, in American lives and treasure, of prosecuting the Cold War. Some of the post-Vietnam innovations in policy continued until the end of the Cold War and even beyond. The chief architects of this midcourse correction were Richard Nixon and Henry Kissinger.

Détente

The thirty-seventh American president professed admiration for Woodrow Wilson[158] and his first inaugural address included some Wilsonian language. He promised, for example, to "consecrate my office, my energies, and all the wisdom I can muster to the cause of peace among nations."[159] In conducting American foreign policy, however, he and his principal foreign policy advisor placed less emphasis than had come to be normal for American administrations on the promotion of American values and more on manipulating and adjusting to the distribution of power in the international system. In rhetoric a Wilsonian, in practice Nixon acted more as a disciple of Theodore Roosevelt.

The agenda with which circumstances presented Nixon upon entering office had less directly to do with values than with power. The United States had too little of it. The Vietnam War, combined with all the other Cold War responsibilities the country had undertaken, had strained the American economy and taxed the patience of the American public. The Nixon administration confronted the task of reducing the costs of waging the contest of systems with the Soviet Union without abandoning the basic American goals.

On July 25, 1969, at a press conference on the island of Guam, the president declared that henceforth the United States would expect its regional allies to bear more of the burden of the common defense.[160] The redistribution of costs and responsibilities within America's global coalitions, which became known as the "Nixon Doctrine," turned out, however, not to be the main vehicle for bringing international commitments into balance with economic and political resources. In his inaugural address, the president identified the mechanism on which he would rely for doing so. "After a period of confrontation," he said, "we are entering an era of negotiation."

The Nixon era was notable for its international negotiations, many of them conducted by Henry Kissinger. The agreement he reached in Paris with North Vietnamese officials did not, in the end, preserve a noncommunist South Vietnam. He and Nixon had greater success, at least for a time, with negotiations with America's major adversary, the Soviet Union.

The new relationship with Moscow that they attempted to create came to be known as "détente," the French word for the relaxation of tensions. Nixon and Kissinger presumed, or at least hoped, that the Cold War had become, or could become, less a mortal ideological conflict and more a historically familiar great-power rivalry—an ongoing jostling for position rather than a clash of competing crusades. Kissinger's best-known book, *A World Restored*,[161] sometimes seen as a kind of road map for the Nixon foreign policy, had dealt with the replacement of ideological fervor by calculations of power as the dominant feature of the international relations of Europe after the Napoleonic Wars.

Détente had its deepest roots in the impulse to lessen the chances of catastrophic war between the two nuclear superpowers. That impulse had prompted the two meetings that Dwight Eisenhower had held with Nikita Khrushchev as well as the measures that the United States and the Soviet Union had taken in the wake of the Cuban missile crisis. These included the establishment of a direct channel of communication between the two capitals, known as the "hot line," and a treaty prohibiting nuclear testing in the Earth's atmosphere, in space, and under the oceans.[162]

Between 1970 and 1972 a similar initiative by the Federal Republic of Germany preceded the Soviet-American détente. The West German government's policy of *Ostpolitik* (literally eastern policy) led to treaties with the Soviet Union, Poland, and East Germany as well as a four-power agreement on Berlin confirming the status quo there.[163] The West German initiative aimed to put the legacy of World War II behind it and establish stable, and if possible productive, relations with its communist neighbors to the east. *Ostpolitik* had the effect of removing Germany and Berlin as contentious issues in the Cold War.

The Nixon administration began its discussions with the Soviet Union in 1969 with the hope that Moscow would exert pressure on North Vietnam to secure a satisfactory conclusion to the Vietnam War. That did not come to pass, but those discussions continued and brought about détente.[164]

Both the United States and the Soviet Union had compelling reasons for seeking to modify their Cold War rivalry. Both wanted to demonstrate their understanding of the perils of the nuclear age. In addition, the United States sought to lighten the burden of the Cold War, and the leaders of the Soviet Union saw détente as an opportunity to affirm their country's international parity with the United States.[165] Détente recognized their country's ascent, in only three decades, from its nadir during the grim months of 1941 and 1942 to the pinnacle of the international system, accepted as a peer by the other global leader.[166] Both countries had, in addition, specific goals for the political, economic, and military negotiations that they conducted in the détente era.

A series of summit meetings between the American and Soviet leaders—so called because they met at the summit of global power—embodied their new relationship. These events differed from previous such meetings after 1945 in that the two sides intended for these meetings to take place regularly and to involve the transaction of serious business, as the Eisenhower and Kennedy summits had not. In fact, summit meetings were held, across three different presidencies, in 1972 and 1973, twice in 1974, and again in 1979. They became media spectacles, broadcast around the world and thereby enhancing the prestige of the two leaders in their own countries and beyond.

Détente also had an economic component. The two countries sought to expand the very modest volume of trade between them. The Soviet regime hoped to improve the country's economic performance by tapping into the resources of the larger and far more productive American economy.[167] The Nixon administration saw expanded trade as part of a strategy of "linkage,"[168] whereby the economic benefits the Soviet Union received would serve as an incentive for restraint in its foreign policy lest policies that offended its American partner cause the reduction of those benefits. Here the administration was following one of the oldest traditions of American foreign policy, attempting to use economic leverage to secure political goals.

In fact, trade between the two did not flourish, partly because political obstacles to it appeared in the United States[169] and partly because the American free-market system and the Soviet centrally planned economy proved to be incompatible. The linkage the administration envisioned did work, but in reverse: good relations in one part of the relationship did not beget good relations in other sectors; but the deterioration of relations in one area did lead to increased friction and less cooperation elsewhere.

In the détente era the two superpowers also tried to improve their political relations. At the 1972 summit meeting in Moscow they issued a "Declaration of Principles" that included promises not to exploit regional tensions or to try to gain unilateral advantages at the expense of the other.[170] This represented their most explicit attempt to reduce the scope and the intensity of the global conflict, an effort that, like linkage, ultimately came to naught because both sides, especially the

United States, came to believe that the other was violating the promises the other had made.

Before and after summit meetings, representatives of the superpowers conducted protracted and complicated negotiations to place limits on the two countries' two nuclear arsenals. The enterprise of arms control, as it came to be called, had begun with the Baruch Plan of 1946, with its aspiration to put all aspects of the bomb-making process under international control. After the Soviet Union rejected the Plan the two sides periodically tabled proposals, usually at the United Nations, for "general and complete disarmament"—the abolition of all weaponry. Neither expected its proposals to be adopted. Each offered them in order to make a favorable impression on international public opinion, engaging in what in a later era came to be called "virtue signaling."

In the wake of the Cuban missile crisis the superpowers concluded the first nuclear arms control agreement: the Limited Test Ban Treaty of 1963. Unlike their plans for disarmament, they negotiated it privately and directly with each other. It had a limited, practical purpose: to restrict nuclear testing, which was jeopardizing public health around the world by spewing toxic radioactive material into the air. The Test Ban Treaty established a pattern for productive negotiations that the two countries followed in the Strategic Arms Limitation Talks (SALT), which began at the end of the Johnson administration and continued during the Nixon years.[171]

The talks yielded the first agreement to control nuclear armaments, which Nixon and Brezhnev signed at their Moscow summit meeting in 1972.[172] It had two parts. An interim agreement placed a cap on strategic—that is, long-range—nuclear-tipped missiles on both sides. The two countries also signed a treaty that put strict limits on systems of ballistic missile defense.[173] This ratified the relationship of mutual assured destruction: each side promised to forswear defense against a missile attack because they had concluded that effective defense was technically infeasible. Neither could ever hope to protect itself against all the nuclear explosives the other could hurl at it; and even a few such explosives landing on its territory would bring unparalleled destruction. They therefore decided that strategic wisdom lay in preventing the competition in developing and deploying missile defenses that would likely have taken place without the Anti-ballistic Missile (ABM) Treaty that they signed, a competition that would have involved increased expenses and would probably have made each less secure while not supplying protection worth having.

The renunciation of defense came more easily to the Soviet Union, which lagged behind its Cold War rival in the kind of technological innovation that building a system of missile defense required, than to the United States. Indeed, American officials and the American public never became entirely comfortable with the commitment to forgo serious efforts at missile defense. Ultimately, in the post–Cold War period, the United States abandoned that commitment.[174]

Arms control affected the two countries differently in another way. For the United States officially to accept the terms of SALT I, as with any treaty, the Senate had to ratify it by a two-thirds majority. The Soviet leaders, by contrast, did not have to answer to a legislative body that they did not control. The Nixon administration did manage to secure the necessary majority. Then, contrary to the initial American expectation that arms control would be confined to a single episode, the negotiations became an ongoing feature of American foreign policy, continuing for the better part of the next two decades. The two countries reached an agreement on offensive weaponry at a summit meeting at Vladivostok, on the Pacific coast of Russia, in November 1974, but never turned it into a final treaty.[175] They did conclude a treaty—SALT II—in 1979,[176] but the American Senate never ratified it, although the United States did informally observe its terms.

Arms control came about through the confluence of technology and politics. It became feasible because, by the early 1970s, the superpowers had nuclear stockpiles of roughly equal size and capability. As Moscow's response to the Baruch Plan demonstrated, the Soviet Union would not have signed an agreement that ratified American nuclear superiority. For the first two decades after 1945 the United States had had a lead in nuclear weaponry. By the time of SALT I in 1972, the Soviet side had caught up.

Another technological advance proved indispensable to arms control: the development of reconnaissance satellites capable of taking high-resolution photographs from space of each side's nuclear forces. The United States would not enter any agreement unless Washington had confidence that it could monitor Soviet compliance with its terms. Since the Soviet Union, unlike the United States, was a closed society that did not permit foreigners to inspect its military facilities, satellite photography was the only way adequate verification was possible for the American side. For that reason, only what could be accurately monitored from space could be included in agreements, which put the emphasis on large items, such as ballistic missiles, that were easier to track from outer space than smaller pieces of military equipment.

Arms control was a political as well as a technical enterprise, in two ways. First, it became the centerpiece of the new political relationship that the United States and the Soviet Union were trying to create. The two superpowers themselves as well as the rest of the world regarded the ABM Treaty and the SALT accord as the outstanding accomplishments of the 1972 summit. Second, whether negotiations were successfully completed depended on the overall condition of the Soviet-American political relationship. When that relationship deteriorated, arms control fell by the wayside; when it improved, agreements became feasible once again.

In the détente era, arms control received a degree of attention, from the two governments directly concerned and from other countries, that seems, in retrospect, excessive.[177] After all, the agreements had only a very minor impact at best on the prospects for war between the superpowers. The attention stemmed from the fact that enterprise involved the most powerful of all weapons, which threatened not only the United States and the Soviet Union but also the entire world; but insofar as peace rested on the nuclear balance between the two, arms control had close to a negligible effect since the agreements the two sides reached imposed only marginal adjustments in the dimensions of their nuclear stockpiles. Without arms control, the two superpowers would likely have spent more money on nuclear weapons—and perhaps a lot more on systems of defense—but it is difficult to envision an arms-control-free scenario in which either would have felt confident enough or insecure enough to start a war.

The danger of war arose from the political rivalry between the two, with its epicenter in Europe. The nuclear arms race was a symptom, not a cause, of that rivalry; but with neither side willing to yield its position on the continent, they could not address the basic cause. With arms control, the United States and the Soviet Union provided symbolic re-assurance that they understood the dangers of the nuclear age.[178]

The superpowers were responsible for negotiating two consequential agreements in this period that other countries also signed and that had purposes other than imposing limits on their own nuclear weapons. The Nonproliferation Treaty (NPT) had two classes of signatories. Countries that already possessed nuclear weapons promised not to furnish them to others, and countries without nuclear arsenals that adhered to the NPT pledged not to acquire these armaments. The treaty was opened for signatures in 1968 and went into effect in 1970. Ultimately it came to include almost every country in the world—190 in all.[179]

The NPT embodied one of the few interests that the United States and the Soviet Union had in common.[180] Besides a shared desire to avoid nuclear war, the two also preferred that as few other countries as possible have the bomb because its spread would reduce their own military advantages over the others. Moreover, it seemed logical to assume that the larger the number of nuclear-weapon states there came to be, the greater would be the chances of a repetition of the 1945 experiences of Hiroshima and Nagasaki.

President Kennedy worried, in 1963, that by 1970 there would be ten countries with nuclear weapons, and by 1975, fifteen or twenty.[181] In the end, the actual numbers turned out to be far lower. For this the NPT deserves some credit. However, most of the countries that could have acquired nuclear weapons but chose not to do so eschewed them for reasons other than the existence of the Treaty: either they calculated that by so doing they would make themselves less secure because their neighbors would follow suit or they considered themselves to be adequately secure already by virtue of the nuclear protection they received from the nuclear armaments of one of the superpowers—for most of the nonproliferators those of the United States.

Another multinational agreement emerged from the Conference on Security and Cooperation in Europe. It began in 1973 at the behest of the Soviet Union, which had long sought international recognition for the adjustments in borders that Stalin had unilaterally made after World War II. The ensuing Europe-wide negotiations yielded an agreement that representatives of thirty-five European countries signed in Helsinki, the capital of Finland, in August 1975.

The Helsinki Final Act had three major parts: the first dealt with the international relations of Europe and included the promise to respect the territorial integrity of the signatory countries, which fulfilled Moscow's goal of securing international recognition of Europe's post-1945 borders. The second had to do with scientific and technical cooperation. The third concerned human rights.[182] When it was concluded, the Helsinki accord was widely regarded as having, at most, minor symbolic importance.[183] Political dissidents in the communist countries of Eastern Europe, however, took up the provisions of the third part and their activities had an impact on the dramatic events in that region of 1989.[184]

As in all democracies, sustaining a major foreign policy of the United States requires public support. This the Nixon policy of détente did not receive, for several reasons. The secrecy with which the administration carried it out alienated some observers and practitioners of American foreign policy. Despite Woodrow Wilson's promise, in his Fourteen Points speech, of "open covenants openly arrived at," American diplomacy, like that of other countries, has normally taken place out of the public eye. Nixon and, at his behest, his chief negotiator Henry Kissinger went further, conducting negotiations without the knowledge of their own government. They often kept the State and Defense Departments, for example, ignorant of matters for which these federal agencies had direct responsibility. To the Cold War trend of concentrating power over foreign policy within the executive branch of the federal government, Nixon added a tendency to concentrate it, within that branch, in the White House. This offended some people who were either directly involved in foreign policy or followed it closely and so were in a position to mount influential opposition to the president's initiatives.[185]

A different and more widely shared criticism of détente weakened support for it in the broader public. By treating the Soviet Union as an equal, and by putting to one side the ideological conflict with Moscow, Nixon was, many Americans came to believe, abandoning the country's supreme political values. This, they thought, constituted a serious betrayal. Two episodes of the Nixon foreign policy provoked discontent for putting what the administration regarded as the country's great-power interests above its highest political values.

In 1971, an election in Pakistan gave a majority of the votes to politicians in its eastern, ethnically Bengali region, which was separated by 2,000 miles from the country's western, predominantly Punjabi territory. West Pakistan had dominated national politics since the country's independence in 1947. The westerners refused to give up power and cracked down brutally in the east. Bengali refugees poured into India, which launched an invasion of East Pakistan, routed the West Pakistani forces there, and paved the way for the Bengalis to secede from the country and form the new country of Bangladesh.[186]

In this conflict, despite the fact that the Punjabis violated the rules of democracy and standards of common decency, the Nixon administration sided with them.[187] It did so for geopolitical reasons: Punjabi-dominated Pakistan was an American ally in the Cold War. Moreover, Nixon and Kissinger were using it as a conduit for a major diplomatic initiative toward China[188] and the president regarded India as overly friendly to the Soviet Union. The administration's willingness to overlook the Pakistani government's gross violations of basic liberties made it the subject of sharp criticism in the United States.[189]

Similarly, the administration sought to oust the government of the Marxist president of the South American country of Chile, Salvador Allende, who had been democratically elected in 1970, albeit with only thirty-six percent of the total vote and with a tiny margin over his nearest challenger. In 1973 the Chilean military overthrew Allende,[190] with the approval, if not the active participation, of the United States.[191] The Nixon administration did more or less what the Eisenhower administration had done in Iran two decades earlier. On the later occasion, however, the policy triggered outrage in some sectors of the American foreign policy community, as had its approach to the crisis in Pakistan two years earlier, because of its apparent indifference to the integrity of the democratic process in a foreign country.

Perhaps the most prominent protest against the priority the Nixon administration accorded to American interests, as it defined them, over the country's cherished values took the form of the Jackson-Vanik amendment. Senator Henry Jackson of Washington and Representative Charles Vanik of Ohio, both Democrats, proposed an amendment to the 1974 Trade Act barring the extension of Most Favored Nation trading status, which the Nixon administration had promised to the

Soviet leadership at the 1972 summit, to countries that did not allow their citizens the right to emigrate. The Soviet Union did not permit free emigration and was preventing an appreciable number of its Jewish citizens from moving to Israel. The administration opposed the amendment but the combination, in the country and in the Congress, of support for the right to emigrate and growing skepticism of, and dissatisfaction with, the overall policy of détente overcame the opposition and the amendment was enacted into law.[192]

The climax of the resistance to the Nixon policy of downgrading American political values in the conduct of foreign policy came with the election to the presidency, in 1976, of the Democratic former governor of Georgia, Jimmy Carter. He defeated Gerald Ford, the Republican former minority leader in the House of Representatives whom Nixon had appointed to the vice presidency upon the resignation of his first vice president, Spiro Agnew.[193] Ford succeeded to the presidency when Nixon himself resigned. In embracing the promotion of American values in the conduct of foreign policy, Carter became the most Wilsonian president since Woodrow Wilson himself. While continuing arms control negotiations with Moscow, he sought to put human rights at the center of America's relations with other countries, thereby reversing the emphasis of the Nixon years.[194]

The preference for advancing values over national interests, as Nixon and Kissinger had not done, found a home mainly on the left side of the American political spectrum, in the Democratic Party. On the more conservative right, a different criticism of détente took hold, an objection not to the way the United States was waging the Cold War, which was the complaint of the proponents of human rights, but rather to what these conservative critics believed to be the fact that the United States was losing it. Some of them found fault with the arms control agreements on the grounds that they conferred strategic advantages on Moscow.[195] President Ford felt compelled to appoint a panel of specialists in military and political affairs from outside the government to conduct an independent audit of the military balance between the two superpowers. Team B, as the panel was called, found the Soviet Union to be in a strategically stronger position, and the United States in a weaker one, than the previous official assessments of the American intelligence community had concluded.[196]

The major piece of economic business that the United States and the Soviet Union did manage to transact also came in for criticism. In 1972 the United States sold one-quarter of the American grain production to the Soviet Union at subsidized prices. The sales caused shortages and raised prices in the United States, and became known as the "great grain robbery."[197]

A major objection to the global strategic consequences of détente concerned events in the Third World, where the United States suffered a series of setbacks, most notably in Vietnam in 1975. The collapse of the Portuguese empire in Africa led to armed conflicts over its constituent parts and a Soviet- and Cuban-backed group gained control of Angola.[198] On the Horn of Africa, Soviet military assistance to Ethiopia, once an American client, enabled it to prevail in a struggle with its neighbor Somalia.[199] On the global chessboard over which the United States confronted the Soviet Union, even the loss of the geopolitical equivalent of pawns such as these African countries, as the Ford administration and other Americans saw it, had negative consequences for the American side.[200]

Détente became so unpopular in the ranks of Nixon's Republican Party that Ford, in his unsuccessful candidacy for election to the presidency in his own right, banned the use of the term in his campaign.[201] His rival for the 1976 Republican presidential nomination, the governor of California, Ronald Reagan, explicitly opposed the policy.[202] Despite President Carter's continued pursuit of arms control with the Soviet Union, by the last years of the 1970s the robust political support in the United States that détente had commanded at its high point in 1972 had eroded considerably. Just as the crises of the 1960s had demonstrated that the destructive power of the military forces the two superpowers deployed against each other made war improbable, so détente's lack of staying power in the United States showed that the deep differences of political values between them made peace, defined as the end of their military and political rivalry, impossible.

Détente counted as the most notable effort in the Nixon years to lighten the burden on the United States of waging the military, political, and economic contest of systems with the Soviet Union and global communism, but it was not the only such effort. The other, similar initiatives involved shocks to the international order. The Nixon administration initiated two of those shocks and had to respond to a third.[203]

Shocks

Richard Nixon gave the world a major geopolitical shock by effecting a political rapprochement with the People's Republic of China.[204] Twenty years of Sino-American estrangement had followed the Chinese entry into the Korean War. During that period the United States hinted at the possibility of direct American military action against China during two crises, in 1954–1955 and 1958, over Quemoy and Matsu, two small islands off the Chinese coast. Chiang Kai-shek's Kuomintang had occupied them and the government in Peking launched attacks against them, mainly through artillery barrages.[205] While they did not go to war again, the United States and the People's Republic of China did not maintain diplomatic relations and had virtually no official contact. The Chinese internal upheavals in the 1950s and 1960s—the Great Leap Forward, when Mao Tse-tung tried to accelerate industrialization, resulting in a famine that killed perhaps forty million people,[206] and the Great Proletarian Cultural Revolution, which Mao provoked by sending student "Red Guards" rampaging across the country—persuaded Americans that China was too unstable, radical, and dangerous for productive relations.

The dramatic change in the relationship between the two countries came about because of hostility between China and the Soviet Union. The Sino-Soviet rift arose from conflicting claims to territory, Chinese resentment at what Peking regarded as unfulfilled Soviet promises of assistance of various kinds, Chinese accusations that Moscow's foreign and domestic policies had strayed from communist orthodoxy, and rivalry for primacy within the global communist movement. In 1969, fighting between the two communist giants erupted along the Ussuri River, which formed part of their disputed border.[207] The Soviet side substantially increased its deployment of troops in the region. These events gave China, then decidedly inferior to its Soviet neighbor militarily, a strong interest in aligning itself with the United States to counterbalance Soviet power.[208]

The United States had a comparable interest in offsetting the power of its chief adversary, and so reducing the burden of opposing it, through an alignment with a country that had previously been a Soviet ally. At the outset of his administration, Nixon hoped that better relations with Peking, as with Moscow, would help the United States arrive at a satisfactory conclusion to the war in Vietnam; but as in the Soviet case, that hope was not realized.[209]

Nixon had broached the idea of improving relations with mainland China even before becoming president, in a 1967 article in *Foreign Affairs*.[210] Once in office, he signaled his wish for a diplomatic breakthrough and the Chinese government reciprocated. On July 9, 1971, Henry Kissinger made a secret trip to Peking to meet with the Chinese leadership; on July 15 Nixon announced that he would visit China; and he spent the period from February 21 to 28, 1972, in that country, meeting with Chinese leaders.

Those meetings achieved their greatest global impact simply by taking place. The striking and, until a few months earlier, unimaginable images of the leaders of the two countries together, which were broadcast around the world, seemed to herald a new era in international relations. Nixon called his visit the "week that changed the world."[211] The most important piece of actual business transacted during the event was the jointly issued Shanghai Communique, which avoided a direct conflict over the most contentious matter in Sino-American relations, the status of Taiwan. The United States had signed a defense treaty with the island republic in 1954 but the communists considered it simply a renegade province of China that should and would be brought under their control. The Communique stated that "all Chinese on either side of the Taiwan Strait maintain that there is but one China and that Taiwan is part of China. The United States Government does not challenge that position."[212] The American side thus asserted that it did not support the independence of Taiwan, or its permanent political separation from the mainland. The Communique also affirmed "the ultimate objective of the withdrawal of all U.S. forces and military installations from Taiwan," while adding that this would happen "as tension in the area diminishes" and stipulating an "interest in a peaceful settlement of the Taiwan question by the Chinese themselves."[213]

The rapprochement with China received a warm reception in the United States.[214] Indeed, it counted as a political masterstroke for Richard Nixon in an election year, a not insignificant reason for his desire to travel to that country.[215] The Chinese government had as little use as did that of the Soviet Union for American political values but, perhaps because China posed the lesser threat, perhaps because unlike the Soviet Union China did not preside over an empire that repressed countries to which Americans had ancestral ties, the rapprochement with Peking did not arouse the kind of opposition that détente did. Nor, for all its concern with human rights, did the Carter administration, which continued that rapprochement, penalize the People's Republic, or even harshly criticize it, for its transgressions on that score.[216]

The outreach to China expressed the non-Wilsonian approach to the conduct of foreign policy to which Nixon and Kissinger subscribed. It comported with the spirit of a classic statement of the approach that Theodore Roosevelt had favored by the nineteenth-century British foreign secretary and prime minister Lord Palmerston: "We have no eternal allies, and we have no perpetual enemies. Our interests are eternal and perpetual, and these it is our duty to pursue."[217] The reconciliation with the communist government in Peking served the American interest of bolstering its position vis-à-vis the Soviet Union, at the cost of joining hands with a government that did not, to say the least, share American political values: Mao Tse-tung had the distinction of being responsible, over the course of his career, for more deaths (almost all of them Chinese) than either Hitler or Stalin.[218]

The China initiative established a triangular relationship among the United States, the People's Republic of China, and the Soviet Union, in which the United States sought to gain leverage on each of the other two by maintaining more cordial relations with each of them than they had with each other. This leverage was on display—or so at least it seemed—during the 1972 Moscow summit meeting. When it took place, the United States was engaged in a punishing attack on Moscow's communist ally, North Vietnam, in response to the North's large-scale assault on the South. Perhaps influenced by the recent Sino-American meeting, rather than canceling or postponing the summit in protest, Brezhnev and his colleagues decided to proceed with it.[219]

In the wake of their political breakthrough, the United States began several kinds of cooperation with China, including the sharing of intelligence and the sale of weaponry.[220] The American government also granted China Most Favored Nation trading status, which the Jackson-Vanik amendment denied to the Soviet Union.[221]

The new relationship strengthened the United States and weakened the Soviet Union by making the world's most populous country part of the global anti-Soviet coalition. It also strengthened—redeemed would not be too strong a word—the American position in East Asia even as the war in Vietnam was being lost. America in effect traded South Vietnam for China, in geopolitical terms a profitable exchange. The rapprochement also rekindled the romantic and proprietary American attitude toward China, the sense of a special relationship between the two countries, that had originated in the eighteenth and nineteenth centuries and that the communist conquest of the mainland had—temporarily as it turned out—extinguished.[222] For all its importance, however, the Sino-American rapprochement did not change the basic structure of the Cold War. It had little effect on the rivalry in Europe, or indeed anywhere beyond East Asia.

Even before it produced a tremor in global security affairs with its rapprochement with China, the Nixon administration had administered a shock to the international economic order by putting an end to the international monetary system the United States had taken the lead in creating at Bretton Woods, New Hampshire, in 1944. The Bretton Woods system had succeeded the gold standard, with the dollar effectively replacing gold at the center of global monetary affairs. The American currency was linked to gold and could be redeemed from the American government for that precious metal at the rate of $35 per ounce. To support their own national currencies and to conduct international transactions, other countries held dollars instead of, or in addition to, gold.

In the new monetary order, the dollar had two contradictory roles, which put increasing strain on the system itself and on American foreign economic policy. On the one hand, the United States felt pressure to limit the creation and outflow of dollars, in order to maintain enough gold to cover those presented for redemption. On the other hand, dollars underpinned economic activity around the world, which put a premium on furnishing the world with a generous supply of them.[223]

After 1945 the outflow of dollars increased, in no small part because of the expense of waging the Cold War by means of American military installations and troop deployments abroad, with a particular increase due to the Vietnam War—for all of which the United States was able to pay in its own currency. The dollar shortage of the immediate postwar years, when the Western Europeans and Japanese could only buy the goods they needed in the United States and required dollars for that purpose, became a dollar glut by the 1960s as these same countries, now prosperous, had to accept more dollars than they wanted. The American government tried in various ways to curtail the "dollar drain,"[224] and America's allies, especially Germany and Japan, refrained from exchanging their dollars for gold, which, because the United States did not have enough gold to purchase all the dollars in foreign hands, would have jeopardized the entire monetary system. As American allies, they treated the accumulation of unwanted dollars as the price of the American military protection that they received.[225]

The United States also paid a price for the operation of the Bretton Woods system. As other countries recovered economically, the dollar became overvalued in comparison with their currencies; but the rules of the system prohibited adjusting the dollar to the new economic realities by devaluing it. Depending as they did on trade, especially with the United States, the Germans and the Japanese were reluctant to increase the value of the deutschmark and the yen, which would have had the same effect as an American devaluation. With an artificially strong dollar, imports to the United States increased, penalizing import-competing American industries, and American exporters struggled. Both consequences had a negative impact on domestic employment.

In response to these mounting pressures, on August 15, 1971, without warning to the rest of the world, the United States announced that it would no longer redeem dollars for gold. "Closing the gold window" removed the central pillar of the Bretton Woods system and freed the United States to devalue its currency. At the same time, the Nixon administration imposed a ten percent surcharge on imports, which it said would only be removed when a satisfactory devaluation of the dollar had been achieved,[226] and announced a freeze on wages and prices at home as a way of stifling inflation.

These decisions had in common with détente and the opening to China the aim of reducing the burden of the post–World War II responsibilities that the United States had undertaken. The centrality of the dollar had imposed risks and costs on the United States that the Nixon administration was no longer willing to pay, as well as restrictions on its freedom to conduct its economic policy by which it was no longer willing to abide.[227]

If the opening to China came as an unexpected and unpleasant surprise to the Soviet Union, the decision to close the gold window shocked America's major trading partners and allies. As both a neighbor of China and a major trading partner of the United States, Japan was shaken by both initiatives, which became known in that country as the "Nixon shocks."[228]

Closing the gold window inspired fears for the future of the international economy. The dollar had anchored it in the same way that American military power underpinned the Western security order. The Nixon initiative left the world without fixed monetary rules—that is, without a stable, wholly predictable monetary system.[229] The last time this had happened, during the Great Depression of the 1930s, the world had suffered severely negative economic effects, and the end of Bretton Woods raised concerns about comparably adverse consequences. Without monetary rules to impart predictability and confidence to international transactions, it was feared, trade would shrivel. Without the discipline of such rules, national governments might feel free to implement inflationary economic policies. In fact, in the years following 1971 the rate of growth of global trade did fall, but the volume of trade continued to expand. Depression-like conditions did not return.[230] The world did suffer a bout of inflation in the 1970s, but not simply because of the end of Bretton Woods.[231]

Despite efforts to do so, the major trading countries did not manage to create a new monetary system to replace the one that ended on August 15, 1971. Governments, traders, and investors learned to live with floating exchange rates rather than the fixed ones that the gold standard and the Bretton Woods system had imposed. In this new monetary world, the dollar, even though no longer linked to gold, continued to play a leading role. As before, central banks of other countries used it as a reserve asset. As before, many global transactions took place in dollars. The world economy, it turned out, needed the equivalent of a global currency and the dollar proved still to be the most suitable choice for that purpose.[232] Even without fixed monetary rules, the Western economic order that the United States had helped to found and done so much to sustain, and that had become a major asset in the contest of systems with the Soviet Union and international communism, held together.

While the Nixon administration initiated the China and monetary shocks, a third seismic event in international affairs originated elsewhere. It differed from the other two in that, while other countries had to adjust to what the United States decided to do in East Asia and with the dollar, the American government was, like others, taken by surprise by, and had to cope with the consequences of, the oil shock.

A war in the Middle East in October 1973, which began when Egypt and Syria attacked Israel, triggered this third shock. The war raged for two weeks and after early gains by the two Arab countries the Israelis launched a successful counterattack against both its assailants, recovering territory initially lost and then capturing more. The Soviet Union sent military supplies to the Arabs. The United States dispatched military assistance to Israel, with which it had developed an increasingly close relationship after the Suez episode of 1956. By ending Nasser's campaign to dominate the Arab Middle East with its sweeping victory in the 1967 Arab-Israeli war, Israel had performed a major service for the United States. Israeli military power enabled America to pursue a policy of offshore balancing in the region. An Israeli defeat in 1973 would therefore have been a setback to the United States as well, and without the American assistance the war might have taken a different and, for the Israelis, less favorable course.[233]

The Arab oil-producing countries of the Persian Gulf supported Egypt and Syria by withholding oil from the United States as well as from other countries. In 1960 they had helped to form a cartel of oil exporters, the Organization of Petroleum Exporting Countries (OPEC), which made coordination among them easier. The market for oil being a global one, the embargo could not target only the United

States. What it could and did do was reduce the world's overall supply of oil, which shook economies everywhere in two ways.

First, with supply diminished and demand unchanged, the price of oil rose sharply, quadrupling between October 1973 and March 1974. Second, the sudden drop in global supply caused shortages, including in the United States, which was seriously affected because so much American transportation took place in gasoline-powered cars, buses, and trucks. Throughout the country motorists had to wait in long lines at gas stations to fuel their cars.[234]

Beyond the inconvenience it caused for individual Americans, the oil shock had a negative impact on the global economy. The rise in the oil price had a deflationary effect, acting as a tax increase by withdrawing purchasing power virtually everywhere, while at the same time stoking inflation because the economic centrality of oil meant that an increase in its price raised the prices of many other items as well. Moreover, the world conducted its oil trade in dollars, and the price increase directed a larger flow of dollars to the oil producers than they could productively invest or even spend. This created a global financial imbalance and thus the need somehow to "recycle" these "petrodollars" in ways that contributed to global growth, or at least did not depress it.

The oil shock had, as well, potential implications for the balance of power in the international system. If other producers of primary products, most of them countries in the Third World, managed to replicate what the oil producers had done, they would accumulate not only much more wealth but also much more international power. In such circumstances, the countries of the West would lose power not to the communist bloc but to the Third World. The contours of geopolitics would shift, to the disadvantage of the United States.

In fact, the West did not suffer serious or lasting economic and political damage from the oil shock. The oil producers used the Western financial system to put their windfall of dollars to, on the whole, productive uses.[235] The oil market adjusted to the sharp rise in price, as markets will, by stimulating more production, much of it in non-OPEC countries, while depressing the price as demand dropped because consumers learned how to use less oil. Greater supply and decreased demand reduced the price. By the first half of the 1980s, allowing for inflation, the global oil price actually fell. Nor did other primary producers follow OPEC's example. For the purpose of forming an effective cartel capable of manipulating global supply and thereby raising global prices, oil proved to be unique. No comparable commodity cartels came into being.[236]

These developments played out over the decade that followed the 1973 oil shock. In that year, however, the world, and especially the United States, confronted more urgent tasks: bringing an end to the oil embargo and preventing the recurrence of the circumstance—a major Arab-Israeli war—that had given rise to it. In the years immediately after the 1973 war, American diplomacy accomplished both.

None of the previous Arab-Israeli wars—Israel's War of Independence in 1948 (when five Arab armies invaded the new state in order to destroy it), the war over Suez in 1956, the Six-Day War of 1967—had put an end to the underlying political conflict. Each war had therefore led to efforts at mediation between and among the warring parties, always with the involvement of the United Nations. In the wake of the 1973 war, in the tradition of Theodore Roosevelt's successful efforts to forge a settlement between Russia and Japan in 1905, the United States became the mediator.

Washington had several good reasons for trying to end the Arab-Israeli conflict, or at least reducing it to the point that it did not erupt in major regional warfare. The most pressing of them was an overriding interest in restarting, and sustaining, the flow of oil from the region without politically motivated interruptions.

The danger of a superpower clash had also come into play in October 1973, near the end of the Arab-Israeli fighting. The Soviet leadership had sent a note to the American government containing a veiled threat to send troops to the region: Israeli forces had surrounded, and seemed poised to destroy, an Egyptian army on the eastern side of the Suez Canal, which occasioned Moscow's message. In response, the Nixon administration put American military forces on a state of heightened worldwide alert but also warned Israel not to proceed further against the trapped Egyptians.[237] The October alert did not bring the United States and the Soviet Union as close to direct armed conflict as the Berlin and Cuban crises had seemed to do; but it caused sufficient alarm to make the Americans anxious to avoid a repetition.[238]

Successful mediation of the conflict offered another benefit to the United States. American policy sought to maintain as cordial relations as possible with both Israel and the Arab countries. Lessening tension between the two would serve that purpose.

Accordingly, when the guns fell silent, Henry Kissinger, now the secretary of state, traveled to the region and brokered an agreement to separate Egyptian and Israeli military forces, lest fighting accidentally begin anew. His success encouraged him to continue his mediation. The Arab countries refused to negotiate directly with Israel, so Kissinger flew back and forth among capitals, carrying out "shuttle diplomacy." In a virtuoso display of empathy, flattery, cajolery, and pressure he secured two disengagement agreements between Israel and Egypt and one between Israel and Syria.[239] Kissinger had received the Nobel Peace Prize for his part in the Vietnam negotiations. He deserved a second one for his Middle Eastern peacemaking.[240]

The Israelis were in no position to resist the diplomatic efforts of their ally and patron and, in any event, had no desire to do so since peace with their neighbors was the highest goal of their foreign policy. The Egyptian leader, Anwar Sadat, aspired, through the American-sponsored peace process, to regain the Sinai peninsula, which his country had lost in 1967. He also wanted to achieve closer relations with the United States, which, he calculated, had more to offer Egypt, especially economically, than did the Soviet Union. The Syrian leader, Hafez Assad, had weaker motivation to settle with Israel. He and the Syrian leadership came from a minority sect, the Alawis, who made up only thirteen percent of the country's population but dominated, through repression, the far more numerous Sunni Muslim Syrians. In these circumstances, the conflict with Israel was a godsend for Assad, enabling him and his fellow Alawis to pose as the champions of all Syrians in confronting their non-Muslim neighbor.

The American mediation between Egypt and Israel culminated during the Carter administration in meetings in September 1978 between the leaders of the two countries at Camp David, the presidential retreat outside Washington, D.C. A formal peace treaty between the two followed the next year. In the various sets of negotiations, the United States not only passed messages between the two sides but also compensated Israel, with political support and economic and military assistance, for the sacrifice of strategically valuable territory the Jewish state had to make to reach a settlement with its Egyptian neighbor.[241]

The Middle East peace process removed the largest Arab country, and the one with the greatest military potential, from the ranks of those willing to go to war with Israel. It thereby eliminated the possibility of a major war in the region on the scale of those of 1948, 1956, 1967, and 1973. This redounded to the benefit of the United States, as did the reduction of Soviet influence in the region owing to the fact that Moscow played no part in the negotiations. The peace process strengthened and expanded American ties with Israel.[242] Because it brought about an Israeli settlement with Egypt but not with its other Arab neighbors, negotiations involving Arabs and Israelis became an ongoing feature of American foreign policy, outliving the Cold War.

By 1978, the adjustments that the Nixon administration had made to the nation's foreign policies for the purpose of lightening the burden of sustaining the American position in the Cold War had, on the whole, succeeded. The Israeli-Egyptian rapprochement was one of them. Elsewhere, in East Asia, the American government had agreed to re-store formal diplomatic relations with China and that country had become the adversary of the erstwhile nemesis of the United States, the communist government of now-unified Vietnam. Indeed, in early 1979 China attacked and occupied a northern slice of Vietnamese ter-ritory.[243] Détente with the Soviet Union, although not in political favor in the United States, remained alive, with the Carter administra-tion prepared to sign a second Strategic Arms Limitation Treaty with Moscow. The global economy had weathered the 1973 oil shock—not, to be sure, without any damage but without damage on the scale of the 1930s.

While much had changed in the world since the end of the Korean War in 1953, and while not all the changes had favored American interests, the overall state of the global competition between commu-nism and the Free World remained more or less stable, with neither side having gained a decisive advantage. The next year, 1979, however, turned out to be the worst one internationally for the United States since 1942, the low point of the country's fortunes in World War II.

This decline in America's fortunes, however, set the stage for another, far more dramatic, reversal. In the following decade the United States recovered its position in the Cold War. By the end of the 1980s and the beginning of the 1990s, almost entirely unexpectedly, the contest of systems had ended and the American side had won.

9

A Superpower Dies in Bed, 1979–1990

Annus horribilis

The year 1979 conformed to an odd twentieth-century pattern. Years ending in "9" tended to produce major international events, which were usually disadvantageous to the United States: in 1919 the post–World War I Paris Peace Conference, with its failures and disappointments; in 1929 the stock market crash; in 1939 the outbreak of war in Europe; in 1949 the communist conquest of China and the first Soviet nuclear explosion.* In the last year of the 1970s, America suffered a series of political and economic setbacks that brought it to its lowest point in the military, economic, and political competition with the Soviet Union and international communism. The troubles of 1979 began in a country, and with a leader, where and with whom the United States had enjoyed, twenty-five years earlier, what had seemed at the time a notable Cold War success—Iran.

After helping to restore the Shah to his throne in 1953, the Iranian monarch became an increasingly important ally of the United States, with his country the anchor of the American position in the Persian Gulf. The strategic significance of that region grew as the industrial

---

* In the 1960s the comparable events came a year early, in 1968, with the Tet offensive in Vietnam and disturbances in American cities as well as upheaval in France and the Warsaw Pact invasion of Czechoslovakia. See Michael Mandelbaum, "1968 Plus Fifty Years: The Irony of History," *The American Interest*, May–June 2018.

world came to depend more and more on its oil, much of which Iran it-self supplied. In 1979 the Shah was overthrown. While he had presided over a respectable national economic performance and his country had received an economic windfall from the spike in the price of oil in 1973, the social and economic changes during his time in power, combined with his authoritarian style of governance, alienated important sectors of Iranian society.[1] In 1978, large public demonstrations against him took place, inspired by a militant exiled Shia Muslim cleric named Ruhollah Khomeini. Increasingly isolated, plagued by the indecisive-ness that was part of his personality,[2] and seriously ill with cancer, the Shah left Iran on January 16, 1979. This time, unlike in 1953, he would not return.[3]

The Carter administration was well aware of the geopolitical stakes for the United States in the Iranian upheavals but was divided inter-nally about the appropriate American response. Some officials sought to conciliate the protesters and Khomeini; others wanted the Shah's government to take a firm stand against them, including the use of force.[4] Even those favoring a firm response, however, believed that the Shah's forces, not American ones, had to carry it out; and this proved impossible.

The fall of the Shah imposed long-term costs on the United States. The opposition to him turned into a genuine revolution, bringing to power not simply an alternative governing elite but a new form of gov-ernment based on an entirely different set of principles. Khomeini pro-fessed a form of Islamic fundamentalism that placed the clergy—above all himself—in control of the country. While he and the government he formed opposed both sides in the Cold War—they were no friends of Marxism-Leninism—they reserved special animus for the United States. America became the object of their wrath and their principal adversary during the rest of the Cold War and thereafter. In 1979, there-fore, the United States not only lost an ally but also gained an enemy.

The hatred of all things American on the part of the officials of what described itself as the Islamic Republic of Iran arose from the close as-sociation of the United States with the despised Shah, whom many in Iran regarded as having been an American puppet. As in China, Cuba, and Vietnam—and although Khomeini himself had pan-Islamic rather than strictly Iranian aspirations—American interests fell victim to local nationalism. The American rather than the Soviet side in the Cold War became the principal target of the clerics because American military and political influence in the Middle East exceeded that of the Soviet Union. Furthermore, Khomeini saw the Western way of life, which the United States both embodied and propagated, as posing a greater threat than did communism to the Iranian people's observance of the harsh laws and customs that he sought to impose on them. The new Iranian ruler called America "the Great Satan," by which he referred to the Satan of the Garden of Eden. Like the serpent in the Book of Genesis, the United States, by its example, tempted Muslims to stray from what Khomeini had ordained as the proper path in life.

The Iranian Revolution caused short-term American losses as well. The Carter administration decided to admit the Shah to the United States for medical treatment despite warnings from Tehran that this could have adverse consequences. True to those warnings, in November 1979, a group of militant Iranian students seized the American embassy and took hostage some fifty-two embassy personnel. What came to be known as the hostage crisis turned into an ongoing humiliation for the United States, as the captors paraded the hostages before television cameras and the American government proved unable to secure their release.[5] Eventually, in April 1980, pessimistic that the ongoing negotiations would free the hostages and persuaded that their captivity was eroding American credibility in the Middle East and beyond,[6] the Carter administration launched a complicated, multistage rescue operation. It involved C-130 transport planes and helicopters, which met at a designated spot in the Iranian desert. The operation went badly wrong. Two helicopters malfunctioned, the president decided to abort the mission, and then a collision in the desert disabled the rest of the fleet of helicopters and caused eight American deaths before the remaining military personnel were flown to safety on the C-130s.[7] To the humiliation of the continuing captivity of the hostages was thereby added the ignominy of the failure of the attempt to rescue them. They were finally released on January 20, 1981, inauguration day in the United States, 444 days after they had been seized.

The Iranian Revolution also did economic damage to the United States, and to the global economy as a whole. It led to a sharp drop in Iran's output of oil,[8] which reduced the global supply. This in turn raised its price even beyond the elevated level it had reached in the wake of the 1973 Arab-Israeli war.[9] The second oil shock, moreover, came at the end of the most economically difficult decade for the United States since the 1930s.

Economic growth slowed and the real wages of most American workers began to fall. At the heart of the decrease in growth lay a decline in the rate of growth of the American economy's productivity—that is, its output per unit of input.[10] This, in turn, had to do with the exhaustion of the gains from a number of basic and unrepeatable innovations, such as widespread electricity and the internal combustion engine, that had powered American growth for a century after 1870.[11]

At the same time, the country suffered from unusually high inflation.[12] The Johnson administration's efforts, in the 1960s, to sustain both the Vietnam War and its ambitious social programs without increasing taxes had raised the levels of prices, and the two oil shocks raised them even further.[13] Moreover, while in the past an expansion of employment had accompanied higher inflation, in the 1970s,[14] as unemployment rose, so did prices. The American economy thus suffered from the worst of both worlds, stagnation and inflation, which came to be called "stagflation."[15]

The hard economic times had a negative impact on American foreign policy, restricting the resources available for initiatives beyond the continental United States, eroding the national self-confidence necessary for a robust international presence,[16] and turning public attention inward.[17] Furthermore, because the conflict with the Soviet Union included a contest of economic systems, the poor economic performance of the United States was a setback in the Cold War.

In July 1979, the pro-American government of a country closer to home than Iran fell and was replaced by a regime hostile to the United States. Anastasio Somoza, a graduate of the United States Military Academy at West Point, had governed Nicaragua, in Central America, as a dictator who was friendly to his country's giant neighbor to the north. The movement that unseated him was named after Augusto Sandino, a Nicaraguan rebel of the 1920s. The Sandinistas had a pronounced political affinity for Fidel Castro's Cuba and, like him, accepted aid from the Soviet Union.[18] The change of government therefore represented another American loss, in the eyes of many Americans, in the global competition with the Soviet Union and Marxism-Leninism.

The Carter administration, with its commitment to the protection of human rights, had, at best, mixed feelings about Somoza, as it had toward the Shah. As in Iran it tried, without success, to find a way to install a government independent of both the dictator and the Sandinistas.[19] Somoza, like the Shah, presented the United States with a problem that came to be known as the "friendly tyrant dilemma."[20] It involved having to decide whether to support a government that did not practice democracy at home but that did align itself with the United States in the international arena. It involved, that is, having to choose, in foreign policy, between the nation's values and its interests. In the early years of the Cold War the choice had been an easy one: Washington had opted to protect the country's interests and had had little compunction about supporting governments in Iran and Central America as well as in countries such as South Korea, South Vietnam, and Pakistan that did not protect liberty or permit free elections but that shared (or professed to share) the American opposition to communism.

In the second half of the Cold War, the long-standing ideological strain in American foreign policy, with its emphasis on the liberty that friendly tyrants did not embrace, assumed a greater prominence. It did so because the contest with the Soviet Union seemed less urgent and precarious and because support for a friendly tyranny but imperfectly democratic regime in South Vietnam had come to grief. The tradeoff between values and interests became more difficult to make, with partisans, especially in the Carter administration, on both sides of the issue. Unfortunately from the American point of view, the regimes that replaced the Shah and Somoza proved to be both tyrannical and unfriendly to the United States.

The most alarming development of an alarming year took place in its final month in Afghanistan, a poor, landlocked, and devoutly Islamic country that shared a border with three central Asian republics of the Soviet Union. A coup in 1978 had brought to power in Kabul, the Afghan capital, a group that signed a twenty-year "treaty of friendship and cooperation" with Moscow. In September 1979, the leader of the regime was assassinated under orders from his second-in-command, who upon taking power showed signs, or so Soviet officials believed, of steering the country's foreign policy away from alignment with Moscow. The Kremlin also feared that the increasingly unpopular Afghan government would fall and be replaced by Islamic fundamentalists.[21] From December 25 to 27, 1979, the Brezhnev government sent 80,000 Soviet troops into Afghanistan.[22] They killed the new leader and replaced him with an Afghan deemed more friendly to them, or at least more pliable.[23]

Records of the deliberations leading up to the decision to intervene among the senior members of the Politburo, the ruling body of the Soviet Union, which became public a decade later, revealed the principal motive behind the Soviet coup to have been defensive.[24] Brezhnev and the other senior (and, like him, elderly) officials feared that Afghanistan would leave the Soviet orbit and join the West.[25] They worried, as both superpowers did during the course of the Cold War, that such a defection would weaken their position around the world.[26]

While the Soviet leadership may have acted in order to preserve the geopolitical status quo, the United States saw its Afghan initiative differently. Viewed from Washington, it appeared to be a provocative and dangerous departure from the norms of the Cold War. For the first time, the Soviet Union had sent troops into a country outside Europe, one that did not belong to the Warsaw Pact. Even more ominously, Soviet control of Afghanistan would move the rival superpower closer to the Persian Gulf, with its large deposits of oil on which Western economies depended.[27] Nor did the events in Afghanistan in late December 1979 alarm only the United States. Other countries considered the invasion a new and threatening departure from the established routines of Soviet foreign policy.

The Carter administration mounted an emphatic response to the invasion. It withdrew from consideration for ratification by the Senate the Strategic Arms Limitation Talks (SALT) II treaty that Carter and Brezhnev had signed in Vienna six months earlier. It imposed sanctions of various kinds on the Soviet Union,[28] including an embargo on the sale of grain and a boycott, joined by most of America's European allies, of the 1980 Olympic Games, which were being held in Moscow. In his 1980 State of the Union address the president issued what came to be called the Carter Doctrine, declaring the Persian Gulf to be a region of particular American interest that the United States would fight to defend.[29]

The Soviet invasion of Afghanistan followed three distinct and recurrent patterns in the history of American foreign policy. First, it galvanized the country, making the world seem suddenly more dangerous for the United States and therefore requiring a major American response, although the events of December 1979 did not propel the United States into a war, at least not directly. Like the launch of Sputnik in 1957, however, the presence of Soviet troops in Afghanistan did lead to a rise in American defense spending. The Carter administration increased its request for the defense budget by five percent.[30]

Second, in the case of Afghanistan an adversary of the United States seriously underestimated the magnitude of the American response to a hostile initiative. While Soviet officials hardly expected Washington's approval for their military intervention, like Nikita Khrushchev and his decision to station missiles in Cuba they did not anticipate the steps the United States would take to raise the costs of their Afghan policy.[31]

Third, the Carter administration's response to the Soviet incursion into Afghanistan provided an example of the historical tendency of the foreign policy of the United States to change abruptly and significantly not when one administration replaces another but rather during the term in office of a single administration that had previously pursued sharply different policies, in response to a dramatic event. Woodrow Wilson was initially determined to keep the United States out of World War I but then presided over American entry into that conflict. Franklin Roosevelt entered office shunning active involvement in European affairs but eventually led the country into World War II. Similarly, at the beginning of 1979 the Carter administration was committed to retaining at least some features of the policy of détente—arms control above all—that his two immediate predecessors had devised. At the end of that year, with the policies that the administration had adopted in response to the events in Afghanistan, the United States had abandoned détente.

Jimmy Carter said that the Soviet invasion of Afghanistan "has made a more dramatic change in my own opinion of what the Soviets' ultimate goals are than anything they've done in the previous time I've been in office."[32] His change of mind, however, and the changes of policy that followed from it, did not save his political career. In the 1980 presidential election his Republican opponent, former California governor Ronald Reagan, defeated him decisively and became the fortieth American president.[33]

Counterattack

Before entering public life, Ronald Reagan had had a successful career in Hollywood as a film actor. His experience in front of the cameras stood him in good stead in politics. He came across more effectively on television than any previous president, thereby earning the nickname "the Great Communicator." While he liked to portray himself as a private citizen temporarily on loan to the government, he was a very ambitious politician, mounting serious candidacies for the presidency three times—in 1968 and 1976 before finally winning the office in 1980. Although his opponents derided him as being out of his depth in the White House, Reagan, having served for a total of eight years as governor of the nation's largest state, had extensive experience that was relevant to conducting the presidency.[34]

He came to the office committed to reviving the American economy by reducing the economic role of the federal government, which had expanded substantially since Franklin Roosevelt's New Deal in the 1930s. Freeing markets to operate with less external interference and freeing entrepreneurs to operate within them would, he was convinced, ignite an upsurge of economic activity that the heavy hand of government was suppressing. His principal domestic initiatives—cutting taxes and easing federal regulations on economic activity—put into practice this commitment.

In foreign policy he had consistently opposed détente. He said, both during the 1980 campaign and before, that that policy had worked to the advantage of the Soviet Union at the expense of the United States. Like John F. Kennedy two decades earlier, Reagan charged that the communist side had taken the lead in the ongoing competition with the United States and the West.[35] He differed from Kennedy, and from other Cold War presidents, in that he did not advocate catching up with the communist bloc simply in order to perpetuate a stalemate in the global competition with it. He believed that the West could and should win the Cold War. In an address to the British Parliament on June 8, 1982, he offered "a plan and a hope for the long term—the march of freedom and democracy which will leave Marxist-Leninism on the ash heap of history. . . ."[36]

Like Kennedy and Truman before him, Reagan emphasized the ideological dimension of the Cold War. His rhetoric expressed this emphasis: he famously called the Soviet Union an "evil empire."[37] His administration established a National Endowment for Democracy to promote the American form of government around the world. By frequently and forcefully invoking American values as underlying the conflict with the Soviet Union, Reagan put himself in opposition not so much to the foreign policy of his 1980 Democratic opponent Jimmy Carter—who had, after all, stressed the protection of human rights—as to that of his fellow Republican Richard Nixon, for whom the pursuit of détente relegated to a distinctly minor role the traditional American interest in spreading liberty and transforming international politics.

To redress what he saw as the Soviet advantage in the military balance with the United States, Reagan added his own substantial increase in defense spending to the increase in the final year of the Carter administration.[38] The new president took a dim view of what nuclear arms control negotiations had achieved, but the United States abided by the terms of the unratified SALT II treaty because American military leaders found it useful to do so.[39] When the Reagan administration eventually resumed negotiations on long-range nuclear weaponry, it sought to reduce rather than simply limit the armaments on both sides and called the negotiations the Strategic Arms Reduction Talks, abbreviated as START.

In the nuclear competition with the Soviet Union, the administration confronted, in its own view, two problems that bore a resemblance to previous strategic challenges. The "window of vulnerability" of the 1980s recalled the purported missile gap of the 1950s.[40] The later challenge stemmed from the fact that the Soviet Union had larger land-based missiles of intercontinental range than did the United States. The Soviet missiles could carry more warheads and so, in theory, might be able to knock out the American missile fleet in a surprise attack by aiming several warheads at each missile. Even in the extremely unlikely event that Moscow successfully executed such an attack, the United

States would retain the capacity for "assured destruction" on which deterrence depended: many American nuclear weapons would remain, carried by long-range bomber aircraft and ocean-going submarines, and could visit massive destruction on the Soviet homeland in retaliation. Nonetheless, some American strategists feared that the theoretical asymmetry between the two missile fleets might be translated into a geopolitical advantage for the Soviet side.[41] It became a major strategic goal of the United States to close the window of vulnerability.

The United States, and not the United States alone, worried as well about the viability of extended deterrence—that is, the credibility of the American commitment to defend Western Europe. In the 1960s response to the presumed Soviet advantage in non-nuclear forces, which some feared undercut that credibility, the Kennedy administration had adopted the strategy of flexible response. That strategy required increases in non-nuclear forces on the continent that America's North Atlantic Treaty Organization (NATO) allies proved unwilling to supply.[42] In the 1970s, the same basic problem arose again, albeit in a different form. The Soviet Union deployed missiles in Eastern Europe capable of reaching targets in Western Europe that came to be called Intermediate-Range Nuclear Forces, abbreviated as INF. NATO had no comparable missiles, which created the possibility, again in the minds of some Western strategists, that the Soviet Union would be able to exploit this advantage for political gain.[†] As with the window of vulnerability, the likelihood of serious political and military damage

---

[†] Strobe Talbott, *Deadly Gambits: The Reagan Administration and the Stalemate in Nuclear Arms Control*, New York: Alfred A. Knopf, 1984, pp. 26–30. Specifically, the nightmare scenario for military planners involved the presumption that in a war in Europe the Soviet side would be able to use its intermediate-range missiles against targets in Western Europe and NATO, having none, would face a choice between giving up or escalating to intercontinental-range missiles, which, if used against the Soviet Union, would invite Soviet nuclear attacks on the continental United States. Since the American government would not take steps that would provoke such attacks, the Soviet side would possess "escalation dominance." Because both sides would know this in advance of any conflict, the American promise to defend Europe through "extended deterrence" would not be credible. Such a scenario was not at all likely, but strategic thinkers and planners tended to concern themselves not only with what was likely but also with what was conceivable. On this point see Robert Jervis, *The Meaning of the Nuclear*

to the West was low but the stakes were high, and addressing the perceived problem did not put a great strain on Western treasuries.

Chancellor Helmut Schmidt of Germany sounded the alarm about this gap in the Western deterrent force and in 1979 the NATO countries agreed to deploy missiles to offset the Soviet ones. Stationing missiles in their countries[43] was not popular with the people of Western Europe, and for that reason the NATO governments also agreed to begin negotiations with the Soviet Union to limit them.[44] The Reagan administration's position in the INF negotiations became known as the "zero option": it mandated that neither side deploy any intermediate-range missiles at all, an unequal bargain because when it was proposed the Warsaw Pact had already installed some and NATO had not yet done so.[45] The plan for deploying such weapons encountered popular resistance, especially in West Germany, which the Soviet Union did all it could to encourage.[46] In November 1983, however, NATO's installation of its own INFs began.

President Reagan introduced the most controversial military initiative of his time in office on March 23, 1983, in a speech proposing the development and deployment of a system of space-based lasers to defend the United States against missile attack. Such a system, Reagan said, would render nuclear weapons "impotent and obsolete."[47] His Strategic Defense Initiative arose from Reagan's discomfort with the condition of Mutual Assured Destruction, which made American security rest on the threat to annihilate the Soviet Union, and vice versa. It stemmed, as well, from his faith in American science and technology, which, he believed, could construct a system effective enough to deflect or destroy the many nuclear warheads the Soviet Union could send to strike the United States.[48]

If Reagan's vision were to come to fruition, it would end the nuclear standoff between the two superpowers, tilting the military balance decisively in America's favor. The president declared his goal to be relieving the world of the threat of nuclear destruction, not achieving nuclear superiority for the United States, and said that he would share

Revolution: Statecraft and the Prospect of Armageddon, Ithaca, New York: Cornell University Press, 1989, pp. 218–221.

the yet-to-be-created technology with the Soviet Union.[49] Soviet officials showed no sign of believing this.

The 1972 the Anti-Ballistic Missile (ABM) Treaty prohibited the kind of defenses that the president sought, but research on missile defense had been an item in the budget of the Department of Defense for many years. Reagan elevated its importance and increased its funding. Before the two sides had to cope with the strategic consequences of a foolproof system of missile defense, however, the United States had to develop one; and it was far from clear that this would ever occur. The Nixon administration had signed the ABM Treaty not because it wanted the United States to be vulnerable to a Soviet nuclear attack but because it concluded that effective defense was not feasible. This was so because in order to be worthwhile, defenses had to work perfectly: only a few Soviet nuclear explosives evading whatever defenses the United States deployed would bring destruction to the country far beyond anything it had ever experienced.[50]

The Reagan administration also devised a response to the gains that the Soviet Union had made in the Third World in the previous decade. For much of the Cold War, insurgents friendly to and sometimes directed by communists had attacked pro-Western governments. The administration sought to turn the tables by supporting insurgents against pro-communist regimes. The policy of encouraging, aiding, and sometimes training and equipping such insurgents came to be known as the Reagan Doctrine.[‡]

The Caribbean and Central America, where the United States had intervened in the past, toward which Americans maintained a proprietary attitude that descended from the Monroe Doctrine, and where Cuba had turned into a Soviet outpost, became a major arena for

---

[‡] Michael Mandelbaum and Strobe Talbott, *Reagan and Gorbachev*, New York: Vintage Books, 1987, p. 62. "In the April 1, 1985 issue of *Time* magazine, conservative columnist Charles Krauthammer hailed the emergence of a 'Reagan Doctrine,' of 'overt and unashamed' aid to 'freedom fighters' seeking to overthrow 'nasty Communist governments.' Although it was given a name only in the second term, and then by a journalist, what came to be called the Reagan Doctrine was established policy from the start." George C. Herring, *From Colony to Superpower: U.S. Foreign Relations Since 1776*, New York: Oxford University Press, 2008, p. 881.

the application of the Reagan Doctrine. On October 25, 1983, 7,600 American troops removed the radical, pro-Cuban government of the tiny Caribbean island of Grenada, where, the administration said, resident Americans, many of them medical students, were in danger.[51] The administration also assisted the government of El Salvador in coping with an insurgency.[52]

Its principal effort in the Western Hemisphere, however, centered on Nicaragua. In December 1981 Reagan authorized $20 million for a covert operation in neighboring Honduras to organize and train an armed force for the purpose of blocking Nicaraguan assistance to the rebels in El Salvador and ultimately for overthrowing the Sandinistas.[53] Initially numbering 500, the Contras, as they were called, grew to a force of 15,000.[54] American support for them became politically controversial. Influenced by the experience in Vietnam, opponents of the Reagan policy objected to the American involvement in a civil war, saw the Contras as uncommitted to democratic principles, and feared that American troopswould be sent to fight in Nicaragua.[55] The opponents succeeded in passing legislation prohibiting the American government from using its funds on behalf of the insurgents.[56] The administration searched for—and ultimately found—money from other sources to sustain them.[57] In 1989, after Reagan had left office, the American government conducted its largest military operation since the Vietnam War to remove the dictator of Panama, Manuel Noriega.[58] The United States applied the Reagan Doctrine beyond Central America as well, in 1985 providing very modest help to a group fighting the Cuban-supported government of Angola in Africa,[59] and to opponents of the Vietnamese-installed government of Cambodia in Southeast Asia.[60]

The Reagan administration also became involved in the affairs of the Middle East, where it discovered that the template of the Cold War was not always relevant. Although governments and other groups in the region were happy to receive military and economic assistance from the superpowers, the chief conflicts there did not pit democratic friends of the West against Marxist-Leninists. Instead, the main cleavages involved differences of sect, religion, tribe, and ethnicity. For this reason, and because the United States used its own military forces rather than sponsoring others, the initiatives in the region do not qualify as instances of the Reagan Doctrine; and in any event, the Reagan Middle East policies did not meet with much success.

In 1980, Iraq, led by a brutal Sunni Muslim dictator named Saddam Hussein, attacked Iran, with its revolutionary, fundamentalist Islamic, Shia Muslim government. Because Iran seemed to pose the greater threat to American interests, and at the behest of the oil-exporting Sunni Muslim monarchies of the Persian Gulf—above all Saudi Arabia—which feared the Islamic Republic, Washington tilted toward Iraq. It provided intelligence to the Iraqi government and, on July 3, 1988, while patrolling the Persian Gulf to ensure the free flow of oil, an American warship accidentally shot down an Iranian airliner, killing 290 people.[61] Whereas in other parts of the world regimes that the United States supported shared at least some American values or American interests, Saddam was so far from sharing either that in the succeeding two decades the United States waged two wars against him.

The Reagan administration also twice became engaged in brief hostilities with Libya, which was led by a mercurial, terrorism-supporting dictator, Muammar Qaddafi. He had overthrown a pro-American monarch in 1969 and styled himself a resolute opponent of the West. On August 19, 1981, two Soviet-made Libyan jets attacked American aircraft over the Gulf of Sidra on the Mediterranean, where the Libyan government claimed exclusive jurisdiction. The American planes returned their fire and shot them out of the sky. In April 1986 Libya was discovered to have sponsored an explosion at a nightclub in Berlin frequented by American servicemen in which one of them died. In retaliation, American warplanes struck targets in Libya.[62]

The United States became even more deeply entangled in Lebanon. The Palestine Liberation Organization (PLO) used the country as a base from which to attack its southern neighbor, Israel. In 1982, in response to the PLO campaign, Israel invaded Lebanon. The leaders of the PLO were forced to leave the country and the Reagan administration dispatched troops to oversee their departure. It withdrew them, but inserted soldiers again when a Lebanese Christian militia perpetrated a massacre in two Palestinian refugee camps in the country.[63] The American forces did not have a clear mission and on October 23, 1983, 241 of them died when terrorists sent a truck loaded with explosives into a compound where they were living. A few months later Reagan withdrew the rest of the troops.

His administration had another misadventure in Lebanon. Pro-Iranian forces in that country took several Americans captive. The president wanted to get them released and to that end members of his government sold weapons to Iran, the proceeds of which were funneled to the Nicaraguan Contras to replace the funds Congress had denied them.[64] What became known as the Iran-Contra Scandal involved the Reagan administration in three violations: of an arms embargo on the Iranian government; of its own principle of not negotiating with terrorists; and of the law prohibiting government assistance to the Contras. When what the administration had done came to light, the president at first denied any knowledge of it but then had to admit that he had in fact authorized arms shipments from Israel to Iran in 1985.[65] His popularity fell to its lowest point in his presidency.[66]

The most consequential campaign of assistance to insurgents took place in Afghanistan, the country where the Reagan Doctrine had its greatest impact on the Cold War. The Soviet invasion and occupation provoked widespread armed opposition in the country. The United States sent arms to the Afghans through neighboring Pakistan, in-cluding, in 1986, Stinger antiaircraft missiles capable of bringing down the helicopters that the Soviet army used in its campaign to pacify the country.[67] Supplying weaponry to the Afghan resistance was perhaps the most significant Central Intelligence Agency (CIA) operation of the second half of the Cold War, although it was hardly a secret one.

In Afghanistan the United States truly did turn the tables on the Soviet Union. With American assistance, Afghanistan became a Soviet version of the American war in Vietnam. The Afghan resist-ance drew its strength less from nationalist sentiment, as in Vietnam, than from tribal loyalties and religious motives; but the Afghans, like the Vietnamese, fought fiercely and absorbed far more casualties than did the much better-armed troops they were fighting. As with the Vietnamese communists, the assistance the Afghans received from other countries enabled them to do painful damage to the foreign forces in their country. Ultimately, the war in Afghanistan had an outcome similar to the end of the war in Vietnam: the Soviet forces withdrew.

The Reagan Doctrine, in its various geographic iterations, did not succeed in overthrowing any of the governments that American-assisted insurgents attacked; but the insurgencies did have an impact. Along with the expansion of the American armed forces that the increase in defense spending purchased, and the potential threat to Soviet security that the Strategic Defense Initiative posed, they exerted pressure on the Soviet Union by raising the cost to Moscow of the competition with the United States and its allies. In the 1980s, however, the important developments in the Cold War took place not in the military rivalry between the superpowers but in the economic, social, and political arenas of the great global contest of systems.

The Crucial Decade

The Cold War changed course during the 1980s. The West escaped the economic doldrums of the 1970s. The communist bloc faltered; its national economies stagnated. The expectation that central planning would prove superior to free markets as a formula for economic growth, an article of faith for two generations of communists, faded away. In addition, another serious challenge to communist rule arose in Eastern Europe. At the same time, an increasing number of countries in the Third World moved toward Western economic and political institutions and practices and away from those similar to the ones in the Marxist-Leninist countries. In the 1980s, in short, while the overall military competition between the superpowers remained a stalemate despite the more aggressive tactics of the Reagan administration, in the economic and political contest the West took a lead that proved, at the end of the decade, to be decisive.

As the decade began, the United States was on its way to overcoming, albeit at considerable cost, one of its major economic pathologies—inflation. Jimmy Carter appointed Paul Volcker to be the chairman of the Federal Reserve and Volcker conquered inflation by raising interest rates to very high levels, reaching 22.4 percent in 1981. This plunged the American economy into recession—unemployment climbed to 10.8 percent in November 1982—but the inflation rate did drop sharply, falling from 12 percent when Carter left office to 3.2 percent in 1983.[68] Thereafter growth resumed, with real gross domestic product increasing by more than a third during the Reagan presidency,[69] partly as a normal rebound from a sharp downturn, partly in response to the stimulus of the Reagan administration's military spending, and partly because of the tax cut—another source of stimulus—that it passed and its easing of regulations on business. In the 1980s, moreover, the remarkable information technologies that were to pervade the West and then the world in subsequent decades began to be available, thanks to the efforts of private American entrepreneurs such as Bill Gates and Steve Jobs.[70]

Western Europe encountered economic difficulties in the 1970s similar to those of the United States. Major sources of the postwar economic upsurge—the adoption of previously untapped American-developed technology and products, for example—had run their course[71] and the two oil shocks dampened economic activity while raising prices, as they did on the other side of the Atlantic. The "trentes glorieuses"—the thirty glorious years of unprecedentedly rapid economic growth—came to an end.[72]

In 1979, however, Margaret Thatcher became prime minister of Great Britain, with the same kind of economic agenda, emphasizing a reduction in the role of government, that Ronald Reagan subsequently brought to the United States. In 1983 the center-right Christian Democrats, with similar inclinations in economic policy, replaced the Social Democrats in power in West Germany. The socialist Francois Mitterrand was elected president of France in 1981 and implemented the opposite kinds of economic policies, raising taxes and nationalizing important sectors of the French economy. His measures provoked a sharp political and economic backlash that caused Mitterrand to reverse course in 1982 and put in practice economic policies more like Reagan's and Thatcher's and less like those to which he had initially been committed.[73]

The major Western European economies did better economically in the 1980s, especially in the decade's second half, than in the 1970s.[74] In addition to the new market-friendly policies, all of Western Europe benefited from the process of formal economic integration that had begun with the formation of the European Coal and Steel Community and continued with the establishment of the European Economic Community. The Single European Act, which went into effect in 1987, set a timetable for the creation of a single European market with the free movement of goods, people, services, and capital,[75] the anticipation of which spurred economic activity in the western part of the continent.[76]

The West as a whole, that is, moved during this crucial decade toward an approach to economic management that came to be called "neoliberalism," giving priority to private institutions rather than government provision and supervision. Reliance on free markets distinguished the Western from the communist economic systems and in the 1980s Western markets became freer. The change of direction produced (or, as critics believed, coincided with) positive economic results. Insofar as the Cold War was a competition between free markets and central planning, in that decade the Western economic system took a substantial, unmistakable lead.

The decade was not free of economic conflict within the West. The economic revival of the countries that World War II had devastated, a revival that had underlain the American decision to close the gold window,[77] continued to exert pressure on American manufacturers. Japanese firms in particular, in industries such as textiles, automobiles, and steel, made inroads into the American market, generating demands for protection by affected industries and especially their workers, beginning in the 1970s.[78] The Democratic Party, to whose coalition labor unions belonged, became the political vehicle for these demands. This reversed the domestic politics of trade. Since the Civil War, the Republicans had supported restrictions on international commerce. In the 1980s the Democrats replaced them in this role while the tariff-supporting Republicans embraced the cause of free trade.[79]

The American government negotiated agreements with Japan (and other countries) to impose limits on trade in some sectors.[80] This violated the principle of free trade but preserved the overall Japanese-American economic relationship—a profitable one for both countries—as well as the cohesion of their military alliance.

Similarly, the United States came to believe, as it had before it ended the Bretton Woods monetary system on August 15, 1971, that Western currencies had become misaligned, with the German deutschmark and the Japanese yen undervalued in relation to the dollar, resulting in American trade deficits. The Plaza Agreement of 1985, named for the New York City hotel where its final details were worked out, realigned

Western currencies in the direction that the American government desired. By reducing the American trade deficit, this helped to relieve some of the domestic political pressure for protection in the United States.[81] Once again, negotiations among the democracies yielded an outcome that preserved overall economic and political harmony in the West. The competition with the Soviet Union put a premium on the maintenance of Western unity; and Western unity in turn fortified the Western position in that competition.

While the Western free-market economies experienced a resurgence in the 1980s, those of the communist countries declined. Between 1978 and 1988 the Soviet economy expanded by a mere seven percent overall, and by the second half of the 1980s its actual annual growth had fallen below one percent.[82] Eastern European growth also fell below one percent in that decade.[83] Such legitimacy as the Moscow-installed governments in Eastern Europe enjoyed rested on the delivery of a rising standard of living. Unable to provide this through domestic economic performance, these governments borrowed heavily from the West, struggled to keep up the required payments, and thus slipped into debt crises.[84]

The Soviet Union labored under several economic handicaps in the 1980s: the price of the oil, on the export of which Moscow depended for its hard-currency earnings, fell sharply;[85] the defense sector claimed a disproportionate share of the country's talent and resources, at the expense of the rest of the economy;[86] and the rigidly hierarchical Soviet system required leadership from the top to instigate change but until 1985 the person at the top of the hierarchy was feeble. Leonid Brezhnev had faded badly in the last years of his life, which ended in 1982.[87] Yuri Andropov, the former head of the secret police, the KGB, succeeded him but developed a debilitating kidney disease and died in 1984. The next in line, Brezhnev's former chief aide Konstantin Chernenko, was infirm when he took power and passed away in 1985.

A broader, deeper problem underlay the decline of the communist economies, however. The model for economic growth on which they relied had, by the 1980s, outlived its usefulness. The institutions and practices that could have delivered growth turned out to be incompatible with the political system the communist parties had imposed and so proved impossible to adopt.

Since the beginning of communist rule these countries had practiced "extensive growth," increasing production through an expanding flow of the ingredients required for it: land, capital, raw materials, and, above all, labor. By the 1980s these ingredients were no longer available in the abundance that had marked the glory years of communist growth. In particular, and as in Western Europe, the Soviet Union and its communist European satellites had run short of underemployed rural workers who became far more productive after moving to cities and working in factories located there.

To sustain economic growth the communist countries would have had to shift to the "intensive" approach, making better use of the ingredients of production at their disposal rather than adding more and more of them. The conditions for intensive growth were present in the West: real prices, so as to allocate resources efficiently; independent firms that could experiment with methods of increasing production; and secure rights of private property to create incentives to develop new and better products and processes of production. The principles and practices of Marxism-Leninism, however, forbade all these things.[88]

The communism that Stalin had created, that is, could not accommodate the necessary bases for economic growth in the late twentieth century. Karl Marx had predicted a conflict between the operations of capitalist economies and the requirements of political stability in the societies in which they were operating, which would, he asserted, lead to revolution. He anticipated, that is, a fatal conflict between economics and politics. Such a conflict did emerge in the 1980s, but in societies governed by parties that professed fidelity to Marx's teachings; and that conflict did lead, ultimately, to revolution.

None of this had anything to do with the United States or its foreign policies, which was the case as well for the major political crisis in the communist bloc in the early 1980s. It occurred in Poland, the country with the largest population of all the members of the Warsaw Pact and the one that had pushed back against communist rule most frequently since 1945.[89] Unlike the rest of Eastern Europe, Poland had some private agriculture and its Catholic Church played a prominent role in everyday life. In 1978 a Pole, Karol Wojtyla, a Cardinal from Krakow, was elected pope, the first non-Italian to hold that office in more than 400 years. Pope John Paul II, as he was known, made a triumphant trip to Poland in June 1979, drawing huge crowds. His visit provided the occasion for a massive public display by the Poles of nationalist—and therefore anticommunist—sentiment.[90]

In August of 1980 workers in the Lenin shipyard in the Polish Baltic city of Gdansk staged a strike. They began with economic demands but soon adopted political ones as well. Strikes broke out across the country and turned into a social movement that was peaceful, well organized, and very broadly based. The government of Poland was forced to do what no ruling Communist Party had ever done before: recognize an independent trade union, which was called Solidarity.[91] The existence of Solidarity violated a fundamental communist taboo against permitting the creation of any organization independent of the state, and the Polish government—headed, in another break with precedent, not by a civilian bureaucrat but by an army general, Wojciech Jaruzelski—ultimately cracked down on it in December 1982, declaring martial law and putting Solidarity's leaders in jail.[92]

The episode demonstrated that communism in Europe had become as decrepit politically as it was economically. Not only could communists maintain themselves in power only through coercion, but also, in Poland at least, the society had found ways to resist the Party, in nonviolent but effective fashion. Furthermore, while communism's Cold War adversary was prospering and it was stagnating, the countries formally part of neither bloc, those belonging to the Third World, were gravitating toward the West. They did not act in concert, nor, in general, did individual countries make economic and political choices for the purpose of aligning themselves with the United States and its allies. Nonetheless, the net effect of the policies they adopted was to tilt the contest of systems further in the direction of the capitalist democracies.

Like the countries of Eastern Europe, in the early 1980s a number of Third World countries, mainly in Latin America, experienced debt crises. The increase in the price of oil caused by the two oil shocks of the 1970s had compelled them to borrow heavily to purchase the imported petroleum required to sustain their economies. As part of the fight against inflation in the United States, as well as the need for the American government to borrow money on a large scale to fund the budget deficits that the Reagan tax cuts and increases in defense spending created, interest rates moved sharply upward and the cost of servicing the borrowers' debts rose beyond what they could pay. They therefore restructured their obligations in negotiations with Western—mainly American—banks and the International Monetary Fund. The new arrangements imposed a harsh austerity on the debtor countries, in which economic growth stalled. The 1980s came to be known as a "lost decade" in much of Latin America.[93]

For the purposes of the global contest of systems, what mattered most about the debt crisis was what did *not* happen. The afflicted countries did not leave the Western financial system. They did not follow the course Cuba had taken two decades previously. Even with the economic pain it caused them, which could be seen in Marxist-Leninist terms as having been inflicted by rapacious capitalists, they judged remaining within the American-centered international economic order to be a better path to economic growth than joining the communist bloc.

Another development in the Third World had an even greater impact in the economic arena of the contest of systems. Two distinct strategies for achieving the economic growth emerged, each of them with affinities to one of the two rival Cold War economic systems. The import substitution approach, like the workings of the centrally planned economies, emphasized the economic role of the government, the development of heavy industry, and a measure of insulation from the global economy—in the case of the Third World countries through protective tariffs.[94] Export promotion, by contrast, relied more on markets, competition, and, as the name implies, exports to foreign markets—an approach more in tune with the free-market economic systems of the United States and its allies.[95]

In the 1980s, the import-substituting countries, like the communist planned economies, faltered: a financial crisis struck the largest of them, India, in 1991 and in response the Indian government adopted free-market policies it had previously eschewed. Export-promoting countries, by contrast, thrived. Japan had pioneered this approach after 1945 and became an economic dynamo, constructing, from the ruins of World War II, the world's second-largest economy. Other East Asian countries, notably South Korea, Taiwan, and Singapore, followed the Japanese example and also achieved impressive economic growth.[96]

At the beginning of the decade the strategy of export promotion made its most significant convert. The People's Republic of China, under Mao Zedong's tyrannical rule an orthodox Stalinist planned economy, began to permit free markets to operate. The Chinese economic reforms started in agriculture, and then quasi-private entities called township and village enterprises appeared and the Communist government in Beijing[97] created special economic zones offering generous terms to attract foreign investment to them. Led by a booming export sector, China's economy soared. Four decades of remarkably rapid economic growth followed.[98]

In the Third World, therefore, the economic practices close to those of the West outperformed those partly resembling the economic patterns of the communist world, even—indeed especially—in the largest communist country on Earth. As the superiority of export promotion over import substitution became ever clearer, countries outside East Asia began to adopt some of the policies it entailed.[99] In this way, the largest and poorest part of the world, which President Kennedy and others had believed would form the crucial battlefield of the Cold War, sided, on the whole, with the West.

While the United States played no direct role in the failure of communist economics, it did contribute to the success of the export-promoting countries. Japan, South Korea, and Taiwan enjoyed the protection that came with an American alliance. More generally, American military power furnished the security in the Asia-Pacific region without which commerce would not take place. Not least important, an appreciable volume of the exporters' exports went to the United States. Export promotion could not have brought the high growth rates it did without access to the American market.

The West also made major gains in the Third World in the 1980s through the spread of its political system. The "democratic wave"[100] of the final decades of the twentieth century actually began in Europe. There, in 1974, the longstanding dictatorship of Portugal fell and, after a turbulent political passage, a democratic government came to power. The wave spread to Asia, where the Philippines, Taiwan, and South Korea abandoned autocratic rule for governments chosen by free elections. It swept over South America as well. In 1980 only two of the countries there qualified as democratic. By 1990, all did.[101]

The United States had close ties with a number of the new democracies and on occasion—in the Philippines, for example—was able to use its influence to promote the transition from autocratic to democratic rule. Democracy spread largely by example, however, as countries admired and sought to emulate the economic prosperity and the stable, liberty-promoting politics of the growing global community of democracies.[102] By virtue of its status as the leader of that community, the United States contributed substantially to the power of its example.

China proved to be the exception to the democratizing trend of the 1980s. In the spring of 1989, a group of students gathered in Beijing's Tiananmen Square to mourn a recently deceased Communist Party leader who had been removed from power for his liberal political views. The initial gathering turned into an ongoing demonstration, with crowds becoming larger every day. Similar demonstrations took place in 341 cities across the country.[103] The causes on behalf of which people were demonstrating varied but included the desire for a democratic rather than a communist political system. The senior communist leaders saw the demonstrations as a threat to their rule and on June 4 sent soldiers to clear out Tiananmen Square by force. Several hundred people were killed.[104]

The setback to democracy in China notwithstanding, the decade of the 1980s was a period of economic and political successes for the West. That ongoing success, as well as the deep difficulties besetting the communist world and the gravitation of the Third World toward Western practices and institutions, were the global conditions that greeted the Soviet leader, Mikhail Gorbachev, who succeeded Konstantin Chernenko in March 1985. They determined his governing agenda. That agenda, as it evolved, had the most profound consequences imaginable. Gorbachev turned out, despite himself, to be the great revolutionary of the second half of the twentieth century. More or less deliberately, he brought about the end of the Cold War. Certainly unintentionally, he put an end to communism in Europe and to the Soviet Union itself. For that reason, he counts as one of the most consequential figures in the history of American foreign policy.

Détente II

Gorbachev was a generation younger than the men who had immediately preceded him as the general secretary of the Communist Party of the Soviet Union and thus the supreme leader of the country.[105] He had a clear mission: to lift the country out of the stagnation—above all the economic stagnation—in which it was trapped. Without economic growth the Soviet Union would fall ever farther behind in the Cold War competition with the United States. At stake was its status as a superpower.[106]

He first sought to improve the country's economic performance through discipline and exhortation. Gorbachev called the new approach "uskoreniye"—acceleration. Workers, managers, planners, and bureaucrats would, in effect, try harder. He attempted to reduce the widespread problem of alcoholism by limiting the sale of vodka, earning himself the title of "the mineral water secretary." This initial approach did not produce the results he wanted. He then adopted a more ambitious program of economic change, which he called "perestroika"—restructuring. When inertia and opposition obstructed the changes he believed necessary he introduced two Western-style political reforms: "glasnost"—freer speech[107]—and democratization.

By 1989 the political reforms had proceeded so far that the country held contested elections for a national legislature, the Congress of People's Deputies.[108] Gorbachev, although not elected, presided over its deliberations, in which the public heard more open discussion of public issues than ever before in the history of the Soviet Union.[109] Two representatives to the Congress became particularly prominent: Andrei Sakharov, an honored scientist turned dissident and Nobel Peace Prize recipient whom the regime had banished to the city of Gorky[110] for declaring his opposition to the invasion of Afghanistan but whom Gorbachev had allowed to return to his home in Moscow,[111] and Boris Yeltsin, once the Communist Party leader in the Siberian city of Sverdlovsk,[112] whom Gorbachev appointed to the Politburo, who tried to resign in protest against what he deemed the unduly slow pace of reform but was fired instead, and who then left the Party and resurrected his political career as an independent.[113]

Gorbachev enjoyed greater success in foreign policy than in domestic affairs. He instigated changes in the Soviet approach to the rest of the world that came to be called "the new thinking." The new ideas— new, that is, to the official doctrines of the Soviet Union—included the proposition that security had to be mutual, with the implication that the policy of amassing ever more armaments, which Brezhnev had instituted, would not make the country more secure. Gorbachev eventually also rejected the precept, which dated back to Lenin, that conflict between the communist and capitalist camps was inevitable. He embraced the principle that sovereign states were entitled to choose their own political systems and international orientations, which canceled the Brezhnev Doctrine[114] and had major repercussions in communist Eastern Europe.

These ideas developed over the course of Gorbachev's time in power. At its outset, his first order of business was to support the economic revitalization that was his principal goal by easing the strain and lowering the cost of the military competition with the United States. He therefore made it a high priority to resume the 1970s policy of détente.

Although he had come to office having opposed the détente of the previous decade, Ronald Reagan also had reasons for wishing to improve relations with his country's great adversary. He had presided over an expansion of American military power, enabling the United States to do what he had long said was necessary:[115] negotiate with the Soviet Union from a position of strength. Moreover, he sensed—correctly—that Gorbachev differed in important ways from his predecessors.[116] Finally, as his Strategic Defense Initiative demonstrated, he wanted to find a way to end the vulnerability of both societies to a devastating nuclear attack.

All told, Reagan and Gorbachev met five times,§ becoming the fifth and final pair of American and Soviet leaders whose interactions helped

---

§ They met in Geneva in 1985; in Reykjavik, Iceland, in 1986; in Moscow in 1987; and in Washington in 1988. The last of their meetings, a brief and informal encounter without a formal agenda, took place in December 1988 at the United Nations in New York, to which Gorbachev had come to deliver a major address. Reagan's vice president, George H. W. Bush, who had won the presidential election in the previous month, also attended the New York meeting. Richard Reeves, *President Reagan: The Triumph of Imagination*, New York: Simon & Schuster, 2005, pp. 482–484. During the Reagan presidency a three-part agenda for Soviet-American relations developed, consisting of arms control, regional conflicts, and, at American insistence, human rights. *Ibid.*, p. 346; Odd Arne Westad, *The Cold War: A World History*, New York: Basic Books, 20017, p. 48.

to shape the history of the twentieth century. Wilson and Lenin offered contrasting views of international order in the wake of World War I. Franklin Roosevelt and Stalin forged a crucial, if temporary, alliance in World War II. Kennedy and Khrushchev presided over the two most dangerous crises of the nuclear age. Nixon and Brezhnev orchestrated the first period of détente, and Reagan and Gorbachev the second.

The two leaders held a get-acquainted session in Geneva in November 1985—the first such meeting in six years—and in October of the next year traveled to Reykjavik, the capital of Iceland, for another encounter. It turned into the most unusual of all Soviet-American summit meetings. Gorbachev proposed what was, by the standards of the nuclear negotiations since the late 1960s, a genuinely radical proposal: to do away—as the Reagan administration's zero option envisioned—with all intermediate-range nuclear missiles in Europe and indeed to go further and reduce all intercontinental-range missiles by half. Reagan countered by proposing the elimination of all ballistic missiles in ten years. The Soviet leader made it a condition of any agreement that the United States not deploy missile defense for ten years. Reagan, committed to his Strategic Defense Initiative, refused. Reykjavik ended without any agreement.[117]

The summit had put the nuclear radicalism of the two leaders on display. As with the American Baruch Plan of 1946,[118] however, it is far from clear that, even if they had reached agreement in principle, the sweeping reductions of which they had spoken would actually have come about. Protracted and undoubtedly contentious negotiations to work out the details would have ensued. Moreover, in the United States influential members of the foreign policy community and of Congress, and even the nation's military leaders, expressed serious reservations about the abolition of all nuclear-armed missiles.[119]

Reagan's vice president, George H. W. Bush, won the 1988 presidential election and succeeded him in the White House. Initially, Bush adopted a cautious approach to the Soviet Union, uncertain that Gorbachev had fundamentally altered its approach to the rest of the world.[120] Soon, however, the new president was carried along by the increasingly radical changes that were taking place in both Soviet domestic affairs and Soviet foreign policy. After the failure at Reykjavik, Reagan and then Bush succeeded in concluding arms control agreements with the Soviet Union that did far more to reshape the nuclear arsenals of the two superpowers than any previous accords.

At their 1987 Moscow summit, Reagan and Gorbachev signed a treaty eliminating, as the United States had wanted, all intermediate-range missiles on the European continent. The INF Treaty broke with precedent in several ways. For the first time, it substantially reduced armaments on both sides and in fact abolished an entire class of weaponry. It had an asymmetrical impact: the Soviet Union gave up more weapons than did the United States.[121] Most importantly, the accord authorized personnel from each side to enter the territory of the other to verify that the terms of the agreement were being carried out.[122] The Soviet regime had never before permitted on-site inspections—hence the reliance, for verifying earlier arms control agreements, on photography by reconnaissance satellites.[123]

At the Moscow summit Reagan made it clear that the political relationship between the two superpowers had changed markedly. Asked whether he still believed the Soviet Union to be an "evil empire," he replied, "No. You are talking about another time, another era."[124]

In the spirit of that new relationship, the two countries subsequently put limits on long-range nuclear armaments as well, in the START I Treaty signed in July 1991 and the follow-on START II accord of January 1993. Together the two led to the decommissioning of a large number of the armaments of this type on both sides. By restricting the Soviet Union's largest missiles, it closed the "window of vulnerability" that had long concerned American officials.** The Soviet government was willing to enter into these agreements because, in the five years since Reykjavik, it had become persuaded that the United States would not, in fact, be able to develop a leakproof shield to protect against

---

** "START I limited each side to a total of 1,600 long-range land- and sea-based ballistic missiles and heavy bombers. Within this overall total, the treaty mandated a 50 percent reduction in the Soviet heavy missiles that Washington regarded as destabilizing. START II went even further: Not only did it stipulate that the nuclear stockpiles on both sides be reduced to within 3,000 and 3,500 warheads over ten years, but also by its terms all multiple warheads on all ballistic missiles were to be eliminated." Michael Mandelbaum, *The Dawn of Peace in Europe*, New York: The Twentieth Century Fund Press, 1996, p. 88.

nuclear attack.[125] Moscow therefore no longer insisted that the United States pledge to forswear missile defense as a condition for such treaties.

In 1990 the two superpowers concluded an agreement to place limits on non-nuclear weapons—the tanks, artillery pieces, combat aircraft, and helicopters that each deployed by the thousands on the European continent. The Conventional Forces in Europe (CFE) Treaty came in the wake of a unilateral decrease in such forces on the Soviet side that Gorbachev had announced in a speech at the United Nations in December 1988.[126] The breakthrough in the procedures for inspection in the INF Treaty made it possible.[127]

Taken together, these late–Cold War arms control agreements gave Europe a more stable, peaceful system of security than it had ever enjoyed. The new "common security" order had two defining features.[128] First, weapons—nuclear and conventional—were configured to be suitable for defense (in the case of long-range nuclear weapons deterrence) but not attack. Second, for both the deployment and the movement of their weapons all European countries and the United States practiced transparency: each could see what weapons all the others had and what they were doing with those weapons. This sharply reduced the chances, and thus the fear, of a successful surprise attack. In these new circumstances, peace rested not merely on the conviction that a military attack could not succeed but also on the confidence that none would be attempted.

The later arms control measures depended, as had the earlier ones, on the state of the political relationship between the United States and the Soviet Union. Because the basic political conflict that had given rise to the Cold War in the first place remained intact in the earlier period, the agreements produced then, for all the time and effort that went into them, had, except for the ABM Treaty, only a marginal impact on the forces the two sides deployed. The arms control of the 1970s had a largely symbolic value. Thanks to the changes that Gorbachev had introduced, by the time of the later treaties the political conflict had become far less sharp, making it possible to achieve much farther-reaching accords. Unlike the earlier agreements, the later ones restructured the two military forces in important ways.

One reason for the improvement in the superpower relationship was that Gorbachev moved to limit or end the Soviet commitments in the

Third World that had had so much to do with the demise of the first period of détente. The Soviet leader concluded that the drain on Soviet resources and the damage to Soviet relations with the West that communist gains in the Third World caused exceeded whatever geopolitical and economic benefits that they brought.[129]

In 1988, Soviet and American diplomats negotiated a Cuban withdrawal from Angola.[130] In 1990, Moscow agreed to reduce its aid to the Sandinistas and support free elections in Nicaragua. The elections were held and a pro-American government won the presidency.[131] Vietnam, which had become a Soviet client, left Cambodia.[132]

The most notable retreat came where the Soviet Union had made the biggest investment in blood and treasure—in Afghanistan. The Soviet officials who had ordered the invasion expected it to last for a few weeks.[133] It went on for a decade. The American-assisted Afghan resistance, while massively outgunned, regularly inflicted casualties on the occupying Soviet forces.[134] In 1986 Gorbachev had called the war there "a bleeding wound." Like President Nixon in Vietnam, he announced that Soviet forces would withdraw from the country[135] and in February 1989 the last Soviet soldier crossed over the border into Soviet Central Asia.

Gorbachev's withdrawal from positions in the Third World that the Soviet Union had won—mainly by force of arms—in the 1970s eliminated a principal American objection to the Soviet conduct of the détente of that period. These initiatives should have riveted the attention of the West, and the rest of the world. In fact, they did not. The major geopolitical development that they represented was overshadowed by a revolutionary sequence of events in Europe.

The End of the Cold War

The Cold War began in Europe. Despite the American and Soviet attention to Asia and the Third World, Europe was its central front and most important stake, and Europe is where it ended. In the extraordinary year 1989, history's most vivid display of the domino principle took place in Eastern Europe. One by one the communist regimes of the region, which Moscow had installed in the three years after the end of World War II, fell from power. Two years later the Soviet Union, the last great multinational empire in Europe, itself collapsed, with its fifteen constituent union republics emerging as fifteen separate, in- dependent, noncommunist countries. These events undid the political consequences of the Russian Revolution and World War II. The prin- ciples and institutions of Marxism-Leninism that had reigned supreme from Berlin to Vladivostok, and from the Arctic Circle to the Black and Caspian Seas, disappeared. With them disappeared the causes of the Cold War, and thus the Cold War itself.

The period from the beginning of 1989 to the end of 1991 forms one bookend, with the years 1945 to 1950 constituting the other, of the third great global conflict of the twentieth century. The later period, like the earlier one, had immense significance for American foreign policy. Unlike the first period, however, in the second the United States assumed the role of bystander, a spectator at rather than a participant in the spectacle of the end of communism in Europe. America and its allies won the two world wars through immense, costly exertions. To the events that ended the Cold War, by contrast, the surviving, victo- rious superpower, with one conspicuous exception—in Germany—di- rectly contributed almost nothing.

Poland was the first domino to fall. With clandestine American as- sistance, Solidarity managed to maintain an underground existence even after the crackdown of December 1982.[136] The country's economy continued to sputter and in 1989 the government sought to reach a compromise with the Polish people through round-table negotiations. The negotiations produced a plan for elections that would be freely conducted but with enough seats reserved for communists to ensure continuing communist control of the government. In the contested seats the communists lost overwhelmingly. They managed, in effect, to lose a rigged election.[137] It was clear in the aftermath that a commu- nist government would have no political legitimacy. In a fundamental and astonishing break with communist political practice, Gorbachev approved the appointment of a noncommunist prime minister, Tadeusz Mazowiecki. This represented the crossing of the Rubicon in commu- nist Eastern Europe. It abandoned the basic principle of governance there since World War II, which in fact lay at the heart of the con- flict with the West: the monopoly of power by the ruling Communist Parties.[138]

Hungary, with the least repressive Eastern European government—"the merriest barracks in the Soviet camp"—came next. The ruling party scheduled free elections for 1990, believing that it could win them. It did not, receiving only eight percent of the vote,[139] and disappeared from Hungarian politics. Before that, it had taken what proved to be an even more dramatic step in the unraveling of European communism: it opened its border with Austria. Visiting East Germans took the opportunity to cross through Austria to West Germany, where they were entitled to automatic citizenship.[140]

This exodus, combined with large demonstrations in East German cities, particularly Leipzig,[141] in the fall of 1989 put heavy pressure on the East German government in Berlin to cope with the rising displays of discontent and flight of its citizens. On November 9 it issued new travel regulations making it easier to visit the West. A government spokesman mistakenly said that anyone could do so without conditions and guards at the Berlin Wall—erected in 1961 precisely to stem the kind of outflow of East Germans that was now taking place through Austria—opened the barrier.[142] People flooded across in both directions: Berlin ceased to be a divided city.[143] Soon it became clear that the division of the country was no longer tenable. The West German chancellor, Helmut Kohl, produced a ten-point plan that pointed to the unification of the two German states.

Unlike the other dramatic episodes of 1989, in the matter of Germany the United States played an important role. In addition to Soviet resistance, both the British and French leaders, Margaret Thatcher and Francois Mitterrand, expressed extreme wariness at the prospect of a larger Germany at the center of Europe—a circumstance that had, after all, led to three major wars between 1870 and 1945. President Bush helped to overcome their opposition by quickly and firmly weighing in on the side of Chancellor Kohl. The United States went on to play a significant part in the merger of the two Germanies. This was the only instance of active American intervention in the collapse of communism in Eastern Europe.

Along with Kohl, Bush and his administration organized a diplomatic framework for determining the German future. The "two plus four" negotiations involved the governments of the two Germanies, which addressed internal German matters, and the United States,

Great Britain, France, and the Soviet Union—the four countries with occupation rights in Berlin stemming from World War II—who concerned themselves with the international consequences of unification. The negotiations settled the details of the union of the German Democratic Republic and the German Federal Republic, which formally took place in October 1990. The new, unified Germany remained part of the NATO alliance.[144]

The revolution in Germany made the end of communism in Eastern Europe all but inevitable. If the Soviet Union was not willing to defend its westernmost outpost in Europe, which was located in the middle of a country from which it had suffered invasion twice in the twentieth century, and after already having permitted a noncommunist government in neighboring Poland, it followed logically that Moscow would not enforce communist rule anywhere else outside its own borders. The turn of Czechoslovakia to discard its Soviet-imposed government came next. The movement to do so was led by the dissident playwright Vaclav Havel, who had organized a group called Charter 77,[145] the goal of which was to promote the principles of the 1975 Helsinki Accords. In Czechoslovakia the legacy of that agreement had its greatest impact.[146]

Finally, Bulgaria and Romania abandoned communist rule. In Bulgaria, Todor Zhivkov, who had led the ruling party for thirty-five years, was shunted aside but veteran communists managed to retain control of the government in the immediate postcommunist period.[147] Only in Romania did violence accompany the end of the old regime. As many as 1,200 people died in the protests against Communist rule in that country. The communist leader Nicolae Ceausescu and his wife, Elena, fled the capital, Bucharest, but were apprehended, given a summary trial, and executed.[148]

In 1989 the political sentiments that communist armed forces had stifled in 1953 in East Berlin, in 1956 in Hungary, in 1968 in Czechoslovakia, and in 1979 in Poland were able to express themselves. Nationalism and anti-communism put an end to Marxist-Leninist rule in Eastern Europe and in so doing removed the fundamental cause of the Cold War. Mikhail Gorbachev's decision not to employ the tactics that Stalin, Khrushchev, and Brezhnev had used made this possible.

With the exception of Romania, the revolutions took place peacefully, the result of the democratic political culture, with its commitment to deciding domestic political questions peacefully, that had seeped into the societies of Eastern Europe despite their regimes' efforts to quarantine them from the West. They were peaceful as well because these regimes could not have been removed by force. The governments, not the people, had the guns; and the guns that the Soviet Union had, especially the nuclear ones, prevented Western military power from removing them. Germany aside, the chief contribution of the United States to the events of 1989 was the Bush administration's careful policy of refraining from "gloating"—that is, from effusively celebrating the demise of communism and Eastern Europe and conspicuously congratulating itself for this outcome.[149] Given the results, which were overwhelmingly favorable to the United States, this was a wise choice.

At the end of 1991 the Soviet Union itself followed communism in Eastern Europe into the dustbin of history. The unraveling began in the three Baltic republics—Estonia, Latvia, and Lithuania—culturally the most western of all the constituent parts of the country and thus the part most directly influenced by the developments in Eastern Europe.[150] Noncommunist parties won the free elections held in 1990 in all three. Lithuania thereupon declared the re-establishment of its independence, which the Soviet Union had extinguished in 1940 in the wake of the Nazi-Soviet pact of the previous year,[151] and the other two followed suit. In the summer of 1990, Russia, the largest of the fifteen constituent republics and the core of the Soviet Union as a whole, also proclaimed itself fully sovereign and Ukraine, the second-largest republic, which had been part of greater Russia for three centuries, did the same.[152] In 1991, Boris Yeltsin won election as Russia's president.[153] Gorbachev accepted none of the union republics' proclamations of effective independence. He was determined that the Soviet Union continue as a unified sovereign state.

The Bush administration adopted the same cautious approach to the unraveling of the Soviet Union as it had toward the falling dominoes in Eastern Europe. On August 1, 1991, the president gave an address in the Ukrainian capital, Kiev, in which he warned that "freedom is not the same thing as independence," and that "Americans will not support those who seek independence in order to replace a far-off tyranny with a local despotism" or "those who promote a suicidal nationalism based upon ethnic hatred."[154] Critics called it his "Chicken Kiev" speech.

The same motive lay behind Bush's caution in both cases: wariness of triggering a backlash against Gorbachev that, in the worst case, would remove him from power and reverse the retreat of communism over which he had presided.[155]

A backlash did, in fact, occur. On August 19, 1991, when Gorbachev was on vacation in the Crimea, a group of Soviet officials opposed to what he had done, and what he had allowed to happen, put him under house arrest and tried to seize power in Moscow. Resistance to the attempted coup rallied around Boris Yeltsin and the coup failed.

Gorbachev was freed, but the coup attempt had seriously diminished his power and dramatically expanded Yeltsin's, accelerating precisely the developments it had been launched to stop.[156] In December, the Russian president and the leaders of Ukraine and the third Slavic union republic, Belarus, signed an agreement effectively dissolving the Soviet Union.[157] The western parts of the country seceded while the Central Asian republics, where nationalist sentiment and European influence were far weaker, had independence thrust upon them. At the beginning of 1992, the Soviet Union was no more.

The downfall of the great Russia-centered communist empire in Eurasia was an event without precedent. Never before had such a powerful state in effect died in bed—that is, expired without suffering a defeat in war or experiencing large-scale revolutionary violence.[158] How could such a thing have happened? The intersection of several forces brought it about.

Not least important was the person, and personality, of Mikhail Gorbachev. The extreme centralization of authority in the Soviet system gave him more power over events than a leader of a democracy could have had. To him, far more than to any other individual, belongs the responsibility for what happened during his time as the supreme Soviet leader, from 1985 to 1991.[159] To what extent Gorbachev actually foresaw, desired, and worked to bring about the world-shaking events of those years is a matter for debate. Was he a man with a plan or a sleepwalker through history?

Clearly, his views changed over time.[160] He moved ever further away from fidelity to orthodox Marxism-Leninism both at home and abroad. By the end, he does seem to have wished to end the Cold War, and that he accomplished. He hoped to foster a more acceptable form of socialism in Eastern Europe[161] but acquiesced in the countries there going their own ways. While he wanted to reform the Soviet Union, he certainly did not wish to dissolve it; but that is what happened.[162]

The decisions he made to initiate some events and accept others arose ultimately from Gorbachev's character, which combined arrogance, ignorance, and decency. His arrogance led to his belief—which the Soviet veneration of the country's leaders, above all its founding leader V. I. Lenin, encouraged—that he had the wisdom and the skill to chart a considerably different and substantially better path for the several hundred million people directly or indirectly under his rule.[163] His ignorance frustrated that project. He had almost no idea of how a modern market economy, some of whose features he aspired to incorporate into the planned economies over which he presided, actually worked. Nor, apparently, was he fully aware that the Soviet-imposed governments of Eastern Europe, as well as those of the Baltic Soviet republics, lacked legitimacy in the eyes of the people they governed.[164] Finally, Mikhail Gorbachev was essentially a decent man who declined to use force to keep communism in power,[165] something that he certainly could have done and that none of his predecessors, from Lenin to Chernenko, would have hesitated to do. Gorbachev's arrogance led him to initiate changes, his ignorance prevented him from understanding their likely consequences, and his decency kept him from suppressing those consequences.

The context in which Gorbachev operated made a contribution to the end of communism equal to, if not greater than, his personal characteristics. When he came to power the Soviet bloc was falling behind the West economically. He took as his task closing the gap by accelerating economic growth. His determination to do so led to the initiatives that dismantled what he was trying to save. In this way, the contest of political and economic systems produced the outcome of the Cold War. Without its course in the 1980s, Gorbachev would not have proceeded as he did—if he had in fact become the Soviet leader— and the Cold War would not have ended, nor would communism in Eurasia have come to an end, as and when they did. They might well not have ended at all.

Communism had fallen behind economically because of the inadequacies of its economic system, which resisted constructive change because of its roots in fundamental Marxist-Leninist political principles. European communism also fell afoul of nationalism, the most powerful political sentiment of the twentieth century. Because communist rule contradicted the national principle by blocking genuine national self-determination from Berlin to Vladivostok, communism in power lacked political legitimacy. Both failures sapped the morale of the communist elite. Their system collapsed, finally, because they did not defend it; and they did not defend it because, by virtue of its failures, they had come to believe—many of them, at least—that it was not worth defending.[166]

While the Cold War did not end, and could not have ended, as previous such conflicts did, with one side defeating the other on the field of battle, its outcome did resemble in significant respects the results of the Napoleonic Wars of the eighteenth and nineteenth centuries and the two world wars of the twentieth. The defeated power in each lost territory and changed its form of government. The great wars of the past have another crucial feature in common with the Cold War: historically, victory almost invariably went to the warring party with "the longest purse"—that is, the most abundant economic reserves.[167] In the Cold War, the contest of systems, victory went to the side—the West—that won the economic competition.

Although the American government was largely a spectator in the great internal drama of European communism that ended the Cold War, when seen in historical perspective the United States did make a major contribution to that remarkable sequence of events. Ronald Reagan's conviction that Mikhail Gorbachev differed from previous Soviet leaders and George Bush's skillful diplomacy in the matter of German unification helped bring the great global conflict of the second half of the twentieth century to a safe and, from the American point of view, welcome conclusion. What the United States did over the long term, however—over the entire course of the Cold War—surpassed in importance its specific policies of the late 1980s. Furthermore, the continuities among the Cold War presidencies, Democratic as well as Republican, mattered more for the outcome of the conflict than their differences. Finally, the American and Western example had at least as much to do with that outcome as concrete American actions. What the United States was counted for as much as—if not more than—what the country did.

In the second half of the twentieth century, American commitments, especially to military protection for commerce and to access for other countries to American capital and American markets, were indispensable to the success of the Western economies. That success, in turn, along with communist failures, created the conditions to which Mikhail Gorbachev responded with the initiatives that led, ultimately, to the demise of communism. The use of economic instruments to affect the policies of other countries, a recurring theme of American foreign policy since the eighteenth century, played a part in the nation's great global conflict two centuries later—although it did so indirectly, through the political and psychological impact of the superior performance of the American economy, rather than by means of direct economic pressure.

Over the long term, as well, successive American administrations remained faithful to the initial Cold War policy of containment. That policy persisted because of the memory of World War II and the perceived cost of retreating from Europe persisted. In addition, both considerations of power and of values—the approaches to foreign policy of both Theodore Roosevelt and Woodrow Wilson—prompted the United States to oppose the Soviet Union and the cost of that policy proved politically tolerable. Containment discouraged the Soviet Union from using force to expand its power and influence westward in Europe. Without containment, the temptation to do so would have been far greater than it was. Had Moscow acted on that temptation, the Cold War would have taken a different and dangerous direction.

Finally, the example of a peaceful community of prosperous democracies, the community that the United States did more than any other country to establish in the second half of the 1940s and to sustain for four decades thereafter, confounded the doctrinal expectations of Marxism-Leninism and created the communists' crisis of confidence, and of faith, in communism that proved fatal to it. That, above all, is how the United States won the Cold War.

The Fourth Age

Hyperpower, 1990–2015

Nothing has ever existed like this disparity of power [between the United States and the rest of the world]. . . . The Pax Britannica was run on the cheap. Britain's army was much smaller than European armies, and even the Royal Navy was equal only to the next two navies—right now all the other navies in the world combined could not dent American maritime supremacy. Charlemagne's empire was merely western European in its reach. The Roman Empire stretched farther afield, but there was another great empire in Persia and a larger one in China. There is, therefore, no comparison [with America's current primacy].

Paul Kennedy[1]

As with the three previous eras in the history of American foreign policy, the end of a major war ushered in the fourth. As with the Revolutionary War, the Civil War, and World War II, the United States was on the winning side and the victory left it with a new and more powerful status in the international system. Unlike the other wars, the international position that the United States assumed in the wake of the Cold War was one no other country held or had ever held.

After the Revolutionary War, the newly independent United States faced the challenges that confront weak states, and history furnishes many examples of such states. After the Civil War the country joined the more exclusive but still familiar company of great powers. The outcome of World War II made America a superpower, along with its peer and competitor the Soviet Union. In the wake of the Cold War, however, the United States had no peer. No other country had, or ever had had, comparable power.

America had more military power by far than any other country. In 2015, twenty-five years after the post–Cold War era began, American military spending still totaled thirty-seven percent of all military expenditures everywhere, which made it equal to the defense budgets of the next seven largest military spenders combined.

Even that statistic does not fully capture the distinctiveness of the American international position. The United States not only had no powerful rivals but also effectively had no rivals at all. This was the defining feature of the new era. Of the potentially powerful members of the international system, Russia had emerged from the wreckage of the Soviet Union shorn of half the population of that communist empire and with its once-mighty armed forces in ruins; China devoted only a modest part of an economy far smaller than the American one to military purposes; and the Europe Union, soon to expand to include the formerly communist countries of Eastern Europe, was the partner and ally of the United States, had only a limited ability to act in united fashion, and deployed little armed might that it could use independently had it wished to do so—as it did not.[*]

Indeed, other countries or groups of countries not only did not have the capacity to challenge the United States militarily but also generally lacked the desire to do so. This meant that the age-old practice of power politics—preparations for war, the anticipation of war, and negotiations and political maneuvering with the prospect of war always in the background[2]—was absent. International relations had become more peaceful than ever before in modern history, which froze in place American supremacy—or so, for a time, it seemed.

The new international configuration inspired new terminology. The world had arrived, it was said, at a "unipolar moment,"[3] unlike the

---

[*] A saying had it that Europe was "an economic giant, a political midget, and a military worm."

bipolarity of the Cold War and the multipolarity of European history before it. In 1998 the French foreign minister, Hubert Vidrine, called the United States a "hyperpower," which implied an international status superior even to that of the two Cold War superpowers.

In another break with historical precedent, the post–Cold War international position of the United States did not bring with it a ready-made foreign policy agenda. As a newly independent weak power the United States had to defend itself against those that were stronger. As one great power among several it carved out its own sphere of influence and contended with its peers in East Asia and ultimately in Europe. As a superpower it prosecuted a global military, political, and economic conflict with the Soviet Union. By contrast, the position of unprecedented supremacy that America assumed after the Cold War did not imply any particular set of international initiatives. Yet over the next quarter century the American hyperpower did conduct a wide-ranging foreign policy.

* * *

At the outset of the post–Cold War era the United States decided, more or less by default, what its foreign policy would *not* be. It did not retreat from most of the policies of the Cold War. Historically, retrenchment had been the country's default postwar foreign policy. After the Civil War and the two world wars the American public had insisted that the large armies assembled for those conflicts be demobilized. The nation did reconstitute a formidable military force after the end of World War II but only because another dangerous rival had appeared. No successor to America's Cold War adversary emerged in its wake but the United States did not abandon the positions and commitments it had acquired during and because of that conflict.

One major reason for this persistence was inertia, an underappreciated force in human affairs. Because the Cold War lasted far longer than previous American conflicts, those positions and commitments had become normal for American society and inertia worked in favor of maintaining them. They did not disrupt everyday American life: they were part and parcel of that life. Nor were they punishingly expensive, and they became less expensive as the end of the Cold War yielded a "peace dividend": defense spending as a percentage of the overall gross domestic product fell by about half.

Moreover, two significant groups favored continuing some form of the American Cold War role in the world. One was the country's foreign policy community, the public officials and private citizens from business, the academy, journalism, and other fields who believed in, and often took part in, the international role that the United States had come to play. Articulate and affluent, its members functioned as a kind of interest group. While seldom of one mind on particular issues, almost all strongly supported the continuation of the major international presence of the United States.

The governments of other countries also wanted the United States to sustain its Cold War policies. While the absence of traditional threats meant that they no longer needed the kind of protection the American alliance system had provided, the continuation of that system gave those who belonged to it a welcome sense of reassurance[4] that no such threat was likely to return. In addition, their participation in the international economic order that the West had created after World War II and for which the United States supplied the security that commerce requires, a lucrative market for exports, and a currency that functioned as the world's money had fostered a prosperity in which they were glad to share.

America furnished to the world what economists call "collective" or "public" goods—valuable services that these countries would not have supplied on their own, like police and fire protection within communities. The hyperpower provided, that is, services that within sovereign states come from the government. In this way the United States acted as the world's government,[5] something that other countries privately appreciated but rarely praised publicly. During the Cold War America had provided these services to an expanding community of countries. When that conflict ended, inertia sustained them. Their continuation formed an important part of the foreign policy of the American hyperpower, but not the entirety of it.

The rest of it, like the foreign policy of every country, had external and internal sources—America's relative power and its particular domestic features, respectively. The external influences were weaker, and therefore far less restrictive, than ever before in the history of the United States and perhaps in the history of any country. With its vast margin of superiority in power over other countries, America had unprecedentedly broad freedom of action in the international arena. In these circumstances, the domestic sources—the characteristically American features of American foreign policy: the country's ideological, economic, and democratic traditions—had an unusually strong impact on that policy.

America's longstanding ideological goals—its aspiration to transform the international order to make it more peaceful and to make other countries more democratic—exercised greater influence on the nation's foreign policy than ever before. In the wake of the Cold War, Americans believed that these benign transformations were possible, indeed were well under way, by virtue of the association of democracy and peace with the second distinctively American feature of American foreign policy: economics.

In the post–Cold War period, international trade and capital flows, which came to be known collectively as "globalization" because they brought virtually every country increasingly into contact with all the others, expanded substantially. Americans had great expectations for globalization because almost every country aspired to be prosperous and the Cold War had persuasively demonstrated that the surest route to prosperity involved the adoption of a free-market economic system and participation in the Western-based international economic order. Furthermore, membership in that economic order, the history of the late–Cold War period seemed to demonstrate, fostered democratic values, democratic practices, and democratic institutions. Democracies, their histories show, in turn have a pronounced tendency to conduct peaceful foreign policies.[6]

In short, there seemed to be a systematic relationship among globalization, free markets, democratic politics, and international peace. This "liberal theory of history"[7] had no canonical texts. It consisted of a widely held set of assumptions about the world in the wake of the Cold War rather than a set of official dogmas. The history of the Cold War seemed to have validated and demonstrated that history was moving in directions favorable to the United States. Post–Cold War American foreign policy sought to assist those favorable historical trends in two ways: by expanding the scope of the Western international economic order, and by suppressing conflict and promoting democratic politics in troubled places around the world.

In carrying out its policy of complementing and assisting the liberal theory of history, the American hyperpower came under the influence of the third historical feature of the foreign policy of the United States: the country's unusually democratic character. In particular, the democratic influence gave post–Cold War prominence to two familiar patterns: the tendency for dramatic external events to galvanize public opinion and drive the nation's foreign policy in new directions, and the propensity for Americans to turn against wars that did not go as they wished or expected.

* * *

In terms of the influence of ideological, economic, and democratic considerations, the fourth age of the foreign policy of the United States resembled the previous three, although the country's enhanced power made them more influential than ever. In one crucial way, however, the fourth period differed from the others. Before the 1990s, through many twists and turns, American international initiatives had enjoyed remarkable success. The foreign policy of the American hyperpower did not.

The American experience in the post–Cold War era in fact divides into two parts. The first, encompassing roughly the decade after the collapse of the Soviet Union, seemed to vindicate the optimism of the liberal theory of history. The global economy expanded. Democracy became the most popular form of government on the planet. Military rivalry among the strongest countries remained dormant.

Then international history turned in a different, less favorable direction. The turn began with the terrorist attacks on New York City and Washington, D.C., on September 11, 2001. They had a familiar effect, pitching the United States into three conflicts that it would not otherwise have waged: shooting wars in Afghanistan and Iraq and an expensive effort to prevent further such assaults that came to be known as the War on Terror.

The attacks of September 11 also began a decade and a half of American international setbacks. In the first three eras of the country's foreign policy the United States had achieved its major goals and expanded its power. In the post–Cold War period the American hyperpower did neither. Its failures had more than one cause. The American government made errors of policy, in part because of the absence of restraints on what it could do in the world. Other countries turned out not to share America's goals and, although far inferior in power, found ways to keep the hyperpower from achieving these goals. Finally, some of what the United States sought to achieve, above all the spread of democracy, lay beyond its power, or indeed that of any country no matter how mighty, to bring about.

The events from 2001 to 2015 undercut the tenets of the liberal theory of history. Increasing integration into the international economic order of the West did not prove irresistible. Instead, the march of globalization stalled. The world did not become steadily more democratic. In some places, with the advent of autocratic rule, it became less so. Most important of all, the deep post–Cold War peace came to an end, and with it ended the fourth age of American foreign policy. By 2015 the United States remained the most powerful of all countries; but the conditions in which it exercised its power were no longer those that the end of the Cold War had bequeathed to the world.

10

The New World Order, 1990–2001

The Gulf War

The first major international event of the post–Cold War era took place while the basic cause of that conflict—the Soviet Union itself—was still in existence. In the latter part of 1990 and the first months of 1991, the United States assembled a broad multinational coalition to wage its largest war since the Vietnam conflict, in the Persian Gulf. The American-led coalition won the war decisively, giving rise to the hope, which verged on an expectation, that the end of the Cold War heralded a new international order that would not only favor American interests but also embody, more than any previous historical period, American values.

The Gulf War came about because of the invasion of tiny, oil-rich Kuwait by its larger neighbor Iraq, with 140,000 troops and 1,800 tanks, on August 1, 1990. Iraq was led by the brutal dictator Saddam Hussein, a man accustomed to the use of violence in pursuit of his personal and political goals at home and abroad. While the Iraqis officially justified the invasion by the claim that Kuwait was in fact a province of their own country, Saddam attacked his neighbor for the same reason that criminals rob banks: for the money. He had started, and waged, a decade-long, costly, and ultimately inconclusive war with the Islamic Republic of Iran. In its wake he needed more funds than his own oil revenues provided for the reconstruction of his country. He took over Kuwait in order to divert income from that country's petroleum to his own uses.[1]

President George H. W. Bush decided that Saddam's forces had to be evicted from Kuwait. "This will not stand," he said of the invasion. Before it took place, however, neither Saddam nor anyone else, including Americans, had reason to expect such a response. Kuwait was neither a formal ally nor a particular friend of the United States and the Americans had sided with Saddam's Iraq in its war with Iran.

As Saddam massed his troops on the border with Kuwait, neither Western nor Arab governments anticipated a full-blown invasion, believing the purpose of the buildup to be the intimidation of Kuwait's ruling family so that it would increase the payments it was already making to Saddam.[2] In a meeting with the Iraqi dictator on July 25, 1990, the American ambassador in Baghdad, April Glaspie, said that the United States "had no opinion" on Iraq's territorial claims on Kuwait, which at that point included strategic islands and oil fields but not the entire country.[3] She gave no hint that the United States would come to Kuwait's rescue in the event of an Iraqi attack. She could not have told Saddam that the United States would defend Kuwait, even if she had wanted to, because Washington had given her no instructions suggesting that it would.[4] Nor would an American security guarantee to Kuwait have commanded broad support in the Congress or the country had the Bush administration chosen to issue one.[5]

The Gulf War thus followed two familiar patterns in the history of American foreign policy. As in the Cuban missile crisis and the Soviet invasion of Afghanistan, the United States responded far more sharply to an initiative by another country than that country had anticipated. And as with the sinking of the battleship *Maine* in 1898 and the attack on Pearl Harbor in 1941, a dramatic event suddenly changed the American government's and the American public's perception of the world, the dangers the country faced, and the policies the United States needed to adopt to meet those dangers.

The Bush administration did in fact have substantial reasons to seek to reverse the Iraqi occupation of Kuwait once it had occurred. Foremost among them was oil. Kuwait produced and exported it. Even more important for the United States was the fact that, by controlling Kuwait, Saddam had put his army on the border of, and in a position to invade, Saudi Arabia, the world's single largest oil exporter. Since the industrial world could not function economically without Saudi oil, an Iraqi seizure of that kingdom,[6] which seemed all too possible once Iraq had conquered Kuwait, would give Saddam Hussein control of a full forty percent of the world's proven oil reserves.[7] With that control would come enormous global power, power that other countries, including the United States, did not want him to have.

The manner in which Saddam took possession of Kuwait's petroleum reserves affected the global and American response to it. Sending troops across a recognized international border constituted a blatant violation of international law. As a clear-cut case of aggression it incurred universal condemnation.[8] As the Bush administration mounted its response to the invasion, its leaders were conscious of setting a precedent for the historical period that the end of the Cold War had begun.[9] They saw an opportunity to establish for the new era a principle that the United States had long endorsed but that was all too seldom observed in practice: the rule of law in international affairs.[10]

Underlying the administration's decision to evict Iraq from Kuwait, finally, was the fact that the Cold War had effectively ended, and with it the restraint that the reflexive Soviet opposition to virtually any American international initiative had imposed on American foreign policy. The United States was now freer to take action against Iraqi aggression than it had been during the forty-five years since World War II.

The American government took the lead in assembling a broad coalition to confront Iraq. A total of thirty-five countries joined it, although few made substantial contributions to its military effort, which was largely an American operation. The king of Saudi Arabia agreed to the deployment of coalition—which meant American—troops on Saudi territory, to protect the kingdom but also as the necessary condition for mounting a successful military campaign to end the occupation of Kuwait. Arab countries, notably Egypt and Syria, also joined,[11] preventing Saddam from successfully portraying the conflict as a neoimperial Western assault on the Arab world.

The Bush administration also played a major role in securing resolutions in the United Nations Security Council, first condemning the invasion (Resolution 660), then imposing sanctions on Iraq (661), and finally authorizing the use of force to expel Iraqi troops from Kuwait (678). These resolutions both created a global political climate favorable to the formation of the anti-Saddam coalition and gave international legitimacy to the attack on the Iraqi army when it came.

After getting the United Nations on record in support of its Gulf policy, the Bush administration, breaking with the precedent of the Cold War years, asked both houses of Congress to approve the use of force in the Gulf, thereby furnishing additional evidence that American foreign policy had entered a new era. The Congress gave its approval—narrowly in the case of the Senate, which registered the closest vote in favor of war in American history, fifty-two to forty-seven.[12]

Crucially, the United States obtained the support of the Soviet Union. When the invasion took place, Mikhail Gorbachev, who was more than a year away from losing both his power and his country, immediately expressed the view that Saddam was in the wrong; and the Soviet Union endorsed the UN resolutions condemning and sanctioning Iraq. Gorbachev and his colleagues turned out to be less than fully committed to the use of force to oust Iraqi troops from Kuwait. Moscow launched several diplomatic initiatives for the purpose of mediating between Saddam and the international community. One of them, which sent a Soviet official to Baghdad, took place after the coalition's military campaign had actually begun, and the Bush administration did not welcome it.[13] In the end, however, and in contrast to its settled Cold War policy, the Soviet Union did not actively seek to inhibit the campaign against Saddam.

Between August and November 1990, the United States sent approximately 250,000 troops to Saudi Arabia, thus successfully deterring Iraqi forces from using Kuwait as a launching pad for the conquest of that country. The American government called this phase of the conflict Operation Desert Shield and hoped that the combination of the blocking force it deployed and the UN-approved economic sanctions would impel Iraq to leave Kuwait. When the Bush high command became convinced that this would not happen, it doubled the number of troops in the region,[14] which reached 543,000, and, on January 16, 1991, launched the war to liberate Kuwait, called Operation Desert Storm.

The war proceeded in two stages. In the first, which continued for forty-two days, coalition warplanes, which had unchallenged control of the airspace in the region, struck targets in Iraq and attacked as well the Iraqi military forces in Kuwait. The air campaign destroyed or crippled an appreciable part of the Iraqi army. It employed for the first time precision-guided munitions, popularly known as "smart bombs," which advanced technology had made far more accurate than the air-launched munitions of previous American wars.[15]

Saddam mounted a limited counteroffensive, firing forty-two Soviet-developed Scud missiles at Israel.[16] He hoped to draw Israel into the conflict and thereby split the coalition. Arab governments, he calculated, would not fight on the same side as the Jewish state. The gambit failed. The Scuds did relatively little damage and Israel, at the urging of the United States, stayed out of the war.[17]

On February 24 the second stage of Desert Storm, the ground campaign, began. Some coalition forces drove straight up the coast of the Persian Gulf to Kuwait's capital. Another detachment executed a flanking maneuver to the west, enveloping a large part of the Iraqi army of occupation. The coalition's superior firepower and mobility, in concert with its complete command of the air, turned the battle into a rout. The Iraqi forces fled homeward in disorderly fashion. With victory assured, the Bush administration decided to stop the fighting after only one hundred hours.

The war ended with Kuwait free but Saddam Hussein still in power in Iraq. To be certain of removing him the coalition forces would have had to drive to Baghdad, and although the Iraqi army could not have prevented this, President Bush and his senior officials decided against it. Invading Iraq would have exceeded the terms of the mandate that the United Nations had given the coalition, which extended only to the liberation of Kuwait. It would have involved the United States deeply in the internal affairs of an Arab country, a prospect that the administration did not find attractive.[18] Besides, the administration expected or at least hoped that Saddam would be ousted without further assistance from the United States, perhaps through a coup by one of his generals.[†]

[†] Michael R. Gordon and Bernard E. Trainor, *Cobra II: The Inside Story of the Invasion and Occupation of Iraq*, New York: Pantheon Books, 2006, p. 11; Herring, *op. cit.*, pp. 910–911; Lawrence Freedman and Efraim Karsh, *The Gulf Conflict, 1990–1991: Diplomacy and War in the New World Order*, Princeton, New Jersey: Princeton University Press, 1993, pp. xxxii, 413. Balance-of-power considerations were also involved in the American conduct of the war. According to National Security Advisor Brent Scowcroft, the United States aimed to

Having retained his power, the Iraqi dictator proceeded to make extensive use of it within his country. Demographically, Iraq consisted of an uneasy amalgam of three groups: Sunni Arabs, led by Saddam; more numerous Arab adherents to the Shia sect of Islam; and Kurds in the north, who were Muslims but not Arabs and spoke Kurdish rather than Arabic. In assembling the country after World War I, the British had given power to the minority Sunni population, and the Sunnis, with Saddam at their head, had retained it by repressing the other two groups. With the Sunni-dominated army's eviction from Kuwait, the Shia and the Kurds rose up against the regime. Using the military forces he had been allowed to keep, Saddam put down both uprisings in brutal fashion. An estimated 60,000 Shia died. The army killed as many as 20,000 Kurds as well,[19] and 2 million of them became refugees, most fleeing to the border with Turkey.

Appalled by the Kurds' suffering, prodded by its ally Turkey to take action to prevent a flood of Kurds from entering Turkish territory, and equipped with a new United Nations Security Council Resolution condemning the repression in northern Iraq—number 688, passed on April 5, 1991—the Bush administration deployed American forces to establish a "safe zone" in northern Iraq.[20] It became effectively independent, with American air power preventing Saddam from further molesting the Kurdish population there. The protection of the Kurds had a different kind of motive from the one that had sent the United States to war in the first place. While Saddam's occupation of Kuwait put in jeopardy American interests—the security of the world's supply of oil and the independence of Saudi Arabia—his subsequent assault on the Kurds offended American values. Although it was not understood at the time, using military force to safeguard the country's values set a precedent for post–Cold War American foreign policy.

The Gulf War differed from the American conflicts in Korea and Vietnam in that the United States achieved its maximal goal—the

"reduce Saddam's military might so that he would no longer pose a threat to the region, yet to do so in such a way that Iraq was secure from external threats and the balance with Iran was preserved." George Bush and Brent Scowcroft, *A World Transformed*, New York: Alfred A. Knopf, 1998, pp. 432–433. See also *ibid.*, pp. 383–384.

liberation of Kuwait—and achieved it on the cheap. Financially, the war cost the American Treasury very little. Countries that joined the coalition but did not send troops to the Gulf region, notably Germany and Japan, made financial contributions to the war effort that came to more than eighty percent of its overall cost. The United States paid $7.3 billion, about twelve percent of the total expenditure.

Unlike in the Korean and Vietnam Wars, the American public did not turn against the Gulf War, because American casualties were far lower than they had been in the two previous conflicts. In the end, the United States suffered only 383 fatalities.[21] Had the war claimed more American lives, popular support would almost surely have declined, perhaps steeply.[22] While the public considered Saddam Hussein both obnoxious and dangerous, it did not have great enthusiasm for going to war with him.[23] The Gulf War had little to do with the Cold War considerations that had initially justified the military efforts in Korea and Vietnam in the eyes of the public. The Bush administration struggled to find a rationale for the conflict that would have broad appeal in the United States, on some occasions asserting that American jobs were at stake, on others stating that a major reason for the war was to prevent Iraq from acquiring nuclear weapons.[24]

The war went as smoothly as it did for the United States and its allies because of their overwhelming military superiority and because the terrain on which it was waged—mainly open desert—and Iraq's decision to engage in battles rather than a guerrilla campaign played to America's military strengths.[25] In addition, Iraq, unlike North Korea and North Vietnam, had no allies or outside sources of supplies and weaponry, because of the end of the Cold War. In this sense the crucial event of the Gulf War occurred ten months before Iraq invaded Kuwait, on November 9, 1989, when the Berlin Wall opened and the end of the great geopolitical rivalry of the second half of the twentieth century came into view.

The Gulf War introduced a major feature of post–Cold War American foreign policy: the enhanced significance of the Middle East. The war also seemed to portend something even more important: the realization of Woodrow Wilson's vision of international affairs[26] seventy years after he had offered it and two centuries after the American Revolution from which it was descended.

The war had proceeded as Wilson had imagined his League of Nations would operate: under the auspices of the United Nations, and with the leadership of the United States, the international community had come together to put right a wrong by ending the illegal Iraqi occupation of Kuwait, thereby vindicating a basic principle of international law. In his State of the Union address on January 29, 1991, just before launching Desert Storm, President Bush said of the impending war:

> What is at stake is more than one small country: it is a big idea: a new world order—where diverse nations are drawn together in common cause, to achieve the universal aspirations of mankind: peace and security, freedom and the rule of law.[27]

The outcome of the war seemed to signify that this new world order had indeed arrived.

George H. W. Bush had performed admirably in the Gulf War, as diplomat in chief assembling the broad anti-Saddam coalition and as commander in chief presiding over a swift, decisive, inexpensive military victory. Nonetheless, his performance did not suffice to earn him re-election in 1992.[28] His successor was more interested in economics than in military matters and found in what had become the dominant trend in the international economy another compelling cause for optimism that the post–Cold War world would guarantee American interests, embody American values, and generally reflect American preferences as no previous historical era had done.

Globalization

Bill Clinton, the governor of Arkansas who defeated George Bush for the presidency, was a full generation younger than his predecessor. He was born, as it happened, in the same year, 1946, as Bush's eldest son, who was himself to succeed Clinton in the office. The new president had no foreign policy experience and so would have had difficulty winning a presidential election during the Cold War, when such experience was considered an important qualification for the job. Clinton became the first American chief executive since Herbert Hoover not to have had any previous association at all with the military.[29]

As the leader of the country that the Cold War's end had made a hyperpower, he had wider latitude to set American foreign policy than any of his predecessors. He entered the presidency with no particular international agenda and that, combined with the absence of any serious external threat, meant that domestic pressures and incentives weighed more heavily on the foreign policies he chose than on those of any other twentieth-century president. In the course of his first two years in office he did, however, find a focus for the nation's relations with other countries: globalization.

The term, which came into widespread use in the 1990s, refers to the process of international economic integration—the increasing cross-border flows of goods, money, and people. Globalization arises from political circumstances that favor international trade, investment, and migration, in combination with technological advances in transportation and communication that make them easier to undertake on an ever-larger scale. The post–Cold War era marked the third period of industrial-era globalization.[30] The first, from the 1870s to the outbreak of World War I, made use of the steamship, the telegraph, and the railroad. The commitment to international commerce of Great Britain, the world's economic leader for much of the nineteenth century, supplied the necessary political underpinning. The second period, which was roughly coterminus with the Cold War, depended on the political cohesion of the West while excluding the communist countries and took advantage of the jet airplane and the automobile as well as long-distance telephone communication and radio and television. Post–Cold War globalization coincided with the time of America's unrivaled international power and with the advent of the revolutionary advances in digital technology.

Globalization became the centerpiece of the Clinton foreign policy partly by default, with the suspension of geopolitical competition,[31] but for other reasons as well. It comported with the new president's highest priority: bolstering the country's economy.[32] It conferred economic benefits on important American industries: American firms dominated international finance and high technology,[33] both of them major elements of globalization's third phase.

The administration also came to see international economic integration as a way not only to enhance Americans' well-being but also to spread American political institutions and values as well. Something similar, after all, had taken place during the Cold War. The superior performance of Western free markets in comparison with that of communist central planning, a difference in part the result of the trade and investment among the Western countries, had made a major contribution to the outcome of that conflict. Moreover, faith in the potentially potent political effects of trade went back to the founding of the republic.[34]

In the wake of the global conflict with communism, virtually every country, including those formerly governed by communist parties, sought to join the international economic order that the United States and the West had established after World War II. Membership in that order was widely regarded as the route to the universally desired goal of prosperity.[35] Engagement with the global economy, Americans came increasingly to believe, acted as a force for the promotion of democracy at home and peaceful relations abroad. "By expanding trade," Clinton said, "we can advance the cause of freedom and democracy around the world."[36] Globalization was therefore central to the informal but widely held set of American views about the post–Cold War world that made up the liberal theory of history. In keeping with this view, the Clinton administration announced as a major aim the "enlargement of the world's community of market democracies."[37]

It did not, however, proceed by first adopting the propositions concerning economics and politics of the liberal theory of history and then seeking to translate them into specific policies. As is often the case in the making of public policy in democracies, the broader principles emerged from specific decisions that the government chose to make.

The first and most important decision concerned the North American Free Trade Agreement (NAFTA) with Canada and Mexico, which the Bush administration had negotiated at the end of its time in office.[38] Clinton had to decide whether to try to persuade the Congress to ratify it. During the presidential campaign he had taken an equivocal position on NAFTA. As he assumed power, while the political climate surrounding trade had in some ways become more favorable than had been the case in the previous two decades,[39] the politics of trade had become more complicated.

For one thing, the argument that trade agreements served a strategic purpose by binding America's allies together and so waging the Cold War more effectively, on which successive administrations had relied since the 1940s, had vanished with the end of the Soviet Union. For another, partisan attitudes toward trade had changed. From the beginning of the nineteenth century Democrats favored expanding it; after the Civil War Republicans advocated restricting it by means of tariffs. By the 1990s, however, the two parties had changed positions. Under the influence of the increasingly protectionist unions that formed an important part of their electoral coalition, the Democrats were prone to skepticism about trade expansion while more and more Republicans supported it. Along with partisan alignments, the political geography of trade politics had also shifted, with the northeastern and midwestern industrial heartland of the country, where the unions had their greatest strength, opposed and the once-Democratic but now Republican (and lightly unionized) South favoring free international trade.[40]

Finally, two new issues had become part of the politics of trade. Unions wanted the countries with which America signed agreements to protect the rights that labor enjoyed in the United States; and the growing environmental lobby insisted that other signatories adhere to high standards of environmental protection.[41] Both the labor and environmental movements generally supported the Democrats. This meant that, to secure passage of NAFTA, Clinton would have to overcome the skepticism, and sometimes outright opposition, of legislators of his own party.

He negotiated agreements on labor rights and the environment that were separate from the formal text of NAFTA and then launched a campaign to secure Congressional approval of it. He had to wage an uphill battle but ultimately won it.[42] That victory laid the foundation of his administration's foreign policy.

The next year the Congress ratified the trade agreement reached by the Uruguay Round of multilateral negotiations, the eighth since World War II and so named because its first meeting took place, in 1986, in Punta del Este, Uruguay. In addition to reducing tariffs on a wide range of items, including services,[43] the agreement included the establishment of a new umbrella body for international trade, the World Trade Organization (WTO).[44] While it had a considerably greater impact on the American economy than did NAFTA, the Uruguay Round passed the Congress more easily because it brought economic benefits to many exporting firms and industries, which organized to lobby to promote it.[45]

Although both measures were enacted into law, and although the Clinton administration embraced trade expansion as fundamental to its vision of American foreign policy, trade was politically more controversial in the 1990s than it had been during the Cold War. Despite having only a modest impact on the American economy, NAFTA became a lightning rod for public dissatisfaction with economic conditions in the United States.[46] In particular, trade took much of the blame for the loss of jobs that was in fact caused more by advances in technology than by cross-border commerce.[47] In his second presidential term Clinton requested "fast-track" authority to submit trade agreements to Congress for an up-or-down vote free of amendments, a necessary condition for passing them. The Congress refused to grant it. In December 1999 the WTO held a major meeting in Seattle, which Clinton addressed. It attracted 50,000 protesters, whose demonstrations turned violent.[48] As the last decade of the millennium ended, and despite its centrality to what Clinton had hoped to accomplish in the world, the cause of trade expansion was on the defensive in the United States.

The Clinton administration welcomed and encouraged the expansion of the cross-border flow of capital for the same reason it sought to increase trade: each promoted—or at least seemed, on the whole, to promote—both prosperity and democracy. In the period between the two world wars the federal government had encouraged "dollar diplomacy" in the hope that private American investment would secure American interests in the countries to which it was directed. In the post–Cold War period American officials believed that investment of all kinds would help promote the kinds of values and institutions that Americans favored.[49] Moreover, the wider the scope for investment, it was logical to assume, the greater would be the chances that capital would be invested where it could have the most productive effects. Expanded capital flows also proved to have drawbacks, however.

Because money can move suddenly and swiftly in very large volume—the German poet Heinrich Heine said that it is "more fluid than water and less steady than air"[50]—capital flows can do serious damage. They can inflate financial bubbles, pushing up the price of an asset dramatically. When the bubble bursts—when investors' confidence in the asset vanishes and they rush to withdraw their money from it—large economic losses can ensue,[‡] especially when borrowed money and banks are involved.[51] The globalization of capital created new opportunities for investment but also greater dangers of sudden, large-scale, destructive capital flight.

Money flowed from the advanced industrial democracies to countries in the Third World that became known, in the post–Cold War era, as emerging markets. Because these new destinations for capital were less familiar, and often less politically stable, than the rich countries to which most cross-border investment had gone during the Cold War, investors in and lenders to emerging market countries were more likely to develop fears, whether justified or not, for the safety of their investments or loans, and withdraw them abruptly.[52] That is what happened in the 1990s. Western banks and investors put a great deal of money into these countries, much of it in the form of loans to banks there, which proved to be bubbles. When the bubbles burst, they triggered financial crises that drew in the United States.

Mexico borrowed on a large scale, promising to pay back the loans, mainly in the form of bonds, in hard currency at a fixed exchange rate. At the end of 1994 the Mexican government devalued its currency, the peso, leading to a flight from it that threatened extensive damage to the country's economy. Such damage had the potential to spill over to its giant northern neighbor, the United States. In 1997 similar crises struck several Asian countries—Thailand, Indonesia, and South Korea—whose banks had borrowed extensively from the West.

[‡] "Bubbles form when investors bid up the price of an asset, believing that it will continue to rise in price. The belief is self-fulfilling: when people believe the price . . . will rise and are willing to invest in it, the price does rise. The fact that others believe this is a good reason to invest: as the price climbs, investors become wealthier, at least on paper. The volatility of money means, however, that bubbles can burst as well as inflate. The price of an asset can fall very rapidly. When investors decide that it is destined to fall (and especially when it actually is falling), they sell, and this belief, too, is self-fulfilling. Selling actually produces the decline in price." Michael Mandelbaum, *The Road to Global Prosperity*, New York: Simon & Schuster, 2014 p. 85.

When the prospect for full repayment began to look shaky, Western lenders withdrew their money from these countries.

The antidote to financial crises such as these is the restoration of lenders' and investors' confidence in the asset and the national currency so that capital does not flee. Such confidence comes from the assurance that they can be repaid in hard currency at any time, which in turn requires hard-currency loans to the stricken country. Since the practice became widely understood in nineteenth-century Britain, the responsibility for acting as the "lender of last resort" in financial crises has fallen to the central bank of the country in distress. The central banks of the emerging market countries could not serve that purpose because they lacked the hard currency needed for the restoration of confidence. These countries therefore turned to the International Monetary Fund (IMF) for loans.[53]

Behind the IMF, and exercising considerable influence on its operations, stood the United States. The American government acted as the moving force in assembling rescue packages for countries experiencing financial crises in the 1990s, and put up some of its own money for Mexico.[54]

The rescue efforts succeeded. The affected countries did suffer economic losses in the short term[55] but by the new millennium they had, thanks in no small part to confidence-inducing IMF loans, returned to economic growth.[56] While the crises illustrated the perils of financial globalization, this outcome also seemed to vindicate the American view of the political impact of economics in the post–Cold War world. The IMF loans came with conditions, which were often imposed at the behest of the United States and some of which involved domestic political as well as economic changes that Washington favored. The long-ruling dictator of Indonesia, Suharto, for example, was forced to step down and ultimately a government chosen in a free election replaced him.[57] In this way participation in the international economy did promote—although not entirely voluntarily and at some economic cost—democratic political change.

In addition to the importance of economics and the dynamics of political change, the financial crises illustrated a third feature of the post–Cold War world: the unprecedented power of the United States. The American hyperpower had, after all, taken the lead in limiting the economic damage from the crises by helping to end them. The cover of the February 15, 1999, issue of the then widely read American news-weekly *TIME* displayed a picture of the three senior American economic officials, Treasury Secretary Robert Rubin, his deputy Lawrence Summers, and Chairman of the Federal Reserve Alan Greenspan, with the caption "The Committee to Save the World."

On the whole, therefore, in American eyes at least, the management of the financial crises vindicated the placement of globalization at the center of post–Cold War American foreign policy. So, too, did the course of relations, during the 1990s, with one particular and very important country: China.

During the Cold War, balance-of-power considerations determined American policy toward that country. The United States overlooked China's radically undemocratic practices at home and aligned itself geopolitically with Beijing against a common adversary, the Soviet Union. Coinciding as it did with the waning of the conflict with international communism, the Chinese government's repression of demonstrators, some professing allegiance to democracy, in Beijing's Tiananmen Square and elsewhere in June 1989 provoked a change in public opinion and a political conflict in the United States over China policy.

President George H. W. Bush wished to maintain the Cold War relationship with the People's Republic. Much of the public, appalled by what the Chinese authorities had ordered done to the demonstrators,[58] wanted the American government to express disapproval of the communists' repression, sentiment that would have been weaker had the Soviet Union still loomed as a major threat.[59] The Democrats in control of Congress voted to deny Beijing Most Favored Nation (MFN) trade status, which the president had regularly granted since the 1970s. Bush blocked this, but Clinton, upon assuming the presidency, announced that he would carry out the China policy that his party preferred. He issued an executive order stipulating that, in the future, China would receive MFN status only if its government did more to protect the rights of the Chinese people. He imposed on China, that is, the same kind of linkage that the Jackson-Vanik Amendment had established for trade with the Soviet Union two decades earlier.

The new policy encountered substantial opposition. The government in Beijing flatly refused to make any kind of concession involving its methods of domestic governance.[60] At the same time, the American business community, unwilling to forgo the opportunities that trade with and investment in China offered, energetically lobbied the administration not to condition their ability to do business there on Chinese internal reform.[61] These efforts doomed to failure Clinton's version of the recurrent American policy of using trade as an instrument of foreign policy.

On May 26, 1994, Clinton reversed course, announcing that his administration would no longer link trade to political change in China. He insisted, however, that he was not abandoning the goal of bringing democratic values and institutions to that country. Rather, the administration had concluded that the best way to do that was to promote rather than restrict American interaction with the vast Chinese market. He advanced as the rationale for his about-face on China policy a central precept of the liberal theory of history: the presumed tendency of engagement with the global economy to promote Western-style politics.[§]

His reasoning smacked of political opportunism, but it was not entirely fanciful. In the previous two decades democracy had made remarkable advances around the world and economic factors had had something to do with that. In the decade since China had opened its economy to the world many of the harshest political practices of the Maoist era had ended.[62] Moreover, communism in Europe had recently expired and it was not unreasonable to believe that communism in China would ultimately meet the same fate, and that American trade and investment could assist this process. In this way the new policy of

---

[§] Douglas A. Irwin, *Clashing Over Commerce: A History of U.S. Trade Policy*, Chicago: University of Chicago Press, 2017, p. 665. Clinton wrote in his memoir that after a meeting with Chinese leader Jiang Zemin he "went to bed thinking that China would be forced by the imperatives of modern society to become more open." Quoted in John Pomfret, *The Beautiful Country and the Middle Kingdom: America and China, 1776 to the Present*, New York: Henry Holt and Company, 2016, p. 562. Clinton's first secretary of the treasury, Lloyd Bentsen, said of China that "one of the ways to promote human rights is to encourage market reform and trade." Quoted in Michael Mandelbaum, *Mission Failure: America and the World in the Post-Cold War Era*, New York: Oxford University Press, 2016, p. 36.

engagement was descended, as well, from the proprietary interest that Americans had adopted toward the Chinese beginning in the nineteenth century.[63]

Accordingly, in 1994 the Clinton administration renewed the annual presidential waiver needed to sustain a normal trading relationship with China[64] and in 2000 persuaded the Congress to make it permanent. The United States also paved the way for Chinese entry into the WTO in 2001. The administration thereby placed globalization at the center of its relationship with the world's largest and its economically fastest-growing country.

Economics did not make up the entirety of America's China policy in the 1990s. Considerations of security played a part as well, notably as they involved Taiwan. The communist government in Beijing continued to claim the right to govern it, but the island's status changed when it underwent a major political transition. From the dictatorship that Chiang Kai-shek had installed on the island upon fleeing the mainland after his defeat in the Chinese Civil War and over which he and his son had presided, the Republic of China on Taiwan transformed itself into a democracy, with its government chosen in free elections.[65]

Beijing's communist authorities objected and showed their displeasure, initially at the visit of Taiwan's president to the United States in 1995 and then, the next year, in response to the first fully free Taiwanese elections, by conducting military exercises in the waters around the island. On the second occasion the American government felt sufficiently concerned to mount a show of force of its own. Washington sent aircraft carriers to the vicinity of the Chinese military exercises as a warning not to attack the newly democratic island.[66]

China also played a part in the confrontation between the United States and North Korea over nuclear weapons. In the four decades after the end of the Korean War, just as in Europe the market economies of the democracies delivered much greater economic growth than did communist central planning, so, too, on the Korean peninsula the noncommunist South far outstripped the communist North in economic terms. To compensate for its relative backwardness and to ensure the continued rule of its longtime communist dictator Kim Il-sung, in 1994 the North threatened to acquire nuclear weapons by shutting down a research reactor and using its fuel rods as the material for atomic bombs.[67] The American government made clear its opposition to such a measure and gave serious consideration to using military means to stop it before a compromise temporarily defused the issue.[68]

As North Korea's only real friend in the world, and because much of the food and fuel that the communist North consumed moved across the border between the two countries, China had considerable leverage over the regime in Pyongyang.[69] While the Chinese government preferred that North Korea not have nuclear weapons, its highest priority was keeping the North Korean regime intact. Beijing was therefore unwilling to apply the kind of economic pressure that had a chance of changing the North's nuclear policy, for fear of triggering its collapse. It also became apparent that, even with the increasing volume of Sino-American trade and investment, having the American government distracted and confounded by North Korea's nuclear maneuvers served Beijing's political purposes in the region.[70]

The developments in Taiwan and North Korea raised the possibility that the American hyperpower would employ military force against a communist country in East Asia, as it had twice done during the Cold War. In the end it did not. Even leaving aside the Gulf War, however, the post–Cold War period did not see the end of American military interventions: the demands of the new world order, as the American government interpreted them, did not require American pacifism. The United States did use force in a number of places around the world, but for a historically novel reason.

Humanitarian Intervention

In the wake of the Cold War, the world became a safer place with the elimination of the threat of a major Soviet-American war but also a more disorderly place, with numerous small-scale conflicts. Some of them came about because of the end of the Cold War, which brought both the disappearance of the communist ideology on which some regimes based their power and the termination of the political support and financial subsidies from one or the other of the superpowers that had helped maintain a measure of stability in otherwise fractious countries.[71]

The United States became involved in several of these lesser conflicts, but for a purpose having little or nothing in common with the American military interventions of the past. Those in the post–Cold War period took place not, as American military operations since the Revolution had taken place, to protect and further American interests. Instead, they were intended to vindicate American values, and in particular in order to defend beleaguered peoples against the depredations of their fellow citizens, or their own governments, or both. Since the eighteenth century, Americans had proclaimed a principled commitment, which was occasionally translated into actual policy, to the defense and promotion, in the international arena, of the values they held dear. Never before, however, had their government gone to war solely for this purpose.

What came to be called humanitarian intervention began in 1991 with the establishment of the protective zone for the Kurds in northern Iraq. Its rationale was distinct from the animating motives for the Gulf War—reversing Saddam Hussein's aggression against a neighbor and preventing him from controlling much of the world's oil reserves. In that war's aftermath the Bush administration was appalled by Saddam's assault on the Kurds (as well as on Iraq's Shia Muslims) and felt a responsibility for their plight, which, after all, had arisen from the insurrection they had mounted that the American defeat of the Sunni-dominated Iraqi government had inspired.[72] Washington received UN authorization for safeguarding the Kurds, a task that proved to be inexpensive in lives and treasure to accomplish. Of all the American post–Cold War humanitarian interventions, the one in northern Iraq turned out to be the most successful. The Kurds remained outside Saddam's control and organized for themselves what was by the standards of the region a reasonably decent, tolerant, and effective government.[73]

While it had its roots in the long-standing ideological strain in American foreign policy, humanitarian intervention differed from previous expressions of that tradition. From the time of the Revolution Americans had hoped to reform the sovereign states of the international system to make them more democratic. Woodrow Wilson had aspired to transform the entire system of sovereign states to make it more peaceful. The latest iteration of the general ideological impulse in the nation's relations with other countries had as its target not the international system or the states that compose it but rather the individuals who populate those states. It sought to secure for them the most basic of human rights: the right to life.

The defining condition of the post–Cold War world made possible this innovation in international affairs. The United States undertook what came to be called humanitarian interventions, in the first place, because it could. As the hyperpower, no other country was in a position effectively to challenge it.[74] America had no pressing alternative uses for its armed forces and the military part of the humanitarian operations in which they engaged proved, like the one in Iraq, to be relatively cheap and easy to conduct.

In addition, humanitarian intervention received the imprimatur of the international community in the form of a new doctrine, "the responsibility to protect." As articulated by UN Secretary-General Javier Perez de Cuellar, it held to be permissible, perhaps even mandatory, setting aside the fundamental international legal precept of the inviolability of sovereignty[75] in favor of intervening in the internal affairs of a sovereign state if and when the inhabitants of that state are subject to acute repression by their governments.[76]

After northern Iraq, the next instance of humanitarian intervention came in December 1992 in Somalia, on the Horn of Africa. There the breakdown of order led to war involving competing clans that threatened many Somalis with starvation. George H. W. Bush, as one of his last acts as president, decided to dispatch 35,000 American troops to the country in order to bring food to those without access to it. The operation succeeded, apparently saving hundreds of thousands of lives.[77]

When the Clinton administration took over responsibility for the operation, which the UN nominally supervised but the United States effectively controlled, it permitted what came to be known as "mission creep." Its goal for Somalia expanded to include what Madeleine Albright, the new administration's ambassador to the UN and its most vociferous proponent of humanitarian intervention, termed "an unprecedented enterprise aimed at nothing less than the restoration of an entire country."[78] Mission creep had a certain logic. To prevent the recurrence of the conditions that the United States had gone to Somalia to end required ending the political conflict that had given rise to them, which led inevitably to involvement in the country's domestic politics.

The resulting efforts at political reconstruction, there and elsewhere, received the title "nation-building."**

In pursuit of this more ambitious goal, American forces launched an assault on the forces of the most troublesome clan leader, Mohammed Farah Aideed, in the Somali capital, Mogadishu, on October 3, 1993. It turned into a fiasco. Two American helicopters were shot down, eight American soldiers were killed, and seventy-four were wounded. The episode provoked a strongly negative reaction in the American public, which had assumed that its country's troops had gone to Somalia simply to distribute food, not to fight. Clinton announced their withdrawal.[79]

Somalia illustrated a paradox of post–Cold War humanitarian intervention that would affect all subsequent episodes of it. Because the geopolitical stakes were negligible as well as because of its status as the world's hyperpower, the United States could engage in these operations without serious external opposition. For the same reason, however—because American interests were not threatened—the American people were willing to pay very little for these interventions, and that imposed a domestic constraint on them. In Somalia, and elsewhere, in the currency of American lives the public proved, in fact, to be willing to pay nothing. The maximum number of politically permissible deaths in humanitarian interventions, the Clinton administration learned, was zero.

Much closer to home, in Haiti in the Caribbean, the United States mounted another operation motivated mainly by values rather than interests. A military junta had ousted the elected president, Jean-Bertrand Aristide. To defend democracy in the hemisphere as well as to stem the flow of Haitian refugees to Florida,[80] the Clinton administration decided to restore Aristide to power. On October 11, 1993, a ship carrying American personnel assigned to help bring about his

---

** "In fact, 'nation-building' was not precisely what the United States mainly attempted in these places. A nation is a group of people bound together by language, or ethnicity, or religion, or some other common cultural feature and thus can only truly develop over time. The more accurate although less frequently used term is 'state-building': what the United States tried . . . to do was to build what each place conspicuously lacked: the institutions of a modern, efficient, democratic, prosperity-supporting state." Mandelbaum, *Mission Failure*, pp. 77–78.

restoration attempted to dock at the port of Haiti's capital, Port-au-Prince. A jeering mob, apparently inspired by what had happened in Mogadishu a few days earlier, prevented it from landing, inflicting yet another painful political humiliation on the administration. Determined to return Aristide to power, Clinton assembled a military force of 25,000 for an invasion of Haiti in September 1994. At the last minute a team of negotiators headed by former president Jimmy Carter brokered an agreement by which the junta agreed to step aside, averting the use of force.[81]

In the spring of 1994, a massacre took place in Rwanda, a small country in the Great Rift Valley region of East Africa. One of its two constituent tribes, the Hutu, slaughtered an estimated 800,000 of the other tribe, the Tutsis.[82] The occasion seemed to call for the implementation of the doctrine of responsibility to protect but, fearful of a political backlash in the United States, the Clinton administration declined to intervene.[83] Senior officials came to regard the decision as a grave error, which increased their determination to protect the people being persecuted in Bosnia-Herzegovina in the Balkans. Although the United States had no interests there, that onetime province of Yugoslavia became a focal point of American foreign policy during Clinton's first term in office.[84]

The Balkans turned out to be one of the places that the end of the Cold War made more violent. The largest country there, Yugoslavia, was, like the Soviet Union, a multinational state held together by communist rule. Like the Soviet Union, with the waning of the power of communist ideology, nationalism broke it apart. Two of its constituent republics, Slovenia and Croatia, seceded without undue upheaval. Bosnia-Herzegovina, a third such republic, was not so fortunate. Unlike the other two, it was not ethnically homogeneous. Instead, forty-three percent of its population consisted of Muslims, thirty-one percent of Serbs—the most numerous group in communist Yugoslavia as a whole, whose own home republic, Serbia, continued to call itself Yugoslavia after communist rule had ended and the other republics had left—and seventeen percent of Croats.[85]

Bosnia's Serbs and Croats wished to join Serbia-Yugoslavia and independent Croatia, respectively, or at least not to remain in a Muslim-dominated independent Bosnia. The Muslims wanted to secede from

Yugoslavia in order to avoid remaining in an essentially Serb country[86] and managed to declare Bosnia independent, which touched off a three-way civil war.[87] In the fighting, each side used its armed forces to evict people of the other two nationalities living in places that they aspired to govern and so wanted to be inhabited only by members of their own ethnic groups, an ugly practice that came to be called "ethnic cleansing." Ultimately the fighting claimed an estimated 150,000 to 200,000 lives and displaced an additional 2.5 to 2.7 million people,[88] making it, by these standards, the worst European conflict since World War II.

As Yugoslavia collapsed, the Bush administration kept its distance on the grounds that, with the end of the Cold War, the United States lacked strategic interests there. As its secretary of state, James Baker, put it: "We've got no dog in this fight."[89] The Clinton administration adopted a different attitude. It regarded Bosnia's fate as consequential for the United States. In the conflict there it sided with the Muslims, for two main reasons. The Clinton officials believed, correctly, that the Muslims' chief enemy, the Serbs, were killing and displacing far more people than the other two nationalities involved in the war.[90] These officials believed, as well, that the war represented unprovoked Serb aggression against a previously peaceful, tolerant, multinational political unit. This was dubious. The different nationalities of Bosnia had never lived, or expected to live, in a separate, independent, multinational sovereign state; and relations among them prior to the collapse of Yugoslavia, particularly during World War II, had been far from peaceful.[91]

As the war proceeded, the Serbs, fortified by assistance from the Serb-dominated Yugoslav National Army, gained the upper hand and conquered much of Bosnia. This disturbed the Clinton administration, which, however, did not manage to develop a policy to oppose them effectively consistent with the president's desire to avoid sending American troops to the Balkans.

Several changes in American policy finally made it possible to end the conflict. Washington brokered an alliance of convenience between the Croats and the Muslims and helped to train and equip a Croat military force that launched a successful offensive against the Serbs, reducing the amount of Serb-controlled territory from two-thirds to one-half of Bosnia.[92] Then Clinton modified the American position on a political settlement of the war to make it more acceptable to the Serbs. He did so for domestic political reasons. The United Nations had dispatched peacekeepers to Bosnia and the president had promised that if it were to withdraw them the United States would provide assistance. When withdrawal began to seem likely, he faced the prospect of sending troops to the Balkans after all, but not to achieve America's professed goal of helping the Muslims but rather to cover an ignominious UN retreat. He feared that such an initiative would impair his chances for re-election in 1996.[93]

Having changed the American position on a Bosnian settlement to bring it in line with the preferences of the leader of Serbia, Slobodan Milosevic, who had assumed responsibility for the Bosnian Serbs as well, and after a brief American bombing campaign against Serb forces in Bosnia,[94] the United States convened a peace conference in November 1995 on an air base in Dayton, Ohio, that hammered out terms to end the war. It created a complicated and unwieldy governing structure that amounted to a three-way partition of the province. The Dayton Accords did not give the Muslims the power or the territory that the Clinton administration had encouraged them to demand,[95] nor did the vast majority of the people who had suffered ethnic cleansing return to their homes. Nor did the settlement create the unified, tolerant, multi-ethnic political community that the administration had made its goal. The Accords did demonstrate the post–Cold War power of the United States, whose active participation was required to reach a settlement, which the European Union had tried but failed to bring about;[96] and the Dayton Accords did end the killing.

The war in Bosnia was followed by yet another Balkan conflict, this one over Kosovo, a part of Serbia rather than a constituent republic of the old Yugoslavia and largely populated by Muslim Albanian Kosovars rather than Serbs. Toward the end of the communist period, Kosovo had enjoyed a measure of autonomy, but the postcommunist Serb leader, the same Slobodan Milosevic with whom the Clinton administration had cooperated to end the Bosnian War, had revoked it and governed the Kosovars in a heavy-handed manner.[97] A group dedicated to resisting the Serbs, the Kosovo Liberation Army (KLA), came into existence and conducted attacks on Serb targets, to which Milosevic responded with severe repression.[98] Between July 1998 and March 1999 a Serb campaign against the Kosovars created 350,000 refugees, most of them displaced within Kosovo.[99]

Bill Clinton was not eager to become involved in another Balkan conflict. As Kosovo descended into violence, however, he was preoccupied with impeachment proceedings against him, the third in American history: he had conducted an affair with a young White House intern and then lied about it under oath. With the president's attention elsewhere, Madeleine Albright, whom he had named secretary of state at the beginning of his second term, who remained an enthusiastic proponent of humanitarian intervention and who harbored a deep animus toward Milosevic, assumed the lead in American policy on Kosovo.

As the fighting between the Serbs and the overmatched Kosovars took place, an international conference convened at Rambouillet, in France, to try to reach a political settlement for Kosovo. Both of the warring parties rejected the terms that were offered, but the American government subsequently persuaded the Kosovars to accept them and used the Serb rejection as the basis for getting NATO to declare war against Yugoslavia—the first time the alliance had gone to war in its fifty-year history.[100] Once again the United States was using its armed forces not to protect American interests—as in Bosnia it had none in Kosovo—but rather in defense of people under assault from their own government.

At its outset, in March 1999, the Kosovo War involved two related but distinct campaigns.[101] NATO forces bombed Serb targets from the air in an attempt to get Milosevic to cease his assault on the Kosovars. Meanwhile, on the ground in Kosovo, Serb forces engaged in a second ethnic cleansing, ultimately displacing another 1.3 million people.[102] The American government believed, wrongly as it turned out, that light bombing would compel Milosevic to give in.[103]

In its fundamental features the Kosovo War reprised the American experience in Vietnam, with a vast advantage in military and economic power in favor of the anti-Serb coalition. The Serbs could not hope to defeat NATO militarily but could hope to achieve their political goal—retaining control of Kosovo—by raising the cost of preventing this beyond what the NATO countries were willing to pay. Since the United States initially made it clear that it was not willing to incur any casualties at all,[104] the Serbs merely had to endure the NATO bombardment in order to succeed; and for a time they were on course to accomplish exactly that goal.

Faced with the prospect of a humiliating failure in its first-ever war, NATO, and specifically the United States, modified its strategy. Having said that he would not send American troops to Kosovo, Clinton hinted that he might change his mind. The alliance intensified its bombing of targets in both Kosovo and the Serb part of Yugoslavia. At the same time, in a diplomatic effort to persuade Milosevic to accede to its terms, NATO enlisted the assistance of Russia, which had opposed the war from the beginning but had concluded that ending the fighting served its interests. On June 2, 1999, eleven weeks after the bombing had begun, the Serb leader finally accepted those terms.

NATO forces entered Kosovo and Serb forces withdrew, effectively severing it from Serbia. Nine years of occupation by Western forces followed, after which the NATO members reversed their wartime assertion that they were not fighting to make possible Kosovar secession from Yugoslavia[††] and granted Kosovo formal independence.

In each of the humanitarian interventions in which the United States engaged—all of them with the goal of rescuing people under assault rather than furthering any American geopolitical interest—the American military easily overcame whatever resistance it met from far weaker opposing forces. During the Cold War, Saddam Hussein, Mohammed Farah Aideed, the Haitian junta, and the Serb leaders could have applied to the Soviet Union for assistance in opposing the Americans and hoped to receive it, as the North Koreans and North Vietnamese had. The end of the Cold War foreclosed that option. On each occasion, American intervention did save some lives, although, in northern Iraq, Somalia, and the Balkans many had already been lost.

[††] "The United States fought on behalf of the Albanian Kosovars and against the Serbs. Yet on the central political issue at stake—whether Kosovo should become independent, as the Kosovars wanted, or remain a part of Yugoslavia, as the Serbs insisted—NATO and the Americans sided with the Serbs. This put the victors in the odd position of having gone to war to vindicate the position of the country against which it was fighting. Victory, in turn, put the members of the winning coalition at odds, on this central issue, with the people it had fought to protect and whose territory it had come to occupy." Mandelbaum, *Mission Failure*, p. 112.

In other respects, however, the interventions could not be counted as successful. They did not establish "the responsibility to protect" as an internationally recognized norm. To do that, the United States would have had to specify precisely when a government's treatment of the people it governs becomes sufficiently brutal to justify violating the country's sovereignty, and to specify, as well, the appropriate mechanism for reaching such a conclusion: the United Nations was the logical candidate for authorizing humanitarian interventions but the NATO and American operations in Bosnia and Kosovo did not have UN approval and important countries such as Russia in fact disapproved of them. The Clinton administration did not provide any relevant standards. It did not even seriously attempt to do so. Nor did it persuade the American public that sending the country's armed forces to protect distressed people far away was a good idea, let alone a solemn duty. The operations in Bosnia and Kosovo did not have Congressional authority. Clinton did not ask for it because he knew he would not have received it.[105]

Nor did the humanitarian interventions of the 1990s transform the countries where they took place, as Madeleine Albright had promised would happen in Somalia, to ensure that the conditions that had prompted the interventions would not recur. The Kurdish enclave in Iraq was the exception, but Somalia remained chaotic, Haiti was still desperately poor and politically unstable, and Bosnia and Kosovo continued to be countries where different national groups disliked, distrusted, and refused to cooperate with one another.[106]

The United States failed to transform the places where it intervened because it was not willing to invest substantial resources in the task but also, and more importantly, for another reason. The pathologies that created the conditions that drew America into their internal affairs had their roots in the political culture—the political history, institutions, practices, and above all values—of the people of the societies in question. Political culture resists change imposed from the outside. Such change ordinarily comes from within, and takes time—time that is usually measured in generations rather than months or years. The resilience of political culture is the enemy of nation-building, as the United States was to rediscover to its cost in the first decade of the twenty-first century.[107]

Still, the American architects of humanitarian intervention could console themselves with the thought that they had done some good in the world—and, as loyal albeit unwitting Wilsonians, they regarded doing good, as they defined it, as the supreme aim of American foreign policy—at little cost to their own country. The interventions did come with costs, however, especially the last one of the decade, the war over Kosovo.

During that conflict the American Air Force accidentally bombed the Chinese embassy in Belgrade, the capital of Yugoslavia, killing three people and injuring twenty-three more. The attack provoked angry demonstrations in Beijing that the communist regime certainly permitted and seems in fact to have encouraged.[108] The Kosovo War did even more damage to relations with Russia. Moscow had no say in the decision to wage it and not only the government but also the Russian public strongly opposed it.[109] By the time it started, however, post-Soviet Russia was already estranged from the United States and the West. Its growing hostility began with a major military and political initiative of the Clinton administration in Europe, which proved to be one of the most serious errors in the history of American foreign policy.

Russia

Even with the Cold War a thing of the past, Russia remained an important country. Its size—geographically it was the largest political unit on the planet—its location, with borders in Europe, East Asia, and the Middle East, its large reserves of oil and natural gas, its economic potential that had gone largely unrealized during the communist era, and not least the large stockpile of nuclear weapons it had inherited from the Soviet Union together endowed it with major significance for the United States and the rest of the world.

History furnished a broad guideline for dealing with the new Russia. After each of the global conflicts of the modern era before the Cold War, the victors' treatment of the defeated power had shaped the international politics of the postwar period. After the Napoleonic Wars and World War II, the winning coalition had made it a point of conciliating the loser—France in the first case, formerly Nazi Germany in the second—and integrating it into the winners' political and economic orders. There followed a long spell of peace with nineteenth-century France and with West Germany in the second half of the twentieth century. After World War I, by contrast, the victors had imposed a harsh peace on imperial Germany, setting in motion a series of events that led to another great war within two decades.[110] In the wake of the Cold War the United States initially followed the first pattern in its relations with Russia. Then it veered off in the second direction, with foreseeably unhappy consequences.

Along with globalization, the relationship with Russia was one of the two issues of foreign policy in which Bill Clinton took a real interest.[111] His Russia policy consisted of supporting, all but unconditionally, the country's first postcommunist leader, Boris Yeltsin.[112] While far from well organized and not always sober, Yeltsin displayed a genuine commitment to democratic politics and to good relations with the West. He seemed to the American government to be the most reliable bulwark against the return of communism or some other form of authoritarian government.[113] Clinton's administration announced a "strategic alliance with Russian reform"[114] and gave as much political assistance to Yeltsin as it could while indulging a number of initiatives by the Russian president that departed from democratic norms—an assault on the Russian parliament building in 1993,[115] a brutal attack on the rebellious Muslim-majority province of Chechnya in 1994, and a "loans for shares" scheme in 1995 in which politically well-connected banks and individuals lent money to the Russian government in exchange for the right to take possession of valuable Russian companies, most of them controlling natural resources, at prices far below their market values.[116]

Under Yeltsin, Russia, like the other formerly communist countries of Europe, embarked on a transition from a centrally planned to a free-market economy. Regarding economic success as the key to creating a peaceful, democratic Russia,[117] the United States endeavored to help the Russians with their transition. George H. W. Bush had been president during the country's first noncommunist year, when economic aid would have had the greatest impact. Fearful that Western funds would be wasted, however, and sensitive, in a presidential election year, to the charge that this president paid too much attention to foreign policy at the expense of domestic matters,[118] the Bush administration's principal economic policy toward the main successor state to its Cold War rival was to insist that Russia continue payment on the Soviet Union's debt.[119]

The Clinton administration took a different approach. It made small grants to Russia and gave the Russian government economic advice, both officially and through American economists who operated independently in Moscow.[120] In addition, the American government encouraged the IMF to make loans to Russia.

In the first half of the 1990s Russia managed to put in place the building blocks of a free-market economy, with private ownership of property and prices set by the ebb and flow of supply and demand rather than by central planners, neither of which had been a feature of the economic life of the Soviet Union. The transition from plan to market proved rockier for Russia than for the countries of Central and Eastern Europe because Russia had more huge, unproductive, state-owned enterprises that had to be dismantled[121] than they, and less recent experience with operating markets. Moreover, while the Eastern European countries, notably Poland, were willing to undergo rapid, massive economic change, known as "shock therapy," Russian reform proceeded more gradually and in piecemeal fashion, which yielded a smaller reward in economic growth. Furthermore, in Russia, more than in the former communist countries to its west, the transfer of assets from the state to private hands enriched a few none-too-honest people and appeared to the vast majority of Russians, not incorrectly, to be a form of state-sponsored theft.

Thus, the Russian public already had reason for skepticism about the Yeltsin economic reforms when, in 1998, the country fell victim to the kind of financial crisis that had already damaged East Asia. The Russian government's expenditures exceeded its revenue from taxes, and after printing money to make up the difference and touching off serious inflation it changed its method of dealing with its deficits. It sold bonds, called GKOs,[122] with short-term maturities and very high yields in hard currency. Russian solvency depended on a continuing flow of bond purchases by investors. The GKOs had the properties of a bubble and in 1998 the bubble burst.

In the second half of that year investor psychology turned against Russia and confidence in the integrity of the bonds it was issuing plummeted.[123] This stemmed not only from the government's fiscal indiscipline but also from circumstances beyond Russia's control: the price of oil, the sale of which provided the country with most of the hard currency it managed to earn, dropped and the financial troubles in Asia had a "contagion" effect, with doubts about the loans there inspiring similar reservations about Russia.[124] Despite an emergency loan from the IMF, on August 17 the Russian government devalued the ruble and suspended payments on the GKOs, inflicting losses on both Russian citizens and foreign investors.[125]

The simultaneous devaluation and default discredited the Yeltsin government's proponents of market reforms,[126] who also happened to be the officials most favorably inclined to close ties with the West. The crash also undermined Boris Yeltsin's political standing, and with it support for the democratic politics he had sought to bring to Russia.[127] The events of August 17 left the United States with the worst of both worlds: the American government and American advisors had not had decisive influence on Russian economic policies, but the Russian public faulted them for the reforms' shortcomings all the same.[128] By 1998, moreover, attitudes toward the United States had already turned negative in Russia because of a major American initiative on European security.

To be sure, some of Washington's initiatives elicited Russian cooperation. The most urgent problem that the collapse of the Soviet Union raised in the United States concerned its military legacy. When it ceased to exist as a sovereign state it had troops stationed in now-noncommunist countries (and in the case of former Soviet republics now-noncommunist and newly independent countries) that did not want them. Diplomatic efforts by the Clinton administration helped to secure the most politically delicate of these withdrawals, from the three Baltic countries, Estonia, Latvia, and Lithuania, that had once been part of the Soviet Union and that all had with borders with Russia.[129] The Soviet collapse had also, in a sudden, massive, unexpected, and unintended act of nuclear proliferation, left its nuclear weapons deployed in what had become four independent countries: not only the Russian Federation but also Ukraine, Belarus, and Kazakhstan. American initiatives helped to concentrate these weapons in Russia through an agreement reached at a conference in Lisbon, Portugal, in 1992 and subsequent negotiations involving Ukraine and Russia as well as the United States.[130]

The disintegration of the Soviet Union created American concerns, as well, about the safety of the many nuclear, chemical, and biological weapons in Russia from loss, theft, and sale to other countries. To address this problem the Congress, led by Senators Sam Nunn, a Georgia Democrat, and Richard Lugar, an Indiana Republican, enacted the Cooperative Threat Reduction program (better known as the Nunn-Lugar initiative), which provided money to help the Russian government to secure these weapons.[131]

Even before the end of the Soviet Union the question of the future of the Western alliance in Europe had arisen, and here the policy the Clinton administration ultimately chose had fateful consequences. The opposing military organization, the Warsaw Pact, had become defunct after the anti-communist revolutions in Central and Eastern Europe of 1989. NATO's reason for being—to deter a communist attack on Western Europe—had disappeared: such an attack was no longer even remotely likely. The American and European members of NATO wanted to keep it in existence as a way to maintain an American presence on the continent. Western officials assured their Soviet and Russian counterparts, however, that while they would not disband NATO, neither would they extend it eastward as Soviet and then Russian forces retreated.[132]

The Clinton administration decided to break this promise and expand NATO to the east,[133] to include first countries that had once belonged to the Warsaw Pact and then newly sovereign states that had once been part of the Soviet Union. Poland, Hungary, and the Czech Republic officially joined the alliance in 1999 and in the next decade seven more countries were added to its ranks: the three Baltic countries plus Slovenia, Slovakia, Bulgaria, and Romania.[134]

Russians were shocked and dismayed by the decision to expand. Across the country's political spectrum, from communists to Western-style liberals, they vehemently opposed it from the outset.[135] They felt both betrayed by the West and treated with disrespect, as if their views about security arrangements on their home continent did not matter—as, in the case of NATO expansion, they did not. Eventually, as a result of expansion, more than a few Russians came to believe that the United States was bent on weakening, isolating, and even destroying their country.

It did not improve Russian attitudes toward expansion that the reasons the Clinton administration gave for it were hollow at best and disingenuous at worst. Clinton officials announced as its principal purpose the consolidation of democratic government in the new members[136] but offered no evidence that membership in a military organization bolsters democratic politics. Moreover, if that were indeed the case, then the country in postcommunist Europe where democracy was shakiest and most in need of reinforcement, and whose membership in the Atlantic alliance would therefore have the greatest value, was Russia.[137] The Russians, however, were informed that they would not be invited to join NATO.[138] The Americans also said that taking the Central and Eastern Europeans into the alliance would prevent the creation of a new, post–Cold War line of division in Europe; but by excluding Russia they were in fact drawing exactly such a line.

Clinton's real motive for expansion seems to have involved domestic politics. He hoped that it would earn him the votes of Americans with ancestral ties to Poland, Hungary, and Czechoslovakia in the 1996 presidential election[139] and feared being outflanked in that election by a Republican candidate more emphatically devoted to the issue.[140] The new member countries, for their part, were happy to receive what they regarded as a guarantee of protection from Russia without having to pay anything for it.

More broadly, as with humanitarian intervention, the United States expanded NATO because it could.[141] Russia lacked the strength to mount effective opposition. Nor did the administration encounter politically potent resistance within the United States, where the Senate ratified expansion, because relations with Russia were no longer considered important. During the Cold War, policies concerning the Soviet Union almost invariably became the subjects of high political interest and sometimes, as with arms control agreements, intense debate. With that conflict in the past, NATO expansion did not achieve comparable notoriety. Insofar as Americans paid any attention at all to it they saw it as a way of doing a favor to new democracies at no expense to the United States.[142]

That perception turned out to be incorrect. NATO expansion persuaded Russians that American promises were not to be believed and that the American government would seek to take advantage of Russian weakness when it could. Those beliefs, which unfortunately were not groundless, when combined with the American-sponsored war in Kosovo that Russia opposed but was unable to prevent, turned Russian public opinion in a sharply anti-American direction.[143] Opposition to Washington's initiatives became the default Russian policy toward the United States, which hardly served American interests.

George F. Kennan called NATO expansion "the most fateful error of American foreign policy in the entire post-Cold War era."[144] The unprecedentedly favorable geopolitical conditions, particularly in Europe, that the end of the Cold War had bequeathed to the United States came to depend for their survival not on active Russian support for them but rather on that country's inability to overturn them because of its weakness. Over time Russia became less weak, and those conditions did not endure.

The Middle East

While attending to economic relations with China, political relations with Russia, and ethnic conflict in the Balkans, American officials in the first post–Cold War decade (and even more so in the second) devoted more attention to the Middle East[145] than to any other part of the world. This emphasis sets American foreign policy after the collapse of European communism apart from its foreign policy during the Cold War.

The Middle East had mattered to the United States during the Cold War: the oil shocks of the 1970s demonstrated the region's importance for the global economy and the need to use American power and American diplomacy to keep its oil available to America's allies. The Soviet Union, whose southern republics bordered on the region, presented a continuing threat to seek dominance there, a contingency that the United States issued the Carter Doctrine to forestall.[146] The American government worried, as well, about the prospect that an unfriendly local power would achieve a commanding position in the Middle East.[147] The sweeping Israeli military victory of June 1967 thwarted the Egyptian leader Gamal Abdel Nasser's aspiration to do so, and the United States itself substantially reduced Saddam Hussein's power in the 1991 Gulf War.

Still, during the four decades after World War II, Europe and East Asia had higher priority for the United States because these two regions were the most populous and economically productive regions on the planet as well as places where Marxist-Leninist ideology and communist power posed the greatest international challenges to the United States. Those challenges largely disappeared with the end of the Cold War, but the problems in the Middle East persisted because they did not stem from the issues that divided the United States and the Soviet Union. The conclusion of the superpower rivalry did not, therefore, eliminate them. Throughout the twentieth century, pressing, unresolved, and potentially explosive geopolitical problems attracted the attention of the United States. In the last decade of that century and beyond, such problems were to be found in the Middle East.[148]

The conclusion of the Gulf War left the United States with two ongoing obligations. Washington undertook to protect the Kurds against Saddam Hussein's forces by maintaining a protective zone for them in their northern Iraqi homeland. In addition, Saddam remained in power in Baghdad and United Nations Resolution 687 required him to abjure weapons of mass destruction and submit to inspections to ensure that he was doing so, conditions that the United States assumed responsibility for enforcing. America also maintained an economic embargo on Iraq and at one point launched a punitive bombing campaign against the country, conducting Operation Desert Fox from December 16 to December 19, 1998, in response to the Saddam regime's refusal to comply with the terms of Resolution 687.[149]

In the wake of the Gulf War, the United States thus carried out the familiar policy of containment, but this time toward Iraq rather than the Soviet Union. In Cold War containment the American government had joined forces with a one-time adversary, China, which also had an adversarial relationship with Moscow. The obvious candidate to play a role analogous to China's in the case of Iraq was Iran, which, while hostile to the United States from the time of the revolution that had put its ruling clerics in power, had waged a bitter, costly, decade-long war with its Iraqi neighbor in the 1980s.

The American government did not, however, align itself with Iran because it regarded the Islamic Republic as posing a threat to American interests in the Middle East on a par with the one that Iraq presented. Furthermore, the American hyperpower felt itself to be sufficiently strong to confront both revisionist countries at the same time. The United States therefore adopted a policy of dual containment in the region.[150]

Another Middle Eastern issue received extensive attention from both the Clinton administration and its two successors. In fact, it preoccupied the American government for the entirety of the post–Cold War era: the Arab-Israeli conflict. All three presidencies sought to build on, continue, and complete the work of Henry Kissinger's shuttle diplomacy and Jimmy Carter's Camp David negotiations of the 1970s. These initiatives had yielded a peace treaty between Israel and the largest Arab state, Egypt, which had fought four wars against each other in twenty-four years.

Two events imparted momentum to what came to be called, simply, "the peace process." In the fall of 1991, in the wake of the victory in the Gulf War, the Bush administration drew upon the political capital it had earned from that conflict to convene a Middle East peace conference in the Spanish capital, Madrid. The conference brought Israeli officials together for the first time with representatives of Arab governments that had refused to deal directly with the Jewish state. The Madrid meeting also included the Palestine Liberation Organization (PLO), an organization with which Israelis had shunned direct contact that claimed to represent all Palestinian Arabs, including those living in territory the Israeli army had captured from Jordan in the 1967 war.[151]

Then, in 1993 in Oslo, Norway, representatives of the PLO and Israelis acting independently but with the knowledge of their government worked out a framework for negotiations between the two parties.[152] The American government embraced the framework and put itself forward as the mediator between the two as well as between Israel and its northern neighbor, Syria. In 1967 Israel had taken Syrian-controlled territory known as the Golan Heights, from which Syria had periodically launched bombardments of Israeli villages after 1948. The goal of the negotiations between the two countries was for Israel to re-turn the Golan in exchange for peace with Syria.

The Israeli prime minister, Yitzhak Rabin, gave priority to a peace agreement with Syria because that country posed a greater military threat than did the Palestinians, and the secretary of state in the first Clinton term, Warren Christopher, made twenty-eight trips to Damascus, the Syrian capital, in pursuit of one.[153] The Syrian dictator, Hafez al-Assad, met with Christopher because he found the peace process a useful way to placate the American hyperpower. Peace itself, however, would have required ending the conflict with Israel, on which Assad, as a member of the minority Alawite sect, relied for such legitimacy as his regime enjoyed among the far more numerous Sunni Muslims he ruled by force.[154] The Syrian talks therefore did not succeed.[155]

The negotiations between Israel and the PLO, which was led by its chairman, Yasir Arafat, did produce five agreements, by the terms of which the Israelis conducted some limited withdrawals from ter-ritory they had conquered in 1967 located between the ceasefire line of their 1948 War of Independence, known as the Green Line, and the Jordan River, the border with the Kingdom of Jordan—without, however, giving up ultimate control over that territory. The ongoing talks with the Palestinians gave the Jordanian king political cover to sign a peace treaty with Israel in 1994.[156] The talks survived the assas-sination of Prime Minister Rabin and the election of a government of the opposing political party, which was less well disposed to making concessions to the Palestinians.

In July 2000, as Clinton's time as president was running out, he brought Arafat and the Israeli prime minister Ehud Barak, a former general who belonged to Rabin's political party, to Camp David for almost two weeks in an effort to reach a final settlement of their con-flict. Barak made sweeping concessions but Arafat rejected them and provoked a violent and deadly campaign against Israeli civilians that lasted for the better part of five years, persuading most Israelis that the PLO had no serious interest in a lasting peace.[157]

Nonetheless, the two presidents who followed Clinton in office, George W. Bush and Barack Obama, both continued American efforts at mediation. They adopted somewhat different approaches to the con-flict: Bush made a Palestinian commitment to democracy a condition for an agreement,[158] while Obama insisted on an end to the building of Israeli housing outside the Green Line.[159] The secretaries of state in the second terms of both presidents[160] made establishing peace between Israel and the Palestinians by creating a Palestinian state a high personal priority. Neither came close to achieving it.

The United States persisted in the enterprise because the relevant officials in successive administrations, who developed personal stakes in the peace process, invariably persuaded themselves that a successful conclusion was close at hand, or at least eventually possible,[161] and because the project cost the United States nothing except the time of senior officials.[162] These officials failed because their basic beliefs about the conflict turned out to be incorrect.

They believed that resolving it would pay major political dividends for the United States. That had been true for the Egyptian-Israeli negotiations in the 1970s, which lifted the Arab oil embargo in the short term and eliminated the possibility of another major Arab-Israeli war, which would have required Egyptian participation, over the long run. The stakes in the Israeli-Palestinian dispute were far smaller and the reward for resolving it far more modest—if it could be resolved at all.[163] It could not, however, be resolved, and believing that it could was the second American mistake.

The Americans convinced themselves that both sides wanted to end the conflict and that the mediator's task was simply to help them arrive at terms for doing so that each could accept. The Israelis did want to end it; they, after all, had not started it. The Palestinians, however, turned out to be unwilling to accept the legitimacy and permanence of a Jewish state in the Middle East.[164] They sought not to end the conflict but to win it, which meant the disappearance of Israel. Their attitude had more than one cause but had its roots ultimately in their political culture,[165] which meant that the American-sponsored Middle East peace process foundered for the same reason that American nation-building in Somalia, Haiti, Bosnia, and Kosovo failed.[166]

Despite the perpetual disappointment of the peace process, as the twentieth century gave way to the twenty-first the American hyperpower could survey the preceding decade of international history with a measure of satisfaction. The new world order that the end of the Cold War had bequeathed was functioning, if not always and everywhere smoothly, then at least tolerably well. The Wilsonian moment that the Gulf War had represented had not endured, but neither had the kind of international aggression that Woodrow Wilson had sought to prevent become a feature of post–Cold War international politics. Humanitarian intervention had not become a global or American norm, nor had the United States made the countries in which it had intervened models of tranquility, good government, and prosperity, but its military operations had saved lives. Globalization had caused financial problems but these had apparently been overcome, and the process of increasing international economic integration seemed destined to proceed.

China had not turned into a rights-protecting democracy but the Americans had reason to hope that its market-based economic growth had set it on the path to becoming one eventually. Russia was disgruntled with NATO expansion but was not imposing unwanted forms of governance on its neighbors, as the Soviet Union had done. Events, in short, had not disproven the liberal theory of history. To the contrary, Americans could plausibly conclude that world history was moving, if not necessarily rapidly or steadily, in their preferred direction.

The decade did bring an unwelcome development, which originated, as it happened, in the Middle East. The United States suffered a series of terrorist attacks: on the World Trade Center in New York in 1993, on an American Air Force barracks in Saudi Arabia in 1996, on two American embassies in Africa—one in Kenya, the other in Tanzania—in 1998, and against the destroyer USS *Cole* in Aden harbor in Yemen in 2000. The American government duly took note of the attacks and promised to deal with their perpetrators in an appropriate way; but terrorism seemed, as the new millennium began, at worst a second-order problem, an annoyance rather than a serious threat. That assessment changed on September 11, 2001.

II

Back to the Future, 2001–2015

September 11 and Its Aftermath

On September 11, 2001, nineteen young men from the Arab Middle East commandeered four American commercial airliners filled with passengers. The hijackers crashed two of the planes into the twin towers of the World Trade Center at the tip of Manhattan and a third struck the Pentagon, the headquarters of the nation's Department of Defense, across the Potomac River from Washington, D.C., in northern Virginia. Passengers in the fourth aircraft managed to overpower the hijackers and that plane crashed in a field in Pennsylvania. All told, 2,977 people died, including everyone on board all four planes, and more than 6,000 were injured.

A shadowy organization called al Qaeda,[1] which a wealthy citizen of Saudi Arabia named Osama bin Laden had founded and led, had planned and carried out the attacks, as it had perpetrated the previous assaults on American targets in Aden, Kenya, and Tanzania.[2] Al Qaeda aspired to spread what it regarded as the original and true form of Islam across the Middle East and around the world. It regarded the ruling governments of the region as heretical and sought to weaken them by striking at their principal foreign supporter, the United States.[3]

The attacks did not come as a complete surprise to the American intelligence community, which had monitored al Qaeda's activities for several years[4] and had even, in the previous month, inserted a warning of the organization's plans to attack the United States into one of the briefings that it provided to the president every day. For the rest of the government, however, and for the country and the world, what happened on September 11 came as a large and nasty shock. Almost no one had even imagined, let alone expected, such a spectacular and horrifying event. The assaults represented the first mass-casualty attacks by foreigners in the continental United States since the War of 1812. To add to the powerful impression they made, they were captured on video. The whole world could see them.

The events of September 11 had the same kind of galvanizing impact on the United States as other, similar events in American history: they made the world suddenly seem a far more dangerous place, they generated a public demand for action to meet the new threat, and the government responded with alacrity to that demand.[5] Like the comparable events in the nation's past, the September 11 assaults propelled the United States into war—in fact, into three different although related wars: in Afghanistan, in Iraq, and into a more diffuse conflict known as the Global War on Terror.

The American president on September 11, 2001, had held office for less than a year. George Walker Bush, the son of Clinton's predecessor in the White House, George Herbert Walker Bush, came to the presidency from the governorship of Texas without any particular experience in international affairs. As a candidate he acquired a measure of credibility in that area of presidential responsibility by surrounding himself with some of the officials involved in his father's notably successful foreign policy.

During the 2000 presidential campaign the second Bush had criticized the Clinton administration for its commitment to nation-building and had promised to conduct a less ambitious, more humble foreign policy.[6] The attacks galvanized him as well as the American public and gave his administration a new direction and a new purpose. On September 11 he said, "We are at war with terror. From this day forward this is the new priority of our administration."[7] Contrary to his campaign assurances, and no doubt to his own initial expectations as well, foreign policy dominated his two presidential terms.

The national effort he launched to combat terrorism qualified as a war in important ways. It involved the mobilization of the nation's resources and the use of force against a foreign enemy. In another way, however, the term "war on terror" was an odd one: it announced a conflict not against a concrete adversary but rather against a tactic, rather as if World War II had been called a war against the blitzkrieg.[8] Awkward as the term was, however, "the Global War on Terror" became established as the principal national undertaking in the wake of September 11. The United States waged it in both defensive and offensive fashion.

The first priority had to be protecting the United States from further such attacks. For this purpose, the government put most of the many federal agencies with relevant responsibilities into a sprawling new cabinet office, the Department of Homeland Security. The Department received generous funding, amounting to more than $1 trillion, in the decade following the attacks.[9] Of this it devoted forty-six percent to protecting people and infrastructure within the United States and forty-four percent to disrupting potential attacks.[10] The total outlays for protecting the homeland seem in retrospect to have exceeded what was needed to defend it against such terrorist threats as it confronted.[11] This was in keeping with American precedent. A rich country, the United States had traditionally funded its wars on a scale lavish by comparison with the expenditures of other countries. Moreover, the incentives policymakers faced favored erring on the side of generosity: the public would blame them for allowing further attacks to occur but not—or at least not as severely—for wasting money.[12]

In the event, no attacks remotely comparable to those of September 11, and very few attacks at all, transpired in the months and years that followed. The near-perfect record of defense may have had something to do with the numerous and costly defensive measures the United States adopted, but it also surely stemmed from the fact that, contrary to the understandable fears that the disasters of that day had inspired, the number of terrorists ready, willing, and able to mount deadly attacks in the United States turned out to be small.[13]

Such people did, however, exist: al Qaeda did have cadres operating around the world. The offensive part of the Global War on Terror involved pursuing and capturing or killing them. The president gave the Central Intelligence Agency (CIA) the major responsibility for carrying out this mission,[14] which involved the liberal use of a new weapon, a pilotless armed aerial vehicle known as a drone. Drones could be remotely guided to distant targets that they could then attack from the air.[15]

The offensive aspect of the War on Terror aroused the criticism, familiar from previous wars, that in attempting to defend the nation the federal government was violating norms of liberty.[16] Unusually for American wars, the liberties being violated according to the critics were those of foreigners, not Americans. Drone attacks, for example, killed people who were not suspected of terrorism as well as those who were. Moreover, captured suspects were incarcerated at the American naval base in Guantanamo, Cuba, or sent to prisons in other countries, where normal American rules governing the treatment of prisoners did not apply (or at least were not applied). A considerable outcry arose over whether torture, illegal under international law, had been employed against some of the detainees.[17]

The War on Terror did, in the view of some, impinge on the liberties of American citizens as well. The government began monitoring telephone calls by Americans, not in order to listen to them but to note any suspicious telephonic contacts.[18] As with other conflicts during which the government's policies eroded civil liberties—Lincoln's suspension of habeas corpus during the Civil War and Franklin Roosevelt's order interning Americans of Japanese descent on the West Coast during World War II, for example[19]—as the nation's sense of emergency dissipated, the policies in question came to an end.[20] While the Global War on Terror was never formally declared to be over, let alone to have been won, the country did eventually return to most of its normal, pre–September 11 routines. Even as it was mounting a campaign against terrorism in the last months of 2001, however, the Bush administration was also launching a more familiar kind of conflict in Afghanistan.

The United States had become involved in that landlocked, mountainous, poverty-stricken Islamic country more than two decades previously, when the Soviet Union had invaded it in 1979 and the American government had supported the Afghan resistance.[21] After the Soviet troops withdrew in 1989, Afghanistan experienced several years of instability and violence until, in 1997, a radical Islamic group that called itself the Taliban[22] consolidated power. The new regime had an affinity for al Qaeda and its leaders welcomed bin Laden to their country and allowed him to establish training camps there. The attacks of September 11 therefore came, in effect, from Afghanistan.

Accordingly, in their wake the American government demanded that the Taliban hand over al Qaeda. When this did not happen, the United States mounted a military campaign in the country that produced a swift and remarkably inexpensive American victory. A mere 400 American personnel entered Afghanistan, most from the CIA. With the aid of monetary inducements they recruited to their side tribes hostile to the Taliban. These local forces, supported by intensive American aerial bombardment, had, by the end of 2001, driven the Islamic radicals from power.[23] The victory proved to be an incomplete one, however: Osama bin Laden and a number of his associates and followers, as well as some of the Taliban leadership, escaped capture by the American forces.

The United States then faced the question of what to do about Afghanistan. Simply leaving seemed inadvisable since that might open the way for the return of the Taliban and the further use of the country as a base for launching terrorist attacks around the world. Although the main motive for the initial military action had to do with considerations of security rather than the desire to rescue distressed people, the United States did in Afghanistan what it had done several times in other countries in the previous decade in the wake of humanitarian interventions: it decided to remain and attempt to refashion the country. Along with other Western countries that had supported the war against the Taliban,[24] the Americans established an interim and then a permanent government for the country, headed, in both cases, by an Afghan with experience in the West, Hamid Karzai.[25]

In the years that followed, the international community, led by the United States, tried to build Western-style political and economic institutions, but with only very limited success. With an economy dependent on near-subsistence agriculture (and the cultivation of poppies for opium), with low rates of literacy, with widespread and often fierce adherence to traditional forms of Islam, and with no experience with political democracy or sophisticated, law-governed free markets, Afghanistan offered poor prospects for the realization of the American ambitions for it.[26]

Also obstructing what amounted to a project of radical modernization was the country's demography. Like Bosnia, several ethnic groups,
not always on good terms with one another, composed it.* Afghanistan
had always been governed in decentralized fashion, which meant that
Karzai had little power to administer it, let alone remake it. It did not
help that he, his family, and many Afghan public officials turned out
to be enthusiastic practitioners of corruption.[27]

Another formidable impediment to nation-building in Afghanistan
came from the insurgency that the defeated Taliban began a few years
after 2001 and that managed, over the course of the next decade, to
gain effective control of much of the country.[28] The insurgency proved
durable: it was still going strong a full two decades after 2001, making
the conflict in Afghanistan the longest shooting war the United States
has ever fought.

To sustain their military and political effort against the American-
sponsored government in the Afghan capital, Kabul, the Taliban drew
on ethnic solidarity among the Pashtun people from whom they came,
on the country's resentment of foreign occupiers, and in particular
on the support they received from the government of neighboring
Pakistan. That country played the same kind of role for the Afghan
insurgents as China had for the Vietnamese communists: it served as
a staging area and a source of supplies. The Pakistani government, although nominally aligned with the United States, strongly preferred an
Afghan government over which it had more sway than it did over the
Karzai regime; and in any case, like the British raj before it, it exercised

---

* "Pashtuns, who live on both sides of the border with Pakistan, are the principal
group in the south, the major city of which is Kandahar. They make up about
40 percent of the country's population. Tajiks, in the north, where the main city
is Mazar-e-Sharif, comprise about 30 percent of all Afghans. This group also
lives in Tajikistan, one of Afghanistan's northern neighbors, which was once a
constituent republic of the Soviet Union. Uzbeks and Turkmen also inhabit the
north of the country and number about 10 percent of the population. Hazaras, in
the west, where the largest city is Herat, are, like the people of neighboring Iran,
Shia Muslims, and speak a dialect of the Iranian language, Farsi. They make up
about 15 percent of all Afghans. All these groups are present in Kabul, the capital,
which dominates the eastern part of the country." Michael Mandelbaum, *Mission
Failure: America and the World in the Post-Cold War Era*, New York: Oxford
University Press, 2016, pp. 158–159.

little authority in the Pashtun-dominated part of Pakistan adjacent to Afghanistan.[29]

The American nation-building exercise in Afghanistan failed to fulfill the initial hopes for it for yet another reason. In the Bush foreign policy it did not command the highest priority. More troops, more money, and more high-level attention went to the third American war that the attacks of September 11 triggered, in Iraq.

Gulf War II

Of all the wars that the United States has fought, the one against Iraq that began in 2003 had the least straightforward origins. It did not come about as a result of a direct or indirect Iraqi attack on either America itself or an American ally or indeed on any country. Since the Gulf War of 1991, Washington had pursued a policy of containment toward Saddam Hussein's dictatorial regime in Baghdad and containment had proven effective: Iraq did not pose an immediate threat to its neighbors. Nor, while the Iraqi dictator egregiously mistreated the people he governed, did the Bush administration decide to remove him from power in order to protect them from him. Nor, finally, did the decision to intervene in Iraq emerge from an orderly process within the American government.[30]

The attacks of September 11 made the war against Saddam possible in the sense that the shock they administered predisposed the American public to support large-scale military operations abroad, as would almost certainly not otherwise have been the case. The attacks had the effect of increasing the Bush administration's political capital and his freedom to spend it, and the president invested it in undertaking the war. In addition, the international standing of the United States as the world's hyperpower meant that no other country could block an American attack on Iraq. While the domestic impact of September 11 and the country's international position explain why the Bush administration had the opportunity to use force to remove Saddam, they do not, by themselves, account for the president's decision to take advantage of that opportunity.

He had personal reasons for a profound dislike of the Iraqi dictator, who had tried to have his father assassinated after the elder Bush had left the presidency; but that was not the reason he took the United

States to war. A number of prominent foreign policy officials, known as neoconservatives, advocated an attack on Iraq immediately after September 11; but the person who made the decision for war, President Bush, did not belong to their camp. A large section of the public believed that Saddam had, in fact, had a hand in the attacks, but no evidence of any direct Iraqi involvement ever came to light.[31] Still, the events of September 11 did bring about the Iraq War, albeit indirectly.

In their immediate aftermath the Bush administration considered the threat of terrorism to be of such magnitude that merely removing the government of remote, geopolitically insignificant Afghanistan did not rise to the level of the response required to deter terrorists worldwide.[32] The terrorists themselves, moreover, were the products of the social and political pathologies of the Arab Middle East. Deposing Saddam, who was both a symptom and a cause of those pathologies, would, administration officials believed, help alleviate them and thus strike at the roots of terrorism.[33]

Finally, Bush officials reckoned that while they had been aware before September 11 that terrorism presented a threat to the United States, they had not realized how serious that threat was. When they asked themselves, as they were bound to do, what other threats they might be underestimating,[34] Saddam came immediately to mind. He had been seeking nuclear weapons before the 1991 war and they had to assume that he would do so again if he remained in power.[35] A bomb in his hands, or a bomb that he made and passed to a terrorist group such as al Qaeda, would pose a major threat to America and the world. It was, therefore, unacceptably dangerous to allow him to continue in power, and September 11 provided the opportunity to end his rule. Thus the United States went to war to dislodge Saddam in 2003 not because of what he had done in the past or was doing in the present but to forestall what he might do in the future.[36] In this way the Iraq conflict counts as an event that is relatively rare historically (and not an example of compliance with international law): a preventive war.[†]

[†] "A preventive war differs from a preemptive attack, which involves striking when an enemy is itself on the verge of attacking and war is inevitable. A preventive war, by contrast, is launched before an attack is imminent in order to forestall a danger that is anticipated to develop at some point in the future." Mandelbaum, *Mission Failure*, p. 199.

Public statements by the president and also by his combative and influential vice president, Richard B. (Dick) Cheney, prepared the American public for a second war in the Persian Gulf region in twelve years; and both houses of Congress voted, in October 2002, in favor of it. The second war differed from the first in that it did not gain the same degree of international support. Ultimately forty-eight other countries joined the anti-Saddam coalition (although only Great Britain made an appreciable military contribution to it) but two important allies, France and Germany, opposed the venture,[37] as did Russia. Moreover, the Turkish parliament declined to allow the United States to launch an attack on Iraq from its country.[38] In November 2002, the United Nations Security Council passed a resolution giving Iraq a "final opportunity" to comply with its disarmament obligations and readmit the UN weapons inspectors that Saddam had evicted in 1997; but when, in early 2003, the Bush administration sought to secure another resolution, this one authorizing war, it failed to do so.

The attack on Iraqi forces proceeded in more or less the same way on the second occasion as on the first. In 1991 American armored columns had swept into Kuwait from Saudi Arabia. In 2003 similar formations, supported, again, by precise and deadly air strikes, entered Iraq from Kuwait. They overcame the resistance that the Iraqi army was able to muster and captured Baghdad in early April 2003, little more than a month after the campaign had begun. Once again, vastly superior American firepower, logistics, training, and morale, in combination with total command of the air, brought a swift and relatively inexpensive victory.[39]

The Bush administration had no serious plan for the aftermath of war other than withdrawing American troops as rapidly as possible.[40] It assumed that the existing Iraqi institutions would continue to function and that they would preserve stability there.[41] That assumption proved to be incorrect. The fall of the Saddam regime brought violent disorder to Iraq, with widespread lawlessness and massive looting in Baghdad, the capital.[42] The president therefore decided that the troops would remain and that the United States would accept at least temporary responsibility for governing the country.

To take charge of Iraq, the Bush administration established the Coalition Provisional Authority (CPA) and appointed as its leader

L. Paul Bremer, a veteran foreign service officer who had never served in the Arab Middle East. He had, in theory, plenipotentiary powers comparable in scope to those that Douglas MacArthur had exercised in Japan after World War II.[43]

The CPA had responsibility not only for the day-to-day governance of Iraq but also for devising a new political system for the country, revamping its economy,[44] and supplying it with modern infrastructure. In Iraq, George W. Bush, the critic of the Clinton administration's nation-building efforts in 2000, became, three years later, the most ambitious American nation-builder of the post–Cold War era and arguably in the entire history of the United States. He became, as well, an ardent Wilsonian. Having won re-election in 2004, in his second Inaugural Address he made a commitment to spreading democracy around the world.[45] Even before that, his administration had launched a "Freedom Agenda" to promote democracy in the Middle East.[46]

The Americans assembled an indigenous government in Iraq and supervised the conduct of several free and largely fair elections there. In other ways, however, the nation-building exercise did not achieve its goals. In its fourteen months of existence, the CPA did not come close to transforming the country into a smoothly functioning, rights-protecting democracy with a flourishing free-market economy. The Authority was not well organized for this purpose: few of its personnel had had extensive experience in the region and many owed their positions to their Republican and conservative political loyalties.[47] More importantly, like Afghanistan, Iraq offered poor prospects for such a transformation. It lacked the relevant institutions, the experience, and the social and political values required to operate them effectively.

Like Afghanistan, it consisted of several ethnic groups that had less than cordial relations between and among them: Sunni Muslim Arabs in the west, non-Arab Muslim Kurds in the north, and Shia Muslim Arabs in the south.[48] In the elections that the United States made possible, Iraqis overwhelmingly practiced ethnic and sectarian solidarity, with Sunnis, Shia, and Kurds supporting candidates from their own groups who were devoted more or less exclusively to these groups' separate and often conflicting interests.

As in Afghanistan, as well, nation-building in Iraq fell afoul of an insurgency.[49] In fact, the end of Saddam's government touched off three violent conflicts. One pitted dissident Sunnis, many of them once part of the old regime,[50] against the occupying Americans. The Sunnis had dominated Iraq until the American invasion, which unsurprisingly aroused their resentment against the invaders and the hope that, by driving them out, the Sunnis could regain their former supremacy. The Shia, who had suffered Sunni repression during the Saddam era and before, had reason to be grateful to the Americans. Since they outnumbered the Sunnis, the elections gave them control of the national government. Still, they formed sectarian militias that opposed and harassed the American forces, creating the second conflict. Neighboring countries assisted the insurgents. Iran and Syria, both with fiercely anti-American governments, provided shelter and weapons to the forces attacking American troops.[51]

The bloodiest of the three conflicts took place between Sunnis and Shia.[52] As they took control of the government and its resources, the Shia gained the upper hand in this conflict. They succeeded in bringing a version of "ethnic cleansing" to Iraq, driving many of the Sunnis who lived in Baghdad out of the capital.

In addition to resisting the Sunni and Shia insurgencies, the United States tried to tamp down the struggle between the two,[53] but suffered from a serious handicap in coping with all three conflicts: it had too few troops to police the country effectively. The secretary of defense, Donald Rumsfeld, was determined to wage and win the second Gulf War with far fewer troops than the United States had deployed in the first one, and he did: 140,000 soldiers defeated the Iraqi army in 2003, compared with 543,000 twelve years earlier. That lower number, however, proved inadequate for keeping order in the country once the battle against Saddam's army had been won, and the Bush administration declined to send reinforcements.[54] So the disorder and the conflicts persisted, which changed the American public's view of the American presence in Iraq.

Like the Cold War conflicts in Korea and Vietnam, the ongoing American war against insurgents in Iraq became unpopular at home. In 2003, just before the invasion, sixty-three percent of the public approved of intervening in that country.[55] By the time of the 2006 midterm elections, fifty-six percent disapproved of it.[56] Public opinion ultimately forced the government to withdraw its troops from the country.

Armed nation-building in Iraq fell victim to the democratic feature of American foreign policymaking.

As with the My Lai massacre in Vietnam,[57] a glaring instance of American misconduct in Iraq came to light: at a prison holding suspected insurgents at Abu Ghraib, American guards mistreated some of the prisoners and photographs of their misdeeds became public.[58] This put the entire American enterprise in Iraq in a bad light, especially in the eyes of Arabs and Europeans. What did most to discredit the Iraq operation in American opinion, however, was what had eroded the popularity of the wars in Korea and Vietnam: American casualties.

As the American death toll in Iraq rose, public approval of keeping Americans in harm's way there declined. It declined more sharply, with deaths reducing public support more rapidly, than had been the case for either Korea or Vietnam. The public had regarded those wars as battles in a larger conflict with the Soviet Union and international communism that it considered to be of supreme importance for the national interests of the United States. The war in Iraq, although associated in the public mind with the Global War on Terror, lacked comparable importance and Americans were consequently willing to pay less—in casualties—to wage it.[59]

As the war became increasingly unpopular, much of the criticism of the Bush administration's policy focused on the failure to locate anywhere in the country the weapons of mass destruction that the administration had asserted Saddam possessed and the presence of which it had used as a justification for the war. The absence of these armaments—which were presumed to be chemical rather than nuclear weapons and that administration officials had genuinely believed to be present[60]—served as a convenient rationale for Democrats who had initially supported the war for shifting their public positions to opposition. It did not, however, drive the public's change of mind.

If the Iraq operation had gone as smoothly as the Bush officials had wrongly foreseen but no chemical weapons had been found, the public would not have turned against American policy. If, on the other hand, American troops had discovered such weapons but the occupation had proved as costly as it did, the public would have abandoned its initial support for the enterprise.[61]

As in the past, public opinion affected policy through elections. Despite the unanticipated disorder in Iraq, in 2004 Bush managed to win re-election; but in the 2006 midterm elections the Democrats, by then more or less unanimously critical of the war, gained control of both houses of Congress and in 2008 the Democratic candidate, who had opposed the Iraq War even before it had begun, won the presidency.

Rather than simply conceding the failure of the war he had launched in 2003, in the face of continuing casualties and growing public dis-affection George W. Bush adopted a new tactic. In what came to be known as "the Surge," he authorized the dispatch of five additional battalions of American troops to Iraq. Two of them went to the Sunni-dominated western part of the country, with the other three being sent to Baghdad.[62] Their mission was not only to combat the anti-American insurgents but also, and what was just as important, to establish good relations with the local tribes in order to wean them from supporting the insurgency.[63] The new approach, along with the losses the Sunnis were suffering at the hands of the Shia and the challenge to the tra-ditional Sunni leadership posed by Islamic fundamentalists, made the Surge successful: tribal leaders adopted a friendlier attitude to the American forces and the level of anti-American violence declined in the target areas.[64]

At the same time as it authorized the Surge, however, the Bush administration, bowing to public opinion, was seeking to end the American military presence in Iraq by negotiating with the Iraqi gov-ernment a deadline for the withdrawal of American troops. The two parties agreed that the Americans would withdraw from the country's cities by June 30, 2009, and leave entirely by December 31, 2011. Bush's successor kept to that timeline.

Like other American wars, the one in Iraq came with a price tag. Ultimately 4,487 Americans died in the country and 32,226 were wounded.[65] In the short term, the economic burden of Iraq was lighter than in previous conflicts: the annual cost amounted to a smaller pro-portion of the overall American gross domestic product than had the wars in Korea and Vietnam. Unlike in past wars, moreover, the Bush administration did not raise taxes to help pay for it. The administra-tion relied on borrowing to make good the budgetary shortfalls that it caused,[66] perhaps calculating that tax increases would make the effort even less popular. Over the long term, however, the price of Iraq, including disability and medical payments for decades into the future, seemed likely to be considerable, perhaps as much as $6 trillion or more.[67]

The war had political costs as well. It weakened America's international standing. It demonstrated that the hyperpower had neither the skills nor the stamina to remake a small, poor Middle Eastern country, and that modestly armed insurgents could challenge its mighty military forces. The failure also diminished public enthusiasm in the United States for the kind of American global role that was central to post–Cold War international politics. Moreover, as the Bush administration drew to a close, an unexpected event imposed, in economic terms, even greater short-term costs on the United States and indeed on the whole world: the worst financial crisis in history.

The Financial Crisis

On September 15, 2008, Lehman Brothers, a large, prominent, venerable investment bank with its headquarters in New York, went bankrupt. Its failure caused a near meltdown of the entire American financial system.[‡] The acute financial distress triggered by that failure spread to Europe.[68] The international financial crisis led in turn to a deep global downturn in economic output, the deepest, in fact, since the Great Depression of the 1930s. To an even greater extent than the Iraq War, the combination of these two events weakened the international position of the United States and in that and other ways undermined the post–Cold War conditions that powerfully favored American interests. The Asian financial crises of the 1990s had inflicted economic damage locally; had had, in the end, relatively modest consequences; and had seemed to reinforce the status of the United States as the world's

---

[‡] According to Ben Bernanke, chairman of the Federal Reserve at the time of the crisis and an academic expert on financial history, this was "the worst financial crisis in global history, including the Great Depression." Quoted in Adam Tooze, *Crashed: How a Decade of Financial Crises Changed the World*, New York: Penguin Books, 2019, p. 163. See also *ibid.*, p. 165.

hyperpower. By contrast, the American-centered financial crisis of 2008 had a negative impact of far greater magnitude that was global in scope and undermined America's post–Cold War standing throughout the world.

The financial crisis had its origins in an enormous real estate bubble in the United States, which owed its size, in the first instance, to the emphasis American social values and therefore the American political system place on encouraging home ownership. Most people who buy homes borrow, often heavily, to finance the purchase, and borrowing both inflated the bubble and made it fragile.[69] Further contributing to its size and its fragility was the "financial engineering" that took place in the decade before the crash, which turned mortgages into complicated securities that could be bought, sold, and insured.[70] This vastly expanded the amount of money invested, directly or indirectly, in American real estate,[71] as did exceptionally low interest rates worldwide.[72]

Financial institutions of all kinds all over the world, as well as governments, put money into these new investment vehicles, which were poorly regulated and, because they were new and complex, poorly understood.[73] Many of the underlying loans were, given the financial positions of the borrowers, unwise. Financial markets operated on the assumption that the proliferation of the new financial instruments made real estate finance more stable. In fact, they turned out to make it much less so.[74]

Like all bubbles, this one required steadily rising prices in the underlying asset in order to sustain itself.[75] American real estate prices stopped rising in 2006 and then began to fall.[76] This set off a negative chain reaction among financial institutions, with losses in one degrading the financial position of others, like falling dominoes. The mechanism of transmission for huge losses from bursting bubbles in the past was people either rushing to sell their shares of the asset—tulips, for example, in the Netherlands in the seventeenth century—or rushing to withdraw their deposits from banks. Such behavior, commonly known as panics, do damage because they are self-fulfilling: the more people who seek to sell the asset, the further the price falls, and thus the more sellers lose; and the more money people withdraw from a bank, the less money the bank has to repay other depositors.

In 2008, the crisis manifested itself in a different and, for the American and European economies, an even more perilous way: financial firms and major corporations had come to depend on large-scale, short-term, very inexpensive financing for their day-to-day operations.[77] As the real estate bubble burst and one institution after another suffered severe losses, such financing seized up. Lenders lacked confidence in the creditworthiness of their borrowers, and even in their own solvency. The flow of capital being the lifeblood of a market economy, the financial crisis of 2008 had the same kind of impact on the affected economies that a severe heart attack does on a human being.[78]

The American government responded swiftly and forcefully to the financial crisis and managed to prevent a complete, calamitous collapse.[79] It bailed out and, in some cases, effectively took control of several large, troubled firms—the insurance giant American International Group, for example, and the two large quasi-governmental organizations dealing in mortgages, the Federal National Mortgage Association (known as "Fannie Mae") and the Federal Home Loan Mortgage Corporation ("Freddie Mac")—each worth billions of dollars before the crisis.[80] The Federal Reserve flooded the financial system with money, which helped to restore confidence in the solvency of the major financial institutions.[81]

The rescue operations in fact demonstrated the reach and the capability of the American hyperpower because the Fed also helped to steady Europe's financial systems by providing dollars to European countries.[82] Over the course of the twentieth century it had become standard practice during financial panics for a country's central bank to act as its "lender of last resort." The American Federal Reserve became the lender of last resort to the whole world.[83]

Still, the role of the United States in the financial crisis of 2008 scarcely qualified as a triumph, and it subverted rather than enhanced America's global standing. After all, problems in the American financial system had caused the crisis in the first place. While the exertions of American officials did avert the worst possible outcome, moreover, the crisis inflicted considerable damage on the Western economies that it engulfed. Further damage came from the deep recession that the crisis touched off: when credit dried up and incomes fell, consumption declined; in response, production contracted, leading to rising unemployment—all combining to create a mutually reinforcing downward economic spiral.[84]

Following the prescription for the appropriate policy in such circumstances, which came originally from the English economist John Maynard Keynes during the Great Depression, the American government acted to increase consumption, production, and economic growth by injecting money not only into the financial system but also into the broader economy. The $700 billion Troubled Asset Relief Program met with initial disapproval in Congress, which had to authorize it, but ultimately was enacted into law.[85] Like the Fed's actions in dealing with the financial panic, the infusion of money made the recession that followed less deep and costly than it might otherwise have been, but did not prevent major losses for the American economy and therefore for the American people.[86]

Like the financial crisis, the deep recession affected countries beyond North America. Just as the interconnections of financial institutions on both sides of the Atlantic spread the financial crisis to Europe, so the dependence of Asian countries on exports to the West meant that the subsequent recession in the United States and Europe reduced their own incomes.[87]

Of all the countries in the world, the People's Republic of China did best at limiting the economic decline that it suffered. The Chinese government marshalled a huge stimulus package that kept economic activity from falling as far, proportionately, as it did elsewhere. The made-in-America crisis, and China's relatively successful response to it, had geopolitical consequences. It planted the idea, especially in the minds of Chinese policymakers, that the American position atop the international hierarchy was shaky and that China might well have the opportunity to make political and economic gains in Asia, and perhaps elsewhere, at the expense of the United States.[88]

In the wake of the chain of events that the failure of Lehman Brothers set in motion, and partly as a consequence of them, Europe experienced a financial crisis of its own,[89] beginning in Greece. When that country joined the European Union's common currency, the euro, it found it easier to sell its national bonds to finance its large budget deficits. Greek bonds became a kind of bubble, and when investor psychology shifted and the country could no longer market them at low interest rates, the result was a financial and economic crisis.[90] It affected other southern European countries—Portugal, Spain, and Italy as well as Ireland in the north—whose debt investors became leery of holding.

The other countries of the EU decided that Greece could not be allowed to fail financially—that is, to default on its obligations[91]—and ultimately provided the funding necessary to prevent this. The rescue packages they provided, however, took time to assemble because the EU, being an association of sovereign countries without a single over-arching authority, unlike the American government did not have the capacity to act quickly and decisively.[92] The terms the Greeks had to accept did not include debt forgiveness and, in large part at the behest of the EU's richest country, Germany, required a prolonged period of severe economic austerity. These policies made the EU unpopular in Greece and indeed in most of southern Europe as well.[93]

The great financial crisis of 2008 and the deep global recession that followed together constitute an episode not only in twenty-first-century economic history but also in the history of post–Cold War American foreign policy. They emanated from the United States and through them America had a strong if unintended and unwelcome impact on other countries. The crisis and the recession tarnished the American image, from which it had emerged from the Cold War and that served as a source of authority in the international system, as an emulation-worthy economic model and a competent global leader. After 2008 the hyperpower appeared to other countries, in economic terms, to be less admirable, less benign, and less effective than before.[94]

The process of global economic integration—globalization—that had played such an important part in international affairs in the wake of the Cold War and on which the United States counted to pro-mote peace and democracy around the world also emerged from the 2008 financial crisis in a weakened condition. It had contributed to the crisis: global demand for safe American assets had encouraged the rapid expansion in the volume of what turned out to be toxic real estate instruments, and the flow of capital from abroad into the United States had helped keep interest rates low, which in turn helped to inflate the real estate bubble.[95] Moreover, the difficulties of the euro and of the EU more generally, each of them both a product and an institutional embodiment of cross-border economic cooperation, put international economic integration in an unflattering light. The crisis and the recession also belied the belief, central to the American conception of globalization, in the supremacy of unfettered markets. The economic disaster of 2008 led to government intervention in Western economies on a massive scale.[96]

Most importantly, the course of the crisis, with financial distress spreading internationally and shocks shaking exporting countries—both of them taking place through the channels of economic interdependence—made globalization, heretofore almost universally popular, suddenly seem dangerous. The widely held assumption that more globalization would improve all lives lost credibility. Unchecked finance in particular came to seem perilous, and individual countries took steps to restrain it.

The post–Cold War international order, and American foreign policy within it, rested in no small part on American power and American prestige, which the wars in Afghanistan and Iraq, and especially the financial crisis, eroded. They rested, as well, on the hopes for the continued expansion of globalization that seemed, in the wake of September 15, 2008, unrealistic. Each of these power- and prestige-sapping developments took place during, and to varying degrees because of, the presidency of George W. Bush. Six weeks after the Lehman collapse a national election produced a new president, from the Democratic Party, who came to office the following January determined to restore American foreign policy to what it had been before September 11, 2001.

The Reset

Like the foreign policies of all post–Cold War presidents, that of Barack Obama, the forty-fourth American chief executive, included a Wilsonian strain. Obama's presidency in fact tracked Wilson's personal experience. Europeans hailed him as a transformational figure as they had Wilson when he arrived in Paris in 1918 in the immediate aftermath of World War I. Obama received the Nobel Prize for Peace from the Norwegian Nobel Committee in his first year in office, in advance of any actual diplomatic achievements. In addition, like Wilson he did not suffer from modesty. He gave a speech in Cairo on June 4, 2009, in which he suggested that, as the son of a Kenyan Muslim father, he was particularly well qualified to repair relations between the United States and the Muslim world, which, he believed, the American wars in two predominantly Muslim countries—Afghanistan and Iraq—had damaged.

Like Wilson, moreover, Obama prophesied a revolutionary alteration of the international system—in the case of the twenty-first-century president not the creation of a world government, which is what Wilson's vision of the League of Nations implied,[97] but something just as ambitious and just as unlikely: the abolition of all nuclear weapons. Obama advanced this idea in a speech in Prague—again with a European audience—on April 5, 2009.

The Obama administration devoted its economic policies largely to trying to mitigate the impact of the deep post-2008 recession. Despite the political backlash against the trade policies of the Clinton administration, however, Obama did engage in multilateral negotiations for two major trade agreements: the Transatlantic Trade and Investment Partnership (TTIP) with Europe and the Trans-Pacific Partnership (TPP) with the major countries of Asia with the conspicuous and deliberate exception of the People's Republic of China. The TTIP remained uncompleted when Obama left office after two presidential terms. He did not submit the TPP for Congressional ratification and his successor in the White House repudiated it.[98] The golden days of globalization did not return.

Of the two wars Obama inherited, extracting the United States from Iraq proved to be easier than leaving Afghanistan. The Bush administration had established a timetable for the withdrawal of American troops from the first country and its successor had merely to keep to it, which it did.

Obama had consistently opposed the Iraq War before becoming president. As a local politician in Illinois beginning a campaign for the United States Senate he had spoken out against going to war in Iraq in October 2002, even before it began.[99] He expressed a different assessment of the conflict in Afghanistan, calling it justified and even necessary. That view may have expressed his genuine belief but it also served his political interests of the moment. Had he opposed both wars, including the one in the country where an attack on the United States had originated, he risked appearing to the American electorate as too reluctant to use force to serve effectively as the nation's commander in chief.[100]

After being elected, he appointed a task force to make recommendations on policy for Afghanistan. Its members were favorably impressed with the results of the Bush administration's Surge in Iraq and recommended a similar effort in Afghanistan. When the military gave the new president its estimates of the personnel needed and the costs required for such an enterprise, however, he balked. His administration labored for almost a year to develop its own approach to the conflict.

Finally, in a speech on December 1, 2009, he announced that he would send more American troops to Afghanistan but only for a limited time, after which he would begin withdrawing them. The contradiction at the heart of the new policy reflected the competing impulses at work in formulating it: on the one hand, the need to fulfill Obama's campaign promises, and on the other, an aversion to prolonging the war there and increasing the costs to American taxpayers, not to mention the desire to avoid the virtual certainty that the longer-lasting and larger the American military presence in Afghanistan was, the greater would be the number of American soldiers who would die there.[101]

Despite the obvious contradiction in Obama's announcement, he had in fact chosen the ultimate direction of his policy toward Afghanistan, which was to reduce the American presence there. He opted, in the end, not for the kind of counterinsurgency campaign that Bush had belatedly launched in Iraq, which had as its goal the establishment of political stability, but rather a counterterrorism strategy, with the more modest aim of limiting the number of terrorists in Afghanistan like those who had attacked the United States on September 11, 2001. The Obama administration did not, however, end the American military presence in Afghanistan entirely, and neither did its successor. Finally, in 2021, Joseph Biden, Obama's vice president who was elected president in 2020, withdrew all American forces from the country, ceding control to the Taliban.[102]

The foreign policy that followed from the disappointments of the Iraq War and was therefore a major theme of the Obama foreign policy was retrenchment in the Middle East. This meant cutting back, if not necessarily terminating altogether, the American engagement in the region. Yet by the end of his time in office it remained a preoccupation of American foreign policy. Obama had authorized a military intervention in yet another country and he had returned the American military to Iraq. These reversals came about as a consequence of a series of events in the region known as the Arab Spring.

On December 17, 2010, Mohamed Bouazizi, a fruit peddler in the Tunisian city of Sidi Bouzid, set himself on fire in protest against his mistreatment by local officials. Anti-government protests in Tunisia followed and spread throughout the Arab world.[103] For a brief, hopeful moment the Arab Spring seemed poised to duplicate, in the Middle East, what had happened in Central and Eastern Europe in 1989[104]— the replacement of dictatorships with democracy.[105] Things did not work out that way. The anti-authoritarian rebellions did not lead to free elections and the establishment of rights-protecting governments anywhere, with the partial exception of Tunisia.[106] Despite its strong inclination to pull back from that part of the world, the Obama administration found itself drawn in (or drawn back in) by the events of the Arab Spring to four Middle Eastern countries.

In January 2011, protests erupted in Cairo against Egypt's long-serving dictator Hosni Mubarak, who had come from, and depended on the support of, the country's armed forces. Because the United States had provided generous economic assistance to Mubarak and his predecessor, Anwar Sadat, since the 1970s, Washington could not ignore events in that country. The protests presented the American government with the "Friendly Tyrant" dilemma familiar from the Cold War era.[107] Egypt aligned with the United States in foreign policy but its domestic politics did not embody American political values. Obama came down on what he believed to be the side of American values: he told Mubarak to leave office.[108]

Mubarak did leave office, but a subsequent election brought to power the Muslim Brotherhood, an organization dedicated to the principles of fundamentalist Islam, not democracy. Its government so alienated Egyptians that in the summer of 2013 mass anti-government demonstrations toppled the Brotherhood and brought to power an army general, Abdul Fattah al-Sisi. With the military back in charge, Egypt had come full circle. The United States had not prevented this, but nor had the American government effectively forced Mubarak from office either: the Egyptian military had dislodged him by denying him its support and then ultimately retaken command of the country. Egypt's political trajectory demonstrated that even the American hyperpower could not control domestic events in a distant and culturally alien country, even one where the economic relationship might have been thought to confer great influence.[109]

In February 2011, a popular uprising also threatened the long-ruling dictator of Libya, Muammar Qaddafi, who, unlike Sadat, did not have a long history of friendship with the United States. Qaddafi struck back against his opponents and seemed on the verge of crushing them. The Obama administration included officials strongly committed to the practice of humanitarian intervention, and they lobbied the president to undertake such an effort in Libya. Other officials disagreed, but when Britain and France decided on military action against Qaddafi, Obama agreed to provide air support for the rebels. He made it clear, however, that the United States would not dispatch ground troops to the country or take responsibility for keeping order there.[110]

With the assist of Western air forces, Qaddafi's enemies deposed and killed him. Disorder followed, with rival claimants to power fighting with one another for the next decade. In the Libyan chapter of the Arab Spring, American intervention did not, in the end, save lives or bring political stability, let alone democracy, to the country.[111]

The worst bloodshed took place in Syria. There the Sunni-majority population rose up against the Alawi ruler Bashar al-Assad, the son of Hafez al-Assad who had died in 2000, and the younger Assad responded with extreme brutality. He almost certainly would have fallen from power but for the military assistance, including combat forces, that he received from the Islamic Republic of Iran, which had a major geopolitical stake in the preservation of his regime.[112] Russia also saw a geopolitical advantage in keeping Assad in power and weighed in with punishing air attacks on rebel strongholds, the most numerous victims of which were civilians.[113] By 2014, after three years of conflict, 200,000 Syrians had died and, out of a prewar population of eighteen million, two million had fled the country and many more had been displaced within it.[114]

In the fall of 2012, Obama's senior foreign policy officials presented him with a plan for arming and training the Syrian resistance. He did not accept it.[115] He did, however, declare that any use by the Syrian regime of any part of its large store of chemical weapons would cross an American "red line" and "change my calculus" about the country.[116] The regime did launch chemical attacks on several cities. Obama initially decided to respond by bombing Syrian military targets. Then he changed his mind. The Russian president, Vladimir Putin, who had succeeded Boris Yeltsin on New Year's Day 2000 but had not pursued Yeltsin's pro-Western foreign policies, said that he was prepared to broker a deal to eliminate Assad's chemical weapons stockpile. Obama agreed.[117] In Iraq, the use of force had weakened the international standing of the United States. In Syria, the failure to use it had a similar effect: the chemical-weapons episode made the United States appear, to the rest of the world, to be a hyperpower with feet of clay.

In Iraq, Sunni Islamist groups in Syria descended from al Qaeda crossed the border between the two countries into Sunni-dominated areas, vanquished the armed forces of the Shia government in Baghdad that opposed them, and proclaimed the establishment of their own Sunni fundamentalist state.[118] Its leaders declared that they were restoring the caliphate of the early Islamic period, but their creation became known in the West as the Islamic State in Iraq and Syria (ISIS).[119] The new regime inflicted harsh repression on those it governed, especially women. It also persecuted religious minorities and publicly executed several Westerners in grisly fashion.[120]

Fearing, among other things, that ISIS would provide a base for anti-American terrorism, the Obama administration decided to supply air power and military advisors to the Iraqi government to help it recapture the territory its troops had lost; and eventually, in 2017, the Iraqi authorities did regain it.[121] In 2014, therefore, only three years after what had seemed to be the final departure of their armed forces from the country, American military personnel returned to Iraq.

In historical perspective, what was notable for international relations about the Obama period was not what his administration's foreign policy did or failed to do but rather what happened around it. During the course of the administration's only partly successful effort to eliminate what it (and much of the American public) considered the mistakes of its predecessor, the global context in which American foreign policy operated changed. It changed emphatically, dramatically, and in ways unfavorable to the United States. These changes brought the fourth age of American foreign policy—the post–Cold War era with America as the universally acknowledged and unchallenged hyperpower—to a close.

The End of the Post–Cold War Era

By 2015 the United States no longer enjoyed the international status with which it had emerged from the Cold War.[122] Its standing as the hyperpower had derived not simply from its military and economic might—both considerably greater than those of any other country— but also from the fact that no other country sought to challenge its position in the global order. Twenty-five years after the beginning of the post–Cold War era, American primacy did face serious challenges: from an ascending China that aspired to displace the United States as the leading power in East Asia and perhaps beyond; from a postcommunist Russia that, while smaller, poorer, and less well equipped militarily than the Soviet Union, was seeking to overturn the military dominance of the United States in Europe and the institutions and rules America had led the way in establishing there; and from two countries—North Korea and Iran—with dictatorial regimes committed to anti-Western ideologies that aspired to enhance their own power and disrupt the politics of their home regions through, among other initiatives, the acquisition of nuclear weapons.

China's remarkable economic growth underlay its challenge to the post–Cold War international order and its leader, the United States. The Chinese gross domestic product (GDP) had grown from $70 billion in 1980 to $9 trillion in 2014. Its per capita annual income had increased from $210 in 1978 to $6,900 in 2016. By a World Bank estimate, 500 million Chinese—approximately the population of the European Union—had risen out of poverty. In 1978, China had had a vanishingly small international economic presence. By 2016 it was responsible for 16.4 percent of global GDP, 20 percent of global manufacturing, 35 percent of global growth, and 11 percent of global trade.[123]

American policy toward China rested on faith in the liberal theory of history—the belief that economic growth would lead to a more liberal, open, tolerant, and ultimately democratic Chinese political system, which in turn would promote a peaceful Chinese foreign policy. The evolution of China's politics and economics furnished some evidence for this belief. Its government became far less repressive, not to mention far less murderous, than had been the case when Mao Zedong wielded power. The scope of individual freedom expanded: the Chinese could travel, own property, and even—within limits—engage in political discussions. Private business and international trade played increasingly large roles in the country's economic life and made major contributions to its rapid growth.[124]

Even when China seemed to be moving in what Americans considered a desirable political direction, its economic growth brought with it costs as well as benefits to the United States. Low wages in China enabled the country's firms to charge less than American producers for products such as toys, furniture, and clothing, leading to the loss of American jobs in these and other industries. China also made a practice of stealing American technology. Its theft of intellectual property took a toll on the American companies that did not receive the compensation to which they were entitled under American and international law when China appropriated their designs.[125]

Then, roughly coinciding with the advent to supreme power in Beijing of Xi Jinping in 2012, the Chinese regime became both more oppressive within its own borders and more aggressive beyond them.[126] Xi narrowed the permitted boundaries of expression and changed the rules of the Chinese Communist Party to allow himself to remain in office indefinitely. He continued the growth of the Chinese military, in particular its maritime capability. The details of the country's naval acquisitions suggested the intention to intimidate, perhaps invade, and certainly subdue Taiwan and to achieve dominance in the South China Sea and the western Pacific Ocean at the expense of the United States.[127]

China also markedly expanded its maritime territorial claims to its south and east, which conflicted with what other countries, with the support of international law, considered to be their own territorial waters. In addition, China constructed artificial islands in the South China Sea, on which it built military installations.[128]

The secrecy in which the Chinese government conducted its affairs made it impossible to know with certainty the reasons for its much more assertive foreign policy, but the new course seemed to stem from the country's deeply rooted nationalism, integral to which was the conviction that its own hegemony in East Asia corresponded to the natural, historically ordained order of things.[129] The assertiveness beyond China's borders also owed something to the increasing reliance of the Xi government on exploiting the same nationalist sentiment in order to reinforce its own domestic political legitimacy and popularity at a time when economic growth, on which it had depended for both for three decades, was slowing.[130] America's post–September 11 setbacks did not create these incentives for a more aggressive Chinese foreign policy, but they surely made the latter part of the second decade of the twenty-first century seem to the Chinese leadership an opportune time to act on them.

As a result, China posed an increasing challenge to the security of the countries of East Asia. It posed an economic challenge to the United States as well. It used its large trade surpluses to purchase American financial assets, giving it, in theory, powerful leverage over American policy. That leverage, however, came from the threat to sell the assets on a large scale, thereby causing economic difficulties for the United States. Since doing so would lower the value of those assets and thus penalize China, however, this aspect of the financial relationship between the two countries was comparable to the Cold War nuclear "balance of terror" between the two superpowers.[131]

The new direction of Chinese foreign policy changed America's overall relationship with the People's Republic. The United States ceased to be a friendly guide, mentor, and partner and instead had thrust upon it the role of counterweight to a rapidly rising power. The other countries of Asia, all of them wary of China and some with bilateral security ties to the United States, looked to Washington to take the lead in checking Chinese regional and global ambitions[132] while at the same time wishing to maintain their profitable economic relations with the People's Republic.

In Russia, Vladimir Putin governed in an increasingly authoritarian manner, effectively suppressing all opposition, bringing more and more of the Russian economy under the control of the government, and making the nation's wealth available to his cronies and supporters. Corruption became the defining feature of the Russian political system, which turned away from democracy and became, instead, a kleptocracy.[133]

Under Putin, Russia's estrangement from the United States, which began with Bill Clinton's decision to expand NATO, widened over the course of the next decade. Even while Yeltsin had held power he had objected to the American-led war in Kosovo, which had received no international approval beyond that of NATO, the organization that waged it. The Russian government also objected to the decision of the George W. Bush administration to withdraw unilaterally from the 1972 Soviet-American Antiballistic Missile Treaty.[134]

In 2007, at a conference in Germany, Putin publicly denounced the United States:

> Today we are witnessing an almost uncontained hyper use of force— military force—in international relations, force that is plunging the world into an abyss of permanent conflicts. . . . One state, and of course, first and foremost the United States, has overstepped its na- tional borders in every way.[135]

The next year, the Bush administration declared that Georgia and Ukraine, both former Soviet republics that were now independent countries, would join NATO.[136] The Western European members had reservations about admitting the two countries to the Atlantic Alliance, and NATO deferred indefinitely the question of Georgian and Ukrainian membership. Shortly after the American declaration, Russian troops engaged in a brief battle with the Georgian army, with the Georgians getting the worst of the fighting.[137] As Putin steered Russian foreign policy away from the alignment with the United States of the immediate post–Cold War years, he moved his country ever closer to China, with the basis for this new orientation being a common animosity toward the hyperpower. Then came an episode that, more than any other, served as both a symbol and a cause of the end of the post–Cold War era: Russia's invasion of Ukraine.

Of all the constituent republics of the Soviet Union that had become independent after 1991, Ukraine had by far the greatest significance for Russia. It was the largest and most economically important of them and had been part of a Russian-dominated state for the longest time—since the eighteenth century.[138] In the 2004 Ukrainian presidential election the prime minister, Viktor Yanukovich, was fraudulently declared the winner. Demonstrations in the capital, Kiev, and elsewhere, known collectively as the "Orange Revolution," ultimately brought to power his opponent, Viktor Yushchenko, who had actually received more votes and was better disposed to cooperation with the West.[139]

Yanukovich won a subsequent election for the presidency and in 2013 announced that, rather than sign an agreement for association with the European Union, he would establish closer economic ties with Russia. This triggered another outburst of protest, and Yanukovich fled the country. Putin denounced what came to be called the Maidan Revolution[140] as an American-led plot.[141] In fact, the United States and the countries of the EU had welcomed the change of government but had not instigated it. In response to the installation of a pro-Western regime in Kiev, Putin sent Russian forces to occupy the Crimean peninsula, a part of Ukraine with a large ethnic Russian population and the location of an important base for the Russian navy. (In 1954 the Soviet government had transferred Crimea to Ukrainian jurisdiction as a good will gesture that at the time had no political or economic significance because both Ukraine and Russia were part of the Soviet Union.) He then went on to sponsor an invasion of the eastern districts of Ukraine, also largely populated by ethnic Russians. In both cases the invaders did not wear Russian army uniforms but there was no doubt that Moscow had launched and was supporting the operations.[142]

Putin had multiple motives for attacking Ukraine. They certainly included the desire to prevent the emergence there of a prosperous democracy, which might inspire Russians to demand as much for themselves, which would have been incompatible with Putin's continuing autocratic rule. He also almost certainly sought to stir up anti-Western sentiment in his country as a way to enhance popular regard for his regime, which, like the Communist government of China, had relied for domestic support mainly on its economic performance. Russia's economic performance, unlike China's, depended on the sale of energy. With energy prices stuck at a level far below their peak, Putin needed some other way to generate support for his kleptocratic regime.[143]

The invasion of Ukraine was a watershed moment for Europe, the clearest case of cross-border aggression since Hitler's rampages of the late 1930s and early 1940s. Angela Merkel, the German chancellor, expressed a widespread sentiment: "Who would have thought it possible 25 years after the fall of the Berlin wall . . . something like this could happen in the middle of Europe?"[144] In response to the invasion, the Western countries imposed economic sanctions on Russia. In so doing they were recognizing that the European political dispensation that the end of the Cold War had produced had come under attack. Like China in East Asia, Russia was seeking to overturn the status quo on the continent and thereby undertaking a serious challenge to the country that served as its ultimate guarantor: the United States.

Two other countries that were less powerful than Russia and China nonetheless mounted challenges to the new post–Cold war order and its American protector. Both made opposition to the United States the dominant feature of their foreign policies. Both had governments committed to radical, anti-Western ideologies. Both had small economies that could not support the kind of major military forces that Russia and China fielded. Both countries, however—North Korea and Iran— had the potential to pose major threats to their neighbors, to American interests, and to the post–Cold War international system through their efforts to acquire their own nuclear weapons, which offer a shortcut to formidable disruptive military power. During the Cold War the two superpowers had cooperated to oppose nuclear proliferation. In the wake of the Cold War the responsibility for doing so fell principally on the American hyperpower.

North Korea did succeed in crossing the nuclear threshold. While the agreement the Clinton administration struck with its government in 1994 was designed to prevent this, in 2002 American intelligence discovered a clandestine North Korean nuclear facility and in 2007 the regime in Pyongyang detonated its first nuclear explosion.[145] Despite disapproving of its communist neighbor's nuclear program, the government in Beijing remained unwilling credibly to threaten to cut off the shipments of food and fuel that passed across their common border in order to compel the North Korean regime to put an end to it.[146] The United States, with overwhelming military superiority over Pyongyang, could have destroyed the North's nuclear facilities through a campaign of aerial bombardment. It never undertook such a campaign, however, because North Korea had the capacity, in retaliation, to do extensive damage to South Korea and in particular to its capital city, Seoul. With that capacity, North Korea effectively deterred the United States.[147]

The United States, however, had the capacity to deter aggression by North Korea as well. America had maintained a military presence in South Korea in the decades after the Korean War for precisely that purpose.[148] That longstanding policy gave the other countries of East Asia, notably South Korea and Japan, confidence that their own safety did not require obtaining nuclear weapons of their own to protect themselves from the communist government in Pyongyang.

Although it had not, by 2015, built its own nuclear weapons, Iran posed a greater threat to the Middle East than North Korea did to East Asia. The upheavals of the Arab Spring enabled Iran to expand its influence in its home region far more extensively than North Korea could do in East Asia. Those upheavals made the centuries-old conflict between the Sunni and the Shia branches of Islam the principal political cleavage in the region. As the largest predominantly Shia country, Iran was able to recruit, train, and deploy Shia militias to act as its military and political proxies in Lebanon, Iraq, Syria, and Yemen.[149]

Iran's regional ambitions received significant if entirely unintended assistance from its foremost adversary, the country it called "the Great Satan." American military power removed three Sunni regimes with murderous hostility toward the Shia in general and Iran in particular: first the Taliban in Afghanistan, then Saddam Hussein's regime in Iraq, and finally the Islamic State in Iraq and Syria.[150]

Like North Korea, Iran launched a secret nuclear weapons program that came to light despite the regime's efforts to conceal it.[151] Unlike in East Asia, the United States did not have a long history of deterring unfriendly regimes in the Middle East. For that reason, other countries in that region would be less inclined to feel confidence in American protection in the face of an Iranian bomb.[152] They were thus more plausible candidates than the East Asians to seek nuclear weapons of their own. Iran's acquisition of the bomb was all too likely to set off a "proliferation cascade," with several Middle Eastern countries building their own nuclear arsenals, thereby increasing the chances for a devastating nuclear war in that region.[153]

American authorities declared that the United States would not permit Iran to get the bomb, but the Obama administration entered into secret negotiations with the regime in Tehran that produced an agreement that fell far short of offering foolproof guarantees on this score. While the terms of the Joint Comprehensive Plan of Action (JCPOA) of 2015 did include some Iranian concessions,[154] it permitted what the United States had previously refused to countenance: an Iranian capacity to enrich uranium—enriched uranium being the fuel for a nuclear explosive and its fabrication the stage of the bomb-making process most difficult to master.[155] Moreover, the JCPOA stipulated that several of the restraints it imposed would expire in ten years, leaving the Islamic Republic free to pursue its nuclear ambitions.[156] Nor did the agreement place restrictions on the many other Iranian activities that threatened its neighbors.

The accord was an odd one for the United States to have concluded with Iran because America had far more military power than the Islamic Republic and the stiff economic sanctions it had imposed on Iran had inflicted serious hardships on the country and its government.[157] In such negotiations the stronger party usually gets the better of whatever deal emerges, but that was not the case with the JCPOA.[158]

America's generosity toward Iran sometimes seemed to stem from Barack Obama's belief that a conciliatory approach[159] could achieve a grand rapprochement with the Islamic Republic, along the lines of Richard Nixon's opening to the People's Republic of China in 1972.[160] At other times he seemed interested less in preventing Iran from getting nuclear weapons than in substantially reducing American engagement in the Middle East[161] so that his country (and his administration) would not have to confront the Islamic Republic when it did acquire them, perhaps having concluded that the American public's disillusionment with the wars in Afghanistan and Iraq had deprived the nation's leaders of the necessary public support for such a confrontation.

Whatever the motives behind it, the Obama policy of conciliating Iran marked a turning point in the history of American foreign policy. The increased assertiveness of China's foreign policy under Xi Jinping, the Russian invasion and occupation of Ukraine, and the North Korean and Iranian quests for nuclear weapons signified the end of the era in which the political and economic arrangements that the end of the Cold War had bequeathed to the world would go unchallenged. The Obama Iran policy denoted the unwillingness of the United States to exert itself to meet the least of these challenges, and so to protect the post–Cold War order. In military and economic terms America remained, in 2015, the most powerful country in the world; but in the Middle East, at least, it was no longer conducting the foreign policy of a hyperpower.

If the end of the Cold War had ushered in a new world order, the international system that had emerged twenty-five years later looked very much like the old one. Political rivalry and the use of force between and among the strongest states had once again become a prominent feature of international relations. As during the Cold War, the United States found itself central to coalitions opposing aggressive countries in Europe and Asia. Unlike during the Cold War, the revisionist powers did not profess a common, well-developed ideology like the Marxism-Leninism of the Soviet Union and Maoist China. Also unlike the Cold War, in the world of 2015 the major revisionists played an active, extensive part in the international economic system that the West had created after World War II: economic interdependence accompanied geopolitical rivalry.

In retrospect, the foreign policy of the American hyperpower in the post–Cold War era presents a paradox. In none of the three preceding periods in the history of its foreign policy did the United States have as much power: yet of all the four eras, the last of them was the one in which the United States had the least success in achieving its goals.[162] In the first era, the country secured and preserved its independence and expanded its territorial scope. In the second, it established a sphere of influence of the kind that other great powers had and combined with several of the others to thwart two German bids for mastery of Europe and a Japanese campaign to dominate Asia. In the third, the United States led the coalition that won the contest of systems with the Soviet Union and international communism. In the post–Cold War period, by contrast, America did not succeed in preserving its own unchallenged primacy, exercised on behalf of its own and its allies' political values and political and economic institutions. What went wrong?

The United States made some errors. NATO expansion needlessly alienated post-Soviet Russia, making opposition to American initiatives the default position of Russian foreign policy and giving Vladimir Putin one of the incentives that lay behind his invasion of Ukraine: by portraying it as a defensive measure in response to American aggression—and after NATO expansion the Russian public was prepared to believe that it was—he enhanced his own popularity at home. Had Russia continued the pro-Western orientation in foreign policy that Boris Yeltsin had adopted, a plausible course in the absence of the American decision to bring the Atlantic Alliance to Russia's new borders while excluding Russia itself, Moscow would likely have supported, or at least not actively opposed, American policies toward China and Iran. This would have powerfully strengthened the American position in dealing with those two countries. Then the Iraq War entangled the United States in a costly quagmire that did not, in the end, produce a decent, competent government there that was friendly to the West.

In both cases America's status as a hyperpower worked against it. The United States expanded NATO and intervened in Iraq because it could: no other country had the means to block either enterprise. In both cases unchallenged power bred overconfidence. American officials were certain that Russians would extract no serious price for NATO expansion and that once Saddam Hussein no longer held power Iraq would become peaceful and ultimately prosperous and democratic.

Overconfidence underlay another costly mistake that undercut America's global influence and its standing in the world and thus contributed to the end of its unchallenged primacy: the great financial crisis of 2008 and the deep recession that followed. American policymakers believed that, fortified by the proliferation of new, complicated real estate assets, the nation's financial system would continue to deliver steady economic growth. Instead, those new instruments caused the system to crash. More generally, faith in the stability and buoyancy of untrammeled financial markets proved to be dramatically misplaced.[163]

Still, just as the Cold War ended because of developments in other countries—specifically in communist Europe—that the United States did not initiate or control, so the post–Cold War era passed away because of trends far from North America that lay beyond even the power of American foreign policy to prevent or to alter.

The nationalism that propelled China's assertive foreign policy had deep historical roots in that country. The Xi Jinping regime could act more forcefully on nationalist sentiment than its predecessors because Xi presided over a more powerful country than they had, with its rising power stemming from its surging economic growth. In theory the United States could have tried to circumscribe that power by inhibiting China's economic expansion.

In practice this was never possible.[164] American businesses and American consumers both derived benefits from China's economic progress. Even if the American government had been willing and able to sacrifice those benefits and adopt measures to set China back economically, other countries would not have followed suit; and Americans themselves would not have felt comfortable opposing an economic trend in Asia that, while it laid the basis for disruptive geopolitical conduct by the communist government in Beijing, also lifted hundreds of millions of people out of poverty.

In China, and elsewhere, the United States counted not only on its own power but also on the dynamics of the liberal theory of history to preserve and strengthen the post–Cold War order. Globalization, Americans believed, would promote economic growth; economic growth would foster democratic governance; and democratic governments would conduct peaceful foreign policies. The history of the twentieth century provided some support for these assumptions, but the post–Cold War histories of Russia and China did not proceed accordingly.

Entrenched and determined ruling elites with their countries' instruments of repression at their disposal—Vladimir Putin and his cronies and allies in Russia, the Communist Party in China—successfully blocked any political changes that threatened to deprive them of their monopolies of power. The United States could only have removed these regimes through unthinkably costly wars. Moreover, the democratic politics and free-market economics at the heart of the liberal theory of history require a particular set of institutions as well as experience in operating them and widely shared values supporting them.[165]

Not every country in the world—and certainly not twenty-first-century Afghanistan, Iraq, China, or Russia—is well endowed with them.

For all these reasons, the United States found itself, in 2015, in a new era of foreign policy, the fifth in 250 years. The specific features of American foreign policy in the new age, as always, could not be known in advance, but one forecast could safely be made. As in the past, that foreign policy would emerge from the interaction of three powerful, timeless forces: the country's position in the international system—that is, its power; the enduring ideological, economic, and democratic features of its approach to the world; and the unpredictable contingencies of human history.

NOTES

———

Preface

1. Useful studies include, among others, George C. Herring's encyclopedic *From Colony to Superpower*, a volume in the magnificent Oxford History of the United States series; Walter LaFeber's graceful *The American Age*; the four volumes in the Cambridge History of American Foreign Policy: Bradford Perkins's *The Creation of a Republican Empire, 1776–1865* (a later edition of the series includes, as the first volume, William E. Weeks, *Dimensions of the Early American Empire, 1754–1865*), Walter LaFeber's *The American Search for Opportunity, 1865–1913*, Akira Iriye's *The Globalizing of America, 1913–1945*, and Series Editor Warren I. Cohen's *America in the Age of Soviet Power*; and Samuel Flagg Bemis's classic *A Diplomatic History of the United States*, originally published in 1936, whose fourth and final edition appeared in 1955 and remains very useful, especially through the nineteenth century. Also worthy of mention in this company are two books that, while not strictly speaking histories of American foreign policy, provide thought-provoking overviews of it: Walter A. McDougall's *Promised Land, Crusader State*, and Walter Russell Mead's *Special Providence*.

Acknowledgments

1. All published by Oxford University Press, they are: Robert Middlekauff, *The Glorious Cause: The American Revolution, 1763–1789*; Gordon S. Wood, *Empire of Liberty: A History of the Early Republic, 1789–1815*; Daniel Walker Howe, *What Hath God Wrought: The Transformation of America, 1815–1848*; James M. McPherson, *Battle Cry of Freedom: The Civil War Era*;

Richard White, *The Republic for Which It Stands: The United States During Reconstruction and the Gilded Age*; David M. Kennedy, *Freedom from Fear: The American People in Depression and War, 1929–1945*; James T. Patterson, *Grand Expectations: The United States, 1945–1974*; James T. Patterson, *Restless Giant: The United States from Watergate to Bush v. Gore*; and George C. Herring, *From Colony to Superpower: U.S. Foreign Relations Since 1776*.

Introduction

1. On the impact of relative power on countries' foreign policies see Michael Mandelbaum, *The Fate of Nations: The Search for National Security in the Nineteenth and Twentieth Centuries*, New York: Cambridge University Press, 1988, especially Chapters 3 and 4.
2. In the nineteenth century the British championed constitutional government and liberty in Europe, although not in their own empire. As the largest trading nation in that era as well as the possessor of the world's most formidable navy, Britain also had occasion to use commerce to further its political aims. And even the aristocratic managers of British foreign policy had to take account of public sentiment.
3. D. H. Fischer, *Albion's Seed: Four British Folkways in America*, New York: Oxford University Press, 1989. See especially the sections on "East Anglia to Massachusetts" (the Puritans) and "North Midlands to the Delaware" (the Quakers).
4. Samuel P. Huntington, *American Politics: The Promise of Disharmony*, Cambridge, Massachusetts: The Belknap Press of Harvard University, 1981, p. 15.
5. "By 1815 America had become the most evangelically Christian nation in the world." Gordon S. Wood, *Empire of Liberty: A History of the Early Republic, 1789–1815*, New York: Oxford University Press, 2009. On the relationship between Protestantism and foreign policy in the United States see James R. Kurth, "The Protestant Deformation," *Orbis*, Spring, 1998, and Adam Garfinkle, "The Anglo-Protestant Basis of U.S. Foreign Policy," *Oris*, Winter, 2018.

The First Age

1. Samuel Flagg Bemis, *A Diplomatic History of the United States,* New York: Henry Holt and Company, *Fourth Edition,* 1955, p. 86.
2. Predators must hunt and kill to survive. This is not the case for the large human collectives known as states, although occasionally, as with Nazi Germany and Imperial Japan in the 1930s and 1940s, their leaders have come to believe that the alternative to conquest is national extinction.

Chapter 1

1. "Altogether the value of colonial exports to Britain in 1775 exceeded by sevenfold the value of those at the beginning of the century." Robert Middlekauff, *The Glorious Cause: The American Revolution, 1763–1789*, New York: Oxford University Press, 2005, p. 36.

2. A. G. Hopkins, *American Empire: A Global History*, Princeton and Oxford: Princeton University Press, 2018, p. 111.

3. Edmund S. Morgan, *The Birth of the Republic*, Chicago and London: The University of Chicago Press, Third Edition, 1992, p. 6.

4. It is sometimes known to Americans as the French and Indian War because those were the colonials' adversaries in the conflict.

5. Sometimes also called the Napoleonic Wars.

6. Fred Anderson, *Crucible of War: The Seven Years' War and the Fate of Empire in British North America, 1754–1766*, New York: Vintage Books, 2001, pp. 5–7.

7. France briefly regained territory in North America in 1800, when Spain ceded land it claimed there to Napoleon's government through the Treaty of San Ildefonso. Three years later the French sold it to the United States in the Louisiana Purchase.

8. The British domination of North America is the reason that Americans and Canadians speak English and that, therefore, English became the global language. The British defeat of France in South Asia in the Seven Years' War is the reason that, even before it became the global language, English became the common language among the diverse peoples of the Asian subcontinent.

9. Brendan Simms, *Three Victories and a Defeat: The Rise and Fall of the First British Empire*, New York: Basic Books, 2007, pp. 504, 533–534.

10. Christopher Columbus, usually credited with being the first European to sail to North America, was trying to reach India, assumed that he had arrived, and designated the people he encountered "Indians."

11. Middlekauff, *op. cit.*, p. 56.

12. Hopkins, *op. cit.*, p. 101.

13. Gordon S.. Wood, *The American Revolution: A History*, New York: The Modern Library, 2002, p. 17.

14. Simms, *op. cit.*, pp. 535–536.

15. The year before Parliament had passed the Sugar Act, which modified the already-existing Molasses Act of 1733, a tariff on foreign molasses, with the aim of reducing smuggling.

16. Douglas A. Irwin, *Clashing Over Commerce: A History of US Trade Policy*, Chicago and London: The University of Chicago Press, 2017, p. 40.

17. "Even if the economic impact of non-importation was modest compared to the recession (in Britain), the political impact was large enough that the protesters achieved their objective: pressure from British manufacturers was an important factor in Parliament's decision to repeal the Stamp Act." *Ibid.*

18. Simms, *op. cit.*, p. 581.

19. The British assumed "that the Americans would shrink from the prospect of force, that the Coercive Acts would isolate Massachusetts from the other colonies, and that, thus isolated, the resistance to imperial authority in the Bay Colony would soon collapse. . . ." Robert W. Tucker and David C. Hendrickson, *The Fall of the First British Empire: Origins of the War*

of American Independence, Baltimore and London: The Johns Hopkins University Press, 1982, p. 329. On the American side "the prevailing expectation was that if the colonies stood united and firm in opposing the Coercive Acts, the government would retreat, draw back from enforcement, and ultimately withdraw the legislation." *Ibid.*, p. 330.

20. See pp. 251-265.

21. This is a major theme of Bernard Bailyn, *The Ideological Origins of the American Revolution*, Cambridge, Massachusetts: The Belknap Press of Harvard University, 1967.

22. Middlekauff, *op. cit.*, p. 51. The events of 1688 triggered conflict that spread even to North America. Steve Pincus, *1688: The First Modern Revolution*, New Haven and London: Yale University Press, 2009, p. 264.

23. Bailyn, *op. cit.*, p. 140.

24. Middlekauff, *op. cit.*, p. 52.

25. Hopkins, *op. cit.*, p. 119; D. W. Meinig, *The Shaping of America: A Geographical Perspective on 500 Years of History, Volume I: Atlantic America: 1492–1800*, New Haven and London: Yale University Press, 1986, p. 296; Simms, *op. cit.*, pp. 540–541.

26. "In a pioneering calculation, Lawrence Harper (1939) tallied up the costs and benefits to the colonies from these trade restrictions for the year 1773. He estimated the total cost to be $3.3 million, only about 2 percent of colonial income." By another calculation, taking into account the benefits of being part of the British Empire, "the net cost to the colonies came to just $0.9 million, a slight 0.6 percent of colonial income." Irwin, *op. cit.*, p. 36.

27. Meinig, *op. cit.*, pp. 287–288; Middlekauff, *op. cit.*, p. 60.

28. Walter LaFeber, *The American Age: U.S. Foreign Policy at Home and Abroad, 1750 to the Present*, New York: W.W. Norton, 1994, Second Edition, p. 15.

29. Britain's trade with the colonies was considerably less valuable than its commerce with the European continent. Simms, *op. cit.*, p. 75.

30. *Ibid.*, pp. 357–358.

31. See pp. 166-167, 172-173.

32. The Americans initially maintained that London had the authority to tax external but not internal economic transactions in North America. As they defined those terms in practice, however, that seems to have been a distinction without a difference. Bailyn, *op. cit.*, pp. 214–215; Tucker and Hendrickson, *op. cit.*, pp. 143, 342–343; Middlekauff, *op. cit.*, p. 128.

33. They were Breed's Hill and Bunker Hill. While most of the fighting took place around the first of them, the episode is known to history as the Battle of Bunker Hill.

34. The British casualties numbered 1,054—226 killed and 828 wounded— the highest number for any single encounter during the entire war. The American toll included 115 killed, 305 wounded, and 30 captured.

35. John Ferling, *Almost a Miracle: The American Victory in the War of Independence*, New York: Oxford University Press, 2007, p. 574.

36. On the Canadian campaign see Eliot A. Cohen, *Captured into Liberty: Two Centuries of Battles Along the Great Warpath That Made the American Way of War*, New York: Basic Books, 2011, pp. 147–160, 174.

37. Wood, *op. cit.*, p. 75.

38. See, for example, John Rodehamel, *George Washington: The Wonder of the Age*, New Haven and London: Yale University Press, 2017, p. 183.

39. Ferling, *op. cit.*, p. 570

40. Wood, *op. cit.*, p. 75.

41. Washington appointed a Prussian, Frederick von Steuben, to train the American troops. Middlekauff, *op. cit.*, pp. 423–425.

42. *Ibid.*, p. 341.

43. The British counted "on helping the good Americans to overcome the bad: the British army would break the power of the rebels, and organise and support the loyalists who would police the country." Piers Macksey, *The War for America: 1775–1783*, Lincoln and London: University of Nebraska Press, 1993. First published, 1964, p. 511. See also Andrew Jackson O'Shaughnessey, *The Men Who Lost America: British Leadership, the American Revolution, and the Fate of the Empire*, New Haven and London, Yale University Press, 2013, p. 354.

44. In the Revolutionary War Britain employed over 32,000 troops from various parts of Germany. John Brewer, *The Sinews of Power: War, Money, and the English State, 1688–1783*, Cambridge, Massachusetts: Harvard University Press, 1988, p. 41.

45. Middlekauff, *op. cit.*, p. 36.

46. Because they were predominantly rural, most Americans were economically self-sufficient, which meant that the colonies "were largely impervious to the workings of sea power." Paul M. Kennedy, *The Rise and Fall of British Naval Mastery*, New York: Charles Scribner's Sons, 1976, p. 114.

47. Quoted in Macksey, *op. cit.*, p. 510.

48. Wood, *op. cit.*, p. 114; Tim Blanning, *The Pursuit of Glory: Europe 1648–1815*, London: Penguin Books, 2007, p. 304.

49. The authoritative account of the making of the Declaration is entitled *American Scripture*. Pauline Maier, *American Scripture: Making the Declaration of Independence*, New York: Alfred A. Knopf, 1997.

50. Bradford Perkins, *The Cambridge History of American Foreign Relations, Volume I: The Creation of a Republican Empire, 1776–1865*, New York: Cambridge University Press, 1993, pp. 19–20; Simms, *op. cit.*, pp. 601–602.

51. Walter A. McDougall, *Promised Land, Crusader State: The American Encounter with the World Since 1776*, Boston: Houghton Mifflin, 1997, p. 5.

52. Middlekauff, *op. cit.*, p. 374.

53. ". . . Burgoyne and his huge, slow-moving entourage from Canada increasingly found their supply lines stretched thin and their flanks harassed by patriot militia from New England. Burgoyne's baggage train was over three miles long, his personal baggage alone took up over thirty carts. By felling trees, destroying bridges, and diverting streams, the patriots did all they could to make the wild terrain even more impassable than it was. Burgoyne had to build over forty new bridges as well as repair old ones. At one point he was covering less than one mile a day. This sluggish pace only worsened the problem of supply. One of his lieutenants declared that for every hour Burgoyne spent thinking about how to fight his army he had to devote twenty hours to figure out how to feed it." Wood, *op. cit.*, p. 81.

54. See pp. 105, 219-220.

55. The poem is "Concord Hymn." It has never been established who, or even which side, fired the first shot.

56. See pp. 44-46.

57. "Ninety percent of the gunpowder used by the colonists during the first years of the war came from Europe, and foreign aid was thus indispensable from the outset." George C. Herring, *From Colony to Superpower: U.S. Foreign Relations Since 1776*, New York: Oxford University Press, 2008, p. 18.

58. Middlekauff, *op. cit.*, p. 404.

59. The phrase is Edmund S. Morgan's, in Morgan, *Benjamin Franklin*, New Haven and London: Yale University Press, 2002, p. 280.

60. From France, during the course of the war, the Americans received "more than $8 million in subsidies and loans. France's ally, Spain, disgorged another $650,000, and, toward the end of the war, Holland extended a loan, guaranteed by France, of $1.8 million." Perkins, *op. cit.*, p. 29. The loans were all the more important because the commercial sanctions against the colonies that Great Britain imposed caused, by percentage, the worst economic downtown in American history, a reduction of an estimated twenty percent of per capita income. Irwin, *op. cit.*, p. 48.

61. Samuel Flagg Bemis, *A Diplomatic History of the United States*, New York: Henry Holt and Company, Fourth Edition, 1955, p. 23.

62. Morgan, *The Birth of the Republic*, p. 83.

63. "The two nations readily agreed not to conclude a separate peace without each other's consent. Each guaranteed the possessions of the other in North America for the present and forever. . . . For the Americans, the indispensable feature of the agreement was a French promise to fight until their independence had been achieved. The United States gave France a free hand in taking British possessions in the West Indies." Herring, *op. cit.*, p. 21.

64. Jonathan Dull, *A Diplomatic History of the American Revolution*, New Haven and London: Yale University Press, 1985, pp. 124–126.

65. "Britain's problems were greatly magnified by France's entry into the war in 1778. The British army had to be scattered even more widely, as it guarded against an invasion of the homeland and was pressed into defending widespread imperial possessions in the Caribbean, India, Africa, and the Mediterranean. The Royal Navy's absolute superiority was instantly jeopardized." Ferling, *op. cit.*, p. 564.

66. Blanning, *op. cit.*, p. 303.

67. Kennedy, *op. cit.*, p. III.

68. Wood, *op. cit.*, p. 83.

69. ". . . [I]n a great many ways the partisan war in the Carolinas and Georgia in 1780–1781 was where the war was won. It saved South Carolina and Georgia from British conquest and may have prevented the loss of the entire South." Ferling, *op. cit.*, p. 574.

70. "[Cornwallis's] problem in the Carolinas had been Howe's and Clinton's in the North: in order to restore the allegiance of America he had to crush the rebellion. And the process of crushing the rebellion simply fed its sources." Middlekauff, *op. cit.*, p. 456.

71. "By the middle of September the two armies had transported themselves some 450 miles along with baggage and supplies. The plan showed Washington's organizational talents at their best. He and a few officers seem to have planned it, selecting the routes and collecting the horses and wagons so vital in the transportation of stores." Middlekauff, *op. cit.*, p. 583.

72. Robert and Isabelle Tombs, *That Sweet Enemy: The French and the British from the Sun King to the Present*, London: William Heinemann, 2006, p. 176.

73. He had initially been secretary of state for home and colonial affairs. When the prime minister, the Marquis of Rockingham, died in office, Shelburne succeeded him.

74. "It is important to realize that Franklin won this victory not because America's bargaining position was so strong, but rather because Shelburne was so anxious for peace. . . . By showering the Americans with concessions he hoped to cause France, Spain, and the Netherlands to face the necessity of concluding peace on reasonable terms lest the Americans make a separate peace, thereby freeing tens of thousands of British troops for military operations against the West Indies." Dull, *op. cit.*, p. 145.

75. Middlekauff, *op. cit.*, p. 594.

76. The Indians who lived in the western territories were neither mentioned in nor consulted about the treaty. *Ibid.*, p. 574.

77. The compensation took the form of East Florida and the Mediterranean island of Minorca. Dull, *op. cit.*, p. 157.

78. See Bemis, *op. cit.*, pp. 62–63, for the details. After the defeat at Yorktown the British recouped their position in the Caribbean with a naval victory in the Battle of the Saints, April 9–12, 1782.

79. H. M. Scott, *British Foreign Policy in the Age of the American Revolution*, Oxford, UK: The Clarendon Press of Oxford University Press, 1990, p. 339.
80. See Chapters 2 and 3.
81. Simms, *op. cit.*, pp. 593–594.
82. Middlekauff, *op. cit.*, p. 599.
83. Wood, *op. cit.*, p. 87.
84. Middlekauff, *op. cit.*, p. 602.
85. The British did successfully cope with one aspect of the difficulty of access to North America: the logistical challenge of transporting "every biscuit, man, and bullet required by the British forces in America . . . across 3000 miles of ocean." Kennedy, *op. cit.*, p. 114. See also Brewer, *op. cit.*, pp. 177–178. Meeting that challenge substantially raised the cost to the British treasury of conducting the war.
86. Perkins, *op. cit.*, p. 57.
87. ". . . Ambassador Jefferson failed to persuade France to reciprocate on matters of trade, while Spain alternately closed the port of New Orleans or charged oppressive fees for its use . . ." McDougall, *op. cit.*, p. 26.
88. ". . . [The American economy was mired in a terrible state throughout the 1780s." Irwin, *op. cit.*, pp. 50–51.
89. Herring, *op. cit.*, p. 44.
90. *Ibid.*, p. 46; Perkins, *op. cit.*, p. 56.
91. Bailyn, *op. cit.*, p. 142.
92. Irwin, *op. cit.*, p. 58; Dull, *op. cit.*, p. 162.
93. Herring, *op. cit.*, pp. 45–46; Bemis, *op. cit.*, p. 73; Morgan, *The Birth of the Republic*, p. 135.
94. Perkins, *op. cit.*, p. 56. In 1783, Barbary pirates seized American ships in the Mediterranean and held their crews for ransom. The American government couldn't raise enough money to free them. Herring, *op. cit.*, pp. 39–40.
95. "Shays's Rebellion also had foreign policy implications since the rebels had reportedly discussed with the British possible separation from the Union." Herring, *op. cit.*, p. 50.
96. James Madison observed in 1787 that "it is not possible that a Government can last long under these circumstances." Irwin, *op. cit.*, p. 56.
97. Catherine Drinker Bowen, *Miracle at Philadelphia: The Story of the Constitutional Convention, May to September 1787*, Boston: Little Brown, 1986. First published, 1966, p. 11.
98. Perkins, *op. cit.*, p. 58; Herring, *op. cit.*, pp. 40, 52.
99. See pp. 99-111. The Convention decided that, for purposes of representation, each slave (almost all of whom lived in the Southern states) would count for three-fifths of a person and that the Congress would have the power to abolish the slave trade (as ten states had already

done) but not until 1808. The Constitution also included a provision for returning fugitive slaves to their owners.

100.   McDougall, *op. cit.*, p. 6.

Chapter 2

1.   In 1792 Washington was unanimously elected to a second term as well.

2.   Eric Hobsbawm, *The Age of Revolution: 1789–1848*, New York: Barnes and Noble Books, 1996. First published, 1962, p. 58; Simon Schama, *Citizens: A Chronicle of the French Revolution*, New York: Alfred A. Knopf, 1989, p. 62.

3.   The Estates-General had last met in 1614.

4.   Gordon S. Wood, *Empire of Liberty: A History of the Early Republic, 1789–1815*, New York: Oxford University Press, 2009, p. 175. "As U.S. Minister in Paris, Thomas Jefferson observed the French Revolution's violent but hopeful beginnings and flattered himself to think the French Declaration of the Rights of Man and the Citizen was inspired by his Declaration of Independence." Walter A. McDougall, *The Tragedy of U.S. Foreign Policy: How America's Civil Religion Betrayed the National Interest*, New Haven and London: Yale University Press, 2016, p. 46.

5.   ". . . European (or indeed world) politics between 1789 and 1917 were largely the struggle for and against the principles of 1789, or the even more incendiary ones of 1793. France provided the vocabulary and the issues of liberal and radical-democratic politics for most of the world. France provided the first great example, the concept and the vocabulary of nationalism. France provided the codes of law, the model of scientific and technical organization, the metric system of measurement for most countries. The ideology of the modern world first penetrated the ancient civilizations which had hitherto resisted European ideas through French influence. This was the work of the French Revolution." Hobsbawm, *op. cit.*, p. 53.

6.   William Doyle, *The Oxford History of the French Revolution*, Oxford, UK: The Clarendon Press of Oxford University, 1989, pp. 416–417.

7.   "The wars of the French Revolution and of Napoleon made the United States the principal carrier of the world until it in turn was involved in the conflict and blockaded by its Embargo and subsequently by the British navy." Samuel Flagg Bemis, *A Diplomatic History of the United States,* New York: Henry Holt and Company, Fourth Edition, 1955. First published, 1936, p. 304. See also Walter LaFeber, *The American Age: U.S. Foreign Policy at Home and Abroad, 1750 to the Present*, New York: W.W. Norton, 1994, p. 71; Douglas A. Irwin, *Clashing Over Commerce: A History of U.S. Trade Policy*, Chicago: The University of Chicago Press, 2017, p. 92; and Robert W. Tucker and David C. Hendrickson, *Empire of Liberty: The Statecraft of Thomas Jefferson*, New York: Oxford University Press, 1990, p. 193.

8. "... [T]hese wars absorbed so completely for a generation the contending
    energies of the principal maritime powers, Great Britain, France and
    Spain, that the United States enjoyed about thirty years of comparative
    unmolestation (except for certain maritime questions that helped
    to bring on the War of 1812). During this fortunate period the new
    republic, essentially a non-military power, was able to consolidate its
    newly established nationality, and to expand its territory, resources,
    and potential strength to a degree reasonably consistent with national
    safety . . . " Bemis, *op. cit.*, p. 95. During this period Napoleon did find
    time to plan to establish a French empire in North America but did not
    succeed in doing so. See pp. 59-61.

9. Wood, *op. cit.*, pp. 101, 103.

10. *Ibid.*, pp. 92–93; Bradford Perkins, *The Cambridge History of American
    Foreign Relations, Volume I: The Creation of a Republican Empire, 1776–
    1865*, New York: Cambridge University Press, 1993, p. 172.

11. "Jefferson envisioned an 'empire of liberty,' a necklace of independent
    republics spread across North America." George C. Herring, *From Colony
    to Superpower: U.S. Foreign Relations Since 1776*, New York: Oxford
    University Press, 2008, p. 2.

12. Perkins, *op. cit.*, p. 93.

13. Wood, *op. cit.*, p. 291.

14. Joseph J. Ellis, *American Sphinx: The Character of Thomas Jefferson*,
    New York: Alfred A. Knopf, 1997, p. 8. See also John Lamberton Harper,
    *American Machiavelli: Alexander Hamilton and the Origins of U.S. Foreign
    Policy*, New York: Cambridge University Press, 2004, p. 1.

15. Wood, *op. cit.*, pp. 189, 192; Tucker and Hendrickson, *op. cit.*, p. 255.

16. Wood, *op. cit.*, p. 644; Herring, *op. cit.*, pp. 99–100.

17. They are the War of 1812, the Mexican War, the Civil War, the Spanish-
    American War, World War I, World War II, the Korean War, the
    Vietnam War, the Gulf War of 1991, the Afghan War, and the Gulf War
    of 2003.

18. Herring, *op. cit.*, p. 65.

19. Wood, *op. cit.*, pp. 179–181.

20. Tucker and Hendrickson, *op. cit.*, p. 58.

21. To justify the proclamation and the president's right to issue it, Alexander
    Hamilton wrote a series of essays under the pen name "Pacificus." James
    Madison responded, arguing for limits on presidential power, using the
    name "Helvidius." Wood, *op. cit.*, pp. 184–185.

22. Felix Gilbert, *To the Farewell Address: Ideas of Early American Foreign
    Policy*, Princeton, New Jersey: Princeton University Press, 1961, p. 117.

23. "One lingering result of Genet's bizarre American adventure was the
    creation of . . . clubs of Jeffersonian Republicans that had come together
    to support Genet and the cause of France." They "held parades, rallies,
    and banquets; campaigned in local elections; drafted petitions; and

worked closely with the opposition press." John Rhodehamel, *George Washington: The Wonder of the Age*, New Haven and London: Yale University Press, 2017, p. 271.

24. The French government tried, unsuccessfully, to tilt the 1796 presidential election away from John Adams, the candidate of Washington and Hamilton's Federalists, believing that a Republican chief executive would adopt policies favorable to France. Bemis, *op. cit.*, p. 104.

25. Herring, *op. cit.*, pp. 74–75; Wood, *op. cit.*, p. 194.

26. Wood, *op. cit.*, p. 195.

27. The pro-British Hamilton exercised considerable influence over the American side of the negotiations. A. G. Hopkins, *American Empire: A Global History*, Princeton, New Jersey: Princeton University Press, 2018, p. 159.

28. Herring, *op. cit.*, pp. 76–77.

29. Quoted in *ibid.*, p. 78.

30. "No other treaty in U.S. history has aroused such hostile public reaction or provoked such passionate debate. . . ." *Ibid.* The dispute over the Jay Treaty contributed to the consolidation of the Federalists and Republicans as political parties, and thus to the formation of the first American party system. *Ibid.*, p. 7.

31. *Ibid.*, p. 80.

32. In the eighteenth century the British Parliament was divided between two political parties, but these tended to be loose associations dominated by aristocrats that were held together by personal ties rather than fixed political principles. See Lewis Namier, *England in the Age of the American Revolution*, London: Palgrave Macmillan, Second Edition, 1961.

33. This was aimed, in part, at the Republicans' affinity for France. Herring, *op. cit.*, p. 83.

34. Quoted in Rhodehamel, *op. cit.*, p. 289. See also Harper, *op. cit.*, p. 177.

35. Wood, *op. cit.*, p. 239; Irwin, *op. cit.*, p. 98.

36. LaFeber, *op. cit.*, p. 51. On the XYZ Affair see Wood, *op. cit.*, pp. 239–243.

37. Wood, *op. cit.*, pp. 247–250.

38. Quoted in *Ibid.*, p. 259.

39. Herring, *op. cit.*, pp. 88–89.

40. Napoleon was trying to end the European war on terms favorable to France and to establish a French empire in North America (see pp. 59-61). To both goals, he believed, conciliating the Americans could make a minor contribution. *Ibid.*, p. 89.

41. *Ibid.*, pp. 89–91.

42. "All aspects of American culture—parades, songs, art, theater, even language—became engines of one party or another promoting France or Britain." Wood, *op. cit.*, p. 255.

43. "The idea of territorial expansion was born when America was born. The charters of most British colonies in America granted them dominion as

far as the Pacific Ocean. The Articles of Confederation explicitly reserved a place in the new nation for Canada." Perkins, *op. cit.*, p. 170.

44. Wood, *op. cit.*, p. 359.

45. Herring, *op. cit.*, p. 101. The eleventh president, James K. Polk, was in this respect Jefferson's equal. See pp. 93–94.

46. Wood, *op. cit.*, p. 357.

47. It was secretly ceded the year before, in the Treaty of Fontainebleau.

48. Spain kept the western part of the territory that France had ceded four decades previously, as well as the Florida territories. The Spanish had another motive for transferring the territory. "Spain believed that France, as the dominant European power, would be better able to maintain a barrier between the Americans and the silver mines of Mexico." Wood, *op. cit.*, p. 367.

49. Herring, *op. cit.*, pp. 102–103.

50. Herring, *op. cit Ibid.*, p. 104. On these general issues see Tucker and Hendrickson, *op. cit.*, pp. 110–122.

51. "The structure of a revived French colonial empire in North America was an inverted pyramid, which rested on the island of Santo Domingo. This rich island and the smaller Guadeloupe and Martinique were expected to furnish a prosperous business in tropical products, which would employ French navigation and, together with the fisheries of Newfoundland, build up sea power. Louisiana would be the necessary continental complement for the islands, an independent source of foodstuffs and lumber; later perhaps the province would be itself extremely wealthy." Bemis, *op. cit.*, p. 134.

52. *Ibid.*, p. 130.

53. *Ibid.*, p. 135.

54. Tucker and Hendrickson, *op. cit.*, pp. 94, 167–171.

55. *Ibid.*, p. 132.

56. American shippers had "developed the legal fiction of the 'broken voyage.' By carrying goods from the French and Spanish colonies to ports in the United States, loading and paying duties on them, and then reloading and receiving rebates on most of the duties before re-exporting them to France as presumably neutral goods," the Americans complied with what the British initially defined as acceptable trade in wartime. Then the British changed their policy. "By the new doctrine of the 'continuous voyage,' American merchants would now have to prove that they actually intended their voyages from the belligerent ports to terminate in the United States, otherwise the enemy goods they carried were liable to seizure." Wood, *op. cit.*, pp. 624, 640.

57. Tucker and Hendrickson, *op. cit.*, p. 190.

58. "Since the Royal Navy needed to recruit at least thirty thousand to forty thousand new seamen every year, it relied heavily on impressing not only British subjects in their own seaports but also those who had deserted to

the American merchant marine—a not insignificant number." Wood, *op. cit.*, p. 642. "As the American government itself would come to realize, there were far more British sailors employed on American ships than American citizens impressed into the Royal Navy." Tucker and Hendrickson, *op. cit.*, p. 194.

59. Jon Latimer, *1812: War with America*, Cambridge, Massachusetts: Harvard University Press, 2007, p. 2.

60. "It was not the actual number of seizures that most irritated Americans; rather it was the British presumption that His Majesty's government had the right to decide just what American trade should be permitted or not permitted. It seemed to reduce America once again to the status of a colonial dependent." Wood, *op. cit.*, p. 641.

61. Paul Schroeder, *The Transformation of European Politics, 1763–1848*, New York and Oxford: The Clarendon Press of Oxford University, 1996 paperback, pp. 435–436.

62. Tucker and Hendrickson, *op. cit.*, p. 203.

63. LaFeber, *op. cit.*, pp. 58–59.

64. Further legislation subsequently supplemented the Embargo Act. See Bemis, *op. cit.*, p. 151, and Wood, *op. cit.*, p. 650.

65. Walter McDougall, *The Tragedy of American Foreign Policy: How America's Civil Religion Betrayed the National Interest*, New Haven and London: Yale University Press, 2016, p. 48.

66. Irwin, *op. cit.*, p. 102.

67. Wood, *op. cit.*, pp. 652, 654; Tucker and Hendrickson, *op. cit.*, pp. 39, 46.

68. Jefferson said, "I place immense value in the experiment being fully made, how far an embargo may be an effectual weapon in future as well as on this occasion." Quoted in Irwin, *op. cit.*, p. 110.

69. *Ibid.*; Schroeder, *op. cit.*, p. 436.

70. Schroeder, *ibid.*

71. Irwin, *op. cit.*, p. 106. *Ibid.*, pp. 102–109, has a detailed analysis of the embargo's economic impact on the United States.

72. As with Prohibition a century later, those seeking to circumvent the embargo made use of Canada in their operations. Herring, *op. cit.*, p. 120.

73. Tucker and Hendrickson, *op. cit.*, pp. 204–205. "In using armed force to enforce the embargo, including dispatching some army regulars, Jefferson was violating all of his beliefs in minimal government." Wood, *op. cit.*, p. 654.

74. The embargo officially ended on March 9, 1809, the day of Madison's inauguration.

75. Wood, *op. cit.*, pp. 664–667.

76. Herring, *op. cit.*, p. 122.

77. "As early as 1809 the president had wondered whether war might be the only real alternative; by 1811 it was his firm conviction." LaFeber, *op. cit.*, p. 60.

78. Wood, *op. cit.*, p. 660.

79. "In my opinion the most unpopular war that this country has ever waged, not even excepting the Vietnam conflict, was our second war with Great Britain." Samuel Eliot Morison, "Dissent in the War of 1812," in Samuel Eliot Morison, Frederick Merck, and Frank Friedel, *Dissent in Three American Wars*, Cambridge, Massachusetts: Harvard University Press, 1970, p. 3.

80. The claim is not uncontested. "It has often been speculated that faster communication in 1812 might have averted an unnecessary war, but this may assume too much. The new British ministry, while more conciliatory, was not prepared to go as far as Madison wished." Herring, *op. cit.*, p. 125.

81. Perkins, *op. cit.*, p. 135.

82. In his war message Madison said there had existed "on the side of Great Britain a state of war against the United States, and on the side of the United States a state of peace toward Great Britain." Quoted in *ibid.*, p. 136.

83. McDougall, *Promised Land, Crusader State*, p. 35; Wood, *op. cit.*, pp. 667, 669–670; Perkins, *op. cit.*, p. 140; Herring, *op. cit.*, p. 126.

84. Perkins, *op. cit.*, p. 138.

85. "The three-pronged American campaign against Canada in 1812 had been a complete failure. What was worse, the failure was due less to the superiority of the Canadian resistance and more to the inability of the United States to recruit and manage its armies." Wood, *op. cit.*, p. 680. On the Canadian campaign see Eliot A. Cohen, *Conquered into Liberty: Two Centuries of Battles Along the Great Warpath That Made the American Way of War*, New York: The Free Press, 2011, Chapter 9.

86. "The scale of the disaster was stupendous. Of the 655,000 troops that had crossed the Vistula only 93,000 remained. Some 370,000 had died as a result of enemy action or disease, or had simply frozen to death; around 200,000, including 48 generals and 3,000 other officers, had been taken prisoner." Blanning, *op. cit.*, p. 664.

87. ". . . [M]any years later Madison confessed that, had he foreseen the French defeat, he would not have supported war in 1812." Perkins, *op. cit.*, p. 137.

88. Daniel Walker Howe, *What Hath God Wrought: The Transformation of America, 1815–1848*, New York: Oxford University Press, 2007, p. 69. At the peace negotiations in Ghent, Belgium, in 1814 the British presented the demand for the establishment of an Indian buffer state in the American Northwest, the area from Ohio to Wisconsin. The American side refused to consider the proposal and the British dropped it.

89. The British did not intend to occupy Washington, D.C. "Strategically, the purpose of the British raid on the Chesapeake had been to distract the Americans from efforts to conquer Canada; psychologically to discredit the Madison administration. Both objectives were

attained." Howe, *op cit.*, p. 66. On the Chesapeake campaign see Donald R. Hickey, *The War of 1812: A Forgotten Conflict*, Urbana and Chicago: University of Illinois Press, 1989, pp. 195–202.

90.   ". . . [T]he evidence suggests that the British were principally motivated to capture New Orleans by the prospect of plunder, and that their occupation of the city, if it had been achieved, would have been short." Howe, *op. cit.*, p. 16.

91.   LaFeber, *op. cit.*, p. 65.

92.   Latimer, *op. cit.*, p. 347.

93.   "If the war and its economic hardships had dragged on much longer, the federal government, the Constitution, and the Republican Party might not have survived intact." Howe, *op. cit.*, p. 73.

94.   Latimer, *op. cit.*, p. 408.

95.   "The opinion of the Duke of Wellington, the future victor at Waterloo, that America could not be easily conquered and certainly not without naval superiority on the Great Lakes clinched the willingness of the British to settle without gaining any of their original terms." Wood, *op. cit.*, p. 695.

96.   Bemis, *op. cit.*, p. 167.

97.   David Cannadine, *Victorious Century: The United Kingdom, 1800–1906*, New York: Penguin Books, 2017, p. 70.

98.   Hickey, *op. cit.*, p. 302.

99.   Howe, *op. cit.*, p. 73.

100.   The competition comes from the Vietnam War in the twentieth century and the second Gulf War in the twenty-first. See pp. 303-313 and 428-435.

101.   Wood, *op. cit.*, p. 693; Morison, *op. cit.*, p. 16.

102.   Andrew Lambert, *Seapower States: Maritime Culture, Continental Empires and the Conflict That Made the Modern World*, New Haven and London: Yale University Press, 2018, pp. 292–293.

103.   Schroeder, *op. cit.*, p. 440; Bemis, *op. cit.*, p. 138.

104.   Tucker and Hendrickson, *op. cit.*, pp. 219–220.

105.   Perkins, *op. cit.*, pp. 145–146.

106.   Latimer, *op. cit.*, p. 400.

107.   Wood, *op. cit.*, p. 699; Herring, *op. cit.*, p. 139.

Chapter 3

1.   Paul Schroeder's *The Transformation of European Politics, 1763–1848*, Oxford, UK: The Clarendon Press of Oxford University Press, 1996paperback, provides an authoritative account of the emergence and operation of the Concert of Europe and the break with precedent in European affairs that it represented. "European international politics was transformed between 1763 and 1848, with the decisive turning-point coming in 1813–1815. A fundamental change occurred in the governing rules, norms, and practices of international politics." *Ibid.*, p. v.

2. Paul M. Kennedy, *The Rise and Fall of British Naval Mastery*,
    New York: Charles Scribner's Sons, 1976, pp. 149–167.

3. On British global hegemony in the nineteenth century see David
    Cannadine, *Victorious Century: The United Kingdom, 1800–1906*,
    New York: Penguin Books, 2017, pp. 45, 102, 185, 266, and Richard Evans,
    The Pursuit of Power: Europe 1815–1914, New York: Viking, 2016, pp. 26,
    132, 140, 292–293.

4. "Economically, the United States was an integral part of the Atlantic
    trading community. Politically, it remained a distant and apparently
    disinterested observer of European internal politics and external
    maneuvering." George C. Herring, *From Colony to Superpower: U.S.
    Foreign Relations Since 1776*, New York: Oxford University Press, 2008,
    p. 177.

5. "Exhausted by a generation of convulsing warfare, Europe required,
    as Castlereagh had said, 'a period of repose.' The period of European
    repose was the period of American expansion." Samuel Flagg Bemis,
    A Diplomatic History of the United States, New York: Henry Holt and
    Company, 1955, Fourth Edition, p. 195.

6. Walter LaFeber, *The American Age: U.S. Foreign Policy at Home and
    Abroad, 1750 to the Present*, New York: W.W. Norton, Second Edition,
    1994, p. 76.

7. See, for example, Bradford Perkins, *The Cambridge History of American
    Foreign Relations, Volume I: The Creation of a Republican Empire, 1776–
    1865*, New York: Cambridge University Press, 1993, p. 151.

8. Michael Mandelbaum, *The Meaning of Sports: Why Americans Watch
    Baseball, Football and Basketball and What They See When They Do*,
    New York: PublicAffairs, 2004, p. 64.

9. Cannadine, *op. cit.*, p. 228.

10. John Darwin, *The Empire Project: The Rise and Fall of the British World-
    System, 1830–1970*, Cambridge, UK: Cambridge University Press, 2009,
    pp. 1, 10; John Darwin, *Unfinished Empire: The Global Expansion of
    Britain*, New York: Bloomsbury Press, 2012, p. 11; Cannadine, *op. cit.*,
    p. 367; Kennedy, *op. cit.*, p. 153; Evans, *op. cit.*, p. 635.

11. Kori Schake, *Safe Passage: The Transition from British to American
    Hegemony*, Cambridge, Massachusetts: Harvard University Press, 2017,
    p. 58; A. G. Hopkins, *American Empire: A Global History*, Princeton, New
    Jersey: Princeton University Press, 2018, p. 127.

12. Andrew Lambert, *Seapower States: Maritime Culture, Continental
    Empires, and the Conflict That Made the Modern World*, New Haven and
    London: Yale University Press, 2018, p. 261.

13. See pp. 317-320. The Rush-Bagot agreement "proved remarkably durable.
    Although the Lincoln administration threatened to abrogate it in
    retaliation for British help to the Confederacy, it persisted until World
    War II, when Canada and the United States agreed that the Great Lakes

could be used for naval construction and training—no longer, of course, directed against each other." Daniel Walker Howe, *What Hath God Wrought: The Transformation of America, 1815–1848*, New York: Oxford University Press, 2007, p. 96.

14. The 1818 accord in fact covered four issues: "fisheries, slaves, boundaries, trans-Atlantic commerce." Samuel Flagg Bemis, *John Quincy Adams and the Foundations of American Foreign Policy*, New York: Alfred A. Knopf, 1965, p. 298.

15. Howe, *op. cit.*, pp. 674–677.

16. The Treaty was "a handsome victory for Zachary Taylor's administration. The British had recognized the United States as an equal in Central America." LaFeber, *op. cit.*, p. 124.

17. Schroeder, *op. cit.*, pp. 628–629.

18. See later, pp. 90–91.

19. Some Americans were skeptical that democracy promotion to the south was feasible, doubting that the Latin Americans would be capable of creating and sustaining the kind of republican government they had installed in the United States. Perkins, *op. cit.*, p. 14.

20. Walter A. McDougall, *Promised Land, Crusader State: The American Encounter with the World Since 1776*, Boston: Houghton Mifflin, 1997, p. 36.

21. Ernest R. May, *The Making of the Monroe Doctrine*, Cambridge, Massachusetts: The Belknap Press of Harvard University Press, 1975, pp. viii–ix; McDougall, *op. cit.*, pp. 74–75.

22. On the American response to the events of 1848 see Howe, *op. cit.*, pp. 792–795, and Herring, *op. cit.*, pp. 152–153.

23. Schroeder, *op. cit.*, p. 630; Bemis, *A Diplomatic History*, p. 203.

24. Howe, *op. cit.*, pp. 112–113. "The immediate Russian threat to Oregon was contained when the Americans and British made separate agreements with the Russians in 1824 and 1825 respectively, defining the southern limit of Alaska as 54 40' north latitude, its present boundary." *Ibid.*, p. 115. See also McDougall, *op. cit.*, pp. 60–63.

25. Cannadine, *op. cit.*, pp. 122, 133.

26. McDougall, *op. cit.*, p. 62; Schake, *op. cit.*, p. 51.

27. Ernest May argues that Adams's position was grounded in his aspirations to win the presidency in 1824. May, *op. cit.*, p. x.

28. A concise overview of the Monroe Doctrine is in LaFeber, *op. cit.*, pp. 84–87.

29. Canning signed a memorandum with the French ambassador in London, Prince Polignac, that "pledged both of them to territorial non-aggrandizement and the renunciation of the use of force in dealing with Latin America." Schroeder, *op. cit.*, p. 634. The Polignac Memorandum rather than the Monroe Doctrine guaranteed the near-term independence of the Latin American republics. McDougall, *op. cit.*, p. 69.

30. Territorial expansion is discussed in the next section of this chapter.

31. *The Statistical History of the United States from Colonial Times to the Present*, Introduction by Ben J. Wattenberg, New York: Basic Books, 1976, p. 8.

32. The fertility rate for white (that is, nonslave) women over this period was as follows: 1820, 6.73 live births per female; 1830, 6.55; 1840, 6.14; 1850, 5.42; 1860, 5.21. Michael Haines, "Fertility and Mortality in the United States," EH.net, https://eh.net/encyclopedia/fertility-and-mortality-in-the-united-states/

33. LaFeber, *op. cit.*, pp. 130–131. In the later period more immigrants came from Ireland, as a result of the great famine of the 1840s, and Germany, in part due to the political upheavals of 1848. "By 1860, among the foreign-born nationwide, the Irish were the most numerous, amounting to 39 percent, followed by the Germans, with 31 percent, while the British-born 'founding stock' fell to 14 percent." Aristide Zolberg, *A Nation by Design: Immigration Policy in the Fashioning of America*, New York: Russell Sage Foundation, 2006, p. 130.

34. Whereas in 1790 only five percent of Americans were urban dwellers, by 1860, twenty percent of a far larger population were. Alan Greenspan and Adrian Wooldridge, *Capitalism in America: A History*, New York: Penguin Press, 2018, p. 58.

35. "America was the first country to be born in an age of growth—an age when the essential economic problem was to promote the forces of change rather than to divvy up a fixed set of resources." *Ibid.*, p. 7.

36. *Ibid.*, p. 41.

37. *Ibid.*, p. 42; Howe, *op. cit.*, p. 505.

38. Howe, *op. cit.*, p. 538.

39. Douglass C. North, *The Economic Growth of the United States, 1790–1860*, New York: W.W. Norton, 1966 paperback, pp. 67–69.

40. Initially the principal industry was textile, which used cotton from the South. Howe, *op. cit.*, p. 132.

41. North, *op. cit.*, pp. 70–71.

42. Also enlarging the scope and speed of communication in this era was the multiplication of newspapers, magazines, and books. Howe, *op. cit.*, p. 2; John Steele Gordon, *An Empire of Wealth: The Epic History of American Economic Power*, New York: HarperCollins, 2004, pp. 158–159.

43. Howe, *op. cit.*, pp. 117–120. The Erie Canal did more than any other single development to make New York City the economic capital of the United States. *Ibid.*, p. 120.

44. "Before the Civil War, foreign investment played a vital role in state-building by funding federal and state institutions, railroads, utilities, and education." Hopkins, *op. cit.*, p. 310. See also *ibid.*, p. 166, and Paul Varg, *United States Foreign Relations, 1820–1860*, East Lansing, Michigan: Michigan State University Press, 1979, p. 25.

45. From 1790 to 1860 tariffs accounted for almost ninety percent of the federal government's income. Douglas A. Irwin, *Clashing Over Commerce: A History of US Trade Policy*, Chicago: University of Chicago Press, 2017, p. 7.

46. ". . . [D]ifferent regions of the country, with their different producer interests, tend to have fairly stable preferences for certain trade policies. Because members of Congress usually reflect the interests of their constituents, Congressional voting patterns also show continuity over time." *Ibid.*, p. 10.

47. Cotton accounted for as much as half the value of total American exports in the first half of the nineteenth century. *Ibid.*, p. 132.

48. The two parties were not always homogeneous on trade issues. Both had national presences, with Northern Democrats and Southern Whigs.

49. Howe, *op. cit.*, p. 84.

50. Irwin, *op. cit.*, p. 128.

51. *Ibid.*, p. 145.

52. Howe, *op. cit.*, pp. 395–400. The 1828 tariff was followed by another in 1832. With the doctrine of nullification Calhoun and the Southerners had the tariff in mind, but they also worried that the Northern states would seek to impose on them the abolition of slavery.

53. *Ibid.*, p. 408.

54. Irwin, *op. cit.*, p. 176.

55. The largest such conflict in the seventeenth century, King Philip's War of 1675 and 1676, was fought in New England.

56. William T. Hagan, *The Indian in American History*, New York: The Macmillan Company, 1963, p. 1.

57. Herring, *op. cit.*, p. 80; LaFeber, *op. cit.*, pp. 48–49.

58. Herring, *op. cit.*, p. 124.

59. Hagan, *op. cit.*, p. 4.

60. David A. Nichols, "U.S. Indian Policy, 1783–1830," *Oxford Research Encyclopedia*, October 2015, p. 6. In 1831 the United States Supreme Court declared that Indian tribes (in this particular case the Cherokees) constituted "domestic dependent" nations and not sovereign states. Howe, *op. cit.*, p. 355.

61. Herring, *op. cit.*, p. 44; Nichols, *op. cit.*, pp. 10–11.

62. Nichols, *op. cit.*, p. 12.

63. Bemis, *A Diplomatic History*, p. 170. "As a result of the War of 1812, foreign nations would never intercede with the Indians again, depriving them of what little leverage they had. The Indians would never again threaten U.S. expansion. From this point, the United States imposed its will on them." Herring, *op. cit.*, p. 132.

64. Howe, *op. cit.*, pp. 75–76.

65. *Ibid.*, p. 386.

66. European-borne diseases, to which they lacked immunity, also severely reduced their numbers. On the various setbacks the Indians experienced at the hands of the federal government see Howe, *op. cit.*, pp. 23, 342–357, 417–423, and 810–811.

67. "The United States early mastered the arts of infiltration and subversion and first employed with Spanish Louisiana the tactics later successfully used in the Floridas, Texas, California, and Hawaii." Herring, *op. cit.*, p. 102.

68. *Ibid.*, p. 180.

69. The most controversial of all was the Mexican War. See pp. 93-99.

70. Howe, *op. cit.*, p. 706.

71. "[Adams] told the cabinet in 1822 that 'the world should become familiarized with the idea of considering our proper dominion to be the entire continent of North America.'" Herring, *op. cit.*, p. 139.

72. LaFeber, *op. cit.*, pp. 80–81.

73. In his largely admiring biography of Adams, Samuel Flagg Bemis called the Transcontinental Treaty "the greatest diplomatic victory won by any single individual in the history of the United States." Bemis, *John Quincy Adams*, p. 340.

74. Spanish possession of West Florida denied the United States access to the Gulf Coast east of New Orleans. The American government claimed that West Florida was included in the Louisiana Purchase, a claim the Spanish denied. Howe, *op. cit.*, p. 301.

75. Bemis, *A Diplomatic History*, p. 186.

76. *Ibid.*, p. 97.

77. *Ibid.*, p. 100; Herring, *op. cit.*, p. 147.

78. Perkins, *op. cit.*, p. 154.

79. Frederick Merck, *Slavery and the Annexation of Texas*, New York: Alfred A. Knopf, 1972, pp. ix–x. The Mexican Congress reversed the policy in 1830. *Ibid.*, p. 178.

80. Howe, *op. cit.*, p. 660.

81. Herring, *op. cit.*, p. 157.

82. *Ibid.*, p. 189.

83. Cannadine, *op. cit.*, p. 235; Herring, *op. cit.*, p. 191.

84. When the agreement was signed in June 1846, British prime minister Robert Peel told the House of Commons, "By moderation [and] by mutual compromise" the two had "averted the dreadful calamity of war between two nations of kindred origin and common language, the breaking out of which might have involved the civilized world in general conflict." Cannadine, *op. cit.*, p. 236. See also Bemis, *A Diplomatic History*, pp. 277–278, and Howe, *op. cit.*, pp. 717–722. The American share of Oregon included "all of the future states of Washington, Oregon, Idaho, and parts of Montana and Wyoming." Herring, *op. cit.*, p. 192.

85. Merck, *op. cit.*, pp. 409–410; Howe, *op. cit.*, p. 719.

86. "The election of 1844 was the only presidential contest in the nineteenth century that depended on an issue of foreign affairs. . . ." Bemis, *A Diplomatic History*, p. 229.

87. The other two goals were domestic in nature: reducing the tariff of 1842 and reviving his predecessor Martin Van Buren's independent treasury so as to ensure monetary stability. These he also accomplished. Robert Merry, *A Country of Vast Designs: James K. Polk, the Mexican War, and the Conquest of the American Continent*, New York: Simon & Schuster, 2009, p. 131.

88. Howe, *op. cit.*, pp. 689–690.

89. ". . . [I]n hindsight it seems likely that the United States would have gained control of the West without fighting for it as the population expansion to the Pacific Ocean had already begun." John S. D. Eisenhower, *So Far from God: The U.S. War with Mexico, 1846–1848*, New York: Random House, 1989, p. 195.

90. Bemis, *A Diplomatic History*, p. 238; Merry, *op. cit.*, p. 256; David Pletcher, *The Diplomacy of Annexation: Texas, Oregon, and the Mexican War*, Columbia, Missouri: University of Missouri Press, 1973, pp. 585–586. In retrospect British intervention in California in any significant way seems unlikely. Pletcher, *op. cit.*, pp. 592–596.

91. To this end Polk helped arrange for the return to Mexico of the exiled leader Antonio Lopez de Santa Anna, believing that he would seize power and conclude a treaty with the United States. Santa Anna did seize power upon his return but continued the war. Howe, *op. cit.*, p. 766. The American government would have the experience of being disappointed, misled, or deceived outright by ostensibly friendly foreign leaders again in the years to come.

92. "Mexico was a dysfunctional, unstable, weak nation whose population wasn't sufficient to control all the lands within its domain." Merry, *op. cit.*, p. 476. "Political instability [in Mexico] was a way of life. . . . Coup followed coup, sixteen presidents serving between 1837 and 1851." Santa Anna himself was president eleven times. Herring, *op. cit.*, p. 196.

93. Bemis, *A Diplomatic History*, p. 237. In addition, "Mexicans enormously underestimated American military power; most believed they could foil an invasion by the U.S. Army, then only a force of seven thousand men." Perkins, *op. cit.*, p. 189.

94. ". . . [W]hen Polk became President, he set forth on a foreign policy of strong stands, overstated arguments, and menacing public pronouncements, not because he wanted war but because he felt that this was the only language which his foreign adversaries would understand." Pletcher, *op. cit.*, pp. 599–600.

95. The tally in the House of Representatives was 174 to 14, with John Quincy Adams one of the dissenters, and 40 to 2 in the Senate. LaFeber, *op. cit.*, pp. 117–118.

96. Eisenhower, *op. cit.*, pp. 209–210.

97. Herring, *op. cit.*, p. 200. The rebels adopted the California grizzly bear as their symbol, which is why the state flag bears an image of one. "The role of a headstrong military leader on the frontier operating with unclear official authorization—the role of Jackson in Florida and Robert Stockton in Texas—was repeated by Fremont in California." Howe, *op. cit.*, p. 754. These freelance operators were known as "filibusters."

98. "Polk pursued all the possible routes to California—purchase, revolution, and war—simultaneously." Howe, *op. cit.*, p. 737.

99. *Ibid.*, p. 772.

100. *Ibid.*, p. 778.

101. Eisenhower, *op. cit.*, p. 284.

102. Thoreau's essay "Civil Disobedience" (which began as a lecture), which heavily influenced Martin Luther King Jr. and the civil rights movement of the 1960s, was inspired in part by the Mexican War and his opposition to it.

103. Howe, *op. cit.*, p. 797; James McPherson, *The War That Forged a Nation: Why the Civil War Still Matters*, New York: Oxford University Press, 2015, p. 22.

104. "Religious leaders, intellectuals, and some politicians denounced [the war] as 'illegal, unrighteous, and damnable' and accused Polk of violating 'every principle of international law and moral justice.'" Herring, *op. cit.*, p. 203. "In the opinion of its numerous critics, the Mexican War was unnecessary, impolitic, illegal, and immoral." John H. Schroeder, *Mr. Polk's War: American Opposition and Dissent, 1846–1848*, Madison, Wisconsin: The University of Wisconsin Press, 1973, p. xiv.

105. Frederick Merck, "Dissent in the Mexican War," in Samuel Eliot Morison, Frederick Merck, and Frank Friedel, *Dissent in Three American Wars*, Cambridge, Massachusetts: Harvard University Press, Fourth Printing, 1971, p. 42; Howe, *op. cit.*, p. 764.

106. Herring, *op. cit.*, p. 203; Eisenhower, *op. cit.*, p. 285.

107. Over 70,000 men enlisted although fewer than 30,000 actually served in Mexico. At the beginning of the war the professional army numbered about 6,000.

108. McPherson, *op. cit.*, p. 18.

109. These were the attempt to appoint Missouri senator Thomas Hart Benton to a position in overall charge of the war and an appropriation to pay for ten additional divisions of soldiers.

110. Howe, *op. cit.*, p. 800.

111. Merry, *op. cit.*, p. 407. "... [M]ost southerners abhorred the idea of 'All Mexico,' which by incorporating millions of Mexican people, mainly of mixed race, and presumably granting them citizenship, would seriously compromise the nature of the United States as an exclusively white republic." Howe, *op. cit.*, p. 798. On this point see also Merry, *op. cit.*, p. 414.

112. Merry, *op. cit.*, pp. 398–400.

113. Howe, *op. cit.*, pp. 802–805.

114. Merry, *op. cit.*, p. 428.

115. Howe, *op. cit.*, pp. 807–808.

116. "Historians have overwhelmingly concluded that Trist made a courageous and justified decision in defying his orders and remaining to secure a peace treaty." *Ibid.*, p. 808.

117. "Polk had successfully discovered the latent constitutional powers of the commander in chief to provoke a war, secure congressional support for it, shape the strategy for fighting it, appoint generals, and define the terms of peace." *Ibid.*

118. In 1854 the Gadsden Purchase added to American territory what would become the southern strip of Arizona and the southwest part of New Mexico, territory that was thought to lie on the optimal southern route for a transcontinental railroad.

119. "The conquest of that large republic [Mexico] by the small armed forces of the United States, despite formidable geographical difficulties and in the face of a hostile population, constituted one of the most amazing military achievements of the nineteenth century. . . ." Howe, *op. cit.*, p. 2.

120. "What later generations would recognize as the characteristic American mode of warfare, emphasizing industry, engineering, and technological proficiency, was already appearing. Though rural America, in the person of the Jacksonian President Polk, made the war, industrial-technological America won it." Howe, *op. cit.*, p. 746. "Total American deaths of 13,283 (seven-eighths of them from disease) constituted 17 percent of all American soldiers, the highest rate for any war except the Civil War." McPherson, *op. cit.*, p. 19. The estimated cost of waging the war was around $100 million. Pletcher, *op. cit.*, p. 579.

121. On the Senate floor the Whigs proposed a peace with no territorial acquisitions except the port of San Francisco. Eighteen of the twenty-one Whig senators voted for the measure, but it did not pass. Howe, *op. cit.*, pp. 806–807.

122. Merck, "Dissent," p. 52.

123. Gordon S. Wood, *Empire of Liberty: A History of the Early Republic, 1789–1815*, New York: Oxford University Press, 2009, p. 518. Patrick Henry, a revolutionary firebrand from Virginia, said of slavery that he looked forward to the time "when an opportunity will be offered to abolish this lamentable evil." Bernard Bailyn, *The Ideological Origins of the American Revolution*, Cambridge, Massachusetts: The Belknap Press of Harvard University Press, 1972 paperback, p. 236.

124. Evans, *op. cit.*, pp. 132–133.

125. Williamson Murray and Wayne Wei-siang Hsieh, *A Savage War: A Military History of the Civil War*, Princeton, New Jersey: Princeton

University Press, 2017, p. 17. At one point fully three-quarters of the world's supply of cotton was grown in the American South. James McPherson, *Battle Cry of Freedom: The Civil War*, New York: Oxford University Press, 1988, p. 39. In 1815 the value of American exports of cotton was $17 million. By 1860 it had risen to $191 million. North, *op. cit.*, p. 233.

126.   "Slavery was in some ways a horrific response to a basic climatic fact: you could not get free men to harvest labor-intensive crops in the heat and humidity." Greenspan and Wooldridge, *op. cit.*, pp. 33–34.

127.   "In 1860, the aggregate value of slaves as property was $3 billion, nearly 20 percent greater than the capital invested in railroads and manufacturing combined, a calculation that excludes the value of land in southern plantations. Slavery generated a stream of income that enabled overall white per capita income in the South to approximate that of northern whites. In the seven cotton states, nearly a third of white income came from slave labor. Thus, slavery was essential to the prosperity and standard of living of many southern whites." Irwin, *op. cit.*, p. 163. See also Howe, *op. cit.*, p. 56, and Greenspan and Wooldridge, *op. cit.*, p. 76.

128.   Howe, *op. cit.*, p. 852; McPherson, *Battle Cry of Freedom*, p. 8.

129.   Howe, *op. cit.*, p. 59; McPherson, *Battle Cry of Freedom*, pp. 209–210.

130.   Greenspan and Wooldridge, *op. cit.*, p. 80.

131.   Most of the immigrants from Europe settled in the North.

132.   For most of the country's history until 1860, the South had controlled national politics. "A Southern slaveholder had been president of the United States two-thirds of the years between 1789 and 1861, and two-thirds of the Speakers of the House and presidents pro tem of the Senate had also been Southerners. Twenty of the thirty-five Supreme Court justices during that period had been from slave states, which always had a majority on the Court before 1861." McPherson, *The War that Forged a Nation*, p. 7.

133.   McPherson, *Battle Cry of Freedom*, pp. vii, 309–310.

134.   McPherson, *The War That Forged a Nation*, pp. 126–127.

135.   McPherson, *Battle Cry of Freedom*, p. 241.

136.   ". . . [U]ntil the last year of the war or so, [the Southern government] retained the support of most slaveless white Confederates. Shoring up that support were widespread devotion to slavery as an institution; an even more widespread and deeply ingrained dedication to white supremacy; religious doctrines and clerical exhortations; local, regional, and family ties; outrage at the wounds inflicted by enemy armies; codes of personal pride and honor; and hopes for eventual victory." Bruce Levine, *The Fall of the House of Dixie: The Civil War and the Social Revolution That Transformed the South*, New York: Random House, 2013, p. 288. ". . . [T]he Northern armies taken as a whole bore a deep

ideological commitment to the cause of the Union, as best seen in a reenlistment rate of close to 60 percent for those battle-hardened Union soldiers whose three-year enlistments expired in 1864." Murray and Hsieh, *op. cit.*, p. 55.

137.   "Southerners were much better represented in the higher ranks of the army than northerners; among antebellum American soldiers prominent enough to be chronicled in the *Dictionary of National Biography*, the South contained twice the percentage of the North despite a smaller population." Greenspan and Wooldridge, *op. cit.*, p. 82. In the Mexican War, two-thirds of the volunteers had come from the slave states. McPherson, *Battle Cry of Freedom*, p. 4.

138.   "The South could 'win' the war by not losing; the North could win only by winning." McPherson, *Battle Cry of Freedom*, p. 336.

139.   *Ibid.*, pp. 313–314, 330–331; Murray and Hsieh, *op. cit.*, p. 8.

140.   "Shiloh launched the country onto the floodtide of total war." McPherson, *Battle Cry of Freedom*, p. 424.

141.   Gary W. Gallagher, *The Confederate War*, Cambridge, Massachusetts: Harvard University Press, 1997, pp. 138–139.

142.   McPherson, *Battle Cry of Freedom*, p. 504. He based this measure on his military authority. He lacked, in his own view, the legal authority to free the slaves in the states that sustained slavery but had remained in the Union—Delaware, Missouri, Kentucky, and Maryland. The liberation of all slaves was accomplished by the ratification of the Thirteenth Amendment to the Constitution in December 1865.

143.   Quoted in Dean B. Mahin, *One War at a Time: The International Dimension of the American Civil War*, Washington, D.C.: Brassey's, 1999, p. 127.

144.   "The proclamation threatened to break up the tenuous coalition of Republicans, War Democrats, and border-state leaders that [Lincoln] had so carefully been building since the outbreak of the war." David Herbert Donald, *Lincoln*, New York: Simon & Schuster, 1995, p. 377. See also *ibid.*, p. 379.

145.   *Ibid.*, p. 380; McPherson, *Battle Cry of Freedom*, pp. 288, 436.

146.   Donald, *op. cit.*, p. 374.

147.   See pp. 108-109.

148.   "After January 1 [1863], Lincoln told an official of the Interior Department, 'the character of the war will be changed. It will be one of subjugation. . . . The [old] South is to be destroyed and replaced by new propositions and ideas.'" McPherson, *Battle Cry of Freedom*, p. 558.

149.   "The capture of Vicksburg was the most important northern strategic victory of the war, perhaps meriting Grant's later assertion that 'the fate of the Confederacy was sealed when Vicksburg fell.'" *Ibid.*, p. 637. On the battle see *ibid.*, pp. 626–638.

150. On Gettysburg see *ibid.*, pp. 652–665, and Murray and Hsieh, *op. cit.*, pp. 272–290.

151. He was promoted to lieutenant general and given overall command of all Union forces.

152. McPherson, *Battle Cry of Freedom*, pp. 733–734.

153. *Ibid.*, p. 771.

154. Murray and Hsieh, *op. cit.*, pp. 460–468, 558.

155. McPherson, *Battle Cry of Freedom*, p. 854. One-quarter of white Southern males of military age in 1860 were killed and another one-quarter were maimed. Gallagher, *op. cit.*, following p. 153.

156. Murray and Hsieh, *op. cit.*, pp. 6–7.

157. Levine, *op. cit.*, p. 284.

158. Gallagher, *op. cit.*, following p. 153.

159. "The implicit purpose of [the North's final] campaigns was not merely the defeat of the Confederate armies, but to bring the war home to the Confederate population, to paraphrase Sherman, to make white Southerners realize that it was in the reach of Northern military power to dispossess them of their homes, their lands, and, if necessary, their very lives." Murray and Hsieh, *op. cit.*, p. 507.

160. Gallagher, *op. cit.*, pp. 126–127.

161. McPherson, *Battle Cry of Freedom, op. cit.*, p. 337.

162. Gallagher, *op. cit.*, p. 115. For the argument that the South lost the war because it developed insufficiently robust nationalist sentiment, see Richard E. Beringer, Herman Hattaway, Archer Jones, and Willian N. Still Jr., *Why the South Lost the Civil War*, Athens, Georgia: University of Georgia Press, 1986, especially Chapter 17. For a rebuttal see Gallagher, *op. cit.*, p. 81.

163. On Lincoln as commander in chief see Eliot A. Cohen, *Supreme Command: Soldiers, Statesmen and Leadership in Wartime*, New York: The Free Press, 2002, Chapter 2.

164. Perkins, *op. cit.*, p. 217.

165. Schake, *op. cit.*, pp. 86, 91, 97–98.

166. "When the Civil War broke out, about one-fifth of the population of Great Britain made a living from the manufacture of cotton, 80 percent of which came from the American South." Herring, *op. cit.*, p. 226.

167. Mahin, *op. cit.*, pp. 86–88; Herring, *op. cit.*, pp. 236–237; McPherson, *Battle Cry of Freedom,* p. 386. Britain also imported a great deal of grain from the North, which partly offset the South's potential leverage from its cotton. *Ibid.*

168. Bemis, *A Diplomatic History*, p. 373; Schake, *op. cit.*, p. 99; Eliot A. Cohen, *Conquered into Liberty: Two Centuries of Battles Along the Great Warpath That Made the American Way of War*, New York: The Free Press, 2011, p. 317.

169. Hopkins, *op. cit.*, p. 231.

170. Bemis, *A Diplomatic History*, p. 365.
171. David Brown, *Palmerston: A Biography*, New Haven, Connecticut: Yale University Press, 2010, p. 451; Mahin, *op. cit.*, pp. 23, 26. The Emancipation Proclamation aided the Northern cause in Britain.
172. "War was considered likely (and privately threatened) by both countries." Schake, *op. cit.*, p. 101. See also Lambert, *op. cit.*, p. 296.
173. Mahin, *op. cit.*, Chapter 5; Bemis, *A Diplomatic History*, pp. 377–380.
174. Bemis, *A Diplomatic History*, pp. 388–392; McPherson, *Battle Cry of Freedom*, p. 682.
175. Mahin, *op. cit.*, Chapters 8 and 17 and Epilogue I.
176. Murray and Hsieh, *op. cit.*, pp. 5–6, 513.
177. Tony Smith, *America's Mission: The United States and the Worldwide Struggle for Democracy in the Twentieth Century*, Princeton, New Jersey: Princeton University Press, 1994, pp. 23–27; David Hackett Fischer, *Albion's Seed: Four British Folkways in America*, New York: Oxford University Press, 1989, pp. 862–863; Hopkins, *op. cit.*, pp. 290–292.
178. McPherson, *Battle Cry of Freedom*, p. 247.

The Second Age

1. Quoted in Bradford Perkins, *The Cambridge History of American Foreign Relations, Volume I: The Creation of a Republican Empire, 1776–1865*, New York: Cambridge University Press, 1993, p. 230.
2. The history of great-power rivalry is the subject of Paul M. Kennedy, *The Rise and Fall of the Great Powers: Economic Change and Military Conflict from 1500 to 2000*, New York: Random House, 1987.
3. In an often-cited memorandum written in 1907 Sir Eyre Crowe, a senior official in the Foreign Office of the United Kingdom, laid out the logic that governed British foreign policy and would, in modified form, guide that of the United States as well. https://en.wikisource.org/wiki/Memorandum_on_the_Present_State_of_British_Relations_with_France_and_Germany
4. On Britain's policy of tending to the European balance in the eighteenth century see Brendan Simms, *Three Victories and a Defeat: The Rise and Fall of the First British Empire*, New York: Basic Books, 2007.

Chapter 4

1. "The history of the rise and later fall of the leading countries in the Great Power system . . . shows a very significant correlation *over the longer term* between productive and revenue-raising capacities on the one hand and military strength on the other." Paul Kennedy, *The Rise and Fall of the Great Powers: Economic Change and Military Conflict from 1500 to 2000*, New York: Random House, 1987, p. xvi.

2. "In the half century between the end of the Civil War and the beginning of World War I in Europe, the American economy changed more profoundly, grew more quickly, and became more diversified than at any earlier fifty-year period in the nation's history." John Steele Gordon, *Empire of Wealth: The Epic History of American Economic Power*, New York: HarperCollins, 2004, p. 205.

3. "A little more than a quarter of the country's population counted as urban in 1870; nearly 40 percent did in 1900." Richard White, *The Republic for Which It Stands: The United States During Reconstruction and the Gilded Age, 1865–1896*, New York: Oxford University Press, 2017, p. 408. See also *ibid.*, p. 501, and A. G. Hopkins, *American Empire: A Global History*, Princeton, New Jersey: Princeton University Press, 2018, p. 307.

4. Arthur Power Dudden, *The American Pacific: From the Old China Trade to the Present*, New York: Oxford University Press, 1992, p. 22. The Russians also believed that the sale would earn the friendship of the United States, and for several decades thereafter Americans did regard Russia favorably, at least in comparison with the prevailing American attitude for most of the twentieth century. *Ibid.*, p. 23.

5. The name originated with the Massachusetts senator and prominent pre–Civil War opponent of slavery Charles Sumner, who based it on what he said was the indigenous term "Al-esk-sa," meaning "great land." *Ibid.*, p. 23.

6. *Ibid.*, p. 61. On Seward see Walter LaFeber, *The Cambridge History of American Foreign Relations, Volume II: The American Search for Opportunity, 1865–1913*, New York: Cambridge University Press, 1993, pp. 7–20

7. Walter LaFeber, *The American Age: U.S. Foreign Policy at Home and Abroad, 1750 to the Present*, New York: W.W. Norton, Second Edition, 1994, pp. 172–173.

8. Samuel Flagg Bemis, *A Diplomatic History of the United States*, New York: Henry Holt and Company, Fourth Edition, 1955, p. 407.

9. LaFeber, *The American Age*, p. 171.

10. *The Statistical History of the United States: From Colonial Times to the Present*, New York: Basic Books, 1976, p. 8.

11. Richard J. Evans, *The Pursuit of Power: Europe, 1815–1914*, New York: Viking, 2016, p. 352.

12. *The Statistical History of the United States*, p. 105.

13. U.S. Census Bureau, *Census of Population, 1850 to 2000*, https://www.census. gov/newsroom/pdf/cspan_fb_slides.pdf. "About two-thirds of immigrants between 1891 and 1920 came from southern, central, and eastern Europe . . ." Hopkins, *op. cit.*, p. 319. See also White, *op. cit.*, p. 706.

14. Kevin H. O'Rourke and Jeffrey G. Williamson, *Globalization and History: The Evolution of a Nineteenth-Century Atlantic Economy*, Cambridge, Massachusetts: The MIT Press, 1999, pp. 124, 127.

15.   *Ibid.*, pp. 159, 166.

16.   White, *op. cit.*, pp. 254, 315–316.

17.   John Taliaferro, *All the Glittering Prizes: The Life of John Hay, from Lincoln to Roosevelt*, New York: Simon & Schuster, 2013, pp. 461, 466–467; George C. Herring, *From Colony to Superpower: U.S. Foreign Relations Since 1776*, New York: Oxford University Press, 2008, pp. 252–253.

18.   John Pomfret, *The Beautiful Country and the Middle Kingdom: America and China, 1776 to the Present*, New York: Henry Holt and Company, 2016, pp. 71, 77–78, 82–83, 118.

19.   *Ibid.*, p. 118.

20.   Walter LaFeber, *The Clash: U.S.-Japanese Relations Throughout History*, New York: W.W. Norton and Company, 1997, pp. 88, 89, 97.

21.   *The Statistical History of the United States*, p. 224.

22.   "By 1913, American output was two and a half times that of the United Kingdom or Germany, four times that of France. Measured per person, American GDP surpassed that of the United Kingdom by 20 percent, France by 77, Germany by 86." David S. Landes, *The Wealth and Poverty of Nations: Why Some Are So Rich and Some So Poor*, New York: W.W. Norton, 1998, p. 307.

23.   Herring, *op. cit.*, p. 340.

24.   After 1873 "the sixty-five-month contraction was the longest in American history." White, *op. cit.*, p. 268.

25.   Jeffry A. Frieden, *Global Capitalism: Its Fall and Rise in the Twentieth Century*, New York: W.W. Norton, 2006, p. 61; LaFeber, *The American Search for Opportunity*, p. 23.

26.   Alan Greenspan and Adrian Wooldridge, *Capitalism in America: A History*, New York: The Penguin Press, 2018, pp. 45–47.

27.   "America's genius lay in three things that are rather more subtle than invention: making innovations more user friendly; producing companies that can commercialize these innovations; and developing techniques for running these companies successfully." *Ibid.*, p. 104.

28.   Daniel Walker Howe, *What Hath God Wrought: The Transformation of America, 1815–1848*, New York: Oxford University Press, 2007, p. 596. The Democratic Party, which had successfully opposed the Whig program, was dramatically weakened in national politics after 1861 because of the secession of the Southern states.

29.   Thomas L. Friedman and Michael Mandelbaum, *That Used to Be Us: How America Fell Behind in the World It Invented and How We Can Come Back*, New York: Farrar, Straus and Giroux, 2011, pp. 37–38.

30.   For Europeans in the years before World War I, "America started to emerge as the image of the future." Evans, *op. cit.*, p. 622.

31.   Landes, *op. cit.*, pp. 301–304.

32.   Greenspan and Wooldridge, *op. cit.*, p. 92. ". . . [N]ow, for the first time in history, even ordinary folk could aspire to ownership of those hard

goods—watches, clocks, bicycles, telephones, radios, domestic machines, above all, the automobile—that were seen in traditional societies as the appropriate privilege of the few." Landes, *op. cit.*, p. 307.

33. Douglas A. Irwin, *Clashing Over Commerce: A History of US Trade Policy*, Chicago: University of Chicago Press, 2017, pp. 7, 209, 211.

34. "The tariff was the most contentious political issue of the age." Herring, *op. cit.*, p. 288.

35. See p. 17.

36. The fact that high tariffs coincided with rapid growth does not necessarily mean that the first caused the second. Irwin, *op. cit.*, pp. 277–278.

37. Evans, *op. cit.*, p. 285.

38. Ronald Findlay and Kevin H. O'Rourke, *Power and Plenty: Trade, War, and the World Economy in the Second Millennium*, Princeton, New Jersey: Princeton University Press, 2007, pp. 378–383; O'Rourke and Williamson, *op. cit.*, Chapter 5.

39. "American exports reduced the cost of food in Europe faster than at any time since the Neolithic era." White, *op. cit.*, p. 220.

40. In 1895 total world trade was worth $8 billion. In 1913 the figure was $18 billion. Frieden, *op. cit.*, p. 19. On the three distinct eras of modern globalization see Michael Mandelbaum, *The Road to Global Prosperity*, New York: Simon & Schuster, 2014, pp. xv–xvi.

41. Irwin, *op. cit.*, p. 298.

42. "After 1874, [American] exports [of goods and commodities] surpassed imports every year except 1875, 1888, and 1893 until the turn downward after 1971." LaFeber, *The American Search for Opportunity*, p. 26.

43. Akira Iriye, *The Cambridge History of American Foreign Relations, Volume III: The Globalizing of America, 1913–1945*, New York: Cambridge University Press, 1993, pp. 13–14.

44. The gold standard became an important political issue because its operation favored holders of capital and disfavored labor and farmers. It was central to the 1896 presidential election. The Nebraskan William Jennings Bryan won the Democratic nomination for president through an impassioned denunciation of the gold standard at the nominating convention that became known as the "Cross of Gold" speech. Bryan lost the election to William McKinley and the United States did not finally abandon the gold standard until 1934. White, *op. cit.*, pp. 842–849.

45. In 1889 tariffs accounted for sixty percent of federal revenues. *Ibid.*, p. 631.

46. See p. 152.

47. See pp. 245-246 and 394-396.

48. "Until the late 1880s the United States was dealt with as a second-rate power." Ernest R. May, *Imperial Democracy: The Emergence of America as a Great Power*, New York: Harcourt Brace and World, 1961, p. 3.

49. "After the Civil War, not only had [the United States] demobilized the army but, more important, scrapped well over half its warships and

allowed the rest to rot." *Ibid.*, p. 7. At the beginning of the twentieth century "the U.S. Army had twenty-eight thousand soldiers at a time when Germany had more than half a million men under arms." White, *op. cit.*, p. 632.

50. "In 1913, only 213 people, including clerks, messengers, and manual laborers, worked for the State Department in Washington, while the entire force of American diplomatic and consular services abroad numbered fewer than 450." John A. Thompson, *A Sense of Power: The Roots of America's Global Role,* Ithaca, New York: Cornell University Press, 2015, p. 37.

51. This is the thesis of Fareed Zakaria, *From Wealth to Power: The Unusual Origins of America's World Role*, Princeton, New Jersey: Princeton University Press, 1998. See, for example, pp. 9, 11, 87–88. The absence of serious threats and the maintenance of a very small government are related. Military threats and actual armed conflict led to powerful governments in Europe, hence Charles Tilly's phrase "war made the state and the state made war." In the United States, war did not make the state. It was the felt need to respond to domestic problems that expanded the scope of the federal government. *Ibid.*, p. 95.

52. In 1856 the Congress passed a "Guano Law" empowering the president to take over islands rich in excrement from sea fowl and bats, which was thought to make good fertilizer. By 1880 fifty of them, almost all uninhabited volcanic islets, had come under American control. Dudden, *op. cit.*, p. 65. Under the same statute the United States took possession of Midway Atoll in 1867. "To the disappointment of the U.S. Navy, Midway proved unsuitable as a deep-water port, though the atoll would play a central strategic role in the Pacific war with Japan once airpower became a factor." Michael J. Green, *By More Than Providence: Grand Strategy and American Power in the Asia Pacific Since 1783*, New York: Columbia University Press, 2017, p. 62.

53. Dudden, *op. cit.*, p. 40

54. In Cook's first voyage he reached Australia and New Zealand.

55. At the time, Secretary of State Daniel Webster said that the United States was "more interested in the fate of the islands, and of their government, than any other nation can be; and this consideration induces the President to be quite willing to declare . . . that the Government of the Sandwich Islands ought to be respected; that no power ought either to take possession of the islands as a conquest, or for the purpose of colonization. . . ." Dudden, *op. cit.*, pp. 58–59.

56. *Ibid.*, pp. 62–63.

57. Herring, *op. cit.*, p. 306.

58. Dudden, *op. cit.*, pp. 67–68.

59. *Ibid.*, p. 65.

60. *Ibid.*, p. 65. The authoritative study of great-power relations in Samoa is Paul M. Kennedy, *The Samoa Tangle: A Study in Anglo-German-American Relations, 1878–1900*, Dublin: Irish University Press, 1974.

61. In the decades between the Civil War and the dawn of the twentieth century, "From Alaska to Hawaii and Samoa, the United States had safeguarded stepping stones across the Pacific. . . . It was an era of quiet power politics, if not outright expansion." Green, *op. cit.*, p. 73.

62. The United States was particularly active—and intrusive—in Cuba, Haiti, the Dominican Republic, and Panama. "The United States repeatedly dispatched warships and landed military forces in the Caribbean-Central America region in the nineteenth century, but after 1898 the pace quickened. Between 1898 and 1920 U.S. Marines entered Caribbean countries no fewer than twenty times." LaFeber, *The American Search for Opportunity*, p. 195.

63. Herring, *op. cit.*, p. 306.

64. *Ibid.*, p. 255; LaFeber, *The American Search for Opportunity*, pp. 62–63; Bemis, *op. cit.*, pp. 411–412.

65. Herring, *op. cit.*, p. 307.

66. Kori Schake, *Safe Passage: The Transition from British to American Hegemony*, Cambridge, Massachusetts: Harvard University Press, 2017, p. 158.

67. "Britain agreed to arbitrate once the United States accepted its conditions for arbitration. The two nations then imposed on an outraged Venezuela a treaty providing for arbitration and giving it no representation on the commission. Britain got much of what it wanted. . . ." *Ibid.*, p. 308. See also Zakaria, *op. cit.*, pp. 151–152.

68. Bemis, *op. cit.*, pp. 523–525; Schake, *op. cit.*, pp. 170–171.

69. https://www.ourdocuments.gov/doc.php?flash=false&doc=56&page=transcript

70. "Within a few years after this [Hay-Pauncefote] treaty Great Britain reduced her permanent garrisons in the West Indies and withdrew her principal naval forces from that area. She rather definitely acquiesced in the predominance of the United States in that part of the world. . . ." Bemis, *op. cit.*, p. 511.

71. David Cannadine, *Victorious Century: The United Kingdom, 1800–1906*, New York: Penguin Books, 2017, pp. 433–446. This is the subject of Aaron L. Friedberg, *The Weary Titan: Britain and the Experience of Relative Decline, 1895–1905*, Princeton, New Jersey: Princeton University Press, 1988.

72. Schake, *op. cit.*, pp. 163–164.

73. Cannadine, *op. cit.*, p. 479.

74. Supporters of tariffs sometimes invoked it, since British-made industrial products tended to be the main competitors of American-made ones. Hopkins, *op. cit.*, p. 294.

75. John Hay, the American ambassador in London from 1897 to 1898 and secretary of state from 1898 to 1905, was among the most prominent of them. Bradford Perkins, *The Great Rapprochement: England and the United States, 1895–1914*, New York: Atheneum, 1968, p. 87.

76. Richard Hofstader, *Social Darwinism in American Thought*, Boston: Beacon Press, 1955. First published, 1944, pp. 172, 179–180; Herring, *op. cit.*, p. 305.

77. Green, *op. cit.*, pp. 53–54.

78. Between 1787 and 1790 American ships made nine trading voyages there. *Ibid.*, p. 22.

79. Stephen R. Platt, *Imperial Twilight: The Opium War and the End of China's Last Golden Age*, New York: Alfred A. Knopf, 2018, pp. xvii–xxvii, 75.

80. The British did not go to war only for commercial reasons. Issues of prestige were at stake as well in the eyes of the government in London. *Ibid.*, pp. 403–404.

81. *Ibid.*, p. 426.

82. Pomfret, *op. cit.*, p. 17.

83. ". . . [A]lthough the China trade never comprised more than a small piece of America's overall commerce—in the early nineteenth century it represented only about 5 percent of U.S. foreign trade—the houses involved in it were few in number, and they were closely held by the families involved, so those Americans who managed to succeed in China were able to accumulate truly fabulous fortunes." Platt, *op. cit.*, p. 203.

84. See pp. 80-81.

85. The British called the American position "jackal diplomacy." Green, *op. cit.*, p. 23.

86. LaFeber, *The Clash*, pp. 20–23; Green, *op. cit.*, pp. 48–51; Herring, *op. cit.*, pp. 213–214.

87. On the Meiji Restoration see Marius B. Jansen, *The Making of Modern Japan*, Cambridge, Massachusetts: The Belknap Press of Harvard University Press, 2000, Chapters 11 and 12.

88. See pp. 151-152.

89. In addition, by the terms of the treaty, "Foreigners could travel anywhere. Christians were protected. Opium was legalized. And, most troubling to the Qing court, Britain and the rest of the Western world were allowed to station representatives in Beijing, implying that foreigners were equal in status to the Son of Heaven." Pomfret, *op. cit.*, p. 51.

90. *Ibid.*, pp. 62–65; LaFeber, *The American Age*, p. 81.

91. "By the 1880s every major Chinese city had at least one Protestant church. YMCAs and YWCAs spread across urban China." Pomfret, *op. cit.*, p. 93.

92. On the Taiping Rebellion see Jonathan D. Spence, *God's Chinese Son: The Taiping Heavenly Kingdom of Hong Xiuquan*, New York: W.W. Norton, 1996.

93. Green, *op. cit.*, p. 69.

94. "Within six months, the Japanese astonished not only the Chinese but the entire world as they utterly destroyed China's fleet and rolled over its armies in Korea, Manchuria, and China proper almost at will." Warren I. Cohen, *America's Response to China: A History of Sino-American Relations*, New York: Columbia University Press, Fourth Edition, 2000, p. 34.

95. Green, *op. cit.*, p. 69.

96. Herring, *op. cit.*, p. 330; LaFeber, *The American Age*, p. 200.

97. "By mid-1899, the Russians and Germans threatened to colonize and close off strategic areas of China." LaFeber, *The American Age*, p. 217.

98. Specifically, he asked for Most Favored Nation status throughout the country. *Ibid.*, pp. 220–224.

99. Herring, *op. cit.*, pp. 333–334.

100. Cohen, *op. cit.*, pp. 38–42; Taliaferro, *op. cit.*, pp. 357–360.

101. Green, *op. cit.*, p. 95.

102. Cohen, *op. cit.*, p. 42.

103. Some influential American figures did argue for territorial acquisitions in China. *Ibid.*, p. 49; Green, *op. cit.*, pp. 92, 93.

104. Taliaferro, *op. cit.*, p. 377.

105. The repression of the Boxers was a brutal, bloody affair that killed, by some estimates, 100,000 Chinese. Ian Kershaw, *To Hell and Back: Europe, 1914–1949*, New York: Penguin Press, 2015, p. 22.

106. LaFeber, *The American Search for Opportunity*, p. 77.

107. ". . . [T]he long-predicted carve-up of China never happened. The European powers had received a severe shock from the [Boxer] uprising. If this was the reaction provoked by the existence of mere treaty ports, what might happen if they tried to take over the whole country? Any further territorial advances seemed ill advised in the circumstances. In addition, two of the powers involved, Russia and Japan, were serious rivals for territorial gains in Manchuria . . . and a peaceful agreement between the two of them over partition was out of the question. . . ." Evans, *op. cit.*, p. 651.

108. The favorable American attitude to Japan was not unrelated to the fact that in the last decade of the nineteenth century the United States exported twice as much to Japan as to China. LaFeber, *The Clash*, p. 59.

109. The treaty provided for "trade on a most-favored-nation basis, the establishment of diplomatic relations, and, as in earlier treaties with China and Japan, extraterritoriality." Herring, *op. cit.*, p. 286.

110. The British, concerned about Russian designs in East Asia, signed a treaty of cooperation with Japan in 1902 that had an anti-Russian purpose. Cohen, *op. cit.*, p. 51. Some Americans did worry about potential challenges from Japan. LaFeber, *The American Search for Opportunity*, p. 102.

111. Thomas Jefferson, for example, expected the "empire of liberty" that he foresaw in North America to include Cuba. Howe, *op. cit.*, p. 703. John Quincy Adams anticipated that the island, once severed from Spain, "could 'gravitate only towards the North American union.'" Herring, *op. cit.*, p. 162. At the close of the Mexican War President Polk offered to purchase it (Bemis, *op. cit.*, p. 313), and in 1858 President James Buchanan urged Congress to appropriate funds for this purpose. LaFeber, *The American Age*, p. 144.

112. Between 1895 and 1898 an estimated 300,000 Cubans died in the uprising. Hopkins, *op. cit.*, p. 399.

113. LaFeber, *The American Search for Opportunity*, p. 131; Bemis, *op. cit.*, p. 442.

114. May, *op. cit.*, pp. 142, 146–147.

115. The slogan often continued "And to hell with Spain."

116. Between March 20 and 28 McKinley sent a series of demands to the Spanish government, which, however, it could not, in the judgment of one historian, have accepted and still remained in office. LaFeber, *The American Age*, pp. 201–202.

117. Herring, *op. cit.*, p. 316.

118. Warren Zimmerman, *First Great Triumph: How Five Americans Made Their Country a World Power*, New York: Farrar, Straus and Giroux, 2002, p. 274. The regiment "had a peculiar composition. Three-quarters of its soldiers were recruited in the Southwest, from Arizona, New Mexico, Oklahoma, and the Indian Territory. Many of the rest were seduced by Roosevelt from the upper-class precincts of Harvard, Yale, Princeton, and the Knickerbocker Club." *Ibid.*, p. 273.

119. May, *op. cit.*, p. 7; Green, *op. cit.*, p. 75.

120. LaFeber, *The American Search for Opportunity*, p. 145. The war left 2,900 Americans dead, 2,500 of whom died from disease. LaFeber, *The American Age*, p. 209.

121. Green, *op. cit.*, p. 86; May, *op. cit.*, p. 244.

122. See pp. 148-152.

123. "'There is, of course, little or no independence left Cuba under the Platt Amendment,' military governor Gen. Leonard Wood candidly conceded." Herring, *op. cit.*, p. 325. One of the bases the United States obtained, at Guantanamo Bay, remained in American hands 120 years later.

124. Hawaii had taken on increased strategic importance as an outpost in the Pacific with the acquisition of the Philippines. Green, *op. cit.*, p. 88. Still, McKinley annexed it with a simple majority vote in the Congress rather than seeking to do so by treaty, which would have required a two-thirds majority.

125. Hopkins, *op. cit.*, p. 400.

126. Cohen, *op. cit.*, p. 37. For a summary of the various explanations of American policy in 1898 see Ernest R. May, *American Imperialism: A Speculative Essay*, New York: Atheneum, 1968, Chapter 1.

127. Zimmerman, *op. cit.*, pp. 251, 262; Frank Freidel, "Dissent in the Spanish-American War and the Philippine Insurrection," in Samuel Eliot Morison, Frederick Merck, and Frank Freidel, *Dissent in Three American Wars*, Cambridge, Massachusetts: Harvard University Press, 1971, pp. 70, 72.

128. Herring, *op. cit.*, p. 311; LaFeber, *The American Age*, p. 198.

129. Herring, *op. cit.*, p. 266.

130. *Ibid.*, pp. 308–309.

131. This is a theme of Ronald Robinson and John Gallagher with Alice Denney, *Africa and the Victorians: The Climax of Imperialism*, Garden City, New York: Doubleday Anchor Books, 1968. First published, 1961.

132. Hopkins, *op. cit.*, p. 284; Evans, *op. cit.*, pp. 643–644; May, *American Imperialism*, p. 196.

133. The most influential such analyses were *Imperialism: The Highest Stage of Capitalism*, by V. I. Lenin, the future leader of the Bolshevik seizure of power in Russia in the wake of the collapse of the tsarist regime in 1917, published during World War I in 1916, and *Imperialism: A Study*, by the English economist J. A. Hobson (1902). For a critique of their theses and related ones see Benjamin J. Cohen, *The Question of Imperialism: The Political Economy of Dominance and Dependence*, New York: Basic Books, 1973.

134. Some Americans subscribed to the "glut" theory, according to which the country could not consume at home all that it produced, and therefore needed foreign markets. Herring, *op. cit.*, p. 270. An economic interpretation of American foreign policy in this period is a principal theme of LaFeber, *The American Search for Opportunity*, as well as other works by this author cited in this chapter.

135. Robert L. Beisner, *From the Old Diplomacy to the New, 1865–1900*, Wheeling, Illinois: Harlan Davidson Inc., 1986, p. 21; Hopkins, *op. cit.*, pp. 358–359, 380; Thompson, *op. cit.*, pp. 16, 19.

136. This is the argument of Hopkins, *op. cit.*, pp. 338–339, 344.

137. Such conflict is a major theme of White, *op. cit.*

138. "The Spanish-American War was one of the most popular conflicts in American history. Every region supported it—especially the south." David Hackett Fischer, *Albion's Seed: Four British Folkways in America*, New York: Oxford University Press, 1989, p. 866.

139. For twenty-first-century examples see Michael Mandelbaum, *The Rise and Fall of Peace on Earth*, New York: Oxford University Press, 2019.

140. Thompson, *op. cit.*, pp. 24, 26.

141. Hopkins, *op. cit.*, p. 508.

142. Walter Russell Mead, *Special Providence: American Foreign Policy and How It Changed the World*, New York: Alfred A. Knopf, 2001, pp. 39–44.

143. Hopkins, *op. cit.*, pp. 362–365, 378. This is a major theme of Zimmerman, *op. cit.*

144. New York: Hill and Wang, 1968.

145. On Mahan and his influence see Green, *op. cit.*, pp. 78–86.

146. Zimmerman, *op. cit.*, pp. 152, 185; Taliaferro, *op. cit.*, p. 342.

147. LaFeber, *The American Search for Opportunity*, p. 149; Hopkins, *op. cit.*, p. 416.

148. Quoted in Dudden, *op. cit.*, p. 84.

149. ". . . [F]ew believe [McKinley's statement] to be the full story or even the true story. . . ." *Ibid.*. p. 84. "The enigma of McKinley's personality makes it exceedingly hard to plumb the motives beneath his policies." May, *Imperial Democracy*, p. 114.

150. Green, *op. cit.*, p. 5.

151. "In 1901 U.S. troops captured [Filipino rebel leader Emilio] Aguinaldo. The back of the revolt was broken, although fighting continued at reduced levels until 1913." LaFeber, *The American Age*, p. 217.

152. *Ibid.*, p. 215.

153. Bemis, *op. cit.*, p. 471.

154. May, *American Imperialism*, p. 201; Thompson, *op. cit.*, p. 41; Hopkins, *op. cit.*, p. 367.

155. Objections to annexation also rested on racial and religious grounds, by both of which criteria the Filipinos were deemed undesirable. Herring, *op. cit.*, p. 323.

156. The "great debate" over imperialism is summarized in *ibid.*, p. 322.

157. Friedel, *op. cit.*, p. 82.

158. LaFeber, *The American Age*, p. 226.

159. Bemis, *op. cit.*, p. 475.

160. Mahan defined imperialism as "the extension of national authority over alien communities." Zimmerman, *op. cit.*, p. 13.

161. "The United States did not want to join the European and Japanese quest for landed, colonial empire. American officials wanted only scattered, relatively small areas of land to serve as bases for their necessary commercial expansionism." LaFeber, *The American Quest for Opportunity*, p. 238.

162. May, *American Imperialism*, p. 14; Hopkins, *op. cit.*, p. 610.

163. Green, *op. cit.*, p. 91.

164. Schake, *op. cit.*, p. 174.

165. Dudden, *op. cit.*, p. 92; Hopkins, *op. cit.*, pp. 627–628.

166. See p. 292.

167. Hopkins, *op. cit.*, p. 659.

168. May, *Imperial Democracy*, p. 264.

169.   Quoted in LaFeber, *The American Search for Opportunity*, p. 178. In 1902 Woodrow Wilson wrote, "No war ever transformed us quite as the war with Spain transformed us. . . . The nation has stepped forth into the open arena of the world." Quoted in Herring, *op. cit.*, p. 335.

170.   ". . . [T]he United States had not witnessed such a conflict [between Roosevelt's and Wilson's views on foreign policy] since the days of Jefferson and Hamilton." John Milton Cooper Jr., *The Warrior and the Priest: Woodrow Wilson and Theodore Roosevelt*, Cambridge, Massachusetts: The Belknap Press of Harvard University Press, 1983, p. xiii.

171.   "Hamilton became a Republican Party icon after the triumph of the Union in the Civil War and the darling of Theodore Roosevelt, Henry Cabot Lodge, and other proponents of an assertive, martial foreign policy at the turn of the century." John Lamberton Harper, *American Machiavelli: Alexander Hamilton and the Origins of U.S. Foreign Policy*, New York: Cambridge University Press, 2004, p. 1. Lodge wrote an admiring biography of Hamilton. Zimmerman, *op. cit.*, p. 164.

172.   "In foreign affairs Roosevelt often did welcome strife, and he frequently stressed practical limitations on diplomatic commitments. By the same token, Wilson did strive to reform international affairs in a more peaceful direction, and he justified his policies with exalted rhetoric that appealed to moral and religious values." Cooper, *op. cit.*, p. xiv.

173.   *Ibid..*, pp. 6, 15.

174.   The third major candidate in that election was the Republican William Howard Taft, who had succeeded Roosevelt as president in 1908. On the 1912 election see James Chace, *1912: Wilson, Roosevelt, Taft & Debs—the Election That Changed the Country*, New York: Simon & Schuster, 2004.

175.   Perkins, *op. cit.*, pp. 289, 290.

176.   LaFeber, *The American Age*, p. 235; Schake, *op. cit.*, p. 178; Cooper, *op. cit.*, pp. 210–211.

177.   Zakaria, *op. cit.*, p. 164.

178.   LaFeber, *The American Age*, p. 233. In 1898 Roosevelt, who had never seen combat, was more eager to go to war with Spain than was McKinley, who, perhaps not coincidentally, had fought in the Civil War. McKinley was the last veteran of that conflict to be president.

179.   Greg Russell, *The Statecraft of Theodore Roosevelt: The Duties of Nations and World Order*, Dordrecht, The Netherlands: Martinus Nijhoff Publishers, 2009, p. 57. ". . . Roosevelt accepted power as a legitimate, and the controlling, element in the relations among major nations. . . . [He] adroitly shifted weights to preserve in Europe and gain in Asia equilibriums tolerable to the United States." John Morton Blum, *The Republican Roosevelt*, Cambridge, Massachusetts: Harvard University Press, 1967, pp. 132–133. " . . . Roosevelt saw world events and policies in terms of power. He was intrigued with power, with the problems of

power, and with rivalries for power." Howard Beale, *Theodore Roosevelt and the Rise of America to World Power*, Baltimore: The Johns Hopkins Press, 1956, p. 449.

180. This was a principal aim of Wilson's policy toward Mexico. See pp. 153-154.

181. See pp. 175-177. Accepting the Nobel Peace Prize in 1906, Roosevelt advocated an "international posse comitatus." Blum, *op. cit.*, p. 137. But what he intended was a far cry from what Wilson had in mind for the League of Nations. " . . . [T]o Roosevelt's way of thinking, international institutions could never provide an alternative to traditional methods of diplomacy." Russell, *op. cit.*, p. xiv.

182. "In world affairs Theodore Roosevelt became the first president to act self-consciously as the leader of a great power, and he was a tireless evangelist for international activism." Cooper, *op. cit.*, p. xii.

183. Herring, *op. cit.*, pp. 348–349.

184. *Ibid.*, p. 349.

185. Hopkins, *op. cit.*, p. 382.

186. LaFeber, *The American Search for Opportunity*, p. 198. Roosevelt disavowed any interest in annexing the Dominican Republic, as the United States had the Philippines. "As for annexing the island, I have about the same desire to annex it as a gorged boa constrictor might have to swallow a porcupine wrong-end-to." *Ibid.*

187. Blum, *op. cit.*, p. 129.

188. Herring, *op. cit.*, pp. 367–369. "Roosevelt did not bother to consult with Congress while he negotiated with the Nicaraguans and then the Colombians, incited Panama to revolt, recognized the new country, and finally drew up a new treaty." Zakaria, *op. cit.*, p. 168.

189. Herring, *op. cit.*, p. 360.

190. *Ibid.*, p. 361.

191. In 1910 Japan formally annexed Korea, which it had dominated since defeating China in 1895. LaFeber, *The Clash*, p. 96.

192. Herring, *op. cit.*, p. 362; Perkins, *op. cit.*, p. 229.

193. Herring, *op. cit.*, p. 362; Pomfret, *op. cit.*, p. 125.

194. "[Algeciras] was not an important accomplishment and the American part was not decisive." Zimmerman, *op. cit.*, p. 473. See also Blum, *op. cit.*, pp. 133–134.

195. Emily S. Rosenberg, *Financial Missionaries to the World: The Politics and Culture of Dollar Diplomacy, 1900–1930*, Cambridge, Massachusetts: Harvard University Press, 1999, pp. 1–2; Herring, *op. cit.*, pp. 372–373.

196. Cohen, *op. cit.*, pp. 64–65; LaFeber, *Clash*, p. 93.

197. In China, dollar diplomacy "failed utterly." Green, *op. cit.*, p. 122.

198. Cohen, *op. cit.*, p. 71.

199. Jan Willem Schulte Nordholt, *Woodrow Wilson: A Life for World Peace*, Translated by Herbert H. Rowen, Berkeley, California: University of California Press, 1991, p. 116.

200. A historian of both Roosevelt and Wilson noted "the resemblance between Wilson's initial diplomatic behavior in 1913 and 1914 and Roosevelt's more than a decade earlier." Cooper, *op. cit.*, p. 266.

201. Patricia O'Toole, *The Moralist: Woodrow Wilson and the World He Made*, New York: Simon & Schuster, 2018, p. 91. "Determined to help other peoples become democratic and orderly, Wilson himself became the greatest military interventionist in U.S. history. By the time he left office in 1921, he had ordered troops into . . . half a dozen Latin American upheavals. To preserve order in some countries, Wilson learned, required military intervention." LaFeber, *The American Age*, p. 277.

202. "By 1910, as the Mexican Revolution was about to erupt, U.S. citizens owned 43 percent of the country's property, or more than did Mexicans." LaFeber, *The American Search for Opportunity*, p. 68.

203. Herring, *op. cit.*, p. 391. "The United States traditionally had recognized governments based simply on whether they held power and fulfilled their international obligations. With Mexico, Wilson introduced a moral and political test." *Ibid.* See also Bemis, *op. cit.*, pp. 546–547.

204. Wilson asked the Congress to approve the use of American forces in Mexico to obtain "the fullest recognition of the rights and dignity of the United States." Nell Irvin Painter, *Standing at Armageddon: The United States, 1877–1919*, New York: W.W. Norton and Company, 1987, p. 291.

205. The occupation turned into a mini-exercise in nation-building. The American military government "built roads and drainage ditches; provided electric light for streets and public buildings; reopened schools; cracked down on youth crime, gambling, and prostitution; made tax and customs collection more equitable, efficient, and lucrative for the government; and developed sanitation and public health programs. . . ." Herring, *op. cit.*, p. 394. These efforts had no lasting effect. ". . . [W]ithin weeks after the marines left it was hard to tell that Americans had been in Veracruz." *Ibid.*

206. *Ibid.*, p. 395; Bemis, *op. cit.*, p. 551.

207. Herring, *op. cit.*, pp. 394–396; Bemis, *op. cit.*, pp. 552–553.

Chapter 5

1. The literature on the origins of World War I is vast. For a relatively brief overview of the outbreak of the war see Richard Evans, *The Pursuit of Power: Europe 1815–1914*, New York: Viking, 2016, pp. 704–713.

2. An estimated twenty million people died as the direct result of World War I, approximately half of them military personnel and half civilian.

3. John Thompson, *A Sense of Power: The Roots of America's Global Role*, Ithaca, New York: Cornell University Press, 2015, p. 58.

4. See pp. 50-51, 52.
5. George C. Herring, *From Colony to Superpower: U.S. Foreign Relations Since 1776*, New York: Oxford University Press, 2008, pp. 406–407.
6. Thompson, *op. cit.*, p. 59.
7. Herring, *op. cit.*, p. 399.
8. Bradford Perkins, *The Great Rapprochement: England and the United States, 1895–1914*, New York: Atheneum, 1968, pp. 306–307.
9. Akira Iriye, *The Cambridge History of American Foreign Relations, Volume III: The Globalizing of America, 1913–1945*, New York: Cambridge University Press, 1993, pp. 23–24.
10. Walter LaFeber, *The American Age: U.S. Foreign Policy at Home and Abroad, 1750 to the Present*, New York: Viking, 1994, p. 285.
11. John Milton Cooper Jr., *Woodrow Wilson: A Biography*, New York: Alfred A. Knopf, 2009, p. 268.
12. Robert W. Tucker, *Woodrow Wilson and the Great War: Reconsidering America's Neutrality, 1914–1917*, Charlottesville, Virginia: University of Virginia Press, 2007, pp. x, 80.
13. *Ibid.*, pp. 6, 8, 205; Thompson, *op. cit.*, pp. 63, 72; Herring, *op. cit.*, p. 399.
14. See p. 66.
15. Tucker, *op. cit.*, pp. x–xi.
16. Herring, *op. cit.*, p. 399.
17. "Before the war, 63 percent of American exports went to countries that would be Entente allies; during the war, that proportion grew to 89 percent." Kori Schake, *Safe Passage: The Transition from British to American Hegemony*, Cambridge, Massachusetts: Harvard University Press, 2017, p. 220.
18. " . . . by the autumn of 1916 almost 40 percent of the British Treasury's war spending was in North America." John A. Thompson, *Woodrow Wilson*, London: Longman, 2002, p. 2. "Altogether some $2.2 billion of arms were sold by the United States to Britain and its allies between August 1914 and March 1917, the period of American neutrality, a considerable sum when one recalls that the export of U.S. merchandise in 1913 had amounted to a little over $2.4 billion." Iriye, *op. cit.*, p. 25.
19. "The allies, with their stronger links to U.S. banks, borrowed $2.5 billion over the next two years [from mid-1915]. . . . The Central Powers received less than one-tenth that amount." LaFeber, *op. cit.*, p. 289.
20. Samuel Flagg Bemis, *A Diplomatic History of the United States*, New York: Henry Holt and Company, Fourth Edition, 1955, pp. 596–600; Tucker, *op. cit.*, p. 140, 211; Thompson, *A Sense of Power*, p. 62.
21. Herring, *op. cit.*, p. 502. "The severity of the note and the warning it held out were striking." Tucker, *op. cit.*, p. 95. "Of all the decisions that the American government made [during the period of neutrality] . . . the most momentous was its unyielding stand against submarine warfare." Thompson, *A Sense of Power*, p. 107.

22. The ship had been carrying munitions for Britain. Herring, *op. cit.*, p. 403.

23. "In the history of American neutrality in World War I, the sinking of the *Lusitania* stands out as the critical event. Its impact was immediate and profound, and although the shock and outrage over the sinking moderated with the passage of time, the effects of the event were to prove lasting." Tucker, *op. cit.*, p. 108.

24. Thompson, *A Sense of Power*, p. 68.

25. Hew Strachan, *The First World War*, New York: The Penguin Press, 2005, p. 225.

26. Herring, *op. cit.*, p. 403; Tucker, *op. cit.*, p. 20.

27. Thompson, *A Sense of Power*, p. 71.

28. The House-Grey memorandum recorded the two men's understanding that President Wilson "was ready, on hearing from France and England that the moment was opportune, to propose that a conference should be summoned to put an end to the war. Should the Allies accept this proposal, and should Germany refuse it, the United States would enter the war against Germany." Quoted in Louis Auchincloss, *Woodrow Wilson*, New York: Viking, 2000, p. 70. Upon being shown the memo Wilson said that it should read "would *probably* enter the war" (emphasis added). The French and the British, for various reasons, did not follow through on this offer. Tucker, *op. cit.*, p. 171.

29. Herring, *op. cit.*, p. 403. This promise was, however, "conditioned on America's persuading the Allies to give up their blockade, which was intended to starve Germany into submission. If the United States did not, Germany would retain freedom of action." William E. Leuchtenburg, *The Perils of Prosperity, 1914–1932*, Chicago: The University of Chicago Press, Second Edition, 1993, pp. 18–19. See also Tucker, *op. cit.*, p. 126. The Allies did not give up the blockade.

30. Tucker, *op. cit.*, pp. 132–133.

31. The sources of tension are listed in Herring, *op. cit.*, p. 404. See also Thompson, *A Sense of Power*, p. 79. The Anglo-American relationship weathered the disputes because it rested "on foundations of mutual trust which had been built up in the *Oregon* and *Alabama* negotiations, in the secretaryships of Hay, Root, Balfour, and Landsdowne, in the intermarriages of families, the interchange of books and travelers, and the interplay of English and American reform movements." Ernest R. May, *The World War and American Neutrality, 1914–1917*, Cambridge, Massachusetts: Harvard University Press, 1963, p. 434.

32. May, *op. cit.*, p. 414. "The German naval leadership reckoned that U-boats could sink 600,000 tons of shipping a month—a rate that would force Britain to a state of collapse within five months, before the USA could make any difference to the outcome of the war." Ian Kershaw, *To Hell and Back: Europe 1914–1919*, New York: Viking, 2015, p. 54.

33. Herring, *op. cit.*, p. 409. The United States broke relations with Germany on February 3.

34. Bemis, *op. cit.*, pp. 612–614.

35. "Wilson even announced that Russia was a 'fit partner' because it had been 'always in fact democratic at heart.'" LaFeber, *op. cit.*, p. 296.

36. Tucker, *op. cit.*, p. 191.

37. *Ibid.*, pp. 2, 202; Thompson, *A Sense of Power*, p. 89. Wilson was also influenced by the thought that American participation in the war would gain the United States more power to shape the postwar settlement. Herring, *op. cit.*, p. 409; Thompson, *A Sense of Power*, p. 82; Thomas J. Knock, *To End All Wars: Woodrow Wilson and the Quest for a New World Order*, Princeton, New Jersey: Princeton University Press, 1992, p. 118.

38. Robert H. Zieger, *America's Great War: World War I and the American Experience*, Lanham, Maryland: Rowman & Littlefield Publishers, Inc., 2000, pp. 57, 58.

39. Nell Irvin Painter, *Standing at Armageddon: The United States, 1877–1919*, New York: W.W. Norton & Company, 1987, p. 331.

40. Robert D. Hormats, *The Price of Liberty: Paying for America's Wars*, New York: Times Books Henry Holt and Company, 2007, p. 125.

41. *Ibid.*, p. 115.

42. Alan Greenspan and Adrian Wooldridge, *Capitalism in America: A History*, New York: Penguin Press, 2018, p. 186.

43. Garrett Peck, *The Great War in America: World War I and Its Aftermath*, New York: Pegasus Books, 2018, p. 107.

44. David M. Kennedy, *Over Here: The First World War and American Society*, New York: Oxford University Press, 1980, pp. 128, 134–135; Peck, *op. cit.*, p. 108.

45. Zieger, *op. cit.*, p. 70.

46. During the war women entered the workforce in larger numbers than ever before. Leuchtenburg, *op. cit.*, p. 158.

47. Peck, *op. cit.*, p. 109.

48. "Symphony orchestras no longer dared to play German music, and the German language and German philosophy were struck from the curriculum of a number of colleges." Jan Willem Schulte Nordholt, *Woodrow Wilson: A Life for Peace*, Translated by Herbert H. Rowen, Berkeley, California: University of California Press, 1991, p. 235.

49. The law made it unlawful to "'cause or attempt to cause' insubordination or resistance in the armed forces or to obstruct recruiting or enlistment." Patricia O'Toole, *The Moralist: Woodrow Wilson and the World He Made*, New York: Simon & Schuster, 2018, p. 293.

50. *Ibid.*, pp. 293–294.

51. *Ibid.*, p. 300.

52. Ronald Steel, *Walter Lippmann and the American Century*, Boston: Little Brown and Company, 1980, pp. 166–167; Painter, *op. cit.*, p. 381; Leuchtenburg, *op. cit.*, pp. 77–78.

53. Knock, *op. cit.*, pp. 144–145.

54. Steel, *op. cit.*, pp. 130–131.

55. Wilson also entertained the hope that the proclamation of liberal war aims would persuade the German people to turn against their government. Steel, *op. cit.*, p. 134.

56. In this speech, given before the United States entered the war, Wilson called for "peace without victory." Thompson, *A Sense of Power*, pp. 76–77; John Milton Cooper, *The Warrior and the Priest: Woodrow Wilson and Theodore Roosevelt*, Cambridge, Massachusetts: The Belknap Press of Harvard University Press, 1983, pp. 312–313.

57. The Fourteen Points are reprinted in Margaret Macmillan, *Paris 1919: Six Months That Changed the World*, New York: Random House, 2001, pp. 495–496.

58. Steel, *op. cit.*, Chapter 11.

59. Point eight also called for the return to France of the provinces of Alsace and Lorraine, which Germany had conquered in the Franco-Prussian War of 1870–1871.

60. At the end of 1917, a full eight months after the United States had entered the war, only 175,000 American troops had arrived in Europe. Few of them had seen combat. Painter *op. cit.*, p. 340; O'Toole, *op. cit.*, p. 308.

61. In the spring of 1918, with Allied forces under pressure from a German offensive, Pershing relented and allowed American troops to fill out depleted European units. Peck, *op. cit.*, p. 164.

62. Zieger, *op. cit.*, p. 92.

63. A total of 10,000 Italians were killed, 30,000 wounded, and more than 250,000 taken prisoner. Peck, *op. cit.*, p. 155.

64. "Hoping to end the standoff on the Western Front, the French and the British launched massive offensives in the spring and summer [of 1917]. Their ground gains were negligible, their casualties appalling—in the range of 500,000." O'Toole, *op. cit.*, p. 302.

65. Zieger, *op. cit.*, p. 95.

66. The major American battles are described in *ibid.*, pp. 97–99. See also Peck, Chapter 6.

67. "In this vast battle, which grew out of the successful effort to thwart the German threat to Paris, [French Marshal Ferdinand] Foch disrupted German plans to renew its assaults north and east of the French capital." Zieger, *op. cit.*, p. 97.

68. "The Meuse-Argonne offensive struck at the Germans' main supply line and involved the largest number of American troops, and casualties, in any engagement the army ever fought—larger than the Battle of the Bulge in World War II." Cooper, *Woodrow Wilson*, p. 438.

69. Herring, *op. cit.*, p. 415.

70. Zieger, *op. cit.*, p. 108. By comparison, "Germany lost 1,800,000 men in the war, Russia 1,700,000, France 1,385,000, Austria-Hungary 1,200,000, and Britain 947,000." Leuchtenburg, *op. cit.*, p. 32. "The lethal influenza pandemic of the fall of 1918 rivaled battlefield action as a killer or incapacitator of soldiers. During the period of September-November 1918, almost 100,000 members of the AEF in France were afflicted. About 10 percent of these men died." Zieger, *op. cit.*, p. 109.

71. "Allies and foes alike attested to the verve, bravery, and enthusiasm of the [American] soldiers and Marines who fought in France." Zieger, *op. cit.*, p. 102.

72. "Although Pershing and his commanders believed that fresh and vigorous American troops could drive back even well-entrenched German veterans, the Meuse-Argonne battlefield soon proved otherwise. . . . Despite repeated frontal assaults, the troops of the First Army were soon stalled well short of their objectives." *Ibid.*, p. 100. See also Peck, *op. cit.*, pp. 186, 190, and Kennedy, *op. cit.*, pp. 173–175.

73. "By the end of 1918, there were over 180,000 foreign troops on Russian soil and several White Russian armies receiving Allied money and Allied guns." MacMillan, *op. cit.*, p. 71.

74. Bemis, *op. cit.*, pp. 686–687; N. Gordon Levin, *Woodrow Wilson and World Politics: America's Response to War and Revolution*, New York: Oxford University Press, 1968, p. 87; Herring, *op. cit.*, pp. 414–415; MacMillan, *op. cit.*, pp. 71, 73.

75. Herring, *op. cit.*, p. 418.

76. LaFeber, *op. cit.*, p. 318.

77. He was the first president to visit Europe while in office. MacMillan, *op. cit.*, p. 3.

78. Herring, *op. cit.*, p. 420.

79. The four—for a time they were three when Orlando temporarily withdrew from the conference in protest against what he considered the slighting of Italy's claims—met in 145 closed sessions in which they made the major decisions.

80. Steel, *op. cit.*, p. 164.

81. Herring, *op. cit.*, p. 419; Thompson, *Woodrow Wilson*, p. 212.

82. Herring, *op. cit.*, p. 420. In fact, the Allies had leverage over Wilson in that they had the power to block the kind of settlement he had promised and in the prospect of which he had invested so much of his personal prestige and political capital. Thompson, *A Sense of Power*, p. 95.

83. Thompson, *Woodrow Wilson*, p. 192; Hajo Holborn, *The Political Collapse of Europe*, New York: Alfred A. Knopf, 1963, p. 100. Wilson was further weakened by the results of the November 1918 national election in the United States, which returned Republican majorities in both houses of Congress.

84. Thus Henry Kissinger gave his 1957 book on the Congress of Vienna the title *A World Restored.*

85. LaFeber, *op. cit.*, p. 316.

86. The economic aspect of the case for generosity toward Germany received notable expression in John Maynard Keynes's widely influential book *The Economic Consequences of the Peace*, published in 1920.

87. Iriye, *op. cit.*, p. 64; MacMillan, *op. cit.*, p. 188.

88. MacMillan, *op. cit.*, p. 189; Thompson, *Woodrow Wilson*, p. 196.

89. Thompson, *A Sense of Power*, p. 91; Holborn, *op. cit.*, p. 95. On the disintegration of the Austro-Hungarian state during World War I see Lewis Namier, "The Downfall of the Habsburg Monarchy," in Namier, *Vanished Supremacies: Essays on European History, 1812–1918*, New York and Evanston, Illinois: Harper Torchbooks, 1958, pp. 122–164.

90. The new states were Finland, Estonia, Latvia, Lithuania, Czechoslovakia, Yugoslavia, Poland, Austria, Hungary, and Turkey. Kershaw, *op. cit.*, pp. 114, 122.

91. Nordholt, *op. cit.*, p. 261.

92. A number of these new countries signed treaties protecting minority rights, which proved at best inconsistently effective. Zara Steiner, *The Lights That Failed: European International History, 1919–1933*, Oxford, UK: Oxford University Press, 2005, p. 607.

93. The treaties with each of the defeated powers were signed in different suburbs of the French capital: besides Sevres with Turkey, Saint-Germaine-en-Laye with Austria, Neuilly-sur-Seine with Bulgaria, Versailles with Germany, and Trianon with Hungary.

94. MacMillan, *op. cit.*, Chapter 29.

95. Lausanne was (and is) a city in Switzerland, not a suburb of Paris.

96. Germany lost thirteen percent of its territory and ten percent of its population. MacMillan, *op. cit.*, p. 465.

97. MacMillan, *op. cit.*, pp. 216, 236. Wilson's Fourteen Points included a promise that a reconstituted Poland would have access to the sea, which gave it territory that included ethnic Germans.

98. *Ibid.*, pp. 69–71. Wilson authorized an attempt to open talks with Lenin's revolutionary government, which went nowhere. LaFeber, *op. cit.*, p. 319.

99. In 1915 Japan had presented China with its "21 Demands," which "sought mainly to legitimize gains made at Germany's expense and expand Japanese influence in Manchuria and along the coast." Herring, *op. cit.*, p. 384. The Chinese government appealed to the United States for assistance in resisting these demands, but the American government did little to support China. *Ibid.*, p. 385; Iriye, *op. cit.*, pp. 31–34.

100. Wilson made the concession to Japan in order to win Japanese membership in the League of Nations, the element of the peace settlement to which he gave the highest priority. In the Nine-Power Treaty of 1922, Japan relinquished Shantung to China. Japan proposed a

clause for the League of Nations charter calling for racial equality. It was not adopted.

101. "The struggle for independence became internationalized and Wilson its unwitting champion. Oppressed people across the world looked to Paris for realization of their aspirations. Failure of the peacemakers even to acknowledge their demands naturally sparked widespread disillusion and anger. Mass protests erupted in India, Egypt, Korea and China, among other places." Herring, *op. cit.*, p. 426.

102. "The mandate system proved little more than annexation in disguise." *Ibid.*, p. 421.

103. Thompson, *A Sense of Power*, p. 104.

104. See p. 170.

105. MacMillan, *op. cit.*, pp. 482, 493.

106. See pp. 182-183, 186-187.

107. The League had forty-three founding members and a further twenty-one countries joined it between 1920 and 1937.

108. Because the United States did not join the League, the Council had four permanent members.

109. After World War II the International Labor Organization became a specialized agency of the United Nations and continues in existence in the present.

110. Greg Russell, *The Statecraft of Theodore Roosevelt: The Duties of Nations and World Order*, Dordrecht, The Netherlands: Martinus Nijhoff Publishers, 2009, p. 162; Bemis, *op. cit.*, p. 646; Herring, *op. cit.*, p. 406.

111. Thompson, *A Sense of Power*, p. 96.

112. Herring, *op. cit.*, p. 423; MacMillan, *op. cit.*, p. 85; LaFeber, *op. cit.*, p. 320.

113. The reservations are set out in Bemis, *op. cit.*, p. 653.

114. Thompson, *A Sense of Power*, p. 99.

115. Lodge wrote to Theodore Roosevelt, "I never expected to hate anyone in politics with the hatred I feel towards Wilson." Quoted in Auchincloss, *op. cit.*, p. 108.

116. Herring, *op. cit.*, p. 433.

117. Thompson, *A Sense of Power*, p. 102.

118. Wilson told the Senate Foreign Relations Committee that the United States "would willingly relinquish some of its sovereignty . . . for the good of the world." Knock, *op. cit.*, p. 233. Taken to its logical conclusion, what Article X implied would have changed the structure of the international system from anarchy to hierarchy, a transformation that sovereign states have never been willing to permit.

119. Thompson, *Woodrow Wilson*, p. 223.

120. The text of the reservation said that "The United States assumes no obligation to preserve the territorial integrity or political independence of any other country or to interfere in controversies between

nations—whether members of the League or not—under the provisions of Article X, or to employ the military or naval forces of the United States under any article of the treaty for any purpose, unless in any particular case the Congress, which under the Constitution has the sole power to declare war or authorize the employment of the military or naval forces of the United States, shall by act or joint resolution so provide." Quoted in Thompson, *Woodrow Wilson*, p. 234.

121. It counted against the reservation that the uncertainty of American support that it fostered would weaken the power of the League to deter aggression. William Widenor, *Henry Cabot Lodge and the Search for an American Foreign Policy*, Berkeley, California: University of California Press, 1880, p. 339; Thompson, *A Sense of Power*, pp. 99–100.

122. Thompson, *A Sense of Power*, pp. 100, 101; Widenor, *op. cit.*, pp. 286, 297, 331; Cooper, *The Warrior and the Priest*, pp. 332, 333; Holborn, *op. cit.*, pp. 115–117.

123. "The bilateral treaty guaranteeing French security was never even reported out of the Foreign Relations Committee." Thompson, *A Sense of Power*, p. 101. See also Leuchtenburg, *op. cit.*, p. 63, and Cooper, *The Warrior and the Priest*, p. 343.

124. "In the history of America's encounter with the world Woodrow Wilson is the central figure." Tucker, *op. cit.*, p. ix. "Wilson towers above the landscape of modern American foreign policy like no other individual, the dominant personality, the seminal figure." Herring, *op. cit.*, p. 379.

125. LaFeber, *op. cit.*, p. 269.

126. Lansing once said of him that "entrenched within the White House, he was impregnable in his self-righteousness and imprisoned within his own certainties." Quoted in Auchincloss, *op. cit.*, p. 113. "Wilson's unwillingness to seek advice, his disinclination to hear what was unwelcome to him, and even more, his penchant for taking an immediate dislike to those who told him what he did not wish to hear were traits recognized by all who served him." Tucker, *op. cit.*, p. 21.

127. Walter McDougall, *The Tragedy of U.S. Foreign Policy: How America's Civil Religion Betrayed the National Interest*, New Haven, Connecticut: Yale University Press, 2016, p. 174; Herring, *op. cit.*, pp. 467–468.

128. "In the 1920s the United States was more profoundly engaged in international matters than in any peacetime era in its history." Warren I. Cohen, *Empire Without Tears: America's Foreign Relations, 1921–1933*, New York: Alfred A. Knopf, 1987, p. xii.

129. Herring, *op. cit.*, p. 440; Leuchtenburg, *op. cit.*, pp. 104–105.

130. Melvyn Leffler, *The Elusive Quest: America's Pursuit of European Stability and French Security, 1919–1933*, Chapel Hill, North Carolina: The University of North Carolina Press, 1979, p. 363; Steiner, *op. cit.*, p. 621. Still, "at around 140,000 the U.S. Army's overall manpower remained

more than 50 percent greater than it had been before the war—and the officer corps was three times as large." Thompson, *A Sense of Power*, p. 115.

131. Herring, *op. cit.*, p. 450; Thompson, *A Sense of Power*, p. 112.
132. Herring, *op. cit.*, p. 472; Thompson, *A Sense of Power*, p. 113. Between 1924 and 1929 American investment in Latin America as a whole more than doubled. LaFeber, *op. cit.*, p. 357.
133. Cohen, *op. cit.*, pp. 72–74.
134. Thompson, *A Sense of Power*, pp. 120–121; Cohen, *op. cit.*, p. 92.
135. Belgian troops also took part in the occupation.
136. Herring, *op. cit.*, p. 458.
137. Locarno is a city in Switzerland.
138. Kershaw, *op. cit.*, p. 180; Steiner, *op. cit.*, pp. 395–404. The United States had helped to engineer the Dawes Plan, which adjusted Germany's financial obligations and paved the way for Locarno. See pp. 186-187.
139. LaFeber, *op. cit.*, p. 347; Steiner, *op. cit.*, pp. 572–574.
140. This is a major theme of Roger Dingman, *Power in the Pacific: The Origins of Naval Arms Limitation, 1914–1922*, Chicago: The University of Chicago Press, 1976. ". . . [P]olitics *within* the capitals of the three major naval nations, far more than international relationships among them, determined the character and assured the success of the first strategic arms limitation agreement in modern times." *Ibid.*, p. xii.
141. Cohen, *op. cit.*, pp. 46–47.
142. Dingman, *op. cit.*, p. 159; Herring, *op. cit.*, p. 452.
143. On Japan see Dingman, *op. cit.*, Chapter 11.
144. Bemis, *op. cit.*, p. 690.
145. Thompson, *A Sense of Power*, p. 113.
146. The ratio among the United States, Britain, and Japan was 5:5:3. A clause of the treaty stipulated that the three would not fortify their bases on the islands they controlled or build new ones. Cohen, *op. cit.*, p. 52. The signatories also promised not to build more capital ships for ten years. Schake, *op. cit.*, p. 236.
147. The Four-Power Treaty superseded the Anglo-Japanese Treaty of 1902. The United States disliked it and the British wanted to conciliate the Americans.
148. See p. 137. By the terms of the treaty Japan relinquished its control of Shantung, which the Paris Peace Conference had ratified. Cohen, *op. cit.*, p. 53.
149. See pp. 317-320.
150. Steiner, *op. cit.*, pp. 588–591.
151. The Qing Dynasty had been established in the seventeenth century by Manchus, who were ethnically distinct from the Han Chinese. The Manchus had conquered all of the country and overthrown the ethnically Han Ming Dynasty.

152. Herring, *op. cit.*, p. 486.

153. Chiang's campaign involved "encouraging Chinese to emigrate to Manchuria, pushing boycotts of Japanese goods, and urging local warlords to construct a railroad line parallel to the Japanese-controlled South Manchurian Railway." Herring, *op. cit.*, p. 488.

154. "Eventually, seventy thousand Japanese troops entered Shanghai. Planes and naval vessels bombarded parts of the city, causing extensive civilian casualties and foreshadowing the carnage that would be inflicted on civilians over the next decade." *Ibid.*, p. 490.

155. On the Manchurian episode and the American response to it see Herring, *op. cit.*, pp. 486–490; Cohen, *op. cit.*, pp. 107–116; and Steiner, *op. cit.*, Chapter 13.

156. Steiner, *op. cit.*, pp. 719–720.

157. Alan Greenspan and Adrian Wooldridge, *Capitalism in America: A History*, New York: Penguin Press, 2018, p. 192.

158. *Ibid.*, p. 194.

159. John Steele Gordon, *An Empire of Wealth: The Epic History of American Economic Power*, New York: HarperCollins, 2004, p. 299.

160. Leuchtenburg, *op. cit.*, p. 108. See also *ibid.*, p. 194.

161. Greenspan and Wooldridge, *op. cit.*, p. 205. Some of these industries had begun before the war. Iriye, *op. cit.*, p. 112.

162. Greenspan and Wooldridge, *op. cit.*, p. 200. For a detailed analysis of the consequences of these two industries see Robert J. Gordon, *The Rise and Fall of American Growth: The U.S. Standard of Living Since the Civil War*, Princeton, New Jersey: Princeton University Press, 2016, Chapters 4 and 5.

163. Greenspan and Wooldridge, *op. cit.*, p. 196.

164. "Without the new automobile industry, the prosperity of the Roaring Twenties would scarcely have been possible: the development of the industry in a single generation was the greatest achievement of modern technology." Leuchtenburg, *op. cit.*, p. 185.

165. Greenspan and Wooldridge, *op. cit.*, p. 202. "The ever increasing use of electricity in the United States is one of the wonders of the twentieth century. In 1902 the United States used 6 billion kilowatt-hours of electricity, about 79 kilowatt-hours per person. In 1929 it was 118 billion, and 960 kilowatt-hours per person, well over ten times as much per capita. Today [2004] usage is a staggering 3.9 *trillion* kilowatt-hours, more than 13,500 per person, more than 170 times as much electricity as was used per person in 1902." Gordon, *op. cit.*, p. 307.

166. Douglas A. Irwin, *Clashing Over Commerce: A History of U.S. Trade Policy*, Chicago: University of Chicago Press, 20017, pp. 352–356.

167. Iriye, *op. cit.*, p. 96.

168. Hormats, *op. cit.*, p. 130.

169. " . . . [T]he foreign loans floated in the United States between 1919 and 1929 amounted to more than that provided by all other capital-exporting nations combined." Thompson, *A Sense of Power*, p. 123.

170. Cohen, *op. cit.*, pp. 38–39. "By 1930, U.S. direct investment exceeded that of France, Holland, and Germany combined." Herring, *op. cit.*, p. 447.

171. Herring, *op. cit.*, p. 450.

172. " . . . [T]he American government, in the course of the world war, had undertaken the role of international lender on an unprecedented scale, which role required it to become involved in the financial affairs of Europe to an unprecedented extent." Cohen, *op. cit.*, p. 21.

173. Herring, *op. cit.*, p. 461.

174. Iriye, *op. cit.*, p. 89.

175. American tariffs did not help matters in Europe. By limiting what the Europeans could sell in the United States they restricted the dollars the European countries could earn to service their debts. Thompson, *A Sense of Power*, p. 116; Leuchtenburg, *op. cit.*, p. 109; LaFeber, *op. cit.*, p. 343.

176. "[Between 1925 and 1929] American banks pumped nearly $1.25 billion of loans into Germany and . . . granted billions more in short-term credits. Americans directly invested $200 million into German plants." LaFeber, *op. cit.*, p. 349.

177. Leuchtenburg, *op. cit.*, p. 111.

178. Steiner, *op. cit.*, p. 240.

179. Cohen, *op. cit.*, p. 33.

180. Steiner, *op. cit.*, p. 615.

181. Kershaw, *op. cit.*, p. 153.

182. Steiner, *op. cit.*, pp. 470–473. " . . . [President] Hoover and [Secretary of State] Stimson gave the scheme no more than lukewarm support." Herring, *op. cit.*, p. 481.

183. For a vivid fictional depiction of the experience of the crash for people heavily invested in the stock market see Upon Sinclair, *Between Two Worlds*, New York: Viking, 1941, Chapters 39 and 40.

184. "Between 1929 and 1933, 40 percent of the nation's banks (9,460) went bankrupt." Greenspan and Wooldridge, *op. cit.*, p. 234.

185. The European banking crisis began with the failure of the Creditanstalt Bank in Vienna in May 1931.

186. In the United States "[g]eneral economic activity declined from late 1929 to the first few months of 1933. By 1932, industrial production, real GDP, and prices had declined by 46 percent, 25 percent, and 24 percent, respectively, from their 1929 levels." Greenspan and Wooldridge, *op. cit.* p. 223.

187. On the causes of the Great Depression see, for example, Irwin, *op. cit.*, p. 397, and Greenspan and Wooldridge, *op. cit.*, pp. 226–237.

188. Barry Eichengreen, *Hall of Mirrors: The Great Depression, the Great Recession, and the Uses—and Misuses—of History*, New York: Oxford University Press, 2015, p. 2.

189. The United States passed the Smoot-Hawley Tariff in 1930. Irwin, *op. cit.*, pp. 371–394.

190. In addition to being in thrall to the wrong ideas, the American federal government lacked the instruments for fighting economic downturns that it would acquire during the course of the twentieth century. David M. Kennedy, *Freedom from Fear: The American People in Depression and War, 1929–1945*, New York: Oxford University Press, 1999, p. 57; Eichengreen, *op. cit.*, p. 155.

191. Steiner, *op. cit.*, p. 803.

192. This is the argument of Charles P. Kindleberger, *The World in Depression, 1929–1939*, Berkeley, California: University of California Press, 1973. ". . . the 1929 depression was so wide, so deep and so long because the international economic system was rendered unstable by British inability and United States unwillingness to assume responsibility for stabilizing it in three particulars: (a) maintaining a relatively open market for distress goods; (b) providing counter-cyclical long-term lending; and (c) discounting in crisis." *Ibid.*, pp. 291–292.

193. ". . . [F]or the world economy to be stabilized, there has to be a stabilizer, one stabilizer." *Ibid.*, p. 305.

194. John Steele Gordon, *op. cit.*, pp. 322–323. In fact, neither type of payment ever resumed.

Chapter 6

1. "He was a man of dauntless optimism, a trait that served him and the nation well during years of economic crisis and war." George C. Herring, *From Colony to Superpower: U.S. Foreign Relations Since 1776*, New York: Oxford University Press, 2008, p. 492..

2. On Roosevelt's style of administration, especially in foreign policy, see, *inter alia*, Robert Dallek, *Franklin D. Roosevelt and American Foreign Policy, 1932–1945*, New York: Oxford University Press, 1979, p. vii; Kent Roberts Greenfield, *American Strategy in World War II: A Reconsideration*, Baltimore: The Johns Hopkins Press, 1963, p. 76; John Lamberton Harper, *American Visions of Europe: Franklin D. Roosevelt, George F. Kennan, and Dean G. Acheson*, Cambridge, UK: Cambridge University Press, 1994, p. 12; and William L. O'Neill, *A Democracy at War: America's Fight at Home and Abroad*, New York: The Free Press, 1993, p. 98.

3. Michael Beschloss, *The Conquerors: Roosevelt, Truman, and the Destruction of Hitler's Germany, 1941–1945*, New York: Simon & Schuster, 2002, p. 88.

4. Quoted in Harper, *op. cit.*, p. 87.

5. Dallek, *op. cit.*, p. 3.

6. John A. Thompson, *A Sense of Power: The Roots of America's Global Role*, Ithaca, New York: Cornell University Press, 2015, pp. 146–147, 156. The second Roosevelt included Wilsonians in his government, if for no other reason than that they were well represented in his Democratic Party. The two most prominent of them were Secretary of State Cordell Hull and another State Department official, Sumner Welles, a personal friend of the president. Dallek, *op. cit.*, p. 421.

7. John Milton Cooper, *The Warrior and the Priest: Woodrow Wilson and Theodore Roosevelt*, Cambridge, Massachusetts: The Belknap Press of Harvard University Press, 1983, p. 360; Dallek, *op. cit.*, p. 16. According to Roosevelt's speechwriter and later biographer Robert Sherwood, "The tragedy of Wilson was always somewhere within the rim of his consciousness. . . . There was no motivating force in all of Roosevelt's wartime political policy stronger than the determination to prevent repetition of the same mistakes." Quoted in Thompson, *op. cit.*, p. 154.

8. Cooper, *op. cit.*, p. xii.

9. David Kennedy, *Freedom from Fear: The American People in Depression and War, 1929–1945*, New York: Oxford University Press, 1999, pp. 107, 157, 375, 388.

10. *Ibid.*, p. 155; Walter LaFeber, *The American Age: U.S. Foreign Policy at Home and Abroad, 1750 to the Present*, New York: W.W. Norton, Second Edition, 1994, p. 372.

11. ". . . [O]f all the people who have left a mark on U.S. [trade] policy, none has had a greater or more lasting impact than Cordell Hull." Douglas A. Irwin, *Clashing Over Commerce: A History of U.S. Trade Policy*, Chicago: The University of Chicago Press, 2017, p. 421.

12. Dallek, *op. cit.*, p. 92.

13. Irwin, *op. cit.*, pp. 8–9, 413.

14. *Ibid.*, pp. 427, 430.

15. Herring, *op. cit.*, p. 464.

16. LaFeber, *op. cit.*, p. 370.

17. Dallek, *op. cit.*, p. 86. See also p. 141.

18. Akira Iriye, *The Cambridge History of American Foreign Relations, Volume III: The Globalizing of America*, New York: Cambridge University Press, 1993, p. 147; Herring, *op. cit.*, p. 499.

19. Iriye, *op. cit.*, p. 161; LaFeber, *op. cit.*, p. 578.

20. Herring, *op. cit.*, pp. 556–561; Iriye, *op. cit.*, p. 195.

21. Samuel Flagg Bemis, *A Diplomatic History of the United States*, New York: Henry Holt and Company, Fourth Edition, 1955, p. 831.

22. It was sometimes called the "Anti-Comintern Pact."

23. "By 1938 most of fertile China, including the valleys of the Yellow and Yangtse rivers, was under Japanese occupation. Both the new capital of Nanking and the old capital of Peking fell to the invaders, and Chiang

Kai-shek, now head of government, withdrew into the interior, to Chungking on the headwaters of the Yangtse." John Keegan, *The Second World War*, New York: Penguin Books, 1990, p. 243.

24. ". . . [T]here was general agreement, at least until the late 1930s, that avoiding involvement in a major overseas war should be the supreme goal of U.S. foreign policy, trumping all others." Thompson, *op. cit.*, p. 135. See also Dallek, *op. cit.*, p. 97.

25. Walter A. McDougall, *Promised Land, Crusader State: The American Encounter with the World Since 1776*, Boston: Houghton Mifflin, 1997, p. 39; Herring, *op. cit.*, p. 502.

26. Kennedy, *op. cit.*, p. 386. "Public opinion polls in 1937 revealed that two-thirds of Americans had come to view entry into the war as a mistake. . . ." Thompson, *op. cit.*, p. 139.

27. Herring, *op. cit.*, pp. 502–503.

28. Thompson, *op. cit.*, p. 133.

29. LaFeber, *op. cit.*, pp. 384–385; Herring, *op. cit.*, p. 501.

30. In October 1937 he said that ". . . we cannot insure ourselves against the disastrous effects of war and the dangers of involvement . . . it [is] impossible for any nation completely to isolate itself from economic and political upheavals in the rest of the world." Quoted in Thompson, *op. cit.*, p. 145. In 1939 he warned members of the Senate Military Affairs Committee, "So soon as one nation dominates Europe, that nation will be able to turn to the world sphere. . . . That is why the safety of the Rhine frontier does necessarily interest us." Kennedy, *op. cit.*, p. 421.

31. "In the aftermath of the Munich settlement, he evidently concluded that Hitler was a 'wild man' whose word could not be trusted and whose limitless ambitions could only be checked by being firmly resisted by superior power." Thompson, *op. cit.*, p. 157.

32. Other considerations also restricted Roosevelt's scope for international activism. His felt need to devote his political capital to protecting his New Deal against conservative opposition was one. His political weakness after his Democratic Party suffered a setback in the 1938 midterm elections was another.

33. Peter Calvocoressi and Guy Wint, *Total War: Causes and Courses of the Second World War*, Harmondsworth, UK: Penguin Books, 1974, p. 71. Appeasement had an economic motivation as well. Ian Kershaw, *To Hell and Back: Europe 1914–1949*, New York: Viking, 2015, p. 321.

34. Dallek, *op. cit.*, p. 130; Thompson, *op. cit.*, p. 148.

35. ". . . [I]n his State of the Union Address in January 1939, Roosevelt openly made a general case for adopting 'methods short of war, but stronger and more effective than mere words, of bringing home to aggressor governments the aggregate sentiments of our own people.' " Quoted in Thompson, *op. cit.*, p. 159.

36. Iriye, *op. cit.*, p. 164; LaFeber, *op. cit.*, p. 389.

37. Thompson, *op. cit.*, pp. 157, 159.

38. Iriye, *op. cit.*, p. 162.

39. Taking advantage of the Nazi-Soviet Pact, in 1940 the Soviet Army occupied the three Baltic countries—Estonia, Latvia, and Lithuania— and attacked Finland.

40. The next year the Germans inflicted military defeats on the British in Norway, North Africa, and Crete.

41. Herring, *op. cit.*, pp. 519–520.

42. On this point see John Lukacs, *Five Days in London: May 1940*, New Haven, Connecticut: Yale University Press, 1999.

43. Gerhard Weinberg, *A World at Arms: A Global History of World War II*, Cambridge, UK: Cambridge University Press, 1994, p. 156; Rick Atkinson, *The Day of Battle: The War in Sicily and Italy, 1943–1944*, New York: Henry Holt and Company, p. 3.

44. See p. 159.

45. Quoted in Thompson, *op. cit.*, p. 165.

46. "Opinion polls in September and October [1939] showed that over 80 percent favored an Allied victory; a similar proportion held Germany, particularly Hitler, responsible for the war." *Ibid*. "While minority groups such as Irish, German, and Italian Americans harbored at least mild sympathies for the Axis, most Americans (84 percent in one poll) and especially the elites concerned about international issues favored an Allied victory." Herring, *op. cit.*, p. 518.

47. See p. 161.

48. Thompson, *op. cit.*, p. 155.

49. Kennedy, *op. cit.*, p. 455; Cooper, *op. cit.*, p. 351; Dallek, *op. cit.*, p. 250.

50. Kennedy, *op. cit.*, p. 463; LaFeber, *op. cit.*, p. 395.

51. "America First was an unwieldy coalition of strange bedfellows, businessmen, old progressives and leftists, and some strongly anti-Jewish groups." Herring, *op. cit.*, pp. 521–522. "The isolationists were strongest in the farming areas of the Midwest and West, and also in Roman Catholic and Lutheran churches, where Irish-Americans, Italian-Americans, and German-Americans worshiped." LaFeber, *op. cit.*, p. 393.

52. Quoted in Kennedy, *op. cit.*, pp. 468–469.

53. Thompson, *op. cit.*, p. 151.

54. *Ibid.*, p. 165; Dallek, *op. cit.*, p. 291.

55. LaFeber, *op. cit.*, p. 395; Herring, *op. cit.*, p. 524.

56. Thompson, *op. cit.*, p. 190.

57. Kennedy, *op. cit.*, pp. 459, 496.

58. *Ibid.*, pp. 469–475.

59. *Ibid.*, pp. 481–482; Thompson, *op. cit.*, p. 154.

60. Quoted in Kennedy, *op. cit.*, p. 496.

61. The statement of Wilsonian principles also responded to the decision to support the Soviet Union, with its decidedly illiberal political system,

in the wake of the German attack on it in June 1941. It was a way of reassuring Americans that their country's foreign policy still reflected its basic political principles. Dallek, *op. cit.*, p. 281.

62. *Ibid.*, p. 274.

63. Thompson, *op. cit.*, p. 189.

64. Kennedy, *op. cit.*, p. 505.

65. *Ibid.*, pp. 510–511; LaFeber, *op. cit.*, p. 398; Dallek, *op. cit.*, p. 275.

66. "Newspaper, public, and official opinion was uniformly opposed to any appeasement of Japan. In September [1941] for example, Roosevelt had learned that 67 percent of the public was ready to risk war with Japan to keep her from becoming more powerful." Dallek, *op. cit.*, p. 502. See also *ibid.*, p. 531; Herring, *op. cit.*, p. 530; and Thompson, *op. cit.*, p. 189.

67. Why did Hitler launch the attack with Britain unsubdued, thereby gratuitously adding to Germany's roster of enemies? "Obsessed by time racing against Germany's best chance of success in its great gamble for European, then world, domination, Hitler turned initial thinking on its head. The way to defeat Britain, he told his generals, was first to defeat the Soviet Union." Kershaw, *op. cit.*, p. 350.

68. On Barbarossa see Richard Overy, *Russia's War*, London: Allen Lane The Penguin Press, 1998, Chapter 3. "By February, 1942, of the 3.9 million soldiers captured up to then by the Germans, the vast majority, some 2.8 million were dead. At least a quarter million had been shot; the others died under the horrible conditions imposed on them by the Germans." Weinberg, *op. cit.*, p. 300.

69. Overy, *op. cit.*, p. 119.

70. "Churchill immediately declared in public the solidarity of Great Britain with the latest victim of German aggression." Weinberg, *op. cit.*, p. 283.

71. Weinberg, *op. cit.*, p. 243. On June 24, two days after Barbarossa began, Roosevelt said, "Of course we are going to give all the aid we possibly can to Russia." Quoted in Robert A. Divine, *The Reluctant Belligerent: American Entry into World War II*, New York: John Wiley & Sons, 1965, p. 123.

72. "Public opinion tended to reflect only a reluctant sympathy for the Soviet Union. In polls taken in late June and early July [1941], George Gallup found that over 70% of those questioned wanted to see Russia defeat Germany. But the ideological distrust of the Soviet Union still influenced many Americans. When asked if they favored the sending of war materials to Russia on the same basis that they were supplied to Britain, only 35% answered yes." Divine, *op. cit.*, p. 125.

73. Overy, *op. cit.*, p. 327. On the general American response to Barbarossa see Dallek, *op. cit.*, pp. 278 and 297, and Weinberg, *op. cit.*, p. 286.

74. Kennedy, *op. cit.*, p. 484.

75. On the negotiations see Weinberg, *op. cit.*, pp. 246–247, 257; Kennedy, *op. cit.*, pp. 508, 513–515; Thompson, *op. cit.*, p. 189; and Dallek, *op. cit.*, p. 302.

76. American officials considered a Japanese attack of some kind likely but "did not know where Japan planned to attack. They assumed that the strike would occur in Southeast Asia and on the large U.S. base in the Philippines." LaFeber, *op. cit.*, p. 403. For a slightly different view see Thompson, *op. cit.*, p. 193. For a rebuttal to the charge that Roosevelt knew the attack on Pearl Harbor was coming and deliberately did nothing to foil it see Ted Morgan, *FDR: A Biography*, New York: Simon and Schuster, 1985, pp. 619–622.

77. Kennedy, *op. cit.*, p. 522.

78. "Roosevelt later told Churchill and Stalin that if 'it had not been for the Japanese attack, he would have had great difficulty in getting the American people into the war.'" Dallek, *op. cit.*, p. 307.

79. The sole dissenter was Jeanette Rankin of Montana, a pacifist and the first woman elected to the House.

80. Kennedy, *op. cit.*, p. 616.

81. On Hitler's attitude toward the United States see John Lukacs, *The Hitler of History*, New York: Alfred A. Knopf, 1997, pp. 153–156.

82. In fact, two and one-half years elapsed between the German declaration of war and the American landings in France.

83. LaFeber, *op. cit.*, p. 418; Dallek, *op. cit.*, p. 324; Herring, *op. cit.*, pp. 570–572.

84. Benn Steil, *The Battle of Bretton Woods: John Maynard Keynes, Harry Dexter White, and the Making of a New World Order*, Princeton, New Jersey: Princeton University Press, 2013, pp. 14, 110, 115; Irwin, *op. cit.*, p. 459.

85. Robert Skidelsky, *John Maynard Keynes: Fighting for Freedom, 1937–1946*, New York: Viking, 2000, p. xxii; Walter A. McDougall, *The Tragedy of American Foreign Policy: How America's Civil Religion Betrayed the National Interest*, New Haven, Connecticut: Yale University Press, 2016, p. 209.

86. Kennedy, *op. cit.*, pp. 576–577, 701. American military leaders strongly opposed this strategy. *Ibid.*, p. 585. See also Dallek, *op. cit.*, p. 372; Keegan, *op. cit.*, pp. 312, 318; and Weinberg, *op. cit.*, p. 682.

87. Rick Atkinson, *The Guns at Last Light: The War in Western Europe, 1944–1945*, New York: Henry Holt and Company, 2013, p. 35.

88. Dallek, *op. cit.*, pp. 378–379, 459–462, 538; LaFeber, *op. cit.*, p. 421; Smith, *op. cit.*, p. 15; Harper, *op. cit.*, p. 113; John Morton Blum, *V Was for Victory: Politics and American Culture During World War II*, New York: Harcourt Brace Jovanovich, 1976, p. 258.

89. Roosevelt cabled Churchill in early 1942 that "I know you won't mind my being brutally frank when I tell you that I think I can personally handle Stalin better than either your Foreign Office or my State Department. Stalin hates the guts of all your top people [including you?]. He thinks he likes me better and I hope he will continue to do so." Quoted in Harper, *op. cit.*, p. 82 note 17.

90. Dallek, *op. cit.*, p. 338; Harper, *op. cit.*, p. 123.

91. Atkinson, *The Day of Battle*, p. 18; Dallek, *op. cit.*, p. 321.

92. Greenfield, *op. cit.*, p. 55.

93. O'Neill, *op. cit.*, p. 144.

94. Eric Larrabee, *Commander in Chief: Franklin Delano Roosevelt, His Lieutenants, and the War*, New York: Harper and Row, 1987, p. 3.

95. Kennedy, *op. cit.*, p. 747. "Three-quarters of them eventually ended up overseas, six times the number that had gone to France with the American Expeditionary Force in 1917–1918." *Ibid.*

96. "Roosevelt disliked the building's architecture and assumed at war's end it would be used for storage." Herring, *op. cit.*, p. 544.

97. The initial members were Admiral William Leahy, the chairman, and General George Marshall, Admiral Ernest King, and General H. H. Arnold, representing the army, the navy, and the army air forces (as the air force was then called), respectively.

98. Larrabee, *op. cit.*, p. 150.

99. Herring, *op. cit.*, p. 542.

100. Williamson Murray and Alan R. Millett, *A War to Be Won: Fighting the Second World War*, Cambridge, Massachusetts: The Belknap Press of Harvard University Press, 2000, pp. 181–182.

101. Eisenhower was born in 1890, MacArthur and Marshall in 1880.

102. "If Ike deserves the accolade of 'great,' it rests on his performance in managing the generals under his command, as fractious and dysfunctional a group of egomaniacs as any war had ever seen." Murray and Millett, *op. cit.*, p. 416.

103. The most prominent naval leaders were Admirals Ernest King, the chief of naval operations; Chester Nimitz, the commander in chief of the Pacific fleet; and William ("Bull") Halsey, the commander in the South Pacific area. Whether because the campaigns they supervised took place far away and in unfamiliar parts of the vast Pacific Ocean or because more Americans served in the army than in the navy, the admirals did not achieve the celebrity of the generals.

104. Marshall had hoped to command the invasion of France but Roosevelt gave the job to Eisenhower. The president explained his decision to Marshall by saying that "I didn't feel that I could sleep at ease with you out of the country." Quoted in Kennedy, *op. cit.*, p. 687. The enormous respect and affection the American public had for Eisenhower stemmed from his role in the European campaign. Had Roosevelt given the responsibility to Marshall, it is unlikely that Eisenhower would have become president.

105. Kennedy, *op. cit.*, p. 655. "By comparison, Germany made 44,857 tanks and 111,767 aircraft; Japan a handful of tanks and 69,910 planes; Britain, over the much longer period of 1934 to 1945, just 123,819 military aircraft." *Ibid.*

106. *Ibid.*, p. 654. The United States excelled at logistics—getting the equipment and other materials to the personnel fighting in the field—as well as production. In the last year and a half of the war in the Pacific, the American government furnished four tons of supplies for each American soldier. The Japanese managed two pounds for each of theirs. *Ibid.*, p. 668.

107. Atkinson, *The Guns at Last Light*, p. 218.

108. Keegan, *op. cit.*, p. 218.

109. "The entire war . . . cost U.S. taxpayers $296 billion—roughly $4 trillion in 2012 dollars." Atkinson, *The Guns at Last Light*, p. 633.

110. Robert Hormats, *The Price of Victory: Paying for America's Wars*, New York: Times Books Henry Holt and Company, 2007, p. 148.

111. *Ibid.*, p. 163.

112. O'Neill, *op. cit.*, p. 215

113. Hormats, *op. cit.*, p. 171.

114. Kennedy, *op. cit.*, p. 647. "In America, consumer spending rose by 10.5 percent from 1940 to 1944 in real terms." Alan Greenspan and Adrian Wooldridge, *Capitalism in America: A History*, New York: Penguin Press, 2018, p. 270.

115. Even before formal American entry into the war, Roosevelt "allowed the FBI to break the law by wire-tapping phones and opening mail of suspected Axis sympathizers; he also let the FBI spy on congressmen who merely criticized him." LaFeber, *op. cit.*, p. 406.

116. Dallek, *op. cit.*, pp. 334–335; Blum, *op. cit.*, pp. 159–163.

117. Kennedy, *op. cit.*, pp. 758–759. "When the Court pronounced on the *Korematsu* case on December 18, 1944, safely after the November presidential election, the camps had already begun to empty. Just the day before the Court's decision was announced, the government had declared that the period of 'military necessity' was ended." *Ibid.*, p. 759.

118. The relevant law was passed in 1988.

119. Greenfield, *op. cit.*, p. 15; Kennedy, *op. cit.*, p. 579. The British favored the North African option. Larrabee, *op. cit.*, p. 133.

120. On Stalingrad see Murray and Millett, *op. cit.*, pp. 283–291; Keegan, *op. cit.*, pp. 227–237; Overy, *op. cit.*, Chapter 6; and Ian Kershaw, *Hitler, 1936–1945: Nemesis*, New York: W.W. Norton, 2000, pp. 534–538.

121. Calvocoressi and Wint, *op. cit.*, p. 477.

122. This is a major theme of Paul Kennedy, *The Rise and Fall of the Great Powers: Economic Change and Military Conflict from 1500 to 2000*, New York: Random House, 1987.

123. In 1961, eight years after Stalin's death, the city reverted to its previous name, Volgograd.

124. After the war the Dutch island possessions in the southwest Pacific became the independent country of Indonesia.

125. "In the six months of 'running wild' between Pearl Harbor and the expulsion of the British from Burma between December 1941 and May 1942, the Japanese had succeeded in what five other imperial powers— the Spanish, Dutch, British, French and Russians—had previously attempted but failed to achieve: to make themselves masters of all the lands surrounding the seas of China and to link their conquests to a strong central position. Indeed, if China is included among the powers with imperial ambitions in the western Pacific, Japan had exceeded even her achievement." Keegan, *op. cit.*, p. 546.

126. LaFeber, *op. cit.*, p. 419.

127. Calvocoressi and Wint, *op. cit.*, pp. 760–761.

128. Keegan, *op. cit.*, pp. 275–278. "Within exactly five minutes, between 10.25 and 10.30, the whole course of the war in the Pacific had been reversed. The [Japanese] First Air Fleet, its magnificent ships, modern aircraft, and superb pilots, had been devastated." *Ibid.*, p. 278. On Midway see also Murray and Millett, *op. cit.*, p. 194.

129. ". . . [D]uring the whole Pacific War, Japan commissioned 14 carriers of all types, the United States 104." Weinberg, *op. cit.*, p. 338. See also Keegan, *op. cit.*, p. 555.

130. Herring, *op. cit.*, p. 552.

131. See pp. 219-220.

132. Keegan, *op. cit.*, p. 425; Greenfield, *op. cit.*, p. 6.

133. Calvocoressi and Wint, *op. cit.*, p. 498.

134. David Kennedy, *op. cit.*, p. 744; Weinberg, *op. cit.*, p. 580; Murray and Millett, *op. cit.*, p. 332.

135. Quoted in Dallek, *op. cit.*, p. 373.

136. David Kennedy, *op. cit.*, pp. 592–593.

137. The best account of the Allied victory in the Battle of the Atlantic is Paul Kennedy, *Engineers of Victory: The Problem Solvers Who Turned the Tide in the Second World War*, New York: Random House Trade Paperback, 2013, Chapter 1.

138. Eight months before Pearl Harbor Roosevelt wrote to Churchill that "I believe the outcome of this struggle is going to be decided in the Atlantic and unless Hitler can win there he cannot win anywhere in the world in the end." Quoted in Larrabee, *op. cit.*, p. 639. See also O'Neill, *op. cit.*, p. 144.

139. Herring, *op. cit.*, p. 539; Greenfield, *op. cit.*, p. 60; LaFeber, *op. cit.*, p. 414.

140. Paul Kennedy, *Engineers of Victory.*, pp. 7, 21–22.

141. *Ibid.*, pp. 34–38; O'Neill, *op. cit.*, p. 149.

142. Weinberg, *op. cit.*, p. 375.

143. Paul Kennedy, *Engineers of Victory*, pp. 52–53.

144. *Ibid.*, pp. 53–54. Also important was the Allied decision to attempt seriously not merely to evade the German submarines but also to attack them. *Ibid.*, p. 40.

145. "During the war as a whole, the casualty rate among the U-boat crews was a staggering 63 percent, or 76 percent if captured sailors are included. No other major service in the struggle came close to these terrible rates of loss." *Ibid.*, p. 71.

146. " 'Roosevelt had come to Teheran determined . . . to come to terms with Stalin,' Harry Hopkins [Roosevelt's longtime advisor] told Lord Moran [Churchill's personal physician] 'and he is not going to allow anything to interfere with that purpose. . . . After all,' Hopkins said, 'he had spent his life managing men, and Stalin at bottom could not be so very different from other people.' " Quoted in David Kennedy, *op. cit.*, p. 676.

147. David Kennedy, *op. cit.*, pp. 679–680; Dallek, *op. cit.*, p. 433.

148. Iriye, *op. cit.*, p. 198. "In Roosevelt's mind, China would serve as a counterweight to Britain and the other European powers in postwar Asia, thus helping to secure permanent decolonization. A strong China would also help protect against a resurgent Japan and would check Soviet ambitions in the region as well. Churchill considered Roosevelt's concept of China as an eventual great power nothing less than ludicrous." David Kennedy, *op. cit.*, p. 670.

149. Stilwell's time with Chiang is described in Barbara W. Tuchman, *Stilwell and the American Experience in China, 1911–1945*, New York: The Macmillan Company, 1971. See also Herring, *op. cit.*, pp. 574–576.

150. David Kennedy, *op. cit.*, p. 814.

151. "The desire to placate Douglas MacArthur, the political need to appear faithful to the dispossessed American colony of the Philippines, and the investment already somewhat adventitiously made in the Southwest Pacific all conspired to [*sic*] the approval of MacArthur's demand that he be allowed to continue up the northern New Guinea shore, liberate the Philippines, and prepare for a further assault on Formosa and the China coast." *Ibid.*, p. 816. MacArthur did reach the Philippines but not Formosa (now called Taiwan) or China.

152. For an excellent account of the operation see Paul Kennedy, *Engineers of Victory*, Chapter 4. "D" stood for day—denoting the day of the operation. The next day was D + 1, and so on.

153. Keegan, *op. cit.*, pp. 373–374; O'Neill, *op. cit.*, p. 344. Allied air forces bombed the transportation grid in northwestern France, obstructing German efforts to rush troops to Normandy. Paul Kennedy, *Engineers of Victory*, p. 252; Murray and Millett, *op. cit.*, pp. 413–416; Keegan, *op. cit.*, p. 376.

154. Atkinson, *The Guns at Last Light*, p. 12.

155. Paul Kennedy, *Engineers of Victory*, p. 273.

156. "By the end of June, American and British units were 20 miles inland and heading south. . . ." Paul Kennedy, *ibid.*, p. 250.

157. Murray and Millett, *op. cit.*, pp. 444–445. "Thirteen U.S. divisions in Europe suffered at least 100 percent casualties—5 more exceeded

200 percent. . . ." Atkinson, *The Guns at Last Light*, p. 633. "Most British and American military deaths, a high proportion of Soviet deaths, half of all German military deaths in the entire war and a majority of civilian deaths occurred during the last eleven months of the conflict." Kershaw, *op. cit.*, p. 354.

158. Murray and Millett, *op. cit.*, pp. 432–433.

159. *Ibid.*, pp. 436–444; David Kennedy, *op. cit.*, pp. 735–736.

160. Murray and Millett, *op. cit.*, pp. 463–471.

161. "Eisenhower justified allowing the Soviets to take Berlin because, first, the Big Three had already agreed [at Yalta in February 1945] to put Berlin in the Soviet occupation zone and, second, he feared that fighting the 200 miles to the capital would kill far too many of his troops to capture a city that he would have to leave anyway." LaFeber, *op. cit.*, p. 443. "Churchill was infuriated by the U.S. decision not to go for Berlin, pleading with Roosevelt and Eisenhower to 'march as far east into Germany as possible' and, 'if open to us,' into Poland." Harper, *op. cit.*, p. 128.

162. ". . . [T]his program of mass killing was from the beginning a major portion of the whole ideological war planned for the East with its intended demographic revolution." Weinberg, *op. cit.*, p. 192.

163. The camps in Germany "were not among the most destructive. They were not extermination camps. The horrors that took place within their confines were on a different plane from the millions of murders committed at Auschwitz, Majdanek, and the four other killing centers, all situated in Poland." David S. Wyman, *The Abandonment of the Jews: America and the Holocaust, 1941–1945*, New York: Pantheon Books, 1984, p. 325.

164. This is the thesis of *ibid.* The principal conclusions are summarized in pp. x–xi.

165. *Ibid.*, p. 316; David Kennedy, *op. cit.*, p. 415; Dallek, *op. cit.*, pp. 167–168.

166. Herring, *op. cit.*, p. 557; Dallek, *op. cit.*, p. 447.

167. "Most likely, it would not have been possible to rescue millions. But without impeding the war effort, additional tens of thousands— probably hundreds of thousands—could have been saved." Wyman, *op. cit.*, p. 331. The author goes on to list twelve steps that could have been taken. *Ibid.*, pp. 331–334.

168. Steil, *op. cit.*, p. 165.

169. Skidelsky, *op. cit.*, pp. 182, 357. Keynes had a less self-interested reason for preferring adjustment by surplus countries. He believed that compelling them to spend their surpluses would expand overall global output, whereas the measures that deficit countries had to take in order to adjust would not.

170. Thompson, *op. cit.*, p. 222.

171. The seats belonged to the Soviet Union itself and to the union republics of Ukraine and Byelorussia.

172. The French thus achieved greater control over Germany in the wake of a war they had lost than had been the case after the previous war, which they had won.

173. David Kennedy, *op. cit.*, pp. 677–678; Thompson, *op. cit.*, p. 224.

174. This was confirmed at Potsdam.

175. Dallek, *op. cit.*, p. 520.

176. "Roosevelt insisted on free elections and the broadening of the Lublin (now Warsaw) government, but with the realization that these were largely matters of form. Form was important for domestic opinion, but did not affect the substance of Soviet control of Poland. . . ." Harper, *op. cit.*, p. 124.

177. Thompson, *op. cit.*, p. 226.

178. "Less than ten years later, in the tense atmosphere of the early Cold War, Yalta became synonymous with treason, fiercely partisan critics of FDR claiming that a dying president, duped by pro-Communist advisers, conceded Soviet control over Poland and Eastern Europe . . ." Herring, *op. cit.*, p. 585.

179. *Ibid.*, p. 584.

180. *Ibid.*, p. 583.

181. Weinberg, *op. cit.*, p. 895.

182. David Kennedy, *op. cit.*, pp. 823–828; Murray and Millett, *op. cit.*, pp. 365–369.

183. David Kennedy, *op. cit.*, pp. 829–834; Murray and Millett, *op. cit.*, pp. 510–516.

184. Murray and Millett, *op. cit.*, pp. 515–516.

185. David Kennedy, *op. cit.*, pp. 846–847.

186. Keegan, *op. cit.*, p. 576; Millett and Murray, *op. cit.*, p. 507.

187. The combined death toll is estimated to have been about 276,000. Herring, *op. cit.*, p. 593.

188. Kennedy, *op. cit.*, pp. 838–840; Herring, *op. cit.*, pp. 591–592.

189. David Kennedy, *op. cit.*, pp. 834–835; LaFeber, *op. cit.*, pp. 447–448.

190. David Kennedy, *op. cit.*, p. 856; Overy, *op. cit.*, p. 288; Keegan, *op. cit.*, pp. 590–592; John W. Dower, *War Without Mercy: Race and Power in the Pacific War*, New York: Pantheon Books, 1986, p. 297; https://en.wikipedia.org/wiki/World_War_II_casualties

The Third Age

1. Credit for coining the term "Cold War" has been ascribed to both the English writer George Orwell and the American financier Bernard Baruch. In 1947 the American columnist Walter Lippmann made it popular by publishing a book entitled *The Cold War: A Study in U.S. Foreign Policy*.

2. On the origin of the term "superpower" see Derek A. Leebaert, *Grand Improvisation: America Confronts the British Superpower, 1945–1957*, New York: Farrar, Straus and Giroux, 2018, p. 6.

3. For the argument that the United States and the Soviet Union would have avoided war after 1945 even if nuclear weapons had never been invented see John Mueller, *Retreat from Doomsday: The Obsolescence of Major War*, New York: Basic Books, 1989.

4. Great Britain, France, and China acquired nuclear weapons. Israel was thought to have them but did not acknowledge possession.

5. The similarities are apparent in the account of a nineteenth-century visit to Russia by a French aristocrat: Astolphe de Custine, *Journey for Our Time: The Russian Journals of the Marquis de Custine*, Washington, D.C.: Gateway Editions, 1987.

6. The term originated before World War II to describe the fascist governments of Germany and Italy. After the war it was applied to communist regimes.

7. Other conflicts had pitted states with differing, and incompatible, political (and religious) ideas against one another, but the Cold War involved a competition of economic systems as well.

8. See pp. 263-265.

9. John Lewis Gaddis, *The Long Peace: Inquiries into the History of the Cold War*, New York: Oxford University Press, 1987.

Chapter 7

1. John Lukacs, *1945: Year Zero: The Shaping of the Modern Age*, New York: Doubleday, 1978. The German term for the immediate postwar state of affairs was "stunde null"—zero hour.

2. "The British had lost about 25 percent of their prewar wealth, had contracted about $14 billion in sterling debt, and had seen the volume of their experts decline by about two-thirds." Leffler, *op. cit.*, pp. 62–63. See also Derek Leebaert, *Grand Improvisation: America Confronts the British Superpower, 1945–1957*, New York: Farrar, Straus and Giroux, 2018, p. 29.

3. Tony Judt, *Postwar: A History of Europe Since 1945*, New York: The Penguin Press, 2005, p. 117.

4. On Stalin's international outlook see Vojtech Mastny, *The Cold War and Soviet Insecurity: The Stalin Years*, New York: Oxford University Press, 1996, Chapter 1; Vladislav Zubok and Constantine Pleshakov, *Inside the Kremlin's Cold War: From Stalin to Khrushchev*, Cambridge, Massachusetts: Harvard University Press, 1996, pp. 7, 12, 27, 34; Vladimir O. Pechatnov, "The Soviet Union and the World, 1944–1953," in Melvyn P. Leffler and Odd Arne Westad, editors, *The Cambridge History of The Cold War, Volume I: Origins*, Cambridge, UK: Cambridge University Press, 2010, pp. 91, 93; John Lewis Gaddis, *We Now Know: Rethinking Cold War History*, Oxford, UK: The Clarendon Press of Oxford University Press, 1997, pp. 15, 25; and Judt, *op. cit.*, pp. 118–119.

5. John A. Thompson, *A Sense of Power: The Roots of America's Global Role*, Ithaca, New York: Cornell University Press, 2015, p. 230. "[America's] GNP was more than three times that of the Soviet Union and almost five times that of Britain. It possessed almost two-thirds of the world's gold reserves, three-fourths of its invested capital, and half of world shipping." *Ibid.*

6. *Ibid..*, p. 235; James T. Patterson, *Grand Expectations: The United States, 1945–1974*, New York: Oxford University Press, 1996, p. 121.

7. Thompson, *op. cit.*, pp. 232–233; Leffler, *op. cit.*, pp. 11, 56.

8. Harry Truman initially shared this view. Melvyn P. Leffler, *For the Soul of Mankind: The United States, the Soviet Union, and the Cold War*, New York: Hill and Wang, 2007, pp. 43–44. "At least through mid-1946, many US leaders spoke and acted as though they truly believed in the continuation of their wartime partnership with Stalin." Judt, *op. cit.*, pp. 108–109.

9. Thompson, *op. cit.*, p. 231; George C. Herring, *From Colony to Superpower: U.S. Foreign Relations Since 1776*, New York: Oxford University Press, 2008, pp. 612–613. Tammi L. Gutner, *The Story of SAIS*, Washington, D.C: School of Advanced International Studies, The Johns Hopkins University, 1987, pp. 4–7.

10. In a speech to students at Princeton University in 1947 George C. Marshall, by then secretary of state in the Truman administration, said, "I think we must agree that the negative course of action followed by the United States after the First World War did not achieve order or security, and that it had a direct bearing upon the recent war and its endless tragedies." Quoted in Benn Steil, *The Marshall Plan: Dawn of the Cold War*, New York: Simon & Schuster, 2018, p. 23.

11. Douglas A. Irwin, *Clashing Over Commerce: A History of US Trade Policy*, Chicago: The University of Chicago Press, 2017, pp. 455–456, 463–465.

12. *Ibid.*, pp. 478–480.

13. *Ibid.*, pp. 480–482.

14. "After six months of negotiations, these original GATT members signed over a hundred agreements, affecting more than forty-five thousand tariffs that covered about half of world trade. The bargainers cut tariffs by greater than one-third on average and agreed not to discriminate among countries." Jeffry Frieden, *Global Capitalism: Its Fall and Rise in the Twentieth Century*, New York: W.W. Norton & Company, 2006, p. 288.

15. Irwin, *op. cit.*, p. 489.

16. *Ibid.*, p. 22.

17. *Ibid.*, p. 486. "World trade exploded after 1950. Exports grew more than twice as rapidly as the economy, 8.6 percent a year. This was an unprecedented increase in world trade. During the glory years of classical liberalism before 1914, world trade volume doubled every twenty to twenty-five years. Over the first twenty-five postwar years, the volume of world trade doubled every ten years." Frieden, *op. cit.*, p. 289.

18. He made the statement in 1947. Quoted in Herring, *op. cit.*, p. 618. In France, Italy, and Great Britain "food was no longer reaching the cities from the country; factories were scrounging for vital raw materials. Gold and dollars with which to import essentials such as fuel were nearly evaporated. Strikes were spreading. Inflation was mounting." Steil, *op. cit.*, p. 94.

19. Herring, *op. cit.*, p. 605.

20. *Ibid.*, p. 617.

21. Between 1948 and 1951 Great Britain received more than twenty-five percent of the total funds distributed. A. G. Hopkins, *American Empire: A Global History*, Princeton, New Jersey: Princeton University Press, 2018, p. 475. From 1945 to 1950 aid to Europe, including the Marshall Plan, totaled $26 billion, the equivalent of ten percent of the annual American gross domestic product. Thompson, *op. cit.*, pp. 230–231.

22. Steil, *op. cit.*, p. 166.

23. *Ibid.*, pp. 192–201.

24. Melvyn P. Leffler, *A Preponderance of Power: National Security, the Truman Administration and the Cold War*, Stanford, California: Stanford University Press, 1992, p. 159; Steil, *op. cit.*, pp. 342–343; William Hitchcock, "The Marshall Plan and the Creation of the West," in Leffler and Westad, editors, *op. cit.*, pp. 159–160.

25. Odd Arne Westad, *The Cold War: A World History*, New York: Basic Books, 2017, p. 112.

26. On Stalin's instructions about Eastern European participation in the Marshall Plan see Norman Naimark, "The Sovietization of Eastern Europe, 1944–1953," in Leffler and Westad, *op. cit.*, p. 189; Mastny, *op. cit.*, pp. 28–29; and Steil, *op. cit.*, pp. 135–137. "The Marshall Plan, in the Kremlin's view, would prove to be a Trojan horse, designed to undermine the centerpiece of its postwar strategic desiderata—the security zone in Eastern and Central Europe." Pechatnov, *op. cit.*, p. 104.

27. The Soviet-style economic system began in the civil war that followed the revolution of 1917. In 1921 V. I. Lenin, the Soviet leader, introduced the "New Economic Policy" that included features of free markets. In 1928 Stalin, his successor, reverted to the wartime economic procedures. Martin Malia, *The Soviet Tragedy: A History of Socialism in Russia, 1917–1991*, New York: The Free Press, 1994, Chapters 4–6.

28. The countries with planned economies (and communist governments) formed the Council for Mutual Economic Assistance in 1949, but this did not lead to the extensive economic interdependence that was practiced among the market economies of the western part of the continent. Frieden, *op. cit.*, p. 274; Ronald Findlay and Kevin H. O'Rourke, *Power and Plenty: Trade, War and the World Economy in the Second Millennium*, Princeton, New Jersey: Princeton University Press, 2007, p. 478.

29. Charles S. Maier, "The World Economy and the Cold War in the Middle of the Twentieth Century," in Leffler and Westad, editors, *op. cit.*, p. 48.

30. *Ibid.*, p. 46; Frieden, *op. cit.*, pp. 275–276.

31. "Gross domestic product per capita, what the income of a typical resident of Europe will buy, tripled in the second half of the twentieth century." Barry Eichengreen, *The European Economy Since 1945: Coordinated Capitalism and Beyond*, Princeton, New Jersey: Princeton University Press, 2007, p. 1.

32. Hitchcock, *op. cit.*, p. 166.

33. Judt, *op. cit.*, p. 93.

34. Steil, *op. cit.*, p. 322. The founding members of the Coal and Steel Community were France, Germany, Italy, Belgium, the Netherlands, and Luxembourg—not coincidentally also the founding members of the European Economic Community.

35. The number fell to twenty-seven in 2020 when Great Britain dropped out.

36. Irwin, *op. cit.*, p. 495. "American officials wanted to assist Europe's ability to import from the United States not simply because it would help maintain exports, but because anything that jeopardized the European recovery and risked economic collapse, political chaos, and possible Communist takeovers would be detrimental to America's national security." *Ibid.*, p. 498.

37. Steil, *op. cit.*, p. 190; Thompson, *op. cit.*, p. 246.

38. Leffler, *A Preponderance of Power*, p. 160.

39. John Lewis Gaddis, *The Cold War: A New History*, New York: The Penguin Press, 2005, p. 32; Westad, *op. cit.*, p. 113; Steil, *op. cit.*, p. 191.

40. Steil, *op. cit.*, p. 229.

41. Westad, *op. cit.*, p. 88; Judt, *op. cit.*, p. 122.

42. David Holloway, *Stalin and the Bomb: The Soviet Union and Atomic Energy, 1939–1956*, New Haven, Connecticut: Yale University Press, 1994, p. 150.

43. *Ibid.*, pp. 218–219.

44. Gaddis, *We Now Know*, p. 260.

45. The Iranian government promised Moscow oil drilling rights in Iran, but then reneged on that promise. On the Soviet-Iranian episode see Ray Takeyh, *The Last Shah*, New York: Oxford University Press, 2020, Chapter 2.

46. Steil, *op. cit.*, p. 24; Gaddis, *George F. Kennan*, p. 254.

47. Michael Mandelbaum, *The Nuclear Question: The United States and Nuclear Weapons, 1946–1976*, New York: Cambridge University Press, 1979, pp. 23–27; Joseph I. Lieberman, *The Scorpion and the Tarantula: The Struggle to Control Atomic Weapons, 1945–1949*, Boston: Houghton Mifflin, 1970, Chapters 13–17; Holloway, *op. cit.*, pp. 161–162; Gaddis, *We Now Know*, p. 97.

48. Judt, *op. cit.*, pp. 134–137.

49. Naimark, *op. cit.*, p. 188.

50. "As Walter Ulbricht, leader of the East German Communists, explained privately to his followers when they expressed bemusement at Party policy in 1945: 'It's quite clear—it's got to look democratic, but we must have everything in our control.'" Judt, *op. cit.*, p. 131. See also Malia, *op. cit.*, p. 298.

51. Naimark, *op. cit.*, pp. 182–183.

52. Westad, *op. cit.*, pp. 79–87; Pechatnov, *op. cit.*, p. 105.

53. Naimark, *op. cit.*, pp. 196–197; Pechatnov, *op. cit.*, p. 94.

54. East Germany, Czechoslovakia, and Poland lay between the western border of the Soviet Union and the eastern border of what became the German Federal Republic.

55. Judt, *op. cit.*, p. 130.

56. Leffler, *A Preponderance of Power*, p. 512; Westad, *op. cit.*, pp. 79–80; Judt, *op. cit.*, p. 168.

57. Leffler, *A Preponderance of Power*, pp. 204–205; Westad, *op. cit.*, pp. 95–96. No Soviet troops occupied Czechoslovakia at the time of the Communist coup there.

58. President Truman himself "was furious over Soviet behavior in eastern Europe, where he felt that Stalin had reneged on promises given to FDR about establishing democracies there." Westad, *op. cit.*, p. 89.

59. *Ibid.*, p. 97.

60. *Ibid.*, pp. 88–89; John Lamberton Harper, *The Cold War*, New York: Oxford University Press, 2011, p. 43; Leffler, *A Preponderance of Power*, p. 7.

61. The British decision came as a shock to the American government because "U.S. officials regarded British strength as critically important to American security interests." Leffler, *A Preponderance of Power*, p. 61. The British-American relationship in this period is a major theme of Leebaert, *op. cit.*

62. Quoted in Herring, *op. cit.*, p. 615.

63. https://www.ourdocuments.gov/doc.php?flash=false&doc=81&page=transcript

64. https://avalon.law.yale.edu/20th_century/trudoc.asp

65. The vote was 67 to 23 in the Senate and 284 to 107 in the House of Representatives. James T. Patterson, *Grand Expectations: The United States, 1945–1974*, New York: Oxford University Press, 1996, p. 129.

66. Herring, *op. cit.*, p. 616.

67. "A vague global policy, which sounds like the tocsin of an ideological crusade, has no limits. It cannot be controlled. Its effects cannot be predicted. Everyone everywhere will read into it his own fears and hopes, and it could readily act as incitement and inducement to civil strife in countries where the national cooperation is delicate and precarious." Quoted in Ronald Steel, *Walter Lippmann and the American Century*,

Boston: Little, Brown and Company, 1980, pp. 438–439. George Kennan agreed with Lippmann's reservations. Gaddis, *George F. Kennan*, pp. 256–257, 268, 279.

68. See pp. 275-276, 308-309.

69. Westad, *op. cit.*, pp. 102–103. Wallace received 2.5 percent of the popular vote.

70. Thompson, *op. cit.*, p. 246. One effect of the Marshall Plan was to undercut the political standing of the Western European Communist Parties, which Stalin instructed to take the unpopular position of opposing accepting the aid. Hitchcock, *op. cit.*, p. 170.

71. "The Soviet leader repeatedly denied assistance to the Greek Communists and often deliberately undermined their policies. Available evidence suggests that Stalin never seriously contemplated a pro-Soviet regime in Greece because he was fearful that it would encroach on what he understood to be an area of vital British and American interests." Svetozar Rajak, "The Cold War in the Balkans, 1945–1956," in Leffler and Westad, editors, *op. cit.*, p. 206.

72. On the centrality of Germany to the Cold War see Marc Trachtenberg, *A Constructed Peace: The Making of the European Settlement, 1945–1963,* Princeton, New Jersey: Princeton University Press, 1999.

73. Thompson, *op. cit.*, p. 240. "None of the occupying powers wanted to contribute more to the German economy than what they were getting out of it—'paying reparations to the Germans,' as the cash-strapped British put it." Westad, *op. cit.*, pp. 107–108.

74. Westad, *op. cit.*, p. 108.

75. *Ibid.*, p. 111.

76. Judt, *op. cit.*, p. 105; Steil, *op. cit.*, p. 161.

77. Steil, *op. cit.*, p. 249.

78. At this point, Stalin seems to have hoped for a united Germany that would become pro-Soviet, or at least not pro-Western, and subject to Soviet influence. Gaddis, *We Now Know*, p. 127; Leffler, *A Preponderance of Power*, p. 204.

79. Pechatnov, *op. cit.*, p. 107; Mastny, *op. cit.*, p. 49.

80. Herring, *op. cit.*, p. 624.

81. Derek Leebaert, *The Fifty-Year Wound: How America's Cold War Victory Shapes Our World*, Boston: Little, Brown and Company, 2002, p. 63. The British Royal Air Force made one-third of the flights.

82. Thompson, *op. cit.*, p. 242; Steil, *op. cit.*, p. 319.

83. Quoted in Herring, *op. cit.*, p. 626.

84. See p. 178.

85. Judt, *op. cit.*, pp. 149–150.

86. On the history of this issue see David P. Calleo, *The German Problem Reconsidered: Germany and the World Order, 1870 to the Present,* New York: Cambridge University Press, 1978.

87. For an account and assessment of this school of Cold War revisionism see Charles S. Maier, "Revisionism and the Interpretation of Cold War Origins," in Maier, editor, *The Origins of the Cold War and Contemporary Europe*, New York: New Viewpoints/Franklin Watts, 1978, pp. 11–14; Harper, *op. cit.*, pp. 84–85; and Thompson, *op. cit.*, p. 252.

88. On the spiral model see Robert Jervis, *Perception and Misperception in International Politics*, Princeton, New Jersey: Princeton University Press, 1976, pp. 62–76.

89. Rajak, *op. cit.*, p. 206.

90. Holloway, *op. cit.*, pp. 151, 368.

91. This theme is to be found, for example, in Leffler, *A Preponderance of Power*. For a critique see Marc Trachtenberg, "Melvyn Leffler and the Origins of the Cold War," *Orbis*, Summer 1995.

92. "All attempts to imagine alternative courses of postwar international relations run up against Stalin himself. It is difficult to think counterfactually about this period without assuming Stalin away. His malevolent and suspicious personality pervades the history of these years." Holloway, *op. cit.*, p. 370.

93. Stalin saw his wartime allies "as selfish and cunning hypocrites, anti-Soviet at heart." He believed "in the need for the Soviet Union to gather strength for an inevitable new showdown." Pechatnov, *op. cit.*, p. 93. See also Gaddis, *We Now Know*, p. 25.

94. "So sharp was the break with what had gone before that one is tempted to treat September 1945 as the end, not of a chapter, but of a story, making all that followed part of a fresh beginning." W. G. Beasley, *The Rise of Modern Japan: Political, Economic and Social Change Since 1850*, New York: St. Martin's Press, 1995, p. 214.

95. "Its wooden cities had been burned to cinders by American firebombs. In Tokyo less than one-third of the city remained standing, and even that was badly damaged by bombs. . . . Everywhere infrastructure was in chaos, millions were homeless or living as internal refugees. Then, as the empire collapsed, almost three million Japanese refugees from abroad came to a home country that many of them had never seen. . . ." Westad, *op. cit.*, p. 134.

96. Walter LaFeber, *The Clash: U.S.-Japanese Relations Throughout History*, New York: W.W. Norton and Company, 1997, p. 261. Churchill called this the bravest "of all the amazing deeds of the war." *Ibid.*

97. Ambassador William Sebald, the ranking American diplomat in Japan, said of MacArthur's authority there: "Never before in the history of the United States had such enormous and absolute power been placed in the hands of a single individual." Quoted in William Manchester, *American Caesar: Douglas MacArthur, 1880–1964*, Boston: Little, Brown and Company, 1978, p. 470.

98. On the American-instituted reforms see Marius B. Jansen, *The Making of Modern Japan*, Cambridge, Massachusetts: The Belknap Press of Harvard University Press, 2000, pp. 680–688.

99. Westad, *op. cit.*, p. 136.

100. Beasley, *op. cit.*, p. 223.

101. Article IX stated that "the Japanese people forever renounce war as a sovereign right of the nations," undertaking not to maintain "land, sea, and air forces, as well as other war potential." Quoted in Beasley, *ibid.*, p. 220.

102. Sayuri Guthrie-Shimizu, "Japan, the United States, and the Cold War, 1945–1960," in Leffler and Westad, editors, *op. cit.*, p. 248.

103. *Ibid.*, pp. 249–250; Herring, *op. cit.*, p. 634; Jansen, *op. cit.*, pp. 698–699; Michael J. Green, *By More Than Providence: Grand Strategy and American Power in the Asia Pacific Since 1788*, New York: Columbia University Press, 2017, p. 264.

104. Jansen, *op. cit.*, pp. 703–704.

105. See pp. 358-359.

106. "Building on understandings at Yalta and Potsdam, U.S. leaders expected that a unified China would fill the vacuum that had drawn in great-power competition in Asia for a century and that China would thus serve as a regional counterweight to Soviet power in the Far East." Green, *op. cit.*, p. 253.

107. Mastny, *op. cit.*, p. 86; John Pomfret, *The Beautiful Country and the Middle Kingdom: America and China, 1776 to the Present*, New York: Henry Holt and Company, 2016, p. 338.

108. "The timing of the conflict was very much determined by the Cold War. In fact, the tenor of GMD (Kuomintang)-CCP (Chinese Communist Party) negotiations had been fluctuating directly in tune with that of US-USSR relations. As the Cold War set in . . . both the GMD and the CCP saw opportunities to take advantage of the contradictions and tensions that became increasingly evident as the superpowers pursued their overall goals." Niu Jun, "The Birth of the People's Republic of China and the Road to the Korean War," in Leffler and Westad, editors, *op. cit.*, p. 226.

109. On the Marshall Mission see Daniel Kurtz-Phelan, *The China Mission: George Marshall's Unfinished War, 1945–1947*, New York: W.W. Norton and Company, 2018. In retrospect it has been argued that the unwavering American support for a united China—Truman charged Marshall with bringing about a settlement that left the country "strong, united, and democratic"—was mistaken. A divided country, along the lines of postwar Germany, goes this argument, would have worked to the advantage of the United States. Green, *op. cit.*, pp. 259–260.

110. "During four months of 1948, Chiang lost nearly 50 percent of his manpower and 75 percent of his weapons. In October alone three hundred thousand Nationalists surrendered." Herring, *op. cit.*, p. 632.

111. On the course of the Chinese Civil War see Jonathan D. Spence, *The Search for Modern China*, New York: W.W. Norton and Company, 1990, Chapter 18.

112. For an assessment of the White Paper see Green, *op. cit.*, pp. 258–262.

113. Pomfret, *op. cit.*, pp. 322–323, 344.

114. Westad, *op. cit.*, p. 144.

115. "Although Soviet aid to Mao never matched American aid to Chiang, it reached substantial levels in the fight's final phase." Kurtz-Phelan, *op. cit.*, p. 349. See also Pomfret, *op. cit.*, p. 359.

116. Pomfret, *op. cit.*, p. 339; Westad, *op. cit.*, p. 139.

117. Shortly after the end of the Civil War, a document issued by the National Security Council "rejected interventionism in Formosa (Taiwan) in favor of 'calculated inactivity.'" Green, *op. cit.*, p. 262. See also Harper, *op. cit.*, pp. 96–97.

118. Thompson, *op. cit.*, p. 239.

119. Don Oberdorfer, *The Two Koreas: A Contemporary History*, Reading, Massachusetts: Addison-Wesley, 1997, p. 3.

120. Westad, *op. cit.*, pp. 162–163.

121. William Stueck, "The Korean War," in Leffler and Westad, editors, *op. cit.*, p. 273.

122. On the reasons for Stalin's change of mind see Westad, *op. cit.*, p. 167, and William Stueck, *Rethinking the Korean War: A New Diplomatic and Strategic History*, Princeton, New Jersey: Princeton University Press, 2002, p. 73.

123. Westad, *op. cit.*, p. 164.

124. Ernest R. May, *"Lessons" of the Past: The Use and Misuse of History in American Foreign Policy*, New York: Oxford University Press, 1976. First published, 1973, pp. 64–67.

125. Herring, *op. cit.*, p. 640.

126. Westad, *op. cit.*, p. 170. The UN had an almost entirely symbolic role in the military effort undertaken in its name in Korea. It exercised no control over the Allied military forces. The United States supplied ninety percent of the troops. *Ibid.*, p. 178.

127. Spence, *op. cit.*, pp. 525–526.

128. Thompson, *op. cit.*, p. 268; Harper, *op. cit.*, pp. 97–98. The principal stated reason was to prevent attacks in either direction across the Strait. Stueck, "The Korean War," p. 275.

129. Westad, *op. cit.*, p. 168; Stueck, *Rethinking the Korean War*, p. 73.

130. "As Secretary of State Acheson put it, decisive action was necessary 'as a symbol [of the] strength and determination of [the] west.' To do less would encourage 'new aggressive action elsewhere' and demoralize

'countries adjacent to [the] Soviet orbit.'" Stueck, "The Korean War,"
p. 276. Dwight Eisenhower, then president of Columbia University, said,
"We'll have a dozen Koreas soon if we don't take a firm stand." Quoted
in Patterson, *op. cit.*, p. 214. See also Green, *op. cit.*, p. 274.

131. Stueck, *Rethinking the Korean War*, p. 81; Gaddis, *We Now Know*, p. 75.

132. Stueck, "The Korean War," pp. 277–279.

133. The North Koreans did experience one significant failure in the war's
first stage. Kim had assured Stalin that Koreans in the south would rise
up to support him. Westad, *op. cit.*, p. 168. They did not.

134. Patterson, *op. cit.*, p. 219; Green, *op. cit.*, p. 276.

135. Thompson, *op. cit.*, p. 269.

136. Stueck, *Rethinking the Korean War*, p. 105; Westad, *op. cit.*, p. 172.

137. ". . . MacArthur called for the bombing of bases in Manchuria,
blockading the Chinese coast, and augmenting his forces with
nationalist troops from Taiwan. He implied that victory could be
achieved without much greater deployment of U.S. troops, possibly
through the use of atomic weapons." Thompson, *op. cit.*, p. 269. See also
Green, *op. cit.*, p. 278.

138. Pechatnov, *op. cit.*, p. 110.

139. The two sides were stalemated over one issue in particular: the fate
of prisoners of war. China and North Korea insisted on compulsory
repatriation. The United States refused. Herring, *op. cit.*, pp. 644–645.

140. Westad, *op. cit.*, p. 181; Mastny, *op. cit.*, p. 172.

141. Stueck, *Rethinking the Korean War*, p. 3. "[A]nother 5 million became
refugees and perhaps double that saw their families permanently
divided." Stueck, "The Korean War," p. 283.

142. Herring, *op. cit.*, p. 645.

143. The phrase is from the constitutional scholar Edward S. Corwin.

144. Arthur M. Schlesinger Jr., *The Imperial Presidency*, Boston: Houghton
Mifflin, 1973, pp. 132–133, 138, 142.

145. ". . . [A] poll in early October 1950 found a large majority in favor of
invading North Korea and forcing its surrender. However, the president's
poll ratings plummeted in November, and by January, 1951 Gallup was
reporting that two-thirds of Americans favored pulling 'our troops out
of Korea as fast as possible,' while 44 percent of those with an opinion
now thought it had been 'a mistake' to intervene in the first place."
Thompson, *op. cit.*, p. 269.

146. This is the argument of John Mueller, *War, Presidents, and Public
Opinion*, New York: John Wiley and Company, 1973.

147. See pp. 309, 432-433.

148. The cases that had the greatest public impact involved Alger Hiss, a
former State Department official, and Julius and Ethel Rosenberg,
who had passed to Soviet agents information relevant to the making
of atomic weapons that Julius Rosenberg had obtained while in the

army. On these cases see Allen Weinstein, *Perjury: The Hiss-Chambers Case*, New York: Alfred A. Knopf, 1978, and Ronald Radosh and Joyce Milton, *The Rosenberg File: A Search for the Truth*, New York: Holt, Rinehart and Winston, 1983.

149. ". . . [I]t is estimated that a few thousand people lost their jobs, a few hundred were jailed, more than 150 were deported, and two, Julius and Ethel Rosenberg (Communists who were arrested in 1950) were executed. . . ." Patterson, *op. cit.*, p. 204.

150. On the period of McCarthyism see *ibid.*, pp. 178–205.

151. "United States military procurement pumped $2.3 billion into a lagging Japanese economy. Exports soared to 50 percent above prewar levels; the GNP increased by 10 percent." Herring, *op. cit.*, p. 646. See also Leebaert, *The Fifty-Year Wound*, pp. 102–103, and LaFeber, *op. cit.*, p. 293.

152. Sheila Smith, *Japan Rearmed: The Politics of Military Power*, Cambridge, Massachusetts: Harvard University Press, 2019, p. 25.

153. Thompson, *op. cit.*, p. 260.

154. Westad, *op. cit.*, pp. 103–105; Herring, *op. cit.*, p. 638.

155. Herring, *op. cit.*, p. 646. The army expanded by fifty percent to 3.5 million soldiers while air force air groups doubled, to ninety-five. *Ibid.*

156. Defense spending increased after the Soviet launch of the first Earth-orbiting satellite Sputnik in 1957, and the Soviet invasion of Afghanistan, in 1979. See pp. 285, 342–343, 345.

157. Gaddis, *We Now Know*, p. 125.

158. Stueck, *Rethinking the Korean War*, p. 136.

159. Gaddis, *We Now Know*, p. 110. On this subject see Robert E. Osgood, *Limited War: The Challenge to American Strategy*, Chicago: University of Chicago Press, 1957.

160. ". . . Stalin did . . . authorize the use of Soviet fighter planes, manned by Soviet pilots, over the Korean peninsula—where they encountered American fighters flown by American pilots. And so there was, after all, a shooting war between the United States and the Soviet Union: it was the only time this happened during the Cold War. Both sides, however, kept it quiet." Gaddis, *The Cold War: A New History*, p. 60.

161. Stueck, *Rethinking the Korean War*, p. 124.

162. Quoted in Patterson, *op. cit.*, p. 224. "In late December [1950], the frightened general [MacArthur] secretly asked Truman to drop atomic bombs on twenty-six targets to stop the Chinese advance. Truman turned down the request. . . ." LaFeber, *op. cit.*, p. 286. The Eisenhower administration considered using nuclear weapons to end the Korean War. Mastny, *op. cit.*, p. 164.

163. Gaddis, *A New History of the Cold War*, pp. 58–60; Gaddis, *We Now Know*, pp. 105–106.

Chapter 8

1. The phrase is from Oscar Wilde's play *The Importance of Being Ernest.*
2. Tony Judt, *Postwar: A History of Europe Since 1945,* New York: The Penguin Press, 2005, p. 523.
3. William McKinley had served with distinction in the Civil War, but as a major. Theodore Roosevelt, with the honorary title of colonel, had come to national prominence through his exploits in the Spanish-American War. See p. 140.
4. James T. Patterson, *Grand Expectations: The United States, 1945–1974,* New York: Oxford University Press, 1996, p. 272.
5. John Lewis Gaddis, *We Now Know: Rethinking Cold War History,* New York: Oxford University Press, 1997, p. 226.
6. See p. 274.
7. Walter LaFeber, *The American Age: U.S. Foreign Policy at Home and Abroad, 1750 to the Present,* New York: W.W. Norton, Second Edition, 1994, pp. 555–556; George C. Herring, *From Colony to Superpower: U.S. Foreign Relations Since 1776,* New York: Oxford University Press, 2008, p. 670.
8. Herring, *op. cit.,* pp. 698–699.
9. Patterson, *op. cit.,* p. 251; Warren I. Cohen, *The Cambridge History of American Foreign Relations, Volume IV: America in the Age of Soviet Power, 1945–1991,* New York: Cambridge University Press, 1993, pp. 81, 86.
10. Michael Mandelbaum, *The Nuclear Question: The United States and Nuclear Weapons, 1946–1976,* New York: Cambridge University Press, 1979, p. 49; David Holloway, "Nuclear Weapons and the Escalation of the Cold War, 1945–1962," in Melvyn P. Leffler and Odd Arne Westad, editors, *The Cold War, Volume I: Origins,* Cambridge, UK: Cambridge University Press, 2010, pp. 385–386.
11. Mandelbaum, *op. cit.,* p. 47.
12. Quoted in Mandelbaum, *op. cit.,* p. 51. See also Patterson, *op. cit.,* p. 287.
13. On the overall Eisenhower military strategy see John Lewis Gaddis, *Strategies of Containment: A Critical Appraisal of Postwar American National Security Policy,* New York: Oxford University Press, 1982, Chapters 5 and 6.
14. Mandelbaum, *op. cit.,* p. 52; Herring, *op. cit.,* p. 659.
15. The number of American nuclear warheads increased from 1,000 in 1953 to 18,000 by early 1961. LaFeber, *op. cit.,* p. 541. The number continued to increase thereafter.
16. Mandelbaum, *op. cit.,* p. 61; Herring, *op. cit.,* p. 692.
17. The author of the article was Albert Wohlstetter, an analyst at the RAND Corporation, a government-funded think tank devoted to military issues. He adapted the article from reports that he and other RAND analysts had written in 1951 and 1955. Mandelbaum, *op. cit.,* pp. 56–57, 66.
18. Patterson, *op. cit.,* p. 420; Herring, *op. cit.,* p. 692; Holloway, *op. cit.,* p. 387.

19. Mandelbaum, *op. cit.*, pp. 74–76.

20. *Ibid.*, p. 77.

21. Patterson, *op. cit.*, p. 290.

22. Mandelbaum, *op. cit.*, p. 59.

23. Francis J. Gavin, "Nuclear Proliferation and Non-proliferation During the Cold War," in Melvyn P. Leffler and Odd Arne Westad, editors, *The Cold War, Volume II: Crises and Détente*, Cambridge, UK: Cambridge University Press, 2010, pp. 398–402; Marc Trachtenberg, "The Structure of Great Power Politics, 1963–1975," in Leffler and Westad, editors, *Crises and Détente*, p. 487.

24. Mandelbaum, *op. cit.*, pp. 90–92.

25. These troops were sometimes called a "tripwire," meaning that a European war in which they became involved (or were supposed to) would bring the United States into the conflict.

26. Judt, *op. cit.*, p. 249.

27. On the various efforts to find a way to conduct a nuclear war see Mandelbaum, *op. cit.*, Chapter 5, and William Burr and David Alan Rosenberg, "Nuclear Competition in an Era of Stalemate, 1963–1975," in Leffler and Westad, editors, *Crises and Détente*, pp. 95, 99.

28. David Holloway, *Stalin and the Bomb: The Soviet Union and Atomic Energy, 1939–1956*, New Haven, Connecticut: Yale University Press, 1994, p. 369.

29. Detailed accounts of the Berlin and Cuban crises are in Lawrence Freedman, *Kennedy's Wars: Berlin, Cuba, Laos and Vietnam*, New York: Oxford University Press, 2000, Chapters 8–9 and 18–24, and Michael Beschloss, *The Crisis Years: Kennedy and Khrushchev, 1960–1961*, New York: HarperCollins, 1991, pp. 215–290 and 377–545.

30. In the past, new presidents had waited until January of their second year in office to deliver this address.

31. Quoted in Mandelbaum, *op. cit.*, p. 70. It was Kennedy who, for Cold-War reasons, pledged to put a man—an American—on the moon.

32. Vladislav Zubok and Constantine Pleshakov, *Inside the Kremlin's Cold War: From Stalin to Khrushchev*, Cambridge, Massachusetts: Harvard University Press, 1996, p. 210; Vojtech Mastny, "Soviet Foreign Policy, 1953–1962," in Leffler and Westad, editors, *Origins*, p. 318.

33. Mastny, *op. cit.*, p. 333.

34. Khrushchev called West Berlin "the testicles of the West." "Every time I want the West to scream," he said, "I squeeze on Berlin." https://erenow.net/ww/the-cold-war-history-in-an-hour/12.php

35. Wilfried Loth, "The Cold War and the Social and Economic History of the Twentieth Century," in Leffler and Westad, editors, *Crises and Détente*, p. 517.

36. Gaddis, *We Now Know*, p. 147.

37. Specifically, Khrushchev "announced that the Western powers had six months in which to negotiate the status of West Berlin with East German authorities. When the deadline passed, the Soviets would sign a separate peace treaty with the East Germans, leaving them responsible for Western access to Berlin. To Dulles's warning that the West would use force if necessary to ensure its access to Berlin, Khrushchev replied that World War III would follow." Cohen, *op. cit.*, pp. 124–125.

38. Odd Arne Westad, *The Cold War: A World History*, New York: Basic Books, 2017, pp. 293–294.

39. Cohen, *op. cit.*, p. 132; LaFeber, *op. cit.*, p. 596; Westad, *op. cit.*, p. 294.

40. Gaddis, *We Now Know*, p. 148.

41. The wall went up on August 13, 1961. On October 17 Khrushchev canceled the ultimatum on Berlin.

42. Westad, *op. cit.*, p. 296. A detailed account of Kennedy's activities during the Berlin crisis is in Richard Reeves, *President Kennedy: Profile of Power*, New York: Simon & Schuster, 1993, Chapter 16.

43. Cohen, *op. cit.*, pp. 130–131.

44. Khrushchev's motives for putting missiles in Cuba have been subject to considerable retrospective scrutiny and speculation. The weight of the available evidence suggests that protecting the Cuban revolution was paramount for him. See James G. Hershberg, "The Cuban Missile Crisis," in Leffler and Westad, editors, *Crises and Détente,* and William Taubman, *Khrushchev: The Man and His Era*, New York: W.W. Norton, 2003, p. 535.

45. The troops were equipped with tactical nuclear weapons. Herring, *op. cit.*, p. 720; Gaddis, *We Now Know*, p. 274.

46. Kennedy had previously declared that the United States would not tolerate "offensive" weapons in Cuba. Cohen, *op. cit.*, p. 138.

47. Gaddis, *We Now Know*, p. 146.

48. "'A missile is a missile,' McNamara is reported to have said. 'It makes no great difference whether you are killed by a missile fired from the Soviet Union or from Cuba.'" Mandelbaum, *op. cit.*, p. 136.

49. In his speech announcing the discovery of the missiles Kennedy invoked the interwar period: "The 1930s taught us a clear lesson: aggressive conduct, if allowed to go unchecked and unchallenged, ultimately leads to war." Quoted in Westad, *op. cit.*, p. 306. The president was also mindful of the political damage Soviet missiles in Cuba could do to his administration and his Democratic Party, which faced Congressional elections in early November.

50. Taubman, *op. cit.*, pp. 531, 553.

51. Westad, *op. cit.*, pp. 307–308. For a retrospective assessment of the chances of a shooting war during the missile crisis see Hershberg, *op. cit.*, pp. 83–84.

52. Taubman, *op. cit.*, p. 568.

53. Mandelbaum, *op. cit.*, pp. 146–148.

54.   The conduit for the promises was the president's brother, Attorney General Robert Kennedy, who established a private channel of communication with the Soviet ambassador in Washington, Anatoly Dobrynin. Westad, *op. cit.*, p. 308.

55.   The closest equivalent to the Berlin and Cuban crises was the military alert the American government ordered in October 1973 in response to what appeared to be a Soviet threat to send troops to the Middle East to intervene in the Arab-Israeli war then under way. See p. 333.

56.   Westad, *op. cit.*, pp. 219–220.

57.   On the Japanese economy see Marius B. Jansen, *The Making of Modern Japan*, Cambridge, Massachusetts: The Belknap Press of Harvard University Press, 2000, p. 729.

58.   Richard N. Cooper, "Economic Aspects of the Cold War, 1962–1975," in Leffler and Westad, editors, *Crises and Détente*, p. 49. On the difficulties of the American economy in the second half of the 1970s see p. 340.

59.   *Ibid.*

60.   Barry Eichengreen, *The European Economy Since 1945: Coordinated Capitalism and Beyond*, Princeton, New Jersey: Princeton University Press, 2007, p. 89; Judt, *op. cit.*, pp. 327–328.

61.   Eichengreen, *op. cit.*, p. 178.

62.   Westad, *op. cit.*, pp. 217–218. Europe was also able to grow rapidly because it had political and economic institutions suitable for this purpose. Eichengreen, *op. cit.*, pp. 3–4.

63.   Cooper, *op. cit.* p. 49.

64.   W. G. Beasley, *The Rise of Modern Japan: Political, Economic and Social Change Since 1850*, New York: St. Martin's Press, 1995, Chapter 5.

65.   Eichengreen, *op. cit.*, p. 180; Douglas A. Irwin, *Clashing Over Commerce: A History of U.S. Trade Policy*, Chicago: University of Chicago Press, 2017, pp. 528, 555.

66.   Gaddis, *We Now Know*, pp. 201, 219–220, 288–289.

67.   Walter LaFeber, *The Clash: U.S.-Japanese Relations Throughout History*, New York: W.W. Norton, 1997, p. 319.

68.   Frederic Bozo, "France, Gaullism, and the Cold War," in Leffler and Westad, editors, *Crisis and Detente*, p. 172.

69.   Cooper, *op. cit.*, p. 49.

70.   Eichengreen, *op. cit.*, pp. 133–146; J. F. Brown, *The Grooves of Change: Eastern Europe at the Turn of the Millennium*, Durham, North Carolina: Duke University Press, 2001, pp. 60–61; Judt, *op. cit.*, p. 427; Westad, *op. cit.*, pp. 187–188; Loth, *op. cit.*, pp. 515–516.

71.   Herring, *op. cit.*, p. 665; Csaba Bekes, "East Central Europe, 1953–1956," in Leffler and Westad, editors, *Origins*, p. 337.

72.   "The negative characteristics of Stalin . . . transformed themselves during the last years into a grave abuse of power . . . which caused untold harm to our party. . . . Stalin acted not through persuasion, explanation,

and patient cooperation with people, but by imposing his concepts and demanding absolute submission to his opinion. Whoever opposed this . . . was doomed to removal from the leading collective and to subsequent moral and physical annihilation." Quoted in Westad, *op. cit.*, p. 199.

73. Bekes, *op. cit.*, pp. 346–347; Judt, *op. cit.*, pp. 312–313; Westad, *op. cit.*, pp. 200–201.

74. Judt, *op. cit.*, p. 320.

75. Bekes, *op. cit.*, pp. 348–351.; Westad, *op. cit.*, pp. 203–205. "Two hundred thousand Hungarians fled west, twenty thousand were arrested, and 230 executed, including Prime Minister Nagy and several of his close associates." Westad, *op. cit.*, p. 205.

76. Charles Gati, *Failed Illusions: Moscow, Washington, Budapest, and the 1956 Hungarian Revolt*, Washington, D.C.: Woodrow Wilson Center Press and Stanford, California, Stanford University Press, 2006, pp. 162–171, 181–186, 199–203.

77. Archie Brown, *The Rise and Fall of Communism*, New York: Ecco, 2009, p. 382.

78. *Ibid.*, p. 385.

79. Dubcek was actually an ethnic Slovak.

80. Judt, *op. cit.*, pp. 442–445. The five invading countries were Poland, Hungary, Bulgaria, East Germany, and the Soviet Union.

81. J. F. Brown, *op. cit.*, p. 45.

82. Mark Philip Bradley, "Decolonization, the Global South, and the Cold War, 1919–1962," in Leffler and Westad, editors, *Origins*, pp. 479–480; Westad, *op. cit.*, pp. 270–271.

83. Westad, *op. cit.*, pp. 435–436.

84. *Ibid.*, pp. 392–393.

85. Herring, *op. cit.*, pp. 680–681.

86. Frederik Logevall, "The Indochina Wars and the Cold War, 1945–1975," in Leffler and Westad, editors, *Crises and Détente*, pp. 290–291; Herring, *op. cit.*, p. 662.

87. Herring, *op. cit.*, p. 673.

88. Counting the Bay of Pigs operation in 1961 as an indirect intervention, the direct American interventions took place in Guatemala in 1954 (see p. 301) and in the Dominican Republic in 1965. On the Dominican intervention see Cohen, *op. cit.*, p. 166, and Herring, *op. cit.*, p. 735.

89. LaFeber, *The American Age*, p. 688; Herring, *op. cit.*, pp. 837–838.

90. On the events in Iran see Ray Takeyh, *The Last Shah: America, Iran, and the Fall of the Pahlavi Dynasty*, New York: Oxford University Press, 2021, Chapters 3 and 4.

91. *Ibid.*, pp. 135–138.

92. *Ibid.*, pp. 146–149, 151.

93. Westad, *op. cit.*, pp. 345–347. The American intervention "did little to alter the course of events inside Guatemala, where Arbenz's regime had made so many enemies among the landowners and the military that it probably would not have lasted in any event." Gaddis, *We Now Know*, p. 178.

94. On the CIA's role in Iraq and Guatemala see Tim Wiener, *Legacy of Ashes: The History of the CIA*, New York: Anchor Books, 2007, Chapters 9 and 10.

95. Herring, *op. cit.*, pp. 674–675.

96. "From the beginning of the crisis, a key assumption had steadily guided [Eisenhower's] thinking: that a war over the canal was the worst option, because it would drive the Arab world, if not the entire developing world, into the arms of the Soviets." Michael Doran, *Ike's Gamble: America's Rise to Dominance in the Middle East*, New York: Free Press, 2016, p. 193.

97. "As [Eisenhower and Dulles] saw it, the Soviet repression in Hungary offered the West a prime opportunity to capture the moral high ground in international politics—an opportunity that the gunboat diplomacy in Egypt was destroying." *Ibid.*, p. 197.

98. Westad, *op. cit.*, p. 273.

99. On the Suez crisis as a whole see Doran, *op. cit.*, Chapters 11 and 12; Douglas Little, "The Cold War in the Middle East: Suez Crisis to Camp David Accords," in Leffler and Westad, editors, *Crises and Détente*, pp. 306–310; and Derek Leebaert, *Grand Improvisation: America Confronts the British Superpower, 1945–1957*, New York: Farrar, Straus and Giroux, 2018, pp. 467–479.

100. Cohen, *op. cit.*, p. 114; LaFeber, *The American Age*, pp. 565–566.

101. Kennedy told "all his top aides to study the address with care. 'Read, mark, learn, and inwardly digest it,' he insisted." Patterson, *op. cit.*, p. 488.

102. On the history of guerrilla warfare see Max Boot, *Invisible Armies: An Epic History of Guerrilla Warfare from Ancient Times to the Present*, New York: Liveright, 2013.

103. On the Kennedy approach to foreign aid and economic development see Robert A. Packenham, *Liberal America and the Third World*, Princeton, New Jersey: Princeton University Press, 1973, pp. 59–74.

104. Cooper, *op. cit.*, p. 62.

105. Herring, *op. cit.*, p. 716.

106. *Ibid.*, p. 712; Westad, *op. cit.*, p. 291.

107. In the final, decisive stage of the Chinese Civil War the Communists fielded a mass army and fought regular battles against the Kuomintang.

108. On the insurgencies in Malaya and the Philippines see Michael Burleigh, *Small Wars, Faraway Places: Global Insurrection and the Making of the Modern World, 1945–1965*, New York: Viking, 2013, Chapters 6 and 7.

109. Michael J. Green, *By More Than Providence: Grand Strategy and American Power in the Asia Pacific Since 1783*, New York: Columbia

University Press, 2017, pp. 268–272; George C. Herring, *America's Longest War: The United States and Vietnam, 1950–1975*, New York: McGraw-Hill, Second Edition, 1986, pp. 5–14, 24.

110. Herring, *America's Longest War*, p. 55.
111. *Ibid.*, p. 68.
112. Patterson, *op. cit.*, p. 510.
113. Ernest R. May, *"Lessons" of the Past: The Use and Misuse of History in American Foreign Policy*, New York: Oxford University Press, 1976, pp. 107–108; Westad, *op. cit.*, pp. 321, 323; Cohen, *op. cit.*, pp. 151–152, 164.
114. Patterson, *op. cit.*, p. 515.
115. LaFeber, *The American Age*, p. 548.
116. Cohen, *op. cit.*, p. 154.
117. See pp. 110-111.
118. Frederik Logevall, *Choosing War: The Last Chance for Peace and the Escalation of the War in Vietnam*, Berkeley, California: University of California Press, 1999, p. 278; Herring, *America's Longest War*, pp. 45–47.
119. Herring, *America's Longest War*, p. 141; Logevall, *Choosing War*, pp. 388–389.
120. The credibility of the threat of massive Chinese intervention was enhanced by the presence, between 1965 and 1968, of approximately 50,000 Chinese troops in North Vietnam. Allen Whiting, *The Chinese Calculus of Deterrence: India and Indochina*, Ann Arbor, Michigan: The University of Michigan Press, 1975, Chapter 6.
121. Frederik Logevall, *Embers of War: The Fall of an Empire and the Making of America's Vietnam*, New York: Random House, 2012, p. 712.
122. Patterson, *op. cit.*, p. 595.
123. LaFeber, *The American Age*, p. 612; Herring, *America's Longest War*, p. 147.
124. Daniel Ellsberg argues that this was true as well of the Vietnam policies of Johnson's predecessors in the White House. Daniel Ellsberg, "The Quagmire Myth and the Stalemate Machine," in Ellsberg, *Papers on the War*, New York: Simon & Schuster, 1972, pp. 71, 78.
125. Patterson, *op. cit.*, p. 599; Herring, *America's Longest War*, pp. 150–151.
126. Herring, *From Colony to Superpower*, p. 770.
127. Herring, *America's Longest War*, pp. 128–129. In August 1964 the United States conducted limited air strikes against North Vietnamese targets in retaliation for what were thought to be attacks on American boats in the Gulf of Tonkin. Patterson, *op. cit.*, p. 603.
128. Herring, *America's Longest War*, p. 152.
129. "By the beginning of 1968 American and South Vietnamese firepower had killed, according to reasonably reliable estimates, some 220,000 enemy soldiers. This was some sixteen times the number of Americans (13,500) slain in Vietnam during the same period." Patterson, *op. cit.*, p. 596.

130. Quoted in Ellsberg, *op. cit.*, p. 30.

131. Herring, *America's Longest War*, pp. 5, 15; Logevall, *Embers of War*, p. xix; Westad, *op. cit.*, pp. 313–314.

132. Logevall, *Choosing War*, p. 376.

133. On Kennan see John Lewis Gaddis, *George F. Kennan: An American Life*, New York: Penguin Press, 2011, pp. 591–594. On Lippmann see Ronald Steel, *Walter Lippmann and the American Century*, Boston: Little Brown and Company, 1980, Chapters 42 and 43.

134. This is the argument of John Mueller, *War, Presidents, and Public Opinion*, New York: John Wiley & Sons, 1973.

135. Although college students made up a large part of the active opposition to the war, only a minority of all American college students took part in it. Patterson, *op. cit.*, p. 627.

136. The antiwar movement became unpopular, to the extent that it set back the cause that was its reason for being in the first place. Its perceived excesses actually increased sympathy for the government's war policies. See Adam Garfinkle, *Telltale Hearts: The Origins and Impact of the Vietnam Antiwar Movement*. New York: St. Martin's Press, 1995, Chapter 1, and Michael Mandelbaum, "Vietnam: The Television War," in *Print Culture and Video Culture, Daedalus*, Fall 1982, pp. 165–166.

137. Herring, *America's Longest War*, pp. 186–191.

138. "Rough estimates of overall casualties during the three weeks following Tet conclude that North Vietnamese and NLF [National Liberation Front, the communist-sponsored guerrilla organization in South Vietnam] battle deaths reached 40,000, compared to 2,300 South Vietnamese and 1,100 Americans." Patterson, *op. cit.*, pp. 679–680.

139. Westad, *op. cit.*, p. 334. On the Tet offensive more generally see Don Oberdorfer, *Tet!*, Garden City, New York: Doubleday, 1971. On the press coverage of Tet see Peter Baestrup, *Big Story: How the American Press and Television Reported and Interpreted the Crisis of Tet 1968 in Vietnam and Washington*, Boulder, Colorado: Westview Press, 1977.

140. "Public approval of Johnson's conduct of the conflict, already low at 40 percent following his public relations blitz in November, fell to 26 percent in the immediate aftermath of Tet." Patterson, *op. cit.*, p. 681.

141. Tad Szulc, *The Illusion of Peace: Foreign Policy in the Nixon Years*, New York: Viking, 1978, pp. 27–28.

142. Henry Kissinger, "The Vietnam Negotiations," in Kissinger, *American Foreign Policy*, New York: W.W. Norton, Expanded Edition, 1974, p. 112.

143. In 1973 military conscription, another source of the war's unpopularity, ended in the United States.

144. Herring, *America's Longest War*, pp. 251–252.

145. Cambodia suffered a terrible postwar fate. The communists who took control of the country, the Khmer Rouge, carried out a murderous policy of emptying the cities, which forced their inhabitants to try

to survive in the countryside. An estimated 1.5 million Cambodians perished—about one-fourth of the population. James T. Patterson, *Restless Giant: The United States from Watergate to Bush v. Gore,* New York: Oxford University Press, 2005, p. 101. For a critical account of American policy toward Cambodia see William Shawcross, *Sideshow: Kissinger, Nixon, and the Destruction of Cambodia,* New York: Simon & Schuster, 1979.

146. By some interpretations the so-called "Christmas bombing" also had the purpose of persuading an unhappy South Vietnamese government to go along with a peace agreement.

147. Among other things, the Paris accords provided for the return of American prisoners of war held in North Vietnam, most of them from the crews of airplanes that communist air defenses had shot down. The status of the prisoners had become an important issue for the American public.

148. Logevall, "The Indochina Wars and the Cold War," p. 300.

149. Herring, *From Colony to Superpower,* pp. 820–822; Herring, *America's Longest War,* pp. 265–267.

150. LaFeber, *The American Age,* p. 668.

151. See pp. 383-390.

152. Herring, *From Colony to Superpower,* p. 812; Patterson, *Grand Expectations,* p. 600.

153. Herring, *From Colony to Superpower,* p. 803.

154. Patterson, *Restless Giant,* p. 99.

155. Herring, *America's Longest War,* p. 273.

156. Patterson, *Grand Expectations,* p. 772; LaFeber, *The American Age,* p. 618. For a detailed account of the Watergate scandal see J. Anthony Lukas, *Nightmare: The Underside of the Nixon Years,* New York: Viking, 1976.

157. Lukas, *op. cit.,* Chapter 4.

158. LaFeber, *The American Age,* p. 636.

159. https://avalon.law.yale.edu/20th_century/nixon1.asp

160. Patterson, *Grand Expectations,* p. 744; Herring, *From Colony to Superpower,* pp. 785–786.

161. New York: Grosset and Dunlap, 1964.

162. Herring, *From Colony to Superpower,* p. 723. See also p. 317.

163. Westad, *op. cit.,* pp. 385–388. A detailed account of Ostpolitik is in Timothy Garton Ash, *In Europe's Name: Germany and the Divided Continent,* New York: Random House, 1993, Chapters II and III.

164. Raymond Garthoff, *Détente and Confrontation: American-Soviet Relations from Nixon to Reagan,* Washington, D.C.: The Brookings Institution, 1985, pp. 248–249, 254, 295.

165. *Ibid.,* p. 10.

166. *Ibid.,* p. 42–43.

167. Svetlana Savranskaya and William Taubman, "Soviet Foreign Policy, 1962–1975," in Leffler and Westad, editors, *Crises and Détente*, p. 142.

168. Garthoff, *op. cit.*, pp. 31–32.

169. See pp. 321, 324-325.

170. Garthoff, *op. cit.*, pp. 289–291.

171. The Test Ban Treaty permitted nuclear testing underground, and the United States and the Soviet Union continued to conduct tests there. On the Treaty see Mandelbaum, *op. cit.*, Chapter 7.

172. A detailed account of the negotiations that produced the 1972 accords is in John Newhouse, *Cold Dawn: The Story of SALT*, New York: Holt, Rinehart and Winston, 1973.

173. The treaty permitted each country to deploy only two systems of defense, one to protect its capital city, the other to guard a major missile site.

174. See p. 449.

175. Burr and Rosenberg, *op. cit.*, p. 108; Herring, *From Colony to Superpower*, p. 819.

176. A detailed account of the negotiations that led to the SALT II agreement is in Strobe Talbott, *Endgame: The Inside Story of SALT II*, New York: Harper & Row, 1979.

177. Gaddis, *We Now Know*, p. 292.

178. Trachtenberg, *op. cit.*, p. 501.

179. In 2015 only five countries were not signatories: India, Pakistan, South Sudan, Israel, and North Korea, which had signed but then withdrew in 2003.

180. Gavin, *op. cit.*, p. 396.

181. *Ibid.*, p. 400.

182. "The nine EC member states insisted that human rights provisions be part of the negotiations. As a result of their persistence, they won agreement in the Helsinki Final Act to Principle VII—'Respect for human rights and fundamental freedoms, including the freedom of thought, conscience, religion or belief'—together with a number of concrete measures to expand human contacts and exchanges under the Basket III provisions of the CSCE." Rosemary Foot, "The Cold War and Human Rights," in Melvyn P. Leffler and Odd Arne Westad, editors, *The Cold War, Volume III: Endings*, Cambridge, UK: Cambridge University Press, 2010, p. 459.

183. Henry Kissinger "did not even bother reading the Helsinki Accords. The American secretary of state, whose lack of enthusiasm for the CSCE was notable throughout the process, at one time even quipped that the Helsinki Final Act might just as well be written 'in Swahili.'" Jussi M. Hanhimaki, "Détente in Europe, 1962–1975," in Leffler and Westad, *Crises and Détente*, p. 214.

184. Judt, *op. cit.*, pp. 501–503.

185.   Garthoff, *op. cit.*, pp. 12–13, 26–27. In a remarkable departure from standard governmental practice, Kissinger and later Nixon "had no American interpreters present for any of their private talks with the Chinese leaders—a practice they also used in the Soviet Union." *Ibid.*, p. 233.

186.   Westad, *op. cit.*, pp. 441–444.

187.   "Nixon ordered the aircraft carrier USS *Enterprise* and three escort vessels into the Bay of Bengal to reassure Pakistan and deter India." Herring, *From Colony to Superpower*, p. 790.

188.   See pp. 325-328.

189.   For a critical account of the Nixon administration's policy during the 1971 war see Gary J. Bass, *The Blood Telegram: Nixon, Kissinger, and a Forgotten Genocide*, New York: Alfred A. Knopf, 2013.

190.   Allende responded to the coup against him by committing suicide.

191.   Westad, *op. cit.*, pp. 356–357.

192.   Herring, *From Colony to Superpower*, pp. 803–804; Cooper, *op. cit.*, pp. 55–56.

193.   Agnew resigned in the face of charges that he had accepted bribes during his pre–vice presidential service as governor of the state of Maryland. See Richard Cohen and Jules Witcover, *A Heartbeat Away: The Investigation and Resignation of Vice President Spiro T. Agnew*, New York: Viking, 1974.

194.   In his inaugural address Carter said that America's "commitment to human rights must be absolute." Quoted in Herring, *From Colony to Superpower*, p. 846.

195.   Garthoff, *op. cit.*, pp. 544–545.

196.   *Ibid.*, p. 551; Herring, *From Colony to Superpower*, p. 551.

197.   Herring, *From Colony to Superpower*, p. 795.

198.   Westad, *op. cit.*, pp. 482–484.

199.   LaFeber, *The American Age*, pp. 690–691.

200.   Garthoff, *op. cit.*, pp. 521–523. The Soviet side made it clear that it intended to continue the competition with the United States, especially in the Third World. "After the signing of the détente agreements of 1972 and 1973 . . . Brezhnev took the occasion . . . to reaffirm that 'revolution, the class struggle, and liberation movements cannot be abolished by agreements.'" Quoted in *ibid.*, pp. 43–44.

201.   Westad, *op. cit.*, p. 484.

202.   In 1975 Reagan said that "all Americans should be against" the Helsinki Final Act, which Ford had signed. Quoted in Robert Schulzinger, "Détente in the Nixon-Ford Years, 1969–1975," in Leffler and Westad, editors, *Crises and Détente*, p. 391.

203.   The phrase "war improbable, peace impossible" (see p. 324) comes from the French political writer Raymond Aron.

204. "For the rest of the world, and especially the rest of Asia, the breakthrough in Sino-American relations amounted to a strategic earthquake." Westad, *op. cit.*, p. 412.

205. Herring, *From Colony to Superpower*, pp. 662–664, 693. In the earlier crisis official American statements suggested the possibility of employing nuclear weapons.

206. During the Great Leap Forward between 1958 and 1961, "at least forty million . . . died, most of them from a combination of overwork and lack of food." Westad, *op. cit.*, pp. 243–244.

207. *Ibid.*, p. 255.

208. On the Sino-Soviet rift see Sergey Radchenko, "The Sino-Soviet Split," in Leffler and Westad, editors, *Crises and Détente*.

209. Green, *op. cit.*, pp. 331, 345; James Mann, *About Face: A History of America's Curious Relationship with China, from Nixon to Clinton*, New York: Alfred A. Knopf, 1999, pp. 34, 39.

210. In the article Nixon wrote that "we simply cannot afford to leave China forever outside the family of nations." Quoted in Green, *op. cit.*, p. 326.

211. Herring, *From Colony to Superpower*, p. 791.

212. Quoted in Mann, *op. cit.*, p. 48.

213. Green, *op. cit.*, p. 353.

214. Herring, *From Colony to Superpower*, p. 793.

215. *Ibid.*, pp. 791, 793.

216. Mann, *op. cit.*, pp. 81–82, 102–103.

217. Remarks in a speech to the House of Commons delivered on March 1, 1848.

218. See Stephane Courtois et al., *The Black Book of Communism: Crimes, Terror, Repression*, Cambridge, Massachusetts: Harvard University Press, 1999.

219. Cohen, *op. cit.*, p. 190; Herring, *From Colony to Superpower*, p. 793.

220. Mann, *op. cit.*, pp. 35, 56, 73–74, 76, 86, 111.

221. In a 1979 visit to the United States by the post-Mao Chinese leader Deng Xiaoping, President Carter is reported to have asked him about his government's policy on allowing Chinese to emigrate. Deng is said to have replied, "How many millions do you want?" The subject apparently did not arise again.

222. Kissinger, in particular, became infatuated with China's two paramount leaders. He described Zhou Enlai in glowing terms: "Urbane, infinitely patient, extraordinarily intelligent, subtle, he moved through our discussions with an easy grace. . . ." Quoted in Mann, *op. cit.*, p. 32. On Mao Tse-tung: "Mao radiates authority and deep wisdom. . . ." *Ibid.*, p. 61.

223. The contradiction between the dollar's two roles was known as the "Triffin Dilemma," after the Belgian-American economist Robert Triffin, who wrote extensively about it. Barry Eichengreen, *Exorbitant*

Privilege: The Rise and Fall of the Dollar and the Future of the International Monetary System, New York: Oxford University Press, 2011, p. 50.

224. This is the subject of Francis J. Gavin, *Gold, Dollars, and Power: The Politics of International Monetary Relations, 1958–1971*, Chapel Hill, North Carolina: The University of North Carolina Press, 2004. On the decline of the American gold stock see Alan Greenspan and Adrian Wooldridge, *Capitalism in America: A History*, New York: Penguin Press, 2018, pp. 307–308.

225. Robert Gilpin, *The Challenge of Global Capitalism: The World Economy in the 21st Century*, Princeton, New Jersey: Princeton University Press, 2000, pp. 60–61.

226. *Ibid.*, p. 70; Eichengreen, *Exorbitant Privilege*, p. 61.

227. This is a theme of Joanne Gowa, *Closing the Gold Window: Domestic Politics and the End of Bretton Woods*, Ithaca, New York: Cornell University Press, 1983. Secretary of the Treasury George Shultz "told the world that America's days as the caretaker of the global payments system were over. 'Santa Claus is dead.'" Gavin, *Gold, Dollars, and Power*, p. 196.

228. Green, *op. cit.*, p. 344.

229. Gilpin, *op. cit.*, p. 70.

230. Gavin, *Gold, Dollars, and Power*, p. 13.

231. Michael Mandelbaum, *The Ideas That Conquered the World: Peace, Democracy and Free Markets in the Twenty-first Century*, New York: PublicAffairs, 2002, pp. 350–351.

232. Michael Mandelbaum, *The Road to Global Prosperity*, New York: Simon & Schuster, 2014, pp. 24–25.

233. Nadav Safran, *Israel—The Embattled Ally*, Cambridge, Massachusetts: The Belknap Press of Harvard University Press, 1978, pp. 482–483.

234. Jeffry Frieden, *Global Capitalism: Its Fall and Rise in the Twentieth Century*, New York: W.W. Norton, 2006, p. 365.

235. Much of the volume of petrodollars was channeled through Western banks to the non-oil-producing Third World countries, which used the loans to purchase the now much more expensive oil that they needed. *Ibid.*, p. 370.

236. *Ibid.*, p. 365.

237. Safran, *op. cit.*, pp. 493–495.

238. On Soviet-American relations during the October 1973 war see Garthoff, *op. cit.*, Chapter 11.

239. Michael Mandelbaum, *The Fate of Nations: The Search for National Security in the Nineteenth and Twentieth Centuries*, New York: Cambridge University Press, 1988, p. 288.

240. Kissinger describes the peacemaking efforts following the 1973 war, and his own involvement in them, in the second and third volumes of his three-volume memoir of his government service. *Years of Upheaval*, Boston: Little Brown, 1982, Chapters XI–XIII, XVII, XVIII, XXI, XXIII, and *Years of Renewal*, New York: Simon & Schuster, 1999, Part Four.

241. Mandelbaum, *The Fate of Nations*, pp. 297, 305–306; Safran, *op. cit.*, pp. 531, 557–558.

242. Mandelbaum, *The Fate of Nations*, pp. 307–308.

243. Mann, *op. cit.*, pp. 98–100.

Chapter 9

1. Amin Saikal, "Islamism, the Iranian Revolution, and the Soviet Invasion of Afghanistan," in Melvyn P. Leffler and Odd Arne Westad, editors, *The Cambridge History of the Cold War, Volume III: Endings*, Cambridge, UK: Cambridge University Press, 2010, pp. 116–117.

2. ". . . [T]he Shah proved weak, vacillating, and suffered from a paralysis of will." Zbigniew Brzezinski, *Power and Principle: Memoirs of the National Security Adviser, 1977–1981*, New York: Farrar, Straus and Giroux, 1983, p. 395.

3. On the downfall of the Shah see Ray Takeyh, *The Last Shah: America, Iran, and the Fall of the Pahlavi Dynasty*, New York: Oxford University Press, 2021, Chapter 8.

4. Generally speaking, the State Department, and its secretary, Cyrus Vance, advocated conciliation, while the National Security Council, led by Zbigniew Brzezinski, preferred firmness. Brzezinski, *op. cit.*, pp. 355, 393; Gary Sick, *All Fall Down: America's Tragic Encounter with Iran*, New York: Random House, 1983, pp. 70–71.

5. Khomeini used the hostage crisis to defeat politically the segments of the coalition that had toppled the Shah that opposed his version of Islamic government. Sick, *op. cit.*, pp. 204–206, 278.

6. Brzezinski, *op. cit.*, p. 517.

7. Sick, *op. cit.*, pp. 296–299.

8. "Iran's oil production fell from 5.8 million barrels per day before Black Friday [September 8, 1978] to 2.3 million barrels in November and, by January [1979] close to zero." Takeyh, *op. cit.*, p. 224.

9. From the end of 1978 to the first quarter of 1980 the price of oil rose by 125 percent. Stephen D. Krasner, *Structural Conflict: The Third World Against Global Liberalism*, Berkeley, California: University of California Press, 1985, p. 106.

10. Alan Greenspan and Adrian Wooldridge, *Capitalism in America: A History*, New York: Penguin Press, 2018, pp. 300–301; James T. Patterson, *Restless Giant: The United States from Watergate to Bush v. Gore*, New York: Oxford University Press, 2005, p. 62.

11. This is a major theme of Robert J. Gordon, *The Rise and Fall of American Growth: The U.S. Standard of Living Since the Civil War*, Princeton, New Jersey: Princeton University Press, 2016.

12. "The cost of living rose between 1973 and 1983 at an average annual rate of 8.2 percent, more than double the rate between 1963 and 1973." Patterson, *op. cit.*, p. 65.

13. Greenspan and Wooldridge, *op. cit.*, pp. 305–306; Patterson, *op. cit.*, p. 65.

14. The Phillips Curve, a widely accepted economic concept that measured the tradeoff between inflation and unemployment, assumed that the two had a stable and inverse relationship. Greenspan and Wooldridge, *op. cit.*, p. 309.

15. The combination of the inflation and unemployment rates was called the "misery index." It was higher, on average, during the Carter years than in any other presidential administration after World War II. https://en.wikipedia.org/wiki/Misery_index_(economics)#Misery_index_by_US_presidential_administration

16. ". . . [T]he mood of the late 1970s was in important ways the gloomiest in late twentieth-century American history." Patterson, *op. cit.*, p. 15.

17. "Spiraling economic problems reinforced already strong tendencies to turn inward. . . . The five issues that most concerned Americans in 1965 all involved foreign policy; nine years later, the top three were domestic." George C. Herring, *From Colony to Superpower: U.S. Foreign Relations Since 1776*, New York: Oxford University Press, 2008, p. 811.

18. *Ibid.*, p. 858.

19. John Cochrane, "The Cold War in Central America," in Leffler and Westad, editors, *op. cit.*, p. 206.

20. On this subject see Daniel Pipes and Adam Garfinkle, editors, *Friendly Tyrants: An American Dilemma*, New York: St. Martin's Press, 1991.

21. Saikal, *op. cit.*, p. 128.

22. Walter LaFeber, *The American Age: U.S. Foreign Policy at Home and Abroad, 1750 to the Present*, New York: W.W. Norton, Second Edition, 1994, p. 699.

23. The Soviet coup in Afghanistan is described in Michael Dobbs, *Down with Big Brother: The Fall of the Soviet Empire*, New York: Alfred A. Knopf, 1997, pp. 18–24.

24. Nancy Mitchell, "The Cold War and Jimmy Carter," in Leffler and Westad, editors, *op. cit.*, pp. 83–84.

25. They saw "a strong indication that [the new leader Hafizullah] Amin wanted to emulate President Sadat of Egypt by sending Soviet advisers home and realigning Afghanistan with the United States, Pakistan, and China." Raymond Garthoff, *Détente and Confrontation: American-Soviet Relations from Nixon to Reagan*, Washington, D.C.: The Brookings Institution, 1985, p. 920.

26. *Ibid.*, p. 930.

27. Saikal, *op. cit.*, p. 129; Garthoff, *op. cit.*, pp. 946, 949. In discussing
     the Soviet invasion with President Carter, his national security advisor
     records that he "stressed that the issue was not what might have been
     Brezhnev's subjective motives in going into Afghanistan but the objective
     consequences of a Soviet military presence so much closer to the Persian
     Gulf." Brzezinski, *op. cit.*, p. 430.

28. Garthoff, *op. cit.*, p. 952, has a list of the measures the Carter
     administration implemented.

29. The relevant sentence read: "An attempt by any outside force to gain
     control of the Persian Gulf region will be regarded as an assault on the
     vital interests of the United States of America, and such an assault will
     be repelled by any means necessary, including military force." Quoted
     in *ibid.*, p. 954. The Defense Department created a special "Rapid
     Deployment Force" to protect the Gulf and its oil fields.

30. Herring, *op. cit.*, p. 855.

31. Vladislav Zubok, "Soviet Foreign Policy from Détente to Gorbachev,
     1975–1985," in Leffler and Westad, editors, *op. cit.*, p. 104; Garthoff, *op.
     cit.*, p. 937; Sick, *op. cit.*, p. 291.

32. Quoted in Garthoff, *op. cit.*, p. 950.

33. Reagan won 50.7 percent of the popular vote to Carter's 41 percent, and
     489 electoral votes to Carter's 49.

34. By comparison, Woodrow Wilson served one two-year term as governor
     of New Jersey and Franklin Roosevelt two two-year terms as governor of
     New York.

35. Raymond Garthoff, *The Great Transition: American-Soviet Relations and
     the End of the Cold War*, Washington, D.C.: The Brookings Institution,
     1994, p. 14.

36. Richard Reeves, *President Reagan: The Triumph of Imagination*,
     New York: Simon & Schuster, 2005, pp. 108–109. A 1982 National
     Security document outlining the strategy toward the Soviet Union made
     it clear that "the President was determined to go on the offensive in the
     Cold War." *Ibid.*, p. 104.

37. LaFeber, *op. cit.*, p. 705.

38. "Less than two weeks after entering office, Reagan approved an
     immediate increase of $32.6 billion in the defense budget over the $200.3
     billion already requested by Jimmy Carter in his last week in office.
     That Carter request had represented a boost of $26.5 billion above the
     preceding year." Garthoff, *The Great Transition*, p. 33. Defense spending
     increased by seven percent per year between 1981 and 1986. Herring, *op.
     cit.*, p. 867.

39. Michael Mandelbaum and Strobe Talbott, *Reagan and Gorbachev*,
     New York: Vintage Books, 1987, p. 119.

40. See p. 285.

41. Mandelbaum and Talbott, *op. cit.*, pp. 114–118.

42. See pp. 288-289.

43. The countries involved were West Germany, Belgium, Italy, the Netherlands, and Great Britain.

44. Odd Arne Westad, *The Cold War: A World History*, New York: Basic Books, 2017, p. 506.

45. Strobe Talbott, *Deadly Gambits: The Reagan Administration and the Stalemate in Nuclear Arms Control*, New York: Alfred A. Knopf, 1984, Chapters 4 and 5.

46. Westad, *op. cit.*, p. 521; Garthoff, *The Great Transition*, p. 552.

47. Mandelbaum and Talbott, *op. cit.*, p. 124.

48. Herring, *op. cit.*, p. 869; Reeves, *op. cit.*, p. 142.

49. Reeves, *op. cit.*, p. 146.

50. Some, both within the administration and outside it, assumed that no system of ballistic missile defense could guarantee the safety of the United States but believed that the prospect of deploying one could be used as a "bargaining chip" in arms control negotiations with the Soviet Union, to be exchanged for Soviet concessions. Warren I. Cohen, *The Cambridge History of American Foreign Relations, Volume IV: America in the Age of Soviet Power, 1945–1991*, New York: Cambridge University Press, 1993, p. 226; Mandelbaum and Talbott, *op. cit.*, p. 128.

51. Patterson, *op. cit.*, p. 206.

52. LaFeber, *op. cit.*, pp. 719–720; Herring, *op. cit.*, pp. 887–888; Reeves, *op. cit.*, pp. 183–189.

53. Herring, *op. cit.*, p. 889.

54. John H. Coatsworth, "The Cold War in Central America, 1973–1991," in Leffler and Westad, editors, *op. cit.*, p. 212.

55. Herring, *op. cit.*, p. 884.

56. *Ibid.*, p. 884; Garthoff, *Détente and Confrontation*, pp. 1057–1058.

57. Herring, *op. cit.*, p. 889.

58. Patterson, *op. cit.*, p. 227.

59. Westad, *op. cit.*, p. 532.

60. Garthoff, *Détente and Confrontation*, p. 1063.

61. LaFeber, *op. cit.*, p. 730.

62. Herring, *op. cit.*, pp. 876–877.

63. Dennis Ross, "American Military Policy Outside Europe," in Michael Mandelbaum, editor, *America's Defense*, New York: Holmes and Meier, 1989, pp. 186–187.

64. Herring, *op. cit.*, pp. 878–879.

65. Reeves, *op. cit.*, p. 375.

66. Reagan's approval rating fell to thirty-six percent. Herring, *op. cit.*, p. 891.

67. *Ibid.*, p. 883.

68. Greenspan and Wooldridge, *op. cit.*, p. 329.

69. *Ibid.*

70. ". . . [T]he number of jobs grew by some 200,000 a month—or by more than 18 million overall—between 1981 and 1989. The Dow Jones industrial average jumped from 950.88 at the time of [Reagan's] first inaugural to 2,239 eight years later." Patterson, *op. cit.*, pp. 169–170.

71. Barry Eichengreen, *The European Economy Since 1945: Coordinated Capitalism and Beyond*, Princeton, New Jersey: Princeton University Press, 2007, p. 224,

72. " . . . [T]he European state could no longer square the circle of full employment, high real wages and economic growth. . . ." Tony Judt, *Postwar: A History of Europe Since 1945*, New York: Penguin Press, 2005, p. 462.

73. *Ibid.*, pp. 549–553.

74. The yearly economic growth rates of the major European countries in the 1980s are listed in John W. Young, "Western Europe and the End of the Cold War, 1979–1989," in Leffler and Westad, editors, *op. cit.*, p. 300.

75. Westad, *op. cit.*, p. 593.

76. The European Community, as it then was, also expanded its membership in the 1980s, with Greece joining in 1983 and Spain and Portugal in 1986.

77. See pp. 328-331.

78. Douglas A. Irwin, *Clashing Over Commerce: A History of US Trade Policy*, Chicago: University of Chicago Press, 2017, p. 559.

79. *Ibid.*, p. 565.

80. *Ibid.*, pp. 575–592; Robert Gilpin, *The Challenge of Global Capitalism: The World Economy in the 21st Century*, Princeton, New Jersey: Princeton University Press, 2000, pp. 233–238.

81. Irwin, *op. cit.*, pp, 605, 610.

82. Jeffry A. Frieden, *Global Capitalism: Its Fall and Rise in the Twentieth Century*, New York: W.W. Norton, 2006, p. 377; Robert Campbell, *The Socialist Economies in Transition: A Primer on Semi-Reformed Economies*, Bloomington, Indiana: Indiana University Press, 1991, p. 123.

83. Jacques Levesque, "The East European Revolutions of 1989," in Leffler and Westad, editors, *op. cit.*, p. 314.

84. John Lewis Gaddis, "Grand Strategies in the Cold War," in Melvyn P. Leffler and Odd Arne Westad, editors, *The Cambridge History of the Cold War, Volume II: Crises and Détente*, Cambridge, UK: Cambridge University Press, 2010, pp. 17–18; Eichengreen, *op. cit.*, pp. 297–298; Wilfried Loth, "The Cold War and the Social and Economic History of the Twentieth Century," in Leffler and Westad, editors, *Crises and Détente*, p. 521.

85. Marshall I. Goldman, *Petrostate: Putin, Power, and the New Russia*, New York: Oxford University Press, 2008, pp. 51–53.

86. ". . . [T]here were, in effect, two Soviet economies: one—privileged and pampered and in a number of areas up to world standards—devoted to military production and defence-related industry; and the other—starved

of capital, new technology and esteem—constituting the civilian industrial sector and supposedly providing for the needs of the ill-served Soviet consumer." Archie Brown, *The Gorbachev Factor*, Oxford, UK: Oxford University Press, 1996, p. 159.

87. Mandelbaum and Talbott, *op. cit.*, p. 68.

88. Campbell, *op. cit.*, p. 141. On intensive and extensive economic growth see Michael Mandelbaum, *The Ideas That Conquered the World: Peace, Democracy and Free Markets in the Twenty-First Century*, New York: PublicAffairs, 2002, pp. 287–293, and Eichengreen, *op. cit.*, p. 6.

89. Levesque, *op. cit.*, p. 312.

90. Gale Stokes, *The Wall Came Tumbling Down: The Collapse of Communism in Eastern Europe*, New York: Oxford University Press, 1993, p. 33; Timothy Garton Ash, *The Magic Lantern: The Revolutions of '89 Witnessed in Warsaw, Budapest, Berlin and Prague*, New York: Random House, 1990, p. 133.

91. On the rise of Solidarity see Timothy Garton Ash, *The Polish Revolution: Solidarity*, New York: Charles Scribner's Sons, 1983, and Dobbs, *op. cit.*, pp. 30–53.

92. Jaruzelski claimed that he had acted to forestall a Soviet invasion. Records of Soviet Politburo deliberations about Poland that became available years later, however, showed that the Soviet leadership was strongly opposed to sending Soviet troops into that country. Zubok, *op. cit.*, p. 100.

93. Frieden, *op. cit.*, pp. 374–375; Westad, *op. cit.*, pp. 572–573. A detailed analysis of the debt crisis is in Miles Kahler, editor, *The Politics of International Debt*, Ithaca, New York: Cornell University Press, 1986.

94. Mandelbaum, *The Ideas That Conquered the World*, pp. 281–282,

95. Frieden, *op. cit.*, pp. 319–320.

96. *Ibid.*, pp. 421–423.

97. The English spelling of the Chinese capital changed from "Peking" to "Beijing" in 1979 with the substitution of the Pinyin for the Wade-Giles system of transliteration. The Communist Party leader until 1976 became Mao Zedong instead of Mao Tse-tung.

98. Frieden, *op. cit.*, pp. 376–377; Westad, *op. cit.*, pp. 556–559; Chen Jia, "China and the Cold War After Mao," in Leffler and Westad, editors, *Endings*, pp. 195–196.

99. Frieden, *op. cit.*, pp. 376, 425.

100. The phrase is from Samuel P. Huntington , *The Third Wave: Democratization in the Late Twentieth Century*, Norman, Oklahoma: University of Oklahoma Press, 1991, which provides a detailed discussion of the increases in democratic government in the 1980s. A chart tracing the historical spread of democracy appears on p. 14.

101. Frieden, *op. cit.*, p. 375.

102. An analysis of the causes of the spread of democracy is in Michael Mandelbaum, *Democracy's Good Name: The Rise and Risks of the World's Most Popular Form of Government*, New York: PublicAffairs, 2007, Chapters 2 and 3. See also Huntington, *op. cit.*, Chapter 2.

103. *The Tiananmen Papers*, Compiled by Zhiang Liang, Edited by Andrew J. Nathan and Perry Link, New York: PublicAffairs, 2002, p. viii.

104. Westad, *op. cit.*, pp. 587–588; Harry Harding, *A Fragile Relationship: The United States and China Since 1972*, Washington, D.C.: The Brookings Institution, 1992, pp. 219–223.

105. Stokes, *op. cit.*, p. 70. Gorbachev was born in 1931, Brezhnev in 1906, Andropov in 1914, and Chernenko in 1911.

106. Martin Malia, *The Soviet Tragedy: A History of Socialism in Russia, 1917–1991*, New York: The Free Press, 1994, pp. 411–413; Mandelbaum and Talbott, *op. cit.*, p. 75.

107. "[Glasnost], usually translated as 'openness' or 'publicity,' is in fact a bureaucratic term dating back to Alexander II and signifying officially encouraged notoriety regarding matters the government wishes to see discussed in a critical but constructive fashion." Malia, *op. cit.*, p. 421.

108. *Ibid.*, pp. 428–429; Brown, *op. cit.*, pp. 188–190.

109. Brown, *op. cit.*, pp. 190–191.

110. Before and then again after the Soviet period the city's name was (and is) Nizhni Novgorod.

111. Westad, *op. cit.*, p. 514; Brown, *op. cit.*, p. 164.

112. In pre- and post-Soviet times Sverdlovsk bore the name Ekaterinburg.

113. On Yeltsin see Leon Aron, *Boris Yeltsin, A Revolutionary Life*, New York: HarperCollins, 2000, Part II.

114. See pp. 298–299.

115. Talbott, *op. cit.*, p. 7.

116. After Prime Minister Thatcher met Gorbachev in 1984, before he became general secretary, she cabled Reagan: "I like Mr. Gorbachev. We can do business with him." Reeves, *op. cit.*, p. 238.

117. Garthoff, *The Great Transition*, pp. 285–291; Reeves, *op. cit.*, pp. 343–358.

118. See pp. 253-254.

119. Reeves, *op. cit.*, pp. 357–358; Mandelbaum and Talbott, *op. cit.*, p. 175.

120. Westad, *op. cit.*, p. 581.

121. Reeves, *op. cit.*, p. 417.

122. Garthoff, *The Great Transition*, p. 327.

123. See pp. 318-319.

124. Westad, *op. cit.*, p. 549.

125. "Five years and more than $12 billion after Reagan's first SDI speech, the Joint Chiefs of Staff were preparing budget proposals based on their own secret studies that the best feasible system, if any system was feasible at all, might have the capacity to block only 30 percent of Soviet warheads in a massive first-strike attack." Reeves, *op. cit.*, pp. 461–462.

126. *Ibid.*, p. 482.
127. On the CFE agreement see Michael Mandelbaum, *The Dawn of Peace in Europe*, New York: The Twentieth Century Fund, 1996, pp. 90–92.
128. On common security see *ibid.*, Part Two.
129. By one estimate, "the Soviets were spending $40 billion annually on their friends abroad." Cohen, *op. cit.*, p. 232.
130. The agreement also recognized the independence of Namibia. Westad, *op. cit.*, p. 568.
131. LaFeber, *op. cit.*, p. 748. An estimated 30,000 people died in the war in Nicaragua. Coatsworth, *op. cit.*, p. 215.
132. Malia, *op. cit.*, p. 417.
133. Dobbs, *op. cit.*, p. 17.
134. "By the end of 1987, more than one million Afghanis had been killed and another three million had fled the country, most to refugee camps in Pakistan, and between twelve thousand and fifteen thousand Soviet soldiers and airmen were dead." Reeves, *op. cit.*, p. 448.
135. As in Vietnam, a peace agreement was signed among the warring parties in Afghanistan that did not, in fact, end the fighting but that did provide cover for Moscow to withdraw its forces. Saikal, *op. cit.*, p. 133.
136. Garthoff, *The Great Transition*, p. 31. "The United States helped the non-Communist opposition group Solidarity stay in contact with the West and promote its cause inside Poland. United States funds purchased personal computers and fax machines and assisted Solidarity members in using them to publish newsletters and propaganda. The covert program helped keep Solidarity alive during the years of martial law. . . ." Herring, *op. cit.*, pp. 881–882.
137. ". . . [I]t was agreed that the opposition would compete for 35% of the 460 seats in the Diet while the other 65% would be left unopposed to the [communists]. A new body, a 100-seat Senate with far less power, was to be elected in free elections. . . . [I]n the first round of the elections, Solidarity's Civic Committee won 92 of the 100 seats in the Senate, far more than predicted. But the biggest surprise was the miserable performance of the [communists] in the competition for the Diet seats reserved for them. Solidarity won 160 of the 161 seats for which it could compete. By contrast, for the 299 seats reserved for the governing coalition, only five candidates managed to garner the 50 percent of the votes required to win. . . . Some people crossed out the names of all the Communists on their ballots; others crossed out the names of the most prominent ones." Levesque, *op. cit.*, pp. 317–318.
138. On the events in Poland see Stokes, *op. cit.*, Chapter 4, and J. F. Brown, *Surge to Freedom: The End of Communist Rule in Eastern Europe*, Durham, North Carolina: Duke University Press, 1991, Chapter 3.
139. Levesque, *op. cit.*, p. 324.

140. On the events in Hungary see Stokes, *op. cit.*, pp. 132–136, and J. F. Brown, *op. cit.*, Chapter 4.

141. Westad, *op. cit.*, p. 591.

142. Helga Haftendorn, "The Unification of Germany, 1885–1991," in Leffler and Westad, editors, *Endings*, p. 339.

143. Stokes, *op. cit.*, p. 136–141.

144. On German unification see Haftendorn, *op. cit.* On the American role, see George Bush and Brent Scowcroft, *A World Transformed*, New York: Alfred A. Knopf, 1998, Chapters 8–12, and Philip Zelikow and Condoleezza Rice, *Germany Unified and Europe Transformed: A Study in Statecraft*, Cambridge, Massachusetts: Harvard University Press, 1995.

145. The name came from the year of its founding, 1977.

146. Levesque, *op. cit.*, pp. 324–327; Stokes, *op. cit.*, pp. 148–157; J. F. Brown, *op. cit.*, Chapter 6.

147. Levesque, *op. cit.*, pp. 330–331; Stokes, *op. cit.*, pp. 141–149; J. F. Brown, *op. cit.*, Chapter 7.

148. Stokes, *op. cit.*, pp. 158–167; J. F. Brown, *op. cit.*, Chapter 8.

149. Michael Beschloss and Strobe Talbott, *At the Highest Levels: The Inside Story of the End of the Cold War*, Boston: Little, Brown and Company, 1993, pp. 85, 86, 91.

150. Alex Pravda, "The Collapse of the Soviet Union, 1990–1991," in Leffler and Westad, editors, *op. cit.*, p. 364.

151. Several violent acts of repression instigated by local Soviet authorities, costing a handful of lives, took place in Lithuania. Archie Brown, *op. cit.*, p. 280.

152. Westad, *op. cit.*, p. 609.

153. As these events were taking place in the western part of the Soviet Union, nationalist conflicts were erupting in its south, in the Caucasus. "In 1989 the Red Army had used force to break up nationalist demonstrations in Georgia. Twenty people were killed. In January 1990, after months of unrest and ethnic clashes between Azeris and Armenians, Soviet special forces took control of the Azerbaijan capital of Baku against strong Azeri nationalist opposition." *Ibid.*, p. 602.

154. Quoted in Garthoff, *The Great Transition*, p. 471.

155. Pravda, *op. cit.*, p. 366.

156. *Ibid.*, p. 373.

157. The events leading to the collapse of the Soviet Union are described in Westad, *op. cit.*, pp. 611–615, and Archie Brown, *op. cit.*, pp. 294–305.

158. Herring, *op. cit.*, p. 913.

159. "It is unlikely that the process that ended in collapse would have started without the drive of an exceptional leader, Gorbachev, determined to reinvigorate the system through radical reform." Pravda, *op. cit.*, p. 358.

160. Archie Brown, "The Gorbachev Revolution and the End of the Cold War," in Leffler and Westad, editors, *op. cit.*, pp. 244–245; Archie Brown, *The Gorbachev Factor*, p. 161.

161. Westad, *op. cit.*, p. 545.

162. Archie Brown, "The Gorbachev Revolution and the End of the Cold War," p. 248.

163. Malia, *op. cit.*, p. 413.

164. J. F. Brown, *op. cit.*, p. 60.

165. Westad, *op. cit.*, p. 614; Pravda, *op. cit.*, p. 370.

166. Ash, *The Magic Lantern*, pp. 141–142.

167. Paul Kennedy, *The Rise and Fall of the Great Powers: Economic Change and Military Conflict from 1500 to 2000*, New York: Random House, 1987, p. xxiv.

The Fourth Age

1. Paul Kennedy, "The Colossus with an Achilles Heel," *New Perspectives Quarterly*, Fall 2001.

2. Michael Mandelbaum, *The Rise and Fall of Peace on Earth*, New York: Oxford University Press, 2019, p. 2.

3. The phrase was coined by the journalist Charles Krauthammer. George C. Herring, *From Colony to Superpower: U.S. Foreign Relations Since 1776*, New York: Oxford University Press, 2008, p. 921.

4. On reassurance see Michael Mandelbaum, *The Case for Goliath: How America Acts as the World's Government in the Twenty-first Century*, New York: PublicAffairs, 2005, pp. 33–35.

5. This is the major theme of *ibid.* See especially Chapter 1.

6. On the "democratic peace" theory see Michael Mandelbaum, *Democracy's Good Name: The Rise and Risks of the World's Most Popular Form of Government*, New York: PublicAffairs, 2007, Chapter 4.

7. The phrase is from Mandelbaum, *The Ideas That Conquered the World*. See Part III, especially p. 275.

Chapter 10

1. Lawrence Freedman and Efraim Karsh, *The Gulf Conflict, 1990–1991: Diplomacy and War in the New World Order*, Princeton, New Jersey: Princeton University Press, 1993, pp. 37–40, 61–62, 429.

2. *Ibid.*, pp. 57–58.

3. Walter LaFeber, *The American Age: U.S. Foreign Policy at Home and Abroad, 1750 to the Present*, New York: W.W. Norton, Second Edition, 1994, p. 760; George C. Herring, *From Colony to Superpower: U.S. Foreign Relations Since 1776*, New York: Oxford University Press, 2008, p. 908.

4. Freedman and Karsh, *op. cit.*, pp. 52–54.

5. *Ibid.*, p. 58.

6. *Ibid.*, p. 71.

7. *Ibid.*, p. 74.

8. *Ibid.*, p. 73.

9. George Bush and Brent Scowcroft, *A World Transformed*, New York: Alfred A. Knopf, 1998, pp. 354, 400.

10. In launching the war Bush said: "We have before us the opportunity to forge for ourselves and for future generations a new world order, a world where the rule of law, not the law of the jungle, governs the conduct of nations. . . ." Quoted in John Mueller, *Policy and Opinion in the Gulf War*, Chicago: University of Chicago Press, 1994, p. 52.

11. Freedman and Karsh, *op. cit.*, pp. 86–97.

12. In the House the vote was 250 to 183. James T. Patterson, *Restless Giant: The United States from Watergate to Bush v. Gore*, New York: Oxford University Press, 2005, p. 233.

13. Freedman and Karsh, *op. cit.*, pp. 376–378; Bush and Scowcroft, *op. cit.*, pp. 470, 479.

14. Freedman and Karsh, *op. cit.*, pp. 196, 210.

15. Precision-guided munitions made up about ten percent of all the bombs dropped on Iraqi targets during the war.

16. Iraq also launched Scud missiles at Saudi Arabia.

17. Freedman and Karsh, *op. cit.*, pp. 307–308, 332–334.

18. The administration of George H. W. Bush's son, George W. Bush, took a different approach to occupying Iraq. See pp. 430-431..

19. Martin Indyk, *Innocent Abroad: An Intimate Account of American Peace Diplomacy in the Middle East*, New York: Simon & Schuster, 2009, p. 35.

20. Freedman and Karsh, *op. cit.*, pp. 420–424. ". . . [S]ome 5,000 American troops were deployed in northern Iraq, together with 2,000 British, 1,000 French and a small Dutch force." *Ibid.*, p. 424.

21. An estimated 35,000 Iraqis were killed. Freedman and Karsh, *op. cit.*, p. 408.

22. ". . . [T]he public's tolerance for American casualties appears to have been quite low, and if there had been substantial costs to American forces, support would probably have dwindled quickly." Mueller, *op. cit.*, p. xvi.

23. *Ibid.*, p. xv.

24. *Ibid.*, p. xvii; Freedman and Karsh, *op. cit.*, pp. 212, 223–224.

25. Freedman and Karsh, *op. cit.*, p. 284.

26. *Ibid.*, p. 430.

27. Quoted in *ibid.*, p. xxix.

28. The impact of the Gulf War, which had ended almost two years before Election Day, on the 1992 presidential election followed a pattern in American history. ". . . [V]oters simply come to neglect the war entirely as they turn to other, more immediate concerns, particularly domestic ones." Mueller, *op. cit.*, p. 99.

29. Clinton's history of avoiding the military draft during the Vietnam War became controversial during the 1992 campaign.

30. Michael Mandelbaum, *The Ideas That Conquered the World: Peace, Democracy and Free Markets in the Twenty-first Century*, New York: PublicAffairs, 2002, pp. 330–331.

31. "'Since we don't have geopolitics any more,' one Clinton adviser pronounced, 'trade is the name of the game.'" Herring, *op. cit.*, p. 926.

32. Early in his administration Clinton promised to "focus like a laser" on the economy. Quoted in Michael Mandelbaum, *Mission Failure: America and the World in the Post-Cold War Era*, New York: Oxford University Press, 2016, p. 16.

33. "By the end of the twentieth century, the United States dominated the information revolution just as thoroughly as it dominated the oil and steel industries in the late nineteenth century." Alan Greenspan and Adrian Wooldridge, *Capitalism in America: A History*, New York: The Penguin Press, 2018, p. 349.

34. See pp. 17-18.

35. Mandelbaum, *The Ideas That Conquered the World*, p. 332.

36. Quoted in Douglas A. Irwin, *Clashing Over Commerce: A History of U.S. Trade Policy*, Chicago: University of Chicago Press, 2017, p. 657.

37. Mandelbaum, *Mission Failure*, p. 17.

38. Irwin, *op. cit.*, pp. 626–632.

39. *Ibid.*, p. 624.

40. *Ibid.*, pp. 658–660. Democrats outside the South, "particularly in the West, represented states with export-oriented industries, such as high technology and aerospace. They clung to the party's traditional position in favor of open trade. The geographic division among Democrats became less North-South than between those states with strong ties to organized labor and those without." *Ibid.*, p. 660

41. Mandelbaum, *The Ideas That Conquered the World*, p. 361.

42. Irwin, *op. cit.*, pp. 631–642. The House approved NAFTA by a vote of 234 to 200, with a majority of Democrats voting against and a majority of Republicans in favor. The Senate voted approval by 61 to 38. *Ibid.*, pp. 641–643.

43. *Ibid.*, pp. 644, 651.

44. A post–World War II proposal for a comparable organization had not secured Congressional approval. *Ibid.*, pp. 504–505. In 1995, the WTO had 128 member countries. By 2015 it had more than 160. *Ibid.*, p. 655.

45. *Ibid.*, p. 652. The tally was 288 to 146 in the House, 76 to 24 in the Senate.

46. *Ibid.*, pp. 635–636.

47. *Ibid.*, pp. 572, 668.

48. *Ibid.*, p. 662.

49. See pp. 396, 398-399.

50. Quoted in Michael Mandelbaum, *The Road to Global Prosperity*, New York: Simon & Schuster, 2014, p. 83.

51. *Ibid.*, pp. 86–87.

52. *Ibid.*, pp. xix, 76.

53. Paul Blustein, *The Chastening: Inside the Crisis That Rocked the Global Financial System and Humbled the IMF*, New York: PublicAffairs, 2001, p. 16.

54. *Ibid.*, p. 78. Critics charged "that the IMF loan to Mexico was essentially going to bail out Wall Street. It was a point the Clinton administration could not deny. American investors and brokerage firms had bought tens of billions of dollars' worth of short-term Mexican government bonds, called *tesobonos*, and the rescue package was providing Mexico with enough dollars to ensure that it could avoid defaulting on any of those bonds. Washington's defense was that the alternative—allowing default—would have dealt an incalculable blow to U.S. interests and conceivably to the global economy in general." *Ibid.*, p. 173.

55. "In order to repay the Western loans the Asian governments had to devalue their own currencies, which increased the cost of their imports and made their firms and people poorer." Mandelbaum, *The Road to Global Prosperity*, p. 89.

56. Blustein, *op. cit.*, pp. 11–12, 372.

57. Mandelbaum, *Mission Failure*, p. 51.

58. *Ibid.*, p. 20.

59. *Ibid.*, p. 24.

60. James Mann, *About Face: A History of America's Curious Relationship with China, from Nixon to Clinton*, New York: Alfred A. Knopf, 1999, pp. 296, 301–303.

61. *Ibid.*, pp. 284–287, 308–309.

62. Mandelbaum, *Mission Failure*, pp. 19, 37.

63. See pp. 135-136.

64. Clinton was able to do this unilaterally because the now-discarded linkage had been imposed by his own executive order rather than by legislation that Congress would have had to repeal. Mann, *op. cit.*, p. 281.

65. Mandelbaum, *Mission Failure*, pp. 32–33.

66. *Ibid.*, pp. 33–35; Mann, *op. cit.*, pp. 328, 335–337. The Taiwan Relations Act of 1979 did not obligate the United States to defend the island but did stipulate that military or other hostile actions against it would be considered "a threat to the peace of the Western Pacific area and of grave concern to the United States." Mann, *op. cit.*, p. 95.

67. Don Oberdorfer, *The Two Koreas: A Contemporary History*, Reading, Massachusetts: Addison-Wesley, 1997, p. 308.

68. Patterson, *op. cit.*, p. 340.

69. Mann, *op. cit.*, pp. 331–332.

70. John Pomfret, *The Beautiful Country and the Middle Kingdom: America and China, 1776 to the Present*, New York: Henry Holt and Company, 2016., pp. 548–549.

71. Herring, *op. cit.*, p. 920. In the wake of the Cold War "the United States conducted large-scale military interventions more, not less, often than during the Cold War, averaging one every eighteen months prior to 9/11." Walter A. McDougall, *The Tragedy of U.S. Foreign Policy: How America's Civil Religion Betrayed the National Interest*, New Haven, Connecticut: Yale University Press, 2016, p. 18.

72. See p. 388.

73. Like other governments in the Middle East and elsewhere, the Kurdish regime was not free of corruption.

74. Rajan Menon, *The Conceit of Humanitarian Intervention*, New York: Oxford University Press, 2016, p. 9.

75. Mandelbaum, *Mission Failure*, pp. 79–80.

76. "But one could—and I would even say, should—inquire whether certain other texts that were later adopted by the United Nations, in particular the Universal Declaration of Human Rights, do not implicitly call into question this inviolable notion of sovereignty. Has not a balance been established between the right of States, as confirmed by the Charter, and the rights of the individual, as confirmed by the Universal Declaration? We are clearly witnessing what is probably an irresistible shift in public attitudes towards the belief that the defence of the oppressed in the name of morality should prevail over frontiers and legal documents." Quoted in *ibid.*, pp. 80–81.

77. *Ibid.*, p. 87.

78. Quoted in *ibid.*, p. 88.

79. *Ibid.*, pp. 88–89.

80. *Ibid.*, p. 91.

81. *Ibid.*, pp. 90–92. Carter was accompanied by Georgia senator Sam Nunn, the long-time chairman of the Senate Armed Services Committee, and Colin Powell, who had stepped down the year before as chairman of the Joint Chiefs of Staff.

82. David Halberstam, *War in a Time of Peace: Bush, Clinton, and the Generals*, New York: Scribner, 2001, p. 273.

83. Mandelbaum, *Mission Failure*, pp. 93–94. One retrospective study concluded that even if the United States had intervened it would not have been able to save most of the Tutsis who died. Alan J. Kuperman, *The Limits of Humanitarian Intervention: Genocide in Rwanda*, Washington, D.C.: The Brookings Institution Press, 2001.

84. Herring, *op. cit.*, p. 924.

85. Steven L. Burg and Paul S. Shoup, *The War in Bosnia-Herzegovina: Ethnic Conflict and International Intervention*, Armonk, New York: M.E. Sharpe, 1999, p. 26.

86. "Bosnia's Muslims, Serbs, and Croats could and did all base their preferences on a well-established international principle, but they were different principles. The one to which the Muslims appealed was the sanctity of existing borders, a concept firmly grounded in international law. . . . [B]y this rule . . . [sovereignty] was being conferred upon . . . [Yugoslavia's] constituent republics, of which Bosnia was one. . . . Bosnia's Serbs and Croats, by contrast, could and did invoke the principle of national self-determination, which the American president Woodrow Wilson had placed at the center of international affairs at

the Paris Peace Conference after World War I." Mandelbaum, *Mission Failure*, p. 97.

87. Burg and Shoup, *op. cit.*, Chapter 3.
88. Mandelbaum, *Mission Failure*, p. 99.
89. *Ibid.*, p. 102; Burg and Shoup, *op. cit.*, pp. 200–201.
90. Burg and Shoup, *op. cit.*, p. 12.
91. *Ibid.*, p. 38. "Opinion polls and election results showed that the majority of those living in Bosnia did not embrace a multiethnic Bosnian identity. . . . Instead, the inhabitants of Bosnia saw themselves, first and foremost, as members of one of the three national groups." Mandelbaum, *Mission Failure*, p. 103. Clinton administration officials also believed that the Serb war against the Muslims constituted an act of genocide, which imposed on the international community a moral obligation to stop it. *Ibid.*, p. 104.
92. Mandelbaum, *Mission Failure*, p. 108; Burg and Shoup, *op. cit.*, pp. 146, 298, 339, 347.
93. Burg and Shoup, *op. cit.*, pp. 316–317, 323, 325, 349, 384.
94. The bombing campaign had a political rather than a military aim. Americans "were able freely to pressure . . .—even threaten—the Muslims only after they had committed themselves to bombing the Serbs. The NATO air campaign protected U.S. policymakers from the charge of having given in to the Serbs. . . ." *Ibid.*, p. 413.
95. In the negotiations the Americans "adopted positions they had earlier criticized European and UN negotiators for adopting." *Ibid.*, p. 383.
96. Mandelbaum, *Mission Failure*, pp. 98–99.
97. *Ibid.*, p. 111.
98. "The KLA had no hope of evicting the Serbs and winning independence on its own. It aimed, rather, to provoke a Serb reaction sufficiently visible and brutal to trigger an intervention by the West, which did have the military means to force the Serbs out of the province. That is exactly what happened." *Ibid.*, p. 113.
99. *Ibid.*, p. 115.
100. *Ibid.*, p. 116. A close aide to Albright said that the Rambouillet meeting had only one purpose: "To get the war started with the Europeans locked in." Quoted in Ivo H. Daalder and Michael E. O'Hanlon, *Winning Ugly: NATO's War to Save Kosovo*, Washington, D.C.: Brookings Institution Press, 2000, p. 89.
101. Daalder and O'Hanlon, *op. cit.*, p. 108; Mandelbaum, *Mission Failure*, p. 117.
102. "Those driven from their homes in 1999 represented nearly three-fourths of the prewar population of roughly 1.8 million ethnic Albanians." Daalder and O'Hanlon, *op. cit.*, pp. 108–109.
103. *Ibid.*, pp. 91, 103–105.
104. Mandelbaum, *Mission Failure*, p. 118.

105. *Ibid.*, p. 126.

106. *Ibid.*, pp. 127–131.

107. On the pervasive role of culture in human affairs see Lawrence E. Harrison and Samuel P. Huntington, editors, *Culture Matters: How Values Shape Human Progress*, New York: Basic Books, 2000.

108. Pomfret, *op. cit.*, pp. 564–565.

109. Daalder and O'Hanlon, *op. cit.*, pp. 125–126, 196–197; Mandelbaum, *Mission Failure*, p. 124.

110. Russians themselves sometimes made reference to this precedent. J. L. Black, *Russia Faces NATO Expansion: Bearing Gifts or Bearing Arms?*, Lanham, Maryland: Rowman & Littlefield, 2000, p. 2.

111. James M. Goldgeier and Michael McFaul, *Power and Purpose: U.S. Policy Toward Russia After the Cold War*, Washington, D.C.: Brookings Institution Press, 2003, p. 89.

112. *Ibid.*, p. 127.

113. *Ibid.*, p. 145.

114. *Ibid.*, p. 94.

115. *Ibid.*, pp. 126–130.

116. Blustein, *op. cit.*, p. 242; Anders Aslund, *How Capitalism Was Built: The Transformation of Central and Eastern Europe, Russia, the Caucasus, and Central Asia*, New York: Cambridge University Press, Third Edition, 2013, p. 61; Daniel Treisman, *The Return: Russia's Journey from Gorbachev to Medvedev*, New York: Free Press, 2011, pp. 204–205.

117. Goldgeier and McFaul, *op. cit.*, p. 12.

118. *Ibid.*, pp. 61, 72, 79.

119. *Ibid.*, Chapter 4, especially pp. 84–86; Anders Aslund, *Russia's Capitalist Revolution: Why Market Reform Succeeded and Democracy Failed*, Washington, D.C.: The Peterson Institute for International Economics, 2007, pp. 116–118. "During the eight years after 1991, Russia's interest payments on the foreign debt came to more than all the aid and new loans the country received." Treisman, *op. cit.*, p. 315.

120. Aslund, *Russia's Capitalist Revolution*, p. 119.

121. Treisman, *op. cit.*, p. 199.

122. The initials stood for "Gosudartsvennye Kratkosrochney Obligatsii— "state short-term obligations." Blustein, *op. cit.*, p. 238.

123. *Ibid.*, p. 229; Goldgeier and McFaul, *op. cit.*, p. 229.

124. Treisman, *op. cit.*, pp. 230–231.

125. On the GKO crisis see Blustein, *op. cit.*, pp. 247–273.

126. Treisman, *op. cit.*, p. 232.

127. Goldgeier and McFaul, *op. cit.*, p. 233.

128. Mandelbaum, *Mission Failure*, p. 64.

129. Goldgeier and McFaul, *op. cit.*, pp. 11–12, 158, 173–174. "Between 1990 and 1996, the number of active troops under Moscow's command fell from 3.4 million to 1.3 million." Treisman, *op. cit.*, p. 316.

130. Goldgeier and McFaul, *op. cit.*, pp. 54–58, 166–171.

131. *Ibid.*, pp. 41, 51, 108; Mandelbaum, *Mission Failure*, p. 66.

132. Jack F. Matlock Jr., *Superpower Illusions: How Myths and False Ideologies Led America Astray—and How to Return to Reality*, New Haven, Connecticut: Yale University Press, 2010, p. 170; Black, *op. cit.*, p. 22; Goldgeier and McFaul, *op. cit.*, pp. 184–185.

133. On the Clinton administration's decision to expand NATO see M. E. Sarotte, "How to Enlarge NATO: The Debate Inside the Clinton Administration, 1993–1995," *International Security* 44:1, Summer 2019.

134. Albania, Croatia, Montenegro, and North Macedonia subsequently joined NATO as well.

135. Michael Mandelbaum, *The Dawn of Peace in Europe*, New York: The Twentieth Century Fund Press, 1996, pp. 58–61; Goldgeier and McFaul, *op. cit.*, p. 203; Black, *op. cit.*, p. 8.

136. Michael Mandelbaum, *NATO Expansion: A Bridge to the Nineteenth Century*, Bethesda, Maryland: The Center for Political and Strategic Studies, 1997, pp. 4–5.

137. *Ibid.*, p. 35; Mandelbaum, *The Dawn of Peace in Europe*, pp. 46–52.

138. Mandelbaum, *NATO Expansion*, p. 5.

139. *Ibid.*, p. 18; Goldgeier and McFaul, *op. cit.*, pp. 193, 202; Treisman, *op. cit.*, pp. 317–318.

140. On the partisan political considerations bearing on the decision to expand see Sarotte, *op. cit.*, pp. 26, 35, 39.

141. Goldgeier and McFaul, *op. cit.*, pp. 16, 206.

142. "The Senate ratified NATO expansion on the basis of the same kind of political calculation that governs the authorization of dams, post offices, and changes in the nation's tax code favorable to a particular industry or firm: some politically significant forces favored it while no one with political clout pressed the negative case." Mandelbaum, *Mission Failure*, pp. 71–72.

143. Black, *op. cit.*, pp. 111, 114.

144. Quoted in Mandelbaum, *Mission Failure*, p. 14.

145. The term for the stretch of largely Islamic territory located roughly between the Mediterranean and the Arabian Sea comes from Great Britain, where it also became known as the Near East in order to distinguish it from East Asia, which, because at a greater distance from the British Isles, became the Far East. For the United States, East Asia, situated as it is on the opposite side of the Pacific Ocean, properly qualifies as the Far West.

146. See pp. 342-323.

147. Mandelbaum, *Mission Failure*, pp. 248–249.

148. *Ibid.*, p. 245.

149. *Ibid.*, pp. 187–188; Michael R. Gordon and Bernard E. Trainor,
      Cobra II: The Inside Story of the Invasion and Occupation of Iraq,
      New York: Pantheon Books, 2006, p. 13.

150. Indyk, *op. cit.*, pp. 36, 41–42.

151. Dennis Ross, *The Missing Peace: The Inside Story of the Fight for Middle
      East Peace*, New York: Farrar, Straus and Giroux, 2004, pp. 80–81.

152. Mandelbaum, *Mission Failure*, p. 263.

153. *Ibid.*, p. 261.

154. *Ibid.*, pp. 261–263; Indyk, *op. cit.*, pp. 279–281.

155. On the Israeli-Syrian negotiations see Itamar Rabinovich, *The Brink of
      Peace: The Israeli-Syrian Negotiations*, Princeton, New Jersey: Princeton
      University Press, 1998.

156. Mandelbaum, *Mission Failure*, p. 264; Ross, *op. cit.*, p. 186.

157. Mandelbaum, *Mission Failure*, pp. 267–270; Indyk, *op. cit.*, p. 342.

158. Elliott Abrams, *Tested by Zion: The Bush Administration and the Israeli-
      Palestinian Conflict*, New York: Cambridge University Press, 2013,
      pp. 1–2.

159. Colin Dueck, *The Obama Doctrine: American Grand Strategy Today*,
      New York: Oxford University Press, 2015, p. 48.

160. They were Condoleezza Rice in the second Bush term and John Kerry in
      the second Obama term. Mandelbaum, *op. cit.*, pp. 282–284.

161. Ross, *op. cit.*, p. 771.

162. "Other than prosecuting wars and managing the great nuclear crisis
      over Soviet missiles in Cuba in 1962, to no other international issue in
      the twentieth century did the American government devote as much
      sustained, high-level attention as it did to the peace process in the year
      2000." Mandelbaum, *Mission Failure*, p. 268.

163. Dennis Ross and David Makovsky, *Myths, Illusions, and Peace: Finding a
      New Direction for America in the Middle East*, New York: Viking, 2009,
      Chapter 2.

164. Mandelbaum, *Mission Failure*, pp. 252, 271. The Palestinians insisted
      that any agreement include a "right of return," according to which
      any Arab who could claim an ancestral connection to what after 1948
      became Israel had a right to return there. This was, and was intended to
      be, a formula for the demographic destruction of the Jewish state. *Ibid.*,
      p. 269; Indyk, *op. cit.*, p. 374. On this point see also Adi Schwartz and
      Einat Wilf, *The War of Return: How Western Indulgence of the Palestinian
      Dream Has Obstructed the Path to Peace*, New York: All Points
      Books, 2020.

165. Mandelbaum, *Mission Failure*, p. 251.

166. The Americans harbored another belief that proved to be erroneous: that
      the process of negotiation would help to bring peace by creating
      familiarity, which would engender trust and ultimately produce a
      settlement. This did not happen.

Chapter 11

1. Al Qaeda means "the base" in Arabic.
2. See p. 421.
3. Michael Mandelbaum, *Mission Failure: America and the World in the Post-Cold War Era*, New York: Oxford University Press, 2016, pp. 139–140.
4. Peter Baker, *Days of Fire: Bush and Cheney in the White House*, New York: Doubleday, 2013, p. 65.
5. Mandelbaum, *op. cit.*, pp. 143–143.
6. Baker, *op. cit.*, p. 50.
7. Quoted in Mandelbaum, *op. cit.*, p. 133.
8. See Michael Howard, "What's in a Name? How to Fight Terrorism," *Foreign Affairs*, January/February 2002.
9. John Mueller and Mark G. Stewart, *Terror, Security, and Money: Balancing the Risks, Benefits, and Costs of Homeland Security*, New York: Oxford University Press, 2011, p. 3.
10. *Ibid.*, p. 160. The balance of the Homeland Security budget went largely to mitigation and resilience. *Ibid.*, p. 167.
11. This is the argument of *ibid.*
12. *Ibid.*, p. 147.
13. "... [T]he total number of people killed in the years after 9/11 by Muslim extremists outside of war zones come to some 200 to 300 per year. ... For comparison, during the same period more people—320 per year—drowned in bathtubs in the United States alone." *Ibid.*, p. 42. See also pp. 53, 95–96, 141–142, 189.
14. Baker, *op. cit.*, p. 148.
15. Mandelbaum, *op. cit.*, p. 151.
16. *Ibid.*, pp. 153–158.
17. Baker, *op. cit.*, pp. 193–194.
18. *Ibid.*, pp. 163–164, 171.
19. See pp. 104, 214-215.
20. See, for example, Baker, *op. cit.*, pp. 483–484.
21. See p. 351.
22. The English translation of Taliban is "students."
23. Mandelbaum, *op. cit.*, pp. 161–162.
24. In the wake of September 11, the countries of the North Atlantic Trade Organization (NATO) invoked, for the first time, Article 5 of the Alliance's charter, which states that an attack on one member is an attack on all of them. *Ibid.*, p. 161.
25. *Ibid.*, pp. 163–164.
26. *Ibid.*, pp. 168–169.
27. *Ibid.*, p. 170.
28. *Ibid.*, p. 165. In August 2021 the Taliban conquered the entire country.
29. *Ibid.*, pp. 171–174.
30. *Ibid.*, p. 194; Baker, *op. cit.*, pp. 207, 215–216.

31. Thomas Ricks, *Fiasco: The American Military Adventure in Iraq*, New York: The Penguin Press, 2006, p. 377.

32. Baker, *op. cit.*, p. 191.

33. Ricks, *op. cit.*, pp. 11, 30.

34. Bush said in an interview, ". . . [W]e were attacked, and therefore every threat had to be reanalyzed." *Ibid.*, p. 375.

35. Evidence came to light after the American invasion suggesting that that assumption was correct. Melvyn Leffler, "The Decider: Why Bush Chose War in Iraq," *Foreign Affairs*, November/December 2020, p. 146.

36. In his 2002 State of the Union address Bush said, "I will not wait on events while dangers gather. . . . The United States of America will not permit the world's most dangerous regimes to threaten us with the world's most destructive weapons." https://georgewbush-whitehouse.archives.gov/news/releases/2002/01/20020129-11.html. See also Baker, *op. cit.*, pp. 109, 176–177, 181, 210–211, 219–224.

37. On the reasons for France's opposition to the Iraq War see Philip H. Gordon and Jeremy Shapiro, *Allies at War: America, Europe, and the Crisis over Iraq*, New York: McGraw-Hill, 2004, p. 11.

38. Michael R. Gordon and General Bernard E. Trainor, *Cobra II: The Inside Story of the Invasion and Occupation of Iraq*, New York: Pantheon Books, 2006, p. 115.

39. *Ibid.*, Chapters 14–21; Ricks, *op. cit.*, Chapter 7.

40. Gordon and Trainor, *op. cit.*, pp. 138, 459; Ricks, *op. cit.*, p. 110.

41. Gordon and Trainor, *op. cit.*, pp. 73, 162.

42. *Ibid.*, pp. 467–468; Rajiv Chandrasekaran, *Imperial Life in the Emerald City: Inside Iraq's Green Zone*, New York: Alfred A. Knopf, 2006, p. 46.

43. Larry Diamond, *Squandered Victory: The American Occupation and the Bungled Effort to Bring Democracy to Iraq*, New York: Times Books/Henry Holt and Company, 2005, p. 37. On MacArthur in Japan see pp. 266-267.

44. Chandrasekaran, *op. cit.*, pp. 61, 115.

45. Baker, *op. cit.*, pp. 374–375.

46. Michael R. Gordon and General Bernard E. Trainor, *The Endgame: The Inside Story of the Struggle for Iraq, from George W. Bush to Barack Obama*, New York: Pantheon, 2012, pp. 8, 46, 112; Baker, *op. cit.*, pp. 290–291.

47. Mandelbaum, *op. cit.*, pp. 207–208.

48. See p. 388.

49. Gordon and Trainor, *The Endgame*, pp. 24, 32.

50. *Ibid.*, pp. 22–23.

51. Gordon and Trainor, *The Endgame*, pp. 230, 315–316; Diamond, *op. cit.*, p. 222. "The insurgents fought on in Iraq armed in no small measure with the sympathy given them by the Arab papers and the satellite channels and by elite and mass opinion in neighboring Arab lands." Fouad Ajami, *The Foreigner's Gift: The Americans, The Arabs, and the Iraqis in Iraq*, New York: The Free Press, 2006, p. 275.

52. Gordon and Trainor, *The Endgame*, pp. 192–194.

53. *Ibid.*, p. 354.

54. Baker, *op. cit.*, p. 332; Chandrasekaran, *op. cit.*, p. 61. Military officers and officials in the Defense Department disagreed among themselves about how many troops were required. Gordon and Trainor, *Cobra II*, pp. 101–104; Baker, *op. cit.*, pp. 248–249.

55. John Mueller, "The Iraq War and the Management of American Public Opinion," in Mueller, *War and Ideas: Selected Essays*, New York: Routledge, 2011, p. 196.

56. Baker, *op. cit.*, p. 326. "By August 2007, three of four expressed pessimism about the conflict, six in ten believed the United States should have stayed out of Iraq, and only 23 percent approved Bush's handling of the war." George C. Herring, *From Colony to Superpower: U.S. Foreign Relations Since 1776*, New York: Oxford University Press, 2008, p. 956.

57. See p. 307.

58. Baker, *op. cit.*, p. 326; Ricks, *op. cit.*, pp. 199–200, 290–293.

59. Mueller, *op. cit.*, p. 200.

60. Richard Haass, *War of Necessity, War of Choice: A Memoir of Two Iraq Wars*, New York: Simon & Schuster, 2009, p. 230; Gordon and Trainor, *Cobra II*, p. 135.

61. Mandelbaum, *op. cit.*, pp. 196–197, 231–232.

62. Gordon and Trainor, *The Endgame*, p. 366.

63. The troops were ordered to "get out, get seen, and let them know you are here." Quoted in Gordon and Trainor, *The Endgame*, p. 373. See also Carter Malkasian, *Illusions of Victory: The Anbar Awakening and the Rise of the Islamic State*, New York: Oxford University Press, 2017, pp. 198–201.

64. Gordon and Trainor, *The Endgame*, p. 430.

65. Michael Mandelbaum, *The Rise and Fall of Peace on Earth*, New York: Oxford University Press, 2019, p. 102. Iraqi deaths may have numbered as many as 100,000. Baker, *op. cit.*, p. 649.

66. Mandelbaum, *Mission Failure*, p. 229.

67. Neta C. Crawford, "United States Budgetary Costs of Post-9/11 Wars Through FY 2020: $6.4 Trillion," Brown University Costs of War Project, November 13, 2019, https://watson.brown.edu/costsofwar/files/cow/imce/papers/2019/US%20Budgetary%20Costs%20of%20Wars%20November%202019.pdf

68. Adam Tooze, *Crashed: How a Decade of Financial Crises Changed the World*, New York: Penguin Books, 2019. , p. 185.

69. *Ibid.*, p. 43.

70. *Ibid.*, pp. 48–55.

71. *Ibid.*, p. 63; Michael Mandelbaum, *The Road to Global Prosperity*, New York: Simon & Schuster, 2014, p. 92.

72. Martin Wolf, *The Shifts and the Shocks: What We've Learned—and Have Still to Learn—from the Financial Crisis*, New York: Penguin Press, 2014, p. 4.

73. Tooze, *op. cit.*, pp. 56–59.

74. Alan Greenspan and Adrian Wooldridge, *Capitalism in America: A History*, New York: The Penguin Press, 2018, p. 383.

75. Tooze, *op. cit.*, p. 65.

76. *Ibid.*, p. 143.

77. *Ibid.*, pp. 60, 146, 149.

78. Mandelbaum, *The Road to Global Prosperity*, pp. 90–91.

79. Tooze, *op. cit.*, p. 207.

80. *Ibid.*, p. 174.

81. Mandelbaum, *The Road to Global Prosperity*, p. 97.

82. Tooze, *op. cit.*, pp. 208, 211.

83. *Ibid.*, pp. 9, 202–203, 214, 219.

84. *Ibid.*, pp. 157, 159–160.

85. The authorization was subsequently reduced to $475 billion.

86. Other countries injected fiscal stimulus into their economies as well. Tooze, *op. cit.*, p. 264.

87. *Ibid.*, pp. 255–261. "How big the costs of these crises will end up being is still unknowable. But, in the cases of the US and the UK, the fiscal costs are of roughly the same scale as a world war. . . . In crisis-hit Eurozone countries the costs would be greater." Wolf, *op. cit.*, p. 325.

88. "According to my Chinese interlocutors, large segments of the Chinese public and elites feel that China's global power has risen quickly since the financial collapse of 2008. . . . The American 'hegemon' had taken a mighty blow when Wall Street collapsed. China, by comparison, seemed stable and strong. . . ." Thomas J. Christensen, *The China Challenge: Shaping the Choices of a Rising Power*, New York: W.W. Norton, 2015, p. 242. See also Edward N. Luttwak, *The Rise of China vs. the Logic of Strategy*, Cambridge, Massachusetts: The Belknap Press of Harvard University Press, 2012, pp. 8, 257, and John Pomfret, *The Beautiful Country and the Middle Kingdom: America and China, 1776 to the Present*, New York: Henry Holt and Company, 2016, p. 599.

89. "The eurozone crisis was a massive aftershock of the earthquake in the north Atlantic financial system of 2008, working its way out with a time lag through the labyrinthine political framework of the EU." Tooze, *op. cit.*, p. 14.

90. Wolf, *op. cit.*, pp. 46–48.

91. Banks in northern Europe held Greek and other southern European debt in appreciable quantities, which gave the governments of northern Europe an interest in protecting them.

92. Tooze, *op. cit.*, p. 112.

93. *Ibid.*, pp. 323–331. On the crisis of the euro see Ashoka Mody, *EuroTragedy: A Drama in Nine Acts*, New York: Oxford University Press, 2018, especially Chapters 4–7.

94. Tooze, *op. cit.*, pp. 2, 4.

95. Both stemmed from a "global savings glut." Wolf, *op. cit.*, p. 151.

96. *Ibid.*, p. 9; Tooze, *op. cit.*, pp. 10, 574–575.

97. See p. 177.

98. Douglas A. Irwin, *Clashing Over Commerce: A History of U.S. Trade Policy*, Chicago: University of Chicago Press, 2017, pp. 685–686.

99. Mandelbaum, *Mission Failure*, p. 179.

100. *Ibid.*, pp. 177–178.

101. *Ibid.*, pp. 179–182; Steven Sestanovich, *Maximalist: America in the World from Truman to* Obama, New York: Alfred A. Knopf, 2014, pp. 304–308; James Mann, *The Obamians: The Struggle Inside the White House to Redefine American Power*, New York: Viking, 2012, pp. 137–140.

102. Obama did complete one piece of previously unfinished business having to do with Afghanistan. He authorized a raid on a villa in Pakistan where American intelligence believed Osama bin Laden was hiding. The American Special Forces conducting the raid found him there and killed him.

103. Mandelbaum, *Mission Failure*, p. 298.

104. See pp. 367-370.

105. Steven A. Cook, *False Dawn: Protest, Democracy, and Violence in the New Middle East*, New York: Oxford University Press, 2017, pp. 17–18.

106. Mandelbaum, *Mission Failure*, pp. 309–310.

107. See p. 341.

108. Colin Dueck, *The Obama Doctrine: American Grand Strategy Today*, New York: Oxford University Press, 2015, p. 77.

109. Mandelbaum, *Mission Failure*, pp. 299–300.

110. Sestanovich, *op. cit.*, pp. 315–317; Mann, *op. cit.*, pp. 289–290. The Libyan intervention was undertaken with the support of a United Nations resolution, number 1973.

111. Mandelbaum, *Mission Failure*, pp. 302–305; Cook, *op. cit.*, pp. 123–132, 148–150.

112. Mandelbaum, *The Rise and Fall of Peace on Earth*, pp. 122–124; Jay Solomon, *The Iran Wars: Spy Games, Bank Battles, and the Secret Deals That Reshaped the Middle East*, New York: Random House, 2016, p. 225.

113. Mandelbaum, *The Rise and Fall of Peace on Earth*, pp. 125–126.

114. Mandelbaum, *Mission Failure*, p. 305. By 2018 the toll had risen to 450,000 dead and eleven million refugees. Mandelbaum, *The Rise and Fall of Peace on Earth*, p. 129.

115. Sestanovich, *op. cit.*, p. 318; Robert S. Singh, *After Obama: Renewing American Leadership, Restoring Global Order*, New York: Cambridge University Press, 2016, p. 31.

116. Mandelbaum, *Mission Failure*, p. 306.

117. *Ibid.*, pp. 306–307; Sestanovich, *op. cit.*, pp. 318–319. Subsequent reports, and chemical attacks in Syria, suggested that Assad did not, in fact, relinquish all of the chemical munitions that he controlled.

118. Mandelbaum, *Mission Failure*, pp. 240–241; Mandelbaum, *The Rise and Fall of Peace on Earth*, pp. 124–125; Malkasian, *op. cit.*, pp. 202–207.

119. It was also known as ISIL—the Islamic State in Iraq and the Levant.

120. On the Islamic State see Cook, *op. cit.*, pp. 195–200.

121. Mandelbaum, *Mission Failure*, pp. 307–308.

122. The end of the fourth period in the history of American foreign policy is the subject of Mandelbaum, *The Rise and Fall of Peace on Earth*.

123. *Ibid.*, pp. 50–51.

124. *Ibid.*, pp. 54–55.

125. Pomfret, *op. cit.*, p. 622.

126. Mandelbaum, *The Rise and Fall of Peace on Earth*, p. 71.

127. *Ibid.*, pp. 66–67; Mandelbaum, *Mission Failure*, p. 348; Pomfret, *op. cit.*, p. 628; Howard W. French, *Everything Under the Heavens: How the Past Helps Shape China's Push for Global Power*, New York: Alfred A. Knopf, 2017, pp. 11, 120.

128. Mandelbaum, *Mission Failure*, pp. 349–350.

129. French, *op. cit.*, p. 266; Mandelbaum, *The Rise and Fall of Peace on Earth*, pp. 56–57.

130. Mandelbaum, *The Rise and Fall of Peace on Earth*, pp. 72–76.

131. Tooze, *op. cit.*, p. 35.

132. Mandelbaum, *The Rise and Fall of Peace on Earth*, p. 86.

133. *Ibid.*, pp. 17–19; Mandelbaum, *Mission Failure*, pp. 357–358. On Russian corruption see Karen Dawisha, *Putin's Kleptocracy: Who Owns Russia?*, New York: Simon & Schuster, 2014.

134. Mandelbaum, *The Rise and Fall of Peace on Earth*, p. 13.

135. Quoted in *ibid.*, p. 26.

136. Baker, *op. cit.*, pp. 585–587.

137. Mandelbaum, *Mission Failure*, p. 360.

138. Rajan Menon and Eugene Rumer, *Conflict in Ukraine: The Unwinding of the Post-Cold War Order*, Cambridge, Massachusetts: The MIT Press, 2015, p. 14; Mandelbaum, *The Rise and Fall of Peace on Earth*, p. 23.

139. Menon and Rumer, *op. cit.*, pp. 32–35.

140. It was named for the central square in Kiev where protesters gathered.

141. The majority of Russians apparently believed him. Menon and Rumer, *op. cit.*, p. 88.

142. *Ibid.*, Chapter 2.

143. Mandelbaum, *The Rise and Fall of Peace on Earth*, pp. 21–22, 30–33.

144. Quoted in Mandelbaum, *Mission Failure*, p. 311.

145. Baker, *op. cit.*, p. 227; Mandelbaum, *Mission Failure*, pp. 331–332.

146. Mandelbaum, *Mission Failure*, p. 334.

147. *Ibid.*
148. *Ibid.*, p. 335.
149. Mandelbaum, *The Rise and Fall of Peace on Earth*, pp. 111–112; Solomon, *op. cit.*, p. 32.
150. Mandelbaum, *Mission Failure*, p. 336.
151. *Ibid.*, p. 337.
152. Mandelbaum, *The Rise and Fall of Peace on Earth*, p. 114.
153. Mandelbaum, *Mission Failure*, p. 342.
154. Solomon, *op. cit.*, p. 294.
155. *Ibid.*, p. 264; Mandelbaum, *Mission Failure*, pp. 328, 339.
156. Solomon, *op. cit.*, p. 277.
157. *Ibid.*, pp. 4, 206–207.
158. Mandelbaum, *The Rise and Fall of Peace on Earth*, pp. 118–119.
159. The American approach to Iran during the Obama years was not entirely conciliatory. The United States inserted the "Stuxnet" virus into the Iranian nuclear weapons program, which set back its progress. David Sanger, *Confront and Conceal: Obama's Secret Wars and Surprising Use of American Power*, New York: Crown Publishers, 2012, pp. 194–209.
160. Michael Doran, "Obama's Secret Iran Strategy," *Mosaic*, February 2, 2015, https://www.hudson.org/research/ 10989-obama-s-secret-iran-strategy
161. Solomon, *op. cit.*, p. 8.
162. Mandelbaum, *Mission Failure*, p. 368.
163. Wolf, *op. cit.*, p. 136; Tooze, *op. cit.*, p. 67.
164. Mandelbaum, *The Rise and Fall of Peace on Earth*, pp. 52–53.
165. See p. 409.

INDEX

＊＊＊

For the benefit of digital users, indexed terms that span two pages (e.g., 52–53) may, on occasion, appear on only one of those pages.